D0847415

Also by Robert Kimball

Also by Barry Day

Also by Miles Kreuger

The Complete Lyrics of

JOHNNY MERCER

ALFRED A. KNOPF   NEW YORK   2009

The Complete Lyrics of

JOHNNY
MERCER

Edited by

ROBERT KIMBALL, BARRY DAY,
MILES KREUGER, and ERIC DAVIS

With gratitude and affection to
Margaret Whiting
Joseph Harris
Michael Feinstein
Howard Green

THIS IS A BORZOI BOOK PUBLISHED BY ALFRED A. KNOPF

Copyright © 2009 by the Johnny Mercer Foundation, Robert Kimball, Barry Day, Miles Kreuger, and Eric Davis

All rights reserved.
Published in the United States by Alfred A. Knopf, a division of Random House, Inc., New York, and
in Canada by Random House of Canada Limited, Toronto.
www.aaknopf.com
Knopf, Borzoi Books, and the colophon are registered trademarks of Random House, Inc.
Copyright information on the lyrics of Johnny Mercer appears in the Index, starting on page 443.

"Johnny Mercer—Too Marvelous for Words" was originally published in the souvenir program for *Dream*,
Luckman Theater, California State University, Los Angeles. Copyright © 2002 by Miles Kreuger.

Library of Congress Cataloging-in-Publication Data
Mercer, Johnny, 1909–1976.
[Lyrics]
The complete lyrics of Johnny Mercer/edited by Barry Day, Robert Kimball, and Miles Kreuger.
—1st ed.
p.   cm.
ISBN 978-0-307-26519-7
1. Songs, English—United States—Texts.   2. Popular music—United States—Texts.   3. Songs—Texts.
4. Musicals—Texts.   I. Day, Barry.   II. Kimball, Robert.   III. Kreuger, Miles.   IV. Title.
ML54.6.M45C66 2009
782.42164'0268—dc22
2009024005

First Edition

The text of this book was set in Bodoni
Composed by Creative Graphics, Allentown, Pennsylvania
Printed and bound by RR Donnelley, China

Photographic Credits

All photographs are courtesy of Special Collections and Archives, Georgia State University Library, except for the following:
The Academy of Motion Picture Arts and Sciences, 96, 120, 136, 264, 341; Billy Rose Theatre Division, The New York Public Library for
the Performing Arts, Astor, Lenox and Tilden Foundations, 157; Photograph by Michael Ochs © Getty Images, 167; The Institute of the
American Musical, xvii, xviii, 12, 21, 42, 85, 106, 195, 247; Courtesy of Photofest, 42, 50, 65, 78, 96, 106, 120, 136, 151, 174, 184, 195, 204,
216, 239, 277, 290, 304, 320, 330, 349; Turner Entertainment Co., a Warner Bros. Entertainment Company. All Rights Reserved, 65.

Contents

OVERLEAF   Old Man Rhythm *at the Lucas in Savannah, Georgia*

JOHNNY MERCER—
TOO MARVELOUS FOR WORDS

He received an astonishing eighteen Academy Award nominations for best song and won four times. He has one of the largest catalogues of hits in ASCAP, for which he served as a board member. Largely a man who wrote lyrics, he also penned the music for some of his best songs, although Margaret Whiting claims that he could barely play the piano with one finger. He appeared as an actor in two movies and had bit roles in several Broadway productions. He co-founded Capitol Records and transformed the neophyte label into a competitor to RCA Victor, Columbia, and Decca. But it was as a familiar radio singer and recording star that Johnny Mercer became by far the best-loved songwriter in history.

John Herndon Mercer was born November 18, 1909, in Savannah, Georgia, to an old and distinguished southern family. His father, George, was an investment banker, who dabbled in real estate, a profession for which young John proved hopelessly inept during the rare occasions when he attempted to help out. His mother, Lillian, encouraged his interest in songwriting and in the activities of local, amateur theatre groups.

In 1922, John entered the prestigious Woodberry Forest School in Madison County, Virginia. When George Mercer's banking business failed in 1927, John was graduated and decided to try his hand in show business in New York. He stowed away on a boat that was headed north but was soon discovered by the crew and forced to work for his passage.

At the time, The Theatre Guild was the finest producing organization on Broadway. Not only did it revive classics and import European plays, but it numbered among its playwrights the leading stage author of the day, Eugene O'Neill. In addition to its stable of established contract actors, The Theatre Guild signed and trained young, aspiring thespians, who were often given walk-on roles.

Film director Vincent Sherman, who was born in Vienna, Georgia, on July 16, 1906, recalls that he and Mercer had bits in the celebrated O'Neill satire *Marco Millions*, which opened at the Guild Theatre (today the Virginia) on January 9, 1928. For reasons that remain a mystery, Mercer used the stage name "John Henry" in his roles as A Dervish and An Indian Snake Charmer. *Marco Millions* was followed at the Guild on April 9 by a revival of *Volpone*, with "John Henry" as Slave to Volpone. Sherman recalls that as two Georgia boys in the big city, there was a bond between them, although they did not become close friends at that time.

Every Mercer biography incorrectly claims that he arrived in New York in 1927 with the Savannah Players to appear in an amateur play, *The Hero*, which won top prize, the Belasco Cup, in a little theatre contest. Unfortunately, except for the 1927 date, not one detail is correct.

During the 1920s, the little theatre movement was very popular. Every season, in one of the smaller Broadway houses, Walter Hartwig, in co-operation with the Manhattan Little Theatre Club, presented a week of competition among amateur groups for the David Belasco Trophy. Three or four short plays were presented each evening. On May 11, 1928, Mercer (this time using his real name) appeared in *Hero Worship* by Frances Hargis at the Frolic Theatre atop the New Amsterdam. The amateur work won a secondary prize (not the so-called Belasco Cup) for the Town Theatre of Savannah, the group's correct name.

On September 9, 1929, at the Knickerbocker, our hero returned to Broadway as one of a group of students in *Houseparty.* Although he used his real name in this collegiate melodrama, he reverted to "John Henry" for one-week revivals of *Marco Millions* (March 3, 1930) and *Volpone* (March 10) at the Liberty. An actor called "John Henry" also had bits in the short lived *She Lived Next to the Firehouse* (February 10, 1931) and *The Sex Fable* (October 20, 1931), but it has not yet been determined that this particular "John Henry" was our boy John Mercer.

Next, we hear the quaint but absurd fable that having just arrived in New York (which he had not), the young man, as a complete stranger in town, tried to get into the cast of The Theatre Guild's third and final edition of the *Garrick Gaieties* (October 16, 1930, Guild) but was informed that the revue was entirely cast; so instead he offered them a song. Far from a stranger, Mercer had been an employee of The Theatre Guild for more than two years and had worked with many of the people mounting the show. However, he did indeed provide them with a song, "Out of Breath (And Scared to Death of You)," his very first published opus and a modest hit at that. Far more significant, he was smitten by a pert, Brooklyn-born chorus girl, Elizabeth Meltzer, using the stage name Ginger Meehan. The couple married on June 8, 1931, and later had two children, daughter Georgia Amanda and son John Jefferson.

The young southerner with his easygoing manner blended quickly into the community of song writers who buzzed around the Brill Building, that remarkable structure just north of Times Square that was home to many of the music publishers and composers.

Over the years, Mercer was to write words to the music of some of the best composers in the country, including Jerome Kern, Harold Arlen, Richard A. Whiting, Harry Warren, Walter Donaldson, Jimmy McHugh, Rube Bloom, Gene de Paul, Johnny Mandel, and Henry Mancini.

In 1933, he hit pay dirt with "Lazybones," with music by Hoagy Carmichael. The boy who has billed himself as John Mercer or John H. Mercer on sheet music was reconstituted as Johnny Mercer in print, on record labels, and soon on the air as well.

Throughout his childhood, the Mercer home had been filled with

The Latest Advance in Recording

Columbia

LONGER PLAYING RECORD

A Practical
Long Playing
Record

Doubles Your
Musical Enjoyment

Plays on
Any Standard
Phonograph

No Attachment
or Adaptor Needed

Up-to-date

Home Entertainment

As You Like It

music. He loved the jazz bands on the many records in the house, so it was natural that, once in New York, he would seek out the company of the actual musicians themselves. From Greenwich Village to Harlem, the town was alive with little clubs and speakeasies that sported the hottest sounds around.

Blessed with a light and smooth baritone that was spiced with a warm, southern accent, Mercer made his recording debut on April 5, 1932, as a vocalist on a Frankie Trumbauer disc and later with the Dorsey Brothers Orchestra.

In 1932, Paul Whiteman, the most popular band leader in America, was on NBC for Pontiac. The program, which was broadcast from the New Amsterdam roof, featured a weekly "Youth of America" segment, a contest for unknown singers. Johnny won the contest and was hired by the "King of Jazz" to sing on the show and write a new piece of special material for each week's broadcast. It was the beginning of a career on radio that lasted until 1954 and made Johnny one of the most popular vocalists in the country, right up there with Bing Crosby and Frank Sinatra.

With fan letters pouring into NBC, it was inevitable that Hollywood would soon come a-calling. In 1935, RKO engaged Johnny not only to write the lyrics for two musicals, *Old Man Rhythm* and *To*

Beat the Band, but to appear on-screen in supporting roles in both pictures. Alas, he was no more successful on-screen than on-stage, but an occasional telecast of the movies reveals a charming, unpretentious performer, who might have been developed, had anyone at the studio cared to pay attention.

Once on the Coast, Johnny's song writing truly began to flourish. He even wrote one song "I'm Building Up to a Awful Let-Down," with Fred Astaire. Although this was simply a popular song, numerous references proclaim that Astaire sang it in a movie called *Fools Rush In*, often dating a picture that was never conceived nor made as 1934, two years prior to the song's composition. It was, in fact, interpolated into a British stage show, *Rise and Shine* (May 7, 1936, Drury Lane).

The studios really took notice, when Bing Crosby added, "I'm an Old Cowhand" (both music and lyrics by Mercer) to *Rhythm on the Range* (Paramount, 1936). Johnny was given a creative haven at Warner Bros. during the height of the musical film craze. In 1937, with Richard A. Whiting, he wrote the words for *Ready, Willing and Able*, in which Ruby Keeler and Lee Dixon danced on the keys of a giant typewriter to the tune of "Too Marvelous for Words"; *Hollywood Hotel*, with Johnny "Scat" Davis and the entire Benny Goodman band introducing "Hooray for Hollywood"; and *Varsity Show*, in which Dick Powell warbled "Have You Got Any Castles, Baby?," "We're Working Our Way through College," and "Love Is on the Air Tonight."

In 1938, Mercer and Whiting gave us "Ride Tenderfoot Ride" in *Cowboy from Brooklyn*; and, with Harry Warren, Johnny wrote "The Girl Friend of the Whirling Dervish" for *Garden on the Moon*; "Jeepers Creepers," introduced by Louis Armstrong in *Going Places*; and "You Must Have Been a Beautiful Baby" for Dick Powell in *Hard to Get*. Meanwhile, a flood of individual songs flowed unabated: "Bob White" with Bernie Hanighen, "And the Angels Sing" with Ziggy Elman, and "Day In–Day Out" with Rube Bloom, among the many.

There was a short-lived Broadway show, *Walk with Music* (June 4, 1940, Ethel Barrymore), with tunes by Carmichael, and back to Hollywood to a new collaborator, Jimmy McHugh, for *You'll Find Out* and *You're the One*. Paramount's *Second Chorus* gave Fred Astaire "Love of My Life" with music by co-star Artie Shaw.

Although Johnny had written one song ("Satan's Little Lamb") back in 1932 with that master of melody, Harold Arlen, their true collaboration began with the 1941 Warner Bros. score to *Blues in the Night*, with its haunting title song, which was nominated for an Oscar and was considered a sure thing. Instead, the award went to Jerome Kern and Oscar Hammerstein's "The Last Time I Saw Paris," which was already an established hit before being added to the score of *Lady Be Good*. Both Kern and Hammerstein apologized to Arlen and Mercer, and the shock waves caused the Academy to clarify its eligibility requirements, that to be nominated a song had to be written expressly for a particular picture.

Johnny and Victor Schertzinger had three big hits in Paramount's *The Fleet's In* (1941): "Arthur Murray Taught Me Dancing in a Hurry," "I Remember You," and "Tangerine." However, the true benefaction of working at Paramount was the developing friendship between Johnny and the studio's head of production, B. G. "Buddy" DeSylva, formerly one-third of the famous song writing team DeSylva, Brown and Henderson. With an electronics whiz named Glenn Wallichs, Mercer and DeSylva decided to found a brand new record label, just as the war was beginning to cause severe shortage in the shellac required to press records.

Undeterred, the trio officially incorporated Capitol Records on April 9, 1942, its name the brain child of Ginger Mercer. At once, Johnny began to engage the best artists he could find, who were not already signed to the big three labels. The first roster sported Paul Whiteman, perky Ella Mae Morse, the lovely Margaret Whiting, daughter of Johnny's collaborator Richard A. Whiting, and, of course, Johnny Mercer himself. With Crosby then reigning at Decca and Sinatra at Columbia, Johnny more than held his own at Capitol. His sides alone helped the baby grow into a giant in no more than five short years. Although the world today celebrates Mercer as a composer and lyricist, one must not forget that throughout the 1940's, he was one of the most popular singers in the nation.

With Capitol and his recording career thriving, Johnny plunged into a writing frenzy that gave us "Dearly Beloved," "I'm Old Fashioned," and the title song from *You Were Never Lovelier* (music by Kern); "That Old Black Magic" and "Hit the Road to Dreamland" from *Star Spangled Rhythm*; "One For My Baby" from *The Sky's the Limit*, and "Ac-Cent-Tchu-Ate the Positive" and "Let's Take the Long Way Home" from *Here Come the Waves* (the three scores by Arlen); and "On the Atcheson, Topeka and the Santa Fe" from *The Harvey Girls* (Warren). Johnny's pop songs include "G.I. Jive" and "Dream" to his own music, and "Trav'lin' Light", composed by Jimmy Mundy and Trummy Young. Johnny also added words to David Raksin's love theme from *Laura* and, with Carmichael, helped to establish Lauren Bacall's screen persona with "How Little We Know" in *To Have and Have Not*, her first film.

Mercer and Arlen returned to Broadway with the rapturously beautiful score to *St. Louis Woman* (March 30, 1946, Martin Beck), which gave the world "Come Rain Or Come Shine," "Any Place I Hang My Hat Is Home," "I Wonder What Became of Me," and, for the Broadway debut of Peral Bailey, "Legalize My Name." The show ran a mere 113 performances.

With composer Robert Emmett Dolan, Johnny was no more successful with *Texas, Li'l Darlin'* (November 25, 1949, Mark Hellinger). Johnny once admitted to me that he always felt that he was not really suited to write for theatre, because he tended to think of lyrics as little poems that were complete in themselves, rather than devices to help further overall story lines. In that regard, he particularly admired Alan Jay Lerner and Oscar Hammerstein II.

The very qualities that he claimed to lack began to surface in his next show, *Top Banana* (November 1, 1951, Winter Garden), a spoof of Milton "Mr. Television" Berle, starring Phil Silvers as a megalomaniacal TV variety-show star. Although not one hit emerged from a score composed and written by Mercer, there was a clear sense that he was attempting to use songs to establish and advance scenes.

A mere five years later, with *Li'l Abner* (November 15, 1956, St. James, music by Gene de Paul), Johnny drew from his southern roots to bring the looney town of Al Capp's Dogpatch deliciously to life. With *Saratoga* (December 7, 1959, Winter Garden, Arlen), *Foxy* (February 16, 1964, Ziegfeld, Dolan), and London's *The Good Companions* (July 11, 1974, Her Majesty's, Andre Previn), Johnny fully embraced the challenge of writing words for characters and situations. Ironically, not one hit song emerged from any of these scores.

That is true also of Stanley Donen's *Seven Brides for Seven Brothers* (M-G-M, 1954) although there is no finer example of Mercer as lyrical storyteller. With a lusty score by Gene de Paul, the songs are finely woven into the story line, help to establish character, and provide Michael Kidd's athletic choreography with spirited and exuberant support. The film is a gem.

In general, however, it was with individual songs, honed to their brilliance, that Johnny's words shone: "In the Cool, Cool, Cool of the Evening," "Glow Worm," "Early Autumn," "Something's Gotta Give," "Satin Doll," "Days of Wine and Roses," and "Moon River," among the best of this period.

Johnny Mercer died in Los Angeles on June 25, 1976, following an operation for a brain tumor. Yip Harburg called him "the greatest of the folk poets." Irving Berlin called him "a great song writer and a wonderful person too." I called him "friend" and miss him dearly.

—Miles Kreuger

MERCER ON MERCER
(WITH A LITTLE HELP FROM HIS FRIENDS)

One day, in fifty, a hundred years' time, the words of Porter, Hart, Wodehouse, Gershwin, Coward,
maybe a few of my own, will be published, recited, analyzed, codified. —JOHNNY MERCER

Music is a life enhancer, like a growing thing. There is no death in it. It is full of life, and the more perfect it is, the more life-giving, the more warming, the more comforting it becomes.

A song is born in excitement, has a robust life climbing the popularity charts and traveling to the ends of the earth, and then, like rare old wine, brings back nothing but sweet memories. And even if the memories are bittersweet, a song takes you back to a time when you were younger, stronger, and the blood was coursing through your veins, the sun seemed to shine brighter, the nights were cooler, and the girls softer and rounder and made to fit in your arm as the music played.

To paint a portrait of Johnny Mercer and his approach to his music, I've drawn on his unpublished 1969 autobiography and on the words of his peers.

Oscar Hammerstein II considered him "the greatest American lyricist alive." He said he could "no more write a lyric like one of his than fly. It's so American."

Hoagy Carmichael refined the definition. "It's home stuff. It sounds like the South . . . like any other place we used to know."

E. Y. "Yip" Harburg—an early mentor—felt that Mercer had "the descriptive flair of a Mark Twain, and the melodies of Stephen Foster seem to be a part of him."

Critic and songwriter Alec Wilder was perhaps the most succinct. "Larry Hart," he concluded, "was an 'indoor writer,' while Mercer was an 'outdoor writer' . . . images of Georgia inhabit all his work."

And indeed, he became the lyrical embodiment of the old phrase. He lived his life "with the South in his mouth."

We lived in the country in the summer. The roads were still unpaved, made of crushed oyster shell, and they wound their way under the trees covered with Spanish moss. It was a sweet, indolent background for a boy to grow up in. Savannah was smaller then and sleepy, full of trees and azaleas . . .

Out on the starlit veranda, I would lie in the hammock and, lulled by the night sounds, the cricket sounds, safe in the buzz of grown-up talk and laughter, or the sounds of far-off singing . . .

Top: *Johnny Mercer with his family, John Jefferson (Jeff), Georgia Amanda (Mandy), and Ginger*
Bottom right: *Ginger and Johnny Mercer*

My eyelids would grow heavy and the Sandman, Japanese or local, was not someone to steal you away but a friend to take you to the "land of dreams" and another day. There to find another glorious adventure to be lived, experienced, and cherished, and—maybe someday—put into a song.

So much has been lost. I miss so many of the old ways, the old days. Maybe it's just being a kid I miss. But I remember Savannah in the old times, and I am overcome by a nostalgia nearly too strong to bear.

Mercer grew up in a South where black and white had learned to coexist, and where there was invariably music—lullabies, work songs, church songs.

I can hardly ever remember there not being music, in town or out. My aunt Hattie swears I hummed back at her at the tender age of six months.

I used to listen with awe and wonder to every kind of music I could get my hands on. Gypsy airs on the accordion or zither, harmonica blues, gems from Broadway, the yodels of Jimmy Rodgers, cowboy songs from the prairies, all reached my ears and touched my heart. Never a more sympathetic listener could they find. I was open, impartial, loving anything that had any kind of story or pleasing air.

Not surprisingly, then, Mercer's later and authentic evocations of those places and times of childhood would stand out from what would become a deluge of sentimental songs extolling "Mammy" and the delights of "Dixie," written, in the words of critic Sidney Carroll, by men "hiking over to Lindy's and ordering some canned cornpone with their lox . . . Their idiom is borrowed or stolen. To these men the South is a place invented by Al Jolson."

One slightly surprising proof of that authenticity came from the Abraham Lincoln Junior Boys' Club of Chicago: "Dear Johnny Mercer: We have taken a vote and are pleased to inform you that you have been voted the most promising young colored singer on the air."

Mercer wrote, "I've still got it somewhere and I treasure it."

Eubie Blake fully endorsed their verdict: "I am an old-timer, and I've seem them all. Ophays, I mean. You are in my estimate the greatest Rhythm Singer of all Ophays I've ever heard."

*   *   *

At the age of six Mercer began singing in the local church choir. By his teens he was listening to every record he could get his hands on, and at the ripe old age of fifteen he felt he was ready to compose his own songs.

His first was called "Sister Susie, Strut Your Stuff."

> Sister Susie, strut your stuff,
> Show those babies you're no bluff.
> Let those fellows see you step,
> Do that dance with lots o' pep.
> Toss your toe—and kick your heel,
> This ain't no Virginia reel.
> Do your walk—and your strut,
> Shake that thing—you know what.
> Ain't she hot, boys?
> That's my gal!
> Sister Susie Brown.

Pilfered it had been, almost in its entirety, but I neither knew nor would have admitted it then. . . .

I believe all creative artists begin by "stealing" from others, possibly even Mozart did. But it's how fast you develop, how high your standards are, and how quickly you find your OWN style that sets you above and apart from your contemporaries.

Nineteen twenty-seven. Eighteen years old and he was ready for New York. Always smitten with one young lady or another, here he found "another girl I was really stuck on . . . New York City!"

Short spells as an actor in bit parts with the Theatre Guild, longer spells looking for jobs and running errands, and even longer ones trying to decide where his future lay—if, indeed, he was meant to *have* a future.

I tried to be a cartoonist and failed. I tried to be an actor and failed. I tried to be a singer and failed. So I just naturally drifted into songwriting.

One evening he and a friend were passing the New Amsterdam Theatre, where Eddie Cantor was starring in *Whoopee*. "I think I'll go in and play him some of my comedy songs," Mercer said.

A couple of nights later, having got the material all neatly written out—no typewriter available—I walked in to the stage door . . . and got on the elevator with a lot of ladies who looked like Aphrodite and were just as naked, during a scene change . . . to Eddie Cantor's dressing room.

The big Broadway star was sitting in his dressing room. . . . His big eyes opened even wider . . . but he seemed little surprised and bade me do my thing. It was a "comedy" song called "Every Time I Shave I Cut My Adam's Apple" and it was not even my title, having been given to me by a friend. Some friend!

Cantor seemed amused at least by the presumption involved. He told Mercer to write at least another half-dozen extra choruses and then send the song to him.

Before the week was over, I had put together about fifteen. But I doubt to this day—as I did then—if they were funny enough for a Broadway star.

Cantor kept in touch with him about the song but never used it. Nonetheless, "his letters actually sustained my determination to be a writer . . . largely due to his encouragement and kindness." (Sadly, these seminal lyrics do not appear to have survived.)

He was beginning to evolve his personal philosophy of writing songs:

There are certain writers who have a great feeling for tunes, no matter where they come from. I think I'm one of them. . . . If I have any gift at all I think it's that I can get the mood of the tune and try to write the words for it. . . . I like it better than writing words first. . . . A melody-less lyric is generally doggerel. I need the melody first to suggest ideas to me. The composer's emotion is his own private business; what I try and do above all is to match the mood. . . . In general, good lyricists are better at hearing the words in music than composers are at hearing the music in words.

When I write alone, I like to get a title first and then find the tune, finishing the lyric at my leisure after the melody is written. This seems the proper sequence to me in the order of their importance: idea first, melody second, and words third.

Just don't write anything below your own intelligence and let the public catch up to you. That way, if you don't compromise . . . you'll never have anything to be ashamed of later. I can't say I am that brave. I've been compromising all my life, I love to have a big hit song, and as long as it seems genuine and honest to me, I'm no snob about its literary quality. Fine, if it has it, but I like "Jeepers Creepers" just as well as "Skylark."

A great lyricist is not necessarily a good music writer. His words will hold up the song, to be sure, but imagine what a Kern tune would have done to it. I escaped that trap long ago. I figured lyric writers were scarce and I concentrated on that. My tunes, while serviceable, were never in the class of Rodgers or Porter, so why not write with men who knew how to really compose?

I simply get to thinking over the song, pondering over it in my mind, and all of a sudden, I get in tune with the Infinite.

I think I absorbed it. I don't think I studied it consciously. . . . I get a lyric idea from anywhere. Maybe from a billboard on the street, or something I read. An idea will hit me and I jot it down. I'm an inside-the-matchcover type of writer.

I'm crazy about songwriters. . . . I can remember being terribly jealous of a few writers when I was a young man, but after I got a few hits of my own, I didn't mind them at all. I've never been jealous, since, of any writer. I love to hear a good song, no matter where it comes from.

When asked about the great moments in a songwriter's life, Mercer answered: "When he first knows that he can write a song, when he gets his first song published, and when he gets his first hit."

No songwriter collaborated with more people than Mercer. Here's what he had to say about a few of those he worked with most regularly.

Oh, sure, I'd studied other people's lyrics. DeSylva, Brown, and Henderson—they had great ideas. Berlin's lyrics—such an economy of words. Cole Porter—such a fund of ideas, such rhyming and style. And Larry Hart was marvelous; he could write beautiful ballads and he'd turn right round and write a funny song. . . . Well, Yip Harburg can do that, too. He can do practically everything.

HARRY WARREN is a professional hit writer. Not everyone is. . . . It's easier writing with them because they don't waste time on obviously inferior tunes. . . . He's probably one of the two or three best popular composers America's ever had. And probably the best movie composer, too.

HOAGY CARMICHAEL . . . Have you ever had a tough teacher whom you appreciated later? That's how it was to write with Hoagy. He is such a gifted lyric writer on his own that I felt intimidated much of the time and tightened up too much to do my best work, but it was always greater later. . . . I considered it a privilege to work with him, still feeling today he is as much responsible for getting me started as anyone in the music business.

RICHARD WHITING had tact to a marked degree, and would go into long, roundabout devices to protect your feelings if he thought a line should be changed. He had a lot of quality, and he was an original. A dear fellow, too, and he was kind of a shy man . . . not at all pushy like a lot of New York writers are.

WALTER DONALDSON was a pip. He'd come to you and say, "Here's a little idea I wish you'd consider working on . . ." And the song would be from 75 to 80 percent finished, words and all. We call him a "rocking chair" writer, because we lyricists had so little to do.

Oh, I loved working with JEROME KERN. He was everybody's favorite composer. Dick Rodgers once said, "There's nobody who hasn't learned from Kern." Little, short man, stood up very straight, took everything very seriously. He was interested in everything that had to do with the project—the scenery, the costumes, the props, everything. That was part of his meticulous craftsmanship. He was the best theatrical writer we've ever had. No seconds. Gershwin and Rodgers are great writers, but Kern's my particular favorite.

HAROLD ARLEN is so sensitive and dear, he reminds me of a violin. He has true empathy and is just as sensitive to music as he is to people. . . . One of our most original composers, he combines his religious background and his experience and feeling for jazz to bring us the most unique music in a long time.

Arlen himself would write, "Our working habits were strange. After we got a script and the posts for the songs were blocked out, we'd get together for an hour or so every day. While Johnny made himself comfortable on the couch, I'd play the tunes for him. He has a wonderfully retentive memory. After I would finish playing the songs, he'd just go away without a comment. I wouldn't hear from him for a couple of weeks, then he'd come around with the completed lyric."

It was this air of abstraction that had Harry Warren christen Mercer "Cloud Boy."

I'd go over to write with CARL SIGMAN, where his little, round, attractive mother would fill me up with blintzes or chopped liver on rye bread. I wished I could have laid some turnip greens or artichoke pickles or divinity fudge on her—but I doubt if she would have dug my Southern reciprocity half as much as I did the smoked sturgeon.

BILLY ROSE was one of the most alert entrepreneurs about new talent. He spotted a couplet of mine in a comedy song, and asked me to write some for his two revues. Little matter that we disagreed over what was funny. I was trying, learning, and being recognized gradually.

JIMMY McHUGH, bless his heart, was an indefatigable worker but at times he drove me up the wall with his method of working. I'd come into the office at the studio and maybe I'd say, "Mornin', Jim, how's it goin?" and he'd start tinkling away on the treble, echoing "Mornin', Jim, how's it going?" to a dozen strains until I thought I'd go daffy. There was no way to break the spell, either, or if you said "I guess I'll go to the men's room" he'd switch to that theme and we'd be going to the men's room for a half hour in waltz time, rhumba, and fox trot. Lunch was the same. That just happened to be his way of working with me, and if it was his way with others, who is to say him nay with all those marvelous melodies that came from his piano?

RUBE BLOOM stutters, sometimes quite painfully for him, but never when he sings, and it was a pleasure to give him a lyric he liked, because not only would his eyes light up, but he would completely forget the impediment while he sang the song over and over like a caress. It was also gratifying to know he liked it because of his superior education and the fact that he is a stickler for correctness in all words, spelling, grammar, information, and syntax. He can be almost a nuisance about it, but not to me, and it is kind of a game with us—for me to not let him catch me in an error.

JOHNNY BURKE was even worse about this. He was a lyric

writer, of course, but he was so particular about it that he could be a real pain in the ass. Poetry, okay. Pedantics, no.

JIMMY VAN HEUSEN is a most gifted composer. Easy to write with. He seems to have a series of chords waiting at his command to which he can fashion a melody the moment his lyricist springs any idea on him. All of the highest quality.

Although the collaboration of HANK MANCINI and me was pretty much of a happenstance, it proved to be a happy one, and his great tunes have kept this old-timer going a little bit longer. I called him one day when I heard a melody he had titled "Joanna." He agreed to let me write a lyric, and though that song achieved no success, it was just about this time that he needed a lyric for a melody he had written for *Breakfast at Tiffany's*. Hank is a disciplined workman, and our big songs together are melodically and harmonically hard to beat, as all his contemporaries agree.

As far as his own ambition was concerned:

I was trying to be as witty as Larry Hart, as sophisticated as Cole Porter, as simple as Irving Berlin, as poetic as Oscar Hammerstein.

In the eyes and ears of some very significant competitors, he obviously succeeded. Irving Berlin wrote: "Johnny Mercer is a great, great songwriter. He's not just a lyricist, he's a songwriter, and there's a big difference. . . . He has a great feel for words. He always knows where to put the right words—sort of like a minister or priest or rabbi who's going to perform the marriage ceremony. He had a good education and so he's literate enough to know all those six- and seven-syllable words, but he's smart enough to know when not to use them. He feels things very deeply—as a matter of fact, he's very sentimental and knows how to use tender corn; there's nothing wrong with good corn, believe me."

People wonder why I haven't written more for the theatre. Having gotten my first published song in a show (*Garrick Gaieties*), so do I. Perhaps it's because in the day-to-day competition of popular songwriting, we have to make continual compromises to the public taste. Give 'em what they want, not too literate, not too diffuse, hardly any satire, etc., etc. Well, that is the exact opposite of writing for the stage, where you should be as literate, as original, and as amusingly theatrical as you can be. If you are a lyric

writer, it is almost a must. I am inclined to make every song, no matter how incidental, fit for popular consumption. . . . Maybe I ought to go off-Broadway . . . like, a couple of thousand miles or so . . . back to Savannah, maybe?

The first complete show score I worked on—*Walk with Music* (with Hoagy Carmichael)—was enough to discourage any writer from trying another. We went from city to city, changing casts, writing new songs, putting in new routines—all to no avail. . . . It was a nice, ineffectual show, out of date and just not vital enough to stand up to *Pal Joey* and the music that was being written then. "Corny" is the word we would have used then—but not Hoagy's tunes. They were ahead of their time, as usual.

His overall verdict? "I'm just not a good show writer."

In analyzing the body of his work, two things become apparent. His best lyrics seem to come from his own emotions and experiences. He is "playing himself" and talking to his audience personally. When he turned to expressing what a particular character was feeling at a dramatic point in a musical, he became self-conscious. *He* was not that person. Then, he writes as much about "love songs" as about love itself. The form of words, the *language* of love is what interests him most.

Everyday words interested him most of all—the language of current speech. He could find poetry in the most ordinary of American words. He was "a timely rhymer," and, as someone once said, he was "spectacular in the vernacular." And being a Southern boy, of course, he never met a "g" he couldn't drop.

Regrets? Certainly he had a few but not too many.

I would have liked to write a hit Broadway show and a hit Christmas song. . . . I would have liked very much to have become more fluent in the techniques of music, so that I could have written more tunes on my own.

John Herndon Mercer (1909–1976) lies in the family plot in Savannah. The headstone on his grave bears the legend:

"And the Angels Sing"
June 25th, 1976

—BARRY DAY

Introduction

I had the privilege of meeting Johnny Mercer twice. The first time I was all of six years old and had no idea who he was. His daughter Amanda (of "Mandy Is Two" fame) was my classmate at the Work and Play School on Manhattan's West Eighty-second Street. We were putting on a class play, and our teacher told us we "better be good" because the man who wrote the then popular "On the Atchison, Topeka, and the Santa Fe" was coming to see us perform the next day. We were all very nervous—but Mr. Mercer turned out to be just another dad who offered us compliments.

By the time I met Johnny Mercer again, his renown was far greater—and, as a musical-theatre historian by then, I knew who he was and his accomplishments as a lyricist and composer. It was early 1972 and several of us, including Johnny, who was a friend of someone in the group, went to the movies to see a Fred Astaire double feature of *Flying Down to Rio* and Johnny's film *The Sky's the Limit*.

After the movie, Johnny told me that he hadn't seen *The Sky's the Limit* (for which he had written wonderful lyrics, among them "One for My Baby" and "My Shining Hour") in almost thirty years. He was gracious and congenial. To my regret, I never saw him again. Four years later he was dead.

I wish I could have foreseen back in 1972 that one day I would be co-editing this book. Compiling Mercer's lyrics has presented its share of challenges, not necessarily unique but unusually daunting compared to the ones I faced working on the earlier volumes in Knopf's Complete Lyrics series. So there are, in retrospect, many questions I would have liked Mercer to answer.

Given the obstacles my collaborators and I encountered trying to organize Mercer's work chronologically, I certainly would have asked him if he remembered when he actually wrote a lot of his lyrics; as we discovered, Mercer did not date many of them, particularly those we found in typescript form. We made educated guesses about the chronology of some of the material but—as I discuss later—in perhaps two hundred cases we could not pin down even an approximate date.

Thinking about *Blues Opera* (also known as *Free and Easy*), a 1959 quasi-operatic reincarnation of Harold Arlen and Mercer's 1946 Broadway musical *St. Louis Woman*, I would have wanted to know from Mercer if it was true that he had almost nothing to do with that later version. Since Mercer's participation in *Blues Opera* is unclear, we—the editors—decided to include only the three lyrics we felt confident might have been intended by him for the project.

And what about the many lyrics of his that appear on lists of his songs under more than one title? Despite cross-referencing and some "eureka" moments that helped us resolve the confusion about numerous duplicate entries, it was still difficult to determine the ultimate title of some songs, precisely how many lyrics Mercer wrote, and how many of them, other than the ones indicated in this volume, are actually missing.

Most of all, I would have wanted to ask Mercer about all those collaborators. Why were there so many? We have tallied well over two hundred—more, to my knowledge, than those of any other major American songwriter. We can only speculate now what prompted Mercer to team up with such a large number of co-writers, often for only one song. Was he restless? Was he lonely and longing for companionship? Perhaps he simply could not resist setting words to a melody he liked. Or was writing lyrics an essential part of his being, even though, as evidenced by drafts of his work, he often had to toil at finding just the right word or phrase to make an impact or express the feeling he wanted to capture?

In fact, Mercer's productivity and his generosity as a colleague were legendary, and, as he knew, many people called him the "lyrics boy." One has the sense that almost anyone with an idea for a song who walked into Mercer's office at Capitol Records or met him somewhere else walked away with a song completed by Johnny Mercer.

In his unpublished autobiography, Mercer casually recalls some of the encounters that led to songs bearing his name. He mentions, for example, how early in his career he met "Al Opler, who walked in one day and whistled a waltz that he needed a lyric for. . . . When I had finished 'While We Danced at the Mardi Gras,' he took it from there." That seems to have been pretty typical of many of Mercer's collaborations.

Elsewhere in his autobiography, he tells the story of "Lost."

One of the more prominent publishers [in Hollywood] at the time was Jack Robbins . . . and nothing pleased him more than to

pub crawl late at night and find some undiscovered tune or singer. He used to like me to go around with him as I was young and interested, coupled with the fact that I would be there in case he needed a fast lyric. [Robbins] heard Phil Ohman playing [a tune] at the Trocadero, learned that it had been written by Ohman and Macy O. Teetor of the Perfect Circle piston ring company when Ohman was sponsored by them on a radio show. It had no lyric, however, so Jack and I dropped by the Troc as one stop on his rounds and, between sets, we went down to the basement and I wrote the lyric to what became the song "Lost."

Recently, songwriter Michael Shanklin described the writing of "El Camino," a 1972 collaboration with Mercer. "My office was downstairs from Mr. Mercer's firm Commander," Shanklin, who was twenty-six at the time, remembers. "One morning he came to my office to listen to a melody I had written. He was holding my cassette of the song, which Marshall Robbins, his administrator, had sent him the previous week. I was shaking from head to foot but managed to hit most of the chords—I think. Mr. Mercer said he liked it and would be pleased to write a lyric for the tune. On his way out he turned to me and said, 'It's good to know who you're getting into bed with.' Six months later I received a phone call from him telling me the lyric was finished. I met him that Sunday morning in his office. There he stood beneath a handsome white straw hat, a true Southern gentleman. In his old Royal typewriter was the lyric titled 'El Camino.' He added a few more words to the song. It was, at last, complete."

Even without his straw hat, Johnny Mercer was a true poet of the South; yet in many ways he was the most quintessentially American of all our songwriters. His range of subjects and moods was awesome, his imagination remarkable. His words evoked summer nights, lives lived at a leisurely pace, images of nature and the natural world that frequently bring to mind Southern landscapes. But he also wrote about giddy college days (even though he never went to college because of the failure of his father's business), angels, trains, dance pavilions, and, often, lost and remembered love. His lyrics were passionate, witty, and colloquial if called for; when nostalgic about the past, they were rarely saccharine. In addition to being an acclaimed lyricist, Mercer was a composer—roughly fifteen percent of his songs had music he wrote himself; on a few occasions he even set other lyricists' words to music. His exceptional achievements included co-founding both Capitol Records and the Songwriters Hall of Fame. And he is the only major songwriter of his era to have a successful career as a singer.

There are more than 1,200 titles in this compilation. To the extent possible, they are arranged chronologically and grouped according to the production—show or film—for which Mercer wrote them. Several hundred are one-off or independent songs, and they too appear chronologically whenever possible. Songs not registered for copyright proved almost impossible to date, since Mercer did not date his lyrics. Hence, there are two large miscellaneous chapters in this book. The first is devoted to early songs of 1930–1932, when Mercer used the name John—rather than Johnny. Toward the end of this book is an even larger miscellaneous section covering the rest of his career. Both sections are arranged alphabetically. Some lyrics we found were too fragmentary to publish.

Each Johnny Mercer show or movie is introduced with information on that production, including creative credits, cast lists, length of run, tryout and tour dates for shows, and release dates for films; the lyrics are prefaced with head notes that give the publication date or the date on which the work was first registered for copyright as an unpublished song, alternate or earlier titles, the names of the artists who introduced the song, and notable recordings. We have also indicated if the music for a lyric is not known to survive. Much of the same information is provided for independent or non-production songs, although for many numbers in this category details are often lacking.

The sources for the lyrics in this compilation are sheet music and piano-vocal scores, show scripts, typed lyric sheets, manuscripts, and sound recordings preserved in the Johnny Mercer archives maintained by the Georgia State University Library in Atlanta in its Special Collections and Archives. Other important sources were the Copyright and Music Divisions of the Library of Congress in Washington, D.C; the Shubert Archive, the Tams-Witmark Library, and the Library for the Performing Arts at Lincoln Center, in New York City; and the Production Files at the Film Academy in Los Angeles.

Mercer material has proved frustratingly hard to track down. While it was disappointing to reach our deadline and realize that there were still lyrics unaccounted for, we could not have assembled as much as we did without the help of several generous and dedicated individuals. They include Michael Feinstein, Steve Taksler, Donald Stubblebine, Max Morath, Ellen Donaldson, Howard Green, Mark Horowitz of the Music Division of the Library of Congress, and, especially, Kevin Fleming of the Georgia State University Library. We extend our profound gratitude to them.

—Robert Kimball

Acknowledgments

In addition to the people thanked in the Introduction, there are many who assisted the editors in the gathering of material for this huge volume. They include Margaret Whiting, who wanted this book for Johnny and patiently awaited its presentation; Joseph Harris, who led the support for the book by the Johnny Mercer Foundation; and the Foundation itself, whose generosity made the book possible.

A number of people found lyrics and shared them with us, including Alan Bergman, Ned Comstock, Robert Emmett Dolan II, Ellen Donaldson, Michael Feinstein, Kevin Fleming of Georgia State University, Aaron Gandy, Richard Harpham of the Harry Warren Archives, Mark Horowitz of the Music Division of the Library of Congress, Rod McKuen, Max Morath, André Previn, Daryl Sherman, Dave Stein of the Kurt Weill Foundation, Donald Stubblebine, Steven Suskin, Stephen N. Taksler, and Caroline Underwood and Claire Osborne of Warner/Chappell.

Thanks to Rosalind Fayne and Caroline Shookhoff for their typing of the manuscript; to Maryann Chach of the Shubert Archive, Jill Packard of the Henry Mancini Enterprises, Geraldine Duclow of the Free Library of Philadelphia, Alan Pally of the Lincoln Center Library for the Performing Arts, and Ron Mandelbaum of Photofest; and to Alvin Deutsch and Jessica Chavkin for obtaining song copyrights and permissions.

We are grateful to those whose books on Johnny Mercer helped light the way for us: Ginger Mercer and Bob Bach for *Our Huckleberry Friend*, Philip Furia for *Skylark*, and Gene Lees for *Portrait of Johnny*; and to Amy Asch, Ken Bloom, Amanda Brown, Lynne Carey Day, the late Blossom Dearie, Will Friedwald, Dick Hyman, Susan Elliott, Herbert G. Goldman, Miranda and Philip Kimball, the late Robert Lissauer, Robert Marks, John Marshall, Richard Norton, Frank Scardino, Michael Shanklin, Charles Tigerman, Joel Whilburn, and the late Jack Wrangler.

We thank others who helped us track down or provided information about Mercer collaborators: Ronald A. Arntz, Louis Diringer, Laurie Fondiler, Gary Giddins, Anthony Gribin, Vern Hansen, Don and Ulla Iavello, Jane Klain, Ashley Locke, Karen Minard, Jim Price, Becky Reed, Andrew Robbins, Edgar Sachs, Stephen Sachs, Ken Samuels, David Sanjek, David Sherr, Ingrid Spiegl, Susan Szilega, André Thomas, Terry Trepper, and especially Jim Steinblatt of ASCAP.

Special thanks to Abigail Kimball, who prepared the index, chronicled Johnny Mercer's many collaborators, and compiled the biographical information about them, and whose editorial experience and perseverance were invaluable to the completion of the book.

Finally, our gratitude to our friends and colleagues at Alfred A. Knopf, who translated our large, often unwieldy manuscript into a book: our editors Katherine Hourigan and Robert Gottlieb, publisher Sonny Mehta, and their cohorts, Kevin Bourke, Jessica Freeman-Slade, Roméo Enriquez, Soonyoung Kwon, Carol Devine Carson, Kathryn Zuckerman, and Patrick Dillon.

—ROBERT KIMBALL AND BARRY DAY,
ON THE EAST COAST

On the West Coast, our primary responsibility was to document Johnny Mercer's contribution to more than ninety motion pictures and to his early attempts to write for musical theatre, almost invariably for shows that closed before reaching Broadway, or were intended for regional houses.

For Johnny's work on the short-lived Boston revue *Tattle Tales*, we were helped by Diane O. Ota, Susan Glover, and Mary Beth Dunhouse at the Boston Public Library, and Rick Wilson at Harvard's Pusey Library. In researching *The Pajama Lady*, we learned about its German source, *Das Gespensterschiff*, from Stefan Kloo at Goethe-Institut Los Angeles, Katherine Lorimer at Goethe-Institut New York, and Brigitte Klein at the University of Frankfurt in Germany. Information about the failed play *The Phantom Ship*, based on the German work and the source for Mercer's *The Pajama Lady*, was supplied by Robert Stewart and Rita Hoffman at the Asbury Park (New Jersey) Public Library; Tom Gilmore of the Asbury Park City Office; Ingrid Bruck, Rudy Primavera, Beatrice Priestly, Jane Birckhead, and Chris Crowder at the Long Branch (New Jersey) Free Public Library; and Tom LaSalle at the Ferguson Library in Stamford, Connecticut.

We received great help on *Paris in Spring* from William B. Secrest Sr. and Jr. at the Fresno (California) County Public Library, Kirsten Tanaka at the San Franscisco Performing Arts Library and Museum, and Eileen King at the Los Angeles Public Library. Gloria Fernandi, Gina Joyce, and Julia de Rosa were all vocal students of the great Cuban diva Carolina Segrera, who starred in *Paris in Spring*.

Patricia Ward Kelly gave us a program for the summer stock revue *Two Weeks with Pay*, choreographed by her husband, Gene Kelly; Hugh Martin remembered working with Johnny on *Three After Three*. Others who shared their reminiscences were the late Fayard Nicholas (*St. Louis Woman*), Rose Marie (*Top Banana*), Charlotte Rae, Julie Newmar, Hope Holiday, the late Edie Adams and (from the film version) Stella Stevens (*Li'l Abner*), and Carol Lawrence, who starred in *Saratoga*, and Ralph Beaumont, who staged its dances.

From Johnny's films, Grace Bradley Boyd recalled *Old Man Rhythm*, and Bill Carey's son Robert showed us his father's scrapbooks. Sally Sweetland talked about giving voice to "My Shining Hour" in *The Sky's the Limit*. For the elusive *The Keystone Girl*, Mark Horowitz at the Library of Congress, Norman Brokaw and Samuel "Biff" Liff at the William Morris Agency, and A. C. Lyles at Paramount all hunted in vain for a screenplay. Howard Greenberg, Charlotte Hall, and Nancy Kunzman at the *Orlando Sentinel* chronicled the premiere of *Johnny Tiger*; and information about *Red Sky at Morning* was supplied by its composer, Billy Goldenberg, and Zoran Sinobad at the Library of Congress. Dave Smith and Ed Ovalle at the Disney archives filled in data about *Robin Hood*.

Herbert G. Goldman, Broadway's most exacting chronicler, traced the tours and other details about all of Johnny's stage shows, including his early, obscure ventures. Leonard and Alice Maltin opened many doors; and Peter Muldavin, the "Kiddie Rekord King," determined that Johnny wrote even for Capitol children's records.

This project could never have been completed were it not for the boundless support and kindness of Howard Green, a dedicated admirer of Johnny Mercer, who supplied prints of all the Mercer films not commercially available; and the great film collector Marvin Eisenman, known to one and all as "Marvin of the Movies." Michael Feinstein, Randy Skretvedt, and Michael Cuscuna, co-founder of Mosaic Records, generously donated many rare Mercer recordings.

Others who helped in many ways include Robert Bader, Lance Bowling, Jelani Bronson, Ray Charles and his son Jon, John Cork, Karen Culbertson and Susan Clore at the William H. White, Jr., Library, Woodberry Forest School, Ellen Donaldson, Shon Encinas, Susanna Erdos, Corky Hale and Mike Stoller, Avie Hern, Huston Huddleston, Jenny, Michael Kerker at ASCAP, Stephen Krentzman, Sandra Joy Lee, and Jonathon Auxier at the USC Warner Bros. Archives, Rachel Lopez, Scott McIsaac, Gregory Powers, Rob Ray, Ranjit Sandhu, Alex Teslik, Gerald Turbow, Marc Wanamaker, Hollywood's most erudite historian, and Dan Wingate.

Special thanks to Mark Heimback-Nielsen, whose scholarly knowledge of the history of Capitol Records brought that aspect of Johnny's career accurately to life; Steven Lasker, with his vast knowledge of early recording and his generous donation of Johnny's very first record; Patty Hall, who graciously provided a copy of her beautiful biography of Johnny Gruelle, creator of Raggedy Ann, and an early Mercer collaborator; and Robert Alonzo Potter, son of the stage and film director H. C. Potter, who was present when Johnny and Don Raye sang "The H. C. Potter's Ball" at the family home in Beverly Hills. We are profoundly grateful for the gift of Mercer materials that found their way into the book, donated by the late Marshall Robbins, who ran Commander Music for Johnny.

But no list of acknowledgments about film can be complete without a deep bow to that glorious institution, the Margaret Herrick Library of the Academy of Motion Picture Arts and Sciences (the Oscar folks). Helmed by Linda Mehr, the staff is uncommonly knowledgeable and helpful to film researchers from all over the world. Of particular help to us were Barbara Hall, Robert Cushman, Faye Thompson, Jenny Romero, Joe Adamson, Howard Prouty, Lucia Schultz, and Galen Wilkes. Please forgive the omission of any other names, as everyone there was remarkably kind and supportive.

And a word of special thanks to Ned Comstock at the USC Doheny Library. There is possibly no librarian in Los Angeles who has quietly and modestly helped more people conduct their research over the years than Ned, a hero to all of us.

Our thanks to one and all.

—MILES KREUGER AND ERIC DAVIS,
ON THE WEST COAST

Left: *Johnny and Ginger Mercer*
Right: *Mercer and Paul Whiteman, March 1932, as Johnny wins the Whiteman Audition*

OUT OF BREATH (AND SCARED TO DEATH OF YOU)

Music by Everett Miller. Published. Copyrighted June 18, 1930. Mercer's first published song. Introduced by Sterling Holloway and Cynthia Rogers in *The Garrick Gaieties* (1930), a revue produced by the Theatre Guild at the Guild Theatre, New York City (June 4–October 8, 1930). Later sung in a revised version of the show by Holloway and Doris Vinton in a sketch entitled "Two Fraidy Cats at Work." Mercer said of this song that "*The Garrick Gaieties* [was] a fork in the road for me and . . . pointed me in the direction I suppose I had to go—towards Tin Pan Alley."

A version of the song (titled "Out of Breath and Scared to Death"), recorded for Brunswick by Doris Vinton and Sterling Holloway (the first "original cast" recording of a Mercer song), is very different from the published song. It was never released. Vinton and Holloway were in the return engagement of *The Garrick Gaieties* (1930), which was presented October 16–25, 1930.

VERSE 1

HE: When tasks superhuman
Demand such acumen
That only a few men possess,
I never have fear to volunteer.
But though others fear me,
Still when you are near me,
And willing to hear me express
Such childish delight,
I'm filled with fright.
Mine's a hopeless case,
But there's one saving grace—
Anyone would feel as I do:

REFRAIN

Out of breath and scared to death of you.
Love was first divined,
Then explored and defined;
Still the old sensation is new:
Out of breath and scared to death of you.
It takes all the strength that I can call to my
    command
To hold your hand.
I would speak at length
About the love that should be made,
But I'm afraid.
Hercules and such
Never bothered me much;

All you have to do is say "Boo!":
Out of breath and scared to death of you.

VERSE 2

SHE: Well, your revelation
Has been a sensation,
A sweet relaxation for me.
And I'd never guess that you'd confess.
But now you have spoken
And shown as a token
That your spirit's broken for me,
Then I will reveal
The way I feel.
Since you must propose,
Then I'll have to disclose
Secrets that I've hidden from view:

REFRAIN 2

Out of breath and scared to death of you.
When we met, my heart
Gave a queer little start
And the feeling's growing into
Out of breath and scared to death of you.
Always I've been used to having my affections
    spurned
And not returned;
Once my passion's loosed,
Then that's the time to be concerned—
You may be burned.
Think I could be made,
But I'm still so afraid—
Hurry and change my point of view:
Out of breath and scared to death of you!

"Original cast" recorded version

HE: Oh, there's no one who's rougher,
No guy can be tougher,
Make more people suffer than me.
SHE: I'm merely to speak.
Strong men grow weak.
HE: But though others fear me,
The thought doesn't cheer me.
And when you are near me, I see
My Waterloo is met in you.

REFRAIN 1

Oh, mine's a hopeless case,
But there's one saving grace.
Anyone would feel as I do:
I'm out of breath and scared to death of you.

Love was first divine,
Then explored and defined.

Still, the old sensation is new:
I'm out of breath and scared to death of you.

Why, it takes all the strength that I can call to my
    command—
Yes, strength to hold your hand.
I could speak at length about the love that should
    be made,
I'm afraid.

Oh, Hercules and such
Never bothered me much,
But all you have to do is say, "Boo"—
Go ahead and say it.

SHE: "Boo."
HE: See? I'm all out of breath and scared to
    death of you.
SHE: Well, now you listen to me.

REFRAIN 2

Since you must propose
That it's time to disclose
Secrets that I've hidden from view,
I'm out of breath and scared to death of you.
When we met, my heart
Gave a queer little start,
But by now it's turning in two,
Out of breath and scared to death of you.

Always I've been used to having my affections
    spurned,
Never returned.
Once my love is loose and that's the time to be
    concerned,
You may be burned.
Oh, I think I could be made
But I'm still so afraid.
Hurry and change my point of view.
I'm out of breath and scared to death of you.

REFRAIN 3

SHE: With a placid face
I would cut my partner's ace,
Something very few would dare to do,
'Cause I'm out of breath and I'm scared to
    death of you.
HE: As for me I would love to roam
Through an old ladies' home,
Give the girls a new thrill or two,
But I'm out of breath and scared to death
    of you.
SHE: When Delilah found her Samson
boyfriend's affair

She cut his hair.
HE: Though my beauty's crowned with golden
     locks, it drives girls wild;
     The price is mild.
SHE: And if I say all right?
HE: Then I'll stay home every night.
SHE: Every night! Oh no, that wouldn't do,
BOTH: 'Cause I'm out of breath and scared to
     death of you.

ANOTHER CASE OF BLUES

Music by Richard Myers. Published. Copyrighted August 5, 1930. Introduced in *Tattle Tales* (1930), which opened at the Wilbur Theatre, Boston, July 15, 1930, and closed out of town. "More and More," another song Mercer is credited with having written for this show, music by Richard Myers and Fred Astaire, is missing.

VERSE

Love meant beauty to me,
I thought of springtime and joy;
But how wrong one can be,
Thinking that love cannot cloy!
I lost the man I longed for,
Prayed in my dreams to find—
How can anyone know
The utter despair in my mind?

REFRAIN

I'll never stand it
Or countermand it
With people thinking the way they do.
Ev'ryone is saying, "Poor child,
Another case of blues."
They've never known it
Or outgrown it,
So nothing they say
Can change my views.
They'd be just the same if
They had "another case of blues."
One day has swept it away from me,
Fate took a hand from above;
One man has twisted life's plans for me,
Posted a ban on love.
I'm through with sorrow,
And from tomorrow
Each man who meets me is bound to lose.
And I know I'll never fall for
"Another case of blues."

THE PAJAMA LADY (1930)

Tryout: National Theatre, Washington, D.C., October 6–11, 1930; Erlanger Theatre, Philadelphia, October 13–25, 1930. Produced (in association with Erlanger Productions Inc.) and directed by George W. Lederer. Originally titled *The Night Owl*. Book by Harry B. Smith and George W. Lederer. Based on the German play *Gespensterschiff* by Rudolf Lothar and Oskar Ritter, which was adapted into English by Owen Davis as *The Phantom Ship* and which closed out of town in 1926. Music by Philip Charig and Richard Myers. Mercer wrote lyrics to three songs; other lyrics were written by Robert B. Smith. The action took place on the freighter *Aurora*, bound from Halifax to New York.

Members of the cast who sang Mercer's lyrics: Lester Allen (Snaggs), Marian Warring-Manly (Flossie), Tom Fant (Bunker), Billy Lytell (Flam), Johnny Dale (Dave), Barbara Newberry (Barbara), and John Barker (John).

DOWN THROUGH THE AGES

Music by Richard Myers and Philip Charig. Published. Copyrighted October 20, 1930. Introduced by Lester Allen (Snaggs) and Marian Warring-Manly (Flossie).

VERSE 1

FLOSSIE: From my youth I have been leery
         Of the truth in Darwin's theory of life.
         I have shelved all idle fancies,
         Never delved into chimpanzees' love
           life.
         But as you conceive it,
         I can quite believe it—
         Now I know for certain
         What's behind the curtain;
         For I feel I've known you somewhere,
         And since you have shown me from
           where,
         Then, dear, it's clear:

REFRAIN 1

Down through the ages by various stages,
I've been calling for you.
From rat to rabbit, I made it a habit

To keep falling for you.
You were a handsome billy goat, dear,
With whiskers all done in curls.
You certainly got the nanny's vote, dear,
Which made me gloat, dear, to all the girls.
So though not a new love,
It has been a true love,
As the poets would say.
Down through the ages by various stages
Right up until the present day!

VERSE 2

SNAGGS: It's a source of fascination
        Just what course this vast creation went
          by,
        What a man and what his place was
        And what plan the human race was sent
          by.
        Often I evolved it,
        Felt that I had solved it;
        Now I find I've known it—
        Meeting you has shown it.
        And to prove my assertation,
        I will make reincarnation
        Clear now—here's how:

REFRAIN 2

Down through the ages by various stages
I've been falling for you.
From caterpillar to mighty gorilla
I fell sprawling for you.
Then as a prehistoric camel,
You had me trembling on the brink;
My love no rival could entrammel
From early mammal to missing link.
Then rising from part man,
Becoming a smart man,
I encountered your charms,
Down through the ages by various stages
Until I held you in my arms.

ONE, TWO, THREE

Music by Richard Myers and Philip Charig. Published. Copyrighted October 20, 1930. Introduced by Tom Fant (Bunker) and Billy Lytell (Flam).

VERSE

Why worry and curse bad breaks?
My system is sound—

I make a stand against them.
You, too, can disperse bad breaks
Or twist 'em around,
When you have planned against them.
You can cause a shake-up of bad news;
It's not hard to break up the blues—
They're really the worst of fakes.
Start making your stand and take a hand
Against them when I count—

REFRAIN

One, two, three, out you go!
One, two, three, watch me throw
Hard luck right out in the cold.
I'll show him danger here;
We want no stranger here—
Black sheep, keep out of the fold.
Give him the air, give him the air,
He'll go flyin' with one good scare.
Lickety split,
Lickety split,
He'll run if you hit him—
One, two, three, out you go!
One, two, three, you can throw
Hard luck right out in the cold!

THREE GUESSES

Music by Richard Myers and Philip Charig. Published. Copyrighted October 20, 1930. Introduced by Barbara Newberry (Barbara) and John Barker (John).

VERSE 1

DAVE: I'm acting queerly,
      I'm nearly deranged—
      You must have noticed how I have
        changed.
BARBARA: First I am normal,
      Quite formal, and then
      I behave like a youngster often again.
DAVE: Things I do and say to you, what are
        they about?
      You've resigned, for you can't find it
        out.

REFRAIN

Guess what makes me shy,
Guess what makes me sigh,
When you are near me.
Three guesses—and the answer's "I love you."

Guess what makes me meek,
Stutter when I speak,
So you can't hear me.
Three guesses—and the answer's "I love you."
Stories of Bo-Peep counting her sheep I find are
  true.
I count them trying to sleep, then when I do—
I talk of you, dear.
Guess why birdies sing
At the sign of spring;
Then guess why I do.
Three guesses—and the answer's "I love you."

VERSE 2

BARBARA: I may have no sense,
      Seem so dense to you
      In that I can't define things you do.
      But if you're clever, one never would
        know,
      For at defining you're just as slow—
        more so.
      Love is blind—in you I find the proof of
        the fact;
      Can't you see how you make me react?

REPEAT REFRAIN

PARIS IN SPRING (1930)

During the 1920s, Louis O. Macloon and his wife, Lillian Albertson, were the most active theatre producers on the West Coast. When they learned of the success of Emmerich Kálmán's newest operetta, *Das Veilchen vom Montmartre* (*The Violet of Montmartre*, March 21, 1930, Johann Strauss Theatre, Vienna), they went to Europe and acquired the English-language stage, film, and television rights from the composer himself. At Harms, Inc., in New York, they were introduced to twenty-year-old John Mercer, who would work cheaply to adapt the libretto by Julius Brammer and Alfred Grünwald for the American stage.

As *Paris in Spring*, "A Romance of Old Montmartre," the production was announced for a two-day tryout at the White Theatre in Fresno, California, to open Friday, October 31, 1930; but that engagement was canceled at the last minute. Instead, the American premiere took place Monday, November 3, at the Curran in San Francisco, where it closed Saturday, November 22. The cast was headed by Broadway star Allan Prior

and Cuban *prima donna* Carolina Segrera (using the stage name Lilli Segrena). Harms published three songs with lyrics by Mercer and an interpolation composed by Walter Jurmann with English lyrics by Desmond Carter.

It was decided to revise the show in part by trimming the score and almost entirely recasting for its Los Angeles debut on February 26, 1931, at the Hollywood Playhouse. Prior was replaced by California favorite Perry Askam, with Albertson discovery June Sumner as Violetta. Popular comedian Eddie Lambert was added. The production was shifted from Hollywood to the downtown Majestic Theatre on Friday, March 13, where it closed soon after on March 21. Despite good reviews, an elaborate production, and planned moves to Chicago and Broadway, *Paris in Spring* had closed forever.

Mercer recalled: "They wanted someone to write English lyrics—and work cheap. That last qualification is probably what got me the job. Anyway, when offered it, I jumped at the chance. Within a week [I was] on the *Chief* and for most of the three days [to the West Coast] I read the translated script, made a few suggestions, and began searching for titles . . . We finally got the show on both in San Francisco and Los Angeles but I was long gone."

The action takes place in Paris circa 1850.

THE MOON SHINES DOWN

Music by Emmerich Kálmán. Published. Copyrighted March 31, 1931. Introduced in San Francisco by Cuban *prima donna* Carolina Segrera (using the stage name Lilli Segrena) (Violetta), Allan Prior (Paul), Russell Scott (Florimond), and Hal Redus (Henri). Sung in Los Angeles by their replacements in the cast: June Sumner, Perry Askam, Charles Boyle, and Harold Stanton.

VERSE

When you're given cause to grumble,
You see only black despair;
When you see your castles tumble
And life seems unfair,
There's always a consolation
If you want to be consoled:
That things could be worse,
For Fate so perverse
Could add to your worries sevenfold.
Don't let misfortune get the better of you,
There is someone in the world to love you,
And there'll always be a moon above you
That will cheer you along.

REFRAIN

See how the moon shines down
On ev'ry countryside and town.
It shines in spring and fall,
It shines upon us all,
No place can be too small,
On both the rich and poor.
If you are famous or obscure,
No matter where you are,
If you are near or far,
You'll see the moon shine down.

VERSE 2

I have in imagination
Been planning what I can do,
Just how as a new relation
I'll take care of you.
Each day I will cook the dinner,
If there will be one to cook;
I'll do ev'ry task,
Each thing that you ask;
There's nothing I will overlook.
And though we never have a lot of money,
And we never live on milk and honey,
When the skies above are not so sunny
Then just think of my song.

REPEAT REFRAIN

UNTIL WE KISS

Music by Emmerich Kálmán. Published. Copyrighted December 5, 1930. Introduced in San Francisco by Allan Prior (Paul). Sung in Los Angeles by Perry Askam.

VERSE

How do we live till we find love?
What good is life till we've divined love?
We go along never knowing
Or caring by what path we're going,
And how can one understand it
Till he awakens to command it?
Seen through a mist, love is partly concealed;
Then when we're kissed, love is revealed.

REFRAIN

Until we kiss, what can we know
Of love or joy, or of despair?
Until we kiss we see the sky above,

But can't see why it's there.
We hear of happiness that comes to lovers,
And yet it's something that we never miss;
For although life can be ideal,
It can't be real
Until we kiss.

DON'T ASK TOO MUCH OF LOVE

Music by Emmerich Kálmán. Published. Copyrighted December 5, 1930. Introduced by Allan Prior (Paul) and Janice Joyce (Ninon). Sung in Los Angeles by Perry Askam and Janice Joyce.

VERSE 1

If a lady fair should make a vow to you,
Don't allow her to take your heart.
Even though she means to keep her pledge to you,
Fate may cause you to drift apart.
So, if she returns and offers her love anew,
Gladly take the heart she proffers; hold it to you.

REFRAIN

Don't ask too much of love when it smiles on you;
To know the touch of love is all one can do.
For love at best is an illusion,
A short intrusion;
And then no chance repeating
That first meeting,
For that first sweetness never can be retraced,
And its completeness never will be replaced.
Hold it, then let it go by;
Don't ever seek to know why,
Don't ever ask too much of love.

VERSE 2

Weak are all men where a lady fair's concerned,
Whether loved or spurned in the end.
What's the diff'rence even though the lady lies?
We will close our eyes and pretend;
We imagine love as something always to last.
When it leaves, we go on living in our past days.

REPEAT REFRAIN

BEYOND THE MOON

Lyrics by Johnny Gruelle and Mercer. (Gruelle was the author of the Raggedy Ann and Raggedy Andy series of children's books.) Music by Gay Stephens. Published. Copyrighted March 3, 1931.

VERSE 1

Beckoning in the night
There is a distant light
Calling to you,
Calling to me,
To the great spirit land.
We will go hand in hand;
There we'll find our daydreams,
The night of love we've planned.

REFRAIN 1

Beyond the moon
I'll sail with hope,
Where dreams come true,
Beyond the moon.
Our fire will gleam
Some night in June
Beside a stream,
Beyond the moon.
Where the moon flower breathes its fragrance
From across a blue lagoon,
We'll climb the skies
To find that soon;
Our sun will rise
Beyond the moon.

VERSE 2

Traveling high and far,
Passing each fading star,
There, high above,
We'll find our love,
Drifting through cloudland's veil,
Out on the rainbow trail,
As the prairie campfires
Glimmer and grow pale.

REPEAT REFRAIN

WHILE WE DANCED AT THE MARDI GRAS

Music by Alfred Opler. Published. Copyrighted December 5, 1931. Alternate title: "Mardi Gras."

VERSE

Romantic, carefree, splendid night,
A gay and glad pretended night,
A magic moon above lighting the way
To our magic love.
I begged for just one dance with you;
Instead I found romance with you.
I should have known not to trust that waltz;
Was it a real love
Or just that waltz?

REFRAIN

While we danced
As we dreamed
At the Mardi Gras,
Was romance
What it seemed
At the Mardi Gras?
Was the love that we made
Just a brief masquerade?
Was it gone with the song
That the orchestra played?
With a sigh,
With a glance
At the moon above,
Was it just by chance
We spoke of love?
Or did you somehow feel
That the wonder was real
While we danced
At the Mardi Gras?

HOW HAPPY IS THE BRIDE

Lyrics by Harold Adamson and Mercer. Music by Vincent Youmans. Written in late 1931 for the musical *Through the Years* which had a brief New York run at the Manhattan Theatre, January 28–February 13, 1932. There are two slightly different versions of this lyric. Not used in show; replaced by a lyric by Edward Heyman with the same title. Earlier title: "Happy as a Bride."

VERSION 1

How happy is the bride
Who takes her wedding vow at eventide,
When day is through!
How lucky is the love
Blessed by the evening star that shines above,
How deep, how true!
What sunshine lies in her smile, revealing joy
As all the while
The moon looks down to light the scene
Where love will crown—ah!
How happy is the bride!
Hear voices ring through all the countryside,
"Moonyean—Moonyean and John!"

VERSION 2

How happy is the bride
Who takes her wedding vow at eventide,
When day is through!
How lucky is the love
Blessed by the stars that twinkle up above,
How deep, how true!
What tender sunshine lies in her smile,
Revealing joy as all the while
The moon looks down to light the scene
Where love will crown another queen.
How happy is the bride!
Hear voices ring through all the countryside,
"Moonyean—Moonyean!"

The year 1932 saw Mercer publish seventeen songs with eleven different composer collaborators—a pattern that foreshadowed the rest of his career.

At the end of the year he would write to his mother that two of them—"Spring Is in My Heart" and "Little Old Crossroad Store"—"look like hits. And, of course, if they are, it won't hurt at all."

SWEET LITTLE LADY NEXT DOOR

Music by Alfred Opler. Published. Copyrighted January 16, 1932.

VERSE

Love is here,
Love is there,
Love is around ev'rywhere;
Though you're a prince or a pauper,
You're bound to get your share.
I am poor,
To be sure,
But do you think that I care?
Love makes my cottage
Look like a castle—
Love makes me a millionaire!

REFRAIN

The neighborhood is not the best,
And the house resembles all the rest,
But it's where I want to be,
As long as I see
The sweet little lady next door.
We've always got a cop on beat
And a trolley running down the street,
But we soon forget the cars
And look at the stars,
The sweet little lady and me.
When we go a-walkin',
There is no sense in talkin',
For we can't hear a word we say.
But somehow we stand it,
For as we hand-in-hand it,
We're a million miles away.
You must come over very soon,
Say around the latter part of June,
And we'll brew a cup of tea,
'Cause then she won't be
The sweet little lady next door.

IT'S ABOUT TIME

Music by Peter Tinturin. Registered for copyright as an unpublished song March 21, 1932. Introduced by Ray Perkins on his radio show.

VERSE

Years may come and years may go,
And after they have gone,
There you'll sit and never know
Just what is going on.

REFRAIN

It's about time
That you see the moon above you,
That you learn to say "I love you."
It's about time
That you feel that certain feeling,
That you start to hit the ceiling—
It's about time.
Why do you suppose
I'm saying the things I am?

Guess you'll never know
Unless I draw a diagram!
It's about time
That you put your arms around me,
That you say you're glad you found me—
It's about time!

JUST LIKE A FALLING STAR

Lyrics by Mercer under the pseudonym Jack Keith.
Music by Ralph W. Bolton. Published. Copyrighted
April 15, 1932.

VERSE

I have heard so many people say
Love can never happen in a day!
I suppose my love affair is diff'rent,
For it simply takes my breath away.

REFRAIN

Just like a falling star,
Falling from the blue,
I discovered you—
Love
Came from up above,
Like a falling star.
Just like a falling star
Lighting up the night,
Making heaven bright,
You
Brought my dreams in view,
Like a falling star.
For even though I hoped you loved me,
You were so far above me,
Something kept us far apart;
Then my hoping ended
And your love descended
Right into my empty heart,
Just like a falling star!
All at once you're here—
Can I keep you near?
Or will you disappear
Like a falling star?

MOUTHFUL O' JAM

Music arranged by Archie Bleyer. Published. Copyrighted May 2, 1932.

There was once a colored boy called Louie;
He was fatter than a sugared ham.
All the smokies worshipped Louie,
'Cause his music drove them screwy,
And he always sang a number with a mouthful o'
    jam.
He was doin' fine until he met Bedelia,
But Bedelia wouldn't let him behave.
He forgot about his playin',
He just left his trumpet layin',
As she led him down the road
That took him right to the grave.

Well, the fatal evenin' started with a party,
And the program wasn't meant to be hot;
But it turned into a riot,
And before the place was quiet,
There was someone on the floor
And he was more than half-shot.
In the meantime Louie hadn't heard the shootin';
He was sleepin' like an innocent lamb.
When he woke and looked around him,
The police had come and found him
With a pocketful of pistols
And a mouthful o' jam.

He was sentenced by a judge and by a jury;
When he heard it he turned cold as a clam.
Though he prayed to be commuted
He was duly executed,
And he got it all from singing
With a mouthful o' jam.

When the devil saw him comin' in the distance,
He said, "Boys, I guess we'd all better scram,
'Cause that smoky's syncopation
Will be much too hot for Satan,
And I know he'll burn up Hades
With his mouthful o' jam.
And he got it all from singin'
With a mouthful o' jam."

WHEN WE RIDE ON THE MERRY-GO-ROUND

Lyrics by Mercer under pseudonym Jack Keith, and Earl McCarron. Music by Ralph W. Bolton. Published. Copyrighted May 3, 1932.

VERSE

Skies are getting clear,
Summertime is here—
You know what I'm thinking of.
Ev'ry mother's son
Knows what should be done—
Now's the perfect time for love!

REFRAIN

Can't we make a date for next Sunday
At a beach that I've found?
You'll forget you gotta be at work on Monday
When we ride the merry-go-round.
Hear that old calliope playin'—
What a wonderful sound!
Do I have to tell you just what I'll be sayin'
When we ride the merry-go-round?
You'll laugh at me,
I'll laugh at you—
Won't it be grand?
You'll start to sing,
I'll grab a ring,
Then I'll put it on your hand,
And, baby,
Maybe when the preacher has seen us,
And a year rolls around,
We will have a little hobby-horse between us,
When we ride on the merry-go-round.

SPRING IS IN MY HEART AGAIN

Music by William H. Woodin (who became President Franklin D. Roosevelt's first Secretary of the Treasury). Published. Copyrighted July 4, 1932.

VERSE

You've been away so long,
And all the world was wrong;
Each little meeting place
Has missed your smiling face.
But now the world is gay

Because you've come to stay;
Those lonely hours
Have passed away.

REFRAIN

Spring is in my heart, for you are here;
Spring is in my heart, and skies are clear.
Life will be the way it used to be
Now that you are back with me.

Ev'ry place I wandered to,
Ev'ry winding street we knew,
Brought me memories of you,
Dreaming of the night you said you loved me
In our little moonlit rendezvous.
I've so many things to say to you;
We will never be apart again—
Spring is in my heart again.

DEEP SOUTH (IN MY HEART)

Music by Archie Bleyer and Mercer. Published. Copyrighted August 25, 1932.

VERSE

Summer's waning,
I'm complaining
Of my loneliness.
Southland's call
Is ringing in my ear.
My heart's paining,
My eyes straining—
It's not hard to guess
They long to see
A place that's far from here.

REFRAIN

I miss the moonbeams,
I miss the sun—
Even though we drifted apart,
I've got the Deep South
Deep down in my heart.

I'd swap the Gulf Stream
For all that I've won,
Leave the town that gave me my start;
I've got the Deep South
Deep down in my heart.

Darkies singin' 'bout the Jordan
May not mean a thing to you,

Darkies, I can hear 'em chordin'
Harmonies that thrill me through.

I start to daydream
When summer's done,
Wondrin' when I'm gonna depart,
Back to the Deep South
Deep down in my heart.

HOW LONG HAS THIS BEEN GOING ON?

Lyric by Mercer and Earl McCarron. Music by Archie Bleyer. Published. Copyrighted August 25, 1932. (Not to be confused with the Gershwins' 1927 song of the same name.)

VERSE

I never heard of love
Or of the moon above;
I never even thought that they were real,
Dear.
But when you came my way
I saw the light of day;
You can't imagine how you make me feel,
Dear.

REFRAIN

All at once you made me see the moon above,
Showed me lots of things that I knew nothing of.
Do you mean to tell me that it's really love?
How long has this been going on?

Never thought my heart would ever start to beat,
Never dreamt that anything could be so sweet,
Never knew a kiss could knock me off my feet,
How long has this been going on?
Hear the birdies singin',
Look at all the lovers a-makin' eyes,
Hear the bells a-ringin',
Guess I'm just beginnin' to realize
The little things that I was missin'.
Look at all the people throwin' shoes and rice.
Don't you think that honeymoons are awf'ly nice?
You can call it love,
I call it paradise.
How long has this been going on?

FALLING OFF THE WAGON

Lyrics by E. Y. Harburg and Mercer. Music by Lewis E. Gensler. Introduced by Tom Harty, Vera Marshe (Marsh), and ensemble in the revue *Ballyhoo of 1932*, Forty-fourth Street Theatre, New York, opened September 6, 1932; 95 performances.

There is some doubt about Mercer's involvement in this song. His name appears on the published sheet music but not in the program. We include it because, at the very least, its theme is "Merceresque."

VERSE

Bacardi, martini,
We're over and finis and through!
I swore off, I laid off—
I paid off my bootlegger, too.
I said, "Not another,"
I promised my mother and dad;
You came along,
And now it's just too bad.

REFRAIN 1

I'm falling off the wagon
And falling into love;
John Barrymore can't compare with you.
I see the ceiling reeling,
I see two moons above;
Sweet applejack, let's go home and brew.
Hail, hail, my heart's all queer!
I don't know from nothin',
And I don't know from bidin' my time.
Here's to love!
Here's to crime!
I'm falling off the wagon,
And I don't need a shove;
I'm staggerin',
Boy, I'm drunk with love!

REFRAIN 2

I'm falling off the wagon,
I think I've lost my oar;
Oh, Wurzburger, stay 'way from my door!
You've got me seeing double,
Two heads, two nose, one eyes;
You're foolin' me, you're two other guys.
Hark, hark, I hear the lark!
And he don't know from hiccoughs,
And he don't know from whiskey or rye;
He just sings
"Hi-de-hi!"
I'll never go to heaven,
But, baby, you will do;

I'll merrily
Go to hell with you!

AFTER TWELVE O'CLOCK

Lyrics by Mercer under the pseudonym Joe Moore. Music by Hoagy Carmichael. Published. Copyrighted September 24, 1932.

When he met Mercer in 1932, Hoagy Carmichael remembered, the lyricist was "a young, bouncy butterball of a man from Georgia. He hadn't a song hit but I could tell that he could write and I was impressed by his personality."

Precisely how they met was never quite resolved. Carmichael thought "through a professional manager at Southern Music or perhaps a song plugger." Mercer remembered that it was through Eddie Wood, a friend of Peer's house arranger, Archie Bleyer, with whom Mercer would also work.

Whatever the circumstances, they began to work together, and these were their first attempts.

After twelve o'clock,
When all is still,
Heaven sends a dream;
Then comes a thrill—
I see you standing before me,
Just as you used to do.

After twelve o'clock
You hold my hand;
Then we steal away
Through Wonderland.
With a word you adore me,
Just as you used to do.

Each night you bring me
Your lovely charms again,
And oh, how real they seem!
I long to take you
In my arms again,
Even though you're only a dream—
I hold you.

After twelve o'clock,
You whisper this:
"I belong to you"—
And then we kiss.
Each night you take me to heaven,
Just as you used to do.

THANKSGIVIN'

Music by Hoagy Carmichael. Published. Copyrighted September 24, 1932.

VERSE

Hallelujah! All the birdies sing;
Hallelujah's my reply,
Life is sweet as almost anything,
Just like pumpkin pie.

REFRAIN

Thanksgivin',
Now I'm livin',
Life is one sweet song.
Boy, howdy,
Skies just can't be cloudy
Since love came along.
Sweet sunshine smiles at me,
Ev'ry day a jubilee.
Oh, Thanksgivin',
Boy, I'm really livin',
Since love came my way.

J. P. McEVOY'S NEW AMERICANA (1932)

Shubert Theatre, New York City; opened October 5, 1932; 77 performances. Produced by Lee Shubert. Book by J. P. McEvoy (third edition of his musical revue). Music by Jay Gorney, Harold Arlen, Richard Myers, Burton Lane, Vernon Duke, Henry Souvaine, Herman Hupfeld. Lyrics mostly by E. Y. Harburg. Directed by Harold Johnsrud.

Cast included: George Givot, Albert Carroll, Don Barclay, Gordon Smith, Rex Weber, Ralph Locke, Lillian Fitzgerald, Francetta Malloy, Peggy Cartwright, Lloyd Nolan, Georgie Tapps, Allan Mann, the Doris Humphrey Dance Group, the Charles Weidman Dancers, and the Musketeers.

"Americana," Mercer recalled, "was notable to me as the first time I worked with Harold Arlen. I had heard of the talented young man who had already had 'Get Happy' and a score of outstanding songs in the Cotton Club revues and I recommended him to Yip Harburg, who was in charge of getting a score together."

WHISTLING FOR A KISS

Lyrics by E. Y. Harburg and Mercer. Music by Richard Myers. Published. Copyrighted September 28, 1932. Introduced by Paul Davin, the Musketeers, Lillian Fitzgerald, Rex Weber, and ensemble.

VERSE

Lackaday, ah, lackaday,
Ah, woe is me—and how.
Silent is the lonely heart
That should be singing now.
Eventide and Whitsuntide
Is woe betide for me.
This my lot—
To be or not to be.

REFRAIN

Whistling for a kiss—umumum—
Who'll hear this sparrow
Whistling for a kiss up to the moon?
Walk through lovers' lane—umumum—
Gee, but it's narrow,
When there's not a soul to hear my tune!
Every lonesome bird must whistle
When there's no one by his side;
I would never need to whistle
If my lips were occupied!
Whistling for a kiss—umumum—
That well-known arrow,
Will it find my heart?
If so, how soon?

SATAN'S LITTLE LAMB

Lyrics by E. Y. Harburg and Mercer. Music by Harold Arlen. Published. Copyrighted September 28, 1932. Introduced by Francetta Malloy and the Musketeers. Recorded by Ethel Merman (Victor).

When the wind goes whip-whip-whip-whip-
    whipping round my floor,
And the rain comes a-rap-rap-rap-rap-rappin' at
    my door,
Give me gin to forget the sin-sin-sinner that I am,
'Cause I'm only Satan's li'l lamb.

Gimme drums that'll start that thump-thump-
    thumpin' in my heart,

Gimme horns that'll blow, blow, blow, blow, blow
   the blues apart,
Gimme thrills that'll break the Ten
   Commandments with a wham,
Doncha know I'm Satan's li'l lamb?

For it's glory, glory, while I'm a-livin',
Purgatory when I'm gone.
What a welcome I will be given
When my soul marches on!

Hi-de-ho
While I'm waitin' for that fatal telegram;
When I go,
Little daisies won't be caring who I am,
'Cause it's heads he wins
And it's tails you lose
When you're Satan's little coal-black lamb!

WOULDJA FOR A BIG RED APPLE?

Music by Everett Miller and Henry Souvaine. Published. Copyrighted September 28, 1932. Previously registered for copyright as an unpublished song December 16, 1930. Introduced by Peggy Cartwright, Gordon Smith, and female ensemble.

VERSE 1

HE: Greater men than I have sought your favor,
   But you merely glance at them and grin;
   You spurn the vermin,
   Who offer ermine and just a bit of sin.
   Even though these propositions bore you,
   Even though you're weary of the chase,
   Let me put a plan before you—
   Maybe it will help my case.

REFRAIN 1

Wouldja for a big red apple,
Wouldja for my peace of mind,
Couldja for a big red apple
Give me what I'm trying to find?

Just imagine you're my teacher,
Teaching me the golden rule—
If I had a big red apple,
Wouldja keep me after school?

Cakes and sweets
And sugar beets

May be what a girl deserves;
Choc'late drops
And lollipops
Are swell on the taste
But hell on the curves!

Wouldja do it just for instance,
Wouldja for my fam'ly tree—
If I had a big red apple,
Wouldja fall in love with me?

VERSE 2

SHE: Better men than you have tried to lure me,
   But I've read the works of El'nor Glyn.
   Once a big German
   Offered me ermine—
   Ah, but the fur was thin!
   You won't find me like the girl from Eden,
   Falling for an apple on a bough.
   I'm more like the girl from Sweden—
   "Ay tank ay go home right now."

REFRAIN 2, LINES 9–15

Gave you sweets and sugar beets
And still you don't give a hoot.
Try a slice of paradise—
Doctors'll tell you
This is the fruit!

WHAT WILL I DO WITHOUT YOU? (WHAT WILL YOU DO WITHOUT ME?)

Lyrics by Mercer and Hilda Gottlieb. Music by Lewis E. Gensler. Published. Copyrighted November 22, 1932. Written for the Warner Bros. film *College Coach* (1933)—the first song Mercer wrote for a film. Not sung in film.

VERSE

I guess we're growing used to each other;
We're sick of the game.
You seem to think you'd like another,
And I feel the same.
Just the same, I feel a little ache;
Only hope it's not a big mistake.

REFRAIN

I'm tired of you,
You're tired of me;
We talked it all over,
Agreed to disagree,
But what will I do without you,
And what will you do without me?
You'll try someone's arms,
I'll try someone's kiss,
And though it seems thrilling,
It all comes back to this:
Just what will I do without you,
And what will you do without me?

I won't let the rest know I'm playing;
I'll make them believe me somehow.
But deep in my heart I'll be saying,
"Oh, I wonder who's kissing you now?"

The moon and the sky,
The land and the sea,
So perfect together—
Apart, what would they be?
So, what will I do without you,
Oh, what will you do without me?

LITTLE OLD CROSSROAD STORE

Music by Peter Tinturin. Published. Copyrighted December 1, 1932. Previously registered for copyright as an unpublished song November 4, 1932.

VERSE 1

Deep in my memory,
One little house I see.
No paint is left on the walls anymore,
But there's Welcome on the door.

REFRAIN

In my dreams ev'ry night
There's a light shining bright
In the little old crossroad store.
And if I wandered in,
They'd say, "How have you been?
Mighty glad that you're back once more!"
I can see ev'ry face round the fireplace,
Just as they were before;
And I'm hoping that there
Will be one vacant chair
In the little old crossroad store.

VERSE 2

Year after year I pray,
Let me go back someday.
I'm growing older, I've been ev'rywhere,
But my heart is always there.

REPEAT REFRAIN

IF I COULD ONLY READ YOUR MIND

Music by Peter Tinturin. Published. Copyrighted July 11, 1934. Previously registered for copyright as an unpublished song December 16, 1932.

VERSE

Even though you say that you belong to me,
And your words sound sincere,
Ev'rything you do seems mighty wrong to me—
Are you fooling me, dear?

REFRAIN

I'm so in love with you,
You seem to love me, too;
And yet you want no ties that bind.
You give your lips to me,
And still your heart is free—
If I could only read your mind!

You promise to be true,
But when there's someone new,
I only tag along behind.
One day you call me dear,
The next you disappear—
If only I could read your mind!

I wonder if I would find
That you'd be the kind
To take me, to love me,

To leave me behind.
If that's the case,
I'll right-about-face,
Look around
For someone else to take your place.

I wouldn't even start
To look into your heart;
I'd be afraid of what I'd find.
I can't believe your eyes,
They're always telling lies—
If I could only read your mind!
If I could only read your mind!

SEVEN LITTLE STEPS TO HEAVEN

Lyrics by Hilda Gottlieb and Mercer. Music by Lewis E. Gensler. Published. Copyrighted December 19, 1932.

VERSE

Ev'rything's set,
Didn't forget,
Paid all the fam'ly calls,
Made a reservation
For Niagara Falls.
Here comes the bride,
Here comes the bride,
This is my lucky day.
There's the organ playing—
Boy, I'm on my way!

REFRAIN

One, two, three, four, five, six, seven,
Seven little steps to heaven,
Headin' right for heaven,
Walkin' up the aisle to you.
Do, re, mi, fa, so, la, si,
Those are not the church bells ringin',

That's my heart a-singin',
'Cause you're gonna say "I do."
And now we'll meet the preacher;
He'll smile at us and then
He'll say, "I'm glad to meetcha—
Hope you never have to call again!"
One, two, three, four, five, six, seven,
Seven little steps to heaven.
I'm in seventh heaven
Walkin' down the aisle with you!

THE ALPHABET OF LOVE BEGINS AND ENDS WITH YOU

Lyrics by Hilda Gottlieb and Mercer. Music by Lewis E. Gensler. Published. Copyrighted December 28, 1932.

VERSE

As a kid in school, everything was Greek to me;
Never knew a rule, couldn't tell an A from Z.
Thought the facts of life would never reach me,
But since you have come along to teach me,
I'm a lucky fool, and I know the mystery.

REFRAIN

The alphabet of love begins and ends with you;
It's A-B-C that no one else will ever do.
L-O-V-E spells "love,"
But all I'm thinking of
Is you and you and you and no one else but you.
My arms could never cling to anyone but you;
They'd never want to cling to anyone but you.
I'm not very smart,
But I've learned this by heart:
The alphabet of love begins and ends with you.

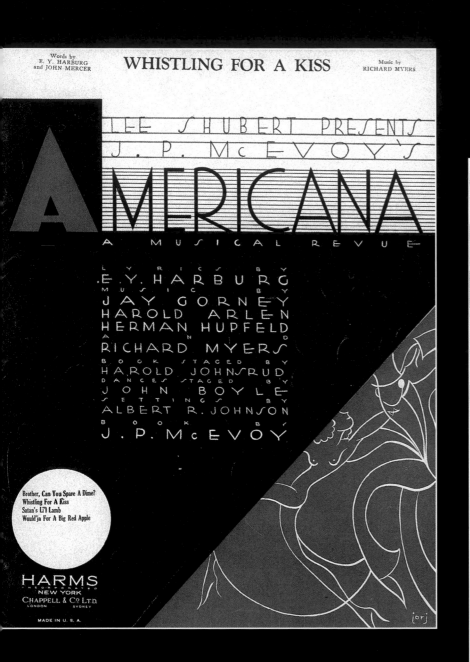

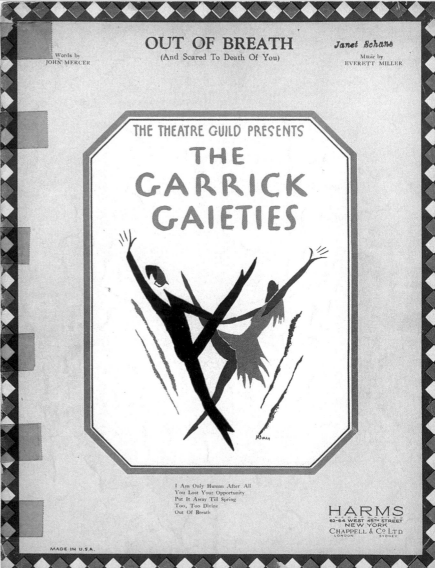

It is impossible to date these lyrics accurately. They are all credited to "John Mercer" or one of several pseudonyms and suggest the period 1930–1932. They were found among Mercer's papers in the Georgia State University Library in Atlanta, Georgia.

ABOUT FACE

Music by Edward Albertson. Written for the unproduced musical *Honor of West Point*.

VERSE

We've got our commands;
A fight is on our hands,
And there's a cause
We must be fighting for.
Though we've done without,
It's time to change about;
We're first in peace,
But we'll be first in war.

REFRAIN

About face—
Give the command!
About face—
Strike up the band!
About face—
We'll make a stand!
About face—
Present arms
With all our might!
Present arms—
We're in the right!
About face—
We will keep Old Glory flying high!
We will either win this war or die!
About face—
Work to be done!
About face—
We'll make 'em run!
About face—
After we've won!
About face—

AFTER ALL THESE YEARS

Music by Mercer does not survive.

You made me happy—
Oh, so happy.
Now it's time for tears,
Because it's over
After all these years.

We stuck together,
Close together,
Sharing hopes and fears.
And now you've left me
After all these years.

You gave me heaven at the start—
To think you'd throw me down!
I used to play the hero's part—
Here I am only the clown.

You left me heartaches,
Lonely heartaches—
They're my souvenirs.
How could you do it
After all these years?

ANNE

Music by Edward Albertson does not survive. Written for the unproduced musical *Honor of West Point*.

Anne,
The army's all in line—
You've made us fall in line
At your command.
Anne,
We're all attention now;
We'd like to mention now
You're simply grand.

I will have to choose somehow,
For I suppose I'm in the army now.

Oh, Anne, in all the dreams we dream
Somehow it seems we dream of Anne!

ARE YOU GONNA THROW ME DOWN?

Music by Mercer does not survive.

They've been talkin' about you,
Talkin' all over town,
And though I hate to doubt you,
Are you gonna throw me down?
You can laugh at the rumor,
But it's makin' me frown;
I've got no sense of humor—
Are you gonna throw me down?
If you've got to deceive me,
Do you have to advertise it so?
If you're planning to leave me,
Needn't be afraid to let me know.
'Fore your kisses grow colder
And you make me the clown,
Tell me straight from the shoulder—
Are you gonna throw me down?

DON'T STOP ME IF YOU'VE HEARD IT

Music by Henry Souvaine does not survive.

VERSE 1

BOY: Let me tell a story
And I am in my glory;
I know at least a million tales or more.
But as an entertainer,
Each day it's getting plainer
That everything I say they've heard before.
Though it would appear that I have none left,
There is one left—just for you.
You may think it either dull or clever,
But whatever you do—

REFRAIN

Don't stop me if you've heard it;
Please let me stumble through.
I've got the grandest story up my sleeve—
I'm in love with you.
I don't know how to word it
To make it really new,
So just as old man Adam said to Eve:
"I'm in love with you."

Although it's a secret
I've been prepared to tell.
Still, you are the first one
I've ever cared to tell,
So—don't stop me if you've heard it,
Don't laugh until I'm through.
Then, if you like it,
Shout it to the skies:
"I'm in love with you."

VERSE 2

GIRL: Sir, you speak too freely!
If I were Horace Greeley,
I'd say, "Go west, where silence is in style!"
But since I've been quiet,
I'll merely say you try it,
And let me speak my speech for just a
while.
I must tell you something now or never
Or forever hold my tongue.
You can never say that these are tame
words—
They're the same words you've sung:

REPEAT REFRAIN

FEVER HEAT

Music by Archie Bleyer does not survive.

Use a slow and lazy motion,
Rocking on your feet;
Take the movement of the ocean,
Bring it to a fever heat.
Let the tom-toms start the rhythm
With a steady beat.
Get your feet in tempo with 'em,
Bring it to a fever heat.
Trouble to learn,
Trouble to toil,
You'll find it hard to master.
But it'll burn,
Bubble and boil,
Hotter than a mustard plaster.
To the slow and lazy motion
Add a tune that's sweet;
By degrees warm up the potion;
Bring it to a fever heat.

FINDERS ARE KEEPERS

Music by Carl Sigman does not survive.

As a child I learned it,
And it still holds true:
Finders are keepers—
And now I've found you.
Wonder who has lost you,
Wonder what they'll do.
Losers are weepers—
I know they'll be blue.
Maybe later on you'll wind up
Having everything your way,
But right now I've made my mind up—
Here you are at last
And here you're gonna stay.
Why should I look further?
Haven't dreams come true?
Finders are keepers—
How close I'll keep you.

GIVE ME BACK MY HEART

Music by Joseph Wiess does not survive.

VERSE

I had saved my hopes,
My every dream for you,
Gave them to you gladly
When you came in view.
In return you gave me
All the love you possessed.
Now perhaps you'll grant me
Just this last request:

REFRAIN

I prayed for romance;
You gave me my chance—
Now give me back my heart.
Love found us, love's gone;
You'll smile and go on—
So give me back my heart.
You'll find somebody new.
Since you're through with me;
I'll find memories of you
In each thing I see.
Those love dreams we knew
You'll carry with you—
So give me back my heart.

HERE YOU ARE

Composer unknown. No music survives.

Here you are—
At last you've come from afar.
I wondered when I'd be near you;
Suddenly,
Here you are!
Here am I—
My heart is yours till I die.
My love is true, though the moon goes,
Not one that soon goes by.
Each moment seemed like a year
Until I saw you appear.
I'm glad I waited,
For I know this was fated,
And now that you are here,
Let all the rest disappear.
I'll always follow your star—
I'm happy, for
Here you are.

HIDEAWAY

Composer unknown. No music survives.

VERSE 1

I've got my heart set
Dead against confusion—
How I want seclusion and the peace it brings!
Let's drop the smart set,
Dining out forever,
Trying to say clever things.
I think the best cure
For our many ills would be a change of scene—
Let's take a rest cure,
Just to see if grass is green.

REFRAIN

There's a place I've prayed to be
Where we both were made to be,
Just the place to find and hide away.
First we'll find a way to go,
Then we'll set a day to go
Leave the world behind and hide away.
Like two children who found one night
They were caged in the wood,
We'll stay hidden from sight
Till we're aged in wood.

Send the time and tide away—
Room for only two
When I find a hideaway with you.

VERSE 2

I've had my fill of
Gazing through a lorgnette—
"My, they haven't gone yet!" said with many
    frowns.
Can't get the thrill of
Going out to soirées,
Wearing Mister Poiret's gowns.
I like your idea of a quiet place
Where we can be alone—
Come, let us fly, dear,
To a corner quite unknown.

REPEAT REFRAIN

HOW I WISH THAT YOU WERE IN MY PLACE

Music by Mercer does not survive.

VERSE

You say that you love me,
But right there it ends,
For you tell a different story
To your friends.
I don't want to hurt you,
But I hope and pray
That you'll feel the things I'm feeling
Some sweet day.

REFRAIN

It's a shame the way you're treating me,
It's a positive disgrace.
Must you say you love me best?
That's a joke to all the rest.
How I wish that you were in my place!
Don't know how you make me string along,
Dreaming of your false embrace.
When you have another date,
I just sit around and wait,
Wishing I could get you in my place.
If you only knew
All the things I'm going through,
If you only knew,
You would change your point of view—
Eating out my heart

Every moment we're apart,
Glad to have the crumbs,
Taking everything that comes.
When my back is turned you laugh at me,
Yet you love me to my face.
You want everyone to see
What a fool you make of me—
How I wish that you were in my place!

I STILL REMEMBER THE MASQUERADE

Composer unknown. No music survives.

I still remember the masquerade;
I remember each song they played.
I remember—do you?
And I remember that no disguise
Could have ever concealed your eyes.
When I saw them I knew
In your glance you were giving me a sign—
Could I help it
If my arms drew you near
And your lips met mine?
Ah, that discovery that we made!
Love was there at the masquerade
And I found it with you.

IF THE MOON COULD TALK

Composer unknown. No music survives.

If the moon could talk,
This is what he'd say:
"Someone's mighty lonely
Since you went away."
Maybe if you heard him
You'd come back someday.
Gee, I wish the moon could talk!
If the moon could talk
Way up in the sky,
We'd be telling secrets,
Just the moon and I;
Then he'd go on and tell you
How I sit and cry.
Gee, I wish the moon could talk!
Here am I, hopelessly blue,
Anxious to pour out my heart.

Here I am—but where are you?
How can we make up when we're far apart?
If the moon could talk
Just a word or two,
Whispering that someone's
Still in love with you,
Maybe you would answer,
"I still love him, too."
Gee, I wish the moon could talk!

I'LL BE FREE

Lyrics by Howard Dietz and John Mercer. Music by Henry Souvaine does not survive.

VERSE

My love dreams used to bloom and flower
Only that they might turn sour
Overnight.
And somehow, though I knew the ending,
I would glory in pretending
I was right.
But now I know
The thrill has gone;
My eyes are opened wide.
From now on I will have no ties that bind,
But see what lies behind
The other side.

REFRAIN

Don't want favors
Or anybody's friendship;
I'll depend on no one but me.
I'll go my way alone
And I'll call my soul my own—
Then I'll be free.
I'll be happy because I'm independent,
I'll depend on no one but me.
I'll hold my head up high,
And you won't hear me cry for sympathy.
All my life I've been just like a silly ingenue,
A clinging vine
Without any spine.
All my life I've been a feather
On a weather vane
In every breeze,
But now by slow degrees
I've discovered a world that's not a shadow—
I'll depend on no one but me.
It may turn out all wrong,
But I know that if I'm strong,
Then I'll be free.

I'M A STRANGER IN THESE PARTS

Music by Henry Souvaine does not survive.

VERSE

Mine was a humdrum quiet life,
Far from questioning looks;
All that I wished to know
I gathered from my books.
Such was the kingdom all my own.
Then some wanderer came,
Talked of a land of love,
Said it was mine to claim,
So I left to win this lovely prize—
Have I blundered or have I been wise?

REFRAIN

I've found a wonderful land,
Nicer than any I'd planned;
But can I be sure that there's no danger?
I'm a stranger in these parts.

How can I possibly tell
If this is heaven or hell?
Like a little infant in a manger,
I'm a stranger in these parts.

Must I look behind me
And blindly roam?
Or will someone find me
And lead me home?

If I had fallen before,
Then I'd know how to explore;
But deep in my heart of hearts
I'm just a stranger in these parts.

I'M SO GLAD YOU'RE YOU

Music by Howard Jackson does not survive.

Mmm—mmm—mmm,
I'm so glad you're you,
I'm so glad I'm me.
And here we are—
Aren't you glad we're we?
Mmm—mmm—mmm,
There is so much time,

There is so much space;
Yet here we are
In a single place.
I guess there're millions who never would like me,
I guess there're millions who wouldn't like you;
Yet with all these around us,
We saw love—it found us—
And my search and your search was through.
Mmm—mmm—mmm,
Why care what they say,
Why care what they do?
Here we are—
I'm so glad you're you.

IN THE AFTERGLOW

Composer unknown. No music survives.

Although it's over, really over,
Dreams of you won't go;
They're all around me
In the afterglow.
The flame we kindled slowly dwindled;
Now it's burning low.
I watch the embers
In the afterglow.
Although you're far away from me,
Somehow you haven't gone,
Because in everything I see
There you are, lingering on.
I'll never hold you as I held you
When you thrilled me so,
But I still have you
In the afterglow.

IN YOUR EYES

Composer unknown. No music survives.

In your eyes
I see the love I'm made for,
In your eyes
Each little dream I've prayed for.
In your glance
I see a promise of heaven.
In your smile
I see the sun shining above.
In my heart

I know that I adored you;
From the start
I've kept my kisses for you.
In my eyes
There's a love I could never disguise.
I think you're grand—
How do I stand
In your eyes?

I'VE GOT A LOT TO LIVE FOR

Music by Ted Helms does not survive.

There were clouds in my sky,
And as love passed me by,
I'd say, "I've not a lot to live for."
Then one day who walked in—
Need I say you walked in?
My heart said, "There's a lot to live for now."
Each thing I did, I did without reason,
But now I know both why and how.
Since I know what to do,
I'll keep on loving you
And make sure I've a lot to live for.

I'VE NOTHING TO HIDE

Music by Alfred Opler does not survive.

Ask me what you want to know;
I've nothing to hide.
Who I am and where I go—
I've nothing to hide.
I'm not ashamed of what I've done,
And I don't want you to be.
I'll bare my secrets one by one;
You can act accordingly.
Love affairs I've had before
Are things of the past,
And if I'm to have one more,
I want it to last.
So let's be sure before we start
That we'll both be satisfied.
Now you see what's in my heart—
I've nothing to hide.

LAZY SONG

Composer unknown. No music survives.

In spring or fall,
In any old season at all,
You'll hear my lazy song.
When the world begins to worry
And I rush to and fro,
I see no use to hurry
When there's no place to go.
Beside a stream
I stop in the evening to dream,
Away from every throng.
When the stars up in the sky go,
Then I go along,
And life is one long lazy song.

MAGIC IN THE MOONLIGHT

Music by Edward Albertson does not survive.

VERSE

Why did you love me
Only to leave me,
Leave me with mem'ries of you?
Why did you thrill me
Only to grieve me?
I only wish that I knew.

REFRAIN

Magic in the moonlight—
On the night I found you,
Love was all around you, dear.
Though we heard no music there,
There was music in the air,
Magic in your glances—
In your eyes you told me
You would always hold me near.
Magic in the things I heard,
Though you didn't say a word;
Magic in the moonlight
As you took my blue dreams,
Turned them into new dreams then.
Surely it was magic,
For you didn't mean it,
And I should have seen it then.
Magic in the moonlight—

Then a word was spoken,
And it meant a broken vow.
Magic in the moonlight then,
Nothing in the moonlight now.

ALTERNATE VERSION OF FINAL EIGHT LINES

Surely it was magic
Seeing you before me,
Having you adore me then.
Magic in the moonlight,
That's what I discovered
When we made a lovers' vow.
Magic in the moonlight then,
Magic in the moonlight now.

RIGHT UNDER MY EYES

Composer unknown. No music survives.

I kept looking around,
Thinking love would never be found;
Then something suddenly arranged it
Right under my eyes.
For when you came along,
My heart started singing a song.
My life was nothing till you changed it
Right under my eyes.
If it's true that love is blind,
Then this must be some other kind,
For I've just begun to see
How nice the world could be.
And so, feeling this way,
There is just one thing I can say.
I'll always do my best to keep you
Right under my eyes.

RING AROUND THE MOON

Composer unknown. No music survives.

We met one night,
The moon was bright,
Our song of love was such a happy tune.
But now the song
Has passed along
And there's a ring around the moon.
The wonderland that we had planned

Was just a dream that ended all too soon.
You broke the spell,
My castle fell,
And there's a ring around the moon.
Stargazing
For the love you've put behind me.
You took along
Our happy song
And made me learn to sing a lonely tune.
I'm waiting here
For skies to clear,
But there's a ring around the moon.

SING ME TO SLEEP

Music by Del Cleveland does not survive.

Sing me to sleep, and as the stars appear,
Hold me near.
No other could sing me to sleep
And hide the world from view,
Only you.
I know that heaven is close beside me
When you whisper soft and low, so
Sing me to sleep
To dream a dream of love and you.

THROUGH TIME AND TIDE

Composer unknown. No music survives.

Through time and tide,
Through shadows that walk at my side,
I'll still go on to you.
Even though the sun keeps setting,
And years disappear,
For me there's no forgetting
That I once held you near.
The road may bend
And suddenly come to an end,
But I'll go on to you,
For I'll never stop my searching,
Though all hope has gone
And the time and tide hurry on.

TIME AFTER TIME

Composer unknown. No music survives.

VERSE

When a girl has made her mind up
That a life of sin will pay,
She is sure to wind up a spinster;
But a girl who tries to show that
She is going virtue's way
Will be dealt a blow that is sin'ster.
Men, instead of talking the wife line,
Will be singing, "Throw out the lifeline!"

REFRAIN

I like the simple life.
I always say the straight and narrow's the only way,
But when I try to walk it I go astray,
Time after time after time,
And though I should be good, I should be firm,
I see no turning for this here worm.
I make a resolution, but out I squirm,
Time after time after time.
I pray I may be led from all temptation,
But there's no salvation for me;
For just before I start to spurn the feasts
And think the thoughts of the purest priests,
I find that I am human and men are beasts,
Time after time.

REPEAT REFRAIN

[*replace final four lines with:*]

For when the devil tries to get my goat,
I've gone to hell by a public vote,
I'm like the fallen Quaker who sows her oat,
Time after time after time.

TOO GOOD TO BE TRUE

Music by Florence Leftwich does not survive.

VERSE

Most of my life I stood alone,
Taking the good and bad alone,
Hoping my little hopes,
Dreaming my dreams.
All of a sudden you appeared.
What of my hopes? They too appeared.

Is this heaven that you've brought me
All it seems?

REFRAIN

You say you love me
As I love you.
You say you love me—
I hope you do.
And yet my heart keeps saying
It's too good to be true.
This world around me
Is so ideal;
This thing's that found me,
I know it's real—
And yet my heart keeps saying
It's too good to be true.
Are you the one I was made for?
Or is it all a mistake?
Is this the dream that I've prayed for?
Seems like a dream,
Yet I'm awake.
I see you walking,
I feel you near;
Your lips are talking,
You're really here.
And yet my heart keeps saying
It's too good to be true.

TWILIGHT

Composer unknown. No music survives.

Twilight
Painting the skies,
Painting a picture for my lonely eyes.
Waiting, watching the view,
Dreaming a dream of you.
Twilight
Stealing away,
Leaving me here at the close of the day.
Lonely, nothing to do,
Dreaming a dream of you.
Somewhere, when shadows fall,
You see the twilight, too.
Dear one, does it recall
Those happy days we knew?
Twilight
Whisp'ring to me,
Making me wonder if I'll always be
Waiting, watching the view,
Dreaming a dream of you.

WATCH A DARKY DANCE

Music by Peter Tinturin.

VERSE

When the blues come hangin' round you,
Don't they make your blood run cold?
Every time they come to hound you,
Don't you feel you're getting kinda old?
When your days and nights are chilly,
There's a way to melt that ice—
You can make hard luck look silly
If you take my advice.

REFRAIN

When you start to feel blue,
And you've got to pull through,
There's one thing you can do—
Watch a darky dance.
Keep an eye on his feet
As he changes the beat;
Take a lesson in heat—
Watch a darky dance.
Let him start the rhythm,
Watch his shoulders sway;
Get in tempo with 'em,
Swing the blues away.
Get a tune you can hum,
Let your heart beat the drum,
Make that grand feelin' come—
Watch a darky dance,
Watch a—darky—dance!

WE STAYED IN LOVE TOO LONG

Music by Archie Bleyer does not survive.

VERSE

Like every pair of lovers,
We said our love would last;
We thought the road to heaven had no turning.
Like every pair of lovers,
We found that love goes past;
That was a lesson we were soon in learning.
We didn't know when we had reached the top,
There was an anticlimax;
We didn't know when to stop.

REFRAIN

We were so happy, but now something's wrong;
The reason seems quite clear enough:
We stayed in love too long.
We both grew tired of love's old sweet song;
But then, instead of ending it,
We stayed in love too long.
We started quarreling and fighting;
That was the writing
Upon the wall.
Still we went on pretending
Instead of ending it all.
Most loves are weak loves, but ours was too
  strong—
Instead of stopping soon enough,
We staycd in love too long.

WE WON'T WORRY TILL FALL

Music by Henry Souvaine does not survive.

VERSE (EARLY VERSION)

SHE: I see by the headlines
    That the latest breadlines
    Are really fine.
    Why don't you get in line?
 HE: I suppose you'd love that.
    Well, I'm quite above that.
    I'll have you know
    I wouldn't stoop that low.
SHE: You may jest, but at your best
    You are just a lousy hobo.
 HE: I am poor, to be quite sure,
    But I'm better far than no beau.

REFRAIN

Pardon my expression,
But spring is here,
So put away your old gray shawl.
To hell with this depression—
We won't worry till fall.
I haven't got a dollar;
I'm unemployed—
But, incidentally, ain't we all?
Let other people holler;
We won't worry till fall.
There are lots of shoulders we could weep on,
Yet there's not a shoulder left to carve;
But as long as there's a bench to sleep on,
We can keep on till we starve.

So come and take a day off,
Forget your cares,
Just wrap 'em with your old mothball—
For wintertime is way off,
And we won't worry till fall.

REPEAT REFRAIN
[*replace final five lines with:*]

Better times are coming—
If we must eat,
The grass will soon be growing tall.
In summer things are humming,
So we won't worry till fall.

VERSE (LATER VERSION)

Why keep talking 'bout Depression?
And why keep walking in the rain?
Love's in our possession,
So let's not complain.
All the world is getting dressed up
In Mother Nature's latest style—
Time to throw your chest up
And put on that smile.

WEARY SHOULDERS

Music by Henry Souvaine does not survive.

VERSE

I'm workin', I'm prayin',
Like the good book say to do,
Each mornin', each evenin',
If it's cloudy, if it's rainin',
I keep a-goin', never thinkin' 'bout complainin'
All day through.
Lord, hear me, stay near me
And make me stronger—
Can't last much longer.

REFRAIN

Weary shoulders, weary shoulders,
Just keep on workin'
Till we gets word to lay the burden down.
Heart is achin', back is breakin',
But that won't matter
When we gets the word to lay de burden down.
Sunup and sundown
And soon a year,
High tide and low tide,
But still we here—

Workin' ever, doubtin' never,
Knowin' for certain
That we'll get word to lay de burden down.

WELCOME, STRANGER

Music by Ted Helms. Mercer later wrote another song with the same title but different lyrics and music (see p. 43).

VERSE

Life's been a merry chase;
I've gone from place to place
To find that loyal friend and true.
While searching high and low
You caught my eye, and lo!
My search is through
Since you hove in view.

REFRAIN

Welcome, stranger,
I've been waiting long for you.
These empty days I spend
Will have an end
If you come in—
Do come in!
Welcome, stranger,
I've prepared the fatted calf.
My cupboard may be bare;
Let's see what's there
And share it half and half.
You're the one that I have looked for,
That my heart is booked for
And now your goose will be cooked for
Eternity—
Wait and see!
Welcome, stranger,
I have opened wide the door,
But if you enter, then I'll
Lock it forevermore.

WE'RE IN WONDERLAND

Music by Carl Sigman does not survive.

VERSE

I wandered on my weary way,
No stars in the sky.

You wandered on your weary way,
And life hurried by.
Now suddenly here we are,
Together how near we are—
Let's both have a look around
This wonderful land we've found.

REFRAIN

I'm the man, you're the maid,
Singing love's serenade;
Hand in hand,
We're in Wonderland.
Not a cloud in the sky
As the world hurries by;
Hand in hand,
We're in Wonderland.
Never dreamt anyone, anything could be so nice;
What was once just a world is paradise.
Can't believe that it's true,
That it's me, that it's you,
Hand in hand,
We're in Wonderland.

WHEN THE MOON IS FULL

Composer unknown. No music survives.

When the moon is full,
Do you feel lonely and blue?
Does it remind you of the night we met?
Have you forgotten what I can't forget?
That wonderful night,
That wonderful thrill;
I wanted you then,
I'm wanting you still.
But now my arms are empty
When the moon is full.

WHERE'S THE HAPPY ENDING?

Music and lyrics by Ted Helms and John Mercer. No music survives.

Where's the happy ending to the perfect day?
Will it come my way at all?
I go on pretending, hoping for my dream,
But my chances seem so small.
Every day I'm lonely,
Every night awake,
Waiting if I'll find it or if I must say
Where's my happy ending gone?

WHY PRETEND?

Composer unknown. No music survives.

We met, we kissed;
I thought that it never would end.
It has, so why pretend?
Why pretend that I can hold you
When all hope has gone?
When my heart says "I told you so,"
I'll never go on.
The road has turned,
The lesson is finally learned;
One thing is clear to me:
As it was in the beginning,
It always will be—
Our love had to end.
Why pretend?

WRAP IT UP

Composer unknown. No music survives.

VERSE

Down in the South
There is a candy kid.
Melt in your mouth,
That's what his candy did.
But here of late
He never makes a sale;
He's out of date,
Folks say his candy's stale.
Now when he meets his customers they all say,
"You'll have to make your candy the modern way."

REFRAIN

Wrap it up in cellophane,
Keep it fresh for me.
Stay home at night and wrap it up tight,
Make it a novelty.
Don't get in a crowded street,
Or on a Ferris wheel;
Take my advice and keep it on ice
Or else you'll break the seal.
There is not a soul who would refuse it
If it were fixed that way;
But if anyone should want to use it,
Keep it to yourself or else you'll lose it.
Hang it in your windowpane
For the world to see,
But if it's wrapped in cellophane
I'll know it's fresh for me.

YOU NEVER MISS THE WATER TILL THE WELL RUNS DRY

Music by Peter Tinturin does not survive.

VERSE

Sisters and brothers, and others,
You can take a tip from me—
After all that I've been through,
Here's some good advice for you,
Here's some extra-good philosophy.

REFRAIN

You never miss the water till the well runs dry;
You never miss the moon until it leaves the sky.
The birdies come in May,
All summer long they stay,
And yet you never notice 'em
Until they fly away.
You never miss the sun until it starts to rain,
And then you want it back with all your might and
    main.
I never missed my honey
Till she said goodbye, 'cause
You never miss the water till the well runs dry.

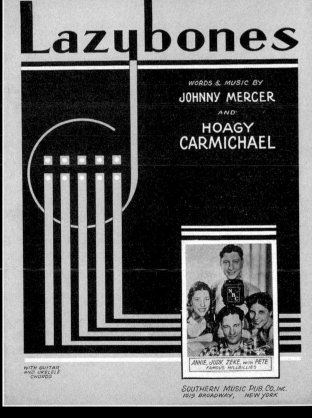

Songs of 1933–1934

DARK IS THE NIGHT

Music by Joseph Meyer. Registered for copyright as an unpublished song January 31, 1933.
   Lyric missing.

IN A CAFÉ IN MONTMARTRE

Music by Joseph Meyer. Published. Copyrighted February 23, 1933. The sheet music contains a note about the word "Montmartre": "pronounced in this song 'Mo-mart.' "

VERSE

Paris in spring,
What a glorious thing!
Paris at night,
What a wonderful sight!
I see you still
In our rendezvous;
I feel the thrill
Of that last night with you.

REFRAIN

In a café in Montmartre
On the night we had to part,
I remember how you sighed "Je t'aime";
Now I am wondering if you're still the same.
At a table set for two
Is there someone close with you?
I'll be coming back again, chérie,
Coming back to find my heart
In a café in Montmartre.

TALKING IN MY SLEEP

Music by Harry Archer and Margot Millham. Published. Copyrighted April 8, 1933.

VERSE

Though I see you nearly ev'ry day,
I can never find a thing to say.
Why should I be so awfully shy

When I'm really not that way?
When it's time to rest my weary head
And I hie me to my trundle bed,
Then I start pouring out my heart,
Saying what I should have said.

REFRAIN

Talking in my sleep,
There's no use talking,
'Cause you never hear the things I say.
Talking in my sleep,
I start in raving
From the moment that I hit the hay.
Talking in my sleep,
My family's sick of hearing
All about your eyes of blue.
When I'm counting sheep,
The sheep keep counting
Ev'ry time I whisper "I love you."
And even if the hour is twelve o'clock,
If the hour is two,
All the neighbors around the block
Have to hear about you.
Walking arm in arm,
The church bells ringing,
And you're about to say "I do"—
When the darned alarm goes ting-a-ling
And I've been talking in my sleep to you.

MUSIC FROM ACROSS THE SEA

Music by Peter Tinturin. Published. Copyrighted June 14, 1933.

VERSE

The sun is down,
The moon is riding high;
I leave the town
And watch the ships go by.
Each little light
Goes sailing out to sea,
And as I stand upon the sand,
I hear a melody.

REFRAIN

Waves are breaking on the shore,
Whispering their song once more,
Bringing back to me
Music from across the sea.
Echo of the long ago,

Song of love we used to know
Never lets me free,
Music from across the sea.
When you tell the waves you're yearning,
When you tell the wind you're blue,
Can't you hear the wind returning,
Telling you, "I'm lonely, too?"
Hope and pray the evening tide
Soon will find you by my side,
Hearing it with me,
Music from across the sea.

LAZYBONES

Music by Hoagy Carmichael. Published. Copyrighted June 15, 1933. Performed in the MGM film *Bombshell* (1933) by Gus Arnheim and His Orchestra.
   Number-one recording by Ted Lewis and His Band (Columbia). Other leading recordings: Don Redman and His Orchestra (Brunswick) and Mildred Bailey (Brunswick). Bailey, who introduced the song, was accompanied by the Dorsey Brothers Orchestra, including Bunny Berigan (trumpet), with an arrangement by Glenn Miller. Also recorded by Ben Bernie (Brunswick); Glen Gray and the Casa Loma Orchestra, with vocal by Pee Wee Hunt (Victor); Irving Aaronson and the Commanders, with vocal by Dick Robertson (Vocalion). Louis Armstrong recorded the song for Decca in 1939.
   Even with only two people involved, accounts of the song's genesis are conflicting. Carmichael wrote to an unidentified friend: "Just now wrote 'Lazybones.' All of a sudden like. That's when they're best." In his autobiography, *Sometimes I Wonder*, he elaborated:

[Mercer] walked in one day and I was sitting in the chair, the door was open, summertime. He knocked, and I said "Come in!" and I'm sitting in the chair, half-dozing. This is the absolute truth. I said, "What's on your mind?" He said, "Well, I thought I'd like to write a song called 'Lazybones.' What do you think of that title?" I said, "With this kind of summer we're having in New York, and what with the Depression, and nobody working, it sounds mighty logical."

Mercer himself recalled it rather differently:

I leapt at the chance to work with Hoagy. He proved an understanding friend and teacher . . . When I say teacher, I mean just that; he broadened my ability with his knowledge and experience. Have you ever had a tough teacher whom you appreciated later? That's how it was to write with Hoagy. He is such a gifted lyric writer on his own that I felt intimidated and tightened up too much to do my best work . . . Hoagy suffered through months of waiting until I came up with the lyrics.

By a separate account Mercer wrote most of the lyric quite easily but was stuck for a pair of lines in the middle. Then a farmer near his country place in New Jersey unconsciously rhymed "prayin' " and "sprayin' " in his presence, and there were the lines needed: "When 'taters need sprayin',/I bet you keep prayin'."

Though the song definitely had "the South in its mouth," its influence was felt far afield. Hitler banned it outright. His new regime was concerned about the popularity of "nigger" songs and considered that "Lazybones" "encourages idleness and does not conform to Nazi ideals."

VERSE

Long as there is chicken gravy on your rice
Ev'rything is nice.
Long as there's watermelon on the vine,
Ev'rything is fine.
You got no time to work,
You got no time to play,
Busy doin' nothin' all the livelong day.
You won't ever change no matter what I say,
You're just made that way.

REFRAIN

Lazybones, sleepin' in the sun,
How you 'spec' to get your day's work done?
Never get your day's work done,
Sleepin' in the noonday sun.

Lazybones, sleepin' in the shade,
How you 'spec' to get your cornmeal made?
Never get your cornmeal made
Sleepin' in the evenin' shade.

When 'taters need sprayin',
I bet you keep prayin'
The bugs fall off the vine.
And when you go fishin',
I bet you keep wishin'
The fish won't grab at your line.

Lazybones, loafin' through the day,
How you 'spec' to make a dime that way?
Never make a dime that way—
Well, looky here,
He never heared a word I say!

DOWN A LONG, LONG ROAD

Music and lyrics by Margot Millham and John Mercer. Published. Copyrighted September 11, 1933.

VERSE

The sky is lonely and blue,
It makes me feel that way too
As I go searching for you.
Low,
I can't afford to be low,
I've got a long way to go.

REFRAIN

Down a long, long road,
Walking all alone,
Down a long, long road
Back to you.
Through a deep blue night,
Not a star in sight,
I go travelin' on
All night through.
Ev'rywhere I go
How I cry,
With no reply!
No one seems to know
Where you've gone
So I go on,
Down a long, long road,
Walking all alone,
Down a long, long road
Back to you.

LIFE'S SO COMPLETE

Music by Richard Himber. Published. Copyrighted September 12, 1933.

VERSE

I've been a lonely rover,
Wandering through the years.
Loneliness now is over;
Love at last appears.

REFRAIN

All is right, the world is bright,
And with you in my arms tonight,

My lips can say, my heart repeat,
"Life's so complete."
Magic seems to fill the air;
Its thrill is more than I can bear.
With your caress, your kisses sweet,
Life's so complete.
The spell of love has never found me;
It came as such a surprise.
But now I see it all around me,
Up in the skies,
Deep in your eyes.
I'm at peace, my search is through;
My journey's end is found in you.
With you the world is at my feet—
Life's so complete.

INDIAN SUMMER

Music by Peter Tinturin. Published. Copyrighted September 13, 1933.

This is not the famous "Indian Summer." That one originally was a 1919 Victor Herbert piano solo. Fifteen years after Herbert's death in 1924, Al Dubin wrote a lyric for it, and the Herbert-Dubin "Indian Summer" became a number-one hit in a recording by Tommy Dorsey and His Orchestra, vocal by Jack Leonard (RCA Victor).

VERSE

Sun has descended,
Faded above;
Summer has ended,
Ended our love.
Whispering shadows sigh,
It's time we said goodbye.

REFRAIN

It's Indian summer;
The leaves are beginning to fall.
It's Indian summer,
And that means the end of it all.
We wandered through clover,
We searched for the moon;
And now it's all over,
So soon, so soon!
The sun fades away in the west,
The swallows are ready to start;
The last one is leaving his nest,
The way that you're leaving my heart.
I just can't believe we're through,
I just can't believe it of you—
Is Indian summer
My winter of love?

THERE'S A RING AROUND THE MOON

Music by Johnny Green. Published. Copyrighted September 29, 1933.

VERSE

Moon is red—
See it shining overhead.
What could be a stranger sign?
It is meant as a danger sign.

REFRAIN

You are in my arms tonight,
And heaven seems so bright,
But there's a ring around the moon.
Love is like a burning flame;
I hope it stays the same—
But there's a ring around the moon.
Does that mean there'll be rain in my heart soon?
Does that mean we'll be drifting apart soon?
I'm so afraid
That love will lose its thrill,
So hold me closer still,
For there's a ring around the moon.

GHOST OF LOVE

Music by Harold Spina. Registered for copyright as an unpublished song October 19, 1933.

VERSE

Twilight appears
Recalling my yesteryears.
Midnight and then
The past comes to life again,
The past comes to life again.

REFRAIN

A ghost of love has found me;
It came to stay
When you went away.
Now that you no longer want me,
A ghost of love will haunt me.
I feel your arms around me—
How real they seem!
And yet it's a dream,
Something that you left to taunt me,

A ghost of love to haunt me.
Blue hallucinations
Stealing across the ceiling
Before my eyes—
What a weird and eerie feeling,
Living in the mist
Where there's nothing existing!
I swear that I'll forget you,
But I can see
It never will be:
Now that you no longer want me,
A ghost of love will haunt me.

YOU HAVE TAKEN MY HEART

Music by Gordon Jenkins. Published. Copyrighted December 20, 1933. Previously registered for copyright as an unpublished song November 22, 1933.

VERSE

Here with your arms around me,
Love in all its mystery has found me.
Here with the moon above you,
Was I meant to be the one to love you?

REFRAIN

You have taken my heart and it's thrilling;
You have taken my heart and I'm willing.
Never have I known a thrill like this,
Like the murmur of rain, soft and tender,
Like the ocean's refrain in its splendor.
If you really want me, I'll surrender:
You have taken my heart.

YOU

Music by Joseph Meyer. Published. Copyrighted November 29, 1933.

VERSE

That certain feeling
I feel in my heart,
That certain feeling—
Just who made it start?
It didn't take me long to know it,
So it's time to show it's—

REFRAIN

You—I can't believe there's a you
Like you.
You're just too good to be true.
Those lips—now I've known them,
Darling, do I own them?
You—you often make me feel blue,
It's true.
Still, I can take it from you,
So you take it from me
That I'm the me for you.

OLD AUNT KATE

Music by Archie Bleyer. Published. Copyrighted December 4, 1933.
     Lyric missing.

FARE-THEE-WELL TO HARLEM

Music by Bernie Hanighen. Published. Copyrighted January 5, 1934. Previously registered for copyright as an unpublished song December 7, 1933.

Introduced and recorded by Paul Whiteman and His Orchestra, vocal by Johnny Mercer (Victor). Jack Teagarden, who was featured on the Whiteman-Mercer disc, recorded it with his band (Brunswick); Benny Morton also recorded the song (Columbia).

By this time Mercer was fulfilling a long-felt ambition to perform as well as write songs. He was hired to sing with Paul Whiteman's currently popular big band at New York's Biltmore Hotel, where he was frequently teamed with trombonist/singer Jack Teagarden in material that was "jazz for the masses."

The Whiteman connection began to be increasingly profitable. Whiteman's band started to broadcast from the Biltmore, giving Mercer and his songs a wider audience than he had previously enjoyed. Not only was he earning a regular seventy-five dollars a week writing songs for Whiteman, but other people of influence were hearing and being impressed by both him and his material. One of them was Irving Berlin, and it was not long before Mercer was signed to a contract with Berlin's music publishing company. Another major figure of the 1930s, Arthur Schwartz (of the songwriting team Dietz and Schwartz), likewise became a Mercer admirer at this time, and later became a Mercer collaborator himself.

VERSE

Mister Jackson, you sho' look cute,
You must have on your trav'lin' suit.
It looks as if
You're really gonna go somewhere.
Mister Budley, you spoke a book;
You just got time for one more look,
'Cuz Mister Jackson
Is leaving you for fair-,
For fair-, for—

REFRAIN

Fare-thee-well to Harlem!
Fare-thee-well to nightlife!
Goin' back where I can lead the right life—
Fare-thee-well to Harlem!

Things is tight in Harlem;
I know how to fix it:
Step aside, I'm gonna Mason-Dix it—
Fare-thee-well to Harlem!

Lately here my soul is reachin'
For the Bible's kindly teachin'
Wants to hear the rev'rund preachin'
"Love each other."
Wants to hear the organ playin',
Wants to hear the folks a-prayin'—
There's a voice within me sayin',
"Ease off, brother!"

So fare-thee-well to Harlem!
All this sin is frighteous;
Goin' back where ev'rybody's righteous—
Fare-thee-well to Harlem,
Fare-thee-well!

MY OLD MAN

Music by Bernie Hanighen. Published. Copyrighted December 22, 1933. Recorded by The Spirits of Rhythm (Brunswick).

VERSE

Sister Kate is cuttin' down expenses,
Brother Gate, you don't see him shirk.
Old Aunt Sue is losin' all her senses,
Try'n' to make a nickel do a dollar's work.
Squeeze a dime
Ev'ry time
And what is the reason why?
It's—

REFRAIN

My old man—
He only works on the one-day plan.
He does his business on Monday
And rests till Sunday,
My old man—
Bless his heart,
He's always tryin' to do his part.
But when it's time to get paid off,
Why, he gets laid off,
My old man.
When he steps out,
Grabs old missus from the washin' tub
And he takes her in a taxi to the Cotton Club,
With a flanky-danky-doodle and a um-ga-ga.
My old man,
He's gonna wind up an also-ran.
He's such a cheerful old loafer,
You're bound to go for
My old man.

FOOL THAT I AM

Music by Matt Malneck and Frank Signorelli. Published. Copyrighted March 16, 1934. Previously registered for copyright as an unpublished song February 16, 1934.

VERSE

So new at the game,
Was I to blame,
Getting my fingers burned?
If love lingers on
After you've gone,
It's because I haven't learned.

REFRAIN

Fool that I am,
I'm still being true.
Fool that I am,
What else can I do?
I want you so,
Though I know we're through—
Fool that I am,
I'm yours.

You told me lies,
But how could I tell?
I wasn't wise;
I loved you too well.
Now here am I

Still under your spell—
Fool that I am,
I'm yours.

No matter if we're apart,
You have my lips,
You have my heart.
No matter what happened then,
I'll do the same again.
Fool that I am,
I can't break away;
I live in hope
You'll come back someday.
That's how I am,
And that's how I'll stay—
Fool that I am,
I'm yours.

MOON COUNTRY (IS HOME TO ME)

Lyrics and music by Hoagy Carmichael and Johnny Mercer. Published. Copyrighted April 13, 1934.

Leading recording by Carmichael (Victor). Other recordings by Glen Gray and the Casa Loma Orchestra with vocal by Pee Wee Hunt (Brunswick), and Gray again (in 1939) with vocal by The Merry Macs (Decca).

Both Mercer and Carmichael were—separately and together—yearning for an America outside the urban sprawl. Hoagy's music, Mercer said, evoked "any place we used to know." Meredith Willson, another midwesterner, called it "our folk music of tomorrow."

VERSE

I know where the peach trees bear
A harvest all the year round.
I know where an old gray mare
Eats blue grass from the ground.
That's where folks never turn a hand,
They just live off the land;
My rockin' chair is waitin' there—
That's why I'm homeward bound.

REFRAIN

I long for that moon country,
That possum and coon country,
That sycamore heaven back South—
I'll lose my mind till I get there.
I long for that ol' country,
That good-for-the-soul country,

Good for cookin' things that melt in your
        mouth—
Oh, Lawd!
When my cousin Cindy Lou
Plays a twilight hymn to you,
She makes that ol' piano
Sound exactly like brand new.
I long for that moon country,
That's where I should be,
'Cause that ol' moon country
Is home to me.

WHEN A WOMAN LOVES A MAN

Music by Bernie Hanighen and Gordon Jenkins. Published. Copyrighted April 18, 1934. Leading recording by Billie Holiday (Vocalion) in 1938.

VERSE

Love to a man is just a thing apart,
To take or leave, according to his whim.
Love to a woman means her very heart—
She only want to live her life for him.

REFRAIN

Maybe he's not much,
Just another man,
Doing what he can;
But what does she care,
When a woman loves a man?

She'll just string along
All through thick and thin
Till his ship comes in—
It's always that way
When a woman loves a man.

She'll be the first one to praise him
When he's going strong,
The last one to blame him
When ev'rything's wrong.
It's such a one-sided game that they play,
But women are funny that way.

Tell her she's a fool,
She'll say, "Yes, I know,
But I love him so,"
And that's how it goes
When a woman loves a man.

HERE COME THE BRITISH

Music by Bernie Hanighen. Published. Copyrighted May 17, 1934. Previously registered for copyright as an unpublished song April 21, 1934, and again on May 12, 1934. Leading recordings by Paul Whiteman and His Orchestra, vocal by Mercer (Victor), and Glen Gray and His Casa Loma Orchestra, vocal by Pee Wee Hunt (Brunswick). Peggy Healy and John Hauser are performers on the Mercer recording.

VERSE 1

Children, open up your history,
Turn to lesson number twenty-three.
Take a look,
Then close the book,
And I will review it rapidly.

REFRAIN 1

Paul Revere, he took a ride,
Just to look around the countryside.
All at once his horse got skittish;
Here come the British,
Bang! Bang!

Washington at Valley Forge
Tried to cross the river—
Look out, George!
All at once his boat got skittish;
Here come the British,
Bang! Bang!

Oh!
Just look around,
No matter where—
Whoa!
You'll find that the British are there.
Napoleon
At Waterloo
Writin' Josephine a billet doux:
"Josie, I've got to close it,
Close this epistle;
There goes the whistle—
Here come the British,"
With a bang! Bang!

Version from Mercer recording

VERSE

Children, open up your history,
Turn to lesson number thirty-three.
Now, Miss Healy, take the floor,
Tell me what the shootin's for.

REFRAIN

Lizabeth, she came to town,
Walter Raleigh laid his coat right down;
All at once the queen got dizzy,
There went Lizzy,
Splash, splash.
Mr. Hauser, answer me,
Who shot who in '63?
Old Wellington shot ten straight passes
There's the classes . . . ah, gee.

Now look out here—
Don't you dare
Talk to your teacher that way.
I'll give you one more chance.
What happened in England today?

The Prince of Wales was in a race,
He was leadin' till he reached the steeple chase.
All at once the horse got skittish,
He starts stallin'
And the horse starts fallin'—
There went the British
With a bang! Bang!

In India the other day,
What did old Mahatma Gandhi say?
Old doctor put me on a diet,
I must be quiet.
What's all the riot?
Here come the British with a bang! Bang!

BENEATH THE CURTAIN OF THE NIGHT (NINFA DE OJOS BRUJOS)

Music and lyrics by Alfredo Brito. English lyric by Mercer. Published. Copyrighted May 14, 1934.

VERSE

Shadows of ev'ning are falling—
See them falling on the sea.
Shadows of ev'ning are calling—
Hear them calling you and me.
Tropical breezes are bringing
Native guitars softly singing;
Come where the music is playing—
Let's wander away.

Love,
The moon is calling from above,
Come
Beneath the curtain of the night.
Love,
The paradise we're dreaming of
Waits
Beneath the curtain of the night—
Where drowsy waters kiss the shore,
You
And I will kiss forevermore.
So let us steal
Where love and love alone is real,
There
Beneath the curtain of the night.

HER FIRST EVENING DRESS

Music by Michael H. Cleary. Registered for copyright as an unpublished song May 14, 1934.

VERSE

He looks at her;
She looks away,
Afraid to meet his glance.
She looks again
In hopes that he may;
He does, and so they dance.

REFRAIN

It's her first evening dress
And his first dance, I guess;
See how grown-up they act,
How matter-of-fact!
See them try to conceal
The excitement they feel;
They pretend not to care,
But they both are aware:
It's her first evening dress;
It's their first love affair.

Earlier version of refrain, lines 1–6

It's her first evening dress
And his first dance, I guess;
How they try to disguise
Their youthful eyes with worldliness—
How they try to conceal
The thrill they feel with each caress!

PARDON MY SOUTHERN ACCENT

Music by Matt Malneck. Published. Copyrighted July 19, 1934. Previously registered for copyright as an unpublished song June 29, 1934.

VERSE

It's a universal moon above you;
Ask the Irish, ask the Greek:
They can always understand "I love you,"
No matter how they speak.

REFRAIN

Pardon my southern accent,
Pardon my southern drawl;
It may sound funny,
Ah, but honey, I love y'all!

If you don't like my accent,
If you don't like my drawl,
Then just don't listen,
Let's start kissin'—
Bet you'll fall!

Come on now,
Let me hear you steal my stuff.
When I say
"Do you love me?"
All you gotta say is "Sho' 'nuff!"

Pardon my southern accent—
Didn't I hear you drawl?
Were you just sighin'
Or replyin' "I love y'all"?

I SAW YOU DANCING IN MY DREAMS

Music by Matt Malneck and Frank Signorelli. Published. Copyrighted July 5, 1934.

VERSE

I dream the hours away,
Dreaming of you all day,
Hoping that my dreams will soon come true.
Though you are far from me,
I know that soon you'll be
Here with me where I can sing to you:

REFRAIN

I saw you dancing in my dreams
And I held you tight.
We sang a love song in my dreams
That wonderful night.
We shared a kiss beneath the Sweetheart Tree,
You whispered that you'd always care for me,
And then I woke up from my dreams
And found you were gone.
But still, I feel your kiss of dreams—
It's lingering on,
And when we meet someday
I'm sure I'll know you,
For I saw you dancing in my dreams.

OLD SKIPPER

Music by Hoagy Carmichael. Published. Copyrighted July 6, 1934.

VERSE

When the waves ran high 'neath an angry sky,
You'd stand before the wheel.
When you met the gale, you would haul the sail
And ride an even keel.
Those days are past and you've left the foam
To an anchor fast in the port of home;
But the waves still call as the shadows fall
And off to sea you sail.

REFRAIN

Dream away, old skipper,
Dream of the days when men were men.
There in your chair and bedroom slippers
Set sail again.
Dream away, old skipper,
Dream of lands so far away;
Sail by the stars and mighty Dipper
To yesterday.
Oh, for a crew that could still pull 'er through
When the north wind moans!
Gone is the crew and the old vessel, too,
Down to Davey Jones.
Dream away, old skipper,
There beside the firelight gleam;
Stand at the wheel of your old clipper
And dream, dream, dream.

IF I COULD HAVE MY WAY

Music by Serge Walter. Published. Copyrighted August 10, 1934.

VERSE

Dear,
If I could own a wishing ring,
And if wishes could come true,
Life
Would never hold too great a thing
To bring to you.

REFRAIN

The moon would light
Your room tonight
If I could have my way.
The breeze would sigh
Your lullaby
If I could have my way.
I
Would gather roses for your bed;
Stars
Would form a halo for your head—
And you would be
In love with me
If I could have my way.

THE BATHTUB RAN OVER AGAIN

Music by Michael H. Cleary. Published. Copyrighted August 22, 1934.

VERSE

I heard dripping, there was something dripping,
It was water dripping on the bathroom floor—
I was dreaming 'bout our eight o'clock date.
I heard dripping, it was plaster dropping,
And I had to pick the pieces up once more—
Now you know the reason why I'm late.

REFRAIN

Oh! The bathtub ran over again
While I was lying there dreaming,
Lying there and dreaming of you—
Yes, the bathtub ran over, as tubs will do.
And the ceiling got soakin' again;
The folks below began saying,

"Dreaming 'bout your baby's okay,
But the house is floating away!"
Yes, I guess I heard the water,
But I didn't bother to look;
I thought we were in the country
And the water was the tinkle of a bubbling brook.
So the bathtub ran over again:
It does whenever I'm dreaming,
And I'm always dreaming of you—
So before I drown the whole darn town,
I think you'd better say "I do!"

TRANSATLANTIC MERRY-GO-ROUND (1934)

Produced by Edward Small for Reliance Pictures, released by United Artists. Released November 1934. Copyright December 12, 1934. Directed by Benjamin Stoloff. Original story by Leon Gordon. Additional dialogue and scenes by Joseph Moncure March and Harry W. Conn. Musical numbers staged by Sammy Lee and Larry Ceballos. Musical director: Alfred Newman.

The cast: Gene Raymond, Nancy Carroll, Jack Benny, Sydney Howard, Mitzi Green, Sid Silvers, Sidney Blackmer, Ralph Morgan, Shirley Grey, Patsy Kelly, Sam Hardy, William "Stage" Boyd, Robert Elliott, Frank Parker, Carlyle Moore, Jean Sargent, Jimmy Grier and His Orchestra, the Boswell Sisters (Martha, Connie, and Vet).

The songs for this film are by Richard A. Whiting (music) and Sidney Clare (lyrics), except for "If I Had a Million Dollars."

Master criminal Lee Lotter has been murdered on a liner and several of the passengers have a motive.

IF I HAD A MILLION DOLLARS

Music by Matt Malneck. Published. Copyrighted September 26, 1934. Previously registered for copyright as an unpublished song August 30, 1934. Introduced by the Boswell Sisters (Martha, Connie, and Vet), accompanied by Jimmy Grier and His Orchestra. Later recorded by them (Brunswick). Other leading recordings were made by Richard Himber and His Orchestra with vocal by Joey Nash (Victor) and by Ozzie Nelson and His Orchestra (Brunswick).

VERSE

Castles with their thrones,
Ships upon the sea,
Gold and precious stones
All belong to me.
Foolish though it seems,
Ev'ry word is true;
Though they're only mine in dreams,
My dreams belong to you.

REFRAIN

If I had a million dollars,
I know just what I would do.
I'd tie a string around the world
And bring all of it to you.
Those little things you pray for,
Whatever they may be,
I'd have enough to pay for
Them all COD.
If I spent a million dollars,
I know I would never care,
Because as long as you were mine,
I'd still be a millionaire.
That's why I'm always dreaming,
Dreaming of what I'd do
If I had a million dollars
And you.

P.S. I LOVE YOU

Music by Gordon Jenkins. Published. Copyrighted September 24, 1934. The leading recording was by Rudy Vallee (Victor); in 1953 the song was revived successfully by the Hilltoppers (Dot).

Mercer later recalled:

One time when Ginger was away on a trip and I naturally desired to write to her. Taking pen in hand, ol' massa Mercer wrote a long letter dealing with just the sort of trivia that occurs to one lonely for another. There it was, completed. I'd written many a love song, and I read it over. I'd left out the real reason I started the letter. So below the great message, I scrawled P.S. I Love You. Immediately, the thought of that phrase as a song title struck me and I dashed off what later, thanks to forgetful me and lucky fate, became a hit tune.

P.S. Mercer claimed this was his favorite song. On other occasions he named "On the Nodaway Road."

VERSE

What is there to write,
What is there to say?
Same things happen ev'ry day.
Not a thing to write,
Not a thing to say;
So I take my pen in hand
And start the same old way.

REFRAIN 1

Dear, I thought I'd drop a line.
The weather's cool;
The folks are fine;
I'm in bed each night at nine.
P.S. I Love You.

Yesterday we had some rain,
But all in all
I can't complain.
Was it dusty on the train?
P.S. I Love You.

Write to the Browns
Just as soon as you're able;
They came around to call.
I burned a hole
In the dining-room table—
And let me see, I guess that's all.

Nothing else for me to say,
And so I'll close—
But by the way,
Ev'rybody's thinking of you.
P.S. I Love You.

REPEAT REFRAIN

[*Replace final eleven lines with:*]

I do my best
To obey all your wishes;
I put a sign up: Think!
But I gotta buy
Us a new set of dishes
Or wash the ones piled in the sink!

Nothing else to tell you, dear,
Except each day seems like a year;
Ev'ry night I'm thinking of you.
P.S. I Love You.

JUST A FAIR-WEATHER FRIEND

Music by Matt Malneck. Published. Copyrighted December 17, 1934. Previously registered for copyright as an unpublished song November 16, 1934.

First version

I thought you'd always stay by me,
Faithful and true to the end;
But you ran away
At the first rainy day,
Just a fair-weather friend.
I had a heart that I gave you;
You only had one to lend:
For when skies were black,
Why, you took it right back,
Just a fair-weather friend.
Like a million others,
Getting all you could,
You were running true to your form.
If a little shower
Sends you off for good,
What would you do in a storm?
Gone is the future I dreamed of,
Those happy days we would spend;
They ended for me
When you turned out to be
Just a fair-weather friend.

Second version

VERSE

No one ever could have told me
You and I would drift apart;
No one ever could have told me—
No one but my heart.

REFRAIN

I thought that you'd stay by me,
True to the very end;
But you ran away
The first rainy day,
Just a fair-weather friend.
I had a heart I gave you,
But you had one to lend;
For when skies were black,
You took it right back,
Just a fair-weather friend.
Foolish me,
I couldn't see
The handwriting on the wall.
Sunny skies
Had dimmed my eyes;

I never thought rain would fall.
Just when I needed someone
On whom I could depend,
You walked out on me—
What else can you be?—
Just a fair-weather friend.

WALKIN' WITH MY SHADOW

Music by Bernie Hanighen. Published. Copyrighted November 21, 1934.

VERSE

Ev'ry night I lay me down to sleep,
And I try to rest my weary head.
Ev'ry day I look to see the sun,
But I find an empty sky instead.
Drifting with the tide,
No one guiding me,
Just a shadow by my side
Keeps me company.

REFRAIN

Walkin' with my shadow,
Sad and blue,
We don't even know where we're walkin' to;
I never seem to find the road
That leads me back to you.
Walkin' with my shadow ev'rywhere,
Askin' ev'rybody if you've been there,
I never seem to find the road
That leads me back to you.
Walkin' to the east,
Walkin' to the west,
Heaven knows where I'm going—
Will my heavy heart ever let me rest?
Must I go trav'lin' on?
Walkin' with my shadow all the day,
Only hopin' sometime you'll come my way—
I never seem to find the road
That leads me back to you.

DOWN T'UNCLE BILL'S

Music and lyrics by Mercer and Hoagy Carmichael. Published. Copyrighted November 26, 1934. Recorded by Frankie Trumbauer and His Orchestra (Victor). The quotation in Verse 2 comes from "When the Frost Is on the Punkin" by the Indiana poet James Whitcomb Riley (1849–1916).

VERSE

When the wind begins a-blowin'
And a-whistlin' in the lock,
Winter's rollin' in.
There's a butter churn a-goin'
And a turkey on the block
Down where the hills begin.

REFRAIN

Come the first snappy weather,
Folks'll get together
Down t'Uncle Bill's,
Down among the hills.
Tables set, and you can bet
Ev'ryone'll get lots of turkey,
Forty-pound.
Then we'll smoke and talk and joke,
Laugh until we choke
When the cider comes round.
All the kids will be yelpin'
For a second helpin'
Down t'Uncle Bill's,
Down among the hills.
Well, it looks like snowin';
Soon we'll all be goin'
Down t'Uncle Bill's
Once more.

VERSE 2

"When the frost is on the punkin
And the fodder's in the shock,"
Winter's rollin' in.
You can bet your coffee dunkin'
There's a turkey on the block
Down where the hills begin.

REPEAT REFRAIN

LAWD, I GIVE YOU MY CHILDREN

Music by Bernie Hanighen. Published. Copyrighted December 13, 1934.

VERSE 1

Lawd, I give you my children;
I done all I can do.
This congregation
Is way beyond salvation,
So I turn them over to you!

REFRAIN 1

Are they livin' in sin?
Yeah, Lawd!
Are they drinkin' their gin?
Yeah, Lawd!
Stayin' up all night?
Yeah, Lawd!
Do they ever do right?
No, Lawd!
Father, Father,
Won't you take them off my hands?

VERSE 2

Lawd, they don't mind their deacon—
Can't you work on them, too?
Please don't destroy 'em,
But if you'll just annoy 'em,
Lawd, I'll sure feel grateful to you!

REFRAIN 2

Are they comin' to church?
No, Lawd!
Leavin' us in the lurch?
Yeah, Lawd!
Are they payin' their dues?
No, Lawd!
Does your parson need shoes?
Yeah, Lawd!
Father, Father,
Won't you take 'em off my hands?

CODA

Lawd, you done hear my story;
Now hear me while I pray,
You better save me
From this flock you gave me—
I can't get to heaven that way.

GAMBLING (1934)

Produced by Harold B. Franklin for Fox Film Corporation. Released December 1934. Copyright November 2, 1934. Directed by Rowland V. Lee. Screenplay by Garrett Graham, from the stage play *Gambling* by George M. Cohan. Lyrics by George M. Cohan and Johnny Mercer. Music by George M. Cohan and Bernard Hanighen. Musical director: Frank Tours. Starring George M. Cohan, with Wynne Gibson, Dorothy Burgess, Theodore Newton, Harold Healy, Walter Gilbert, Cora Witherspoon, Joseph Allen, Percy Ames, Six Spirits of Rhythm, David Morris, E. J. DeVarney, Robert Strange, John T. Doyle, Fred Miller, and Hunter Gardner.

DR. WATSON AND MR. HOLMES

Music by Bernie Hanighen. Introduced by Six Spirits of Rhythm and recorded by them as The Spirits of Rhythm (Decca).

Gangway for that famous sleuth!
Must be Sherlock—that's the truth.
"Elementary, Doctor Watson."
"You are amazing, Mister Holmes."

No detective stands a chance.
"Well, How about this Philo Vance?
He's a good man, Doctor Watson."
"As a jurist, Mister Holmes."

"When they have a crime wave
And the papers all rave
And they're hollering for a showdown,
The inspector can see
That he's got to have me—
'Quick, quick, Sherlock, the lowdown.' "

"Cops can't even solve a crime,
Bound to miss it every time.
Ain't it awful, Doctor Watson?"
"Simply lousy, Mister Holmes."

"Now, when policemen have a case
Where they raid some gambling place,
How they muff it, Doctor Watson!"
"What's the reason, Mister Holmes?"

"By the time the cops catch on,
All the evidence is gone.
Must be dummies, Doctor Watson."
"They're morons, Mister Holmes."

"While they're looking around,
Not a thing to be found,
And the gambling rooms are lobbies.
And the rattle of dice
Is the tinkle of ice."
"Look, Sherlock—the bobbies!"

"Why, Inspector, how d'ye do?"
"Sherlock, I'll be seeing you."
"Now where are you going, Doctor Watson?"
"To China, Mister Holmes!"

OLD MAN RHYTHM,
TO BEAT THE BAND,
and Other Songs of 1935

THE LITTLE MAN WITH THE HAMMER

Music by Bernie Hanighen. Registered for copyright as an unpublished song January 3, 1935. Recorded by Glen Gray and His Casa Loma Orchestra, vocal by Pee Wee Hunt (Decca). This song was also performed in a 1943 two-reel Universal short called *Glen Gray and His Casa Loma Orchestra in "Smoke Rings,"* with a vocal also by Hunt. Lyric transcribed from recording.

Now there are great men of wisdom,
Lawyers and doctors and such,
And even great politicians,
But even they don't amount to much
In comparison with a certain man
Who really has what it takes—
He's the leading purveyor of bad dreams
And a connoisseur of headaches.

When the little man with the hammer
Starts to hit you with all his might,
You can bet your boots
And your Sunday suits
You got a little tight.
When the little man with the hammer
Starts to reorganize your head,
Then there ain't no pills
Gonna cure your ills;
You might as well be dead.
When it's after one
And you're having fun,
You never give a hang,
But I'll bet you say
At the break of day,
"Here come the British with a bang bang!"
It's the little man with the hammer,
Always trying to pick a fight.
So it's lift your cup
With the bottoms up,
We'll wear 'em out tonight.

[*Drum solo.*]

Yeah, there he goes startin' to pound.
Maybe someday I'll get used to that sound.
Pretty soon trumpets will start to blow
And old Gabriel will say, "Pee Wee, you better go."
Then that little man will try to make me wait,
But I'll get away before it's too late.
Then you know just what that little rascal will do?
He'll pick someone else. Boy, I sure hope it's you.
He'll try to get you, you better look out,
That little man with the hammer that I'm talkin'
  about.

FOR LOVERS ONLY

Music by Harry Warren. Lyrics by Al Dubin and Mercer. Registered for copyright as an unpublished song January 15, 1935. The song was intended for the Warner Bros. film *Broadway Gondolier* but was not used. It is the earliest known Warren-Mercer collaboration.

VERSE

The little dreams you love to cling to,
The words you sing to,
A serenade,
The magic of the night above you,
The words "I love you,"
They all were made—

REFRAIN

For lovers only.
The shadows fall
And bring the darkness
That hides them all.
The twilight hides the stars
Along the Milky Way,
And their design
Looks like a sign
That seems to say
For Lovers Only.
The way is clear;
The moon is lonely,
He wants you here.
The sun's for ev'ryone,
But night will always be
For lovers only,
Like you and me.

THE KEEPER OF MY HEART

Music by Matt Malneck. Registered for copyright as an unpublished song January 21, 1935. Recorded by Benny Goodman with a vocal by Helen Ward (Columbia) and by Mercer himself (Capitol).

You will be the keeper of my heart
Forever,
Even though we both may drift apart
Forever.
Just as long as there's a sky above,
You will be the keeper of my love.
I don't know if you will love me, too,
Forever,
Or if I may keep your heart from you
Forever.
I just know that you will always be
The keeper of my heart
For me.

THE DIXIELAND BAND

Music by Bernie Hanighen. Published. Copyrighted March 8, 1935. Benny Goodman recorded the song for Columbia, with vocal by Helen Ward, and also for Victor. Other leading recordings were made by Bob Crosby, with vocal by Joe Harris (Decca); by Kay Starr (Crystalette); and by Mercer himself (Capitol).

Dj'ever hear the story of the Dixieland Band?
Let me tell you, brother,
That the music was grand!
They had piano and clarinet;
Only thing they needed was a second cornet—
And that's what led to the ruin,
Ruin of the Dixieland Band.

When the folks would holler for the "Maple Leaf
  Rag,"
They would get to swinging,
But the trumpet would drag.
They had to keep him 'cause he played so sweet,
But they needed someone who could give them
  the beat,
Someone who swung with the rhythm,
Rhythm of the Dixieland Band.

He'd play so sweetly.
'Stead of playin' [*musical riff*]
He'd play so sweetly,

Old Man Rhythm: *Johnny is in the baggage rack.*
Standing, from left to right: *Sonny Lamont, Betty Grable, Douglas Fowley, Grace Bradley, and Bill Carey*

They'd be sayin' [*musical riff*]—
Sure enough, he got 'em so they couldn't play
  right.
Finally he fixed 'em on a Saturday night:
He hit a figure that was off the chord,
Apoplexy got 'em and they went to the Lord.
And that's the pitiful story,
Story of the Dixieland Band.

Now they're up in heaven and they're happy at
  last,
'Cause they found a trumpet man who really can
  blast.
The way he swings 'em is an awful shame;
He can really do it—Gabriel is his name.
And now, folks, here is a sample,
Listen to the Dixieland Band.

If you hear a trumpet start to play,
Don't you be afraid it's the Judgment Day,
'Cause it's just Mister Gabriel soundin' his A
And the Dixieland Band is fixin' to play!

OLD MAN RHYTHM (1935)

Associate producer: Zion Myers for RKO Radio Pic-
tures. Released August 1935. Copyright August 2, 1935.
Directed by Edward Ludwig. Screenplay by Sig Herzig
and Ernest Pagano, from a story by Lewis E. Gensler,
Sig Herzig, and Don Hartman. Additional dialogue by
H. W. Hanemann. Music by Lewis E. Gensler. Lyrics by
Johnny Mercer. Dance numbers staged by Hermes Pan.
Song numbers staged by Sam White. Musical director:
Roy Webb.

With Charles "Buddy" Rogers, George Barbier, Bar-
bara Kent, Grace Bradley, Betty Grable, Eric Blore,
Erik Rhodes, John Arledge, Johnny Mercer, Donald
Meek, and Evelyn Poe.

A wealthy businessman becomes a college freshman
to prevent his son marrying a gold digger. Mercer's first
film score.

THERE'S NOTHING LIKE A COLLEGE EDUCATION

Published. Copyrighted July 22, 1935. Previously registered for copyright as an unpublished song May 21,
1935. Introduced by Douglas Fowley, Joy Hodges, John
Arledge, Margaret Nearing, Bill Carey, Betty Grable,
Sonny Lamont, Johnny Mercer, Eric Blore, Evelyn Poe,
and ensemble.

VERSE

ALL: Rah! Rah! Rah! Sis boom bah!

DOUGLAS
FOWLEY: Mister Jones, I've got a proposition.
  It's not a job,
  Not insurance,
  It's none of those.

ALL: Rah! Rah! Rah! Sis boom bah!

FOWLEY: Mister Jones, a man in your position
  Will understand
  Just what I'm selling—
  Here goes!

REFRAIN 1

JOY
HODGES: If you've never had a college education,
  Then you ought to have a college
    education,
  'Cause there's nothing like a college
    education
  To teach you how to fall in love.
  If you never took a stroll around the
    campus,
  Then you ought to take a stroll around
    the campus,
  'Cause there's nothing like a stroll
    around the campus
  To learn about the moon above.
  Now, if you speak in Latin or Greek,
  She'll think you're simply grand.
  If you say "I-ove-lay ou-yay,"
  Just hold her hand—she'll understand.
  This normally should lead to osculation
  (For which "kissing" is the literal
    translation),
  And to be the master of the situation—

ALL: Oh, there's nothing like a college
    education!

JOHNNY
MERCER: [*spoken*] Yeah.

REFRAIN 2

JOHN
ARLEDGE: My brother says
  You can cram until you go into a coma,
  You can write a million themes for
    your diploma,
  But until you learn to write that letter
    home-a,
  Then you'll never be a college man.

If you don't pick out a roommate
  who's a scholar,
One who's always glad to lend you half
  a dollar,
And a guy who wears the same size
  shirt and collar,
Then you're dumb as when you first
  began.

MARGARET
NEARING: Well, I can't dance,
  And as for romance,
  I don't know what that is.
  I can't flirt
  Or wear a short skirt,
  But I'm a whiz at an algebra quiz.

UNKNOWN
SINGER: [*as* BING CROSBY] You may learn about
    the problems of the masses;
  In chemistry you'll study poison
    gases;
  But until the day you learn to cut your
    classes—

ALL: Oh, you haven't got a college
    education!

MERCER: [*spoken*] Yeah!

REFRAIN 3

BILL
CAREY: You can study pharmacy till you're the
    berries,
  You may be one of the great
    apothecaries,
  But until you learn to mix a super
    chocolate whip with cherries,
  You might as well stay home and
    play—
  You'll never make a dime that way!

BETTY
GRABLE: So you learn to cook and marry some
    baloney
  Who comes home to every meal with
    some old crony,
  And there's nothing in the house but
    macaroni—
  Oh, you'll never keep a man that way!
  Now you must cram for every exam,
  And learn a lot of facts;
  But it's great when you graduate:
  You just relax—

FOWLEY: And pay income tax!

SONNY
LAMONT: Each professor says that I'm his worst
    tormentor,
  I'm the dumbest guy in every class I
    enter,
  But as long as I'm an old collegiate
    center—

ALL: Oh, you'll always have a college
  education!
MERCER: [*spoken*] Yeah.

REFRAIN 4

MERCER: Oh, I left my old plantation in the
  South-a
  With my southern accent drippin' from
  my mouth-a
  Just to hear you Yankees talk to one
  a-nouth-a,
  But I can't understand a word.
  When my German teacher tries to make
  me *sprechen*,
  And it's time to give the class a final
  check-in,
  I've got everybody sayin', "Well, I
  reckon,"
  It's the darndest thing you ever heard!
  I endorse our lovemaking course;
  I never pass it by.
  Every day my mark is an A;
  I'll tell you why: I satisfy!
  Any time those coeds wanna pet, I pets
  'em;
  If they want to cuddle in my arms, I lets
  'em;
  It's my southern hospitality that gets
  'em—
ALL: Oh, there's nothing like a college
  education!

ERIC
BLORE: I'm the handyman, the valet, and the
  waiter;
  I'm the registrar, the kingfish, the
  dictator;
  I'm the pater of the dear old alma
  mater—
  I've been here since enrollment day.

  This is Andy, he's my first-assistant yes
  man,
  Or in England, as we'd say, my
  acquiesce man,
  But the blighter's nothing but a
  blooming guess man,
  And "I won't talk" is all he'll say!

EVELYN
POE: Mama said I ought to be wed—
  Well, kid, I'm nearly twenty-two!
  Get some poise, go out with the boys;
  You'll find a few that are dumber than
  you.
ALL: So you go to school to find your true
  vocation—
  So what happens when you're through
  with graduation?

So you wind up in a diff'rent
  occupation—
Oh, there's nothing like a college
  education, yeah!
Rah! Rah! Rah!
Sis! Boom! Bah!
Roberts! Roberts! Rah!

Additional lyrics (not used in film)

You can study salesmanship and self-reliance,
You can get your bizness course down to a
  science,
But if you can't go and get yourself some clients,
You may as well stay home and play.

If you're broke, the money's a joke,
Don't let it worry you;
Your old man will do what he can—
If he's true blue he'll work your way through!

Attention, please, you budding M.D.'s,
I've got a cure for nerves.
Engineers, just lend me your ears—
He who observes will learn about curves!

BOYS WILL BE BOYS, GIRLS WILL BE GIRLS

Published. Copyrighted July 22, 1935. Previously registered for copyright as an unpublished song June 4, 1935. Introduced by Betty Grable, Evelyn Poe, Joy Hodges, Grace Bradley, Ronald Graham, John Arledge, Barbara Kent, and ensemble.

VERSE

BETTY
GRABLE: I betcha when your father was a
  youngster,
EVELYN
POE: I betcha when your mother was a maid,
JOY
HODGES: I betcha that he stood beneath her
  window,
GRACE
BRADLEY: I betcha that he sang this serenade:

REFRAIN

GRABLE: Pardon me, but can't you see
  That there's a moon above?
ALL: Boys will be boys,

Girls will be girls,
Love will be love.

GRABLE: Why deny that you and I
  Have dreams we're dreaming of?
ALL: Boys will be boys,
  Girls will be girls,
  Love will be love.

GRABLE: What strong arms you have, darling—
  The better to hold me near!
  What sweet lips you have, darling—
  The better to kiss me, my dear!

  So hold me tight,
  It's quite all right—
  Just ask the moon above:
ALL: Boys will be boys,
  Girls will be girls,
  Love will be love.

Additional lines for refrain [lines 11 to end of lyric]

JOHN
ARLEDGE: Ah, Juliet, you're a prisoner;
  I think it's a doggone crime!
BARBARA
KENT: [*as* MAE WEST] Well, Romeo, if you
  think so,
  Come up and free me sometime!
  Hold me tight,
  It's quite all right—
  Just ask the moon above.
  He'll wink his eye, and he'll reply,
  "Boys will be boys,
  Girls will be girls,
  Love will be love."

COMES THE REVOLUTION, BABY

Published. Copyrighted July 22, 1935. Previously registered for copyright as an unpublished song June 4, 1935. Introduced by Joy Hodges and Grace Bradley, duo pianos, with Johnny Mercer and Evelyn Poe. Danced by Betty Grable and Sonny Lamont.

VERSE

JOHNNY MERCER: Sensational, spectacular,
  Swell, elegant you,
  I'll upset your apple cart.

Inferior, innocuous,
Impossible me,
Rebellion is in my heart.

REFRAIN 1

I'm sick of being your Mickey Mouse;
That ain't the way it should be.
Comes the revolution, baby,
You'll belong to me!
I'll head the family in our house;
Just stick around and you'll see.
Comes the revolution, baby,
You'll belong to me!
Let one be for all,
Let all be for one—
Let's be thataway, too.
Then you'll be for me
And I'll be for me
And three for a nickel
And none for you!
So just remember the smallest axe
Can wreck the mightiest tree.
Comes the revolution, baby,
You'll belong to me.

REFRAIN 2

EVELYN POE: I see your game and I call your bluff,
You're just the way you should be.*
Comes the revolution, baby,
You'll belong to me!
Forget the Harry Houdini stuff,
I'm still the gal with the key.
Comes the revolution, baby,
You'll belong to me!
Whatever we have,
We'll share what we have,
Just the way that we do.†
Then I'll take the soup
And I'll take the steak
And I'll leave the payment
Of the check to you!
So, don't forget when you're up in
    arms
Whose arms they're goin' to be.
Comes the revolution, baby,
You'll belong to me!

_____

* *Alternate line:*
    You're all I want you to be.
† *Alternate lines:*
    We'll share with each other,
    Just like poor kids do.

I NEVER SAW A BETTER NIGHT

Published. Copyrighted July 22, 1935. Previously registered for copyright as an unpublished song June 4, 1935. Introduced by Charles "Buddy" Rogers, Grace Bradley, Johnny Mercer, Douglas Fowley, and John Arledge.

VERSE

Gee whiz,
What a lovely night it is!
Hey, Toots,
Goin' my way?
Gee whiz,
What a lovely night it is!
Hey, Toots,
Is it okay?
Where do we go?
What do we do?
When do we start?
How's about you?
Hey, Toots,
Whaddaya say?
[*Whistle.*]

REFRAIN 1

I never saw a better night
For ringin' doorbells
Or shootin' marbles*
Or eatin' peanuts!
Or maybe makin' love is best—
Now, what would you suggest?

I never saw a better night
For climbin' fences†
Or stoppin' streetcars
Or throwin' snowballs!
Or maybe makin' love is best—
Now, what would you suggest?

My! My! My!
You're the apple of my eye,
And I want to be with you!
Why, why, why
Should we let the night go by
When there's so much to do, do, do?

I never saw a better night
For swimmin' channels

_____

* *Alternate line:*
    Or turnin' cartwheels
† *Alternate line:*
    For climbin' flagpoles

Or playin' hopscotch*
Or pitchin' horseshoes.
Or maybe makin' love is best—
Now, what would you suggest?

REFRAIN 2

GRACE
BRADLEY: I never saw a better night
For shootin' pistols—
An automatic
Is most emphatic.
You'd better make your last request—
Now, what would you suggest?

I never saw a better night
For swingin' blackjacks
To manufacture
A little fracture.
I'll put a lily on your chest—
Or what would you suggest?

Say your prayers;
Send a letter to your heirs,
Tell 'em that you done me wrong.
Spread your wings
While the congregation sings,
"Get along,
Little Dogie, get along!"

I never saw a better night
For using poison;
But then carbolic
Might give you colic.
So, maybe making up is best—
And that's what I suggest.

OLD MAN RHYTHM

Published. Copyrighted July 22, 1935. Previously registered for copyright as an unpublished song June 4, 1935. Introduced by Grace Bradley, Betty Grable, Margaret Nearing, Joy Hodges, Ronald Graham, Johnny Mercer, Bill Carey, Evelyn Poe, and danced by Bradley, Sonny Lamont, Grable, and Frank Edmunds, and reprised in the finale by the ensemble.

REFRAIN 1

Beat that drum,
Old Man Rhythm!

_____

* *Alternate line:*
    Or shootin' tigers

Make things hum,
Old Man Rhythm!
Wave your hand,
Start that band—
With a rum-tum-tum
On your big bass drum,
All the world goes crazy!

Pat your feet,
Old Man Rhythm!
When they beat,
We go with 'em!
Get movin',
Start provin'
That you're the king!
Make the sun start shinin',
And birds start singin',
And clocks start tickin',
And trains start puffin',
And feet start dancin',
And hearts start thumpin'—
And we'll go places,
And we'll be happy!
So, Old Man Rhythm,
Old Man Rhythm,
Old Man Rhythm, swing!

MUSICAL INTERLUDE

VERSE

Ev'ry bolero we hear—
Ah!—
Needs you for its atmosphere—
Ah!
You're in the tangoes of Spain,
You're in three quarter refrain,
But what's that, what's that?
Hear that tom-tom!

REFRAIN 2

[*Same as* REFRAIN 1 *except lines* 3–6:]

Where are you from,
Old Man Rhythm?
Here and there,
Ev'rywhere!

WHEN YOU ARE IN MY ARMS

Published. Copyrighted July 22, 1935. Previously registered for copyright as an unpublished song May 21, 1935. Introduced by Charles "Buddy" Rogers (Johnny).

This song was filmed, and announced in the RKO press materials, including stills, but is not sung in the current print as released for television—possibly a truncated print. The melody is heard several times in the background.

VERSE

Once love's mystery was secret to me,
A thing I could not see through.
Now love's mystery
Is clear as can be,
Since I found you.

REFRAIN

When you are in my arms,
There's music in the air.
There's music in the air
And moonlight ev'rywhere
When you are in my arms.
When you are by my side,
I walk along the street,
I walk along the street
With roses at my feet,
When you are by my side.
But when you go away,
The music doesn't play;
The moonlight fades away
Off in the sky.
My heart forgets to beat;
I walk along the street,
The roses at my feet
Wither and die.
So, when you're in my arms,
I say a little pray'r
I say a little pray'r
That I may keep you there
Forever in my arms.

IT'S A NIGHT IN A MILLION

Music by Harry Warren. Registered for copyright as an unpublished song June 20, 1935. Not used in film.

REFRAIN

It's a night in a million,
Stars were never so bright;
And you're one in a million
On this wonderful night.
Through the ages before us,
Through the ages to be,
It's a night in a million

That was saved from all eternity
And sent to you and me.

TO BEAT THE BAND (1935)

Original title: *If You Were Mine*. Associate producer: Zion Myers for RKO Radio Pictures. Released November 1935. Copyright November 8, 1935. Directed by Ben Stoloff. Screenplay by Rian James, from a story by George Marion, Jr. Music by Matt Malneck. Lyrics by Johnny Mercer. Musical numbers staged by Sam White. Musical director: Alberto Colombo. With Hugh Herbert, Helen Broderick, Roger Pryor, Fred Keating, Eric Blore, Phyllis Brooks, Evelyn Poe, Johnny Mercer, Ray Mayer, Joy Hodges, and the Original California Collegians.

Herbert plays a middle-aged incompetent who stands to inherit a multimillion-dollar estate, as long as he marries a widow— any widow—within three days.

I SAW HER AT EIGHT O'CLOCK

Music by Matt Malneck. Published. Copyrighted October 15, 1935. Previously registered for copyright as an unpublished song September 12, 1935. Introduced by Fred Keating, Johnny Mercer, Evelyn Poe, Hugh Herbert, Phyllis Brooks, Eric Blore, and the Original California Collegians. Alternate title: "Time Marches On."

FRED
KEATING: The Senate votes a million more
To end the war on crime;
Time marches on.
Professor Einstein says that there is
No such thing as time;
Time marches on.
Another earthquake rocks Japan
But be that as it may,

JOHNNY
MERCER: Here's the biggest news flash
Of the day—

REFRAIN 1

I saw her at eight o'clock;
I felt my heart jump.

I met her at nine o'clock,
Like any old chump,
I wasted till ten o'clock
Before I could talk;
Then I timidly suggested
That we oughta take a little walk.
Eleven o'clock came round;
She said it was late.
Along about twelve o'clock
We stopped at her gate.
And then at one o'clock I kissed her;
The moon fell out of sight.
Now, here it is two o'clock—
What a beautiful night!

REFRAIN 2

EVELYN

POE: I saw him at eight o'clock,
      A nice-lookin' guy.
      I met him at nine o'clock;
      I gave him the eye.
      Along about ten o'clock
      We went to a show—
      Don't you know he bought a pair of
          tickets in the ninety-second row!
      Eleven o'clock came round;
      He ordered a Coke—
      He could have got one for me,
      But then he was broke.
      He climbed the stairs to my apartment,
      He tried to hold me tight,
      So I kicked him right down again—
      What a terrible night!

REFRAIN 3

HUGH

HERBERT: I'll see you at eight o'clock,
          A definite date.

PHYLLIS

BROOKS: I'd rather say nine o'clock—
          You're sure to be late.

HERBERT: Well, how about ten o'clock—
          That is, if you can?
          I forgot I've got to go and see a
          Dog about a man!

BROOKS: Eleven o'clock suits me—
          Don't put yourself out!

HERBERT: Let's make it twelve o'clock,
          Thereabout.

BROOKS: Perhaps you'd rather make it Tuesday
          At five o'clock instead?

HERBERT: What time did you say it was?
          I'm going to bed.

SANTA CLAUS CAME IN THE SPRING

Music by Mercer. Published. Copyrighted October 15, 1935. Previously registered for copyright as an unpublished song July 17, 1935. Introduced by Roger Pryor.

VERSE

Is it April?
Is it snowing?
Have I lost my head completely?
Have blossoms turned to snowflakes on the ground?
Are they robins,
Are they sleigh bells
That I hear sing out so sweetly?
Has someone turned the calendar around?

REFRAIN

Santa Claus came in the spring,
Santa Claus came when the skies were blue—
I heard his sleigh bells ting-a-ling
The day that I met you.
Santa Claus came in the spring,
Riding along through the daffodils,
And I just saw him vanishing
Across the distant hills.

I heard his reindeer on the ground;
I thought I caught a glimpse of red—
But suddenly I whirled around,
And there you were instead!
What if he hurried away?
Santa Claus came when the skies were blue,
And now it's Christmas ev'ry day,
Because he brought me you.

EENY, MEENY, MINEY, MO

Music and lyrics by Matt Malneck and Mercer. Published. Copyrighted October 15, 1935. Previously registered for copyright as an unpublished song August 28, 1935. Introduced by Johnny Mercer, Ronald Graham, Evelyn Poe, and the Original California Collegians. Key recording by Benny Goodman (Victor). Other leading recordings by Ginger Rogers and Johnny Mercer (Decca), Bob Crosby (Decca), and Billie Holiday with Teddy Wilson (Brunswick).

Published version

VERSE

Round the town
What are they sayin'?
On the air
What are they playin'?
Something to teach to babies in nurseries.
Way back home
We howdy-do it,
And in France
They parlez-vous it—
You learned the phrase along with your ABCs:

REFRAIN

Eeny, meeny, miney, mo,
Catch a trouble by the toe,
If it hollers, let it go,
Let it fly away!

Eeny, meeny, miney, mo,
It's the saying high and low—
Hear it everywhere you go,
Any time of day.

Big Ben rings it,
Vallee sings it,
Whiteman swings it,
Even Mister Crosby Bings it.

Eeny, meeny, miney, mo,
Catch a trouble by the toe,
If it hollers, let it go,
Let it fly away!

Film version

EVELYN POE: Eeny, meeny, miney, mo,
             What's the use of feelin' low?
             Might as well be hi-de-ho,
             It's your lucky day!
             Go to meetin',
             Take your seatin',
             Keep repeatin'
             Everything is okey-dokey.

WHAT'S THE USE OF LIVING?

Music and lyrics by Mercer and Matt Malneck. Introduced by Ronald Graham. Sung separately and then simultaneously with "Eeny, Meeny, Miney, Mo."

What's the use of living
With no one to love?
What's the use of seeing
Cloudy skies above?
Why pretend I'm happy
When I'm not that way?
What's the use of living
With no one to love?

IF YOU WERE MINE

Music and lyrics by Mercer and Matt Malneck. Published. Copyrighted October 15, 1935. Previously registered for copyright as an unpublished song July 17, 1935. Introduced by Roger Pryor. Leading recording by Teddy Wilson and His Orchestra, with vocal by Billie Holiday (Brunswick). Other recordings were made by Lanny Ross (Brunswick), Jan Garber (Victor), and Jerry Cooper (Rainbow).

VERSE

When I make a wish,
When I say a prayer,
You are always in each one.
Not another thing for which I care,
Not a thing beneath the sun,
My one dream-come-true,
My one wish is you.

REFRAIN

If you were mine,
I could be a ruler of kings;
And if you were mine,
I could do such wonderful things!
I'd say to a star,
"Stop where you are,
Light up my lover's way,"
And ev'ry star above you
Would obey.
Say,
If you were mine,
I would live for your love alone;
To kneel at your shrine,
I would give up all that I own,
Yes, even my heart,
Even my life,
I'd trade it all for you,
And think I was lucky, too,
If you were mine.

MEET MISS AMERICA

Music and lyrics by Mercer and Matt Malneck. Published. Copyrighted October 15, 1935. Previously registered for copyright as an unpublished song August 28, 1935. Introduced by Joy Hodges, Johnny Mercer, the Original California Collegians, and ensemble; danced by Nick Condos.

Sheet music version

VERSE

Ladies and gents,
Ladies and gents,
This little lady is simply immense.
Is she terrific?
Is she colossal?
Is she a sight to see?
Ladies and gents,
Ladies and gents,
Now the big show is about to commence.
It's not a quarter,
It's not a nickel,
It's absolutely free!

REFRAIN

She's a local gal, but remember, pal,
Cinderella came from the sticks—
Meet Miss America
Nineteen thirty-six!
With her baby stare and her savoir faire,
She can do the fanciest tricks—
Meet Miss America
Nineteen thirty-six!
She can wear a gingham gown
Like it came from New York town;
She's a breath of Hollywood
Right here in the neighborhood!
When she waltzes by,
All the yokels sigh
And the city slickers are hicks—
Meet Miss America
Nineteen thirty-six!

Additional verses for film version

With some wampum belts,
Very little else,
She subdued Columbus and crew—
Meet Miss America
Fourteen ninety-two!

Back at Plymouth Rock
This one got the block
'Cause she sat on anyone's knee—

Meet Miss America
Sixteen twenty-three!

She can dig more gold
Than a bank could hold,
And she didn't have a mine—
Meet Miss America
Eighteen forty-nine!

With a cashmere shawl
And a southern drawl
She's the gal who started the war—
Meet Miss America
Eighteen sixty-four!

When she bustled in
With her bustle out,
Every fellow wanted a date
Meet Miss America
Eighteen ninety-eight!

You remember me.
I'm the girl you'd see
On the arm of ev'ry marine.
Meet Miss America
Nineteen seventeen!

You can have the rest
But I've got the best.
Here's the girl who everyone picks—
Meet Miss America
Nineteen thirty-six!

Additional lyric (dated August 21, 1935)

You can have the rest,
But I've got the best,
And I'm gonna have her for life—
Meet Miss America,
Privately my wife!

CENTRAL PARK

Music by Matt Malneck. Published. Copyrighted December 6, 1940. Previously registered for copyright as an unpublished song July 17, 1935. Originally written for *To Beat the Band* but unused. Finally used in *Let's Make Music* (1940), where it was introduced by Bob Crosby and His Orchestra.

VERSE

In Manhattan at the close of day
Lights are flickering on old Broadway.

Crowded ferry boats are bright,
Pushing along through the night.
While the shadows of the dusk grow long
And the city sings a noisy song,
In the bustle and the sound
There in the dark will be found—

REFRAIN

Central Park,
It will be our lover's lane
In the middle of Manhattan,
It will be our heart's domain.

Central Park
In the traffic's busy whirl
Is a meadow full of daisies
For a city boy and girl.

The stars can leave the sky,
We'll still go on dreaming;
For fifty stories high
The bright windowpanes
Will be gleaming.

Close your eyes
And you're under tropic skies
On an island in the dark,
Our island called
Central Park.

MAYBE YOU KNOW WHAT I MEAN

Music by Hoagy Carmichael. Registered for copyright as an unpublished song October 23, 1935.

VERSE 1

HE: Babe, ain't nature grand?
     All her tricks are neatly planned;
     Every creature has some feature to admire.
     Though you're none too swift,
     Maybe you can get the drift.
     Here's the point I would suggest—
     We're no different from the rest.

REFRAIN 1

Monkeys have tails
And fishes have scales,
And what do they have these charms for?
What are my great big arms for?
Maybe you know what I mean?

Camels have humps
And gooses have bumps
The moment they see a gander.
Why does a cat philander?
Maybe you know what I mean?

Why does the springtime bring fever?
Does a beaver work for fun?
What does a moon in the blue do?
Tell me who do rabbits run to?

Each unicorn is proud of his horn,
For that is his main attraction—
Think of the mare's reaction.
Maybe you know what I mean

INTERLUDE

Speaking of you and speaking of me,
Say, doncha think it's lovely weather?
S'posin' we get to get together?

VERSE 2

SHE: You believe I'm dense,
      And I think you've no sense—
      On these two points
      Both our viewpoints
      Coincide.
      I'll admit I'm green
      And my wits are none too keen,
      But as hopeless as I am,
      I don't need no diagram.

REFRAIN 2

Peacocks have plumes
And hotels have rooms
To lure in the wayward couple.
Why is a snake so supple?
Maybe I know what you mean.

The best of frogs
Will go to the dogs,
And I can explain their downfall.
Why did that Roman down fall?
Maybe I know what you mean.

While deer are shy in demeanor,
The hyena loudly laughs.

What do you make of the word "necks"—
Those absurd necks on giraffes?

Lovers have lanes
And lions have manes
And I know why men have muscles,
Why grandmama wore bustles—
Maybe I *know* what you mean.

WRAP YOURSELF IN CELLOPHANE

Music by Hoagy Carmichael. Registered for copyright as an unpublished song October 23, 1935.

VERSE

From your head to your feet,
You are sweet enough to eat,
So you'd better take care.
From your head to your toes,
You are mighty like a rose,
So you'd better beware.
Those kisses I have tasted,
They're sweet as they can be.
I hate to see them wasted,
Save each one for me.

REFRAIN

Wrap yourself in cellophane,
Fresh as you can be;
Tell everyone you're saving all your love for me.
If you get caught in the rain,
That will be all right,
You'll never lose that honey flavor, wrapped up
     tight.
You're my little chocolate candy bar,
Gotta keep an eye on you;
You're my little sugar hot-cha-cha,
Gotta tell you what to do-do-do-do-do.
Wrap yourself in cellophane,
Fresh as you can be;
Tell everyone you're saving all your love for me.

ON THE NODAWAY ROAD

Music by Charles Bates. Published. Copyrighted November 4, 1935. Mercer recalled: "It's a simple thing.

Just the story of a farmer riding down the road in his buggy and the things he thinks about. That's all there is to it. But it's my favorite." The song was a flop.

Ploddin', ploddin',
Ol' Betsy's head keeps a-noddin', noddin',
Ol' Betsy's hoofs are a kickin' up the dust along
   the road,
Haulin' a load down the Nodaway Road.
Creakin', creakin',
Ol' wagon wheels keeps a-squeakin', squeakin',
Groanin' a tune while the crickets sing their song,
Go 'long, go 'long
Haulin' a load down the Nodaway Road.

Got to get a load o' hay to town,
Hurry back before the sun goes down.
Smoke in the chimney as we climb the hill
Round evenin' time, round evenin' time.
Ol' Betsy hurries goin' past the mill
Round evenin' time, round evenin' time.
I can hear the dogs bark
As I open up the gate,
Ain't missed meetin' me yet;
And the lights through the dark say,
"You'd better not be late,
Supper table is set."

Night is creepin', creepin',
I'll bet ol' Betsy is sleepin', sleepin',
Dreamin' away of another dusty day
To toil away,
Haulin' a load down the Nodaway Road,
Haulin' a load down the Nodaway Road.

GOODY GOODY

Lyrics and music by Mercer and Matt Malneck. Published. Copyrighted January 14, 1936. Previously registered for copyright as an unpublished song December 20, 1935. The top-selling recording—number one on the charts—was by Benny Goodman and His Orchestra, with vocal by Helen Ward (Victor). Other significant recordings were made by Freddy Martin (Brunswick) and Bob Crosby (Decca). Frankie Lyman and the Teenagers made a successful recording in 1957.

Legend has it that Mercer saw the words on the menu of a Chinese restaurant, made a note of them, then filed them away and lost them. Years later they resurfaced and struck him as being a good title for a song for the Benny Goodman band. Lead singer Helen Ward hated it but was persuaded to sing it—and it became one of her biggest hits.

VERSE

You told me that
There wasn't a lesson in lovin'
That you hadn't learned.
Oh yeah?
Oh yeah?
You told me that you keep playin' with fire
Without getting burned.
Oh yeah?
Oh yeah?

REFRAIN

So you met someone
Who set you back on your heels—
Goody goody!
So you met someone
And now you know how it feels—
Goody goody!
So you gave him your heart too,
Just as I gave mine to you,
And he broke it in little pieces,
Now how do you do?*

So you lie awake
Just singin' the blues all night—
Goody goody!
So you think that love's
A barrel of dynamite.
Hooray and hallelujah,
You had it comin' to ya.†
Goody goody for him,
Goody goody for me,
And I hope you're satisfied,
You rascal, you!

———————

* *Alternate version of lines 9–10 of refrain:*
   And he stuck it in his collection,
   Section ninety-two.
† *Alternate version of line:*
   Now you don't like it, do ya?

BING CROSBY'S OUTSTANDING HIT

I'm An Old Cowhand

(FROM THE RIO GRANDE)

Words and Music by
JOHNNY MERCER

AS SUNG BY
BING CROSBY
in his latest Paramount Picture
"RHYTHM ON THE RANGE"
musical direction by BORIS MORROS.

Leo Feist inc.   1629 BROADWAY · NEW YORK · N.Y

Adolph Zukor presents

"RHYTHM ON THE RANGE"

with
BING
CROSBY
Frances
FARMER
Bob BURNS

Directed by Norman Taurog
A PARAMOUNT PICTURE

LEW LESLIE'S BLACKBIRDS OF 1936 (London) and Other Songs of 1936

RISE AND SHINE (1936)

Produced at the Theatre Royal, Drury Lane, London. Opened May 7, 1936: 44 performances. Directed by Ralph Reader. Cast included: Irene Browne, Binnie Hale, Clarice Hardwicke, Syd Walker, Jack Whiting, Grace Lane, Eileen Penberthy, Meriel Forbes, John Kevan, Geoffrey Sumner, Viola Compton, D. Hay Petrie, Alexander Butler, Leonard Thorne, Mary Honer, David Garry, Fred Hearne, Reg Smith, and Gordon Crocker.

I'M BUILDING UP TO AN AWFUL LETDOWN

Music by Fred Astaire. Published. Copyrighted December 30, 1935. Previously registered for copyright as an unpublished song November 22, 1935. Introduced by Binnie Hale, Jack Whiting, and ensemble.

Recorded by Fred Astaire (Brunswick), Red McKenzie (Decca), and The Little Ramblers (Bluebird).

It's generally thought that Mercer's first song with Fred Astaire was the result of a chance encounter in 1935 at a Hollywood recording studio, where Mercer was recording "Eeny, Meeny, Miney, Mo" with Ginger Rogers. In fact, they had worked together as far back as 1930, on a song called "More and More" (lyric missing). Throughout his career Astaire remained an aspiring songwriter, and the chance meeting triggered their decision to collaborate again.

VERSE

I'm like Humpty Dumpty
Upon the garden wall:
I'm riding high,
And who can deny
That whatever goes up must fall?
Poor old Humpty Dumpty,
He got the toughest break;
And yet his fall
Was nothing at all
Like the tumble I'm gonna take.

REFRAIN

I'm building up to an awful letdown
By playing around with you.
You're breaking down my terrific buildup
By treating me as you do.
My castles in the air,
My smile so debonair,
My one big love affair,
Is it just a flash?
Will it all go smash,
Like the nineteen twenty-nine market crash?
I'm building up to an awful letdown
By falling in love with you.

WELCOME, STRANGER

Music by Mercer. Published. Copyrighted March 16, 1936. Previously registered for copyright as an unpublished song February 12, 1936. An earlier song bears the same title but different lyrics and music (see p. 19).

VERSE

If I saw an angel
On a busy street,
It would cause me no surprise.
Ordinary angels,
They're not any treat
After you came true
Before my very eyes.

REFRAIN

Welcome, stranger—
Fancy meeting you here!
Welcome, stranger—
There's just room for two here.
Even though it's humble
For such magic charms,
Make yourself at home, dear,
Right in my arms.
Welcome, stranger—
Oh, how I have missed you!
You're no stranger;
In my dreams I've kissed you.
My love has been your love
From the very start.
Welcome, stranger—
Welcome to my heart!

LOST

Music by Phil Ohman. Lyrics by Mercer and Macy O. Teetor. Published. Copyrighted February 28, 1936. Previously registered for copyright as an unpublished song February 12, 1936. Leading recordings by Guy Lombardo (Victor), Jan Garber and His Orchestra (Decca), Hal Kemp and His Orchestra (Brunswick), Ruth Etting (Bluebird), Vincent Lopez (Melotone), and Peggy Mann (Coral).

VERSE

It pays to advertise,
That's what they say;
And so I'll advertise
My heart's gone astray.
I missed it first of all
The day we met.
For your information,
Here's the situation . . .

REFRAIN

Lost—a heart as good as new.
Lost—the moment I met you.
Lost or strayed or stolen away—
Finders keepers, losers weepers.
Lost—two lips that look like mine.
Found—two lips that look divine.
Lost—my heart;
But I was lucky, too,
Because I lost my heart to you.

THE BELLS OF HONOLULU

Music by Franz Steininger. Published. Copyrighted February 28, 1936.

VERSE

The natives were singing "Aloha";
The vessel was ready to start;
The chapel bells rang out their sad goodbye.
A maiden was kissing her sailor
And begging him not to depart
As there on the shore
He kissed her once more
And whispered with a sigh:

REFRAIN

When the bells of Honolulu
Sing their twilight melody,

I'll be sailing far away from you,
So pray for me.
Let the bells of Honolulu
At the close of ev'ry day
Ring a message of my love to you
While I'm away.
Let's kiss and say "Aloha,
Aloha, till we meet again."
Then the bells of Honolulu
Will ring out their sweetest song,
For they'll see me in your arms again,
Where I belong.

RHYTHM ON THE RANGE (1936)

Produced by Benjamin Glazer for Paramount Pictures. Released July 1936. Copyright July 31, 1936. Directed by Norman Taurog. Screenplay by John C. Moffitt, Sidney Salkow, Walter DeLeon, and Francis Martin, based on a story by Mervin J. Houser. Musical director: Boris Morros. With Bing Crosby, Frances Farmer, Bob Burns, Martha Raye, Samuel S. Hinds, Warren Hymer, Lucille Webster Gleason, George E. Stone, James Burke, Martha Sleeper, Clem Bevans, Leonid Kinskey, Charles Williams, and Beau Baldwin, 50th (a bull).

The songs for this film are by Leo Robin, Sam Coslow, Frederick Hollander, Richard A. Whiting, Ralph Rainger, Billy Hill, and J. Keirn Brennan, except for "I'm an Old Cowhand (from the Rio Grande)."

A hired hand saves the boss's daughter when she is kidnapped by local bad men.

I'M AN OLD COWHAND (FROM THE RIO GRANDE)

Music by Mercer. Published. Copyrighted May 26, 1936. Introduced by Bing Crosby, Martha Raye, Leonid Kinskey, Bob Burns, the Sons of the Pioneers, and Louis Prima on trumpet. Crosby's recording with Jimmy Dorsey and His orchestra (Decca) became a number-two hit on the popular-music charts.

Mercer remembered:

Between movie assignments Ginger and I took a trip down to Savannah in a little car. We took three days out of six just to cross Texas, and I saw all those guys down there in those spurs and ten-gallon hats driving cars around. That struck me as kind of funny and so I thought maybe I should put it all into a song. Bing put the song into a picture, and I really think he saved my Hollywood career because I began to get more offers after that.

It was to be the first of several collaborations with Crosby, that other ex-Whiteman band singer, over the next forty years.

According to music historian Will Friedwald, "I'm an Old Cowhand," while "credited entirely to Johnny Mercer," was "partially written by" Harry Warren.

Published version

VERSE

Step aside, you ornery tenderfeet—
Let a big bad buckaroo past!
I'm the toughest hombre you'll ever meet,
Though I may be the last.
Yessirree,
We're a vanishing race;
Nosirree,
Can't last long.
Step aside, you ornery tenderfeet,
While I sing my song.

REFRAIN 1

I'm an old cowhand
From the Rio Grande,
But my legs ain't bowed
And my cheeks ain't tanned.
I'm a cowboy who never saw a cow,
Never roped a steer 'cause I don't know how,
And I sho' ain't fixin' to start in now.
Yippy-I-O-ki-ay,
Yippy-I-O-ki-ay.

REFRAIN 2

I'm an old cowhand
From the Rio Grande,
And I learned to ride
'Fore I learned to stand.
I'm a ridin' fool who is up to date—
I know ev'ry trail in the Lone Star State,
'Cause I ride the range in a Ford V-Eight.
Yippy-I-O-ki-ay,
Yippy-I-O-ki-ay.

REFRAIN 3

I'm an old cowhand
From the Rio Grande,
And I come to town
Just to hear the band.
I know all the songs that the cowboys know,
'Bout the big corral where the dogies go,
'Cause I learned them all on the radio.
Yippy-I-O-ki-ay,
Yippy-I-O-ki-ay.

REFRAIN 4

I'm an old cowhand
From the Rio Grande,
Where the West is wild
'Round the borderland,
Where the buffalo roam around the zoo,
And the Indians make you a rug or two,
And the old Bar X is a bar-be-que.
Yippy-I-O-ki-ay,
Yippy-I-O-ki-ay.

Additional lyrics used in film

REFRAIN 1

I'm an old cowhand
From the Rio Grande—
Come and see me soon
Round the borderland.
I can teach you all that you want to know,
How to brand a calf, how to rope and throw,
'Cause I learned it all from the pitcher show.
Yippy-I-O-ki-ay,
Yippy-I-O-ki-ay.

REFRAIN 2

I'm an old cowhand
From the Rio Grande,
But I done retired—
Livin' off the land.
I spend all my time at the hotel bar
With a Planter's Punch and a big cigar,
'Cause my old ranch horse is a movie star.
Yippy-I-O-ki-ay,
Yippy-I-O-ki-ay.

REFRAIN 3

I'm an old cowhand
From the Rio Grande,
And my campin' grounds
Is the soda stand.
Well, I don't know much 'bout a snaffle bit,
And I ain't sure there's such a thing as it,
But I give a strawberry float a fit.
Yippy-I-O-ki-ay,
Yippy-I-O-ki-ay.

REFRAIN 4

I'm an old cowhand
From the Rio Grande,

And there ain't so much
I don't understand.
Now I don't pretend to be awful smart,
But I know the horses go before the cart,
'Cause I read that once in the racing chart.
Yippy-I-O-ki-ay,
Yippy-I-O-ki-ay.

REFRAIN 5

MARTHA

RAYE: I'm an old cowgal,
Just a reg'lar pal—
They don't call me Emma,
They just call me Al.
We're so gosh-darn horsey around our
way
That we don't say "howdy," we just say
"hay,"
And we never answer—we all just
neigh.
Yippy-I-O-ki-ay,
Yippy-I-O-ki-ay.

DUET

CROSBY: I'm an old cowhand
RAYE: And we sing duet in the cowboy band.
CROSBY: You should hear us make with the
hi-de-ho!
RAYE: You should hear us make with below-
below-below-below!
CROSBY: And both join in with—
BOTH: Wo-ho-ho-yippy-O-yippy-I-O-ki-ay,
Yippy-I-O-ki-ay.

A WORD TO THE WISE
WILL DO

Music by Archie Bleyer. Registered for copyright as an unpublished song June 17, 1936.

VERSE

Did you mean it, darling,
Or did you not?
After all, it's just about the same.
Have I seen it, darling?
You ask me what?
Why, the finish of our silly little game.

You have cleared my mind of every doubt;
Bit by bit you've let your secret out.

REFRAIN

Just a word said by chance,
But it meant the ending,
And though quite a surprise,
A word to the wise will do.
Just a casual glance,
But so condescending—
How it opened my eyes!
A word to the wise will do.
I didn't need to be told that we would part;
I merely looked in your eyes and saw your heart.
Just a word when we met,
Yet how well I knew it!
Now the same rule applies—
A word to the wise will do.

DREAM AWHILE

Music by Phil Ohman. Published. Copyrighted July 9, 1936.

VERSE

While the music is playing,
While the lights are soft and blue,
Listen to the thing my heart is saying,
Whispering to only you.
Listen to the thing my heart is saying,
Ev'ry word it says is true.

REFRAIN

Dream awhile—
We've only a while to dream.
Love is sweet,
But swift as a candle's gleam.
Close your eyes;
The music is soft and low.
Dream awhile,
Before it is time to go.
Darling, can't you see
Nothing is ever quite the same?
Give your lips to me
And let our hearts burst into flame.
Hold me tight,
For that is the thrill supreme.
Dream awhile—
We've only a while to dream.

LEW LESLIE'S BLACKBIRDS OF 1936

Presented by Charles B. Cochran and produced by Lew Leslie. Tryout: Opera House, Manchester, England; opened June 12, 1936. London run: Gaiety Theatre; opened July 9, 1936; 124 performances. Music by Rube Bloom. Lyrics by John Mercer.

Cast included: Lavaida Carter, Lucille Watson, Harold and Fayard Nicholas, Maude Russell, Emmett Wallace, Emery Smith, Tim Moore, Eunice Wilson, John Garth, Gallie de Gaston, Jules Bledsoe, and Una Carlisle.

The previews in Manchester contained two numbers that were dropped in London and replaced by "Jo-Jo, the Cannibal Kid." Leslie's later New York production, *Blackbirds of 1939* (Hudson Theatre; opened February 11, 1939; 9 performances), included two of the Bloom/Mercer songs written for the 1936 show.

Mercer recalled:

We found ourselves with fifty Blackbirds (for it was a colored show) on a ten-day Cunard boat headed for Old Blighty. Leslie, a good-hearted man of a "dese, dem and dose" guy, affected a beret and French phrases that he must have made up, as I've never found anyone who could translate the words he used to lay on us . . . Every other spare minute Ruby and I were writing, because this show was to turn out like a back-stage movie. Leslie had talked everybody into everything. Rube and I, and the cast, including the Nicholas brothers—Harold Nicholas being about ten years old and adorable as well as fantastic—and the late Tim Moore, the famous "Kingfish" of TV fame, marvelous even then at getting his laughs. Even English producer Charles B. Cochran agreed to work on the merest shoestring. Leslie had no money . . .

The cast was rehearsing the numbers as they came hot off the piano . . . They pitched in with a will and no company ever gave a more energetic, enthusiastic opening night. We were fairly well received and considering our lack of experience and the mediocrity of the production, we were lucky to run the six months we did.

Immediately after *Blackbirds* opened, Mercer left for Hollywood to take up a contract with Warner Bros.

THE SWING IS THE THING

Published. Copyrighted September 28, 1936. Introduced by Una Carlisle in Manchester. Introduced by Lavaida Carter and Lucille Watson in London.

VERSE

This crazy age we're living in
Will cut our lives in half;
It really takes an iron man to stand the gaff.
This crazy age we're living in
Is sure to drive us mad—
I'm positively goin' nuts, but ain't I glad?

REFRAIN

The whole world is saying
The swing is the thing.
The dance bands are playing;
The swing is the thing.
Someone pulled a lever,
Someone pulled a string;
Now we've got the fever
To swing, swing, swing.
The trumpets are blowin'
And, oh, what a sound!
The whole world is goin'
Around and around.
So join in the chorus,
Give out with a zing,
'Cause you know and I know
The swing is the thing!

YOUR HEART AND MINE

Published. Copyrighted July 30, 1936. Introduced by Maude Russell and Emmett Wallace.

VERSE 1

I knew when I met you
That our love would bloom,
Just as surely as I know
We are in this room.
You know the same thing, too,
And deep down inside,
Both our hearts began to tell us
They would never be denied.

REFRAIN

Your heart and mine,
They belong together,

Just like April weather and skies of blue.
Your heart and mine
Told us at their meeting
By their very beating how well they knew.
And though a thousand oceans divide us,
A thousand centuries, too,
If you should need me,
My heart would lead me to you.
The oldest stars in the sky
May have seen some true hearts,
But they won't find two hearts
Like your heart and mine.

KEEP A TWINKLE IN YOUR EYE

Published. Copyrighted July 31, 1936. Introduced by Harold Nicholas and the Blackbirds Beauty Chorus. Alternate title: "I've Got a Twinkle in My Eye."

VERSE 1

I feel happy and I stay happy,
No matter what the season.
They're all as nice as they can be
To me.
No blue Mondays for this young chappie,
And there's a darned good reason—
It's quite a simple recipe.

REFRAIN

Just keep a twinkle in your eye
And a twinkle in your toe
And you'll be steppin' mighty high
Wherever you go.
'Cause with a twinkle in your eye
And a twinkle in your toe
Nobody's goin' to pass you by
Without a hallo.
Just throw your head back
And stick your chin out,
Bring your best Sunday grin out—
You know you can win out soon.
Thanks to the twinkle in your eye
And the twinkle in your toe,
You'll find that life is just like pie,
Wherever you go.

VERSE 2

When you tell me that you feel gloomy,
I can't be sympathetic;
There's no excuse for you to stay

That way.
Simply pay close attention to me,
And though it's not poetic,
There's still a lot in what I say.

REPEAT REFRAIN

JO-JO, THE CANNIBAL KID

Published. Copyrighted September 28, 1936. Introduced by Lavaida Carter and company in the London production. Sung in the New York production *Blackbirds of 1939* by Laurene Hines and Hamtree Harrington and danced by Taps Miller, Joyce Beasley, and ensemble.

VERSE

Gather round me, you explorers,
Buck and Admiral Byrd—
Here's a story,
One you never heard.
There's a fellow in the jungle,
Someone you never knew—
You won't get him
But he might get you.

REFRAIN

Who's the talk of ev'ry table
From Chicago to Madrid?
Who's the African Clark Gable?
Jo-Jo, the Cannibal Kid.

All the tribe eat roots and berries.
He's the one who never did.
He prefers his missionaries.
Jo-Jo, the Cannibal Kid.

He could always pass
On his manner and his savoir-faire,
Mix with ev'ry class,
Meet the finest people ev'rywhere.

Circuses send offers daily;
Billy Rose made him a bid—
But he's holding out for Barnum and Bailey,
Jo-Jo, the Cannibal Kid.

DIXIE ISN'T DIXIE ANY MORE

Published. Copyrighted September 28, 1936. Introduced by Lavaida Carter. Sung in New York production of *Lew Leslie's Blackbirds of 1939* by Laurene Hines.

VERSE

I just paid a visit to the sunny South,
Looking for the sights I used to see.
But I didn't recognize the sunny South—
Nothing there is what it used to be.

REFRAIN

There are steamers running up and down the
    Swanee River
And a trolley going by the cabin door.
And the famous old plantation
Has become a filling station—
Dixie isn't Dixie anymore.

There is no more bridle path among the sweet
    magnolias
Where the ladies used to drive their coach and
    four;
Far away down south in heaven
Now is Highway Ninety-Seven—
Dixie isn't Dixie anymore.

You won't hear those darkies in the fields as white
    as cotton,
'Cause they're all too busy singing on the radio.
On the spot where all the traders used to sell their
    cotton
There is now a Woolworth five-and-ten-cent store.
And where aunty had a shanty
There's a poster of Durante—
Dixie isn't Dixie anymore.

HARLEM TO HOLLYWOOD

Published. Copyrighted December 21, 1936. Introduced by Emery Smith and ensemble.
    Lyric missing.

WHY CAN'T IT BE ME?

Published. Copyrighted July 30, 1936. Introduced by Eunice Wilson and Emmett Wallace.

VERSE

If I were Romeo and you were Juliet
And Mister Shakespeare wrote this play,
"By yonder moon above"
Is what I'd say.
I'm not a Romeo, you're not a Juliet,
And Mister Shakespeare writes no more,
So I'll ask you the question
That I've asked you before.

REFRAIN

You've got to belong to somebody,
So why can't it be me?
Why shouldn't I be
That somebody you see?
You've got to be sweet to somebody,
'Cause how else could you be?
I'd like to suggest
No one but me.
You should have someone who'd like to be your
    slave
Waiting at your beck and call.
You should have someone who'd never misbehave
And wouldn't mind it at all.
Since I know that I'm able to qualify
In every degree,
I want to know why—
Can't it be me?

I KNEW

Published. Copyrighted September 28, 1936.

VERSE

I don't believe in telling fortunes
Or seeing visions in the sky.
I've never been to a Gypsy,
I pass astrologers by.
I never tried to see the future
And yet the moment I met you,
I saw what I always pictured,
I saw what I always knew.

REFRAIN

I knew your eye would have a twinkle,
I knew you'd talk the way you do,
I knew your nose would have a wrinkle
When the laughter broke through.
Your fam'ly tree must go back
Somewhere in the sky,
And you must be a throwback
To the angels on high.
I knew the way you'd put your hand out
When you were introduced to me,
I knew that you would be a standout
Any place you might be.
I knew that you'd be perfect,
Perfect through and through.
Yes, I knew a lot of things,
But never knew there was anything
Just like you.

SOUTH WIND

Published. Copyrighted July 30, 1936.

VERSE

Ain't it funny what your end can be?
Makes no difference how you start.
Fate has a way of playing
With most ev'rybody's heart.
Ain't it funny who your friend can be
When you're trav'lin all alone?
I'm talkin' to the one friend
That I can still call my own.

REFRAIN

South Wind,
Can't I hitch a ride with you?
If you're passin' over Georgia
That's the way I'm headin', too.
South Wind,
Let me rest my weary head.
Drop me in a field of cotton
Softer than a feather bed.
I know my heart is heavy,
My spirit's mighty low,
But if they're not too heavy,
Pick me up and take me where I long to go.
South Wind,
Ain't you kind of lonesome, too?
Can't we go along together,
Can't I hitch a ride with you?

PETER PIPER

Music by Richard A. Whiting. Published. Copyrighted September 8, 1936. Recorded by Red Norvo and His Orchestra (Brunswick).

This was Mercer's first collaboration in an eighteen-month working relationship with Whiting, which ended with Whiting's death at age forty-six on February 10, 1938.

VERSE

I'm in the middle of solving a riddle
That no one can do.
That goes for Albert Einstein,
The League of Nations, too.
So, my fine and feathered friend,
I'll leave it up to you.

REFRAIN

If Peter Piper picked a peck of pickled peppers,
How much do I love you?
Then what have I got to pick
To turn the trick
And make you love me, too?
If Simple Simon sat beside a shallow saucer,
Tryin' to catch a whale,
Then what have I got to try
To make you buy
The heart I've got for sale?
How much wood would a woodchuck chuck
If a woodchuck could chuck wood?
I'd chuck double with no trouble
If it did me any good.
If Peter Piper picked a peck of pickled peppers,
I'll tell you what I'd do:
I'd pick a peck of peppers,
Sit beside a saucer,
I'd even be a wood-chuck chuckin'
All I could chuck,
Just to make you love me, too.

JAMBOREE JONES

Music by Mercer. Published. Copyrighted November 24, 1936. Previously registered for copyright as an unpublished song September 17, 1936. Recorded by Paul Whiteman, with vocal by Mercer (Decca), and later by Mercer again (Capitol). The songwriter recalls: "I wrote it for Benny Goodman . . . just a kind of admiration for the way he played. But he didn't play it much, because I

don't think he liked it. It's kind of a put-on of 'Casey Jones' and 'Steamboat Bill,' don't you think?"

REFRAIN 1

I begin my story out in West Virginia
In a little college.
All the student body only cared for football,
Never mind the knowledge.
Never mind the sheepskin,
They preferred the pigskin—
Seemed to have it in their bones.
They knew all about it,
Couldn't live without it,
All except a certain Mister Jamboree Jones.
And—
He played the clarinet with all his might;
He studied night and day,
He practiced day and night.
No running up the field for Mister Jones;
He'd rather run up and down the scale—
What tones!

REFRAIN 2

Even though his buddies
Always cut their studies
To attend a rally,
While they all were rootin'
You could hear him tootin'
"What became of Sally?"
How they used to hate him,
Co-eds wouldn't date him,
Thought he was an awful bore.
But he liked his rhythm
More than bein' with 'em,
So he only grinned and went to practice some
    more.
And—
Meanwhile, the team marched on to greater fame,
Till they were asked to play
The famous Rose Bowl game,
And on that day of days the students beamed—
What did they do when the team marched on the
    field?
They screamed.

REFRAIN 3

Startin' from the kickoff
They pulled ev'ry trick off,
But they couldn't win it.
'Stead of goin' forward
They were goin' backward
'Bout a mile a minute.
Seein' their position
They called intermission,
And they heard the ref'ree say,

"Seventeen to nothin' ain't exactly nothin',
And you've only got about a minute to play."
And—
Then from the stands there came a distant wail,
And it was Jamboree
A-swingin' "Hold 'em, Yale."
And then the students all began to yell,
The players marched up the field and down the
    field,
Pell mell.
Rah rah rah rah,
Sis boom bah bah
Bop de oddle-da,
Yea, Bo, watch 'em go.

CODA

Now on a certain West Virginia hill
There stands that college still,
Just as it always will;
And there's a picture in its Hall of Fame.
You'll see the boy in the frame
Who won the game.
Jamboree Jones is the gentleman's name!

DO MY EYES DECEIVE ME?

Music and lyrics by Mercer and Dave Dreyer. Registered for copyright as an unpublished song October 30, 1936.

VERSE

Am I enchanted with the magic of a lovely
    evening?
Is this a miracle that's sure to disappear from
    view?
Has some magician put me in a spell for just this
    evening?
Or has the most exciting dream I ever dreamed
    come true?

REFRAIN

Do my eyes deceive me
Or is this really you in my arms—
Like a sweet, mysterious, delirious dream come
    true?
Do your sighs deceive me?
Am I fooled by your wonderful charms
And the inspirational, sensational things
    you do?
One wave of your hand, the stars sing a tune.
One kiss from your lips and my heart jumps over
    the moon.

If my eyes deceive me and I'm fooled by your
    wonderful charms
Let them keep deceiving me by having me in your
    arms.

MISTER T. FROM TENNESSEE

Music by Matt Malneck. Registered for copyright as an
unpublished song December 12, 1936. Performed at the
Hickory House, New York City, December 11, 1936, by
"The Three T's"—Jack Teagarden, Frank Trumbauer,
and Charlie Teagarden.

I'm Mr. T from Tennessee,
I was southern aristocracy.
I just keep singin' all the livelong day
Just as happy as can be.

There's Mr. T with his trombone
And his very uncommercial baritone.
You can't understand a word he says,
But it sure is a pretty tone.

And I got music,
And I got rhythm,
And I got sweet dreams,
I got everything but dough.

Any time you're on a spree
And they're givin' out a few drinks free,
I'll play it for you till the cows come home,
Mr. T from Tennessee.

JUST REMEMBER

Music by Carl Sigman. Published. Copyrighted January 28, 1937. Previously registered for copyright as an
unpublished song December 12, 1936.

    Recorded by the Australian singer-violinist Brian
Lawrance and His Lansdowne Orchestra (Rex), Henry
Hall and the BBC Orchestra, and Henry Jacques and
His Correct Tempo Dance Orchestra (HMV).

VERSE

We've never known such happiness,
Watching our dreams come true;
If we would keep our happiness,
Here's what we both must do.

REFRAIN

Just remember
I'm in love with you;
Just remember
That you love me, too.
We'd be foolish letting trouble come between us;
We'd be foolish when we know
We love each other so.
Just remember
Love is give and take;
Smile at each mistake
For the other's sake.
Hope I never make you blue,
But if I ever do,
Just remember
That I love you.

49

CTIVE SWEETIE:

too marvelous, I don't know any words

READY, WILLING AND ABLE; VARSITY SHOW; HOLLYWOOD HOTEL; and Other Songs of 1937

READY, WILLING AND ABLE (1937)

Produced by Hal B. Wallis for Warner Bros. Released March 1937. Copyright February 5, 1937. Directed by Ray Enright. Screenplay by Jerry Wald, Sig Herzig, and Warren Duff, based on a *Saturday Evening Post* story by Richard Macaulay. Music by Richard A. Whiting. Lyrics by Johnny Mercer. Musical numbers directed and staged by Bobby Connolly. Orchestrations by Ray Heindorf. Musical director: Leo F. Forbstein. With Ruby Keeler, Lee Dixon, Allen Jenkins, Louise Fazenda, Ross Alexander, Carol Hughes, Hugh O'Connell, Wini Shaw, Teddy Hart, and Adrian Rosley.

Two songwriters import an English leading lady for their new show.

THE WORLD IS MY APPLE

Introduced by Lee Dixon.

The world is my apple,
The moon is my lucky dime—
I'm higher than the stratosphere
Just because you are near.
The moment I met you
My stock took a rise;
Just look at the chart—
My happy heart is hittin' new highs.

The world is my apple,
And I picked a bunch of stars
That I'm stringing to a lucky charm
Just to fit round your heart.
To put it quite briefly,
There's nothing I can't do—
The world is my apple,
And it's all for you.

Top: Ready, Willing and Able: *Ruby Keeler and Lee Dixon dancing in "Too Marvelous for Words"*
Bottom: Varsity Show: *Ford L. Buck and John W. Bubbles, from the reprise of "Have You Got Any Castles, Baby?"*

THE LITTLE HOUSE ON THE HILL

Introduced by Lee Dixon, Ross Alexander (dubbed by James Newill), and Adrian Rosley.

There's a little old house
On a little old hill
And a little old mortgage
That I'm payin' still.
There's a little old cellar,
No coal in the bin,
And a little old chimney
That's crumbling in.

There's a little old man
Who comes round every day
To take all the little old fixtures away.
But sell it? I wouldn't.
Or rent it? I couldn't.
I can't even give it away.

MY FATHER'S WEDDING SUIT

Comic fragment introduced by Lee Dixon.

All wrinkled and crinkled,
In an old trunk I found it,
My father's wedding suit.

HANDY WITH YOUR FEET

Introduced by Ruby Keeler, Louise Fazenda, and female ensemble. Alternate title: "If You're Handy with Your Feet."

RUBY
KEELER: Ladies, dry your tears
And lend me your ears.
Little Jane is gonna get you
A swell beau.
Ladies, I've a plan
To get you a man,
But you've got to know
Your foot from your elbow.

You can always rate
As a dinner date,
Really give the fellas a treat;
They'll be sendin' flowers and candy,
If you're handy with your feet.

You can be the champ
As a local vamp,
Just the type they're dyin' to meet;
And you'll soon be drinking their brandy,
If you're handy with your feet.

Take my tip and tap-tap—
That is the way to start.
Take my tap and tiptoe
Into your baby's heart.

When your big romance
Takes you out to dance,
Cuddle up and tell him he's sweet—
You'll be close as Amos 'n' Andy,
And won't that be dandy!
Just remember to be handy with your feet.

You know that game called Handies
That everyone was playing?
You use your hands to illustrate
A picture or a saying.
For instance, here's a handy saying—
Perhaps it's rather barmy—
I heard it from an Englishman:
It's "Moon Over My Army."

GIRLS: That game went out with Pyramids
As far as we're concerned.
KEELER: I know, but now I'll teach you all
Another game I learned.
Just relax and give yourselves a treat
While I do a Handy with my feet.

[*She taps.*]

Do you get it?
GIRLS: Yes, it's a Highland Fling.
KEELER: No, it's Chaplin doin' the Buck and Wing.
ALL: Now, this one doesn't need second sight:
It's a husband sneaking in drunk at night.

[*All dance.*]

This step may have a Spanish feel,
But it's really only a Cuban heel.

[*All dance.*]

Here's a simple one, but it's very nice—
It's 'S On Ya Heinie on a Block of Ice.

[*All dance.*]

On your mark!

LOUISE
FAZENDA: Why, that's Jesse Owens, the racing
man!

ALL: No, it's Ariel chasing her Caliban.
If you haven't learned it by Sunday,
We'll be here till Monday
Just to teach you to be handy with your
feet.

TOO MARVELOUS FOR WORDS

Published. Copyrighted January 25, 1937. Introduced (spoken) by Ross Alexander; reprised by Alexander (dubbed by James Newill); performed in finale by Alexander (dubbed by Newill), Wini Shaw, Lee Dixon, and female ensemble and danced by Ruby Keeler, Dixon, and dance ensemble. Number-one-selling recording by Bing Crosby, with Jimmy Dorsey and His Orchestra (Decca). Another leading recording came from Leo Reisman and His Orchestra (Brunswick).

Technically, this promised to be one of the most difficult lyrics Mercer had yet faced. The film's producer, Hal Wallis, told him and Whiting that he planned to use several reprises of the song in the film and that Mercer would be required to write a different set of lyrics for each of them. Mercer angrily replied that he'd "never find the words" and went home. Later that day Whiting arrived and handed him a dictionary. His own words to Wallis—and the copy of *Webster's*—gave him the clue, and he wrote a song about a man who can't find the right words to describe the girl he loves. The staging in the finale, one of the best-loved production numbers of the era, had Ruby Keeler and Lee Dixon tap dance on the keys of a giant typewriter, while sixteen chorus girls in black stockings kick their legs up and down to suggest the key hammers, as they type out the lyrics. The song was also a homage to Ira Gershwin's " 'S Wonderful."

Published version

VERSE

I search for phrases
To sing your praises,
But there aren't any magic adjectives
To tell you all you are.

REFRAIN

You're just too marvelous,
Too marvelous for words,

Like "glorious," "glamorous,"
And that old standby, "amorous."

It's all too wonderful,
I'll never find the words
That say enough,
Tell enough—
I mean, they just aren't swell enough.

You're much too much
And just too very very,
To ever be in *Webster's Dictionary*.

And so I'm borrowing
A love song from the birds
To tell you that you're marvelous,
Too marvelous for words.

Film version (Finale)

ROSS
ALEXANDER: Now is the time for all good girls to
come to the aid of the boss.

GIRLS: The boss is in a quandary,
The boss is at a loss.

ALEXANDER: If I can land this prospect, girls,
It may mean a contract for life.

WINI SHAW: To whom is the letter going?

ALEXANDER: To my prospective wife.
"My dear prospective wife—"

SHAW: No, no.

ALEXANDER: "My dear prospective sweetie:
As I reply to yours of recent
date . . ."

SHAW: You sound as though you're
drawing up
A statistician's treaty.
Suppose I help you out as you
dictate.

BOTH: [*he speaks as she repeats, singing*]
You're just too marvelous,
Too marvelous for words,
Like "glorious," [and]
"glamorous,"
And that old standby, "amorous."
It's all too wonderful,
I'll [You'll] never find the words,
That say enough,
Tell enough,
I [You] mean, they just aren't swell
enough.
You're much too much
And just too very very
To ever be in *Webster's Dictionary*.
And so I'm [you're] borrowing
A love song from the birds
To tell you that you're marvelous,
Too marvelous for words.

ALEXANDER: May I express just one P.S.?
[*sung*] You're just too marvelous,
Too marvelous for words—

GIRLS: Like "rapturous," "fabulous,"

ALEXANDER: Your voice is tintinnabulous.
It's all too wonderful,
An ordinary word—

GIRLS: Like "magical," "mystical,"

ALEXANDER: Seems just too apothistical.

GIRLS: The sweetest words
In Keats' or Shelley's lyrics—

ALEXANDER: Aren't sweet enough—
To be your panegyrics.

SHAW: And so you're borrowing
A love song from the birds
To tell you that you're marvelous,
Too marvelous for words.

ALEXANDER: [*spoken*] Please send it off without
delay—
She's got to get it right away.

RUBY KEELER
& GIRLS: [*she reads letter aloud; they repeat*]
You're just too marvelous,
Too marvelous for words,
Like "rapturous," "fabulous,"
Your voice is tintinnabulous.

KEELER: Now what on earth can that word
be?

GIRLS: Why don't you call him up and see?
[*spoken to Alexander*] You've written
such obscure words,
I can't understand your letter.

ALEXANDER: I know they're very poor words.
Perhaps you'd like these better:
"Adorable"
And "amorous"
And "glorious"
And "glamorous"
Are insufficient when applied to
you.
To be euphemistical,
To be eulogistical,
I have to originate a million words
That no one ever knew.
I try to be logical and sensible,
But I'm incomprehensible
Whenever I begin to find a phrase;
For they never say enough
And they never tell enough—
I've already told you
No vocabulary's swell enough.
What'll I do to say
The things I have in mind?
It's really absurd
There isn't a word to fit you.
No matter where I look,
I only seem to find
"Delectable,"

"Delirious,"
"Magnificently mysterious."
You're simply too spectacular
To be in my vernacular,
And so you see
I'm forced to go to the birds.
The reason must be quite apparent,
That you are just too
Utterly, utterly wonderful
And marvelous for words.

KEELER: I don't know what he's driving at,
But I'll just have to answer that.
You're just too marvelous,
I don't know any words . . .

[KEELER *and* LEE DIXON *dance on typewriter.*]

[ALEXANDER *enters and points to the words* "I am sorry."]

ALEXANDER: "Dear Jane,
I'm writing this to tell you I was
wrong.
I think you're just colossible—
You've made this whole thing
possible."
SHAW: You fought. She threw you down.
DIXON: This'll kill you, he gave her the air.
KEELER: And you did it very well.
ALEXANDER: Ah, but you came through like
Frank Merriwell.
KEELER: In spite of all our acting and
pretending,
Now boy meets girl and there's a
happy ending.
SHAW &
DIXON: And so he's [she's] borrowing
A love song from the birds—
ALEXANDER: To tell you that you're marvelous,
GIRLS: Marvelous!
ALL: Too marvelous for words.

Michael Feinstein's version

Michael Feinstein adapted the film version and recorded it on his 1993 album *Forever* (Elektra), with a musical arrangement by Ralph Burns.

After the published refrain's final "too marvelous for words":

Like adorable
And amorous
And glorious
And glamorous,
They're insufficient when applied to you.
To be egotistical
To be eulogistical,

I have come up with a million words
I never thought I knew.
I'd rather be logical and sensible
But I'm incomprehensible
Whenever I begin to find a phrase.
But they never say enough,
They never tell enough
And I've already told you
My vocabulary's not swell enough.
What do I do to say
The things I have in mind?
It's really absurd,
There isn't a word to fit you.
No matter where I look,
I only seem to find
Delectable,
Delirious,
Magnificently mysterious.
You're simply too spectacular
To be in my vernacular,
And so, you see,
I'm forced to go to the birds.
The reason must be quite apparent,
You're just too
Utterly, utterly wonderful
And marvelous for words.

You're just too marvelous,
Too marvelous for words
Like rapturous, fabulous,
Your voice is tintinnabulous.
It's all too wonderful
That ordinary words
Like magical, mystical
Seem much too apothistical.
The sweetest words in Keats and Shelley's lyrics
Aren't sweet enough to be your panegyrics.
And so I'm borrowing
A love song from the birds
To tell you you're colossible,
You've made my whole life possible
And too marvelous for words.

JUST A QUIET EVENING

Published. Copyrighted January 25, 1937. Introduced by Ross Alexander (dubbed by James Newill) and danced by Lee Dixon and Ruby Keeler. Leading recordings by Eddy Duchin, with vocal by Jerry Cooper (Victor); Shep Fields (Bluebird); and Orlando Roberson (Variety).

VERSE

Going out to parties
Is only making us
Blasé and bored.
And if we were smarties,
We'd overlook the fuss
We can't afford
And thank the Lord—

REFRAIN

For just a quiet evening,
No celebration,
Just conversation
Alone with you.
I'm the type
Who smokes a pipe
With charm and finesse;
You can cook
Or read a book
Or mend an old dress.
Just a quiet evening—
No band with trumpets,
Just tea with crumpets,
That's what we'll do.
I can't tell you how much
I've been looking forward to
Just a quiet evening
Alone with you.

Additional lyrics from film

Just a quiet evening,
No celebration,
Just conversation
Alone with you.
Won't you say
You'll let me stay
A moment or two?
It'll let me
Really get
Acquainted with you.
Just a quiet evening—
There'll be no smart talk,
Just heart-to-heart talk,
That's what we'll do.
I can't tell you how much
I am looking forward to
Just a quiet evening
Alone with you.

SENTIMENTAL AND MELANCHOLY

Published. Copyrighted February 3, 1937. Introduced by Wini Shaw.

INTRODUCTION

Sentimental and melancholy
Whenever I think about you . . .

VERSE

The swift-moving years
Have altered my tears
To only a sweet regret;
But somehow the spell that we captured
Lingers around me yet.
It's as easy for me to remember
As it was for you to forget.

REFRAIN

Sentimental and melancholy
Whenever I think about you—
It's only a mood,
A brief interlude
That's better described
As just feelin' blue.
I suppose it's just my folly
To keep it alive as I do,
But it's a kind of sugar-coated misery,
And foolish as it seems,
I sort of like to be
Sentimental and melancholy
Whenever I think about you.

READY, WILLING AND ABLE

Not sung in film.

VERSE

They say that ev'ry bird on a limb
Has some little bird that's nuts about him—
And if a bird can have it,
Why can't I?
They say that ev'ry bee in a hive
Has some little bee who's glad he's alive—
And if a bee can have it,
I can try.

REFRAIN

I'm ready, willing and able.
Yes! I've got what it takes,
But nobody takes what I've got.
I'm ready, willing and able.
Yes! There's lots that I like,
But none of them like me a lot.
Here am I
Feelin' like a firecracker
Just about to ignite
With no matches in sight.
Hey! Brother, can you spare a light?
I'm ready, willing and able.
Yes! I've got what it takes,
But no one'll take what I've got.

WHEN A BLUES SINGER FALLS IN LOVE

Lyric missing.

GASOLINE GYPSIES

Registered for copyright as an unpublished song March 23, 1937. Not used in film.

VERSE

I have always envied the delights of
The knights of the road,
Happy-go-lucky tramps
Living in tourist camps
In a little cottage that is streamlined,
A dream-lined abode.
Darling, if you just agree,
Can't you see that both of us should be—

REFRAIN

Just a couple of gasoline gypsies,
And the happy-go-luckiest kind,
Hummin' a love song
And joggin' along
Waggin' our trailer behind.
Just a couple of gasoline gypsies
In a regular palace on wheels,
Over the hilltops
Without any cops
Taggin' along at our heels!

In the fall to Mexico
And in the spring to Lake Louise—
Thanks to Mister Texaco,
We can go any place that we please!
Just a couple of gasoline gypsies
Only stopping to ask for advice
"How do the roads lay?
Is this the right way
That leads to Paradise?"
As we ride off in the twilight
And the taillight faintly gleams
Everyone'll be watching our trailer
Winding down the trail o' dreams.

THE SINGING MARINE (1937)

Produced by Hal B. Wallis for Warner Bros. Released July 1937. Copyright June 3, 1937. Directed by Ray Enright. Screenplay by Delmer Daves. Musical numbers created and directed by Busby Berkeley. Orchestrations by Ray Heindorf. Musical director: Leo F. Forbstein. With Dick Powell, Doris Weston, Lee Dixon, Hugh Herbert, Jane Darwell, Allen Jenkins, and Larry Adler.

The songs for this film are by Harry Warren (music) and Al Dubin (lyrics), except for "Night Over Shanghai."

A young marine (Powell) is helped by his colleagues to go to New York to compete in an amateur singing contest, but personal and professional complications ensue.

Al Dubin, Warren's regular lyricist, contributed five of the film's six songs, but Mercer and Warren's "Night Over Shanghai" made it into the final cut.

NIGHT OVER SHANGHAI

Music by Harry Warren. Published. Copyrighted April 8, 1937. Previously registered for copyright as an unpublished song March 5, 1937. Introduced by Dick Powell, Doris Weston, and ensemble, with Larry Adler on harmonica.

VERSE

Lighted lanterns in the doorways of the Shanghai
  shops,
Slant-eyed merchants counting up their yen,
Tired coolies padding homeward as the daylight
  stops,

And the twilight fills the winding streets with
     ragged beggar men—
So the sleepy city goes to sleep again.
And then—

REFRAIN

Night over Shanghai,
Moon on the rise,
Pale yellow faces with sad old eyes.
Night over Shanghai,
Lips painted red
Smile from the windows
Just overhead.
Oh! Where are the dreams gone up in smoke?
Where are the dreamers who never awoke?
They're gone, like the driftwood,
Gone out of sight,
In the darkness over Shanghai
In the night.

VARSITY SHOW (1937)

Produced by Hal B. Wallis for Warner Bros. Released September 1937. Copyright July 14, 1937. Directed by William Keighley. Screenplay by Jerry Wald, Richard Macaulay, Sig Herzig, and Warren Duff, based on an original story by Warren Duff and Sig Herzig. Music by Richard A. Whiting. Lyrics by Johnny Mercer. Additional songs by Tom Waring, Don Raye, Roy Ringwald, and Paul Gibbon. Finale created and directed by Busby Berkeley. Orchestrations by Frank Perkins, Steve Mougin, and Virgil Davis. Vocal arrangements by Roy Ringwald and Frank Perkins. Musical director: Fred Waring. Starring Dick Powell and Fred Waring and His Pennsylvanians, with Ted Healy, Rosemary Lane, Priscilla Lane, Walter Catlett, Johnny "Scat" Davis, Sterling Holloway, Mabel Todd, Lee Dixon, and Buck and Bubbles.
     Collegians stage a revue.

THE VARSITY SHOW'S REHEARSING

The film's opening number. Introduced by Fred Waring and His Pennsylvanians, Mabel Todd, Sterling Holloway, Johnny "Scat" Davis, Priscilla Lane, Rosemary Lane,

Walter Catlett, Tom Waring, Poley McClintock, Gene Conklin, George MacFarlane, Lee Dixon and ensemble.

FRED
WARING: Listen to me, you varlets,
     And harken, all ye starlets,
     The Varsity Show's rehearsing in
        the gym!
MABEL TODD: Well, I'll appear
     To let 'em hear
     My ocarina!
BOY: And wait till I play "Nola"
     On my concertina!
GIRL: Just wait till Professor Biddle
     Hears me play my fiddle!
STERLING
HOLLOWAY: And I've been taking magic
        through the mail—
     Say, I can saw a man in half!
     But I've forgotten whether
     I ever got that lesson
     Where I put him back together . . .
JOHNNY
DAVIS: Gimme some dough and I'll get
     My trumpet out of hock—
1ST STUDENT: The Varsity Show's rehearsing
     Today at three o'clock!
2ND STUDENT: The Varsity Show's rehearsing
     Today at three o'clock!
LEE DIXON: The Varsity Show's rehearsing
     Today at three o'clock!
4TH STUDENT: The Varsity Show's rehearsing
     Today at three o'clock!
THREE
STUDENTS: Say, if they need a trio
     We can harmonize it too.
GENE
CONKLIN*: With my tenor voice I'll sing
     About a night in June!
TOM
WARING*: My lusty baritone will surely make
        the ladies swoon!
PRISCILLA
LANE: And I can sway!
     And I can swing!
POLEY
MCCLINTOCK*: And I can sing like the birdies
        sing—
     Tweet, tweet, tweet, TWA, TWA.
ROSEMARY
LANE: My talents are more dramatic
     And slightly operatic—
     La-la-la-la-la-la—

---
* *Members of the Pennsylvanians.*

La-la-la-la-la-la—
La-la-la-la-la-la!
TWO BOYS: We can do an act we call
     ventriloquism.
1ST BOY: I'm the straight man.
2ND BOY: I'm the dummy.
BOTH: Boy, we'll whiz 'em!
GIRLS: Just wait till the movies vamp
        us—
     They'll take us off the campus
     And they'll put us on a train for
        Hollywood!
WALTER
CATLETT: I only hope the boys and girls
     Recite some pretty sonnets
     Instead of all this ha-cha-cha
     Like André Kostelanetz!
ALL: Mister Opportunity, at last we
        hear you knock—
     The Varsity Show's rehearsing
     Today at three o'clock!
CATLETT: No, no, no, no, no,
     That type of dancing's out!
     I don't want any trickery
     But dignified Terpsichore!
     Here, here, what's this?
LANE: We're just rehearsing a scene
     Where I'm supposed to mother
        him.
CATLETT: But you're not supposed to
        smother him!
     Bravo! Bravo! Now there's a
        glorious voice,
     With resonance and clarity
     And none of this vulgarity!
     With talent such as yours,
     The show begins to shape up.
GEORGE
MCFARLAND*: I wish we had a Tarzan here
     So he could shut that ape up!
WARING: Shhh!
     Now please be quiet, children,
     While I call the roll
     But first Mister Bolton singing
        "Old King Cole."
CATLETT: Old King Cole?
DAVIS: Yeah!

[*Segue into "Old King Cole."*]

---
* *Member of the Pennsylvanians.*

OLD KING COLE

Registered for copyright as an unpublished song February 18, 1937. Introduced by Johnny "Scat" Davis accompanied by Fred Waring and His Pennsylvanians.

VERSE

When I was a tot,
I thought quite a lot
Of the famous people in
The story books I got.
As I grew in size,
So did I grow wise,
And I learned some things
That really opened up my eyes.
But, in spite of ev'rything I've learned,
There's one old guy
Who's still ace high
As far as I'm concerned.

REFRAIN

Old King Cole was a merry old soul,
And the old boy loved to have his fling.
Old King Cole was a very old soul,
But he waved his scepter with a swing.
He called for his pipe
To kick the gong around;
He called for his bowl of tea-N-T.
And he always liked
To have a song around,
So he called for his fiddlers three,
And they all went out on a spree.
Old King Cole was a merry old soul,
That's all, as far as I can see,
But because he had his fling,
And because he liked to sing,
He went down in history—
So perhaps there's a chance for me!

WE'RE WORKING OUR WAY THROUGH COLLEGE

Published. Copyrighted July 26, 1937. Previously registered for copyright as an unpublished song March 23, 1937. Introduced by Dick Powell, Ted Healy, Rosemary Lane, and ensemble.

REFRAIN 1

We're working our way through college
To get a lot of knowledge
That we'll probably never ever use again.
It helps a lot to know
You've got a nice diploma,
But will it pay the mortgage on the home sweet home-a?
We're getting an education
To run a filling station,
For they never take anyone but college men.
Oh, you've got to know your Cicero,
Your Hannibal and Caesar,
To turn the crank
And fill the tank
And say, "How many, please, sir?"
And mathematics is the thing we've gotta know,
Working our way through college on the old man's
Dough, re, mi, fa, sol, la, ti . . .

PATTER

The guy who is a perfect whiz
In engineering science
Will get a lot of prizes,
But he won't get any clients.
And the guy who writes a composition
Will never write a check.
We feel the noose around our neck;
We know we're licked, but what the heck!

REFRAIN 2

We're working our way through college
To get a lot of knowledge
That we'll probably never ever use again.
And do we study, do we toil?
Don't you think it!
And do we burn the midnight oil?
No, we drink it!
The study of economics
Will never fill our stomicks
If we finally have to be insurance men.
Oh, the Sigma Chi may rate you high
And ask you to their rushes,
But no one's gonna ask you when
You're selling Fuller brushes.
Hooray for history and Greek and algebra!
We're working our way through college
With a Rah! Rah! Rah! Rah! Rah! Rah!

Additional lyrics used in film

We're working our way through college
To get a lot of knowledge
That we'll probably never ever use again.
It's swell to tell
What parallel
And parallax is,
But after graduation
Will it pay our taxes?

The study of economics
Will never fill our stomicks
If we finally have to be insurance men.
It's a cinch to cram for each exam
And make yourself a scholar,
But if you go in business
Can you make yourself a dollar?
Hooray for history and Greek and algebra!
We're working our way through college
With a Rah! Rah! Rah!

When we get out of school,
We'll vote the Democratic ticket.
The Republicans made promises
That weren't exactly cricket.
You recall they said we'd have
A couple of chickens in the pot.
We wonder where the chickens got;
We haven't even got the pot!

We're working our way through college
To get a lot of knowledge
That we'll probably never ever use again.
And do we study, do we toil?
Don't you think it!
And do we burn the midnight oil?
No, we drink it!
The fellas who need their classes
Will sit upon their chassis,
And the dopiest guys will all be millionaires.
Yes, the Sigma Chi
May rate you high
And ask you to their rushes,
But no one's going to ask you when
You're selling Fuller brushes!
Hooray for history and economics, too!
We're working our way through college with a
    boola-boo!
Rah! Rah! Rah! Rah!
Do, re, mi, fa, sol, Rah! Rah!

ON WITH THE DANCE

Published. Copyrighted July 15, 1937. Previously registered for copyright as an unpublished song March 23, 1937. Introduced by Rosemary Lane and Dick Powell, accompanied by Fred Waring and His Pennsylvanians; reprised by Buck and Bubbles.

VERSE

ROSEMARY
    LANE: I believe
        There is a tune the piper plays;

There is a price the dancer pays.
But what do I fear
As long as you're near?

REFRAIN

On with the dance—
Let the melody be mellow,
And let it weave a spell over you and me.
On with the dance—
When they play a love song for us,
My heart will sing the chorus
So tenderly.
Then from the ceiling
Let it come stealing,
That flood of colored light,
Like a rainbow in the night.
When there's romance in each note the band is
    playing,
You can't blame me for saying,
"On with the dance!"

Additional lyrics used in film

DICK
POWELL: There's a very charming roundelay,
And maybe that's the trouble:
Charm is simply out of place today—
We want speed,
We want swing,
We want bubble!

First you pick the tempo up—
Bring the drum in,
Take the fiddles out!
Let the brass come in!

On with the dance—
Let the trumpets blow the roof in,
Give us some room to hoof in,
And watch us sing!
On with the dance!
When the music is staccato,
Oh, what an obbligato
Our feet can swing!
We don't care what notes
Long as they're hot notes!
We'll even take a waltz
Just as long as it has schmaltz!
We'll take a chance,
And we don't care where we land up—
So, leader, strike that band up
And on with the dance!

PATTER

Let me see you really bear down,
Trip the light fantastic right;

Get in there and let your hair down—
Curfew shall not ring tonight!
I don't know just what you're doing,
But to make it really keen
Do a little Suzi Q–ing,
Mix it with a tap routine!

DANCE

Swing your arms around and bingo!
Throw your head back on the beat.
In the dance-director lingo,
Get the lead out of your feet!

Give me something like Nijinsky
With a little rhumba dance;
Then perhaps a dash of Minsky—
Boy, I think you've got something there!

YOU'VE GOT SOMETHING THERE

Published. Copyrighted July 15, 1937. Previously registered for copyright as an unpublished song March 23, 1937. Introduced by Dick Powell and Rosemary Lane. Reprised by Buck and Bubbles. Recorded by Dick Powell (Decca).

VERSE 1

DICK
POWELL: You don't seem to understand
The power you command—
No,
You don't seem to know what you can do!
If fair Helen's lovely lips
Could launch a thousand ships,
You could split the universe in two—

REFRAIN 1

With those stars in your eyes,
You've got something there.
They advertise—
You've got something there.
That frown so stormy,
That smile so sunny,
They're worth a million dollars
In anybody's money.
And those Come-kiss-me lips—
You've got something there.
I'm getting tips-
Y, so much do I care!
And as for this young and foolish heart,

You should be aware
That you've really got something there,
Yes, you've really got something there!

VERSE 2

ROSEMARY
LANE: You don't seem to understand
The power you command;
No, you don't seem to know what you
    can do.
You don't seem to understand—
One movement of your hand
Could split this little universe in two!

REFRAIN 2

When you smile with your eyes,
You've got something there.
You can't disguise
You've got something there.
Those sweet, sweet nothings,
The way you word them,
It doesn't really matter
How many times I've heard them!
And the charm you reveal,
You've got something there—
I have a feeling I'm starting to care.
And so I've told my young and foolish heart,
"Better be aware!"
'Cause you've really got something there,
Yes, you've really got something there!

HAVE YOU GOT ANY CASTLES, BABY?

Published. Copyrighted July 15, 1937. Previously registered for copyright as an unpublished song March 23, 1937. Introduced by Dick Powell and Priscilla Lane. Reprised by Priscilla Lane and ensemble with Fred Waring and His Pennsylvanians and by Buck and Bubbles. Recorded by Dick Powell (Decca). Other leading recordings by Tommy Dorsey and His Orchestra, with vocal by Jack Leonard (Victor); Dolly Dawn and Her Dawn Patrol, conducted by George Hall (Vocalion); and Gus Arnheim and His Orchestra (Brunswick).

VERSE 1

DICK
POWELL: I have dreamed about romance a lot—
Men like Galahad and Sir Lancelot
Always did the things I'd like to do.
Physic'ly I'm not as durable,

But romantically I'm incurable,
And I'd like to do the same for you.

REFRAIN 1

Have you got any castles
That you want me to build,
Baby?
Have you got any dragons
That you want to have killed,
Baby?
I'll get into my seven-league boots;
I'll get into my bulletproof suits;
I'll get out my revolver that shoots,
And rat-a-tat-tat—
Down they'll go!
Have you got any mortgages
You want to have paid,
Baby?
Have you got any villains
That you want to have laid
To rest?
After all my adventures are through
And I bring home a dragon or two,
You can tell all the papers
That I did it because
I love you!

VERSE 2

PRISCILLA

LANE: Men are really men no longer now,
For the weaker sex is the stronger now;
We compete in ev'ry single thing.
Gents belong in the Smithsonian,
Since we gals are all Amazonian,
And the Queen has now become the
King!

REFRAIN 2

Have you got any mountains
That you want to have clumb,
Baby?
Have you got any oceans
That you want to have swum,
Baby?
I'll get out of my bonnet and shawl,
I'll get into my nothing-at-all,
I'll give out with my Weissmuller crawl,
And over the waves I'll go—
Splash! Splash!
Have you got any continents
You want me to fly,
Baby?
Oh, there just isn't anything

That I wouldn't try
For you!
After all my adventures are through,
And I hang up a record or two,
You can tell all the papers
That I did it because
I love you!

MOONLIGHT ON THE CAMPUS

Published. Copyrighted July 15, 1937. Previously registered for copyright as an unpublished song April 15, 1937. Introduced by Dick Powell. Recorded by Dick Powell (Decca).

VERSE

No lights are on in the dormitory;
They've all been put out for the night.
But in heaven's second story
There still remains a brighter light.

REFRAIN

There's moonlight on the campus tonight,
And here it is another June;
And even when we're strolling by,
Another year's gone rolling by
So soon,
Too soon.

There's moonlight on the campus tonight;
It nearly makes the teardrops start.
To leave it all behind us both
And know a year may find us both
Apart, sweetheart.

There will be another June,
Another night, another moon,
For some lucky pair,
But we won't be there
To help share it.

There's moonlight on the campus tonight,
So, darling, give tonight to me—
One dream to put our finger on,
A magic dream to linger on
In memory.

LOVE IS ON THE AIR TONIGHT

Published. Copyrighted July 15, 1937. Previously registered for copyright as an unpublished song March 23, 1937. Introduced by Dick Powell and Buck and Bubbles with Fred Waring and His Pennsylvanians.

VERSE

Up in Maine or on the western plain,
Makes no diff'rence where you go,
Cinderella and her fella
Have the parlor lights turned low,
List'ning to the radio.

REFRAIN

Love is on the air tonight,
And it's on a heart-to-heart hookup.
Love is ev'rywhere tonight—
Better look your coziest nook up.
Each station throughout the nation
Will have a song coming through;
So, if your set works,
The major networks
Will do your wooing for you.

You should never sing to her
If a song is not up your alley—
You may sound like Bing to her,
But suppose she likes Rudy Vallee?
If some crooner from old Altoona*
Can tell her better than you,
Why should you care,
Long as love is on the air tonight?

---

* Alternate lines:
    If some gypsy from old Poughkeepsie
    or
    If some fellow who's selling Jell-O
    Or some basso from old El Paso,
    Or some phony from old Tyronee,
    Or some wacky from Nagasaki
    Can tell her better than you,
    What do you care,
    Long as love is on the air tonight?

WHEN YOUR COLLEGE DAYS ARE GONE

Registered for copyright as an unpublished song March 23, 1937. Not used in film.

When the world lies before you
And your college days are through,
Will the bright college years fade away?
Will the old college songs
Bring back the faces that you knew
Or the friends you left on graduation day?
Will the moon through the treetops
Make your memories start
Of the men on the campus
And the girl who had your heart?
And will time, that old gypsy,
Bring you back, off and on,
When the world lies before you
And your college days are gone?

HOLLYWOOD HOTEL (1937)

Produced by Hal B. Wallis for Warner Bros. Released January 1938. Copyright December 27, 1937. Directed by Busby Berkeley. Screenplay by Jerry Wald, Maurice Leo, and Richard Macaulay, from an original story by Jerry Wald and Maurice Leo. Music by Richard A. Whiting. Lyrics by Johnny Mercer. Musical numbers staged by Busby Berkeley. Orchestrations by Ray Heindorf. Musical director: Leo F. Forbstein. With Dick Powell, Rosemary Lane, Lola Lane, Hugh Herbert, Ted Healy, Glenda Farrell, Johnny "Scat" Davis, Alan Mowbray, Mabel Todd, Allyn Joslyn, Grant Mitchell, Edgar Kennedy and the Hollywood Hotel Program with Louella Parsons, Frances Langford, Raymond Paige and His Orchestra, Jerry Cooper, Ken Niles, Duane Thompson, and Benny Goodman and His Orchestra.

HOORAY FOR HOLLYWOOD

Published. Copyrighted February 7, 1938. Previously registered for copyright as an unpublished song July 31, 1937. Introduced by Johnny "Scat" Davis, Frances Langford, and Benny Goodman and His Orchestra, including Hymie Schertzer, Red Ballard, Harry James, and Gene Krupa. Reprised in Finale by Dick Powell, Rosemary Lane, Johnny "Scat" Davis, Ted Healy, Mabel Todd, Frances Langford, Lola Lane, Glenda Farrell, and ensemble. Recorded by Johnny "Scat" Davis (Universal).

If a song can become an instant anthem, this one certainly did. It pleased the denizens of the Dream Factory and confirmed the convictions of the happily paying customers. It became the unofficial theme song of the movie capital. You'll hear it to this day in any context that has any claim to represent Hollywood.

At the time Mercer said of it: "Hollywood seemed to me like a big put-on and I had to make a little fun of it."

Published version

Hooray for Hollywood!
That screwy, ballyhooey Hollywood,
Where any office boy or young mechanic
Can be a panic
With just a good-looking pan,
And any barmaid
Can be a star maid
If she dances with or without a fan.
Hooray for Hollywood!
Where you're terrific if you're even good,
Where anyone at all from Shirley Temple
To Aimee Semple
Is equally understood.
Go out and try your luck—
You might be Donald Duck!
Hooray for Hollywood!

Hooray for Hollywood!
That phony, super-Coney Hollywood,
They come from Chillicothes and Paducahs
With their bazookas
To get their names up in lights,
All armed with photos from local rotos
With their hair in ribbons and legs in tights.

Hooray for Hollywood!
You may be homely in your neighborhood,
But if you think that you can be an actor,
See Mister Factor;
He'd make a monkey look good—
Within a half an hour
You'll look like Tyrone Power!
Hooray for Hollywood!

Film version

JOHNNY
"SCAT" DAVIS: Hooray for Hollywood!
That screwy, ballyhooey
Hollywood,
Where any office boy or young
mechanic
Can be a panic
With just a good-looking pan.

FRANCES
LANGFORD: And any shopgirl
Can be a top girl
If she pleases the tired
businessman.

HYMIE SCHERTZER,
HARRY JAMES
& RED BALLARD: Hooray for Hollywood!
You may be homely in your
neighborhood,
Bom, bom, bom, bom, bom,
bom, bom—

GENE KRUPA: —to be an actor,
See Mister Factor
He'll make your kisser look
good.

DAVIS: Go out and try your luck—
You may be Donald Duck!
Hooray for Hollywood!
Hooray for Hollywood!
That bully, wild and wooly
Hollywood!

LANGFORD: They hire cowboys and they
hang their chaps up
And all their maps up
And give them all that they
lacked.
Now ain't it funny,
They pay them money?
Shows what you can do
If your horse can act!

DAVIS: Hooray for Hollywood!
They hire fellas whose
physiques are good
And then they tell them
they're the perfect-shape
men
To act like ape men,
And they convince them
they should.
They make them grunt and
yell—

FIVE BAND
MEMBERS: And people think you're swell!

DAVIS: Hooray for Hollywood.
It's really got me.
Hooray!

FIVE BAND
MEMBERS: Hooray!

DAVIS: Hooray for Hollywood.

Additional lyrics for Finale

DAVIS: Hooray for Hollywood!
That screwy, ballyhooey
Hollywood!

TED HEALY &
MABEL TODD: Where any office boy or young
mechanic
Can be a panic—

DICK POWELL &
ROSEMARY LANE: With just a good-looking pan.

LANGFORD,
LOLA LANE,
GLENDA FARRELL
& 2 MEN: And old vaudevillians
Are making millions . . .

ENSEMBLE: It doesn't matter if you're five
or fifty—
If you look nifty.
Then leave the old
neighborhood!
You've got a chance to win—
You might be Rin Tin Tin
Hooray for Hollywood!

DICK POWELL &
ROSEMARY LANE: It makes your dreams come true
Just like the movies do,

ALL: Hooray for Hollywood!

I'M LIKE A FISH OUT OF WATER

Published. Copyrighted November 3, 1937. Previously registered for copyright as an unpublished song August 28, 1937. Introduced by Dick Powell, Rosemary Lane, Ted Healy, and Mabel Todd. Recorded by Dick Powell (Decca).

Published version

VERSE

Ev'rybody says I'm witty;
I can even please my boss.
I took Pelmanism
To give me magnetism
So I could put myself across.
And so it really seems a pity
You put me at a total loss;

REFRAIN 1

I'm like a fish out of water
When you're around.
I feel like a jockey
Playing a game of hockey
Or like a monkey without a zoo
Ev'ry time that I'm with you.

I'm like a fish out of water,
I don't know why.
I feel like a sailor
Traveling in a trailer—
I'm on the most unfamiliar ground
Whenever you're around.

I feel so small
And I get red as a beet;
I trip and fall,
I'm all hands and feet.

I'm quite a card and a cutup
Around the boys,
But you make me shut up
And lose my poise.
It's a funny thing what love can do—
I'm like a fish out of water with you.

REFRAIN 2

I'm like a fish out of water
When I'm with you,
As helpless as Morgan*
Swingin' it on the organ
Or Mae West playing an ingénue,†
Ev'ry time that I'm with you.

I'm like a fish out of water
When you're around;
I'm like Eddie Cantor
Doing a Van Devanter
Or Charles A. Lindbergh
Upon the ground
Whenever you're around.

I feel so small *etc.*

[*Lyric continues as in Refrain 1.*]

Film version

VERSE 1

DICK
POWELL: Oh no, I'm not witty.
But would you believe it,
I took Pelmanism

_____
* *Alternate lyric:*
    Just like J. P. Morgan
† *Alternate lyric:*
    Or Dizzy Dean
    With no ballyhoo

To give me magnetism,
So I could put myself across.
And so it really seems a pity
You put me at a total loss.

REFRAIN 1

I'm like a fish out of water
When I'm with you.
Just like J. P. Morgan
Swingin' it on the organ
Or Dizzy Dean with no ballyhoo
Every time that I'm with you.
I'm like a fish out of water
When you're around—
I'm like Eddie Cantor
Doing a Van Devanter
Or Colonel Lindbergh
Upon the ground
Whenever you're around.
I feel so small
And I get red as a beet;
I trip and fall,
I'm all hands and feet.
I'm quite a card and a cutup
Around the boys,
But you make me shut up
And lose my poise.
It's a funny thing what love can do.
I'm like a fish out of water with you.

VERSE 2

ROSEMARY
LANE: Though I'm good at conversation,
Though I've been around a lot,
Though I make a showing
To keep the party going
When the party's not so hot.
In spite of my sophistication
You've put me in an awful spot.

REFRAIN 2

I'm like a fish out of water
When I'm with you,
Like Marion Talley
Doing a Rudy Vallee
Or Mickey Mouse playing an ingénue,
Every time I'm with you.
I'm like a fish out of water
When you're around.
I'm like Ginger Rogers
Running the Brooklyn Dodgers.
I'm on the most unfamiliar ground
Whenever you're around.
My whole life through
I've always known what to say,
But now with you

It all goes away.
Exactly like Man o' War as an also-ran
Or like Sally Rand if she lost her fan.
I feel all wet and it's no wonder I do.
POWELL: That's how I get when I'm out with you,
BOTH: So if I act like a dummy and seem insane
And won't even come in out of the
rain—
POWELL: It's a funny thing what love can do—
BOTH: I'm like a fish out of water with you.

Additional film lyrics for Ted Healy and Mabel Todd

Not used in film.

TED
HEALY: I'm like a fish out of water when you're
with me,
Like Popeye the Sailor
Doing a Robert Taylor,
The Chrysler Building in Kankakee,
Every time that you're with me.
I'm like a fish out of water—I don't know
why.
I'm like Mischa Auer
Copying Tyrone Power
Or like Mack Sennett without a pie,
Each time I catch your eye.
I start to speak,
My tongue gets twisted and tied.
You touch my cheek,
I blush like a bride.
So if I act like an oyster without a shell
Or like John L. Lewis in the AFL,
You can blame it on the things you do—
I'm like a fish out of water with you.

MABEL
TODD: You're like a fish out of water—you're
tellin' me!
You look kinda pashful,
Why do you be so bashful?
You're as sly as a guy can be
Every time that you're with me.
You're like a fish out of water when I'm
with you—
You act like a spinster
Standing before a min'ster,
Only you never say I do,
Whenever I'm with you.
Come over here—
Don't be a kid out of school.
Come closer, dear—
Ain't you ever heard of the golden rule?
I want to see you cheek to cheek,
But you want to see me week to week.
Tell Doctor Jekyll what to do,
Start lettin' Mister Hyde come through,

You're like a fish out of water when I'm
with you.

SILHOUETTED IN THE MOONLIGHT

Published. Copyrighted November 3, 1937. Previously registered for copyright as an unpublished song August 28, 1937. Introduced by Rosemary Lane. Reprised by Frances Langford and Jerry Cooper with Raymond Paige and His Orchestra. Recorded by Frances Langford (Decca), Benny Goodman's Trio (Victor), and Glenn Miller and His Orchestra (Brunswick).

VERSE

Looking as you do,
You're a dream tonight,
Standing as you are
In this silver light,
A vision that will never leave my sight,
Looking as you do tonight.

REFRAIN

I'll remember this moment,
I'll wrap this picture in a dream,
For silhouetted in the moonlight,
How sweet you seem!
Through the long night of waiting
I'll hardly know that you are gone,
For silhouetted in the moonlight,
You'll linger on.
Your actions,
Your expressions
Will fill my heart
And thrill my heart
Ev'ry single moment we're apart.
So, I'll never be lonely,
Though there be shadows ev'rywhere,
For silhouetted in the moonlight,
You'll be there.

LET THAT BE A LESSON TO YOU

Published. Copyrighted November 3, 1937. Previously registered for copyright as an unpublished song March 23, 1937. Introduced by Johnny "Scat" Davis,

Dick Powell, Rosemary Lane, Harrison Greene, Mabel Todd, Ted Healy and ensemble, Benny Goodman and His Orchestra. Originally intended for *Varsity Show* but not used in that film. Recorded by Benny Goodman and His Orchestra (Victor).

Published version

VERSE 1

Oh! Columbus was the discoverer of America,
And he sailed the sea in fourteen ninety-two,
But the good Queen Isabella
Found a more attractive fella,
And Columbus wound up in the jugeroo!

REFRAIN

Oh! Let that be a lesson to you—
Ev'rybody meets his Waterloo.
He wasn't too big to end up behind the eight ball,
And remember, buddy, there is still a lot of room
for you!

VERSE 2

Raleigh met Queen Elizabeth on a muddy street,
And he wanted to protect her dainty tread,
So he took his coat and hat off,
But the Queen took more than that off—
Now, don't get me wrong, she took off Walter's head!

REPEAT REFRAIN

Film version

VERSE

JOHNNY
"SCAT" DAVIS: Oh! Columbus was the discoverer of
America,
And he sailed the sea in fourteen
ninety-two,
But the good Queen Isabella
Found a more attractive fella,
And Columbus wound up in the
jugeroo!

REFRAIN

Oh! Let that be a lesson to you,
Ev'rybody meets his Waterloo.
He wasn't too big to end up behind
the eight ball,
And remember, buddy, there is still a
lot of room for you!

DICK
POWELL: Ronnie Bowers once was a singer in
Benny Goodman's band

And he came to Hollywood to be a
    star,
But his screen career was halted
By a double-chocolate malted—
Now his spotlight is the headlight of
    a car.
Oh! Let that be a lesson to you,
Ev'rybody meets his Waterloo.
He wasn't too big to end up behind
    the eight ball,
And remember, honey, string along
    and you will be there too.

ROSEMARY
    LANE: What's the difference if you're a
        waiter or you're a movie star?
    Don't you know that I'm all for you
        anyhow?
    That's the kind of girlfriend I am,
    In the words of Omar Khayyam
    Give me ham on rye, a lemonade, and
        thou.
    Oh! Let that be a lesson to you,
    Now things are not so tough in
        Waterloo.
    You really don't have to end up
        behind the eight ball
    Give a good kiss, honey, and watch it
        roll away from you.
    Oh, let that be a lesson to you—
    GIRL: That shows you what the old love bug
        will do!
    MAN: Kinda looks as though she's puttin'
        you behind the eight ball.
    POWELL: What do I care, Pop, if there's room
        enough for baby too?
    2ND MAN: Pardon me, young man, can you
        bring me a soda right away?
    3 KIDS: You can make our orders just the
        same as Pa's.
    POWELL: That'll be one, two, three, four
        drinks.
    2ND MAN: Kids, you'll have to pay for your
        drinks.
    1ST BOY: Well, in that case bring him his drink
        and three more straws.
    POWELL: Oh! Let that be a lesson to you.
    3 BOYS: Oh, yeah?
    POWELL: I can see your Pa knows what to do.
    3 BOYS: Says you!
    1ST GROUP: You're never too great to end up
        behind the eight ball.
    2ND GROUP: So, remember, buddy, there's still a
        lot of room for you.
    POWELL: And you!
    2ND GROUP: And you.
    POWELL: Who, me?
    2ND GROUP: Yeah, there's still a lot of room for
        you!

POWELL: Oh! Let that be a lesson to you,
4 MEN: Certainly, everybody meets his
        Waterloo.
    You're never too big to end up behind
        the eight ball
    And remember, buddy, there's a lot
        of room for you!
MABEL
    TODD: Mister Samson was the mightiest man
        upon the earth,
    He could lift a building forty times
        his size,
    But his muscles couldn't save him,
    'Cause he let Delilah shave him,
    When she got through he couldn't lift
        his eyes.
    Now let that be a lesson to you,
    Just remember what a gal can do.
    Little Delilah put him, put him
        behind the eight ball.
    Why don't you please remember,
        Buddy, la-da, la-da.
    Please remember, Buddy, la-da, la-da.
    That's what I'm going to do to you,
    Tee-da-dee-dah-dah-dah-dah,
    I'm going to do to you.
TED
    HEALY: Listen, sister, don't you remember
        Jonah and the whale?
    The whale thought he was quite an
        eater, too.
    I don't know about your figger,
    But the whale's was even bigger,
    And he found out he bit off more
        than he could chew,
    Oh, hallelujah!
    Oh, let that be a lesson to you,
    There's nothing that the whale, he
        could do.
    He wasn't too big to end up with
        indigestion.
    Take it easy, sister, you're gonna be
        the same way too!
    ALL: Oh! Columbus discovered our
        America.
    He sailed the sea in fourteen ninety-
        two—
    LANE: But the good Queen Isabella
        Found a more attractive fella—
    POWELL: And Columbus wound up in the
        jugeroo!
    ALL: Oh! let that be a lesson to you.
    Ev'rybody meets his Waterloo,
    He wasn't too big to end up behind
        the eight ball,
    And remember, buddy, there's a lot
        of room for you!

I'VE HITCHED MY WAGON TO A STAR

Published. Copyrighted November 3, 1937. Previously registered for copyright as an unpublished song August 28, 1937. Introduced by Alan Mowbray (dubbed by Dick Powell). Reprised by Powell with Raymond Paige and His Orchestra. Recorded by Dick Powell (Decca) and Benny Goodman and His Orchestra (Victor).

VERSE

It's a proven theory of all astrology
That human beings cannot fly through space.
If I differ, let me offer my apology,
But I can prove that such is not the case.

REFRAIN

I've hitched my wagon to a star,
That lucky little star
That watches over you.
And now no ties can bind me,
I'll go where you go;
I've left the world behind me,
And I want the world to know,
If it wants me it can find me—
In your afterglow.
I've tied my heartstrings to a dream,
That lucky little dream
That introduced me to you.
I've made my heart a guiding chart
To lead me where you are;
I've hitched my wagon to a star.

SING, YOU SON OF A GUN

Registered for copyright as an unpublished song September 10,1937. Finale: Introduced by Dick Powell, Johnny "Scat" Davis, Rosemary Lane, Frances Langford, Jerry Cooper, Ted Healy, Mabel Todd, Lola Lane, Glenda Farrell, and Raymond Paige and His Orchestra.

Stand up and sing, you son of a gun—
You know it's spring, you son of a gun!
The skies are blue,
The birds are twittering, too;
There's lots and lots of moon about,
And that's enough to croon about.
Go have your fling, you son of a gun—
Let romance ring, you son of a gun!
Go and get someone to make a duet—
Get in the swing and sing, you son of a gun!

INTERLUDE

Doves are cooing,
Cows are softly mooing,
Owls are whooing,
They're all I-love-you-ing,
Two-by-two-ing,
Can't you see that it's your opportunity
To join the community?

Sing, sing, sing, sing, you son of a gun—
Just be like Bing, you son of a gun!
Sound your A and sing your worries away,
You know it's spring, so sing, you son of a—
Swing! You son of a—
Sing! You son of a gun.

CAN'T TEACH MY OLD HEART NEW TRICKS

Published. Copyrighted November 12, 1937. Previously registered for copyright as an unpublished song August 26, 1937. Not used in film. Recorded by Frances Langford (Decca), Benny Goodman's Trio (Victor), and Margaret Whiting, the composer Richard Whiting's daughter.

REFRAIN

Can't teach my old heart new tricks—
It won't believe that we're through.
It keeps on beating for you—
Can't teach my old heart new tricks.
I tell my old eyes it's spring;
They won't believe what I say.
They say it's raining all day—
Can't teach my old eyes a thing.
I tell my lips they'll soon be singing a song;
I tell my arms a new love's coming along;
But oh! I'm so wrong!
For something inside still ticks
Although it's broken in two;
It keeps on beating for you.
Can't teach my old heart new tricks,
Can't teach my old heart new tricks.

Alternative lyrics from Mercer archive

Can't teach my old heart new tricks,
Can't make it love someone new.
Can't teach my old heart new tricks—
Keeps on beatin' just for you.

I tell my old eyes it's spring;
They tell me it's cold and gray.
Can't teach my old eyes a thing,

Keep cryin' night and day.
Oh, why can't I forget you
As you've forgotten me?
But something inside still ticks,
Not knowing it's snapped in two.
Can't teach my old heart new tricks—
Keeps on beatin' just for you.

SINGIN' IN THE MOONLIGHT

Music by Mercer. Registered for copyright as an unpublished song October 1, 1954. Not used in film.

Singin' in the moonlight,
Meetin' all the gang out
Down around the hangout,
Evenin' in its prime.*
Singin' in the moonlight,
Arm around your baby,
Kissin' later, maybe,
When there's time.
Singin' with the top down
Where the waves can sing
Their old familiar song.
Wanna be in heaven?
Spend yourself a June night
Singin' in the moonlight
All night long!

LOVE IS A MERRY-GO-ROUND

Music by Rube Bloom. Published. Copyrighted May 27, 1937. Previously registered for copyright as an unpublished song April 24, 1937. Possibly written earlier for *Blackbirds of 1936*.

---

* *Alternative lyric, lines 1–4.*
   Singin' in the moonlight,
   Kinda harmonizin',
   While the moon is risin'
   On its lazy climb.

VERSE 1

I have heard the poets sing of love
In a million different ways.
Some of them are quick to blame it,
While some acclaim it
With praise.
I am just an ordinary soul,
Never knew what love could be.
Darling, you made my mind up for me.

REFRAIN

Love is a merry-go-round;
It gets you dizzy, I know.
Love is a merry-go-round,
But here I go.
I was just fooling around,
Like ev'rybody I know;
Now I'm on a merry-go-round
Since I met you.
Although the chance is
I'll never get the old ring,
I'm gonna try till I do.
And though it seems like
The most impossible thing,
One in a million comes through!
Say—
I may be Paradise bound;
You are the one who would know.
Love is a merry-go-round,
But here I go!

VERSE 2

I recall that back in childhood days
When the circus came to town,
All the children used to go there
To see the show there,
I found.
I don't have to see a circus now,
'Cause I'm on the carousel—
One look at you and dear, how I fell!

REPEAT REFRAIN

BOB WHITE (WHATCHA GONNA SWING TONIGHT?)

Music by Bernie Hanighen. Published. Copyrighted September 21, 1937. Number-one recording by Bing Crosby and Connie Boswell with John Scott Trotter's

Orchestra (Decca). Other leading recordings by Mildred Bailey, accompanied by Red Norvo (xylophone) and His Orchestra (Vocalion); Johnny Mercer (Brunswick); Benny Goodman's Orchestra, with vocal by Martha Tilton (Victor); and Gene Kardos, with vocal by Bea Wain (Melotone).

Mercer "swung" this one on a record with his old friend Bing Crosby in the great tradition of the famous vaudevillians Gallagher and Shean. He was to repeat the feat twenty-five years later with a younger partner—Bobby Darin—and a suitably updated (1961) lyric, on the album *Two of a Kind* (Atco).

(For the benefit of non-ornithologists, the bobwhite is a genus of North American quail.)

VERSE

Mister Bob,
Don't you know things have changed?
You're behind time
With the melody you always sing;
All the birds
Have their songs rearranged.
Better get smart—
Whatcha gotta do today is swing!

REFRAIN

I was talkin' to the whip-poor-will;
He says you got a corny trill,
Bob White!
Whatcha gonna swing tonight?
I was talkin' to the mockingbird;
He says you are the worst he's heard,
Bob White!
Whatcha gonna swing tonight?
Even the owl
Tells me you're foul,
Singin' those lullaby notes.
Don't be a bringdown—
If you can swing down,
Gimme those high notes!

There's a lotta talk about you, Bob,
And they're sayin' you're off the cob.
Fake it, Mister B,
Take it, follow me,
Bob White!

[*Whistle.*]

We're gonna break it up tonight!

From top left:
Hard to Get: *Dick Powell and Olivia de Havilland*
Going Places: *Louis Armstrong serenading Jeepers Creepers*
Garden of the Moon: *John Payne and Margaret Lindsay*
Gold Diggers in Paris: *Rudy Vallee and Rosemary Lane*

GARDEN OF THE MOON,
GOING PLACES,
and Other Songs of 1938

IF YOU CAN TAKE IT

Song dated January 19, 1938. Music by Harry Warren. Music and lyrics found in the Harry Warren Archives.

VERSE

Ask any lover and you'll discover:
Love isn't always sunshine and spice.
Read any poet; his lines will show it,
That all your smiles
Can turn to tears
Before you know it.
But still I hope
You think it's worth the price.

REFRAIN

The same old sighs—the moon above,
This funny business called love:
If you can take it,
Take it from me.
Those little words that go amiss,
But always end in a kiss:
If you can take it,
Please take it from me.
If your heart can stand to stop its beat
Taking the bitter and taking the sweet,
If it wants to ache like mine,
Won't you come in? The water's fine.
And all these nights of wond'ring when
I'll ever see you again:
If I can take it so willingly,
Then you can take it,
So take it from me.

OUR HEARTS WILL NEVER GROW OLD

Song dated February 1, 1938. Music by Harry Warren. Music and lyrics found in the Harry Warren Archives.

Our hearts will never grow old;
They'll manage to hold
This feeling of spring.
While stars are aging above,
We'll still keep our love
A permanent thing.
This thing that has bound us,
This warmth that has found us,
Will linger around us

And never grow cold.
How sweetly another day starts
When we know our hearts
Will never grow old.

JEZEBEL (1938)

Produced by Hal B. Wallis for Warner Bros. World premiere March 10, 1938, Radio City Music Hall. Copyright January 26, 1938. Directed by William Wyler. Screenplay by Clements Ripley, Abem Finkel, and John Huston, based on the play by Owen Davis Sr. Music by Max Steiner. Musical director: Leo F. Forbstein. Starring Bette Davis, Henry Fonda, George Brent, with Margaret Lindsay, Donald Crisp, Fay Bainter, Richard Cromwell, Henry O'Neill, Spring Byington, and John Litel.

In the Deep South before the Civil War, a Southern belle stirs up the local menfolk before an outbreak of plague brings out her true worth.

JEZEBEL

Music by Harry Warren. Published. Copyrighted February 21, 1938. Not used in film. Not to be confused with the 1951 song with the same title by Wayne Shanklin, which was recorded and popularized by Frankie Laine.

VERSE

You're a thousand women
All rolled into one,
You play almost any kind of part.
You're a thousand women,
Yet you're really none,
For you can't be human
If you haven't got a heart.

REFRAIN

Jezebel,
I see the devil in your eyes,
But it doesn't matter,
When you tell me those milk-and-honey lies.
Jezebel,
I see an angel in your face,
But it's like a siren
That is calling me to your embrace.
I wish I could hate you,
I wish I could hate you.
And yet it's a feeling I can't define,

I know that I love you,
I know that I love you.
Your heart is a magnet
That's forever pulling at mine.
You know so well
That you can keep me in your spell,
And I know it, too,
For I would die without you,
Jezebel.

WALTZ OF THE FLOWERS

Lyrics by Al Dubin and Mercer. Music by Harry Warren.

REFRAIN

The daisies are dancing,
A rose is romancing
A shy little violet blue;
Carnations are swaying,
The lilacs are playing
The waltz that I'm dancing with you.
The bluebells are ringing,
The tulips are singing
An old-fashioned song that is new.
Flowers glide
Side by side*
While I waltz with you.

INTERLUDE

Springtime blossoms
All dressed in white,
And jolly hollyhocks
Put on their gayest frocks;
Morning glories
Dance through the night,
There's one forget-me-not
That all the rest forgot.

REPEAT REFRAIN

_____

* *Repeated refrain replaces the last two lines with:*
    And it all comes true
    When I waltz with you.

GOLD DIGGERS IN PARIS (1938)

Produced by Hal B. Wallis and Sam Bischoff for Warner Bros. Released June 1938. Copyright April 8, 1938. Directed by Ray Enright. Screenplay by Earl Baldwin and Warren Duff. Story by Jerry Wald, Richard Macaulay and Maurice Leo, from an idea by Jerry Horwin and James Seymour. Music by Harry Warren. Lyrics by Al Dubin. Additional lyrics by Johnny Mercer. Musical numbers created and directed by Busby Berkeley. Orchestrations by Ray Heindorf. Musical director: Leo F. Forbstein. With Rudy Vallee, Rosemary Lane, Hugh Herbert, Allen Jenkins, Gloria Dickson, Melville Cooper, Mabel Todd, Fritz Feld, Curt Bois, and the Schnickelfritz Band.

Three girls chase rich husbands in Paris.

DAY DREAMING (ALL NIGHT LONG)

Music by Harry Warren. Published. Copyrighted April 22, 1938. Introduced by Rudy Vallee and Rosemary Lane. Recorded by Rudy Vallee (Victor).

VERSE

Although a day with you
Is quickly gone,
You have a way with you
That lingers on;
And like a sweet encore,
I see your face once more, for:

REFRAIN

All night long
I'm daydreaming,
Daydreaming of wonderful you;
Constantly
I can see you before me,
Then we kiss
And you whisper you adore me;
And though I know
I'm only daydreaming,
Please tell me I'm not play-dreaming,
Tell me I'm not wrong,
While I'm daydreaming
All night long.

Earlier unused version of refrain

All night long
I'm daydreaming,
Daydreaming of you and your love.
I repeat
Every sweet thing you told me;
And I pray
That some day you will hold me.
And even though I know
I'm daydreaming,
Please tell me I'm not play-dreaming.
Tell me I'm not wrong
While I'm daydreaming
All night long.

MY ADVENTURE

Music by Harry Warren. Registered for copyright as an unpublished song November 27, 1934, and again February 17, 1938. Not used in film.

I found my one big adventure
The moment you came in view
The thrill of searching for treasure
Couldn't measure up to you.
Your kiss would be more exciting
Than anything I could do
And all my dreams of sailing the seas
Are memories.
You're my island in the blue,
My adventure is you.

COWBOY FROM BROOKLYN (1938)

Also known as *The Dude Rancher*. Produced by Hal B. Wallis for Warner Bros. Released July 1938. Copyright May 18, 1938. Directed by Lloyd Bacon. Screenplay by Earl Baldwin, based on the play *Howdy Stranger* by Robert Sloane and Louis Pelletier Jr. Music by Richard A. Whiting. Lyrics by Johnny Mercer. Additional music by Harry Warren. Orchestrations by Adolph Deutsch. Musical director: Leo F. Forbstein. With Dick Powell, Pat O'Brien, Priscilla Lane, Dick Foran, Ann Sheridan, Johnny Davis, and Ronald Reagan.

A boy from Brooklyn finds himself in a small western town, where the only work he can get is as a cowboy, a job for which he is ill-suited. Being Dick Powell, he sings and is discovered by a talent scout, Pat O'Brien, and soon becomes America's favorite singing cowboy.

I'VE GOT A HEARTFUL OF MUSIC

Music by Richard Whiting. Published. Copyrighted April 22, 1938. Previously registered for copyright as an unpublished song August 26, 1937. Introduced by Dick Powell, Harry Barris, and Candy Candido. This was originally written for Busby Berkeley's film *Hollywood Hotel* (1937) but was not used.

VERSE

Jeeves, get out my Sunday suit,
Lay out my Sunday style,
And pardon me while
I put on my Sunday smile.
Pardon me for singing, Jeeves,
But words are rather weak
And I am much too happy
Just to speak.

REFRAIN

Yes! I've got a heartful of music
And I've gotta burst into song.
Oh! Little robin red-breast
Hasn't got a thing on me.
No! I've got a heartful of sunshine
And I've gotta pass it along.
Come on, you hurdy-gurdies
And you birdies above,
Tune in to my heartful of music.
Tune in to the music of love.

RIDE, TENDERFOOT, RIDE

Music by Richard Whiting. Published. Copyrighted April 1, 1938. Previously registered for copyright as an unpublished song January 19, 1938. Introduced by Dick Powell and Priscilla Lane; reprised by Powell and male ensemble.

Recorded by Powell (Decca) and Dick Todd (Victor). Also recorded by the bands of Eddy Duchin (Brunswick), Freddy Martin (Bluebird), Orrin Tucker (Vocalion), and Guy Lombardo (Victor).

Ride, tenderfoot, ride tonight,
Let the old range riders here at your side, tonight.
They're fast company,
So, if you wanna be a cowboy,
Then you gotta ride, tenderfoot, ride!
You gotta hit the trail
In Oklahoma when the moon is pale,
And get to Texas with the mornin' mail,
'Fore you can be a cowboy.
You gotta rope and throw,
You gotta get your share of buffalo
And win the money at the rodeo,
'Fore you can be a cowboy.
You gotta tend your cattle the best you can,
Hold your likker like a man,
And ride, tenderfoot, ride tonight!
Let the old range riders here at your side tonight.
They're fast company,
So, if you wanna be a cowboy,
Then you gotta ride, tenderfoot, ride!
Ride, ride, ride!

I'LL DREAM TONIGHT

Music by Richard A. Whiting. Published. Copyrighted April 1, 1938. Introduced by Dick Powell.

VERSE

My nights have all been peaceful,
I left the world behind,
I never had a dream disturb my peace of mind.
But they're no longer peaceful,
For now there's something wrong,
Your image haunts me all night long.

REFRAIN

I'll dream tonight,
I'll toss the whole night through.
I'll dream tonight,
And all because of you.
The trees will dance,
The chimney tops go reeling,
A million stars will swing upon the ceiling.
My eyes will see
A rainbow-colored sky.
The moon will be a place for us to fly.
I'll have the sweetest nightmare
That I ever knew.
I'll dream because I fell in love with you.

HOWDY, STRANGER

Music by Richard A. Whiting. Registered for copyright as an unpublished song January 19, 1938. Introduced by Dick Powell and ensemble.

Way out where I come from
The dogs are ten feet high,
And a man can light his cigar
From the moon up in the sky.

Way out where I come from
The corn grows up so tall
That there ain't no one to pick it—
We just wait for it to fall.

Howdy, stranger!
Howdy do to you!
Step right up and call me "pard."
I'm the roughest, toughest maverick
That you ever knew,
And the whole darn world
Is my backyard.

Way out where I come from
The cows are like a dream,
But they ain't much good for milkin'
'Cause they only give us cream.

Way out where I come from
The chickens are our pride.
They lay eggs the way we want 'em—
Some are scrambled, some are fried.

Howdy, stranger!
Howdy do to you!
Step right up and call me "pard."
If you ever come out my way
Say you're a friend of mine,
And the whole darn world
Is your backyard.

On February 10, 1938, Richard Whiting died. Though only forty-six he had suffered from heart trouble for some time.

Mercer was devastated. Whiting had been the composer with whom he was most at ease. He was in the habit of sitting at Whiting's piano and working with him side by side, while with other collaborators he would take the melody from the composer and work on it on his own.

He now had to find a new partner and one who would satisfy Warner Bros., since he and Whiting had been hired as a team. The studio suggested that he should fulfill his contract by working with their top composer, Harry Warren, with whom he had worked previously on a few songs, and collaborating on the lyrics with Warren's longtime lyricist, Al Dubin.

Dubin was not pleased by this development. With his record he felt he didn't need a collaborator. Nonetheless, he went along with the arrangement and he and Mercer did write a few songs together and eventually became good friends.

Now Mercer and Warren were a team, too; a team that would produce some of the biggest hits of the next decade or so.

COWBOY FROM BROOKLYN

Music by Harry Warren. Published. Copyrighted April 22, 1938. Previously registered for copyright as an unpublished song February 17, 1938. Played instrumentally.

When I was just a little shaver back in Brooklyn,
I always thought that I would like to be a cowboy,
Because I loved to see 'em in the movin' pictures,
A-ridin' and a-shootin' away.
And so, as I grew up,
I saved a lotta money,
I bought a saddle and I bought a buckin' bronco,
I said goodbye to all the fellas back in Brooklyn
And went to Arizona one day.
But I'll tell you, pard,
I worked so hard
And ev'rybody played so rough;
That they always had me waitin' on the table,
Sweepin' out the stable and stuff!
And so I sold my saddle and my buckin' bronco
And you won't ever catch me near another cowboy,
'Cause I can always see 'em in the movin' pictures
A-ridin' and a-shootin' away,
Okay!
But I belong in Brooklyn,
Hangin' round the drugstore,
Roundin' up the sodas all day.

BOY MEETS GIRL (1938)

Produced by Hal B. Wallis for Warner Bros. Released August 1938. Copyright May 12, 1938. Directed by Lloyd Bacon. Screenplay by Bella and Sam Spewack, from their stage play. Music by M. K. Jerome. Lyrics by Jack Scholl. Additional songs by Harry Warren and Johnny Mercer. Musical director: Leo F. Forbstein. Starring James Cagney and Pat O'Brien with Marie Wilson, Ralph Bellamy, Frank McHugh, Dick Foran, Bruce Lester, Ronald Reagan, Paul Clark, Penny Singleton, Dennie Moore, Harry Seymour, Bert Hanlon, and James Stephenson.

Two Hollywood scriptwriters make a star of a child that has yet to be born.

BOY MEETS GIRL

Music by Harry Warren. Registered for copyright as an unpublished song February 15, 1938. Played instrumentally.

VERSE

M is for moonlight,
P is for park,
B is for benches
There in the dark.
K is for kisses,
S is for swell.
Put 'em together,
What do they spell?

REFRAIN

Boy meets girl,
Moon above,
Steals a kiss,
Falls in love.
Boy meets girl
Out one night,
Someone else—
There's a fight!
Boy feels blue
All day long,
Girl does too,
Says she's wrong.
Boy meets girl,
Same moon above,
There's a kiss,
Back in love.

SOMETHING TELLS ME

Music by Harry Warren. Published. Copyrighted March 18, 1938. Leading recordings by Louis Armstrong (Decca) and Kay Kyser (Brunswick).

VERSE

Haven't read it in your eyes,
Haven't heard it in your sighs,
Couldn't tell you why it's so,
Nevertheless, I only know:

REFRAIN

Something tells me
I'm falling in love.
Something tells me
You're sent from above.
Not the stars or the man in the moon,
Though I'm certain
They set the stage and opened the curtain.
Something tells me
My waiting is through.
I hope something
Is telling you, too.
Something whispers
That we'll never part,
And something tells me it's my heart.

THE WEEKEND OF A PRIVATE SECRETARY

Music by Bernie Hanighen. Published. Copyrighted March 21, 1938. Introduced and recorded by Mildred Bailey with Red Norvo's Orchestra (Brunswick).

I went to Havana
On one of those cruises,
For forty-nine fifty
To spend a few days.
I went to Havana,
To look at the natives,
To study their customs,
Their picturesque ways.

In searching for some local color,
I ran across a Cuban gent,
And he was such a big sensation,
I forgot the population.
He showed me the city,
He taught me the customs;
My trip to Havana
Was quite a success.

We had Bacardi,
I forgot the clock,
So we were tardy
In returning to the dock.
Though I delayed it,
Even dropped my shawl,
The Cuban made it,
As they gave the final call.
Darn it all!

I'm back in the office,
I'm punching the time clock,
But you can bet my mind
Is not on my work.
Instead of Bacardis,
I'm ordering Bromos;
Instead of the Cuban,
I'm stuck with a clerk.

The other girls can go to Europe,
And marry into royalty,
And they can get an earl or pasha
Or a gent with lots of casha.

But when I get married
And settle in Brooklyn,
He may be a slicker,
He may be a hick or a Reuben,
But you can bet that he'll be Cuban.

MR. CHUMP (1938)

Produced by Bryan Foy for Warner Bros. Released July 1938. Copyright June 24, 1938. Directed by William Clemens. Screenplay by George Bricker. Music by Bernie Hanighen. Lyrics by Johnny Mercer. With Johnny "Scat" Davis, Lola Lane, Penny Singleton, Donald Briggs, Chester Clute, Frank Orth, Granville Bates, and Spencer Charters.

A small-town boy would rather play the trumpet than work.

AS LONG AS YOU LIVE (YOU'LL BE DEAD IF YOU DIE)

Music by Bernie Hanighen. Published. Copyrighted July 27, 1938. Introduced by Johnny "Scat" Davis (vocal and trumpet) and men in band.

VERSE

I'm gonna leave you, 'cause it's high time;
Somebody else is beatin' my time.
But you'll never hear me cry,
'Cause long as you live, you'll be dead if you die.
You had your fun and now you rush off;
You're givin' me an awful brush-off.
You'll be sorry bye and bye,
'Cause long as you live, you'll be dead if you die,

Oh, yes! Oh, yes!
Take the good advice I give,
Oh, yes! Oh, yes!
As long as you live, you'll be dead if you die.
If you die, you'll be dead, just as long as you live.
So here's a final word of warning,
You're gonna wake up dead some morning.
Then you'll cry, "How 'bout that guy?
I do believe he wasn't tellin' a lie!"
So take it from me—
As hard as you try,
As long as you live, you'll be dead if you die.

MR. CROSBY AND MR. MERCER

Mercer supplied new lyrics for the comedy-patter song "Mr. Gallagher and Mr. Shean," written by Ed Gallagher and Al Shean for the *Ziegfeld Follies of 1922*. The Crosby-Mercer version was recorded for Decca on July 1, 1938, accompanied by Victor Young's Small Fryers (including Spike Jones on drums).

Mercer and Crosby reveled in this apparently improvised Gallagher and Shean–type to-and-fro. In fact, the lyric was too complex for them to memorize and they had to bring cue cards into the studio.

The number was such a success that Crosby made the format part of his repertoire and continued to perform variants of it with his regular partner Bob Hope for years to come. It also relaunched Mercer's own singing career, which had rather languished since his days with the Whiteman band, and had in any case been sidelined by his remarkable output of lyrics.

JOHNNY
MERCER: Oh, Mister Crosby,
Oh, Mister Crosby,
All the orchestras are swinging it today,
And I wanted to find out
What the noise is all about—
Do you really think that swing is here to stay?

BING
CROSBY: Oh, Mister Mercer,
Oh, Mister Mercer,
Swing is really much too ancient to condemn:
In the jungles they would play
In that same abandoned way.
MERCER: On the level, Mister Crosby?
CROSBY: On the downbeat, Mister M.
MERCER: Oh, Mister Crosby,
Oh, Mister Crosby,
I've been reading in the latest magazine
That a jivin' jitterbug
Blew his top and cut a rug—
Will you tell me what that language really means?
CROSBY: Oh, Mister Mercer,
Oh, Mister Mercer,
As a student of the slang they use pro tem,
That just means a solid gait—
Cut a murderistic plate.
MERCER: That's amazin', Mister Crosby!
CROSBY: Elementary, Mister M!
MERCER: Oh, Mister Crosby,
Oh, Mister Crosby,
Is it true that swing's another name for jazz?
And the first place it was played
Was in a New Orleans parade,
And the southern negro gave it all it has?
CROSBY: Oh, Mister Mercer,
Oh, Mister Mercer,
I believe that its foundation came from then.
They just slowed the tempo down
And they really went to town.
MERCER: Allegretto, Mister Crosby!
CROSBY: Alligators, Mister M!
CROSBY: Mister Mercer,

Well, I trust that I have made the matter clear.
So, when someone plays a thing,
You will understand it's swing
And appreciate the rhythm that you hear.
MERCER: Oh, Mister Crosby,
Oh, Mister Crosby,
I'm afraid that type of rhythm's not for me.
I prefer my music plain
À la Schubert's "Serenade."
CROSBY: Sort of ritardo, Mister Mercer?
MERCER: Sort of Lombardo, Mister C.

GARDEN OF THE MOON (1938)

Produced by Hal B. Wallis and Lou Edelman for Warner Bros. Released September 1938. Copyright July 22, 1938. Directed by Busby Berkeley. Screenplay by Jerry Wald and Richard Macaulay, based on a *Saturday Evening Post* story by H. Bedford-Jones and John Barton Browne. Music by Harry Warren. Lyrics by Al Dubin and Johnny Mercer. Orchestrations by Ray Heindorf and Frank Perkins. Musical director: Leo F. Forbstein. With Pat O'Brien, Margaret Lindsay, John Payne, Johnny "Scat" Davis, Melville Cooper, Mabel Todd, and Jimmie Fidler.

Pat O'Brien is a tough nightclub owner who tries to take advantage of an aspiring band leader and, predictably, a girl is involved.

GARDEN OF THE MOON

Lyrics by Al Dubin and Mercer. Music by Harry Warren. Published. Copyrighted July 20, 1938. Introduced by Mabel Todd; reprised by John Payne, Johnny "Scat" Davis, and band. Leading recordings were made by Red Norvo (Brunswick); Jimmy Dorsey, with vocal by Bob Eberly (Decca); and Skinnay Ennis (Victor).

VERSE

There are flowers April showers never help at all,
And sunny skies make them fade away;
For their place is an oasis,
Where the moonbeams fall,

And they begin to blossom,
When twilight fades away.

REFRAIN

There's a garden where the flowers
Are sentimental hours
That bloom eternally
Down the lane of love
In the garden of the moon—
Where a couple never misses
A chance to pick some kisses
From off the sweetheart tree,
Blossoms from above
In the garden of the moon.
Sweet, sweet nothings
I'll gather on our way—
Sweet, sweet nothings
To put in your bouquet.
Oh, it's time that we were going
To where a dream is growing;
So come along with me
Down the lane of love
To the garden of the moon.

LOVE IS WHERE YOU FIND IT

Lyrics by Al Dubin and Mercer. Music by Harry Warren. Published. Copyrighted July 20, 1938. Introduced by John Payne and Johnny "Scat" Davis. Leading recordings by Jimmy Dorsey and His Orchestra, with vocal by Bob Eberly (Decca); and Kay Kyser, with vocal by Harry Babbitt (Brunswick). Not to be confused with the 1948 song of the same name by Nacio Herb Brown (music) and Earl K. Brent (lyrics).

VERSE

Clouds are in the sky above,
And fish are in the sea;
If it's birds you're looking for,
You'll find them in a tree.
Nature put her wonders
In their natural habitat,
But the wonder of them all
Just doesn't work like that.

REFRAIN

Oh! Love is where you find it,
No matter where you go.
You may be in Kalua
Or Kokomo;

You may be on the ocean
Or by a wishing well;
The street lights may be blinking
When you feel that sinking spell—
Cupid gets around, back and forth.

Now it's North Carolina,
Then it's China—
Doesn't seem to matter at all.
You can fall on a hayride
Or a sleigh ride,
So wear a suit of armor
When you go out to play—
'Cause love, love, love is where you find it,
And you'll find it out someday.

Additional lyrics for film

JOHNNY
"SCAT" DAVIS: You may be sewin' buttons
Or learnin' how to swing;
I might be playin' cornet
When I feel that hornet's sting
Maybe we will meet
As we come into some coliseum—
JOHN PAYNE: Or museum.
DAVIS: Maybe in the next candy shop
Where I stop
You'll be workin'—
PAYNE: Soda jerkin'!
So wear your suit of armor
When you go out to play
'Cause love, love, love is where you find it,
And you'll find it out someday.

LOVE IS WHERE YOU FIND IT

Although Mercer gave these lyrics the same title as above, this is a different song. No music is known to exist.

I never thought the night would bring
A thrill I never knew;
But love is where you find it,
And I found it here with you.
I never dreamt my heart would sing
Before the day was through;
But love is where you find it,
And I found it here with you.
A country lane, a city street—
It doesn't matter where;
You never know when you will meet

Your lover waiting there.
I never thought the dreams I dreamed
Could possibly come true;
But love is where you find it—
And I hope you've found it too.

THE LADY ON THE TWO-CENT STAMP

Lyrics by Al Dubin and Mercer. Music by Harry Warren. Published. Copyrighted July 20, 1938. Introduced by John Payne, Ray Mayer, Jerry Colonna, Joe Venuti, Johnny "Scat" Davis, and band.

REFRAIN 1

I'm in love with a lady in a stamp collection,
Yes sirree! She's the lady on the two-cent stamp.
Late one night, looking through the Caribbean
section,
There she was sittin' pretty on a two-cent stamp.
And like a dope,
I keep her inside an envelope
In order to hide her eyes
From guys.
And soon I hope
I'm able to snag a microscope
That really magnifies
Those eyes.
I'll take a boat that is traveling in her direction,
Just to look for the lady on the two-cent stamp.
Where the blue sea is rolling
I'll drop a sentimental hint,
And through life we'll go strolling—
That's if she isn't out of print.
Oh! Woe is me if it's nothing but a vain
affection—
I'm in love with the lady on the two-cent stamp.

REFRAIN 2

I've been told she's a Caribbean institution;
Ev'ryone loves the lady on the two-cent stamp.
People say she's the reason for the revolution;
They would die for the lady on the two-cent stamp.
From ev'ry town,
The mountains and plains, they hurry down
On buses and trains to see
Marie.
The native sons
All gather at night and grab their guns;
They're ready to fight for her,
Yes sir!

When politicians are coming up for reelection,
They all call on the lady on the two cent-stamp.
At a conf'rence or parley
You oughta see the way she vamps!
She's got more drag than Farley—*
Besides, she sells a lot more stamps.
Oh! Woe is me if she really has a green
    complexion—
I'm in love with the lady on the two-cent stamp.†

CONFIDENTIALLY

Lyrics by Al Dubin and Mercer. Music by Harry Warren.
Published. Copyrighted July 20, 1938. Introduced by
John Payne; reprised in the film's finale by Payne and
band.

VERSE

Have you heard the startling news?
It's an exposé.
I'll tell you,
But don't give me away—
Won't you kindly listen to
All I have to say?
It may not please you;
Then it may.

REFRAIN

Confidentially, I'm so in love,
I go floating through the skies,
Confidentially, the stars above
Have seen the secret in my eyes.
Though I know
That everybody's guessing,
I'm not confessing who.
But, darling,
You are bound to know eventually,
So confidentially,
It's you.

_____

* *Postmaster General James A. Farley.*
† *Film version of Refrain 2 ending:*
    It looks like everyone
    Seems to want to have her in their stamp collection—
    They would die for the lady on the two-cent stamp.
    I hope and pray that she hasn't got a green
        complexion—
    We're in love with the lady on the two-cent stamp!

Additional lyrics for Finale

JOHN PAYNE: Confidentially, I'm so in love,
             I go floating through the skies.
   BAND: Oh, Don,
          How you carry on!
  PAYNE: Confidentially, the stars above
          Have seen the secret in my eyes.
   BAND: Listen, Toni,
          That's no baloney.
  PAYNE: Though I know
          That everybody's guessing,
          I'm not confessing who.
   BAND: You can go ahead and shout it—
          Ev'rybody knows about it!
  PAYNE: You are bound to know eventually,
          So, confidentially, it's you.
   BAND: Wo-ho, confidentially,
          Confidentially, it's nobody else but
          you!

THE GIRL FRIEND OF THE WHIRLING DERVISH

Lyrics by Al Dubin and Mercer. Music by Harry Warren.
Published. Copyrighted July 20, 1938. Introduced by
John Payne, Jerry Colonna, Ray Mayer, Johnny "Scat"
Davis, Joe Venuti, and ensemble. Leading recordings by
Guy Lombardo and His Orchestra (Decca); Van Alexan-
der, with vocal by Butch Stone (Bluebird); and Skinnay
Ennis (Victor).

VERSE

One fine day I chanced to stray
On a little side street in old Bombay
And met a sentimental Oriental.
She saw me and I saw she
Had a manner too bold and much too free;
Her eyes were positively detrimental.
When I asked about this gay coquette,
I discovered much to my regret:

REFRAIN

She's the girl friend of the whirling dervish;
She's the sweetest one he's found.
But ev'ry night in the mellow moonlight,
When he's out dervishing with all his might,
She gives him the runaround.

All the boy friends of the whirling dervish
Are his best friends to his face,

But there's no doubt, when he isn't about,
They all come hurrying to take her out—
She leads him a dizzy pace.

He dreams of a Hindu honeymoon;
He doesn't dream that
Ev'ry night when he goes out
To make an honest rupee,
She steps out
To make a lotta whoopee.

Oh! The love song of the whirling dervish
Has a sweet and tender sound.
But will he burn if he ever should learn
That while he's doing her a real good turn,
She gives him the runaround!

She's got a nervish
Throwin' him a curvish,
Which, of course, he doesn't deservish,
Poor old whirling dervish!

Additional lyrics sung in film

People say she likes to stay
With the phonograph playing all the day;
She likes to hear those hot musicians jivin'.
So they come with the fife and drum,
The clarinets goin' rum, tum, tum—
You'd think that Benny Goodman was arrivin'!
All night long they try to win her hand,
Serenadin' her to beat the band.
Alabama tried to win her affection
On his brand-new flugelhorn—
Oh, yeah!
She says he's full of corn.
Then the swami took up the "Song of India"—
You could hear the others shout,
"Oh, yeah!"
She got up 'n' threw that oboe out!
The noise reached the maharaja,
And you could hear him holler,
"Listen, I played bass when
I was down in Cuba,
I bet I could win her on the tuba!"
So she listened to the maharaja
As he tried to, he tried to go to town;
Then she cried, "Everybody one side,
Wo-ho, let me play it on the trombone slide,
'Cause I'll really mow you down!"

KEEP AWAY FROM THE SWINGING DOORS

Music by Harry Warren. Registered for copyright as an unpublished song August 28, 1938. Not used in film.

The barkeep's a bully, a knave, and a lout,
So, dearie, you mustn't go hanging about—
Your father may be the next tramp they throw out.
Keep away from those swinging doors!

HARD TO GET (1938)

Produced by Hal B. Wallis for Warner Bros. Released November 1938. Copyright October 8, 1938. Directed by Ray Enright. Screenplay by Jerry Wald, Maurice Leo, and Richard Macaulay, from an original story by Wally Klein and Joseph Schrank, based on the short story "Stuffed Skirt" by Stephen Morehouse Avery. Music by Harry Warren. Lyrics by Johnny Mercer. Orchestrations by Ray Heindorf. Musical director: Leo F. Forbstein. With Dick Powell, Olivia de Havilland, Charles Winninger, Allen Jenkins, Bonita Granville, Melville Cooper, and Isabel Jeans.

Spoiled young heiress and her entanglements with a young man (Powell) who runs a motor court.

THERE'S A SUNNY SIDE TO EVERY SITUATION

Published. Copyrighted October 14, 1938. Introduced by Dick Powell. It was later used in the Broadway musical *42nd Street* (opened August 25, 1980), with its score of Harry Warren songs, where it was introduced by Karen Prunczik and ensemble.

Published version

REFRAIN

Long ago, one fine day,
Some philosopher was heard to say:
"There's a sunny side to ev'ry situation."
And the same applies to you;

His philosophy's still true—
There's a funny side to ev'ry complication.
When you're broke through and through,
Folks can't borrow anything from you—
That is what we call the law of compensation.
When it's raining cats and dogs,
Think how swell it is for frogs—
Ev'ry situation has a sunny side.

Sing tra-la, la-la-la-la-la-la,
The sun may never, never shine;
But tra-la, la-la-la-la-la-la,
Somewhere the weather's fine!

You've no dough, so relax,
You don't have to pay an income tax—
You've no job, so just pretend it's your vacation.
Though some eggs are dark outside,
They look diff'rent when they're fried—
Ev'ry situation has a sunny side.

REFRAIN 2

When it rains, when it pours,
Think how nice it is to stay indoors—
There's a sunny side to ev'ry situation.
When your rent is overdue,
Let the landlord fret for you—
There's a funny side to ev'ry situation.
When you lose all you own
And they take away your telephone
And you feel that you are out of circulation,
Say you're lucky after all:
Those insurance men can't call—
Ev'ry situation has a sunny side.

Sing tra-la, la-la-la-la-la-la,
The sun may never, never shine;
But tra-la, la-la-la-la-la-la,
Somewhere the weather's fine!

With no bonds and no stocks
In your little safe-deposit box
You can never be affected by inflation.
When your car is out of gas,
Then no red lights can you pass—
Ev'ry situation has a sunny side.

Film version

PARTIAL REFRAIN

When your work's hard to do,
Think how wonderful it is for you—
There's a sunny side to every situation.
Though your arms begin to ache
And your back's about to break

When you finish, it's the sweetest relaxation.
Sweep the floor, dust the wall,
You may never get a dime at all,
But at least you'll learn an honest occupation!
Do your job and thank your stars
That you're not behind the bars—
Ev'ry situation has a sunny side.
Sing tra-la, la-la-la-la-la-la,
The sun may never, never shine;
But tra-ha-ha-ha-ha-ha-ha, ha-ha-ha-ha,
Somewhere the weather's fine!
Oh . . .

Additional lyrics

Make the beds, beat the rugs,
And exterminate the little bugs—
Never waste your time in idle conversation,
If you work the way you should,
You can keep the job for good—
Every situation has a sunny side.

REFRAIN 3

There's a run in her hose
And a little smudge upon her nose
That she picked up in the nasty filling station.
Such a horrid little girl
Probably needs a change of erl,
And her chassis should be spanked in moderation.
Is she sad? Is she blue?
Well, we'll make you just as good as new
With our special wash and grease and lubrication.
When we've Simonized your face,
They'll accept you anyplace—
Every situation has a sunny side.

Back to work, back to toil.
But you're doing it for Federal Oil—
Don't forget that Gold Star on your graduation.
When you can't pay for your gas,
Then no red lights can you pass—
Every situation has a sunny side.

As you go your merry way,
Just remember what I say—
Every situation has a sunny side.

YOU MUST HAVE BEEN A BEAUTIFUL BABY

Published. Copyrighted October 10, 1938. Introduced by Dick Powell. Number-one recording by Bing Crosby with Bob Crosby's Orchestra (Decca); other leading recordings were made by Tommy Dorsey and His Orchestra (Victor) and in the 1960s by Bobby Darin (Atco) and the Dave Clark Five (Epic).

The song supposedly had its origins in a visit Johnny and Ginger paid to the Mercer family home in Savannah. Ginger used similar words on seeing a picture of the infant Mercer on a bearskin rug. No mother could fail to pick up such a cue: Lillian Mercer immediately went to fetch the blue ribbon young Johnny had won in a baby contest.

VERSE

Does your mother realize
The stork delivered quite a prize
The day he left you on the fam'ly tree?
Does your dad appreciate
That you are merely super-great,
The miracle of any century?
If they don't, just send them both to me.

REFRAIN

You must have been a beautiful baby,
You must have been a wonderful child.
When you were only startin'
To go to kindergarten,
I bet you drove the little boys wild.

And when it came to winning blue ribbons,
You must have shown the other kids how.
I can see the judges' eyes
As they handed you the prize—
I bet you made the cutest bow!
Oh you must have been a beautiful baby,
'Cause, baby, look at you now!

GOING PLACES (1938)

Produced by Hal B. Wallis for Warner Bros. Released January 1939. Copyright December 15, 1938. Directed by Ray Enright. Screenplay by Sig Herzig, Jerry Wald, and Maurice Leo, based on the play *The Hottentot* by Victor Mapes and William Collier Sr. Music by Harry Warren. Lyrics by Johnny Mercer. Orchestrations by Ray Heindorf and Frank Perkins. Musical director: Leo F. Forbstein. With Dick Powell, Anita Louise, Allen Jenkins, Ronald Reagan, Walter Catlett, Harold Huber, Louis Armstrong, and Maxine Sullivan.

A store clerk poses as a famous jockey for an advertising stunt but finds himself taken at his word and riding a dangerous horse (Jeepers Creepers) in a big race.

JEEPERS CREEPERS

Published. Copyrighted November 2, 1938. Introduced by Louis Armstrong. Al Donahue and His Orchestra's recording (Vocalion) reached number one on the popular-music charts. Louis Armstrong also recorded the song (Decca).

Mercer recalled:

I think I heard Henry Fonda say something like "Jeepers Creepers" in a movie . . . It just rang a little bell in my head and I wrote it down when I got out of the movie. ('Cause, you know, in America in those days it was a polite way of saying "Jesus Christ!") . . .

I thought it would be a cute idea for a song. I searched around quite a bit and then found that it fit so well as a title for that melody of Harry's. It was lucky casting that we got Louis Armstrong to sing it, although it wasn't written for him.

The song brought Mercer's first Academy Award nomination, but it lost to "Thanks for the Memory" by Leo Robin and Ralph Rainger, from *The Big Broadcast of 1938*.

VERSE 1

I don't care what the weatherman says—
When the weatherman says it's raining,
You'll never hear me complaining,
I'm certain the sun will shine.
I don't care how the weather vane points—
When the weather vane points to gloomy,
It's gotta be sunny to me
When your eyes look into mine.

REFRAIN

Jeepers Creepers!
Where'd ya get those peepers?
Jeepers Creepers!
Where'd ya get those eyes?
Gosh all git up!
How'd they get so lit up?
Gosh all git up!
How'd they get that size?
Golly gee!
When you turn those heaters on,
Woe is me!
Got to put my cheaters on.
Jeepers Creepers!
Where'd ya get those peepers?
Oh! Those weepers!
How they hypnotize!
Where'd ya get those eyes?

VERSE 2*

Sugarplum, I just haven't a chance
When you look round and show those eyes-es.
You sure hand out great surprises—
One melting look and I'm done.
Somehow they lead me, and do they lead
Down the road to complete disaster?
Each new day I'm fallin' faster—
You're the rock I perish on.

REPEAT REFRAIN

SAY IT WITH A KISS

Lyrics by Al Dubin and Mercer. Published. Copyrighted November 2, 1938. Introduced by Dick Powell and Walter Catlett. Recordings by Maxine Sullivan (Victor); Teddy Wilson (Brunswick); Gene Krupa, with vocal by Irene Daye (Brunswick); and Artie Shaw, with vocal by Helen Forrest (Bluebird).

VERSE

My eyes have looked at you and found you fair;
My heart's been asking me if you could care.
And now my heart and I are standing by—
We await your reply.

REFRAIN

Let me hear you say it,
Say it with a kiss.
If you mean that look I've seen,
Say it with a kiss.
There is wine and candle shine
And music in your lips,
Magic in the touch
Of your fingertips.
Words may not convey it;

In English edition only.

Say it with a kiss.
And your look might speak a book
That my eyes might miss.
You don't have to know the words
To love's familiar tune;
Say it with a kiss
And say it soon.

OH, WHAT A HORSE WAS CHARLIE

Lyrics by Al Dubin and Mercer. Introduced by Dick Powell, Walter Catlett, Harold Huber, and Allen Jenkins; reprised as "Oh, What a Horse Was Jeepers" by Jenkins and Huber.

DICK POWELL: Oh, what a horse was
Charlie—
POWELL &
WALTER CATLETT: Till he got a charley horse!
POWELL: Crowds used to cheer him;
They stood on their chairs.
CATLETT: No horses got near him
Excepting the mares.
HAROLD HUBER: He'd have a meal of barley
And then he'd burn up the
course.
ALLEN JENKINS: They're off at Saratoga.
HUBER: They're off at Tanforan.
CATLETT: They're off at Caliente—
But Charlie's on his [inaudible]
POWELL: Can you imagine?
It had to happen to Charlie.
JENKINS: God bless her and keep her,
A Mother Macree . . .
ALL: Oh, what a horse was Charlie
Till he got a charley horse!
HUBER: They made him a gelding
To increase his pace—
But he needed welding
To place in a race.
JENKINS: He never won a parley—
HUBER: [spoken] Wait a minute! It's
"par-lay"!
JENKINS: [spoken] It won't rhyme!
POWELL: [spoken] Fellas, wait a minute!
I think it'll work.
Please, just try it again now.
JENKINS: [sung] He never won a parlay;
He ran out on every course.
POWELL: Now, here's how Charlie's crew
works.
They get him out on the track.

JENKINS: [spoken] All right, funny man,
say something!
CATLETT: Me?
They simply mention glue works
And nothing could hold him
back.
ALL: Oh, what a horse was Charlie
Till he got a charley horse!
POWELL &
HUBER: The crowds cheered and sang
Tales of his form and speed.
CATLETT &
JENKINS: He led all the bangtails
When they went to feed.
Don't place the blame on
Charlie,
You must consider his source.
HUBER: His father gave up racing—
POWELL: To join a polo team.
JENKINS: His mother had a dairy—
CATLETT: Delivering milk and cream.
ALL: Oh, what a horse was Charlie
Till he got a charley horse!
HUBER: He still is the strongest.
POWELL: He still is the best.
JENKINS: He still is the bravest.
CATLETT: He chases the rest.
ALL: He is particularly
The horse the jockeys endorse.
POWELL: [spoken] They're at the post.
CATLETT: [spoken] There they go!
JENKINS: [as horse] I'm leading at the
quarter!
HUBER: [as horse] I'm leading at the half!
JENKINS: You're way out at the finish!
HUBER: Wait out the photograph!
ALL: Oh, what a horse was Charlie
Till he got a charley horse.

REPRISE

JENKINS: Oh, what a horse is Jeepers—
HUBER: To run in a steeple chase!
JENKINS: The grandstand will cheer him;
He'll jump high and wide.
HUBER: And Randall will ride him
Or go for a ride.
BOTH: Oh, what a horse was Jeepers
Till he got a charley horse!

MUTINY IN THE NURSERY

Music by Mercer. Published. Copyrighted November 28, 1938. Introduced by Louis Armstrong and His Orches-

tra, Maxine Sullivan, Dick Powell, Anita Louise (dubbed by Etta Jones), Vivian Dandridge, Dorothy Dandridge, and ensemble.

VERSE

There's mut'ny in the nurs'ry,
There's mut'ny in the nurs'ry,
'Cause Mother Goose is on the loose—
Her kids are swingin' out!
There's mut'ny in the nurs'ry
And music in the nurs'ry,
'Cause Mother Goose is on the loose—
You ought to hear 'em shout—
If you could see Miss Jennie Jones,
You'd find her swingin' lightly.
And lazy Mary won't get up,
Won't get up,
No, lazy Mary won't get up—
She stays out too late nightly.

There's mut'ny in the nurs'ry,
There's mut'ny in the nurs'ry,
'Cause Mother Goose is on the loose—
Her kids are swingin' out!
Little Bo Peep has lost her sheep,
But she knows just where to find them,
For they all stand around the band,
Waggin' their tails behind them.
One little, two little, three little jitterbugs,
Four little, five little, six little jitterbugs,
Seven little, eight little, nine little jitterbugs,
Ten little jitterbug boys.
Ten little, nine little, eight little jitterbugs,
Seven little, six little, five little jitterbugs,
Four little, three little, two little jitterbugs,
One little jitterbug girl.

There's mut'ny in the nurs'ry,
There's mut'ny in the nurs'ry,
'Cause Mother Goose is on the loose—
Her kids are swingin' out!
Little Jack Horner came to their corner,
Playing his clarinet.
He stuck in his thumb and played it so dumb,
He ruined their hot duet.
There was mut'ny in the nurs'ry
When they all got loose,
They began to yell for old Mother Goose.
Goosey Goosey Gander,
Take a tip from me—
Better truck on home before you miss the
jamboree!

There's mut'ny in the nurs'ry,
There's mut'ny in the nurs'ry,
'Cause Mother Goose is on the loose—
Her kids are swingin' out!

Additional lyrics sung in film

DICK
POWELL: Hey diddle diddle,
The cat has a fiddle;
The cow is beginning to croon.
The little dog laughs
And laughs and laughs
Because they're never in tune.

ANITA
LOUISE: Mary had a little lamb,
Little lamb, little lamb,
Mary had a little lamb;
He said, "I'll see you later."

POWELL: He went off to hear them jam,
Hear them jam, hear them jam.
Mary had a little lamb—
Now he's an alligator.

ALL: Oats, peas, beans, and barley grow;
Oats, peas, beans, and barley grow.
Can you or I or anyone know
How oats, peas, beans, and barley
grow?

LOUIS
ARMSTRONG: Now grab yourself a partner,
Grab yourself a partner;
Open the ring and choose one in
While we all dearly laugh and sing.
Oats, peas, beans, and barley grow;
How they do it I don't know.
But if you will give me my horn
I promise I won't blow no corn.

[*He plays.*]

ALL: Mut'ny, mut'ny, a bad mutiny
Right in the nursery, yeah,
nursery—
Can it be that mutiny
Right in the nursery?
BOYS: A, B, C, D, E, F, G, H, I, J, K, L, M,
N, O, P—
3 GIRLS: Q, R, S, and T, U, V,
W, and X, Y, Z!
BOY: Well, they can swing in any key—
ALL: A, B, C, D, E, F, G!
LOUISE: Little Miss Muffet
Sat on a tuffet
Playing her big bass viol.
Along came a spider
And sat down beside her
So he could jam a while.
POWELL: Little Jack Horner
Came to their corner
Playing his clarinet.
He stuck in his thumb
And played it so dumb
He ruined their hot duet.

BOYS: One little, two little, three little
jitterbugs,
Four little, five little, six little
jitterbugs,
Seven little, eight little, nine little
jitterbugs—
GIRL: Ten little jitterbug boys!
BOYS: Ten little, nine little, eight little
jitterbugs,
Seven little, six little, five little
jitterbugs,
Four little, three little, two little
jitterbugs—
BOY: One little jitterbug girl!
MAXINE
SULLIVAN: I better close the window,
I better close the window,
I better close the window
And go and join the boys.
ARMSTRONG: You'd better lock the window,
You'd better latch the window,
You'd better nail the window
To keep out those floy-floys.
SULLIVAN: Rock-a-bye baby,
In the treetops,
When the wind blows,
The cradle will rock.
When the bough breaks,
The cradle will fall
And down will come baby,
Cradle and all.

[ARMSTRONG & SULLIVAN *scat to* "*Rock-a-bye Baby.*"]

GIRLS: Three little kittens
Have lost their mittens
And just from clapping hands.
And the grown-up cats
Have lost their spats
From dancing to those bands.
ARMSTRONG: If you don't think these cats can
swing,
I'll let them show you how.
BOYS &
GIRLS: Meow, meow, meow, meow,
Meow, meow, meow, meow, meow.
POWELL: They sang a song of sixpence,
A pocketful of rye,
Four and twenty blackbirds
Baked in a pie.
When the pie was brought in,
Opened by the king,
All the blackbirds flew around
And started in to swing.
ALL: There was a mut'ny in the nurs'ry
When they all got loose—
They began to yell for
Old Mother Goose.

Goosey Goosey Gander,
Take a tip from me—
Better truck on home
Before you miss the jamboree!
Yeah, yeah, yeah, yeah!
Mut'ny, mut'ny,
Mut'ny in the nurs'ry!

COULD BE

Music by Walter Donaldson. Published. Copyrighted December 5, 1938. Leading recordings by Johnny Messner and His Orchestra (Bluebird); Bob Haymes (King); Glen Gray and the Casa Loma Orchestra, with vocal by Pee Wee Hunt (Decca); Barry Wood (Brunswick); and Sammy Kaye and His Orchestra (Victor).

VERSE

Am I seein' things
Ever since I looked at you?
Do the flowers blossom
On the wall?
Does a cat have wings?
Mustn't say it isn't true;
Anything can happen,
'Cause after all—

REFRAIN

Could be that yellow moon
Is just a big balloon
And not that yellow moon above.
Could be that angel face
Is something out of space
And not that angel face I love.
Could be this heart of mine
Is just a valentine
And not this heart of mine at all.
Could be a dream I see,
But if you're asking me—
Could be I'm in love.

CUCKOO IN THE CLOCK

Music by Walter Donaldson. Published. Copyrighted January 18, 1939. Previously registered for copyright as an unpublished song December 21, 1938. Principal recordings by Kay Kyser and His Orchestra (Brunswick); Benny Goodman and His Orchestra, vocal by Johnny Mercer (Victor); and Glenn Miller and His Orchestra, vocal by Marion Hutton (Bluebird).

VERSE

Tick tock
In the parlor
Was the only sound;
Tick tock
On the mantel,
Nothing else around.
Boy and girl were close as they could be—
Never dreamt that they had company.

REFRAIN

There they were, there they were,
He was baby-talkin' her,
And the cuckoo in the clock went "Cuckoo."
Ev'ry fifteen minutes he crew,
"Cuckoo, cuckoo, cuckoo."
"Be a pal, be a pal,"
Said the fella to the gal,
And the cuckoo in the clock went "Cuckoo—
I believe they're startin' in to woo,
Woo-woo! Woo-woo! Woo-woo!"
They didn't know that ev'rything
They said was overheard;
They didn't hear that little birdie
Givin' them the bird.
So he said with a sigh,
"Who's your little peachy pie?"
And the cuckoo in the clock went "Cuckoo—
Though I'm just a little cuckoo,
I'm not as cuckoo as you!"
Then he closed the door and withdrew—
"Cuckoo, cuckoo, cuckoo."

WINGS OF THE NAVY,
NAUGHTY BUT NICE,
and Other Songs of 1939

In January 1939 Mercer was invited to join the cast of CBS's New York–based radio show *Camel Caravan*, which featured Benny Goodman and His Orchestra. (Goodman "believed in me long before others did," Mercer later noted.) So successful was the combination that very soon he was not only singing but replacing the emcee and writing special comedy material. When the show came from Pittsburgh, for example, Mercer parodied the song "You Ought to Be in Pictures" as "You Ought to Be in Pittsburgh," with lyrics such as

> George Washington surveyed it
> And made a mental note,
> He WPA'd it.

The film had the tag line: "For all the world to witness that America will not be unprepared."

WINGS OF THE NAVY (1939)

Produced by Hal B. Wallis for Warner Bros. Released February 1939. Copyrighted February 8, 1939. Directed by Lloyd Bacon. Screenplay by Michael Fessier. Musical direction: Leo F. Forbstein. With George Brent, Olivia de Havilland, John Payne, Frank McHugh, John Litel, Victor Jory, Henry O'Neill, John Ridgely, John Gallaudet, Donald Briggs, Edgar Edwards, Regis Toomey, Albert Morin, Jonathan Hale, Pierre Watkin, Don Douglas, Max Hoffman, Alan Davis, and Larry Williams.
Jerry and Cass are competitive flyers.
The film had the tag line: "For all the world to witness that America will not be unprepared."

WINGS OVER THE NAVY

Music by Harry Warren. Published. Copyrighted November 3, 1938. Unused except instrumentally.

Naughty but Nice: *Dick Powell, Ann Sheridan, and Helen Broderick*

VERSE

A sailor is a guy they call a gob;
A gob's a guy who has a deck to swab.
But listen, all you country boys,
If ever you come to town,
And Uncle Sammy offers you a job,
Pick out the aviation when you put your moniker
 down!

REFRAIN 1

Wings over the navy, wings over the sea,
We're top o' the service, the navy's cavalry,
High over the oceans, flying wide and free.
The soldiers, sailors, and marines
Are demons at eating pork and beans
Or posing in the magazines;
But we're the navy's eyes,
The adm'ral's fireflies,
We're high-sky-ridin' aeronautical guys,
Wings over the navy, sailing the seven skies.

REFRAIN 2

Wings over the navy, wings over the sea,
We're top o' the service, the navy's cavalry,
High over the oceans, flying wide and free,
The soldiers, sailors, and marines
Are demons at eating pork and beans
Or posing in the magazines,
But if there's gonna be
A fightin' jamboree,
The thing to do is let the enemy see
Wings on the horizon, wings of the old navee!

LEW LESLIE'S BLACKBIRDS OF 1939

Tryout: Majestic Theatre, Boston, November 8–19, 1938. It then shut down for nearly two months for rewrites and rehearsals. New York run: Hudson Theatre, opened February 11–18, 1939; 8 performances. Conceived and staged by Lew Leslie. Produced by Lew Leslie. Music by Rube Bloom. Additional music by George Gershwin, Sammy Fain, Louis Haber, Vic Mizzy. Lyrics by Johnny Mercer. Additional lyrics by Mitchell Parish, Dorothy Sachs, Irving Taylor. Sketches by Nat Dorfman, Fred H. Finklehoffe, John Monks Jr. Dances by Eugene Van Grona. Settings by Mabel A. Buell. Costumes by Frances Feist. Orchestrations by Ferde Grofe and Ken Macomber. Vocal arrangements by J. Rosamund Johnson.

Cast featured Lena Horne, Hamtree Harrington, Dewey "Pigmeat" Markham, Rosalie King, Tim Moore, Bobby Evans, Joe Byrd, Ralph Brown, Laurene Hines, Kate Hall, Norman and Blake (Norman McConny and Atta Blake), Taps Miller, Eugene Van Grona's Swing Ballet featuring Beryl Clarke and Al Bledger, J. Rosamund Johnson's Choir, the Blackbirds Beauties, a dancing chorus, Whitey's Lindy Hoppers, and the specialty act—Dr. Sausage and His Five Pork Chops. There were ninety performers in the cast. The show featured three numbers by Bloom and Mercer, two of which, "Jo-Jo, the Cannibal Kid" and "Dixie Isn't Dixie Anymore," were premiered in London in *The Blackbirds of 1936*. The third song introduced in *Blackbirds of 1939* was "I Did It for the Red, White and Blue." This was the sixth and last version of *Lew Leslie's Blackbirds*.

I DID IT FOR THE RED, WHITE, AND BLUE

Music by Rube Bloom. Registered for copyright as an unpublished song October 22, 1938. Introduced in *Blackbirds of 1939* by Tim Moore and Rosalie King.

VERSE

America was once the champ of champions,
But England has begun to get her goat.
Their golfers are a menace,
They've taken back the tennis,
And now they're built the largest boat afloat.
We didn't mind them taking all the laurels,
But when the Dionne babies came along
Then ev'ry U.S. father got in a frightful bother
And straightaway began to right the wrong.

REFRAIN

Me and Dinah talked the situation over
And we thought it was the decent thing to do.
People said I'd be a traitor
To refuse to be a pater,
So I did it for the red, white, and blue.

I'll admit I had my eyes upon the record,
But I never even dreamt that I'd come through,
Or that she'd be so prolific,
Or that I'd be so terrific,
But I did it for the red, white, and blue.
Of course, you can see that I'm proud,
But one thing has taken me aback;
There isn't a boy in the crowd
And brother is my face black!
You may wonder how on earth I ever did it

And to be quite truthful, somehow I do too.
Well, the really honest fact is
It took quite a lot of practice,
But I did it for the red, white, and blue.

(GOTTA GET SOME) SHUT-EYE

Music by Walter Donaldson. Published. Copyrighted January 18, 1939. Previously registered for copyright as an unpublished song called "Shut Eye" December 21, 1938. Leading recordings by Kay Kyser, with vocal by Ginny Simms (Brunswick); Glen Gray and the Casa Loma Orchestra, with vocal by Pee Wee Hunt (Decca); and Glenn Miller and His Orchestra, with vocal by Marion Hutton (Bluebird).

VERSE

You folks want to go out to the movies;
I've seen the movies all over town.
You folks want to go out to a party;
Have a nice party—
I'll run along
And be a smarty.

REFRAIN

Gotta get some shut-eye,
Give the world the go-bye;
Got an awful lot of dreamin' to do.
Gotta catch some shut-eye,
Where the kisses flow by,
Got an awful lot
Of dreams to come true.
Gonna let that sandman
Sprinkle me with stars;
Only hope that old lamp lighter
Lets me hold my baby tighter.
So I'm goin' bye-bye,
Catch myself some shut-eye;
Got an awful lot of dreamin' to do.

NAUGHTY BUT NICE (1939)

Produced by Hal B. Wallis for Warner Bros. Released June 1939. Copyright July 1, 1939. Directed by Ray Enright. Screenplay by Richard Macaulay and Jerry Wald. Music by Harry Warren. Lyrics by Johnny Mercer. Orchestrations by Ray Heindorf. Musical director: Leo F. Forbstein. With Ann Sheridan, Dick Powell, Gale Page, Helen Broderick, Ronald Reagan, Allen Jenkins, ZaSu Pitts, and Maxie Rosenbloom.

A classical-music professor writes a popular song—without meaning to.

MILLIONS OF DREAMS AGO

Music by Harry Warren, based on "I Dreamt I Dwelt in Marble Halls" from *The Bohemian Girl* by Michael William Balfe. Written September 29, 1938. Introduced by Gale Page.

I knew that you'd come along some sweet day,
Millions of dreams ago.
I knew exactly the words you would say
Millions of dreams ago.

REMEMBER DAD (ON MOTHER'S DAY)

Music by Franz Schubert, from his "Unfinished" Symphony (no. 8). Registered for copyright as an unpublished song August 27, 1956. Introduced by Jerry Colonna and Allen Jenkins.

Lonely,
Somebody's lonely—
Remember Dad on Mother's Day.
Say!
Mother would have no other,
So cheer him up and make him gay.
Candy would be dandy
Some kind thought to convey,
So, pet him and don't forget him—
Remember Dad on Mother's Day.

HOORAY FOR SPINACH

Published. Copyrighted February 1, 1939. Introduced by Ann Sheridan. In 1928 *The New Yorker* published a cartoon (drawn by Carl Rose and captioned by E. B. White) that resonated with every family with strong-willed children. A small child looks up from her plate and mutters, "I say it's spinach, and I say the hell with it." Mercer saw it as an opportunity for a neat topical twist—and for all we know, he agreed with the *New Yorker* kid. Recorded by Skinnay Ennis and His Orchestra (Victor).

VERSE

As a kid, I hated
Spinach and all its ilk;
I abominated
Cod liver oil and milk—
That was simply that,
And I'd leave them flat,
Though you stuck a gat
At my brow.
But I must admit
My opinion's different now.

REFRAIN

Hooray for spinach!
Hooray for milk!
They put the roses in your cheek soft as silk.
They helped complete you
Till I could meet you, baby!

Hooray for sunshine!
Hooray for air!
They put the permanent in your curly hair.
They helped to raise you
Till I could praise you, baby!

Bless the summer that freckled your nose,
Those galoshes that sheltered your toes.
Bless the fellow who taught you to kiss,
If he taught you to kiss like this!

Hooray for spinach!
It took you far!
Bless all the nourishment in each candy bar!
They helped you grow up
Till I could show up
And love you as you are.

I'M HAPPY ABOUT THE WHOLE THING

Published. Copyrighted February 1, 1939. Introduced by Dick Powell and Gale Page. Recorded by Maxine Sullivan (Victor) and Sammy Kaye and His Orchestra (Victor).

VERSE

DICK POWELL: I'm rather English as regards
emotion;
I'm so afraid to say the things I
mean.
I have a quaint and silly notion
You'd be embarrassed by a scene.
So though I feel a very deep
devotion,
I'll simply tell you, old bean—

REFRAIN

I'm happy about the whole thing.
You have the right looks,
You're sweet to my friends,
You keep the right books
Between your bookends—
I'm happy about the whole thing.
Whenever we dance,
You're seen and not heard;
You offer your glance,
But never a word—
What's more,
You let me sing!
Your disposition
Is like old Sol;
You're sunny as a politician.
Whereas, to wit,
I really must admit
I'm happy about the whole thing.
GALE PAGE: When your attitude
Is one of despair,
I get in the mood
And not in your hair.
BOTH: You're always right in the swing—
I'm happy about the whole thing.

IN A MOMENT OF WEAKNESS

Published. Copyrighted February 1, 1939. Introduced by Gale Page and Ann Sheridan. Recorded by Dick Powell (Decca).

VERSE

Pity the stars and the moon,
Shining for ages above,
Casting a spell
And doing it well,
Setting the scene for love.
Pity the stars and the moon—
They can get nowhere with you.
I pity them,
For I'm the same way, too.

REFRAIN

In a moment of weakness
Could you let those lips be kissed?
Could you let that feeling get you
That you simply can't resist?
In a moment of moonlight
Could you let your heart go free?
If you should let go
In a weak, weak moment,
Fall in love with me!

I'M UP A TREE

Music by Harry Warren, based on Robert Schumann's "The Merry Farmer" from *Album für die Jugend*. Introduced by Allen Jenkins.

I'm up a tree,
And here's what puzzles me—
Won't someone tell me
What came first,
The chicken or the egg?

CORN PICKIN'

Published. Copyrighted February 1, 1939. Introduced by Ann Sheridan. Danced by the National Jitterbug Champions and Dick Powell.

VERSE

To gain entrée into any New York club,
Ya don't have to have a million or two;
In all honky-tonks right up to the Stork Club,
The one thing they want is somebody who can
do—

REFRAIN

Corn pickin',
I'm crazy 'bout pickin',
There ain't any trick in pickin',
Corn pickin',
Just shuffle a few feet,
By makin' your two feet slew feet,
You reach out and you get your gal and you hold her,
You bend down and grab an ear from the stalk,
You raise up and throw it over your shoulder,
And then you sashay round her
And start in to walk,
I'm talkin' 'bout
Corn pickin',
It's better than chicken—
So, hurry and pick that corn!

I DON'T BELIEVE IN SIGNS

Introduced by Ann Sheridan.

I don't believe in signs,
But when the moon is always new,
Whenever I am out with you
And stars are multiplied by two,
I know this is love.
I don't believe in signs,
But when the birds go tweet, tweet, tweet,
And my poor heart goes beat, beat, beat,
And I feel wings upon my feet,
I know this is love.
I'm not suspicious of any magic art
And I'm not superstitious,
But still I'll cross my heart;
For there's a million signs
That started on the day we met;
My little world is all upset—

I don't believe in signs, and yet,
I know this is love.

HAVE A DREAM ON ME

Music by Harry Warren, adapted from Mozart's *The Magic Flute*. Registered for copyright as an unpublished song September 17, 1938. Not used in film.

Why that wistful smile?
Do you want a castle on the Nile?
Would you like the stars that gleam?
Then have a dream on me—
It's free.
And, darling, take a glance,
We are really in the south of France.
Things are only what they seem,
So have a dream on me.

That coach and four,
Those footmen at the door—
It's really true,
They all belong to you.
That house with many spires,
You'll have ev'rything your heart desires—
All you have to do
Is have a dream on me.

LALITA

Music by Harry Warren, based on Franz Liszt's "Second Hungarian Rhapsody." Intended for Jerry Colonna. Not used in film.

Lalita, I'd love to linger longer,
Languidly with you,
Lalita, beneath a banyan branch
Where balmy breezes blew.
Lalita, the only señorita
Neater and sweeter than Rio Rita,
Lalita, your Yank is yearning for
Those yesteryears with you.
Chiquita, don't dare defer the day you say
You do, do, do.
In Spanish, I long to tell you so,
My sweet Lalita, *yo te amo.*

YOU GROW SWEETER AS THE YEARS GO BY

Music by Mercer. Published. Copyrighted February 21, 1939.

VERSE

When I look at you
Standing there beside me,
I am filled with pride,
I am happy, too,
When the winter lies upon the meadow;
I don't mind if summertime is through
When I look at you.

REFRAIN

You grow sweeter as the years go by;
You grow sweeter as the twilights fly,
I need never dream of our first kiss
When I know our last one is as sweet as this.
Though September takes the place of June,
In September there's the harvest moon.
Let the leaves start falling, darling—
What care I,
When you grow sweeter as the years go by?

HOLY SMOKE (CAN'T YA TAKE A JOKE?)

Music by Royal Marsh. Published. Copyrighted November 17, 1939. Previously registered for copyright as an unpublished song February 25, 1939. According to copyright records, this song was registered as an unpublished song seven times with seven different composers. The music for the published version was written by Royal Marsh, who submitted the winning entry in a contest for amateur songwriters sponsored by the Song Hit Guild.

VERSE

Looks like I'm in the doghouse,
Looks like I pulled a bloomer—
And this thing of being behind the eight ball
Is more than a rumor.
Well, baby, all I can say is,
Where's your sense of humor?

REFRAIN

What if I showed up kinda late,
Comin' from another date?
Holy smoke!
Can't ya take a joke?

That was no lipstick on my tie—
That was only cherry pie!
Holy smoke!
Can't ya take a joke?

Bet if you wrote to Beatrice Fairfax,
Asked her what to do,
Bet if you only gave her the bare facts,
She'd say I love you.

Honey, I didn't tell those lies,
Must have been two other guys!
Holy smoke!
Can't ya take a joke?

YOU AND YOUR LOVE

Music by Johnny Green. Published. Copyrighted March 11, 1939. Recorded by Count Basie, with vocal by Helen Humes (Vocalion); Bob Crosby, with vocal by Teddy Grace (Decca); Gene Krupa, with vocal by Irene Daye (Brunswick); and Ozzie Nelson, with vocal by Harriet Hilliard (Bluebird).

You and your love
Are the only things that I am conscious of,
And the only things I can see
Or breathe or feel
Are you and your appeal.
You caught my eye
Like a shooting star that tumbles through the sky,
And the little streets and buildings
That made up the view
Are gone, just leaving you.
Where is the fun I used to get
From seeing a show or winning a bet?
My simple life is all upset;
It has no kick for me,
Because, you see, there's you and your kiss,
And the world can hold no greater thrill than this.
So I gladly give up ev'rything I ever knew,
Because now I have you.

AND THE ANGELS SING

Music by Ziggy Elman. Published. Copyrighted April 11, 1939. Previously registered for copyright as an unpublished song March 23, 1939.

Working with Benny Goodman, as he did throughout the late 1930s, gave Mercer the opportunity to get to know Goodman's trumpet player, Ziggy Elman, and to put words to a Hebrew melody Elman had adapted as "Fralich in Swing" and recorded with his orchestra (Bluebird). Benny Goodman's recording of "Angels" (Victor), featuring Elman on trumpet, with vocal by Martha Tilton, was the number-one recording in America for five weeks during the spring of 1939. Other leading recordings were made by Glenn Miller (Bluebird); Jan Savitt, with vocal by Bon Bon (Decca); Count Basie, with vocal by Helen Humes (Vocalion); and Alec Templeton (Victor).

Mercer had suggested to Goodman that if the melody were to be slowed down, it could be "kind of a Gershwin tune." The decision was clearly justified. When the song was released, Bing Crosby wrote to say that he thought it was Mercer's best song to date. "You're getting practically poetic."

We meet,
And the angels sing;
The angels sing
The sweetest song
I ever heard.
You speak,
And the angels sing—
Or am I reading music
Into ev'ry word?

Suddenly
The setting is strange:
I can see water and moonlight beaming,
Silver waves
That break on some undiscovered shore;
Then suddenly
I see it all change—
Long winter nights with the candles gleaming.
Through it all your face that I adore.

You smile,
And the angels sing;
And though
It's just a gentle murmur
At the start,
We kiss,
And the angels sing
And leave their music ringing
In my heart.

SHOW YOUR LINEN, MISS RICHARDSON

Music by Bernie Hanighen. Published. Copyrighted May 5, 1939. Previously registered for copyright as an unpublished song March 24, 1939.

REFRAIN

Show your linen, Miss Richardson,
Show your linen to ev'ryone.
Dance in a gay, ladylike way,
And we can have a barrel of fun.
Show the lace on your petticoat,
Kick your heels at the proper note.
Show ev'rybody that you're really hep,
Give 'em that revolving step!
This is your innin',
Show your linen,
Dear Miss Richardson!

INTERLUDE

See all the elder ladies
With their noses kinda turned up,
Burned up.
See all the elder gentry—
Ev'ry one of them is plumb struck
Dumbstruck.
Ev'rybody's beau
Formin' in a row
Strut along the aisle
Kitchen-style.
Look at all the elder ladies in the eye
And let your hair down,
Bear down.
Show your linen and show your lace;
Put a smile on your bashful face.
Pay no attention to the chaperone;
Listen to the slide trombone,
'Cause they close up the hall at one—
Yes, ma'am,
Show your linen, Sister Richardson!

DAY IN—DAY OUT

Music by Rube Bloom. Published. Copyrighted August 9, 1939. The recording by Bob Crosby and His Orchestra, with vocal by Helen Ward (Decca), reached number one on the charts. Other important recordings were made by Tommy Dorsey (Victor), Artie Shaw (Bluebird), Al Donahue (Vocalion), and Tony Martin (Decca).

Day in—day out,
The same old hoodoo follows me about,
The same old pounding in my heart
Whenever I think of you,
And, darling, I think of you
Day in and day out.
Day out—day in,
I needn't tell you how my days begin,
When I awake I awaken with a tingle,
One possibility in view,
That possibility of maybe seeing you.

Come rain—come shine,
I meet you and to me the day is fine.
Then I kiss your lips
And the pounding becomes
The ocean's roar,
A thousand drums.
Can't you see it's love?
Can there be any doubt,
When there it is
Day in   day out.

BLUE RAIN

Music by Jimmy Van Heusen. Published. Copyrighted October 13, 1939. Leading recordings by Mildred Bailey (Vocalion) and Glenn Miller, with vocal by Ray Eberle (Bluebird).

VERSE

Clouds cover up my horizon with blankets dark as
    night;
Skies haven't cleared since you disappeared from
    sight.
Ev'rything I lay my eyes on
Reminds me that you're away;
Here in my room
It's always a gloomy, gray day.

REFRAIN

Blue rain
Falling down on my windowpane,
But when you return
There'll be a rainbow
After the blue, blue rain.
And there's a blue star
Looking down, asking where you are,

But when you return
There'll be a sunbeam
Hiding the blue, blue star.
Skies will be much brighter than they were
    before
When you and love come strolling through the
    door.
Then there'll be no more blue rain,
Just the sound of my heart's refrain,
Singing like a million little bluebirds
After the blue, blue rain.

I THOUGHT ABOUT YOU

Music by Jimmy Van Heusen. Published. Copyrighted October 13, 1939. Introduced and recorded by Benny Goodman, with vocal by Mildred Bailey (Columbia). Other recordings were made by Hal Kemp (Victor); Will Bradley, with vocal by Carlotta Dale (Vocalion); Bob Crosby, with vocal by Teddy Grace (Decca); and, a decade later, Nellie Lutcher (Capitol).

Nineteen thirty-eight had been a year of considerable change for Mercer. The death of Richard Whiting led him to form a working partnership with Harry Warren, among others; and among the most successful others was Jimmy Van Heusen, with whom he turned out a number of hits, this one being the first. He liked working with Van Heusen: "He seems to have a series of chords waiting at his command to which he can fashion a melody the moment his lyricist springs any ideas on him." This particular song was also the first of Mercer's signature "train" songs; the idea, he said, came to him on the journey from California to New York.

VERSE

Seems that I read
Or somebody said
That out of sight is out of mind.
Maybe that's so,
But I tried to go
And leave you behind—
What did I find?

REFRAIN

I took a trip on the train
And I thought about you;
I passed a shadowy lane
And I thought about you.
Two or three cars
Parked under the stars,
A winding stream,
Moon shining down
On some little town,
And with each beam
Same old dream:
At ev'ry stop that we made,
Oh, I thought about you!
But when I pulled down the shade,
Then I really felt blue;
I peeked through the crack
And looked at the track,
The one going back to you,
And what did I do?
I thought about you.

MAKE WITH THE KISSES

Music by Jimmy Van Heusen. Published. Copyrighted October 13, 1939. Leading recordings by Benny Goodman, with vocal by Mildred Bailey (Columbia); Will Bradley, with vocal by Carlotta Dale (Vocalion); Les Brown and His Orchestra (Bluebird); and Bea Wain (Victor).

VERSE

Those skies on that horizon,
Ain't any flies on them;
They came right from a Technicolor show.
It's grand here,
Yet you stand here
Wastin' the whole p.m.
When any dummy knows that we should get
    chummy.

REFRAIN

Make with the kisses,
Make with the sighs,
Make with the baby talk,
Give with the eyes!
Here am I making with the "I'll be true,"
And ev'ryone's making love to someone—
What goes with you?

Make with the kisses,
Make with the thrills,
Make with the snuggle-up
That brings the chills!
The sky is making with the moon above;
It couldn't be brighter—
Hold me tighter,
Make with the love!

SMARTY PANTS

Music by Walter Donaldson. Published. Copyrighted October 27, 1939.

VERSE

At the races your horses come in one-two;
At a party you mix a fine drink;
In the moonlight you really know what to do.
Do I mind it? I don't think.

REFRAIN

You old smarty pants,
Where'd you learn to dance?
Where'd you learn to throw that line?
How'd you learn to say the things you say
And say them in that city-slicker way?
You old smoothie pie,
Who taught you to sigh
With that honey in your glance?
When you do the things you do,
How can I help lovin' you,
You old smarty pants?

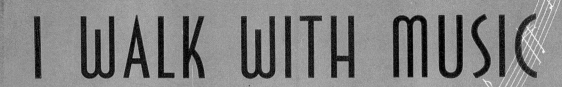

THREE AFTER THREE/ WALK WITH MUSIC | 1939–1940

THREE AFTER THREE / WALK WITH MUSIC (1939–1940)

Original title: *Three After Three.* Tryout: Shubert Theatre, New Haven, November 24–25, 1939; Shubert Theatre, Boston, November 27–December 9, 1939; Ford's Opera House, Baltimore, December 11–16, 1939; Forrest Theatre, Philadelphia, December 25, 1939–January 6, 1940; National Theatre, Washington, D.C., January 8–13, 1940; Nixon Theatre, Pittsburgh, January 15–20, 1940; Royal Theatre, Toronto, January 22–27, 1940; Erlanger Theatre, Chicago, January 29–February 24, 1940; American Theatre, St. Louis, February 25–March 2, 1940; English's Opera House, Indianapolis, March 4–6, 1940; Taft Auditorium, Cincinnati, March 7–9, 1940; Cass Theatre, Detroit, March 10–16, 1940. Title changed to *Walk with Music.* New York run: Ethel Barrymore Theatre, opened June 4, 1940; 55 performances. Produced by Ruth Selwyn (in association with the Messrs. Shubert). Lyrics by Johnny Mercer. Music by Hoagy Carmichael. Book by Guy Bolton, Parke Levy, and Alan Lipscott. Based on the comedy *Three Blind Mice* by Stephen Powys. Production under the supervision of Rowland Leigh. Book staged by R. H. Burnside. Dance collaboration by Anton Dolin and Herbert Harper. Orchestra under the direction of Joseph Littau. Vocal arrangements by Hugh Martin.

Critical opinion of *Three After Three* in its ever-changing embryonic form was summed up by *Variety's* critic, "Bone":

> Whether this new Selwyn-Shubert musical becomes a job for the undertaker or just the doctor is entirely up to its producers . . . Score is not outstanding but fills the bill adequately . . . Tendency of the lyrics is toward a mere rhyming of lines rather than inspired wordage.

By the time the show arrived at the Ethel Barrymore Theatre on June 4, 1940, many things had changed. Simone Simon had left the cast and had been replaced by Kitty Carlisle. Mitzi Green had returned. The Martins had left to join the cast of *Louisiana Purchase* and had been replaced by another singing group, the Modernaires.

Heading the cast during the New York run were Kitty Carlisle (Pamela), Mitzi Green (Rhoda), Betty Lawford (Carrie), Art Jarrett (Steve), Donald Burr (Wing), Frances Williams (Polly), Marty May (Conrad), Ted Gary (Bellboy), the dancers Alice Dudley and Kenneth Bostock, and the Modernaires (Ralph Brewster, Bill Conway, Harold Dickinson, and Chuck Goldstein).

The lyrics to some songs from this show have not been found. "Put Music in the Barn," music by Mercer and lyrics by Mercer and Hugh Martin, and "Happy New Year to You," music by Carmichael.

GREETINGS, GATES

Introduced by the ensemble.

BOYS &
GIRLS: Greetings, gates
And sophisticates,
And all you tardy inebriates.
Stop rustling your bustles and your stays about
And we will try to tell you what the play's about.
It's been fun.
Since it first was done
By Mr. Hans Christian Andersen—
In fact before the days of Mr. Andersen—
Frank Crumit played it once with Julia Sanderson.
GIRLS: The action starts on a farm
With not one Cinderella but three.
They feel they're wasting their charm in the sticks,
For the males there are all R.F.D.
BOYS: They're sick of hearing their hired men say
That they've got prizewinning eggs.
GIRLS: Eggs!
BOYS: They long to hear an inspired man say
That he never saw nicer legs.
BOYS &
GIRLS: Now you know how the plot will go,
So don't say we didn't tell you so.
If you don't like the idea or the rest of it,
T' hell with ya, you'll have to make the best of it.
Just relax; make your nasty cracks
Out in the lobby between the acts.
Don't say it has a reminiscent smell f' ya.
The critics told us that in Philadelphia.
Before we show the play to you,
We really ought to say to you
BOYS: In manner most conventional,
ALL: That any similarity to any low vulgarity
BOYS: Is really quite intentional.
ALL: Now we'll step back into character and say,
Ladies and Gents—
The play.

Added verse

BOYS &
GIRLS: There's no harm
If a girl has charm,
But who can use charm upon a farm?
So as their interest in eggs and butter dies,
Our caterpillars turn to social butterflies.
Now you know we intend to show
Three Cinderellas who seek a beau,
So watch the little sisters,
Hand-in-hand with guilt,
Attempt to land an Astor or a Vanderbilt.

Opening of Act 2 of *Three After Three*

BOYS &
GIRLS: Greetings, gates and sophisticates,
And all you tardy inebriates.
You've had your intermission drink of brandy now.
You ought to think that everything is dandy now.
What a spot. Things are not so hot.
Our little Vivi upset the plot.
Just goes to show you what prevarication does.
Now you can see what this administration does.
GIRLS: Miss Gibson has a notorious name
After that episode in the bed.
But Palm Beach now has a glorious name—
It is filled up for seasons ahead.
BOYS: Just try and guess what the play will do now,
As acted by our little troupe.
If you can tell us what they will do now,
You will not win a Plymouth Coupe.
BOYS &
GIRLS: Here we go with our monster show,
With snappy patter and jokes you know.
If some things in the first act made you drowsier,
We promise you the second act is lousier.
Hip, hooray. Everything's okay.
We're only glad this is not L.A.
Out there they know by heart what Cinderella says,
And we would have to read the things Louella says.
Before we show the act to you,
We're pointing out a fact to you—
BOYS: In case you like things lyrical—
BOYS &
GIRLS: That any similarity to Porter is a rarity
BOYS: And in this show, a miracle.

BOYS &
GIRLS: Now we'll get the hell out of your view.
Ladies and Gents, Act Two!

TODAY I AM A GLAMOUR GIRL

Introduced by Kitty Carlisle (Pamela), Betty Lawford (Carrie), Mitzi Green (Rhoda), Glamour Girls, and ensemble. During the pre-Broadway tryout (as *Three After Three*) it was sung by Simone Simon (Vivi), Mary Brian (Carrie), and Mitzi Green (Rhoda).

TRIO: There are things we never could afford
The clothing we wear are strictly from
Montgom'ry Ward.
PAMELA: We wouldn't dare to buy a Lincoln or a
Cord.
CARRIE: We've been the perfect picture of poor
propriety.
RHODA: Well—we got our hands upon some
dough,
And we hear tell that dough was only
made to blow,
So what the hell! Off to the city we will
go.
Today we're moving in on society.
GIRLS: They go to Jackels for their sables and
minks;
They've learned to get along on thirty-
nine winks;
Just ask them anything—they'll answer,
"It stinks!";
For today they are the glamour girls.
They don't eat anything—for eating's
passé;
They'll take a brandy or a small
Dubonnet;
They have their salads made by Lily
Daché;
For today they are the glamour girls.
TRIO: Speaking of possessions;
We never say how many farms—or
ranches—we own,
But when it comes to indiscretions . . .
CARRIE: You ought to see the souvenirs of
Franchot's
We own.
PAMELA: I spend my weekdays giving things to the
poor.
CARRIE: I spend my Sundays in the rotogravure.
RHODA: And once a month I go away for the cure.

ALL: We're the darlings of the social whirl,
For today I am a glamour girl.
RHODA: I read the latest books—I'm really well
versed.
PAMELA: I see the newest plays before they're
rehearsed.
CARRIE: I study singing with Cobina the First.
ALL: For today I am a glamour girl.
PAMELA: My physiognomy is ghostly and white,
CARRIE: As though somebody dug her up for the
night
RHODA: But has to put her back before it gets
light.
CARRIE: One of my parlor tricks is swinging a
hymn.
RHODA: If something's funny I just murmur,
"How grim."
TRIO: For today I am a glamour girl.
ALL: We shop at Abercrombie's.
We only go to clubs that keep inferiors
out.
We just adore to order Zombies.
RHODA: We like to dance around with our
posteriors out.
VIVI: I love Cole Porter's "Got You Under My
Skin."
CARRIE: My favorite tune is his "Beguine the
Begin."
RHODA: If Peter Arno calls me up—I ain't in.
TRIO: I'm the darling of the social whirl,
For today I am a glamour girl.
Once we were farm girls
Living in an aura of propriety.
Now we are charm girls
And we're moving in on society.
VIVI: Am I from Dixie?
TRIO: Today I am a glamour girl.
CARRIE: Without my shoes on.
TRIO: Today I am a glamour girl.
RHODA: I need a punch line—
TRIO: Today I am a glamour girl,
Today I am a glamour girllllllll.
Page David Selznick!

EVEN IF I SAY IT MYSELF

Introduced by Donald Burr (Wing), The Modernaires (Ralph Brewster, Bill Conway, Harold Dickinson, and Chuck Goldstein), and ensemble. Burr replaced Jack Whiting during the pre-Broadway performances.

QUARTETTE: Chook—a chook—a chooka's blowin'.
Chook—a chook—a choo-choo-train.

Charleston, Tampa,
WING: I'm going north again,
QUARTETTE: Get aboard 'er if you're goin'.
Better get aboard this train.
Hold your hats, kids,
WING: Here I go again.
WING &
QUARTETTE: Even if I say it myself,
I'm the hap-hap-happiest one.
I'm like the swallow—
I like to follow the sun.
Even if I say it myself,
I'm a chip-chip-chipper chap.
Don't need a diamond pin on,
'Cause I've got my Sunday grin on.
Got a special kind of shelf,
Where I stick my troubles away.
Even though love hasn't got me,
I'm not the least upset,
'Cause even if I say it myself,
It's gonna get me yet.

I WALK WITH MUSIC

Published. Copyrighted February 16, 1940. Introduced by Kitty Carlisle (Pamela), Donald Burr (Wing), and Glamour Girls.

VERSE

If you see the heavens full of nightingales,
And they are all singing as they fly;
Then you'll know, my dear,
What I always hear
Ev'ry time that you pass by.

REFRAIN

There's a love song floating on the soft summer
air;
When you spoke, you left it there.
From this day I walk with music,
For your voice will follow me everywhere.*
Your sweet sigh
Will come singing through the sky.
I will hear and understand—and
Though I wander past the last distant star,
It will never seem too far;†
For from this day on I walk with music
And the song will lead me to where you are.

* So I know I'll always follow you everywhere.
† Though the miles between us are from here to a star,
   I will never think them far;

OOH, WHAT YOU SAID

Published. Copyrighted December 12, 1939. Introduced by Mitzi Green (Rhoda), Marty May (Conrad), Ted Gary (Bellboy), and The Modernaires. In the pre-Broadway version *(Three After Three)* it was sung by Mitzi Green (Rhoda), Ted Gary (Master of Ceremonies), and the Martins (Hugh Martin, Ralph Blane, Jean Rogers, and Phyllis Rogers). Leading recordings by Glenn Miller and His Orchestra, with vocal by Marion Hutton (Bluebird); Hal Kemp, with vocal by the Smoothies (Victor); and Bob Crosby, with vocal by Marion Mann (Decca).

REFRAIN

RHODA: [*to* STEVE] Ooh, what you said
Got me all flustered—
Face is red.
Ooh, what you said
When you said what you said.

Ooh, what you did
Got me all bashful like a kid.
Ooh, what you did
When you did what you did.

Fun is fun,
But look at what you've done.
Ain't you the naughty one!
Talking that way—
Say, are you jokin' or just outspoken?

Ooh, what you said!
Oughta go cover up my head.
When you whispered,
"I love you—oo."
Ooh, ooh, what you said!

VERSE

Where did ya get such a big moustache?
You durned old villain scarin' young
    chillun.
How in the world can ya be so rash,
Turnin' on all that Hollywood pash?
CONRAD: [*to* RHODA] Ooh, what you said!
Lady, you sure can use your head.
Ooh, what you said when you said what
    you said.
Ooh, what you did when you did what
    you did.
If you should
Go out to Hollywood,
I know that you'd be good
Talkin' that way.

And with your glamour,
T' hell with drammer.
Ooh, what you said!
If you can make my face red,
Then there's nothing you can't do—so,
Ooh, what you said.

Jeep, jeep, I'm a jeep from Jersey.
Jeep, jeep, I'm a jeep from Jersey.
'Lizbeth, Englewood, Weehawken,
Hackensack, Paterson, Hoboken.

Ooh, how they sing, all of these people
    who like swing.
Ooh, how they sing, when they sing what
    they sing.
Landsakes alive, where do they think up
    all of this jive?
In every dive, sakes alive, how they jive.
They go

[*Scat vocalese.*]

Keep right on till the jive is callin'

[*Scat vocalese.*]

Ooh, how they sing

[*Scat vocalese.*]

Though we don't know what they do,
Ooh, how they sing.

Are you jazzy or razz-matazzy?
Are you dippy or rip-tip-tippy?
Are you corny or are you corny?
Are you onyx or philharmonics?

Ooh, what you said! Ought to go cover
    up my head.
When you whisper I love you-oo,
Then it means we're almost through-oo.
So, if you don't like what we do-oo,
Say, can anything be new-oo?
We can say the same for you-oo.
Incidentally, that's our cue-oo.
Ooh, what you said.

EVERYTHING HAPPENS TO ME

Registered for copyright as an unpublished song, January 18, 1940. Introduced by Frances Williams (Polly).

VERSE

POLLY: Scorpio's child is full of grace.
Gemini's child is fair of face.
And if you're born under Capricorn,
    you'll shine.
Scallions to mother and to dad;
Maybe their luck was just as bad,
For one dark morn their child was born
Under the Indian sign.

REFRAIN

Everything happens to me,
Happens to me so darn regularly.
Long about spring,
I meet a new prince,
I have everything
Done over in chintz.

Alternate lyrics

Everything happens to me,
Happens to me but continually.
My room looks gay
In crimson and white,
My sheer *negligee*
Won't last out the night.

My maid is dismissed after tea,
And under the mat there's a skeleton key.
I'll have it known
This night is my own.
Lower the lights.
Turn off the phone.
Then he sneaks in but doesn't sneak in alone.
Everything happens to me.

Other alternate lyrics

VERSE

And then I arrange a large tea,
But just when it's going so beautifully,
Surer than sin,
Some floozy walks in.
Quick as a flash
He's in a spin.
And so I take another sock in the chin—
Everything happens to me.

REFRAIN

Everything happens to me,
Happens to me so darned regularly.
I met a gent not so long ago
Who loved Rockwell Kent
And owned a Van Gogh.
His etchings he said were divine
And would I come up any evening to dine.
I dressed like mad—I didn't look bad—
Went to his rooms; but what a cad.
He had the etchings, but that's all that he had—
Everything happens to me.

ENCORE

Everything happens to me,
Happens to me but continually.
I met a guy—an Argentine beau.
Well, why should I lie—a real gigolo.
He cost me a dollar a dance,
And five if I wanted a bit of romance.
Kisses—one—oh, ten dollars.
And, boy, did I go.
But, darn it all, wouldn't you know,
When it got interesting
I ran out of dough—
Everything happens to me.

Extra choruses

POLLY: Everything happens to me,
   Happens to me, but particularly.
   I met a man
   With snow in his hair—
   It's a catch as catch can,
   But now I don't care.
   He seemed the most eager of grooms,
   So after the wedding we went to our rooms.
   Shyly he sighed,
   "I'll just step outside,
   Then I'll come back,
   Back to my bride."
   But somewhere between his room
   And my room—he died.
   Everything happens to me.

   Everything happens to me.
   Leaving the wedding with spouse number
      three,
   Up comes a storm,
   I'm wet as a rag,
   We stop at a farm—
   Yes, it's the old gag.
   The rain on the roof is divine,
   And he has the bedroom connecting with
      mine.
   Over the transom

I sneak a glimpse,
And there he stands
My big romance
Clad in pajamas—not the tops but the pants.
Everything happens to me.

Reprise

Introduced by Stepin Fetchit (Chesterfield).

CHESTERFIELD: Everything happens to me.
   If it ain't one thing it's two or it's
      three.
   People been travellin' land and
      feet since Adam raised Cain,
   And they wait 'till I'm born to
      start travellin' by plane.
   They said 'taint no danger when
      you take a flight,
   And they won't call your number
      if you've been livin' right,
   But suppose that pilot drivin'
   Has been livin' wrong all last
      night—
   I ain't goin' up with dat man.

   They say you travel faster by air,
   But who found out I'm in such a
      hurry to git somewhere?
   They say if that plane decides to
      slip,
   You can dive out in a parachute
      before it tip,
   But supposin' that rip cord don't
      rip—

[*Clarinet effect.*]

   I ain't goin' up with dat man.

   The other day I went out to see
      my best girl.
   When I got there I seen
   A big pair of shoes lyin' sideways
   Underneath the bed,
   So I pulled out my razor.
   She say, "Honey, what you gonna
      do with dat razor?"
   I say, "Well if dere ain't no one in
      dem shoes
   I'm just gonna shave."

   The other day I was standin' on
      the corner
   And saw a big policeman
   Take out his billy and tap a little
      boy
   Alongside the head.
   I said, "Ain't you ashamed

Hittin' a little boy with dat old
   folk stick?
Why don't you hit someone your
   size—hit a man?"
And as I went to turn around,
If it hadn't o' been for the back o'
   my head
He'd a knocked all my eyes out.

WAIT TILL YOU SEE ME IN THE MORNING

Registered for copyright as an unpublished song, December 27, 1939. Introduced by Kitty Carlisle (Pamela) and Art Jarrett (Steve). In *Three After Three* it was sung by Simone Simon (Vivi) and Earl Oxford (Wing).

The song was clearly tried briefly and dropped from *Three After Three*, since there is a "Special Chorus" for Vivi and Steve that would have ended it.

PAMELA: Women have a way to lure
   The unsuspecting male;
   Strong perfume around the room
   Will hardly ever fail.
   Can that be the reason
   That you seem to care for me,
   Or are you attracted
   By my state of dishabille.

   Wait 'till you see me
   In the morning
   About ten—around then;
   Wait until you see me in the morning,
   Then say it again.
   There in the cold, gray light of dawning,
   When the last hour has fled,
   Wait 'till your glamour girl is yawning
   With my cold cream on,
   My lipstick gone,
   My hair up in curlers on my head.
   Though this is quite my nicest evening
   Since I can't tell you when,
   Wait until you see me in the morning—
   Then say it again.

SPECIAL CHORUS

STEVE: Now that I've seen you in the morning,
   This is more than a yen.
   Now that I have seen you in the morning,
   I'll say it again.
VIVI: Though it is past the witching hour,
   I'm still certain you'll do.

Fresh from your early morning shower—
Now that I have seen you in the morning,
I'll say it again.

Though it is past the witching hour,
I'm still certain you'll do.
Fresh from your early morning shower—
You've a rosy cheek
A fine physique.
And not only that—you're pretty, too.

STEVE: Now that I've seen you in the morning,
I'll say it and say it again.

When the only glimmer
Is the glimmer of a star
Whether I'm out dancing
Or in Ma'moiselle's boudoir—
I can understand
How things take on a rosy hue.
I can even understand
How I look good to you—but—

Wait 'till you see me in the morning.
Don't decide until then.
Wait until you see me in the morning,
Then say it again.
If you should see me with my pants off,
Take a look at my shins;
I'll bet you call
The whole romance off,
For you're sure to find
The night is kind,
It covers a multitude of chins.
I'm not so positive this evening
If it's me—or just men.
Wait till you see me in the morning,
Then say it again.

Adapted version*

VERSE 1

If you think that you look bad when you arise
    from bed,
Just to cheer yoruself up some day look at me
    instead.
Soldier, when you wake up any morning around
    five,
Take a squint at me and wonder if I am alive.

REFRAIN 1

Wait 'till you see me in the morning,
Any reveille time.
Wait until you see me in the morning,

---

* "For non-profit performance only, in military and
naval establishments by United States Armed
Forces" in World War II.

My face is a crime!
There, in the cold, gray light of dawning,
When the last star has fled,
Just watch this glamour boy keep yawning;
Op'ning as I rise
Those blood-shot eyes,
My hair standing straight up on my head.
Whether it's clear or it's storming,
And the sky's gray or blue,
I look just the same on any morning,
I look worse than you!

VERSE 2

When the only glimmer is the glimmer of a star,
Whether I'm out dancing or in somebody's
    boudoir,
Ev'ry woman will conform and fall in love with me,
Maybe it's my uniform and well-groomed
    dignity.

REFRAIN 2

But, if they could see me in the morning,
Any reveille time.
Oh, if they could see me in the morning,
I'm hardly sublime!
If they should see me with my pants off
And would look at my shins,
I'll bet they'd call the romance off.
They'd be sure to find the night is kind—
It covers a multitude of sins!
They're very positive each evening
That I'm tops of all men,
But, if they could see me in the morning,
They'd murder me then!

BREAK IT UP, CINDERELLA

Registered for copyright as an unpublished song, January 18, 1940. Introduced by Mitzi Green (Rhoda), Frances Williams (Polly), Marty May (Conrad), Ted Gary (Bellboy), the Modernaires (Ralph Brewster, Bill Conway, Harold Dickinson, Chuck Goldstein), the Glamour Girls, and ensemble. During the tryout it was sung by Jack Whiting (Wing), Mitzi Green (Rhoda), Frances Williams (Polly), and Marty May (Conrad).
    It was later revised when the war broke out as "Break It Up Now, Buck Private" and used in the military show *At Ease* (1942).

WING: What is a gent supposed to say when a
    pretty maid looks so glum?
    He says, "Cheer up—old chum."

RHODA: What is a girl supposed to say when a
    gentleman heaves a sigh?
    She says, "Chin up—white tie."
WING: Laugh, clown, laugh—
RHODA: Pip pip, old bean, and so on.
WING: When they call your act, you put a show
    on—go on.
    Break it up, Cinderella,
    Every night now is open shop.
    Break it up, Cinderella,
    Your prince is a flop.
    Break it up, Cinderella.
RHODA: This is my evening on the loose,
    Seems that I lost my fella
    And I'm a dead goose.
    Only a dope would sit and mope
    When everyone's drinkin' hearty.
WING: Plenty of gents think you're immense,
    So why should you leave the party?
    Break it up, Cinderella.
RHODA: Innocent dancing ain't no crime.
WING: Break it up, Cinderella 'n'
    Have a good time.
    Make a champagne dipper
    Outta your slipper,
    Pass it around the hall.
    Break it up, Cinderella,
    You're Queen of the Ball!
CONRAD: Oh, Happy, Happy New Year.
    Hope it's not a blue year.
    Oh, Happy, Happy New Year.
RHODA: Maybe I'm not so gay as I could be,
    Maybe I'm not as gay as I should be,
    Maybe, oh maybe, I'm not.
POLLY: We'll go round and see the town
    And try to scare some fun up
    And won't start home
    'Till break of dawn,
    In time to see the sun up.

Alternate lyrics

POLLY: Gentlemen, take this angel cake
    And waltz her around till sunup;
    Take her to meet the town's elite,
    While I go and scare some fun up.

    Break it up, Cinderella,
    Every night now is open shop.
    Break it up, Cinderella,
    Your prince is a flop.

"Break It Up Now, Buck Private" (1942)

VERSE

What is a pal supposed to say when a buck private
    looks so glum?

He says, "Cheer up, old chum!"
What is a pal supposed to say when a buck private
    heaves a sigh?
He says, "Chin up, head high!"
Drag him out of camp into the city;
Get a girl for him, then sing this pretty ditty:

REFRAIN

Break it up now, buck private,
Get in the spirit, don't feel blue—
I'm sure that if you try it, you'll feel good as new.
Break it up now, buck private,
Make this your evening on the loose—
I'll bet ya' you'll survive it;
Don't be a dead goose.
Only a dope would sit and mope while everyone's
    drinking hearty.
Plenty of guys think you're a prize, so why don't
    you join the party?
Break it up now, buck private,
Leaving your barracks ain't no crime.
Break it up now, buck private, and have a good time.
Just forget your rifle,
And grab this eyeful,
Give her a kiss or two.
Break it up now, buck private,
You'll feel good as new!

SMILE FOR THE PRESS

Introduced by Kitty Carlisle (Pamela), Donald Burr (Wing), Art Jarrett (Steve), the Modernaires (Ralph Brewster, Bill Conway, Harold Dickinson, Chuck Goldstein), and the Glamour Girls.

QUARTETTE: Smile for the readers of the
        Telegram.
    Smile for the readers of the *Post*.
    Frown for the readers of the *Tribune*
        and the *Times*—
    They never publish pictures,
    And very few crimes.
PAMELA: Suppose that we look very, very
        solemn.
QUARTETTE: We might get your picture in Walter
        Lippman's column.
STEVE: Smile for the readers of the daily
        press—
    They're your public and you simply
        can't refuse.
QUARTETTE: And now bare your calf,
    For this photograph

Is going in the *Daily News*.
PAMELA: My, what an age!
    We have lost the printed page
    And the world's as full of cameras
    As a dog has fleas.
STEVE: I can recall,
    No one used the things at all
    But the *National Geographic* and a
        few Japanese.
GIRLS: *Life, Look, Click,*
    They're causing a big sensation.
    It's a hell of a situation.
PAMELA: Whatever became of the *Nation*?
QUARTETTE: *Time, Tide, Pic,*
    They come when you're looking
        crummy
    Or you're beating your sweet old
        mummie
    Or print a chart in color of your
        tummie—
    Yummy!
    Won't you look pretty, Miss Gibson,
    Look pretty for the press?
PAMELA: I hate this old dress,
    And my face is a mess.
GIRLS: Quite true—but she needn't confess.
QUARTETTE: Then won't you say something, Miss
        Gibson,
    Say something for the press?
PAMELA: I'm marrying for love and not for
        money.
GIRLS: Very funny.
PAMELA: I'm sure that we'll be awfully, awfully
        happy.
GIRLS: Very snappy.
PAMELA: And I haven't another thought in my
        head.
GIRLS: And she hasn't another man in her
        bed.
STEVE: I'd like to say
    We'll be married right away,
    And you all must come and see us
        take our marital vow.
WING: I shall be there
    To escort the happy pair
    And to kiss the bride with no
        detective telling me how.
QUARTETTE: Thanks from the readers of the
        Telegram.
    Thanks from the readers of the *Post*.
WING: Just let me know if Stevie doesn't
        treat you right.
GIRLS: She ought to write a column
    And call it "My Night."
WING: I'll come around to see how you are
        faring.
STEVE: Yes, do come to see us and we can tear
        a herring.

QUARTETTE: Thanks from the readers of the daily
        press.
    Though we hate to have to bid you
        toodle-oo,
    We'll come back in force
    To cover the divorce
    And thank you for the interview.

A FRIEND OF THE FAMILY

Introduced by Art Jarrett (Steve), Donald Burr (Wing), and Kitty Carlisle (Pamela).

STEVE: You can be a friend of the family.
    And when I'm working late,
WING: I can have a date.
PAMELA: We can go to Radio City.
    Won't that be great?
WING: I can hardly wait.
STEVE: You can be a friend of the family.
    When Pam is all alone,
WING: I can telephone.
PAMELA: I'll be sure to bring my Aunt Kitty
    As chaperone.
WING: I will bring a bone.
    We can take in all the same old bars.
STEVE: I'd rather you took in the old aquarium.
WING: Maybe take a walk beneath the stars.
PAMELA: Why, Wing, I'd just adore to see the
        Planetarium.
STEVE: So while I learn to be the big breadwinner,
WING: I can be the Man Who Came to Dinner.
PAMELA: Though you can't be part of the family,
STEVE: You still can be
WING: The family's friend.

WAY BACK IN 1939 A.D.

Published. Copyrighted December 12, 1939. Introduced by Mitzi Green (Rhoda), Marty May (Conrad), Alice Dudley, and Kenneth Bostock and ensemble. Sung in *Three After Three* by Art Jarrett (Steve) and Mitzi Green (Rhoda).

STEVE: What a panorama for a couple to survey:
    Perispheres and Jitterbugs and F.H.A.
    All of which is leading up to what I want
        to say—
    I will love you in December as in May.

Thou art the girlfriend,
I fell for thee
Way back in 1939 A.D.
Thy lips made hist'ry
Sweet unto me
Way back in 1939 A.D.

Nights were in flower, you may be sure.
Not knights in armour—nights of sweet
    amor.
Canst thou remember long, long ago
I'd serenade you with my radio?
There was no balcony too high for me,
If I could watch a *Mickey Mouse* with thee
Back in 1939 A.D.

RHODA: Thou art a wolf, sir,
I saw through thee
Way back in 1939 A.D.
My lips detected when thou kissed me
Traces of bourbon in the family.
Thy mistress shed thee for non-support,
Told your nights errant in King's County
    Court.
There was no jousting bout too rough for
    me
Way back in 1939 A.D.

HOW NICE FOR ME

Published. Copyrighted December 12, 1939. Introduced by Kitty Carlisle (Pamela). Also sung in *Three After Three*, but the program does not indicate who introduced it.

Original version

PAMELA: You left the moonlight—
How nice for me.
You left the starlight—
How nice for me.
You left a heart that won't beat—
How perfectly sweet,
How perfectly lovely.

You left me moments we might have
    known,
You left me sweet dreams to dream alone.
You left a memory, too.
How thoughtful of you—
How nice for me.
You didn't even take the touch of your
    lips,
So much of your lips is right here.
You even left me with most of your love,

The ghost of your love
Spends every night here.
You made a package of everything,
The rains in autumn, the stars in spring.
You left it here without a single string,
Then you left me fancy free—
How nice for me.

Could there be someone in quest of you?
If not, then give me the rest of you.
No, you want me to have the best of you
In holding your memory—
How nice for me.

When you came by you brought the
    moonlight—
How nice for me.
Now my world is rolling in moonlight
    constantly—
How nice for me.
Now there's starlight glowing on
    everything I see.

Blow, breezes, blow.
Blow, rain and snow.
I walk through daisy fields wherever I go,
For you've shown me
Just how enchanting love can be.
I see sweetheart roses on every tree.
How perfectly swell of you—
How nice for me.

Version from libretto

PAMELA: You left the moonlight—
How nice for me!
You left the starlight—
How nice for me!
You left the world at my feet.
How perfectly sweet—
How perfectly lovely.

You left me moments to spend alone.
The dreams we started, I end alone.
So here am I, fancy free,
How lucky for you,
How ducky for me!
You even left the old desire in my heart.
The fire in my heart burns brightly.
Though you've departed with most of
    your love,
The ghost of your love will haunt me
    nightly.

And so your step down the hall is mine,
That first "hello" when you'd call is mine,
You gave back ev'rything—it all is mine,

Including a memory.
How nice for me!

WHAT'LL THEY THINK OF NEXT (NOW THAT THEY'VE THOUGHT OF YOU)?

Published. Copyrighted January 19, 1940. Introduced by Mitzi Green (Rhoda) and Art Jarrett (Steve). Sung and danced in *Three After Three* by Simone Simon (Vivi), Mitzi Green (Rhoda), Earl Oxford (Wing), the Martins (Hugh Martin, Ralph Blane, Jean Rogers, and Phyllis Rogers), and ensemble.

WING: If you see a speechless yokel standing
    saucer-eyed,
It is I, completely mystified.
Almost any other bloke'll tell you much
    the same,
For I'm not the only one
Who's become unvocal.
Thomas Alva Edison would hang his
    head in shame.

CHORUS &
RHODA: What'll they think of next,
Now that they've thought of you?
Now that they've thought of your sweet
    face,
What is there left to do?
What'll they think of next?
What are things coming to?
Now that they've thought of your
    embrace,
Miracles must be through.
Maybe your eyes aren't really new eyes,
But they're better—they're true eyes.
Maybe your arms aren't streamlined,
But they're better—
They're dreamlined.
Who wouldn't be perplexed
Seeing what they can do?
Telephones, talkies, television, too.
Now they're even making dreams come
    true.
What'll they think of next,
Now that they've thought of you?

THE RHUMBA JUMPS

Published. Copyrighted December 12, 1939. Previously registered for copyright as an unpublished song November 15, 1939. Introduced by Frances Williams (Polly), the Modernaires, the Glamour Girls, and ensemble. Sung in *Three After Three* by Frances Williams (Polly) and the Martins.

POLLY: There's a Harlem band 'way down in San
    Domingo,
A very talented group.
They kicked 'em off of a sloop.
Even though the band can't understand
    the lingo,
They're never down in the dumps,
For when the drummer boy thumps,
THE RHUMBA JUMPS!

"Hep, hep!"* they hollered the moment
    they landed,
"We've got a rhumba the king once
    commanded."
Then they passed the tin and started in to
    play
The way they learned to play
Back in the U.S.A.

Now they're on the air and San Domingo's
    lappin' it up,
And I do declare those Harlem boys are
    wrappin' it up;
Folks in every land tune in on San
    Domingo.
They're never down in the dumps,
For when the drummer boy thumps,
THE RHUMBA JUMPS!

"Hep, hep!"† they holler. "Stay right in
    your villa,
We're on the air for a brand of vanilla."
If you wanna dance and wanna dance in
    style,
You better turn the dial
To San Domingo Isle,
And when you hear "Aye-aye,
Hi-de-aye,"
You'll know the reason why
THE RHUMBA JUMPS!

---

* *Or:* "Dig us!"
† *Or:* "Cool it!"

DARN CLEVER THESE CHINEE

Registered for copyright as an unpublished song December 27, 1939. Introduced in *Three After Three* by Simone Simon (Vivi), Mitzi Green (Rhoda), Mary Brian (Carrie), and the Martins. Dropped from the show before the New York opening of *Walk with Music*. Later in the run this would be re-named "Darn Clever These Chinese," presumably for reasons of early political correctness.

VERSE

Fortune tellers are often fakes,
Cards and dice make mistakes,
So we're keeping Confucius right beside us, to
    guide us,
As we go traveling about.
Any time we're in doubt
If we read his philosophy, he'll help us out.

REFRAIN 1

VIVI: Darn clever are these Chinee.
    They makee fine philosophy.
    They say a lady must look her best,
      'cause*
    Plain girl like museum—
    Velly nice but who come see um?
CARRIE: Chinee philosopher also state
    To catch fine fish,
    Get fine bait.
RHODA: These catchee lotta fine fish, they tell
    me.
    Do you dig me, Gate?
VIVI: Pheasant must look pleasant
    To catch other pheasant.
    Girls wear clothes, Lord bless um—
CARRIE: To catchee man who then undress
    um.
RHODA: Darn clever fella are these Chinee.
    They make fine philosophy.
ALL: And if it's naughty,
    Don't blame us three, 'cause
    We read it—
    They said it.
    Darn clever, these Chinee!

REFRAIN 2

RHODA: Darn clever fella are these Chinee.
    They make fine philosophy.

---

* *Alternate line:*
  They get together and they agree that

They get together and they agree
That nice girl catch rich marriage,
Naughty girl catch baby carriage.

Chinee philosopher oft exclaim,
If man make bed
Girls sleep in same.
That's what is known in the best of
    circles
As the Army Game.

VIV, CARRIE
& RHODA: They say man like rooster:
    He his own best booster,
    But for all his braying
    His makes hen do all the laying.
    Darn clever fella are these Chinee.
    They make fine philosophy.
    And if it's naughty,
    Don't blame us three
    'Cause we quote it—
    They wrote it.
    Darn clever, these Chinee.

Alternative lyrics

When it comes to intelligence
Chinee have plenty sense.
Plenty bright when it comes to writing
    fable,
Most able!
If you take "Hon'able" advice,
Slant your eyes,
Look real nice,
You'll wind up at a wedding,
Ankle deep in rice.

CARRIE: Darn clever fella are these Chinee.
    They make fine philosophy.
    They got together and they agree:
    Girl look for rich daddy,
    But they cook for Harvard laddie.

They got together and they agree
That when love catchee dumb lawyer,
Lawyer have to see Max Steuer.
Chinee philosopher always say,
Possession make nine-tenths of law.
Shall I call a deputy with a shotgun,
Or shall I call paw?
Must I stare at your puss
Till my head gets noddy?
Whisper "*habeas corpus*":
At least it means "give up the body."
Darn clever fella are these Chinee.

Darn clever these Chinee.
They make fine philosophy.
They got a lotta their stuff from me,

Like nice girl catch
Rich marriage,
Naughty girl catch baby carriage.
Chinee philosopher once inferred
A bird in bush
Worth two in herd.
Some fella tried to show me his garden,
Boy, he was a bird.

When man start appealing
And girl feel that feeling,
Don't relax one smidgeon
Give him an inch and you dead pigeon.
Darn clever these Chinee.

If you're in doubt, rely on me.
Pay no attention to this fine trio.
They kid it,
I did it.
Darn clever these Chinee.

NEWSY BLUESIES

Introduced in *Three After Three* by Frances Williams (Polly) and Marty May (Conrad). Dropped from show before the New York opening of *Walk with Music*.

CONRAD: Well, I've learned through bitter
experience
That being a chump doesn't pay.
I won't be naïve,
I won't even believe
What I read in the papers each day.
I see by the *New Haven Courier*
We've come to a new way of living.
The twenty-third, they say,
Was Thanksgiving Day.
Well, I'd rather call it "Franksgiving."
POLLY: At least FDR has done one thing
That Hoover and comp'ny could not.
Now Franklin can brag
He topped Hoover's gag
With two *turkeys* in every pot.
CONRAD: Republicans can't seem to mind it;
In fact, it has made them feel quite
perky,
For most of them feel
The famous New Deal
Has merely brought forth one more
"turkey."
POLLY: We taxpayers feel that as usual
Politicians have had the last word.
They still hold the ace,

Except in this case
They couldn't wait to give us the bird.
CONRAD: Reporters have interviewed gobblers
To try to find out how they judge it.
And one turkey cracks,
"We're getting the axe
That should have been used on the
budget."

I'M OFF THE WAGON (BOOM, I'M OFF THE WAGON)

Registered for copyright as an unpublished song January 18, 1940. Introduced in *Three After Three* by Art Jarret (Steve), Jack Whiting (Wing), and ensemble. Dropped from show before the New York opening of *Walk with Music*. Alternate title: "We're Off the Wagon."

STEVE: You've been such a playboy
And you've always said
You would never let a pretty face go to
your head.
WING: Boom! I'm off the wagon. No wagon for
me.
Boom! I'm off the wagon. The wagon's
fini.
Boom! I've got a whiff of it. One sniff of
the spring.
Boom! I'm getting tipsy on love.
Happy days meet my gaze and there's
love in my eye.
Boom! Boom! Boom! I'm off the wagon,
that's why.
RHODA: I've been such a good girl,
Kept myself in line.
Lips that sipped of other lips
Could never sip of mine.
I've been such a good girl
Till, the other night,
Someone knocked my good intentions
Higher than a kite.

AMAZING WHAT LOVE CAN DO

Registered for copyright as an unpublished song January 18, 1940. Introduced in *Three After Three* by Jack Whiting (Wing). Dropped from show before the New York opening of *Walk with Music*.

VERSE

STEVE: Say, can you spy
The gleam in my eye?
You should, for it shines like the moon
through the trees.
Feet off the ground,
I'm waltzing around.
I feel like the man on the flying trapeze.

REFRAIN 1

I once was a gay boy,
A lone wolf, a playboy.
I tried to be one of those cynical lads.
Now I'm even believing the magazine ads.
Amazing what love can do.
My trousers are higher
Like those in *Esquire*,
I've asked Arthur Murray to teach me to shag,
And I never drink coffee—I drink Kaffee Hag.
Amazing what love can do.
At one time my haircut
Resembled a square cut,
But now I go in for the most debonair cut.
I read Noël Coward
And watch Willie Howard.
I tell all their stories but in my own style.
And I've even developed a Roosevelt smile.
Amazing what love can do.

REFRAIN 2

My step has a new surge,
My teeth shine like blue serge,
I slick down my hair till I'm practically bald,
And whenever she's mentioned, I sit there enthralled.
Amazing what love can do.
My figure is slimmer,
My profile is trimmer.
I wish you could see how my waistline's decreased.
And it's half due to handball and half
Fleischman's yeast.
Amazing what love can do.
My soap is Life Buoy,
My hairline is crew-y,
I've planned a moustache 'cause she loves Thomas
Dewey.

I don't go with fellers,
I haunt Bonwit Teller's
So I'll understand anything she might say.
And I only read *Harper's Bazaar* and *My Day*.
Amazing what love can do.

Come on, let's arm against trouble.
Remember your cares are a bubble
And that goes double
If you'll just sing an' shout.
Sing your way out.

CHARM AGAINST TROUBLE

Introduced in *Three After Three* by Jack Whiting (Wing). Dropped from the show before the New York opening of *Walk with Music*.

VERSE

WING: An ounce of charm, like prevention,
Is worth a pound of cure.
There ain't no harm in mirth,
I've found. And I'm sure—
Shucks, I'm positive—

REFRAIN

I've got a charm against trouble.
I'm holdin' a charm against trouble.
Remember that your care is a bubble
If you keep singin' a song.
There ain't no harm
Just to be a gendarme against trouble.
Remember that goes double.
Oh, there ain't no trouble
That you can't sing your way out.

GLAMOUR BOYS

Written for Jack Whiting (Wing), Art Jarrett (Steve), and Marty May (Conrad) to perform in *Three After Three*. Unclear whether it was used in the show. Not used in *Walk with Music*.

STEVE: You must admit we are the social elite.
CONRAD: By that I mean we're dumb but
frightfully sweet.
WING: With just sufficient brains to drink and
to eat.
ALL: For today we are the Glamour Boys.
STEVE: The women love to dine with us tête-a-
tête.
WING: We stop at Pierre's because the beds
there are great.
CONRAD: And James McKinley Bryant gets us a
rate.
ALL: For today we are the Glamour Boys.
Speaking of our relations—
Our blood is thin but then it's of the
bluest, of course,
And when it comes to implications

We're always implicated in the newest
divorce.
STEVE: If I got married lots of tears would be
shed.
WING: I'm always quoted for the smart things
I've said.
CONRAD: And Jerry Zerbe's photographed us in
bed.
ALL: We are short of cash but full of poise,
For today we are the Glamour Boys.
WING: So this is Cuba—we're in debt to our
necks.
CONRAD: These people never heard of traveler's
checks.
STEVE: We have to get along on certified sex.
ALL: For today we are the Glamour Boys.
CONRAD: The girls down here are like the girls in
New York.
STEVE: The same old faces that you see at the
Stork.
WING: The only difference is, they're wearing
burnt cork.
ALL: That's no difference when you're
Glamour Boys.
So we are rhumba dancers,
Although it means we'll have to pay the
piper someday.
And we've become the gay romancers,
Although it means we'll have to change a
diaper someday.
WING: I'll stay in Cuba just to keep out of reach.
STEVE: I'll stay to search for Pam and patch up
the breach.
ALL: It's a life that every guy enjoys,
For today we are the Glamour Boys.

YOU'LL FIND OUT,
SECOND CHORUS,
and Other Songs of 1940

MISTER MEADOWLARK

Music by Walter Donaldson. Published. Copyrighted May 6, 1940. Previously registered for copyright as an unpublished song April 17, 1940. Leading recordings by Bing Crosby and Johnny Mercer (Decca); Ted Weems, with vocal by Perry Como and whistling by Elmo Tanner (Decca).

VERSE

I'm in the country but I dunno why,
'Cause I am strictly a city-lovin' guy.
I'm sittin' there
When a little bird flies my way one day.
I look at him and he's lookin' at me,
Both satisfyin' our curiosity.
Quick like a rabbit
I get me a thought,
So I up to him and say,
"Hey!"

REFRAIN

"Mister Meadowlark,
We've got an awful lot of serenadin' to do.
Mister Meadowlark,
I'm just a city slicker and I'm counting on you—
She's got a country guy who whistles.

My whistle is thin,
So when I begin—

[*Whistle.*]

That's where you come in—

[*Whistle.*]

Mister Meadowlark,
If you should cop a gander
When I'm kissin' my chick,
Needless to remark
I hope you'll have the decency to exit
But quick!
And if Missus M thinks you're out steppin',
I'll make it all right.
Mister Meadowlark,
Meet me in the dark
Tonight.

Top: Second Chorus: *Burgess Meredith, Fred Astaire, and Paulette Goddard*
Bottom: You'll Find Out: *Kay Kyser and His Band*

LITTLE COWBOY BLUE

Music by Walter Donaldson. Registered for copyright as an unpublished song April 17, 1940.

Breeze seems to sigh
Woo-woo-oo, hush-a-bye.
Stop your weepin', little fella,
Sandman's creepin' through the sky.
Time to count your sheep,
Little Cowboy Blue—
Hit the trail to Sundown Town,
Where they all are waitin' for you.
When you go to sleep,
Worries all skidoo.
Say your "Now I lay me down"
While my heart goes dreamin' with you,
Little Cowboy Blue.

FOOLS RUSH IN (WHERE ANGELS FEAR TO TREAD)

Music by Rube Bloom. Published. Copyrighted May 6, 1940. The recording by Glenn Miller and His Orchestra, with vocal by Ray Eberle (Bluebird), reached number one on the popular-music charts. Other important recordings were made by Tommy Dorsey, with vocal by Frank Sinatra (Victor); Mildred Bailey (Columbia); Harry James, with vocal by Dick Haymes (Variety); Kay Kyser, with vocal by Ginny Simms (Columbia); and, much later, Brook Benton (Mercury, 1960) and Ricky Nelson (Decca, 1963).

The song had an interesting genesis. Bloom originally wrote it as a purely instrumental track and called it "Shangri-La," inspired by the 1937 film *Lost Horizon.* Mercer's title comes from Alexander Pope's *Essay on Criticism.* Mercer said of the song: "I think it's one of my better lyrics—a simple way to a big, almost operatic kind of tune."

VERSE

"Romance is a game for fools,"
I used to say,
A game I thought I'd never play.
"Romance is a game for fools,"
I said and grinned;
Then you passed by,
And here am I
Throwing caution to the wind.

REFRAIN

Fools rush in
Where angels fear to tread,
And so I come to you, my love,
My heart above my head.
Though I see
The danger there,
If there's a chance for me
Then I don't care.
Fools rush in
Where wise men never go,
But wise men never fall in love,
So how are they to know?
When we met,
I felt my life begin;
So open up your heart
And let this fool rush in.

ON BEHALF OF THE VISITING FIREMEN

Music by Walter Donaldson. Published. Copyrighted May 6, 1940. Leading recording by Bing Crosby and Johnny Mercer (Decca). The alternate version was written during World War II.

VERSE

Blow me down—
Look at who's in town!
Pull up a chair—
There's one over there.
How've you been?
How's the next of kin?
Fellas, look who just blew in!

REFRAIN 1

On behalf of the visiting firemen from Kansas City,
Let's have a smile on me!
On behalf of the gentlemen slicked up and
    lookin' pretty,
Let's make it two or three!
Like the governor of Carolina North
Told the governor of Carolina South,
On behalf of the firemen from any city,
Let's have a smile on me.

REFRAIN 2

[*Repeat first 4 lines.*]

We're all gathered here on this auspicious day,
And we'd . . . Bless my soul,

There's Elmer! Whatcha say?

[*Repeat last 2 lines.*]

REFRAIN 3

On behalf of the visiting firemen from Minnesota,
Let's have a smile on me!
On behalf of the citizen just in from North
    Dakota,
Let's make it two or three,
Just as our forefathers always tried to show,
"Give us Liberty or give us . . ."—well, let it go!
On behalf of the visiting firemen who filled their
    quota,
Let's have a smile on me.

Alternative version

On behalf of the visiting airmen from Buna-Gona,
Let's have a smile on me.
On behalf of the bombardiers training out in
    Pomona,
Let's make it two or three!
As the bey of Tunis told the bey of Algiers,
"I don't know where these guys came from, but
    three cheers!"
On behalf of the visiting Yankees from this old
    groana,
Let's have a smile on me.

On behalf of the visiting tigers from Chunking,
    China,
Let's have a smile on me.
On behalf of the officers just back from Asia Mina,
Let's make it two or three!
For you servicemen there isn't any charge
And we welcome you to our . . . why, hello, Sarge!
On behalf of our fightin' men, than which there
    ain't no fina,
Let's have a smile on me!

NIGHTCAP SONG

Music by Walter Donaldson. Registered for copyright as an unpublished song June 19, 1940, and again November 15, 1940.

There's a snowcap on the mountain,
There's a redcap on the train,
There's a hubcap on an auto
And a pink cap on Champagne.
There's a skullcap on a freshman

At the university,
There's a white cap on the cream,
But the nightcap's on me!

HOMECOMING

Music by Walter Donaldson. Published. Copyrighted May 15, 1942. Previously registered for copyright as an unpublished song June 28, 1940.

VERSE

Red leaves of autumn and geese in the sky
Set me to dreaming of things,
Things I discovered when I was so high
My heart stops beating and it sings.

REFRAIN

Soon I'll be home coming.
Picture me home coming:
Same home, same house, same folks
Running to the door;
Same smiles, same kiss, that kiss
I've been waiting for.
Easy chair, fire gleaming,
Dozin' there half-dreaming,
And then I'm a kid again.
Slowly up the stairs I climb,
Homecoming time.

PRETTY PLEASE

Music by Walter Donaldson. Registered for copyright as an unpublished song June 28, 1940.

VERSE

Midnight kisses ocean,
Ocean kisses shore.
With all this emotion
What are we waitin' for?

REFRAIN

Heaven sent us
Nights like these—
Cuddle closer,
Pretty please!

Stars a-spinnin'
Through the trees—
Please, my pretty,
Pretty please!
Ask any bird
On any bough:
Love's gonna get you eventually,
Why not now?
Time's a-wastin',
Breezy breeze.
Kiss me, pretty,
Pretty please!

THE LEGEND OF OLD CALIFORNIA

Music by Harry Warren. Registered for copyright as an unpublished song August 13, 1940.

REFRAIN

When campfire lights grow pale,
They tell the strangest tale
In California.
As April fills the lanes,
A phantom rides the plains
In California.
Beneath the moon above,
He searches for his love
In California.
They parted long ago
When diamond stars hung low
In California.
He told her the night he left her,
That he would return someday;
She waited and waited and waited without him,
Dreaming about him riding away.
But fate can never wait
And he returned too late
To California.
As April fills the lanes,
You'll see him ride the plains.

TWO WEEKS WITH PAY (1940)

Tryout: Ridgeway Theatre, White Plains, New York; opened June 24, 1940; closed two weeks later. Produced by Dorothy and Julian Olney. Conceived by Ted Fetter and Richard Lewine. Sketches by Peter Barry, David Gregory, and Charles Sherman. Directed by Felix Jacoves. Dances by Gene Kelly. Set design by Lawrence L. Goldwasser. Costumes by Marion Herwood. Vocal arrangements by Harold Cooke. With Marie Nash, Eugene Hari, Pat Harrington, Bill Johnson, Ruth Mata, Earl Oxford, Hiram Sherman, and Remo Bufano's Puppets. The show contained one Mercer song.

WITH YOU WITH ME

Music by Johnny Green. Published. Copyrighted March 15, 1957. Previously registered for copyright as an unpublished song August 27, 1956. Introduced by Marie Nash and Bill Johnson, danced by Dawn Roland and Maurice Kelly.

VERSE

When I rise and open my eyes
To find that the skies say, "Rain!"
I never sigh or pace the floor
Or open my umbrella, for
You're here, and I
Shall nevermore complain.

REFRAIN

With you with me
The day breaks merrily;
The world
Goes spinning gaily on.
With you
I walk on thistledown;
This dreary old town
Puts on a new gown!
And just between you and me,
It's seventh-heavenly
To know
My heart is finally gone!
And love
Is all they said it would be;
It's sugar and spice
And ev'rything nice

And all of that twice
With you with me.

THE AIR-MINDED EXECUTIVE

Music by Bernie Hanighen. Registered for copyright as an unpublished song October 26, 1940.

VERSE

Life, Look, Pic, Peek
Always print a beautiful calf,
And another thing they love
Is a certain photograph.
You take the *Time, Tide, Newsweek,*
Ev'ry editorial staff—
Over a beer, they agree
The man of the year was the—

REFRAIN

Air-minded executive;
He dearly loved to fly.
He was an up-to-date go-getter;
His lady friend was even better—
She went along to take a letter,
Way up in the sky.

Air-minded executive
Would take off on the sly,
He was a most romantic feller,
And oh, the things he used to tell her
Above the roar of his propeller
Somewhere in the sky!

Foggy or fair,
They would be there
Lightin' a flare at the airport,
Fillin' the tanks,
Callin' the banks,
Tellin' 'em
"Hold up the contract!" . . . "Contact!"

The air-minded executive
Became a wealthy guy.
And so he wed his secretary;
They settled down in Waterbury,
And they commute by stratosferry.

My, they love to fly,
Even as you and I!

LONG TIME, NO SEE

Music by Walter Donaldson. Registered for copyright as an unpublished song November 15, 1940.

Long time, no see,
Long time, no laughs,
Long time for me to be looking
At nothing but photographs.
Long time, no moon,
No stars above,
Long time for me to be sitting
And waiting for words of love.
It's the funniest thing,
Yes indeed,
How quick the time passes.
It's the funniest thing—
When you go,
It's as slow as molasses.
Long time, no see—
"Long time" is right,
But I'll be ever so glad
When you're back in my arms tonight.

YOU'LL FIND OUT (1940)

Produced and directed by David Butler for RKO Pictures. Released November 1940. Copyright November 22, 1940. Screenplay by James V. Kern, after a story by David Butler and James V. Kern. Special material by Monte Brice, Andrew Bennison, and R. T. M. Scott. Music by Jimmy McHugh. Lyrics by Johnny Mercer. Orchestrations by George Duning. Musical director: Roy Webb. Starring Kay Kyser, with Peter Lorre, Boris Karloff, Bela Lugosi, Helen Parrish, Dennis O'Keefe, Alma Kruger, Joseph Eggenton, and Kay Kyser and His Band, featuring Ginny Simms, Harry Babbitt, Ish Kabibble, and Sully Mason.

Kay Kyser and His Band are hired to play at a party for a young girl in a gloomy old house and end up saving her life.

LIKE THE FELLA ONCE SAID

Music by Jimmy McHugh. Published. Copyrighted November 7, 1940. Introduced by Harry Babbitt, Sully Mason, Ginny Simms, Jack Martin, Roscoe Hillman, Kay Kyser, Ish Kabibble, and the men of Kay Kyser's Band; danced by Kay Kyser and Kay Kyser's Band.

VERSE

I've been saving epithets and epigrams to show
    you
How dull you are,
The lull you are.
Are they stationhouse remarks that I'm about to
    throw you?
I fear they are,
But here they are:

REFRAIN 1

Like the fella once said
Who sat on a hat,
"I'm tellin' you, baby,
I'm leavin' you flat."
Like the bale o' hay said
That dropped from a load,
"I'm tellin' you, baby,
I'm hittin' the road."

Admitted you fooled me
For a spell,
But just like the farmer
Told the well,
"I dug ya."
Like the bicycle pump
Once said to the spare,
"I'm tellin' you, baby,
I'm givin' you air—
So there!"
I loved you, but our love is dead,
Like the fella once said.

Additional lyrics

REFRAIN 2

Like the fella once said
To the mule who was sick,
"I'm tellin' you, baby,
You're losin' your kick!"

[spoken] You know what the short chair said to the
    tall chair?
No, what'd the short chair say to the tall chair?
"Hi, chair!"

[sung] Like the fella once said while shavin' his
    mush,
"I'm tellin' you, baby,
You're getting' the brush!"

[spoken] Hey, you know what the bug said to the
    windshield?
"That's me all over!"

[sung] Like the mirror says
When you've added a pound,
"I'm tellin' you, baby,
Be seein' you round!"

It's just like the trumpet
Told the drum,
"I don't care how much
You rum-tum-tum—
I'm blowin'!"

Like the warden once heard
The prisoner shout,
"I'm tellin' you, baby,
I'm cuttin' on out,
No doubt!"
Like the fella once said.

REFRAIN 3

Like the baker said
When he looked at the bun,
"I'm tellin' you, baby,
It's over and done."

Like the cook in the kitchen
Said to the cup,
"I'm tellin' you, baby,
You're all washed up!"

It's just like the tree
Said to the ground
The moment that autumn
Rolled around—
"I'm leavin'!"

Like the fella said
'Bout his old Panama,
"I'm tellin' you, baby,
You've been the last straw,
Haw, haw!"
Like the fella once said.

YOU'VE GOT ME THIS WAY (WHATTA-YA-GONNA DO ABOUT IT?)

Music by Jimmy McHugh. Published. Copyrighted November 7, 1940. Introduced by Harry Babbitt and Kay Kyser's Band and recorded by them (Columbia). Other leading recordings were made by Glenn Miller and His Orchestra, with vocal by Marion Hutton (Bluebird); Tommy Dorsey and His Orchestra, with vocals by Jo Stafford and the Pied Pipers (Victor); and Jimmy Dorsey and His Orchestra, with vocal by Helen O'Connell (Decca).

VERSE

I say hello
To the people I know
In a vague sort of way;
Baffled and blue,
I go wandering through
The day.
Don't ask me what ails me,
What I'm thinking of;
One look reveals
That I'm head over heels
In love.

REFRAIN

You've got me this way—
Say,
Whattaya gonna do about it,
Whattaya gonna do about it?
You've got me this way,
Crazy for you.
You kissed me one day,
Then,
Seein' that I was true about it,
Wha' did you go and do about it?
You left me this way,
Bluer than blue.
You thought it was funny,
My fallin' so hard;
I'm laughin' my sides off, honey,
You're really a card.
You've got me this way—
Say,
Now that I'm in a stew about it,
What am I gonna do about it?
I'm just gonna stay
Crazy for you.

(TING-A-LING) THE BAD HUMOR MAN

Music by Jimmy McHugh. Published. Copyrighted November 7, 1940. Introduced by Harry Babbitt, Kay Kyser, and the men of Kay Kyser's Band, including Sully Mason, Jack Martin, Roscoe Hillman, and Ish Kabibble, and recorded by them (Columbia).

Published version

VERSE 1

Up ev'ry morning at the break of day—
What a life, what a life, what a life!
Cold cup of coffee on the breakfast tray—
What a wife, what a wife, what a wife!
All day long
Things go wrong.
So, as I wander on my weary way,
I sing this song.

REFRAIN 1

Ting-a-ling, ting-a-ling, ting-a-ling,
I'm the Bad Humor man,
Ting-a-ling, ting-a-ling, ting-a-ling,
Got a frown on my pan.
Oh, I don't like anything, nosiree—
I hate people and they hate me,
So I sing, "Ting-a-ling, ting-a-ling"
As I go on my way;
With my wagon rumbling
I keep grumbling,
"Gee, it's an awful day!"

VERSE 2

Hey, little kiddies, do you hear that noise?
Better fly, better fly, better fly!
Here comes the enemy of girls and boys—
What a guy, what a guy, what a guy!
Hear him yell,
Hear his bell—
Drop your velocipedes and drop your toys
And run pell mell!

REFRAIN 2

Ting-a-ling, ting-a-ling, ting-a-ling,
It's the Bad Humor man,
Ting-a-ling, ting-a-ling, ting-a-ling,
With a frown on his pan.
Oh, he hates his job and he hates his beat;
He hates everyone on the street.
So he sings, "Ting-a-ling, ting-a-ling,"

As he goes on his way;
With his wagon rumbling
He keeps grumbling,
"Gee, it's a lousy day!"

VERSE 3

When the old umbrella man says hello,
I say, "Ain't gonna rain no mo'!"
When the peanut vendor says, "Hi, what's new?"
I look up and yell, "Nuts to you!"
When the man comes by with the mandolin,
I just wrap it around his chin.
When I see that shabby old cabby guy,
I spit right in his kindly eye.
When I meet my very good friend Ned Sparks,
We pass three or four sour remarks.

Film version

HARRY
BABBITT: Ting-a-ling, ting-a-ling, ting-a-ling.
It's the bad humor man.

MEN IN
BAND: Hey, little kiddies, do you hear that noise?

SULLY
MASON: Better fly, better fly, better fly!
BAND: Here comes the enemy of girls and boys—
MASON: What a guy, what a guy, what a guy!
3 MEN: Hear him yell,
Hear his bell!
MASON: Drop your velocipedes and drop your toys—
BAND: And run pell mell!
BABBITT: Ting-a-ling, ting-a-ling, ting-a-ling,
It's the Bad Humor man.
Ting-a-ling, ting-a-ling, ting-a-ling,
With a frown on his pan.
MASON: He's a gloomy Gus,
He's a grouch on wheels,
He's one of America's
Foremost heels.
3 MEN: Ting-a-ling, ting-a-ling
As he goes on his way—
MASON: With his wagon rumblin'
He keeps grumblin',
"Gee, it's an awful day!"
BAND: [*variously; speaking and singing like kids*]
Oh, boy! School is out! School is out!
London Bridge is falling down—
Three Blind Mice,
See how they run!—
London Bridge is falling down!
—I wanna play too!
—Old McDonald had a farm!

—Throw me that ball, Rusty!
—Hey, look, kids, the Bad Humor Man!
—I want a chocolate one!
—Can you give me vaniller?
—I want a little peach!
—Can you give me a raspberry, mister?

ISH
KABIBBLE: With pleasure, kiddie!
Up ev'ry morning at the break of day.
What a life, what a life, what a life!
Cold cup o' coffee on the breakfast tray.
What a wife, what a wife, what a wife!
BAND: All day long things go wrong
KABIBBLE: So, as I wander on my weary way
I sing this song:
BAND: Ting-a-ling
Ting-a-ling
Ting-a-ling,
KABIBBLE: I'm the bad humor man.
BAND: Ting-a-ling
Ting-a-ling
Ting-a-ling,
KABIBBLE: With a frown on my pan.
BAND: He's mean as Simon, I mean, Lagree.
KABIBBLE: Yes, I hate people and they hate me!
BAND: So he sings,
Ting-a-ling, ting-a-ling, ting-a-ling,
As he goes on his way.
KABIBBLE: With my wagon rumbling
I keep grumbling,
"L-ow, what a wow-sy day."

KAY
KYSER: That's no way to act.
Now, why be mad?
KABIBBLE: My fitness is good,
But my humor's bad.
KYSER: Then, come on, kids,
With your musical toys.
They'll make you
One of the Happiness Boys.
KABIBBLE: Well, thank you, kiddies,
For the helping hand.
You've made me smile
And it sure feels grand.
KYSER: Then keep on smiling
And join the band!

101

I'D KNOW YOU ANYWHERE

Music by Jimmy McHugh. Published. Copyrighted November 7, 1940. Introduced by Ginny Simms and Kay Kyser and His Band; reprised by Harry Babbitt and Kay Kyser and His Band (with Sonovox). Recorded by Simms and Babbitt with Kyser's Orchestra (Columbia). Also recorded by Glenn Miller and His Orchestra (Bluebird). Nominated for an Academy Award as Best Song but lost to "When You Wish Upon a Star" from *Pinocchio*.

VERSE

Sunday-school picnic,
Rotary luncheon,
Army and Navy game—
Darling, any place would be the same.
Here in the city,
Out in the country,
Up in the land of Oz—
Darling, wouldn't matter where it was,
Because—

REFRAIN

I'd know you anywhere;
I'd know that grin.
I'd know you anywhere
When you walked in;
I would tingle
With a single
Glance in your eyes;
Watching the starlight
Dance in your eyes.
You saw my vacant stare,
You understood;
I'd love you anywhere,
Honest, I would.
I was certain
This would happen,
Strange as it seems,
I'd know you anywhere
From my dreams.

I'VE GOT A ONE-TRACK MIND

Music by Jimmy McHugh. Published. Copyrighted November 7, 1940. Introduced by Ginny Simms, Harry Babbitt (with Sonovox), danced by Kay Kyser and His Band. Recorded by Kyser and His Band (Columbia).

VERSE

I'm in what's known as a pickle:
I should be fickle,
I must be true;
For having my mental setup,
There is no letup
From loving you.

REFRAIN

I've got a one-track mind;
It's got a point of view:
All the day long
It's busy with thoughts of you.
I've got a one-track heart,
Can't call my heart my own;
Early or late,
It's beating for you alone.
I've got the stubbornest pair of arms
That reach in your direction;
I've got a pair of lips
That long for your affection.
But having a one-track mind
Has its advantage, too.
It keeps telling me
To tell you that I love you,
And I must do
What my one-track mind
Tells me to do.

DON'T THINK IT AIN'T BEEN CHARMING

Music by Jimmy McHugh. Published. Copyrighted November 7, 1940. Not used in film.

VERSE

Fare-thee-well and stuff,
Time to whisper bye-bye;
How the minutes fly by
When the moon is bright.
Can't thank you enough,
Lovely to have known you—
S'pose I telephone you,
Say, tomorrow night?

REFRAIN

Ta-ta, old bean,
Don't think it ain't been charming,
Holding you close to my heart.
By that I mean

Don't think it ain't been charming,
Even though we have to part.
Such a frightfully lovely nightful
Couldn't be more complete;
I found it most delightful,
Which prompts me to repeat,
Ta-ta, old bean,
Maybe I [you] acted freshly,
'Speshly by holding you [me] tight;*
But don't think it ain't been charming
Tonight.

YOU'LL FIND OUT

Music by Jimmy McHugh. Published. Copyrighted July 2, 1941. Not used in film.

You'll find out
Without a doubt,
You'll find out some night;
You'll discover what it's all about
When stars are shining bright.
Every peach
That's out of reach
Drops from off the bough;
You'll discover what a sigh can do,
What a moon up in the sky can do†—
You'll find out right now.

SECOND CHORUS (1940)

Produced by Boris Morros and Robert Stillman for Paramount Pictures. Released December 1940. Copyright January 3, 1941. Directed by H. C. Potter. Screenplay by Elaine Ryan and Ian McLellan Hunter, from an original story by Frank Cavett. Contributions to screenplay by Johnny Mercer. Music by Artie Shaw, Bernard Hanighen, and Hal Borne. Lyrics by Johnny Mercer. Dance director: Hermes Pan. Associate musical director: Eddie Paul.

Starring: Fred Astaire and Paulette Goddard, with

---

* *Alternate lyrics:*
  Really, it's quite alarming
  Ling'ring till dawn's early light;
† *Alternate lyric:*
  What a breeze that passes by can do—

Artie Shaw and His Band, Charles Butterworth, Burgess Meredith, Frank Melton, Jimmy Conlon, Don Brodie, Marjorie Kane, Joan Barclay, and Willa Pearl Curtis.

Two trumpeters and their lady manager try their luck on Broadway.

I AIN'T HEP TO THAT STEP (BUT I'LL DIG IT)

Music by Hal Borne. Published. Copyrighted January 7, 1941. Previously registered for copyright as an unpublished song October 5, 1940. Introduced by Fred Astaire, men in band, and Paulette Goddard; danced by Astaire and Goddard. Recorded by Fred Astaire (Columbia).

Published version

VERSE

I've seen some people on the dance floor,
And that's what keeps me off the dance floor.
To ev'ry ball or dancing hall with fear I go,
But you want to go,
So even though
On my ear I go,
Here I go.

Film version

PAULETTE
GODDARD: It seems to me—
FRED
ASTAIRE: It seems to you?
GODDARD: I said it seems to me—
ASTAIRE: You said it seems to you?
GODDARD: Seems to me I smell a mouse—
ASTAIRE: Somewhere about the house.
I said it seems to me—
BAND: You said it seems to you—
ASTAIRE: I said it seems to me—
BAND: You said it seems to you—
ASTAIRE: That such an embarrassing
situation
Calls for concentration.
Do you dig me, Jack?
BAND: We dig you, Jack!
ASTAIRE: Can you think of a plan?
BAND: We solid can!
ASTAIRE: To get me out of this mess?
BAND: Ah, yes, yes, yes!
We'll start the music
And play it back.
ASTAIRE: Solid, Jack!
BAND: Solid, Jack!

MAN IN BAND: Can you sing and dance?
ASTAIRE: I'll take a chance.
MAN IN BAND: Are your boots on right?
ASTAIRE: I've got 'em laced up tight.
MAN IN BAND: Is Miss Miller a killer?
ASTAIRE: From Spanish villa.
MAN IN BAND: Is her dancin' mellow?
ASTAIRE: Why, mellow as a cello!
BAND: Then it seems to me,
Obviously,
Why not go right into your
terpsichory?
ASTAIRE: What will it be?
GODDARD: Don't look at me!
ASTAIRE: Now, let me see,
What will it be?
I never could do the conga,
Could never get through the
conga,
But if you say, "Do the conga,"
I ain't hep to that step, but I'll dig
it!
I never could see mazurkas,
They're poison to me, mazurkas,
But if it's to be mazurkas,
I ain't hep to that step, but I'll dig
it!
BAND: When they invented the
Charleston,
He was a total flop.
ASTAIRE: Right, but I say, if you wanna
Charleston,
I'll never stop, I'll dance till I
drop!
I never could dig the polka,
The corniest jig, the polka.
But if you say, "Dig the polka,"
I ain't hep to that step, but I'll dig
it.

LOVE OF MY LIFE

Music by Artie Shaw. Published. Copyrighted November 4, 1940. Previously registered for copyright as an unpublished song October 5, 1940. Introduced by Artie Shaw and His Band and Fred Astaire; reprised in fake comic Russian by Astaire. Leading recordings were made by Astaire (Columbia) and by Artie Shaw, with vocal by Anita Boyer (Victor). Nominated for an Academy Award for Best Song but lost to "When You Wish Upon a Star" from *Pinocchio*, music by Leigh Harline, lyrics by Ned Washington.

VERSE

Were you the girl most likely to succeed?
And have you thought of what you'd like to be?
A DAR?
A suffragette?
A movie star?
If nothing yet,
Would you consider just a hint from me?

REFRAIN

Would you like to be the love of my life?
For always,
And always watch over me?
To square my blunders
And share my dreams,
One day with caviar,
Next day a choc'late bar?
Would you like to take the merry-go-round?
I'll lead you,
I'll need you—
Just wait and you'll see.
I hope in your horoscope
There is room for a dope who adores you;
That would make the only dream of my life
Come true—
For the love of my life
Is you.

Comedy version

Vodka bublichki de love uff my life
Stassnia
Krassnia
Bla-bla-bla
With no more caviar
Hershinsky chocolate bar?
Would you like to be the love of my life
For always,
And always
Watch over me?
Oh, play a peek and a plook
On the string of your old
Balalaika!
Vodka bublichki de loff uff my life
Da-da
For the love of my life
Is you.

POOR MISTER CHISHOLM

Music by Bernie Hanighen. Published. Copyrighted November 4, 1940. Previously registered for copyright as an unpublished song October 5, 1940. Introduced by Fred Astaire and Burgess Meredith; reprised by Astaire. An earlier title: "The Blues Sneaked in Every Time." Recorded by Fred Astaire (Columbia).

VERSE

Got a mandolin,
Bought it secondhand
From a Mister Chisholm in the balalaika band.
Had the sweetest tone,
Resonant and low;
Often made you wonder
Why he let it go.
If you have the time,
How they parted comp'ny and he offered it for sale
Makes a fascinating tale.

REFRAIN

Poor Mister Chisholm
Play'd on the mandolin,
But he couldn't win,
'Cause he tried to swing
And he broke a string
Ev'ry time.
Poor Mister Chisholm
Just couldn't dig the jive—
When he did arrive
At the proper note,
He arrived by boat
Ev'ry time.
He tried to jazz up his mandolin
But never could quite control it,
He always brought Bach and Handel in.
When he took a lick,
He always broke a pick!
Poor Mister Chisholm
Still gave it all he had,
But he played so bad
That they yelled, "He's tight!"
And they threw him right in the can—
What a man!
He disgraced his kin
On the mandolin
Ev'ry time.

Alternative lyrics

Poor Mister Chisholm,
You're quite a gay old blade
With your serenade,

But you're corny, Jack,
Better truck on back to Dubuque,
Get a uke—
You disgraced your kin
On the mandolin
Ev'ry time.

Earlier version ("The Blues Sneaked in Every Time")

VERSE

Once I had a horn,
Bought it secondhand
From a Mister Chisholm in the local band.
Blew the sweetest tone
Any horn could blow;
Often made me wonder
Why he let it go.
If you have the time
How they parted company and he offered it for sale
Makes a fascinating tale.

REFRAIN

Poor Mister Chisholm
Played in the Elks parade,
But the way he played
Is a downright sin
'Cause the blues sneaked in
Ev'ry time.
Poor Mister Chisholm,
He tried to please the crowd,
But he blew so loud
That he raised a din,
'Cause the blues sneaked in
Ev'ry time.
Though everyone kept in step but him,
He nonchalantly ignored 'em,
And thinking no one was hep but him
Took a firmer grasp,
Swung out and split his lip.
Poor Mister Chisholm
Still gave it all he had,
But he played so bad
That they yelled, "He's tight!"
And they threw him right in the can—
What a man!
He disgraced his kin
'Cause the blues sneaked in
Ev'ry time.

ME AND THE GHOST UPSTAIRS

Music by Bernie Hanighen. Published. Copyrighted November 4, 1940. Previously registered for copyright as an unpublished song October 5, 1940. Intended for Fred Astaire and Hermes Pan but cut from the film before its release. Recorded by Fred Astaire (Columbia).

VERSE

Oft upon a midnight dreary,
While I ponder, weak and weary,
From a long trip on the Erie,
Comes a rapping at my chamber door.
It's an ectoplasmic tapping
That disturbs my nightly napping,
Like a shroud that's gently flapping,
Emanating from the second floor.

REFRAIN

Buddies are we,
Me and the ghost upstairs,
Sipping our tea,
Me and the ghost upstairs.
But he's inclined to moan when left alone,
So I think of things
That'll tickle his funny bone,
Lonely old ghost upstairs.
Regular folks,
Dropping our worldly cares,
Swapping our jokes,
Me and the ghost upstairs.
And then he slaps his shroud
And laughs out loud
And he says, "Oh, boy!
That'll paralyze all the crowd,"
Jolly old ghost upstairs.

He's quite a cook;
He serves a beautiful drink.*
He wrote a book,
And in invisible ink.
I took a look,
And the title,
'Pon my faith,
Was *The Groups of Wraith.*
Once in a while
He brings a gang of friends;
Does it in style,
Careless of what he spends.

———————
* *Alternate line:*
  He serves a delightful drink.

And though the place is small,
We have a ball,
'Cause you know those spooks
Don't require no room at all.
We have some mighty fine affairs,
Me and the ghost upstairs.

OVERLEAF

Top: Blues in the Night: *from left to right, Billy Halop,*
Peter Whitney, Richard Whorf, Jack Carson, Priscilla
Lane, and Elia Kazan
Bottom: Birth of the Blues: *standing left to right,*
Brian Donlevy, Perry Botkin, Bing Crosby, Mary
Martin, Harry Barris, and Danny Beck; seated with
his trombone, Jack Teagarden

YOU'RE THE ONE, NAVY BLUES, BIRTH OF THE BLUES, BLUES IN THE NIGHT,
and Other Songs of 1941

CALLING ALL SQUARES

Music by Bernie Hanighen. Registered for copyright as an unpublished song January 3, 1941.

Honk, honk, there's the horn,
Honk, honk, bring your corn,
Honk, honk, calling all squares!
Crew cuts, grab your chicks,
Round cuts, all your "icks,"
Short cuts, calling all squares!
We are here to dig a little jive,
Elect a president at quarter after five;
And when the membership decides on the weekly
    square,
We'll shoot the lingo
And swing some bingo.
Quonk, quonk, beat your chops,
Quonk, quonk, look out, pops,
Honk, honk, calling all squares.

I BOOGIED WHEN I SHOULD HAVE WOOGIED

Music by Bernie Hanighen. Registered for copyright as an unpublished song January 14, 1941. Recorded by the Will Bradley Orchestra, featuring Ray McKinley (vocal) (Columbia).

I boogied when I should have woogied
And I woogied when I should have boogied.
My straight beat should have been an eight beat
And my eight beat should have a gate beat.
I rumbled the drum,
I rattled the snare,
I tickled the big cymbal.
It went to my head,
The customer said,
You shouldn't be so nimble.
You boogie when you're supposed to woogie.
Now, the customer's right,
And I know that I'm
Gonna please him if he's got a dime.
I boogie when I'm supposed to woogie
And I will boogie woogie all night long.

LOCA ILLUSION

Music by Xavier Cugat.
    Lyric missing.

YOU'RE THE ONE (1941)

Produced and written by Gene Markey for Paramount Pictures. Released January 1941. Copyright February 7, 1941. Directed by Ralph Murphy. Music by Jimmy McHugh. Lyrics by Johnny Mercer. Musical numbers staged by LeRoy Prinz. Musical arrangements of "Yogi" and "Strawberry Lane" by Jule Styne. Musical director: Phil Boutelje. With Bonnie Baker, Orrin Tucker, Albert Dekker, Jerry Colonna, Edward Everett Horton, Lillian Cornell, Walter Catlett, Don Castle, Teddy Hart, Renie Riano, Eddie Conrad, and Orrin Tucker's Orchestra.

    An agent attempts to place his client as a singer in Orrin Tucker's Orchestra, and eventually succeeds.

YOU'RE THE ONE (FOR ME)

Published. Copyrighted November 7, 1940. Introduced and recorded by Orrin Tucker and His Orchestra (Columbia).

VERSE

Ev'ry creature underneath the sun
Has a feature that some other creature adores.
Ev'ry creature has a certain face that it feels a glow
    for,
And the face I go for is yours.

REFRAIN 1

You're the one for me.
Just as ev'ry fish
Has a lovely dish
That he swims with in the sea,
You're the one for me.

You're the one for me.
Just as ev'ry bat
Who's as blind as that
Has a bat that he can see,
You're the one for me.

Nightingales all practice their scales
When love goes by;
Fireflies get stars in their eyes,*
And so did I,
So it's plain to see,
Just as ev'ry moose
Who is on the loose
Finds his m-o-o-s-e,
You're the one for me.

REFRAIN 2

You're the one for me.
Just as ev'ry gnat
Likes to hang his hat
Where a certain gnat may be,
You're the one for me.

You're the one for me.
Just as ev'ry seal
Gets the old appeal
From a girlfriend's symmetry,
You're the one for me.

Camels blink and run for a drink
When love goes by;
Geese, the chumps, get covered with bumps,
And so did I.
So it's plain to see,
Just as ev'ry goat
Makes a mental note
When he spies his dream goatee,
You're the one for me.

You're the one that fills the bill;
Fell head over heels like Jack and Jill—
Something tells me
You're the one for me.

Extra refrains

You're the one for me
Just as orioles
Warble barcarolles
To prospective brides-to-be,
You're the one for me.

You're the one for me.
Just as every loon
Is inclined to swoon
In another's company,
You're the one for me.

---

* *Alternate line:*
    Chickadees get weak in the knees,

Chickadees get weak in the knees
When love goes by;
Even shrimp are prone to get limp
And so did I.
So it's plain to see,
Just as ducks and drakes
Have their angel cakes
In the feathered family,
You're the one for me.

You're the one for me.
Just as every monk
Goes from trunk to trunk
Till he finds his baby's tree,
You're the one for me.

You're the one for me.
Just as each giraffe
Keeps a photograph
Of a ravishing Missus G,
You're the one for me.

Antelope come out in the ope
When love goes by;
Porcupines get quills up their spines,
And so did I.
So it's plain to see
Just as each gazelle
Runs to beat all, well,
It's as plain as A-B-C,
You're the one for me.

You're the one for me.
Just as kangaroos
Hop around in twos
When the spring is o'er the lea,
You're the one for me.

You're the one for me.
Just as every fly
Has a Lorelei
That he worships privately,
You're the one for me.

Woolly lambs say, "Look at those gams!"
When love goes by;
Katydids get goofy as kids
And so did I.
So it's plain to see
As the tsetse fly
Murmurs "Tootsie, I
Guess it simply had to be,"
You're the one for me.

You're the one for me.
Just as every roc
Searches every flock

For a roc that's fancy free,
You're the one for me.

You're the one for me.
Just as every snipe
Finds a certain type
That he loves exclusively,
You're the one for me.

Dinosaurs would gather in scores
When love passed by;
Unicorns would toot their horns,
And so will I.
So it's plain to see,
Dragons spouted fire
For their heart's desire
And I'd do the same for thee—
You're the one for me.

You're the one for me.
Just as buffalo
Keep a gal in tow
When they roam the lone prairiee,
You're the one for me.

You're the one for me.
Just as every yak
Makes a witty crack
To arouse his lady's glee,
You're the one for me.

Grizzly bears come out of their lairs
When love goes by;
Chipmunks, too, chip in to woo-woo
And so did I.
So it's plain to see
Just as every swine
Has his Valentine
That he bounces on his knee,
You're the one for me.

You're the one for me.
Just as crocodiles
Crawl for miles and miles
So they'll meet eventually,
You're the one for me.

You're the one for me
Just as octopi
Roll a glassy eye
When they meet that certain she,
You're the one for me.

Terrapins go head over fins
When love goes by;
Even whales go head over tails
And so did I.

So it's plain to see
Even though I've gone
From the Amazon
To the distant Zuider Zee,
You're the one for me.

Alternate verse

His arms were empty,
My nights were free,
And the want ad in his eyes
Seemed to advertise
He was looking for someone like me.

I COULD KISS YOU FOR THAT

Published. Copyrighted November 7, 1940. Introduced and recorded by Bonnie Baker and Orrin Tucker and His Orchestra.

VERSE

There's a Neolithic man in me,
Spencer Tracy and Tarzan in me.
They appear
Ev'ry time you're near.
It's not easy to convey to you,
Reasons why I feel that way to you;
Words are weak—
But we the people speak!

REFRAIN

'Cause you're sweet and you're swell
And a smoothie as well,
I could kiss you for that.
'Cause you're simple and shy
And a regular guy,
I could kiss you for that.
That marvelous face
Takes over the place
Wherever we two have gone.
We walk in a room,
You give 'em the zoom
And boom!
The panic is on.
'Cause you never insist
That you ought to be kissed,
I could kiss you for that.
For the way that you fib
And the cut of your jib,
I could kiss you for that.

Whenever I spy
That gleam in your eye,
I get an electric chill,
'Cause I know where I'm at—
I could kiss you for that,
And I think I will.

STRAWBERRY LANE

Published, Copyrighted November 7, 1940. Introduced by Bonnie Baker and children. Recorded by Bonnie Baker with Orrin Tucker and His Orchestra (Columbia).

Published version

VERSE

Blind man's bluff is a game you can play
With a handkerchief round your eyes;
And sometimes if you lose your way,
You discover a big surprise.
I played once and I found the land
Where the wise old sandman goes;
To this day I'm the only one who knows.

REFRAIN

If you wanna go down to Candy Town
Through a jungle of sugar cane,
Turn right with me at the cinnamon tree,
Down Strawberry Lane.
Oh, the stop and go signs are Valentines
And the letters are very plain.
The cars all stop for the gingerbread cop,
Down Strawberry Lane.
Just hop in my car,
It's a big choc'late bar,
And we'll be there in forty winks,
It isn't very far.
If we ever see crowds of ice cream clouds,
How the peppermint drops will rain!
So grab a cup and we'll gobble 'em up,
Down Strawberry Lane.

Film version

VERSE

BONNIE
BAKER: Long ago when the lights were low,
 I was hurrying home one day;
 In the park it was awfully dark
 And I happened to lose my way.
 And I walked and walked till I found the
 town

Where the soda fountain flows.
To this day I'm the only one who knows.

REFRAIN AND PATTER

3 KIDS: [*reciting lines to musical meter*] We'd
 like to go to a taffy pull!
TOOTHLESS
BOY: I'd like a marshmallow soft as wool!
BAKER: There's a dish for ev'ry wish.
SISSY: Is ev'ry day a choc'late Sundae?
LITTLE BOY: Ha, ha, that's a rich one!
LITTLE GIRL: I'd like the little Christmas tree with
 a candy-coated star!
BLACK BOY: I wants a choc'late, cocoanut,
 caramel, butterscotch five-cent
 cigar.

REFRAIN

LITTLE GIRL
TRIO: [*sung*] If you wanna go down to
 Candy Town
 Through a jungle of sugar cane,
 Turn right with me at the cinnamon
 tree,
 Down Strawberry Lane.
ALL: Oh, the stop and go signs are
 Valentines,
 And the letters are very plain.
 The cars all stop
 For the gingerbread cop,
 Down Strawberry Lane.
BLACK BOY: When I blow my whistle, they gotta
 stop,
 'Less they buys me a drink of soda
 pop!
BAKER: Come sit beside me in my car;
 It's a very 'normous choc'late bar.
 If you all behave we'll be there in a
 flash—
 It really isn't very far.
ALL: If we ever see crowds of ice cream
 clouds,
 How the peppermint drops will rain!
 So grab a cup and we'll gobble 'em
 up,
 Down Strawberry Lane.
BAKER: If you wanna go down to Candy
 Town
 Through a jungle of sugar cane,
 You turn right here at the cinnamon
 tree,
 Down Strawberry Lane.

THE YOGI (WHO LOST HIS WILLPOWER)

Published. Copyrighted February 17, 1941. Introduced by Orrin Tucker and His Orchestra, Lillian Cornell, Jerry Colonna and ensemble. Recorded by Jerry Colonna with Orrin Tucker and His Orchestra (Columbia).

VERSE

ORRIN
TUCKER: A yogi is a man who thinks and
 thinks
 And never has a time for forty winks.
 He seldom eats and rarely drinks—
BODYGUARDS: And he's usually from Rangoon.
TUCKER: A yogi is a man who takes a pin
 And casually sticks it through his
 skin—
 You'll always find his picture in—
BODYGUARDS: A "Believe It or Not" cartoon.
TUCKER: With him it's mind over matter.
 But I know one who lost his mind
 And became as mad as a hatter.

REFRAIN

There was a yogi who lost his willpower;
He met a dancing girl and fell in love.
He couldn't concentrate
Or lie on broken glass.
He could only sit and wait
For her to pass.
Unhappy yogi,
He tried forgetting,
But she was all that he was conscious of.
At night when he stretched out
Upon his bed of nails,
He could only dream about
Her seven veils.
CHORUS: His face grew flushed and florid—
TUCKER: Ev'ry time he heard her name.
CHORUS: And the ruby gleaming in her
 forehead—
TUCKER: Set his Oriental soul aflame.
 This poor old Yogi,
 He soon discovered
 She was the maharajah's turtle dove,
 And she was satisfied.
 She had an emerald ring,
 An elephant to ride—
CHORUS: And ev'rything.
TUCKER: He was a passing whim—
 That's how the story goes.
CHORUS: And what became of him?
TUCKER: Nobody knows.

LILLIAN
CORNELL: Ah!
CHORUS: As he stretched out upon his bed of
nails,
He could only dream about her seven
veils.
TUCKER: His face grew flushed and florid
Ev'ry time he heard her name;
And the ruby that gleamed on her
forehead
Set his Oriental heart aflame.
CHORUS: And so this yogi, this poor old yogi,
He soon discovered she belonged to the
maharajah.
TUCKER: She was so satisfied
She had an emerald ring—
CHORUS: She had a Sudan sedan to ride and
ev'rything;
She was a passing whim.
JERRY
COLONNA: [spoken] Ah, women!
CHORUS: That's how the story goes.
CORNELL: And just like old man Mose—
TUCKER: What became of him?
COLONNA: [spoken] What became of him?
Puzzling, isn't it?
[sung] Nobody knows—
CHORUS: What became of the yogi.
What became of the yogi,
Nobody knows!

GEE, I WISH I'D LISTENED TO MY MOTHER

Introduced and recorded by Orrin Tucker and His Orchestra (Columbia).

VERSE

Curses on the day I ran away from school.
What a dope,
What a fool!
Curses on the girl that I turned out to be,
My IQ's N.G.

REFRAIN

Gee, I wish I'd listened to my mother,
My sister,
My brother!
Gee, I'd like to think of what they've shown me
Before they disown me!
Mother told me everything

She ever knew;
She even told me
What a little kiss could do.
Gee, I wish I'd listened to my mother
Before I met you.

MY RESISTANCE IS LOW

Introduced by Bonnie Baker. Recorded by Orrin Tucker and His Orchestra (Columbia). There is a well-known later song (1951) by Hoagy Carmichael and Harold Adamson with the same title.

The song presented worries for Luigi Luraschi, Paramount's head of censorship. On September 28, 1940, he wrote to Joseph Breen, director of the Motion Picture Production Code Administration, "Will you please phone us as soon as possible regarding the enclosed lyrics . . . as Bonnie Baker is scheduled to record this song tomorrow?" Breen replied: "Lyric rejected as too suggestive."

You say you want to see me every night,
But every time you see me you wanna hold me
tight.
I ought to say no,
Ought to make you let me go,
Oh, but my resistance is low!

You say you love me truly,
But when you proceed to act so unruly,
I ought to say no,
Make you let me go,
But my resistance is low.

I used to dream of a true love,
Of raptures so sweet and divine;
Oh, but you brought me a kind of new love
And it's taken full possession of my mind!

I like to go to dances or a movie with you,
But you just wanna park the car and pitch a little
woo.
I ought to say no,
Make you let me go,
Oh, but my resistance is low!

My mother always tells me a kiss is all right;
But when it's dark and after twelve you turn out
the light.
I ought to say no,
Make you let me go;
My resistance is low.

My mother always tells me I can let you hold my
hand,
But holding hands is very dull when kisses are so
grand.
I ought to say no,
Make you let me go—
My resistance is low.

Revised lyrics

I once had no one to dream of,
No kisses, no love that was divine,
Oh, but you brought me a kind of new love
If the flutter in my heart is any sign!

I get the strangest feeling
Whenever I'm with you;
There's a look in your eye
I ought to criticize,
But it seems there's really nothing I can do.

P.S. I GOT THE JOB

Not used in film.

This lyric, like "My Resistance Is Low," caused concern in the offices of Joe Breen and Luigi Luraschi. A memo to Breen from Luraschi (September 16, 1940) states, "The line 'He wanted a kiss that was more than a kiss' has been changed to 'He wanted a kiss that was really a kiss.' Please advise if this substitution meets with your approval."

In a subsequent memo (December 27, 1940), a Mr. Arthur Houghton told Luraschi that he could not okay the following lines:

He wanted a thrill
That was really a thrill.
Did I sell a bill?
P.S. I got the job.

He wanted a sigh
That was more than a sigh.
Did I qualify?
Well, yessiree, Bob.
P.S. I got the job.
He wanted a date
That would keep him out late.
Did I hesitate?
Well, nosiree, Bob.
P.S. I got the job.
He was the type who was ripe
For a smile and a big baby stare;
I made my eyes twice their size
And I gave him that

"Tch, I declare!"
He wanted a kiss
That was more than a kiss.
Did I stop at this?
Well, nosiree, Bob.
P.S. I got the job.

HONOR BRIGHT

Not used in film. There are two versions of the refrain.

VERSE

Every Scout and Camp Fire Girl
Is taught in early youth,
If they speak at all,
To always speak the truth.
That's the way I've always been
Since I was in Troop A.
Since I'm on the square,
Believe me when I say—

REFRAIN

Honor bright,
By the moon above,
You're the one I love—
At least tonight.
Honor bright,
I can feel a thrill,
And I always will—
At least I might.
I'll be true forever
And forevermore—
That is, if forever
Means till three or four.
Honor bright,
By the stars that gleam,
You're my only dream—
At least tonight.

ALTERNATE REFRAIN

Honor bright,
By the moon above,
You're the one I love—
At least tonight.
Honor bright,
By the stars that gleam,
You're my only dream—
At least tonight.
On my reputation
As an Eagle Scout,
I won't ever leave you—

Till the tide goes out.
Honor bright,
By the moon above
You're the one I love—
At least tonight.

I'LL GET YOU IN THE END

Not used in film.
  Lyric missing.

IN A MOMENT OF SURRENDER

Not used in film.
  Lyric missing.

THIS IS THE NIGHT OF MY DREAMS

Not used in film.
  Lyric missing.

PEEKABOO TO YOU

Music by Mercer, Carl Sigman, and Joseph Meyer. Published. Copyrighted March 24, 1941. Previously registered for copyright as an unpublished song March 1, 1941.

VERSE

Is this the way to Main Street?
Or: Can you change a dime, please?
I don't know how to say it,
But have you the time, please?

REFRAIN

Peekaboo to you, you dreameroo,
Who ever let you out alone?
Peekaboo to you with all that woo-woo,
Walkin' in a danger zone.
Don't ya know that big bad wolves are out,
Prowlin' the neighborhood?
And you look mighty good,
Little Red Riding Hood.
Take a look at how they hold a powwow;
Take a listen to the sighs.
Take a look at me and you can see
I'm jealous with light green eyes.
Mom! Hand me my fowlin' piece,
I'll police those charms;
Then I'll say "Peekaboo to you"
In my arms.

NAVY BLUES (1941)

Produced by Hal B. Wallis, Jerry Wald, and Jack Saper for Warner Bros. Released September 1941. Copyright September 13, 1941. Directed by Lloyd Bacon. Screenplay by Jerry Wald, Richard Macaulay, Arthur T. Horman, and Sam Perrin, from a story by Arthur T. Horman. Music by Arthur Schwartz. Lyrics by Johnny Mercer. Musical numbers staged by Seymour Felix. Orchestrations by Ray Heindorf. Musical director: Leo F. Forbstein. Starring Ann Sheridan, Jack Oakie, Jack Haley, Martha Raye, with Herbert Anderson, Jack Carson, Jackie Gleason, William T. Orr, Richard Lane, John Ridgely, and the Navy Blues Sextette (Kay Aldridge, Georgia Carroll, Marguerite Chapman, Peggy Diggins, Leslie Brooks, and Claire James).

  Sailors get into hot water in Honolulu.

NAVY BLUES

Introduced by Ann Sheridan, Martha Raye, the Navy Blues Sextette (Kay Aldridge, Georgia Carroll, Marguerite Chapman, Peggy Diggins, Leslie Brooks, and Claire James, all dubbed by Trudy Erwin and the Music Maids), and ensemble; reprised by ensemble in the finale.

Film version

ANN
SHERIDAN: Ship ahoy there, ev'ry sailor boy
there—

My, but you're lookin' fine!
Army, Navy, or Marines—
If I had to choose,
You would find I'm inclined to
    be partial
To the guys called the Navy
    Blues.

MEN &
WOMEN: Here they come, those Navy
    Blues,
Faces all ashine!
Step aside for the pride of the
    Navy,
For the Navy that's yours and
    mine!
They're spick-and-span from
    stem to stern,
What a sight to see!
Every son of a gun in the Navy
Is a son of a gun for me!

SHERIDAN: Ship ahoy there, every sailor boy
    there—
My, but you're lookin' fine!

MEN &
WOMEN: Army, Navy or Marines—
If I had to choose,
You would find I'm inclined to
    be partial
To the guys called the Navy
    Blues.

MARTHA
RAYE: [spoken] Cigars! Cigarettes! Nuts!
[sung] Here they come, those
    Navy Blues—
That's where I came in.
Step aside for the bride of a sea
    wolf,
And his name isn't Errol Flynn!
Other girls at least get men:
I'm a hard-luck dame:
Mine's a drip
From the ship Mississippi
And a droop on the poop of
    same.
It's a struggle getting him to
    snuggle;
He's the old-fashioned kind.
From a half a million men that a
    girl could choose,
I elope with the dope of the
    Navy—
That's why I got the Navy blues.
I'll drop your anchor!
I've got the Navy blues.
I'm in dry dock!
I've got the Navy blues.
Ah, Heathcliff!

[RAYE sees SHERIDAN.]

Pipe the kiddie,
Venus in the middie,
Get a load o' those lines!

SHERIDAN: What's the difference who you
    are,
If you win or lose.
No romance has a chance with
    the Navy—

BOTH: That's why we've got the Navy
    blues.

SHERIDAN: They have a gal in every port—
RAYE: Who sits upon her davenport—
BOTH: While her lawyers all report
Another year of nonsupport!

1ST GIRL: They're home a week and gone
    for ten
To Devonshire or Duna.
So what if Uncle Sam needs
    men—

RAYE: What do we need—tuna?
2ND GIRL: Ev'ry time the fleet returns,
They've got new tattoo marks.
That's all right if when they
    leave—

SHERIDAN
& RAYE: We've got black-and-blue marks!
The Navy lies over the ocean—

SHERIDAN: The Navy lies over the sea.
RAYE: It's perpetual lack of emotion—
BOTH: And that's what's ruining me!
TWO GIRLS: Why should they make such a
    fuss
'Cause Dewey took Manila?
I'm sure that any one of us—
RAYE: Could take a whole flotilla!
THREE GIRLS: The admiral says the
    strangest things
To make them do his bidding.
"Man the lifeboats!" "Man the
    guns!"

SHERIDAN
& RAYE: What is he doing—kidding?
SHERIDAN, RAYE
& THREE GIRLS: Sailing, sailing over the
    bounding foam—
RAYE: That can't be my boy coming
    home?

SHERIDAN,
RAYE & MEN: Here they come, those Navy
    Blues,
Faces all ashine!
Step aside for the pride of the
    Navy,
For the Navy that's yours and
    mine!

They're spick-and-span from
    stem to stern,
What a sight to see!
Every son of a gun in the Navy
Is a son of a gun for me!
Ship ahoy there, every sailor boy
    there
My, but you're lookin' fine!
Army, Navy, or Marines—
If I had to choose,
You would find I'm inclined to
    be partial
To the guys called the Navy
    Blues!

Additional lyrics not used in film

Can it be there's something wrong
With the face I use?
It appeals to the heels in the Navy—
That's why I've got the Navy blues.
I need launching!
I've got the Navy Blues.
Drop your anchor!
I've got the Navy Blues.
I'm in dry dock!
I've got the Navy Blues.
Replace your divots!
I've got the Navy Blues.

They have a gal in every port,
But don't ever sell the ladies short.
Look at the gals they left behind
And this is what you find:
When they do reach the harbor, they're physical
    wrecks,
And though we agree that they're all in,
We're supposed to believe it's from scrubbing the
    decks
Or laying a little tarpaulin.
They may look well in the middies
And be swell on some destroyer,
But they're just little kiddies
When you get 'em in the foyer.

Heaven help the enemy,
He'd better keep his distance.
It requires ten o' me
To weaken his resistance!
He said, "Cuddle closer—
Oh, by the way, are you a minor?"
So, I answered, "No, sir"—
I thought he meant a forty-niner!

WHEN ARE WE GOING TO LAND ABROAD?

Introduced by Jack Haley, Jack Oakie, and male ensemble; reprised in finale by Oakie and Haley.

VERSE

JACK
HALEY: I'm walkin' down the street one day,
Admirin' the view,
When suddenly a poster makes me linger.
The poster's lookin' right at me
And saying "I Want You!"
It's Uncle Sammy pointin' with his finger.
Well, natur'lly, I'm goggle-eyed
And slightly droopy-jawed
At all the propositions that he makes me.

JACK
OAKIE: The meals are free, the pay is good,
With lots of time abroad.
HALEY: And that's the paragraph that really takes
me.

REFRAIN 1

BOTH: We've stood up on the poop
From Guadalajara to Guadeloupe,
But when are we gonna land abroad?
We've seen Japan and Hindustan,
They're really in existence.
Seen Peru and China, too,
But always from a distance.
Talk about your views
Of Venezuela and Vera Cruz—
We gotta admit they ain't no fraud.
HALEY: I meet all the residents.
OAKIE: Holler at ev'ry doll I see,
HALEY: That's to help the President's—
BOTH: Pan-American policy!
We think the world's a whiz,
But nevertheless the question is—
When are we gonna land abroad?

REFRAIN 2

We've helped the Navy go
From Montevideo to Mexico,
But when are we gonna land abroad?
HALEY: We've seen a sheik, a Mozambique,
An Arab and a Pygmy—
OAKIE: Maybe soon we'll visit
Goona-Goona, do you dig me?
HALEY: Our horizons lie
From Paramaribo to Paraguay.
BOTH: No wonder we're simply overawed,

There is such a lot we've seen—
Photographie from Paris, France.
We could tell you what we've seen,
Only we mustn't embarrass France.
We'll never shake the jinx,
We visited Egypt and its Sphinx—
When are we gonna land abroad?

Film montage

SAILORS: No longer will we go
From Boston to Burma to Borneo.
We're finally gonna land abroad.
It ain't no fun
To gaze upon a Zuni or a Zulu.
Glory be,
We're glad that we arrived in Honolulu.
We see-sawed on the sea
And finally landed in Waikiki.
The commodore always hemmed and
hawed
And so we seed and sawed.
If we're daffy-loco-nuts,
That's how it all has gotten us.
Just a glimpse of coconuts
Wouldn't be half as monotonous.
We wish to make it clear
To everyone in the fleet that we're
Finally gonna land abroad.

[*Sung to the tune of "Navy Blues."*]

Oh, here they come, those Navy Blues,
Faces all ashine.

[*Return to "Abroad."*]

Dizzy,
Daffy,
Loco,
Nuts,
No wonder we're off our coconuts!
We've heard Hawaii call
But nevertheless and after all,
When are we gonna land abroad?

Additional lyrics for finale

HALEY &
OAKIE: We've felt the salty spray
From British Honduras to Bantham Bay,
But when are we gonna land abroad?
We've seen the East,
We've seen the West,
The Earth is very big, folks,
Pretty, too,
Especially through
The windows of the brig, folks.
We think the world's a whiz,

But nevertheless the question is:
When are we gonna land abroad?

Additional lyrics not used in film

We've gazed upon the shore
Of Santa Maria and Salvador,
But when are we gonna land abroad?

IN WAIKIKI

Published. Copyrighted August 13, 1941. Introduced by Ann Sheridan, the Navy Blues Sextette (dubbed by Trudy Erwin and the Music Maids), and ensemble; reprised in finale by Martha Raye, the Navy Blues Sextette, and male ensemble.

Published version

VERSE

Gangway,
You folks on that steamer!
Gangway,
You folks on that train!
Gangway
For this city dreamer—
Take a look at my smile;
Take a listen
And I'll explain.

REFRAIN

When I get my summer vacation,
You can bet I'm going to be
Far away from civilization
In Waikiki.
Where the flowers grow in the forest,
And I might get stung by a bee,
But I won't get stung by the florist
In Waikiki.
Lying on a pillow
By a lazy sea,
You can have a date with a cutie
And be sure it's on the QT—
Walter Winchell's never on duty
In Waikiki.

Oh, the days are really seraphic,
And they pass angelically,
And there ain't no five o'clock traffic
In Waikiki,
Where those ukuleles
Play a tune for me.

While you city dwellers are tortured
By the lack of vitamin B,
I'll be picking mine from an orchard
In Waikiki.

Oh, it's not considered so shocking
If your skirt is over your knee,
And you can't get runs in your stocking
In Waikiki.
You won't meet some out-of-town buyer
Who insists on pitching spree,
So you're never under a dryer
In Waikiki.
Blue Hawaiian moonlight
Through a mango tree,
There's no baby carriage to hurdle,
And no supper dishes to see,
And we never put on a girdle
In Waikiki.

There's a view that's certain to thrill you
Where the mountains look at the sea
And the air's so fresh it'll kill you
In Waikiki.
Every shrub and bush in the garden,
Every single flower and tree,
Smells just like Elizabeth Arden
In Waikiki.
Clouds go by above you,
Driftin' lazily,
Steel guitars play tropical dream songs,
While the men sing rapturously.
And you don't hear BMI theme songs
In Waikiki.

You can make a comf'table living
From the things that you fish from the sea,
You can get a lot without giving
In Waikiki.
You can sit around and just stagnate
And collect a lot of debris
Or an old utilities magnate
In Waikiki.
Beach boys on a surfboard,
That's the type for me—
Be they butchers, bankers, or sailors,
They must be O.K. or N.G.
Without benefit of their tailors
In Waikiki.

Film version

GIRLS: When I get my summer vacation,
You can bet I'm going to be
Far away from civilization
In Waikiki.
Where the flowers grow in the forest,

And you might get stung by a bee,
But you won't get stung by the florist
In Waikiki.
Lying on a pillow
By a lazy sea,
You can have a date with a cutie
And be sure it's on the QT—
Walter Winchell's never on duty
In Waikiki.
Oh, it's not considered so shocking
If your skirt is over your knee,
And you can't get runs in your
    stocking
In Waikiki.
There's no baby carriage to hurdle
And no supper dishes to see,
And we never put on a girdle
In Waikiki.
Oh, blue Hawaiian moonlight
Shining through a mango tree.
While you city dwellers are tortured
By the lack of vitamin B,
We'll be picking ours from an orchard
In Waikiki.

ANN
SHERIDAN: There's a view that's certain to thrill
    you
Where the mountains look at the sea,
And the air's so fresh it'll kill you
In Waikiki.
Where I'm apt to see a flamingo
Underneath a coconut tree,
And there ain't no Monday-night
    bingo
In Waikiki.
Clouds go by above you
Drifting lazily.
Steel guitars play tropical dream songs
While the men sing rapturously,
And you don't hear radio theme songs
In Waikiki.
You can make a comf'table living
From the things you fish from the sea.
You can get a lot without giving
In Waikiki.
You can sit around and just stagnate,
And collect a lot of debris
Or an old utilities magnate
In Waikiki.
Tall and dark and handsome,
That's the type for me.
Be they butchers, bakers, or sailors
They must be O.K. or N.G.
Without benefit of their tailors
In Waikiki.

Additional lyrics for finale

MARTHA
RAYE: Well, I tried to get me a man there,
And I tried vociferously—
All I did was get me a tan there
In Waikiki.

GIRLS: Though the grass skirts never did wear
    well,
But they fit so glamorously,
That regretfully we say farewell
To Waikiki!

YOU'RE A NATURAL

Published. Copyrighted August 12, 1941. Introduced by Herbert Anderson and Ann Sheridan and reprised by them in finale.

Published version

VERSE

Like Don Budge with a racquet,
Like Joe Louis with a glove,
So are you when it comes to love.
Bette Davis is in movies,
Venus shining up above;
Like any tip-top star,
I'll tell you what you are.

REFRAIN

You're a natural—
You're a meadow of new-mown hay,
You're a whip-poor-will singin' to the moon.
You're a natural—
You're the end of a perfect day
And the murmur of a Sunday afternoon.
Doggone it,
You're as sweet as you seem!
And I'll tell you something too—
You're a little boy's dream come true.*
It's a miracle
And I'm thanking the stars that shine
You're a natural
And you're mine!
You're a natural—
You're a harvest moon in July,
You're as handsome and graceful as . . . a cow.
You're a natural—
You're a Plymouth Rock flyin' by,

* *Alternate line:*
    Back in school I thought of you.

You're a cantaloupe hangin' on a bough.
Doggone it,
Needn't tell me I'm wrong!
You're a silo full of corn,
You're a nightingale song at morn—
It's a miracle
And I'm thanking the stars that shine
You're a natural
And you're mine.

You're a natural—
You're the bark of a friendly dog,
You're a settin' hen, settin' on a nest.
You're a natural—
You're a champion Berkshire hog,
You're a seven-pound chicken, stuffed and
    dressed.
By jeepers,
You're a cute little pig,
Fat and young and full o' curves—
You're my grandmother's fig preserves!
It's a miracle
And I'm thanking the stars that shine
You're a natural
And you're mine.

STRIP POLKA

Music by Mercer. Published. Copyrighted August 11,
1942. Rejected by the film censor Joseph L. Breen, who
wrote Warner Bros. chief Jack L. Warner, "The entire
lyrics for 'The Strip Polka' are unacceptable because of
their low moral tone." Not used in film.

Introduced and recorded by Mercer (Capitol).
Number-one recording by Kay Kyser, with vocal by Jack
Martin (Columbia); other leading recordings by the An-
drews Sisters (Decca) and Alvino Rey, with vocal by the
Four King Sisters (Bluebird).

VERSE 1

There's a burlesque theaytre where the gang loves
    to go,
To see Queenie, the cutie of the burlesque show,
And the thrill of the evening is when out Queenie
    skips
And the band plays the polka while she strips!

REFRAIN 1

"Take it off, take it off!"
Cries a voice from the rear.
"Take it off, take it off!"

Soon it's all you can hear.
But she's always a lady,
Even in pantomime,
So she stops—
And always just in time!

VERSE 2

She's as fresh* and as wholesome as the flowers in
    May,
And she hopes to retire to the farm someday,
But you can't buy a farm until you're up in the
    chips,
So the band plays the polka while she strips!

REFRAIN 2

"Take it off, take it off!"
All the customers shout,
"Down in front, down in front!"
While the band beats it out.
But the State Board of Censors
Have declared it a crime,
So she stops—
And always just in time!

VERSE 3

Oh, she hates corny waltzes and she hates the
    gavotte,
And there's one big advantage if the music's
    hot—
It's a fast-moving exit just in case something r-r-
    rips,
So the band plays the polka while she strips!

REFRAIN 3

"Take it off, take it off!"
Cries the bald-headed gent
Down in front—"Atta girl!"—
It's a real compliment.
It's a buck's entertainment
For the price of a dime.
But she stops—
And always just in time!

REFRAIN 4

Drop around, take it in,
It's the best in the west—
"Down in front!" "Take it off!"
You can yell like the rest.
Take her out when it's over;

_____

* *Alternate wording:*
    She's as sweet . . .

She's a peach when she's dressed,
But she stops—
And always just in time!

Queenie, queen of them all,
Queenie, someday you'll fall,
Someday church bells will chime
In strip-polka Time!

It's the polka time,
Church bells will chime,
It's the Polka time!

TURN OUT THE LIGHTS (AND CALL THE LAW)

Breen objected to the line "He's in the groove and won't
withdraw" "because of its sex suggestiveness." Not used
in film.

VERSE

Long about 4 a.m.,
When Harlem cats are tall,
Even the best of them all
Suddenly are mighty small
When a certain cat comes lurkin' there-abouts,
'Cause they know there'll be a shambles and a
    rout.
So when he appears, in toto they all shout—

REFRAIN

Turn out the lights and call the law—
Here comes the man from Omaha!
He's in the groove and won't withdraw,
And the only way to stop his syncopation
Is eliminatin' all illumination!
Turn out the lights and call the man,
We got to stop him if we can—
He'll blow us over to Japan,
So get ready with the Edison and call the man!
He's as high
As a bird can fly;
Lights his big cigar
From the evenin' star.
Off he trots
To the brightest spots.
He's the killer of the kilowatts!
Turn out the lights and call the law—
Here comes the man from Omaha!
He's in the groove and won't withdraw—
Start protesting the Westinghouse and call the law!

HAWAIIAN PARTY

Music by Arthur Schwartz. Not used in film. Lyric missing.

BIRTH OF THE BLUES (1941)

Produced by B. G. DeSylva and Monta Bell for Paramount Pictures. Released November 1941. Copyright November 7, 1941. Directed by Victor Schertzinger. Screenplay by Harry Tugend and Walter DeLeon after a story by Tugend. Dances directed by Eddie Prinz. Dixieland arrangements by Joe Glover. Musical director: Robert Emmett Dolan. With Bing Crosby, Mary Martin, Brian Donlevy, Carolyn Lee, Eddie "Rochester" Anderson, J. Carrol Naish, Warren Hymer, Horace MacMahon, Ruby Elzy, Jack Teagarden, Danny Beck, Harry Barris, Perry Botkin, Minor Watson, Harry Rosenthal, Donald Kerr, Barbara Pepper, Cecil Kellaway, and Ronnie Cosbey. The songs for this film are by a wide variety of writers. "The Waiter and the Porter and the Upstairs Maid" has both music and lyrics by Johnny Mercer.

The plot involves the problems of a jazz band in New Orleans.

THE WAITER AND THE PORTER AND THE UPSTAIRS MAID

Music by Mercer. Published. Copyrighted August 18, 1941. Introduced by Bing Crosby, Jack Teagarden, Mary Martin, and band and recorded by them (Decca).

VERSE

BING
CROSBY: As your genial host,
May I offer a toast
To the wine-buying guest on my
    right.
[spoken] The best in the house for the
    old colonel.
[sung] May his bank account grow
Heavy laden with dough.
BAND: May he spend it in here every night,

Every night.
CROSBY: Seeing this night in its glory,
You people so loyal, so true,
Puts in mind of a story—
BAND: Tell us about it, pray do.

CROSBY: The people in the ballroom
Were stuffy and arty,
So I began to get
Just a little bit afraid.
I sneaked into the kitchen
And found me a party:
The waiter
JACK
TEAGARTEN: And the porter
MARY
MARTIN: And the second-story maid.
CROSBY: I peeked into the parlor
To see what was a-hatchin'
In time to hear the hostess
Suggest a charade.
MARTIN: And who was in the pantry
A-laughin' and scratchin'?
CROSBY: The waiter
TEAGARTEN: And the porter
MARTIN: And the upstairs maid.
TEAGARTEN: When they heard the music
That the orchestra played,
MARTIN: The waiter and the porter
Grabbed a hold of the maid,
CROSBY: Then they all proceeded
To go into a clog—
ALL: Hot diggety dog!
CROSBY: If ever I'm invited
To some fuddy duddy's,
I ain't gonna watch
Any harlequinade.
TEAGARTEN: You'll find him in the kitchen
Applaudin' his buddies,
CROSBY: The waiter
TEAGARTEN: And the porter
MARTIN: And the upstairs maid.

Pardon me, ma'am, you look just
    right,
Your hair's in place,
Your corset's tight.
TEAGARTEN: Pardon me, sir, there's lots of ice,
The fire is banked,
I fixed it twice.
CROSBY: Pardon me, folks, the roast is
    carved,
The wine is served,
You must be starved.
ALL: Pardon me, sir, may we be free—
The kitchen crowd is havin' a
    Jamboree.

MARTIN: I went and got a dishpan
To use as a cymbal.
CROSBY: The porter found a regular
Glass that he played.
TEAGARTEN: The fingers of the waiter
Were each in a thimble.
ALL: You should-a heard the music
That the combination made.

[Instrumental break.]

Marching' through the kitchen
To the pantry and back,
Man, you should-a seen us,
We were ballin' the jack.
Once a half an hour passed
Without any call—
Jack, we had a ball!
MARTIN: The waltzes and mazurkas,
We hate 'em, we spurn 'em.
TEAGARTEN: We got a lot of rhythms
We wanna hear played,
CROSBY: And we know where to go to
If we want to learn 'em:
ALL: The waiter
And the porter
And the upstairs maid.

Additional lyrics not used in film

TAG

It's pretty hard to cakewalk
Or tickle a toe to
The ordinary music you always hear played.
But if you wanna dance,
We advise you to go to
The waiter and the porter and the upstairs maid.

BLUES IN THE NIGHT (1941)

Produced by Hal B. Wallis and Henry Blanke for Warner Bros. Released November 1941. Copyright October 6, 1941. Directed by Anatole Litvak. Screenplay by Robert Rossen, based on the play *Hot Nocturne* by Edwin Gilbert. Music by Harold Arlen. Lyrics by Johnny Mercer. Orchestrations by Ray Heindorf. Musical direction: Leo F. Forbstein. With Priscilla Lane, Betty Field, Richard Whorf, Lloyd Nolan, Jack Carson, Wally Ford, Elia Kazan, Peter Whitney, Billy Halop, Howard Da Silva, Joyce Compton, Herbert Heywood, George Lloyd,

Charles Wilson, Matt McHugh, Jimmie Lunceford and His Band, and Will Osborne and His Band.

A traveling jazz band and its professional and emotional problems.

BLUES IN THE NIGHT

Published. Copyrighted September 18, 1941. Introduced by William Gillespie and small Negro group. Extensively recorded, by (among others) Jimmie Lunceford and His Orchestra, with vocal by Willie Smith (Decca); Artie Shaw and His Band (Victor); Dinah Shore (Bluebird); Cab Calloway and His Band, Dizzy Gillespie on trumpet (Okeh); and Benny Goodman and His Sextet (Okeh). Woody Herman and His Orchestra had a number-one recording (Decca). The song was nominated for an Academy Award as Best Song, but lost to Jerome Kern and Oscar Hammerstein II's "The Last Time I Saw Paris."

Mercer's peers truly appreciated the song's unique quality, though Mercer himself claimed, "to me it was just another Southern song."

Among their accolades:

Arthur Schwartz: "Probably the greatest blues song ever written—and that includes 'St. Louis Blues.' "

Robert Emmett Dolan: "I was in New York and Kern and Hammerstein's 'The Last Time I Saw Paris' had just won the Academy Award over 'Blues in the Night.' Oscar said to me, 'When you get back to Hollywood, tell Johnny he was robbed.' He was robbed of an Oscar by an Oscar."

Harold Arlen: "It was a jail sequence in the movie, and I wanted to write it as authentic as possible. It took a day and a half to write and I couldn't wait to get over to Johnny's house to play it for him. He's not much of a re-actor and so we fussed around with it for quite a while. I remember he had lots of phrases and lines written down but none of them seemed to fit the opening phrase right. But then I saw those words 'My mama done tol' me,' way down at the bottom of the pile and I said, 'Why don't we move them up to the top?' It sure worked." (In fact, Mercer's original opening line was "I'm heavy in my heart, I'm heavy in my heart.")

Arlen even suggested they change the song's title to "My Mama Done Tol' Me." Mercer disagreed, and they went to Irving Berlin for an opinion. Berlin said the song should remain "Blues in the Night"—and the title of the film was changed to match it.

Mercer's own mama, Miss Lillian, lived near Five Mile Bend, where the trains turned, and she always remembered the sad sound of their whistles ("A-whooee-duh-whooee"). "Trains are a marvelous symbol," Mercer noted. "Somebody's always coming in or leaving on one, so it's either sadness or happiness."

My mama done tol' me
When I was in knee pants [pigtails]*
My mama done tol' me—son [hon],
A woman'll [man's gonna] sweet-talk
And give ya the big eye,
But when the sweet talkin's done
A woman's [man is] a two-face,
A worrisome thing who'll leave ya t'sing
The blues in the night.

Now the rain's a-fallin',
Hear the train a-callin',
Whooee!
(My mama done tol' me.)
Hear that lonesome whistle
Blowin' 'cross the trestle,
Whooee!
(My mama done tol' me.)
A-whooee-duh-whooee,
Ol' clickety clack's
A-echoin' back
The blues in the night.

The evenin' breeze'll start
The trees to cryin'
And the moon'll hide its light
When you get the blues in the night.

Take my word, the mockingbird'll
Sing the saddest kind of song;
He knows things are wrong,
And he's right.

[*Whistle.*]

From Natchez to Mobile,
From Memphis to Saint Joe,
Wherever the four winds blow—
I been in some big towns
An' heard me some big talk,
But there is one thing I know:
A woman's [man is] a two-face
A worrisome thing
Who'll leave ya t'sing
The blues in the night.

[*Hum.*]

My mama was right,
There's blues in the night.

---

* *Alternate lyrics for female vocalist are given in brackets.*

HANG ON TO YOUR LIDS, KIDS (HERE WE GO AGAIN)

Published. Copyrighted September 18, 1941. Introduced by Priscilla Lane, Jack Carson, Richard Whorf, Billy Halop, Elia Kazan, and Peter Whitney.

VERSE

Cheer up, fellas,
Stop complaining—
Your umbrella's dry!
Snow ain't snowing,
Rain ain't raining,
Clouds are going by.
One more word
And I'll punch you in the eye.

REFRAIN 1

Hi-diddle-dee-dum-dum-dum,
So what if we're busted, chum?
Hang on to your lids, kids,
Here we go again.

So what if we're on the cuff
And fresh outa things and stuff?
Hang on to your lids, kids,
Here we go again.

Hi-diddle-dee-dum-dum-dum,
My, but it's adventuresome!
Hang on to your lids, kids,
Here we go again.

Why say
That we're on the ropes?
I say
"Hang on to your hopes, dopes!"

So what if we're in a spin?
That's really where we came in,
We're livin' and that ain't tin.
Hang on to your lids, kids,
Here we go again.

REFRAIN 2

Hi-diddle-dee-dum-dum-dum,
So what if we're on the thumb?
Hang on to your lids, kids,
Here we go again.

Move over there,
Here we come.

Hang on to your cappies, chappies,
Here we go again.

Hi-diddle-dee-dum-dum-dum,
My, but it's adventuresome!
Hang on to your hats, cats,
Here we go again.

We're not
Gonna ditch the law.
Fear not—
"Hang on to your straw, Ma!"

Around and around we go.
So what if we got no dough?
Hang on to your old chapeau.
Here we go again, men,
Here we go again.

So maybe we got no moo—
Some cows are the same way too.
Hang on to your tops, Pops,
Here we go again.

Why cry
When we hit the curb?
We cry,
"Hang on to your turb, purr baby!"

Ben Franklin said it all.
"Divided, we gotta fall—
United, we'll have a ball!"
Hang on to your lids, kids,
Here we go again.

THIS TIME THE DREAM'S ON ME

Published. Copyrighted September 18, 1941. Introduced by Priscilla Lane. Reprised by Betty Field (dubbed by Trudy Erwin). Leading recordings by Woody Herman (Decca) and Glenn Miller, with vocal by Ray Eberle (Bluebird).

Mercer said of the song: "It's one of Harold's nicest tunes. It's kind of a poor lyric, I think. Built on the thing about 'the drink's on me.' I think it's too flip for that melody. I think it should be nicer. I was in a hurry . . . I remember the director didn't like it . . . I could have improved it, I really could. I wish I had. But, you know, we had a lot of songs to get out in a short amount of time, and we had another picture to do."

Somewhere, someday
We'll be close together,
Wait and see.
Oh, by the way,
This time the dream's on me.
You'll take my hand
And you'll look at me
Adoringly,
But as things stand,
This time the dream's on me.
It would be fun
To be certain that I'm the one,
To know that I at least supply
The shoulder you cry upon,
To see you through
Till you're everything you want to be.
It can't be true, but
This time the dream's on me.

WAIT TILL IT HAPPENS TO YOU

Introduced by Betty Field (dubbed by Trudy Erwin).

REFRAIN

You can tell me love's a phony,
A lotta baloney,
But wait'll it happens to you.
You can tell me I'm a dilly
Who's just bein' silly,
But wait'll it happens to you.
You can give me good advice
About payin' the price
And I'd better forget it, you say.
You're talkin' through your hat;
How d'ya get that way?
You can laugh at me
For singin' those
"If I Can't Have Him, Then I Don't Want
    Anyone" blues.
You can laugh and say
That love'll never knock you
For that well-known twister,
Say I'm a big weak sister—
But, mister,
Wait until it happens to you.

SAYS WHO? SAYS YOU, SAYS I!

Published. Copyrighted September 18, 1941. Introduced by Mabel Todd, male quartet, and Will Osborne and His Band.

VERSE

There must be brownies
And there must be pixies
And there must be goblins
Beyond the beyond.
I never thought they'd respond
But someone certainly waved a wand.

REFRAIN

'Tis spring today and love is on the way.
Says who? Says you, says I!
'Tis spring and skies are full of butterflies.
Says who? Says you, says I!
That daisy crew is breaking through,
They're making quite a try;
They're hoping to
Get a gander at you, says I!
'Twas gray, 'twas cold,
But now as I behold,
The trees all wear bouquets,
And way up high
The moon's an apple pie,
The clouds are egg frappés.
Within this dream of cake and cream,
Just who is the lucky guy*
'Tis me, says you—
'Tis gotta come true,
Says I!

MANDY IS TWO

Music by Fulton McGrath. Published. Copyrighted January 23, 1942. Previously registered for copyright as an unpublished song June 4, 1941. Leading recordings by Bing Crosby (Decca) and Guy Lombardo, with vocal by Kenny Gardner (Decca).

* *Alternate line:*
    Just who is the Lorelei?

In 1939 Johnny and Ginger Mercer adopted a little girl they called Georgia Amanda. On May 12, 1941, Mandy turned two—and if that wasn't enough to bring on a song from a fond father . . .

VERSE

Look at the ribbon and look at the curl,
Look at the pinafore.
Here's to the beautiful birthday girl—
May she have many more!

REFRAIN

Mandy is two.
You ought to see her eyes of cornflower blue—
They really look as if they actually knew
That she's a big girl now.

Mandy is two.
You ought to see how many things she can do:
She knows her alphabet and ties her own shoe,
And no one showed her how.

If you could see Her Majesty
With braids in her hair,
Almost as though her Sunday beau
Came around and brought her
An orchid to wear!

Mommy is blue
Because her little girl is going on three;
But Miss Amanda's just as proud as can be
That she's a big girl now.

MANDY IS THREE

A year later Mercer wrote new words to the same music.

Mandy is three.
She isn't half the child we thought she would be.
She doesn't take after her mommy or me
And she's a big girl now.

Mandy is three,
You oughta see how really square she can be.
She knows her alphabet but just up to C—*
She simply "don't know how."

If you could see Her Majesty
With braids in her hair,
She looks as though her Sunday beau
Came and got a gander
And gave her the air!

Mommy is sore
Because her little girl is going on four
But can't do anything at all anymore,
And she's a big girl now.

SKYLARK

Music by Hoagy Carmichael. Published. Copyrighted February 10, 1942. Previously registered for copyright as an unpublished song November 15, 1941. Leading recordings by Dinah Shore, accompanied by Rosario Bourdon's Orchestra (Bluebird); Glenn Miller and His Orchestra, vocal by Ray Eberle (Victor); Harry James and His Orchestra, vocal by Helen Forrest (Columbia); and Bing Crosby (Decca). The greatest of Mercer's "bird" songs, "Skylark" stayed on radio's *Your Hit Parade* for nearly three months.

Hoagy Carmichael had written an instrumental he called "Bix Licks," after his friend the jazz cornetist Bix Beiderbecke. It was intended for a musical that was never produced. Later he played the tune for Mercer: "I didn't hear from him for six months. He's the original 'Don't call me, I'll call you' guy." By the time the lyric was finished, Carmichael had forgotten the melody, so Mercer sang it to him over the phone. "Quite some kick to sit back comfy like that at the telephone and listen."

No mean lyricist himself, Carmichael jotted down some ideas of his own on a worksheet and passed them on to Mercer:

> Skylark,
> Have you anything to say to me?
> Is it all the way it used to be?
> Over the meadow where we kissed
> Does there remain a golden mist?
> And later . . .
> And in your lonely flight
> Haven't you heard the music of the night?
> (Haven't you heard it?)
> (Wonderful music)
> Soft as a lullaby, crazy as a loon,
> Sad as a gypsy serenading the moon . . .

Whether he was playing with something Mercer had started, or vice versa, we probably shall never know.

Skylark,
Have you anything to say to me?
Won't you tell me where my love can be?
Is there a meadow in the mist
Where someone's waiting to be kissed?
Skylark,
Have you seen a valley green with spring
Where my heart can go a-journeying
Over the shadows and the rain
To a blossom-covered lane?
And in your lonely flight,
Haven't you heard the music in the night?
Wonderful music,
Faint as a will-o'-the-wisp,
Crazy as a loon,
Sad as a Gypsy serenading the moon!
Oh Skylark,
I don't know if you can find these things,
But my heart is riding on your wings,
So, if you see them anywhere,
Won't you lead me there?

---

* *Alternate line:*
   Her mental processes are something to see—

OVERLEAF
Left: You Were Never Lovelier: *Rita Hayworth and Fred Astaire dancing to "I'm Old-Fashioned"*
Top right: The Fleet's In: *from left, Dorothy Lamour, William Holden, Betty Hutton, and Eddie Bracken*
Bottom right: Star Spangled Rhythm: *"A Sweater, a Sarong, and a Peek-a-boo Bang," Paulette Goddard, Dorothy Lamour, and Veronica Lake*

THE FLEET'S IN,
YOU WERE NEVER LOVELIER,
STAR SPANGLED RHYTHM,
and Other Songs of 1942

ALL THROUGH THE NIGHT (1942)

Produced by Hal Wallis and Jerry Wald for Warner Bros. Released January 1942. Copyright January 10, 1942. Directed by Vincent Sherman. Screenplay by Leonard Spigelgass and Edwin Gilbert, from a story by Leo Rosten (as Leonard Q. Ross) and Spigelgass. Music by Arthur Schwartz. Lyrics by Johnny Mercer. Musical director: Leo F. Forbstein. Starring Humphrey Bogart, Conrad Veidt, and Kaaren Verne, with Jane Darwell, Frank McHugh, Peter Lorre, Judith Anderson, William Demarest, Jackie Gleason, Phil Silvers, Wally Ford, Barton MacLane, Edward Brophy, Martin Kosleck, Jean Ames, Ludwig Stossel, Irene Seidner, James Burke, Ben Welden, Hans Schumm, Charles Cane, Frank Sully, and Sam McDaniel.

Gangsters act like patriotic Americans to detect Nazi spies in World War II New York.

ALL THROUGH THE NIGHT

Published. Copyrighted December 19, 1941. Introduced by Kaaren Verne (dubbed by Vera Van).

VERSE

When the sun has sunk beneath the willows,
When a star or two tells me another day is
    through,
Here's a dream that waits upon my pillow,
So I live through the day
Knowing you'll come my way.

REFRAIN

All through the night you are mine,
Deep in star-spangled dream you are mine.
All through the dream violins sing to me,
And all through the song I feel you cling to me.
Though all through the day I'm alone,
I know that twilight will make you my own.
Who cares if dreams never do come true?
I share them all through the night with you.

CAPTAINS OF THE CLOUDS (1942)

Produced by Hal B. Wallis and William Cagney for Warner Bros. Released February 1942. Copyright January 21, 1942. Directed by Michael Curtiz. Screenplay by Arthur T. Horman, Richard Macaulay, and Norman Reilly Raine, from a story by Horman and Roland Gillett. Lyrics by Johnny Mercer. Music by Harold Arlen. Musical score by Max Steiner. Musical director: Leo F. Forbstein. Starring James Cagney, with Dennis Morgan, Brenda Marshall, Alan Hale, George Tobias, Reginald Gardiner, Air Marshal W. A. Bishop, Reginald Denny, Russell Arms, Paul Cavanagh, Clem Bevans, J. M. Kerrigan, J. Farrell MacDonald, Patrick O'Moore, Morton Lowry, Squadron Leader Owen Cathcart-Jones, Frederick Worlock, Roland Drew, Lucia Carroll, George Meeker, Benny Baker, Hardie Albright, Ray Walker, Charles Halton, Louis Jean Heydt, Byron Barr, Michael Ames, Willie Fung, and Carl Harbord.

A wisecracking Canadian pilot proves himself when the bullets start flying.

CAPTAINS OF THE CLOUDS

Published. Copyrighted January 14, 1942. Introduced by male chorus and danced by female ensemble.

Mercer had his doubts about this one, but "we played it for some Canadians and they liked it"—so much so, in fact, that the Royal Canadian Air Force adopted it as a march and made it their official song during World War II.

VERSE

On with your helmets,
On with your motors,
Tune 'em up and let 'em sing,
Take 'em off and let 'em swing high,
Painting a V across the sky,
A V for a victory by and by!

REFRAIN

You're off for the big show tonight;
So fly 'em wing to wing.
You're angels of hell and you fight
For country and for king.
You're Captains of the Clouds—
Let 'er roll,

You're on your way.
Hit the sky again,
Fly again,
Try again,
Till the flag's on high again,
Captains of the Clouds!

Original refrain

We fly with the angels tonight;
You'll find us wing to wing.
We're angels of hell and we fight
For country and for king.
We're Captains of the Clouds—
Let 'er roll,
We're on our way.
Hit the sky again,
Fly again,
Try again,
Till the flag's on high again,
Captains of the Clouds.

THE FLEET'S IN (1942)

Produced by B. G. DeSylva and Paul Jones for Paramount Pictures. Released March 1942. Copyright April 7, 1942. Directed by Victor Schertzinger. Screenplay by Walter DeLeon, Sid Silvers, and Ralph Spence, based on the 1928 Paramount screenplay by Monte Brice and J. Walter Ruben and the 1933 play *Sailor, Beware!* by Kenyon Nicholson and Charles Robinson. Lyrics by Johnny Mercer. Music by Victor Schertzinger. Dances staged by Jack Donohue. Musical director: Victor Young. With Dorothy Lamour, William Holden, Eddie Bracken, Betty Hutton, Leif Erickson, Betty Jane Rhodes, Barbara Britton, Cass Daley, Gil Lamb, Jack Norton, Roy Atwell, Robert Warwick, Lorraine and Rognan, and Jimmy Dorsey and His Orchestra, with Bob Eberly and Helen O'Connell.

A sailor on leave takes on a bet that he can kiss the glamorous singer in a ritzy nightclub.

THE FLEET'S IN

Published January 28, 1942. Introduced by Betty Jane Rhodes; reprised by Eddie Bracken and male chorus.

Hey there, mister,
You'd better hide your sister,
'Cause the fleet's in,
The fleet's in!

Hey there, mister,
Don't say nobody's kissed her,
'Cause the fleet's in,
The fleet's in!

If they do as well on the sea
As they do on the shore,
Hey there, Congress!
You can tax us some more!
And charge it to production.
Get me, I'm always kiddin'.

Hey there, rookie,
You'd better call your cookie
And your sweets in—
The fleet's in!
They'll take anything*
If it isn't nailed down.
She may be dark or fair,
But sailors don't care
As long as she's wearing a gown.
So if you love her,
Keep under cover—
The fleet's in town!

TANGERINE

Published. Copyrighted January 28, 1942. Introduced by Bob Eberly, Helen O'Connell, and Jimmy Dorsey and His Orchestra, who also made a number-one-selling recording (Decca). Aother leading recording was made by Vaughn Monroe (Bluebird). In 1976 a disco version by the Salsoul Orchestra (Salsoul) enjoyed popularity.

VERSE

South American stories
Tell of a girl who's quite a dream,

––––––––
* *Alternative of last eight lines:*
    They'll take anything
    That is wearing a gown.
    So, sister, I suggest
    Have everything pressed,
    Get dressed in your best hand-me-down,
    Tonight we show off,
    'Cause it's the blow-off—
    The fleet's in town!

The beauty of her race.
Though you doubt all the stories
And think the tales are just a bit extreme,
Wait till you see her face.

REFRAIN

Tangerine,
She is all they claim,
With her eyes of night
And lips as bright as flame.
Tangerine,
When she dances by,
Señoritas stare
And caballeros sigh.
And I've seen
Toasts to Tangerine*
Raised in every bar†
Across the Argentine.
Yes, she has them all on the run,
But her heart belongs to just one—
Her heart belongs to
Tangerine.

REFRAIN 2

Tangerine,
She is all they say,
With mascaraed eye
And chapeau by Daché.
Tangerine
With her lips of flame—
If the color keeps
Louis Philippe's to blame.
And I've seen
Clothes on Tangerine
Where the label says,
"From Macy's Mezzanine."
Yes, she's got the guys in a whirl,
But she's only fooling one girl—
She's only fooling
Tangerine.

––––––––
* *In the film the three lines "Toasts . . . Argentine"
  were replaced by:*
    Times when Tangerine
    Had the bourgeoisie
    Believing she was queen.
† *Another alternate line:*
    Drunk in every bar

WHEN YOU HEAR THE TIME SIGNAL

Published. Copyrighted January 28, 1942. Introduced by Dorothy Lamour and Jimmy Dorsey and His Orchestra.

VERSE

BAND: Operator, operator, whadda you say,
       Can we get a little information today?
       If you're on the Erie,
       And you're hep to [diggin'] the jive,*
       Tell the leader gentleman we wanna take
         five!
       Quick, before our nickel changes into a
         dime—
       Operator, operator, what is the time?

REFRAIN

DOROTHY
LAMOUR: When you hear the time signal, the
         time will be
       Time to fall in love with me.
       Hear those bells ring merrily,
       "I love you."
       When you hear the time signal the tone
         will say,
       "Time's a-wastin' ev'ry day,
       One more minute's slipped away."
       That won't do.
       I can hear bells in my sleep,
       Bells when I look at a menu.
       Ev'ry engagement I keep
       The clock goes a-tickety-tock, a-tickety-
         tock.
       When you hear the time signal the time
         will be
       Time to end my misery.
       Come on, baby, follow me—
       I love you.

Additional lyrics for refrain

I know that I'm really in deep,
'Cause now I attend every fire,
And then when I do get to sleep,
The clock goes a-brring.
But my one desire is to hear the chimes
Ring out those weddin' rhymes.
What a day for you and me
When they ring out that killer-diller!
Baby, we'll go and buy a raft,

––––––––
* *Alternate phrase:*
    And you're diggin' the jive

Just forget that heavy craft;
Tell your captain that you've been drafted.
Come on, baby, follow me!
I love you,
I love you.

IF YOU BUILD A BETTER MOUSETRAP

Published. Copyrighted January 28, 1942. Introduced by Betty Hutton and Jimmy Dorsey and His Orchestra. Reprised by Bob Eberly, Helen O'Connell, and Jimmy Dorsey and His Orchestra. Leading recording by Dorsey and His Orchestra, with vocals by Eberly and O'Connell (Decca).

VERSE

Back in your chairs,
You unfortunate squares,
While a lady
Tries to sell her wares!

REFRAIN 1

If you build a better mousetrap,
Bake a better bun,
Mix a better toddy,
You'll have everybody
Comin' on the run.
If you wash a better window,
Sweep a better floor,
Climb a higher steeple,
You'll have all the people
Knockin' at your door.
That's the way to be successful,
So I'm gettin' wise.
I'm kissin' better kisses,
Sayin' sweeter nothin's,
Lyin' bigger lies,
And I'm squeezin' better squeezes,
Teasin' better teases,
Ev'rything pleases,
But gee!
Why doesn't anything happen
To me?

REFRAIN 2

If you build a better mousetrap,
Crank a better crank,
Make a better matzoh,
You'll be puttin' lots o'
Money in the bank.

If you dig a deeper oil well,
Stake a richer claim,
Pick a lot of winners,
You'll be havin' dinners
Given in your name.
That's the way to be successful,
So I'm gettin' hep,
I'm snugglin' better snuggles,
Strugglin' better struggles,
Gettin' quite a rep.
And I'm cooin' better cooin',
Doin' better wooin',
Goin' to ruin,
But gee!
Why doesn't anything happen
To me?

Film reprise (for Eberly and O'Connell)

BOB
EBERLY: If you build a better mousetrap,
Grin a better grin,
Roll a better eye, too,
All the boys'll try to
Chuck you neath the chin.

HELEN
O'CONNELL: If you make a better moon face
When you're with the chicks,
Whisp a better whisper,
How you gonna miss persuading five
or six?

BOTH: That's the way to be successful,
So we're gettin' wise.
We're kissin' better kisses—

O'CONNELL: Sayin' sweeter nothin's—

EBERLY: Lyin' bigger lies.

BOTH: And we're squeezin' better
squeezes,
Teasin' better teases,
Positively amorous!

O'CONNELL: Why doesn't anything ever occur?

EBERLY: Why can't I make an impression on
her?

BOTH: Why doesn't anything happen to us?

NOT MINE

Published. Copyrighted January 28, 1942. Introduced by Dorothy Lamour, Betty Hutton, Eddie Bracken, Bob Eberly, and Jimmy Dorsey and His Orchestra. Leading recording by Dorsey and His Orchestra, with vocals by Bob Eberly and Helen O'Connell (Decca). Alternate title: "Somebody Else's Moon (Not Mine)."

VERSE

Harvest moons may come and harvest moons may
go;
Stars may light your heaven with a silver glow.
But as for me,
I'd sooner see a show.

REFRAIN 1

DOROTHY
LAMOUR: It's somebody else's moon above,
Not mine.
It's somebody else's night for love,
Not mine.
A heart to someone else
Is a thing that melts;
To me it's just a comic valentine.
Let somebody else's tears be shed,
Not mine.
Let somebody else's nose get red,
Not mine.
I like playing solitaire,
But until I draw a pair,
It's somebody else's moon up there,
Not mine.

REFRAIN 2

BETTY
HUTTON: It's somebody else's moon above,
Not mine.
It's somebody else's night for love,
Not mine.

EDDIE
BRACKEN: A lady should resist,
When at first she's kissed

or

HUTTON: I know I should resist
When at first I'm kissed.

HUTTON: Oh, gee, I never get the chances to
decline.
There's somebody else's bitter tears,
Not mine,
That fall into someone else's beers.
Not mine!!
I can't even get a beau.

BRACKEN: Why not hire Romeo?

HUTTON: He'd wind up with someone else's
dough,
Not mine.

Alternative lyrics

HUTTON: I can't even land a clerk
Or a guy who is out of work.
But if you should see me with some jerk
He's mine.

REFRAIN 3

HUTTON: They're somebody else's eyes of blue,
Not mine.
They're somebody else's muscles, too,
Not mine.

BRACKEN: The kind of girl I seek
Should be warm and weak,
But, baby, you overdo the clinging
vine!

HUTTON: You're somebody else's game of tag,
Not mine.

BRACKEN: And somebody else's punching bag,
Not mine.

HUTTON: Some girls miss a wedding cake
Just because of an old mistake.
That's somebody else's lucky break,
Not mine.
Though I've found a man or two,
It's the same story when I'm through.
The body is someone else's, too,
Not mine.

I REMEMBER YOU

Published. Copyrighted January 28, 1942. Introduced by
Dorothy Lamour, Bob Eberly, Helen O'Connell, and
Jimmy Dorsey and His Orchestra. Reprise danced by
Lorraine and Rognan accompanied by Dorsey and His
Orchestra. Leading recordings by Eberly with Dorsey
and His Orchestra (Decca) and by Harry James and His
Orchestra, with vocal by Helen Forrest (Columbia). Im-
portant later recordings were made by, among others, the
George Shearing Trio (MGM) and Frank Ifield (Vee-Jay).

Mercer always claimed that he wrote the song "very
fast, ten minutes, half an hour at the most."

VERSE

Was it in Tahiti?
Were we on the Nile?
Long, long ago,
Say an hour [a year]or so,
I recall that I saw
Your smile.

REFRAIN

I remember you—
You're the one
Who made my dreams come true
A few kisses ago.
I remember you—
You're the one

Who said, "I love you, too,
I do,
Didn't you know?"
I remember, too, a distant bell
And stars that fell
Like rain out of the blue.
When my life is through
And the angels ask me
To recall
The thrill of them all,
Then I shall tell them
I remember you.

ARTHUR MURRAY TAUGHT ME DANCING IN A HURRY

Published. Copyrighted January 28, 1942. Introduced
by Betty Hutton and Jimmy Dorsey and His Orchestra.
Recorded by Helen O'Connell with Dorsey and His Orchestra (Decca) and by the King Sisters (Bluebird).

Film version

VERSE

Life was so peaceful at the laundry,*
Life was so calm and serene,
Life was très gay
Till that unlucky day
I happened to read that magazine.
Why did I read that advertisement
Where it said,
"Since I rumba, Jim thinks I'm sublime"?
Why oh why
Did I ever try?
I didn't have the talent,
I didn't have the money,
And teacher did not have the time!

REFRAIN

Arthur Murray
Taught me dancing
In a hurry;
I had a week to spare.
He showed me the groundwork.
The walk-around work,
And told me to take it from there.
Arthur Murray
Then advised me

_____
* Alternate wording (published):
  . . . at the drive-in,

Not to worry;
It would come out all right.
To my way of thinkin',
It came out stinkin'—
I don't know my left from my right.
The people around me can all sing
"A-one and a-two and a-three";
But any resemblance to waltzing
Is just coincidental with me.
'Cause Arthur Murray
Taught me dancing
In a hurry,
And so I take a chance.
To me it resembles
The nine-day trembles,
But he guarantees it's a dance.

Later version

REFRAIN 1

[Same as in film version except for final three lines.]

You've heard of Pavlova,
Well, Jack, move ovah!
Make way for the Queen of the Dance!

REFRAIN 2

My tango resembles a two-step;
My rumba makes people turn pale;
My conga goes into a goose step
Till the FBI is doggin' my trail.
'Cause Arthur Murray
Taught me dancing
In a hurry—
Maybe the stars were wrong,
If I ain't a menace
To Ruth St. Denis,
I'll do until one comes along!

TAG

Turkey trot or gavotte,
Don't know which,
Don't know what,
Jitterbug, bunny hug,
Long as you cut a rug,
Walk the dog, do a clog,
Lindy-hop till you drop,
Ball-the-jack,
Back to back,
Cheek to cheek,
Till you're weak!
You've heard of Pavlova,
Well, Jack, move ovah—
Make way for the Queen of the Dance!

TOMORROW YOU BELONG TO UNCLE SAMMY

Published. Copyrighted October 22, 1942, under the title "Uncle Sammy." Introduced by Cass Daley and Jimmy Dorsey and His Orchestra. Alternate title: "Uncle Sammy."

REFRAIN 1

Oh, tomorrow you belong to Uncle Sammy,
But tonight you belong to me.
You may never get your chevrons walkin' me in
    the park,
But I can guarantee you'll get a black-and-blue mark.
Even though the Navy is your alma mammy,
Mammy's turning you over to me.
The commodore appointed me to save a few lives;
He says a guy who has a date with me and survives
Is a cinch to have a picnic when the blackout
    arrives—
So tonight you belong to me.

MEDLEY

I was home on the range
And in need of a change,
For there weren't any men out my way;
And I'm tellin' you, pal,
It's no fun for a gal
Where the deer and the antelope play.
Then he came from out of nowhere—
He was the yardbird of Company B—
And he said, "Please,
Won't you put a fella at ease?
I'm one of those lonesome draftees,
And I'd like a date with you—
We might enjoy a pop or two
At some secluded rendezvous."
But I said, "Nothin' doin', *mon chérie*,
It's gotta be a cocktail or two."
That's how we spent an hour or two—
And then his girlfriend came into view.
With a twist of the wrist
She hit me with her fist,
And in her fist was a bottle of
Ice-cold cola—*
It knocked out every molar.
I had a sweet little headache,
But she wasn't through with me,
'Cause she started reaching
For all the silverware.
She threw it all without a compromise.
I tried to see the nearest exit,

---
* *Or:* Pepsi-Cola—

But a spoon got in my eye.
My eye was all red;
My complexion was white;
All blue was my anatomy.
I shouted "I am an American!"
That's the Broadway melody.

REFRAIN 2

Oh, tomorrow you belong to Uncle Sammy,
But today you belong to me.
You can put your plans of national defense on the
    shelf
And figure out a personal defense for yourself.
They may need you on the S.S. *Alabammy*,
But that ain't where you're gonna be.
In any grave emergency, when worst comes to
    worst,
Somebody always hollers, "Save the womenfolk
    first!"
What the heck's the use of savin' us? Let's get it
    rehearsed!
Oh, tonight you belong to me.

REFRAIN 2 (ALTERNATIVE)

Oh, tomorrow you belong to Uncle Sammy,
But tonight you belong to me.
You can save your country's honor when the bugle
    has blown,
But for the next few hours you'll be savin' your own.
They may need you on the S.S. *Alabammy*
But that ain't where you're gonna be.
I'll show you some maneuvers but they won't be a
    sham,
Instruct you in the tactics of the battering ram,
And tomorrow they can wheel you back to your
    uncle Sam—
But tonight you belong to me.

ON THE FRIENDLY SIDE

Not used in film.

On the friendly side,
Perhaps we ought to keep it
On the friendly side,
For it's easy to see
What happens to me with you.
I get starry-eyed,
I feel a million little wheels
Go round inside,
And before I can count up to ten,

I'm a dead pigeon again.
So I'm sure that I'd be better off
If it were on the friendly side.
It's so friendly like this—
A casual kiss or two,
That's all I need to start a stampede;
So maybe we'd better
Keep it on the friendly side.

I'M COOKING WITH GAS

Not used in film.
    Lyric missing.

YOU WERE NEVER LOVELIER (1942)

Produced by Louis F. Edelman for Columbia Pictures. Released December 1942. Copyright October 19, 1942. Directed by William Seiter. Screenplay by Michael Fessier, Ernest Pagano, and Delmer Daves, based on the film *Los Martes Orquídeas* by Carlos Olivari and Sixto Póndal Ríos. Music by Jerome Kern. Lyrics by Johnny Mercer. Dances directed by Val Raset. Orchestrations by Conrad Salinger and Lyle "Spud" Murphy. Musical director: Leigh Harline. Starring Fred Astaire and Rita Hayworth, with Adolphe Menjou, Isobel Elsom, Leslie Brooks, Adele Mara, Gus Schilling, Barbara Brown, Douglas Leavitt, and Xavier Cugat and His Orchestra.

A South American hotel tycoon has three daughters; according to tradition, the two younger girls can marry their boyfriends only if their older sister marries first. The tycoon tries to interest her in a phantom admirer . . . but then Fred Astaire comes along.

The film was a follow-up to the successful pairing of Astaire and Hayworth in the previous year's *You'll Never Get Rich* (songs by Cole Porter).

DEARLY BELOVED

Published. Copyrighted July 6, 1942. Introduced by Fred Astaire with Xavier Cugat and His Orchestra; reprised by Rita Hayworth (dubbed by Nan Wynn). Recorded by Fred Astaire (Decca); Xavier Cugat and His Orchestra (Columbia); Dinah Shore, accompanied by Paul Weston's Orchestra (Victor); Alvino Rey and His Orchestra (Bluebird); and Glenn Miller and His Orchestra, vocal by Skip Nelson (Victor). The song was nominated for an Academy Award but lost to Irving Berlin's "White Christmas."

VERSE

Tell me that it's true,
Tell me you agree:
I was meant for you,
You were meant for me.

REFRAIN

Dearly beloved,
How clearly I see,
Somewhere in heaven
You were fashioned for me.
Angel eyes knew you,
Angel voices led me to you.
Nothing could save me;
Fate gave me a sign;
I know that I'll be yours
Come shower or shine.
So I say merely,
Dearly beloved, be mine.

TAG

You were meant for me,
I was meant for you.
Tell me you agree,
Tell me that it's true.

Alternative lyrics for refrain

Dearly beloved,
Sincerely I say
Life would be emptiness
If you went away.
So I say merely,
Dearly beloved, please stay,
Stay, stay.

WEDDING IN THE SPRING

Published. Copyrighted September 1, 1942. Previously registered for copyright as an unpublished song April 13, 1942. Introduced by Leslie Brooks and Adele Mara. Reprised by Lina Romay and chorus with Xavier Cugat and His Orchestra and danced by Rita Hayworth, Fred Astaire, Adolphe Menjou, Gus Schilling, and ensemble. Recorded by Fred Astaire (Decca).

Published version

Ding, dong, dell,
The bells in the steeple go,
Ding, dong, dell,
Around the countryside.
Ding, dong, dell,
And off all the people go,
Off to kiss the bride.
All the donkey carts are driving
To the wedding in the spring.
All the neighborhood's arriving
To see the wedding ring.
Now they're forming in a column,
For the service has begun.
Although the padre's solemn,
He's the only one.
Down the aisle, the pages and flower girls;
In a while the happy bride and groom.
The ladies smile—
"We'll give her a shower, girls!
Dishes and a broom!"
All the gentlemen are jolly,
For the wine is flowing free;
All the ladies melancholy
For days that used to be.
When the carriage that's been waiting
Takes the newlyweds away,
The crowd keeps celebrating
Till the break of day.
Ding, dong, dell,
The bells in the steeple go,
Ding, dong, dell,
Around the countryside.
Ding, dong, dell,
Toast the bride, then farewell,
Off they ride.
Oh, what fun
Comes under the heading
Of "Wedding in the Spring"!

Additional lines for film version

Listen to the birdies
Loud in the treetops,
Puffing their cheeks out*
All around the place.
Little hurdy-gurdies
Sounding so merry,
Getting so very
Blue in the face.
Surely there's a reason
Everybody's gay.
It must be the season
For a wedding day.

* *Alternate line:*
  Letting those squeaks out

When the carriage that's been waiting
Takes the early birds away . . .

Oh, woe is me,
I'll never be
A beautiful, blushing bride.
Our family has sisters three,
Perhaps we should subdivide
"Father."

I'M OLD-FASHIONED

Published. Copyrighted July 9, 1942. Previously registered for copyright as an unpublished song April 1, 1942. Introduced by Rita Hayworth (dubbed by Nan Wynn) and Fred Astaire. Leading recordings by Astaire (Decca); Xavier Cugat (Columbia); and Glen Gray and the Casa Loma Orchestra, with vocal by Kenny Sargent (Decca).

Mercer recalled Kern playing the song's melody "and I had an idea for it. I brought it in and he played it over. And he got up and hugged me. He called 'Eva, Eva!' and . . . his wife . . . ran downstairs and he kissed me on the cheek and he said, 'Wait'll you hear this lyric!' Well, of course, you know, that makes you feel like a million dollars. It's just a fair lyric, but he was pleased."

A one minor discordant note in the film: Rita Hayworth, at her most gorgeous, is required to sing the lines

> I admit I was never one
> Adored by local lads . . .
> I'm the type that they classify
> As quaint.

VERSE

RITA
HAYWORTH: I am not such a clever one
           About the latest fads.
           I admit I was never one
           Adored by local lads.
           Not that I ever try to be
           A saint,
           I'm the type that they classify
           As quaint.

FRED
ASTAIRE: Quaint that they mother you,
           Quaint that they brother you,
           Must be another you—
           I like the other you.

REFRAIN

HAYWORTH: I'm old-fashioned,
           I love the moonlight,

I love the old-fashioned things:
The sound of rain
Upon a windowpane,
The starry song that April sings.
This year's fancies
Are passing fancies,
But sighing sighs,
Holding hands,
These my heart
Understands.
I'm old-fashioned,
But I don't mind it;
That's how I want to be,
As long as you agree
To stay
Old-fashioned
With me.

THE SHORTY GEORGE

Published. Copyrighted September 1, 1942. Previously registered for copyright as an unpublished song May 1, 1942. Introduced by Fred Astaire, Rita Hayworth (dubbed by Nan Wynn), chorus, and Xavier Cugat and His Orchestra. Recorded by Fred Astaire (Decca).

FRED
ASTAIRE: Just heard of the Shorty George,
Got word of the Shorty George.
Seems that it's a kind of jig
Named for someone about so big.
He rambles around the town,
Preambles around the town,
Then steps on a crowded street
'N' beats his feet till his feet is beat.
CHORUS: Watch him go! And he can
Like a real nach'l man.

ASTAIRE: High stepper is Shorty George,
Black pepper is Shorty George,
He dances to pay the rent,
And to see that you're solid sent.

Say, mister, can you spare a penny?
Lady, can you spare a dime?
He makes I don't know how many,
'Cause he's dancin' all the time.
Papa's dressed up mighty sporty—
RITA
HAYWORTH: Mama's snoozin' in the shade;
But while Mama's catchin' forty,
Shorty sees the rent is paid.
ASTAIRE: Get hip to the Shorty George,

Hop-skip to the Shorty George.
Directions are short and sweet—
HAYWORTH: I know:
You beat your feet till your feet is beat.
CHORUS: So catch on to Shorty George,
And latch on to Shorty George—
Good people, I'm tellin' you
That the Shorty George is the dance to do.

YOU WERE NEVER LOVELIER

Published. Copyrighted July 13, 1942. Previously registered for copyright as an unpublished song April 13, 1942. Introduced by Fred Astaire. Leading recordings by Astaire (Decca), Vaughn Monroe (Victor), and Paul Whiteman and His Orchestra (Capitol).

VERSE

I was never able
To recite a fable
That would make the party bright.
Sitting at the table,
I was never able
To become the host's delight.
But now you've given me my after-dinner story;
I'll just describe you as you are in all your glory.

REFRAIN

You were never lovelier,
You were never so fair;
Dreams were never lovelier—
Pardon me if I stare.
Down the sky the moonbeams fly to light your face;
I can only say they chose the proper place.
You were never lovelier,
And to coin a new phrase,
I was never luckier
In my palmiest days.
Make a note, and you can quote me, honor bright,
You were never lovelier than you are tonight.

THESE ORCHIDS

Registered for copyright as an unpublished song July 16, 1956. Introduced by four young delivery boys (names unknown).

These orchids, if you please,
With apologies
And another note.
We're obliged to sing
What the sender wrote,
Quote:
"Oh, sí-sí-sí, sí-sí-sí-sí, Mama,
See how I love you!
Oh, sí-sí-sí-sí
Comma,
Say you love me, too!"

ON THE BEAM

Published. Copyrighted September 1, 1942. Previously registered for copyright as an unpublished song April 13, 1942. Intended for Fred Astaire. Cut before the film's release. Originally called "Dancing on Air." Recorded by Fred Astaire (Decca).

I'm dancing on air,
Haven't a care,
I'm on the beam.
Time's flyin' by,
And I'm flyin' high.
I'm walking on wings,
And ev'rything's peaches and cream;
Blind flying's all gone,*
I'm really on the beam.
I'm like the B-Nineteen
Loaded with Benzedrine:
When I come on the scene,
I bust a hole in the sky.
One foot is in the groove,
The other's on the move,
Which only goes to prove
I'm a remarkable guy.
Big grin on my face,
You can't erase
My self-esteem,
There's no pro and con,
I'm really on the beam.

* *Alternate line:*
Storm signals are gone,

WINDMILL UNDER THE STARS

Music by Jerome Kern. Published. Copyrighted June 17, 1942. Previously registered for copyright as an unpublished song April 28, 1942. Intended for *You Were Never Lovelier*, but not used in film. Recorded by Russ Morgan and His Orchestra (Decca) and Johnny Johnston (Capitol).

There's a windmill
Under the stars,
Waiting for spring,
Waiting to swing
Under the stars.
In Granada
There are guitars,
Silent and still
Under the silver stars.
And there are poppies
And fleurs-de-lis
That wait to blossom
In Brittany;
They raise their faces,
Hoping to see
And breathe the sweet air
Of liberty.
And that great day
Surely will come;
Poppies will grow,
Breezes will blow,
Windmills will hum.
On some perfect spring again,
All the world will sing again
With the windmill
Under the stars.

BARREL-HOUSE BEGUINE

Music by Jerome Kern. Registered for copyright as an unpublished song April 1, 1942. Not used in film.

REFRAIN

SHE: Somewhere between Cape Horn and Saint
          Augustine
      Someone invented a dance
      Known to the natives
      As the beguine.
HE: But as it went forth
      And blazed a trail to the north,

It couldn't stand
The change of scene.
Folks in Memphis said,
"That's too sweet!"
So they waylaid it and played it
And made it a barrel-house beat.
SHE: Well, all reet!
BOTH: Now if you lean
      Or brush against any nickel machine,
      Out comes that beat,
      Off go your feet,
      Tapping the Barrel-House Beguine.

THE BIRTH OF CAPITOL RECORDS

At the start of the 1940s, there were three major record companies in America: Columbia (the oldest), Victor (the most prestigious), and Decca (with most of the popular radio and film stars of the day). All three were headquartered in New York.

With Hollywood churning out musical films faster and faster and using big bands for specialties, and the radio networks establishing large studios on the Coast, there was a westward flow of talented musicians and singers that cried out for a California-based record company.

Johnny Mercer discussed the idea first with Harold Arlen and bandleader Bobby Sherwood and expressed the feeling that a new label could be free from what he perceived as the old-fashioned musical arrangements and business-as-usual policies of the big three. He later suggested starting a new record company with an old friend, Glenn Wallichs, who in 1940 had built the biggest record store in Los Angeles, Wallichs Music City, at the northwest corner of Sunset Boulevard and Vine Street, right in the heart of Hollywood. Wallichs was an electronics whiz with an aggressive business sense and a perfect partner to run the business end of a record enterprise, while Johnny handled its creative aspects.

Now, all they needed was capital. Early in February 1942, Wallichs and Mercer met at Lucey's Restaurant on Melrose Avenue with Buddy DeSylva, who in the 1920s had been one-third of the celebrated songwriting team DeSylva, Brown, and Henderson. In the 1930s, DeSylva became a film producer at Fox and now was an executive producer at Paramount, when he was not mounting successful shows on Broadway with scores by Cole Porter and Irving Berlin.

When Mercer and Wallichs asked DeSylva if he thought Paramount would be interested in investing in a new record label, DeSylva said that he could not speak for the studio, but he personally would give them a check

for $10,000, soon followed by another for $15,000. On March 27, the three partners had a statement notarized that they had applied to found a company called Liberty Records. Because the name conflicted with the label owned by New York's Liberty Music Shops, it was changed on June 1 to Capitol at Ginger Mercer's suggestion.

On April 6, Johnny ran the company's first recording session, Martha Tilton singing a new Mercer song, "Moon Dreams"; and on July 1, Capitol Records made its first release of nine ten-inch 78 rpm discs, numbered 101 through 109. Of these, number 102, "Cow Cow Boogie" with seventeen-year-old singer Ella Mae Morse and Freddie Slack's Orchestra, became the label's first million-dollar seller, while number 103, Johnny's own recording of "Strip Polka," was not far behind.

Among the artists on the first release were Connie Haines, Johnnie Johnston, Dennis Day, and the orchestras of Bobby Sherwood, Gordon Jenkins, and Paul Whiteman. These were soon joined by Nat "King" Cole, Stan Kenton, Les Baxter, Les Brown, Benny Goodman, Betty Hutton, and Peggy Lee, and later by Jo Stafford, Paul Weston, the Pied Pipers, and Margaret Whiting.

Despite the wartime shortage of shellac for pressings and the impending year-long musicians' strike that began on August 1, Capitol Records, with its sassy musical styling and superior pressings, was an instantaneous hit. Now, America had the Big Four.

STAR SPANGLED RHYTHM (1942)

Produced by B. G. DeSylva for Paramount Pictures. Released December 1942. Copyright December 29, 1942. Directed by George Marshall. Screenplay by Harry Tugend. Sketches by George S. Kaufman, Arthur Ross, Melvin Frank, and Norman Panama. Music by Harold Arlen. Lyrics by Johnny Mercer. Dances staged by Danny Dare and George Balanchine. Vocal arrangements by Joseph J. Lilley. Musical director: Robert Emmett Dolan. With Bing Crosby, Bob Hope, Fred MacMurray, Franchot Tone, Ray Milland, Victor Moore, Dorothy Lamour, Paulette Goddard, Vera Zorina, Mary Martin, Dick Powell, Betty Hutton, Eddie Bracken, Veronica Lake, Alan Ladd, Eddie "Rochester" Anderson, William Bendix, Jerry Colonna, Macdonald Carey, Walter Abel, Susan Hayward, Marjorie Reynolds, Betty Jane Rhodes, Dona Drake, Lynne Overman, Gary Crosby, Johnny Johnston, Gil Lamb, Cass Daley, Ernest Truex, Katherine Dunham, Arthur Treacher, Walter Catlett, Sterling Holloway, Cecil B. DeMille, Preston Sturges, Ralph Murphy, Ellen Drew, Sherman Sanders, the Golden Gate Quartette, and Walter Dare Wahl and Company.

The doorman of Paramount studios pretends to his son that he is a big-time producer.

HIT THE ROAD TO DREAMLAND

Published. Copyrighted November 25, 1942. Introduced by Dick Powell, Mary Martin, and the Golden Gate Quartette. Recorded by Freddie Slack and His Orchestra, with vocals by the Mellowaires (Capitol).

VERSE

DICK POWELL: Twinkle, twinkle, twinkle, twinkle
Goes the star.
MARY MARTIN: Twinkle, twinkle, twinkle, twinkle,
There you are.
Time for all good children
To hit the hay.
Cock-a-doodle, doodle, doodle,
Soon will be another day.
POWELL: We should be on our way!
MARTIN: [*yawns*] Pardon me.
POWELL: [*yawns*] Me, too. Waiter, two more,
please.

REFRAIN

MARTIN: Bye-bye, baby,
Time to hit the road to Dreamland.
You're my baby,
Dig you in the Land of Nod.
POWELL: Hold tight, baby,
We'll be swinging up in
Dreamland,
All night, baby,
Where the little cherubs trod.
MARTIN: Look at that knocked-out moon,
Been a-blowin' his top in the blue.
POWELL: Never saw the likes of you!
MARTIN: What an angel!
Bye-bye, baby,
Time to hit the road to Dreamland,
Don't cry, baby,
It was divine.
POWELL: But the rooster has fin'lly crowed,
BOTH: Time to hit the road.
POWELL: Bye-bye, baby,
Time to hit the road to Dreamland.
[*spoken*] Waiter, could I have a
little more water, please?
MARTIN: [*sung*] Hold tight, baby—
We'll be swinging up in
Dreamland!

[*spoken*] Waiter, could I have a
spoon, please?

GOLDEN GATE
QUARTETTE: Pardon me, ma'am,
And pardon me, sir,
This is not a job that we prefer,
But it's strictly the railroad
regulation
That we close this car before we
reach the station.
So, if you'll forgive our effrontery,
We'll be as brief as we can be.

Yes, yes, good children
Gettin' on,
Time to hit the road.

King Solomon once in his wisdom
said,
"There's nothin' quite like a good
feather bed!"
That may not be just the written
word,
So don't quote me cause I only
heard,
And then, I coulda misunderstood,
But if he didn't say that then he
certainly should,
'Cause in this world with its killin'
pace
A man's gotta find a good restin'
place.
There's early to bed, early to rise
Makes a man healthy, wealthy, and
wise!

Yes, yes, good children,
Gettin' on,
Time to hit the road.

With everything electric and
mechanized
If you do get nervous I ain't
surprised.
But listen, good people, you can't
cure ills
With capsules, tablets, and vitamin
pills,
And the only thing to rest your head
Is a good night's sleep in a quilted
bed.
So just resolve to be good and firm
'Cause the early bird's a-gonna
catcha the worm.

Yes, yes, good children,
Gettin' on,
Time to hit the road.

Now see that moon shinin' way up
there?*
His chops are all beat and he ain't
nowhere.
He's dyin' to get some shut-eye,
too,
But he's got to stay up and light
the way for you.
So be good children and treat him
right
And he'll shine like a lantern
tomorrow night.
It's half past two and that ain't no
crime
And we hope you had a most
enjoyable time.
We surely do thank you for your
friendly call,
But we're forced by law to say good
night all.

Yes, Yes, good children,
Gettin' on,
Time to hit the road.
MARTIN: They say, baby,
Time to Hit the Road to
Dreamland.
POWELL: Okay, baby.
BOTH: Don't think that we all need a
building to fall on us.
MARTIN: Time to dim the lamp.
POWELL: Time to hit the ramp.
MARTIN: Back to our abode.
BOTH: Time to hit the road.
QUARTETTE: Yes, yes, good children,
Gettin' on.
It's getting time to hit the road.
Yes, Yes, good children
Gettin' on.
It's getting time to hit the road.
BASS: It's gettin' on,
It's gettin' on.

ON THE SWING SHIFT

Published. Copyrighted November 25, 1942. Introduced by Dona Drake, Betty Jane Rhodes, Marjorie Reynolds, Sherman Sanders (square dance caller), and dance ensemble.

---

* *Alternate line:*
So take a tip from the moon up there—

VERSE

DONA
DRAKE: Like some old tabby
Who sleeps in the sun,
I dream all day of the night that is
done.
Not that we frequent the same
habitat,
But in a way I'm a cat.

Life is fine with my baby on the swing
shift,
On the line with my baby on the
swing shift.
Oh, it's the nuts there among the nuts
and bolts
Plus the hundred thousand volts
shining from his eyes.
He's an interceptor.
What care I if they put me in the
wing shift?
He's nearby in the fuselage.
Overtime?
Here's why I'm doing it free—
Baby's with me on the swing shift
jamboree!

BETTY JANE
RHODES: Life is fine with my baby on the swing
shift,
On the line with my baby on the
swing shift.
He's for me, he's the whole darn
factory.
Gets the love machinery working in
my heart!
He's a beautiful bomber!
What care I if they put me in the
wing shift?
He's nearby painting camouflage.
Overtime?
Here's why I'm doing it free—
Baby's with me on the swing shift
jamboree!

SQUARE DANCE

Forward all and fall back all.
First and third forward and back.
Forward again and sides divide.
Swing in the center and swing on the
side.
Meet your partner promenade eight
round the old track
And you'll come out straight.
Ladies to the center and back to the
bar.
Gents to the center and form a star.

Left hands back—grab your partner
promenade.
Gents swing out, ladies swing in.
Ladies swing out and all eight swing.
Sashay fancy and trip it light
All rest, all rote, all root, all right.
DRAKE: Jack be nimble, Jill will fly,
Buckets lively keep your benders high.
Swing your chick on the double quick.
Blow my topper and button my socks,
When the cats start jumpin'
The dance hall rocks.
DRAKE &
RHODES: What care I if they put me in the
wing shift?
He's nearby in the fuselage.
Overtime?
Here's why I'm doing it free—
Every one of you come join us
At the swing shift jamboree!

I'M DOIN' IT FOR DEFENSE
(THE JEEP SONG)

Published. Copyrighted November 25, 1942. Introduced by Betty Hutton.

VERSE

BETTY
HUTTON: Because I tell you you're a buster,
Needn't think you are Gen'ral Custer;
So when I whisper that you're my
adored,
Don't go overboard!
Before you start to be commanding,
We had better have an understanding:
If this is gonna be romance,
I'm gonna wear the pants.

REFRAIN 1

Mister Bones,
Get this right:
I'm your date
For tonight,
But when I
Hold you tight,
I'm doing it for defense!

Months and months
You've been drilled;
Now it's time

You were thrilled.
Start from here,
Then we build—
I'm doing it for defense!

If you kiss my lips and you feel me respond,
It's because I just can't afford a bond.
If you think you're Cary Grant, brother, relax,
You're just the rebate on my income tax!
Don't be hurt,
Don't be sore—
I'm a pal,
Nothing more.
This ain't love,
This is war.
I'm doin' it for defense!

REFRAIN 2 (NOT USED IN FILM)

HUTTON: Once I start I can't quit;
I said I'd do my bit.
Sorry, bud, but you're it—
I'm doing it for defense!
Orders are for today.

EDDIE
BRACKEN: Just relax, come what may.
Duty calls, I obey!
HUTTON: I'm doing it for defense!
Your morale needs building up, you
must agree.
BRACKEN: Please forget morale and consider
me.
HUTTON: Put your face starboard and give us a
kiss.
BRACKEN: Heaven help a sailor on a night like
this!
HUTTON: Let's pretend I'll attack—
Your defense mustn't crack.
BRACKEN: This ain't war, it's murder, Jack!
HUTTON: I'm doing it for defense!

A SWEATER, A SARONG,
AND A PEEK-A-BOO BANG

Published. Copyrighted November 25, 1942. Introduced by Paulette Goddard, Dorothy Lamour, Veronica Lake (dubbed by Martha Mears), Arthur Treacher, Walter Catlett, and Sterling Holloway.

Submitting the lyric to the censor, Paramount's
Luigi Luraschi wrote (June 5, 1942): "Please advise if
the enclosed lyrics meet with your approval. The tag line
has been omitted as the producer is afraid of its being
publicized and, therefore, losing its punch. For your in-

formation the line is—'Mussolini, Hirohito and a Peeka-boo Bang.' "

VERSE

PAULETTE GODDARD,
DOROTHY LAMOUR
& VERONICA LAKE: In us you see
Three very unhappy ladies of
the silver screen.
Our lives should be
A wonderful bed of roses but
they're just routine.
LAKE: Sleep at ten.
GODDARD: Wake at dawn.
LAMOUR: Get up and put the glamour
on.
ALL: In us you see
Three very unhappy ladies of
the silver screen.

REFRAIN 1

We came out to make the
grade in moving pitchers;
We came out to mingle with
the glamour gang.
But we're sorry that we
came,
For our only claim to fame—
GODDARD: Is a sweater—
LAMOUR: A sarong—
LAKE: And a peek-a-boo bang!
LAMOUR: Oh, the money that we spent
to learn dramatics,
Oh, the vocal exercises that
we sang,
All went scootin' down the
drain
When they met us at the
train—
GODDARD: With a sweater—
LAMOUR: A sarong—
LAKE: And a peek-a-boo bang.
LAMOUR: We've played in chases,
Tender embraces,
And ev'ry sort of scene—
GODDARD: But the disgrace is
So far our faces
Haven't got on the screen.
LAKE: You can have your picture
taken with a panther—
GODDARD: Or perhaps adopt a small
orangutang!
LAMOUR: Are you ladies telling me
I've been living in a tree
In sarongs that aren't as long
as a peek-a-boo bang?

REFRAIN 2

ALL: Our vocabularies rate with
Ronald Colman's;
We've eliminated ev'ry trace
of slang.
Ev'ry day we go to school
Right beside a swimming pool
In a sweater, a sarong, and a
peek-a-boo bang.

We have always kept our
figures looking sylphlike,
But it's only proved to be a
boomerang,
For the only clothes we wear,
Even at a large affair,
Are a sweater, a sarong, and a
peek-a-boo bang.

Our situation has no salvation,
No matter where we go.
Metro to Goldwyn, Goldwyn
to Warners,
Where the wind machines
blow.

LAKE: All I ever see is sweaters on a
campus.
GODDARD: All I ever see is jungles in
Penang.
LAMOUR: Well, you're luckier than me—
Both of you at least can see!
LAMOUR AND
GODDARD: Yes, a sweater must be better
than a peek-a-boo bang.
Yes, a sweater must be better
than a peek-a-boo bang!

REFRAIN 2 (ALTERNATE LINES)

ALL: If you mothers have another Shirley Temple,
You can save the little darling quite a pang,
If before you make the trip
You are sure to pack her grip
With a sweater, a sarong, and a peek-a-boo
bang.

[*They come to a dead stop at the word "grip" and lead
out three little girls dressed exactly like them to join in
the title line.*]

REFRAIN 3

ARTHUR TREACHER,
WALTER CATLETT &
STERLING HOLLOWAY: We were bathing beauties in
the time of Sennett,

When they hit you in the
kisser with meringue.
Throwing pastry is passé,
So we earn our dough
today
TREACHER: With a sweater—
CATLETT: A sarong—
HOLLOWAY: And a peek-a-boo bang!
ALL THREE: Once we had our wardrobes
made by custom tailors,
But these outfits seemed to
add a little tang.
And the public fairly begs
For a chance to see our
legs—
TREACHER: In a sweater—
CATLETT: A sarong—
HOLLOWAY: And a peek-a-boo bang.

[*Dance interlude.*]

GODDARD,
LAMOUR
& LAKE: For the costumes that we
wear we take no credit,
And we'd like to tell you
all from whence they
sprang.
Three designers that are
know
Set the fashions long
ago—
GODDARD: Mussolini—
LAMOUR: Hirohito—
LAKE: And a peek-a-boo bang.

THAT OLD BLACK MAGIC

Published. Copyrighted November 25, 1942. Introduced by Johnny Johnston; danced by Vera Zorina. Number-one recording by Glenn Miller and His Orchestra, with vocals by Skip Nelson and the Modernaires (Victor). Other leading recordings were made by Johnny Johnston (Capitol); Freddie Slack and His Orchestra (Capitol); Horace Heidt and His Orchestra (Columbia); and, more than a decade later, Sammy Davis Jr. (Decca); Louis Prima and Keely Smith (Capitol); and Bobby Rydell (Cameo).

The personal side of Mercer's life overlaps with the professional in this and several subsequent songs. At this time he was involved in an on-again-off-again affair with Judy Garland, and "That Old Black Magic," while not dedicated to Garland, was intended for her.

Mercer recalled:

Harold had this tune and it impressed me as being a very elegant tune, a natural hit. It occurred to me that perhaps "black magic" would be a good idea, because Cole Porter had written a song called "You Do Something to Me," and it went, "Do do that voodoo that you do so well." And I thought, gee, that's a great idea to be wasted on one word in a song. I've always loved Porter—those early songs of his were so clever, and later on his melodies became so right and full. Anyway, that thing about voodoo must have stuck with me. And I thought perhaps if I could incorporate that into a tune someday, it might work. Well, this tune just seemed to fill the bill.

That old black magic has me in its spell,
That old black magic that you weave so well.
Those icy fingers up and down my spine—
The same old witchcraft when your eyes meet mine.

The same old tingle that I feel inside,
And then that elevator starts its ride,
And down and down I go,
Round and round I go,
Like a leaf that's caught in the tide.

I should stay away,
But what can I do?
I hear your name
And I'm aflame,
Aflame with such a burning desire
That only your kiss
Can put out the fire.

For you're the lover I have waited for,
The mate that fate had me created for,
And ev'ry time your lips meet mine,
Darling, down and down I go,
Round and round I go
In a spin,
Loving the spin I'm in
Under that old black magic called love!

SHARP AS A TACK

Published. Copyrighted November 25, 1942. Introduced by Eddie "Rochester" Anderson, Katherine Dunham, Slim Gaillard and Slam Stewart, male vocal trio, and dance ensemble.

INTRODUCTION

MALE TRIO: Hey, look at that aurora borealis,
That boy must live in Buckingham Palace!
All resplendent in scarlet and gold,
That cat is a solid joy to behold.

VERSE

ROCHESTER: Comp'ny zoot!
I'm out Sunday strollin'.
Comp'ny voot!
Dig this suit
With a belt t'boot.

REFRAIN

Whadda they say
When they see me* comin' their way?
Boy, draped to the bricks
Muggin' lightly, killin' the chicks,
J-J-J-Jackson, I'm as sweet as a beet
With a pleat in the seat.
Payin' no mind
To the conversation,
With my nose in the air,
Nevertheless, I swear they holler,
"He ain't only classy,
He is fat and he's sassy."
What do they shout
When they see me cuttin' on out?
"J-J-J-Jackson, h-h-h-hurry on back,
'Cause, Papa, you're sharp as a tack
With a belt in the back!"

KATHERINE
DUNHAM: You ain't only classy,
You're Haile Selassie!
ROCHESTER: With a belt in the back!

TAG

What'll they yell
When they see me wavin' farewell?
"J-J-J-Jackson h-h-h-hurry on back,
That uniform's sharp as a tack
With a belt in the back!"

OLD GLORY

Published. Copyrighted April 20, 1942. Introduced by Bing Crosby and chorus, with actors Eddie Marr, Irving Bacon, Peter Potter, and Matt McHugh.

* Or: When they dig me

BING
CROSBY: From a forest clearing in the north Maine woods
Or a wagon crossing in Ohio,
There started a song.
Someone added a note,
Someone added a word,
And soon the wide world heard—

REFRAIN

Old Glory, Old Glory,
Our dreams are in you.
Tall timber, blue prairie,
They're part of you, too.
Love made you,
Tears kept you,
Brave hearts that are gone:
We hail them
And we won't fail them—
Old Glory flies on!
CHORUS: Old Glory, Old Glory,
Our dreams are in you.

SCENE

CROSBY: [spoken] "I pledge allegiance to the flag and to the Republic for which it stands . . ." We used to say that when we were kids—that and a lot of other words we didn't understand. We didn't know what they meant then. None of this crowd knew.
VOICE: Yeah? What do they mean now, buddy?
CROSBY: What do they mean now? Why, everybody knows that, mister! Here's a man from New Hampshire—let's ask him.
NEW
HAMPSHIRITE: No need to ask me, son! It means gettin' up early in the cold, lightin' lanterns, milkin' . . . cuttin' notches in maple trees for syrup . . . goin' to school to read about Washington and the Redcoats . . . followin' rabbit tracks in the snow . . . an attic room that wind 'ud come whistlin' through . . . It means that, son, and a whole lot more.
CROSBY: I pledge allegiance to the flag
And to the Republic for which it stands
VOICE: Go on! Can't fool me with that flag wavin'!
CROSBY: How 'bout it, Georgia boy?

He says I'm "flag wavin'," mean anything to you?

GEORGIAN: Sho' does, big boy—specially from them thirteen stripes. One o' them stands for Georgia, and like the man says, a lot more.

CROSBY: Such as?

GEORGIAN: Such as red clay hills—Folks say Confederate blood stained 'em—and marsh grass and big oak trees with moss on 'em . . . watermelons in the hot sun, and spiritual singin' in the evenin'!

CHORUS: Sometimes I feel like a motherless chile!
Sometimes I feel like a motherless chile!

GEORGIAN: That's it!

CHORUS: I'm a ramblin' wreck from Georgia Tech
And a hell of a, hell of a, hell of a, hell of a,
Hell of an Engineer

GEORGIAN: That's right! That's it too!
Oglethorpe and Bobby Jones and Ty Cobb and "Come in and stay awhile, we're delighted to have you!"

VOICE: [laughs] Anybody can dramatize things!

CROSBY: Think so? Where you from, lady?

IOWAN: I'm from out where the tall corn grows . . . Iowa!

CROSBY: Grow anything else out there?

IOWAN: Sure do. Americans, for one thing.
Cattle, too, and hogs—
Some of 'em direct descendents of the hogs
That came by covered wagon.
Took a heap o' drivin' to get there safe.
Grandpa used to tell us about the Indians
And blizzards
Waitin' for them porkers.

CROSBY: Anything else out there ma'am?

IOWAN: Sure! Ranchers, haystacks, Greyhound buses,
Filling stations, hamburger stands, motels.
It's all there in the flag, third star from the right,
Fourth row, Iowa!

CROSBY: And where are you now, mister? Still listenin'?

VOICE: Right here. Keep talkin'.

CROSBY: Anybody here like to talk to this fellow?

CLAUDETTE
COLBERT: Yeah! Were you ever in Brooklyn, mac? Did you ever see steam comin' out of the sidewalk, or get packed like a herring into a Flatbush Express? or go to Coney on Sunday, or throw a pop bottle at an umpire?— "Aaaaah—gid oudda dere, ya bum!"? Did you ever see the Empire State Building? It's higher than some towns are wide. Do you know of any other country where a Brooklyn girl can get to be a movie star? Ah! There it is—top-right-hand corner—Brooklyn!

CROSBY: What d'ya say now, mister?

VOICE: Well . . .

CROSBY: Convinced?

VOICE: Well . . .

CROSBY: Well, there's lots more!

[*Sing-song, increasing pace.*]

Longhorns from Texas and apples from Oregon,
Mountains and rivers

OVERMAN: And buckboards and flivvers,
And minutemen and trappers

BETTY
HUTTON: And jitterbugs and flappers!

CHORUS: And John Brown's body and Gen'ral Lee's sword
And Vanderbilt and Carnegie and Edison and Ford!

ROCHESTER: And how about Washington?
I mean all three—
George and Martha and Booker T.
Will Rogers, Nathan Hale,
Union Pacific, Oregon Trail.
"Hi, Captain!"—"Howdy, Doc!
Didn't we meet at Plymouth Rock?"
America, the cornucopia—
Buddy, this the way to Utopia!
This is your future, yours and mine,
And there ain't any Germans, Italians, or Japs
Who are gonna push us off our
Hard-won, homemade Rand-McNally maps.

PRINCIPALS: Alamo, Gettysburg, Château-Thierry—
Hit 'em hard!
"How do I get to Freedom City?"
"Keep on going where you're

headed!"
"Thank ya, buddy!"
"Okay, pard!"

CHORUS: Meet me in Saint Louis, Louie,
Meet me at the fair!
This way to balloon ascension—
"Howdy, neighbor, put 'er there!"
Boston Tea Party, Sitting Bull,
Four of a kind will beat a full!
Bataan Peninsula, Shiloh Ridge,
Crossword puzzles and contract bridge!
[*whispering*] Over the meadow and through the woods
To Grandmother's house we go,

PRINCIPALS: Down to the neighborhood movie,
Where we'll catch the early show!
Floyd Collins, Al Capone,
Union Pacific, Franchot Tone!
Hi Captain! Howdy Doc!
Didn't we meet at Plymouth Rock?
America, the cornucopia
Buddy, is this the way to Utopia?
How do I get to the Promised Land?

CROSBY: Follow the lines in Uncle Sam's hand.
Lincoln saw 'em, John Hancock, too.

PRINCIPALS: When the whirlwind comes a-blowing,
Keep right on the way you're goin'—
Follow the markers, follow the sign,
It's as plain as Highway Ninety-nine
This is your future—yours and mine
And there ain't any Germans, Italians, or Japs
Who can push us off our hard-won, home-made,
Rand-McNally map;
For these are our rivers—our prairie lands

ENSEMBLE: We pledge allegiance to the flag and to the Republic for which it stands.

VERSE

From a forest clearing in the north Maine woods
Or a wagon crossing Ohio,
There started a song,
Someone added a note,
Someone added a word,

CHORUS: And soon the wide world heard.
Old Glory, Old Glory,
Our dreams are in you.
Tall timber, blue prairie,
They're part of you, too.
Love made you,
Tears kept you,
Brave hearts that are gone:
We hail them
And we won't fail them—
Old Glory flies on!

HE LOVED ME TILL THE ALL-CLEAR CAME

Published. Copyrighted November 25, 1942. Intended for Betty Hutton, but not used in film. Later used in the 1943 Paramount film *Riding High* starring Dick Powell and Dorothy Lamour, where it was introduced by Cass Daley and the Milt Britton Band.

VERSE

I was strolling in the park
Just as it was getting dark
When I heard the sirens moan.
I ducked into a shelter,
Willy-nilly, helter-skelter,
To find that I was not alone.
There was someone next to me,
And though neither one of us could see,
We sensed each other close at hand,
And there within the gloom
Of that little blackout room
Love and I played a one-night stand.

REFRAIN

He loved me till the all-clear came,
He loved me till the all-clear came.
He had the strongest yen
In the dark and then
Suddenly the all-clear came.
He loved me till the lights went on;
I looked around and he was gone.
Our story seemed to go
Like a picture show—
Suddenly there came the dawn.
While I was brave as could be
And trying to be merry,
There in the cozy dark
I don't know if it was he
Or an incendiary,

But something found its mark.
I didn't even get a scratch,
And incident'ly, there's the catch—
But still they've listed me
As a casualty.
Isn't that an awful shame?*
And I think he really loved me,
He really, really loved me,
Till the all-clear came.

SPOKEN INTERLUDE

We sat and spoke of many things,
My life and cabbages and kings.
He had been all around the world.
He told me of the Taj Mahal
Shining in the moonlight!
I drew closer.
He told me of the Nile;
I drew closer still.
He whispered,
"How about a game of gin rummy, kid?"
How can you play gin rummy in the dark?
He grew restless;
I tried to amuse him.
I said, "Shall we rumba?"
But he was a square
From Delaware,
So we waltzed!
He said, "You dance divine."
Them's his words, not mine.
My, his grammar was a shame!
He held me tenderly
And drew close to me.
Suddenly the all-clear came.
All through the raid
He was a civilian inspector
Telling me what to do,
But in the light
He was a con-she-en-si-ous objector—
I mean to pitching woo!
Of course, I didn't come to harm;
The air raid was a false alarm.
And confidentially, ladies,
So was he.
My lawyer's gonna file a claim†
And to think I nearly loved him,
I really, nearly loved him,
Till the all-clear came.

---

* *Alternate line:*
    I intend to file a claim.
† *The censor insisted that the original line—"I found out his name was Mame"—be changed, "to get away from any possible 'pansy' suggestion."*

LET'S GO, SAILOR

Registered for copyright as an unpublished song under the title "Let's Go, Sailor" June 18, 1968. Not used in film. Alternate title: "Shore Leave."

REFRAIN 1

Let's go, sailor,
Shore leave startin' tonight.
Let's go, sailor,
See that your buttons are bright.
Come on, sailor,
Get that foldin' dough out.
Come on, sailor,
We're gonna kick it about!

Yessirree,
When we pitch a spree,
It's a jamboree
Of world renown.
Down to get you in a rowboat, honey,
Shore leave tonight!

REFRAIN 2

Yessir, sailor,
We've got evenings to spend.
Call her, sailor,
Ask her if she's got a friend.
Heave ho, sailor,
Be a jolly jack-tar,
You know, sailor,
That's what we think we all are!

Yessirree,
When we pitch a spree,
It's a jamboree
Of world renown.
Down to get you in a convoy, honey.
Sailor, let's go!

Alternative version

Shore leave, sailor,
Get that foldin' dough out!
Shore leave, sailor,
We're gonna kick it about!
Heave ho, sailor,
Be a jolly jack-tar—
You know, sailor,
That's what they think we all are!
Yessiree! When we pitch a spree,
It's a jamboree
Of world renown.
Yessiree! Be yourselves when we

Hit the town.
Don't let the Navy down.
Call up Mabel,
Yell with all your might,
"I'll be down to get you in a rowboat, honey,
Shore leave tonight!"

OLD ROB ROY

Music by Robert Emmett Dolan. Recorded by Freddie
Slack and His Orchestra, vocal by Ella Mae Morse (Capitol).

Cheeks like a cherry pie,
Big twinkle in his eye,
He's got a grin you can't destroy,
Sir, I refer to Old Rob Roy.

Eighty if he's a day,
But does he act that way?
You'd think that he was still a boy.
He has a picnic,
Old Rob Roy.

He's up with the early sun,
Gets his business done,
Has his nap at six
For kicks.

He's got jazz, a Harlem flat,
He's everybody's daddy.
If life's a thing that you'd enjoy,
Latch onto Mr. Old Rob Roy.

SONGS OF DELTA DELTA DELTA

Music by Johnny Mercer.
    Lyric missing.

OVERLEAF
Top: The Sky's the Limit: *Fred Astaire dancing to
"One for My Baby (and One More for the Road)"*
Bottom: Laura: *Dana Andrews looking at the portrait
of Laura (Gene Tierney)*

THE SKY'S THE LIMIT,
HERE COME THE WAVES,
and Other Songs of 1943–1945

THEY GOT ME COVERED (1943)

Produced by Samuel Goldwyn for Samuel Goldwyn Productions, released by RKO Radio Pictures. World premiere January 27, 1943. Copyright December 31, 1942. Directed by David Butler. Screenplay by Harry Kurnitz, after an original story by Leonard Q. Ross and Leonard Spigelgass. Additional dialogue by Frank Fenton and Lynn Root. Lyrics by Johnny Mercer. Music by Harold Arlen. Musical score by Leigh Harline. Musical director: Constantin Bakaleinikoff. Starring Bob Hope and Dorothy Lamour, with Lenore Aubert, Otto Preminger, Eduardo Ciannelli, Marion Martin, Donald Meek, Phyllis Ruth, Philip Ahn, Donald MacBride, Mary Treen, Bettye Avery, Margaret Hayes, Mary Byrne, William Yetter, Henry Guttman, Florence Bates, Walter Catlett, John Abbott, and Frank Sully.

A bumbling foreign correspondent accidentally breaks up a German spy network in Washington.

PALSY-WALSY

Published. Copyrighted March 31, 1943. Introduced by Marion Martin (dubbed by Martha Mears) and female dancers.

VERSE

I need a friend to see me through,
Someone who is tried and true,
Someone who will keep the wolves away.
Nothing is wrong with baby's eyes,
Nothing is wrong with baby's size,
Which makes me romantically One-A.
So, you see, I need to be protected,
And, my turtle dove, you are elected.

REFRAIN

Palsy-walsy,
My old pie face,
Since I met you
I'm a dead duck.
Palsy-walsy,
You old sly face,
Can't forget you,
Reckon I'm stuck.
Through thick, through thin
Or any "How've you been?"
We'll grin and take it on the chin.

Who's excited?
Plan your campaign,
You'll get my vote.
I'll take champagne or beer,
Because you're my
Palsy-walsy, dear.

THE SKY'S THE LIMIT (1943)

Produced by David Hempstead for RKO Radio Pictures. Released September 1943. Copyright August 21, 1943. Directed by Edward H. Griffith. Screenplay by Frank Fenton and Lynn Root. Lyrics by Johnny Mercer. Music by Harold Arlen. Dances created and staged by Fred Astaire. Musical director: Leigh Harline. Starring Fred Astaire and Joan Leslie, with Robert Benchley, Robert Ryan, Elizabeth Patterson, Marjorie Gateson, and Freddie Slack and His Orchestra.

A test pilot on leave falls for a lady news photographer.

MY SHINING HOUR

Published. Copyrighted July 2, 1943. Introduced by Joan Leslie (dubbed by Sally Sweetland), female trio, and Freddie Slack and His Orchestra. Comedy reprise by Leslie (dubbed by Sweetland) and Fred Astaire. The song was nominated for an Academy Award but lost to "You'll Never Know" by Harry Warren and Mack Gordon. A best-selling recording was made by Glen Gray and the Casa Loma Orchestra, with vocals by Eugenie Baird (Decca).

VERSE

This moment, this minute
And each second in it
Will leave a glow upon the sky,
And as time goes by,
It will never die.

REFRAIN 1

This will be my shining hour,
Calm and happy and bright;
In my dreams, your face will flower,
Through the darkness of the night.

Like the lights of home before me
Or an angel watching o'er me,
This will be my shining hour
Till I'm with you again.

REFRAIN 2

This will be my shining hour,
Calm and happy and bright.
I recall the Chrysler Tower
Tall and ghostly in the night;
Not a sign and not a flicker
As we watch the Times Square ticker.
This will be my shining hour
Till I'm with you again.

Comedy reprise

This will be my shining hour,
Lonely though it may be,
Like the face of Mischa Auer
On the music-hall marquee.
Were they stingers or Bacardis?
Was it Tony's? Was it Sardi's?
This will be my shining hour
Till I'm with you again.

A LOT IN COMMON WITH YOU

Published. Copyrighted July 7, 1943. Introduced by Joan Leslie, Fred Astaire, and Freddie Slack and His Orchestra. Alternate title: "I've Got a Lot in Common with You."

Published version

VERSE

Psychiatrists have said
A man who's slightly cracked
Can like a maid who's tetched in the head.
And so it goes with me—
My addled brain can't see
Why a love such as ours shouldn't be.
Think it over:
Two noble souls designed above,
Two silly characters in love.

REFRAIN 1

You're average,
I'm so-so.
Not too-too,
Or oh-so,

Thank heavens
We know so!
Lonesome, stranded,
Truthful, candid,
Silly or dappy,
Long as we're happy—
I've got a lot in common with you.

REFRAIN 2

BOY: You're tender.
GIRL: You're tasty.
BOY: You're hurried.
GIRL: You're hasty.
BOY: You're pale and—
GIRL: You're pasty.
BOTH: You tarry. I'm tardy.
GIRL: You're Laurel. I'm Hardy.
BOY: Martini.
GIRL: Bacardi.
BOTH: We seem to have a lot in common, we two.
Two noble souls with one desire—
When can we buy an extra tire?
GIRL: You're scrawny. I'm skinny.
BOY: You're tone-deaf. I'm tinny.
GIRL: You're Mickey. I'm Minnie.
BOY: Tender. Tasty.
GIRL: Pale and pasty.
BOY: People will find us
As fate designed us.
BOTH: I have a lot in common with you.

REFRAIN 3

GIRL: You stammer. I stutter.
BOY: You fidget. I flutter.
GIRL: You're super.
BOY: You're utter.
BOTH: I seem to have a lot in common with you.
BOY: You're lissome. I'm lanky.
GIRL: You're cross. I'm cranky.
BOY: You're hanky. I'm panky.
BOTH: We seem to have a lot in common, we two.
So noble are our horoscopes
You'd never guess that we are dopes.
GIRL: You're aces. I'm deuces,
Which gives us excuses—
BOY: To raise some papooses.
GIRL: Must be married.
BOY: Motion's carried.
Then, if you're sleepy,
You share my teepee.
BOTH: I have a lot in common with you.

CHORUS

You're lonesome, I'm stranded.
You're truthful. I'm candid.

And we're both left-handed.
I seem to have a lot in common with you

Film version

FRED
ASTAIRE: You're lonesome, I'm stranded.
JOAN
LESLIE: You're truthful, I'm candid,
And we're both left-handed.
ASTAIRE: I seem to have a lot in common with you.
LESLIE: You slay me, I floor you.
ASTAIRE: You vex me, I bore you.
LESLIE: But I can't ignore you.
BOTH: We seem to have a lot in common, we two.
ASTAIRE: Two noble souls designed above.
LESLIE: [spoken] Get outta here, will ya!
ASTAIRE: [spoken] I will not.
[sung] Two silly characters in love.
LESLIE: You're woozy, you're whacked up.
ASTAIRE: I saw you, I cracked up.
LESLIE: You're breaking my act up.
ASTAIRE: Lonesome, stranded.
LESLIE: Truthful, candid.
ASTAIRE: Silly or sappy,
Long as I'm happy.
BOTH: I've got a lot in common with you.

ASTAIRE: The stage was my born field.
I've made it my sworn field.
LESLIE: Get back in that cornfield!
I think that we're slipping.
ASTAIRE: You'd better start stripping.
LESLIE: My zipper ain't zipping.
ASTAIRE: Perhaps we'd better tell a gag.
LESLIE: Perhaps we'd better wave the flag.
What's all the horseplay worth?
ASTAIRE: These eggs that we lay worth?
LESLIE: Where's Cagney?
ASTAIRE: Where's Hayworth?
BOTH: I've got a lot in common with you.

ONE FOR MY BABY (AND ONE MORE FOR THE ROAD)

Published. Copyrighted July 2, 1943. Introduced by Fred Astaire. Recorded by (among many others) Lena Horne, with Horace Henderson's Orchestra (Victor); Johnny Mercer (Capitol); Tony Bennett (Columbia); and Frank Sinatra (Capitol).

Arlen called the melody one of his "tapeworms," since it exceeded the traditional thirty-two bars. "Johnny took it and wrote it exactly the way it fell. Not

only is it long—forty-three bars—but it also changes keys. Johnny made it work."

Astaire reflected later: "The funny thing about these two songs was that, while the picture was in operation, neither of them registered as an immediate hit, but several months later 'My Shining Hour' became the number-one song of its day, and 'One for My Baby' has become a standard classic popular song and one of the best pieces of material that was written specially for me."

Incidentally, the role of Joe the Bartender is played by Victor Potel.

It's quarter to three,
There's no one in the place except you and me;
So set 'em up, Joe,
I've got a little story you oughta know.
We're drinking, my friend,
To the end of a brief episode—
Make it one for my baby
And one more for the road.

I've got the routine,
So drop another nickel in the machine.
I'm feelin' so bad,
I wish you'd make the music dreamy and sad.
Could tell you a lot,
But you've got to be true to your code—*
Make it one for my baby
And one more for the road.

You'd never know it,
But, buddy, I'm a kind of poet,
And I've got a lotta things to say,
And when I'm gloomy,
You simply gotta listen to me
Until it's talked away.

Well, that's how it goes,
And, Joe, I know you're getting anxious to close;
So thanks for the cheer,†
I hope you didn't mind my bending your ear,‡
This torch that I've found,‡
Must be drowned or it soon might explode,
Make it one for my baby
And one more for the road—
That long, long road.

* Alternate line from film:
    But that's not in a gentleman's code—
† Alternate wording from film:
    So thanks for the beer,
‡ Alternate lines from film:
    Don't let it be said
    Little Freddie can't carry his load.

HARVEY, THE VICTORY GARDEN MAN

Copyrighted July 7, 1943. "Harvey" originally was named "Shorty" and also occasionally was called "Hector." Introduced by Ella Mae Morse and Freddie Slack and His Orchestra but later deleted.

VERSE

Early and late, I love to frolic
Out where the atmosphere's bucolic,
Rural and rustic.
You will find me all the day long
Here in the garden plot I labor,
Due to the fact I have a neighbor
And to the fact he always sings this song—

REFRAIN

Tomatoes, tomatoes,
He's talking about tomatoes,
Potatoes, persimmon,
He hollers to the women,
"Come and help yourself,
Just pick 'em off the pantry shelf,
'Cause I'm Harvey, the Victory Garden Man."

He spends all his hours
Among the cauliflowers;
They say ev'ry room in
His little home is bloomin',
And his windowsill
Looks like an Oklahoma hill,
'Cause he's Harvey, the Victory Garden Man.

"Come on, you cats,
Aristocrats,
And dig, dig, dig—
Pretty soon that little ol' seed
Gets big, big, big!
Forget your troubles
Among the vegetubbles
And rake 'em
And hoe 'em,
But if it's hard to grow 'em,
You can call on me—
Delivery is rural free!"
He's a home front man,
But he's doin' all he can,
Harvey, the Victory Garden Man.

Additional lyrics

VERSE

Squash and peas, peas and beans,
Everything, including turnip greens—

As he goes on his way,
Hear him cry his patriotic rondelay.

PATTER

When you make out your daily market list,
Call on this happy horticulturist.
His produce is extremely succulent
And grown to musical accompaniment.
He blows his horn and plants his corn;
In the place of Tuesday's hash
Harvey advises succotash.
This gastronomic gadabout is quite a gourmet
He likes his victuals full of vitamin A
From early bright till late at night
You'll hear him chortlin' with sheer delight.

HANGIN' ON TO YOU

Not used in film.
    Lyric missing.

TRUE TO LIFE (1943)

Produced by Paul Jones for Paramount Pictures. Released October 1943. Copyright August 9, 1943. Directed by George Marshall. Screenplay by Don Hartman and Harry Tugend, after a story by Ben Barzman, Bess Taffel, and Sol Barzman. Lyrics by Johnny Mercer. Music by Hoagy Carmichael. Musical director: Victor Young. Starring Mary Martin, Franchot Tone, Dick Powell, and Victor Moore, with Mabel Paige, William Demarest, Clarence Kolb, Beverly Hudson, Raymond Roe, Ernest Truex, and Harry Shannon.

    The writer of a soap opera goes to live with a "typical" family to get local color.

MISTER POLLYANNA

Published. Copyrighted August 30, 1943. Introduced by Mary Martin.

VERSE

Trouble's just a bubble;
Trouble's only in your mind.
Life is what you make it,

So make it work for you.
And if winter comes
Then spring can't be so far behind.
Bundle up and take it
And you'll come smiling through.
This is my philosophy,
But I shouldn't take the credit;
For a wise old friend of mine
Is really the one who said it.

REFRAIN

Mister Pollyanna
Is the man
Who writes those sunny little rhymes.
Mister Pollyanna
Is the one
Who tells us "Any times are happy times."
He's the merry fellow
Who believes that
Sunshine follows the rain,
"So you mustn't complain,
Whatever you do—*
Let a smile be your umbrella."
When you're feelin' gloomy,
There are times you'd like to sock him in the eye,
'Specially when he tells you,
"Things'll clear up by and by."
But he's a wise old guy.
When you tumble out of bed next morning,
Everything's bonny and bright,
That's when you discover
Mister Pollyanna's nearly always right.

INTERLUDE

This is my philosophy,
And it's the one to follow,
Though I must admit at times that
It's pretty hard to swallow.

REPEAT REFRAIN

SUDSY SUDS THEME SONG

Registered for copyright as an unpublished song April 4, 1968. Introduced and reprised by male quartet.

Alternate line:
    If the world's all wet

Sudsy Suds, Sudsy Suds,
S-U-D-S-Y—
It cleans the dishes
Feeds the fishes,
Satisfies your washing wishes
And besides, it is delicious
Sudsy Sudsy Suds,
Soapy Sudsy Suds
Soupy Sudsy Suds!

THE OLD MUSIC MASTER

Published. Copyrighted August 30, 1943. Introduced by Dick Powell.

One thing Mercer and Carmichael had in common was their passion for jazz. Hoagy had been a great admirer of jazz trumpeter Bix Beiderbecke (1903–31) and Mercer had been a fan from childhood. Words like "hip" and "jive" may sound dated today but in 1943 they were—well, hip.

As the years went by something else began to date, politically. It was no longer appropriate to talk about "a little colored boy," and the line was revised to read "little Harlem boy." But even that didn't solve it. Nor did "a little curly boy." The final revision—"a swingin' little boy"—couldn't have pleased Mercer.

Now almost totally forgotten, Reginald de Koven (1859–1920) was a music critic, conductor, and composer of opera and operetta. The reference was probably a little obscure even in 1943, but at least it gave Mercer a rhyme for "Beethoven"!

VERSE

One night long ago by the light of the moon,
An old music master sat composing a tune.
His spirit was soaring and his heart full of joy
When right out of nowhere stepped a little
    colored boy.

REFRAIN

"You gotta jump it, music master,
You gotta play that rhythm faster,*
You're never gonna get it played
On the Happy Cat Hit Parade.†
You better tell your friend Beethoven
And Mister Reginald de Koven
They better do the same as you
Or they're gonna be corny too!

———
* *Alternate line:*
    Yuh gotta swing that music faster,
† *Or:* On the Lucky Strike Hit Parade

Long about nineteen seventeen
Jazz'll come upon the scene;
Then about nineteen thirty-five,
You'll begin to hear swing,
Boogie woogie, and jive.

"You gotta show* that big broadcaster
That you're a solid music master,
And you'll achieve posterity—
That's a bit of advice from me."

The old music master simply sat there amazed
As wide-eyed and open-mouthed he gazed and he
    gazed.
"How can you be certain, little boy? Tell me
    how."
"Because I was born," he said,
"A hundred years from now!"
He hit a chord that rocked the spinet
And disappeared into the in-fin-ite.
And up until the present day, you can take it from
    me
He's as right as can be,
Ev'rything has happened thataway!

THERE SHE WAS

Introduced by Dick Powell.

VERSE

I stepped to the hall
For a view of the ball,
Feeling sharp as a ? vest. (checkered?)
No thought of romance,
Just began to dance
And he seemed then like all the rest.
And then in a glance it all happened—
When I looked to my right,
Guess what happened?

Alternative verse

I was glad to be living
And free as a lark—
Last night at a party
Where I chanced to be,
Guess what happened to me?

———
* *Or:* You better tell

WHEN LOVE WALKS BY

Published. Copyrighted August 3, 1944. Previously registered for copyright as an unpublished song March 14, 1944. Lyric dated December 11, 1942. Not used in film.

Bells, faraway and chimelike,
Ring off in the sky,
I guess it's at a time like
This when love walks by.
You think you hear footsteps
No louder than a sigh;
Though you know it isn't so,
Your heart could swear
Love has just been there.
Dreams wander from a pillow
To walk on the hill;
Birds singing in a willow
Trees grow shy and still.
Though only a poet
Could ever tell you why,
I'm certain you will know it
When love walks by—
And so will I.

TRAV'LIN' LIGHT

Music by Jimmy Mundy and Trummy Young. Published. Copyrighted December 7, 1943. Recorded by Paul Whiteman and His Orchestra, vocal by Billie Holiday (Capitol).

I'm trav'lin' light
Because my man has gone,
And from now on
I'm trav'lin' light.

He said goodbye
And took my heart away,
So from today
I'm trav'lin' light.

No one to see,
I'm free as the breeze—
No one but me
And my memories.

Some lucky night
He may come back again,
But until then
I'm trav'lin' light.

G.I. JIVE

Music by Mercer. Published. Copyrighted January 21, 1944. Previously registered for copyright as an unpublished song December 24, 1943. Number-one recording by Louis Jordan and his Tympany Five (Decca); another leading recording was Mercer's own (Capitol).

At the outbreak of the war, Mercer had immediately volunteered, but had been told that the Army thought it best for him to stay where he was and work on troop entertainments. He recalled:

Every weekend we were off to [one of the camps] to play a show for the enlisted men . . . As a matter of fact, that is one of the reasons for the song "G.I. Jive." It was written for a soldiers' network program of the same title. Paramount was doing patriotic pictures like *Star-Spangled Rhythm* and *Here Come the Waves*, which I wrote the songs for also, so while Frank Loesser and Irving Berlin wrote the outstanding war songs in "Praise the Lord and Pass the Ammunition" and "This Is the Army, Mr. Jones," I was following orders and doing my bit when I turned out "G.I. Jive." It was during these times when we played all those bases that I realized how popular and how big Capitol was becoming. There wasn't a jukebox in any PX that didn't have "G.I. Jive" or some other Capitol recording of one of my songs on it.

Dave Dexter, the publicity director of the fledgling Capitol Records, gave his own account of how the song came about: "Mercer got the idea for 'G.I. Jive' while waiting for the traffic light at the corner of Sunset and Vine. He noticed all the servicemen on the streets around that busy intersection. So he drove that one block to where our offices were, came upstairs, sat down at the typewriter and dashed the whole thing off in a couple of minutes. It was one of our biggest hits that year."

Many people considered the song the World War II equivalent of Irving Berlin's "Oh, How I Hate to Get Up in the Morning."

VERSE

This is the G.I. Jive,
Man alive!
It starts with the bugler
Blowin' reveille over your head
When you arrive.

Jack, that's the G.I. Jive!
Root-tee-tee-toot,
Jump in your suit,
Make a salute—voot!
After you wash and dress,
More or less,
You go get your breakfast
In a beautiful little café
They call the mess.
Jack, when you convalesce,
Out of your seat
Into the street,
Make with the feet—reet!

If you're a P-V-T, your duty
Is to salute the L-I-E-U-T,
But if you brush the L-I-E-U-T,
The MP makes you KP on the QT—
This is the G.I. Jive!
Man alive!
They give you a private tank
That features a little device
Called fluid drive.
Jack, after you revive,
Chuck all your junk
Back in the trunk
Fall on your bunk—clunk!
Soon you're countin' Jeeps,
But before you count to five,
Seems you're right back diggin' that
G.I. Jive.

LOOK IN THE MIRROR

Music by Allie Wrubel. No copyright information.
   Lyric missing.

PROPAGANDA

Music by Mercer.
   Lyric missing.

PEPSODENT COMMERCIAL (POOR MIRIAM)

Music by Mercer. Written for Bob Hope's radio show. Pepsodent had just started introducing the "magic ingredient" Irium into its toothpaste.

Ooh, Miriam,
Poor Miriam,
Neglected using Irium*
When the telephone rings—

[*Sound of phone ringing.*]

   MIRIAM: Hello.
   MALE VOICE: Sorry, wrong number!

[*Phone gag is repeated.*]

It's the saddest thing!
Don't be like Miriam—
Use Irium!

MOON DREAMS

Music by Chummy MacGregor. Published. Copyrighted January 3, 1944. Previously registered for copyright as an unpublished song March 1, 1941. Recorded by Mercer in 1942 (Capitol).

Moon dreams
Dancin' on my pillow,
Moon dreams
Recall a night of paradise
With you.
Out of the blue dark
Love came strolling,
Over the white sand
The silver waves were rolling,
And in the distance a tango started,
Floated like a feather,
Gay and summer hearted.
We never once questioned whether

---

* *Mercer sang "neglected to use Irium" at the "Lyrics & Lyricists" program at the 92nd Street Y in New York City on March 14, 1971. Another alternate: "Who forgot to use her Irium."*

Our night of love together
Would ever die.
Blue mountains,
Waves rolling,
I see them when the moonbeams shine,
And once again in moon dreams
You are mine.

THE TAILGATE RAMBLE

Music by Wingy Manone. Published. Copyrighted August 14, 1944. Previously registered for copyright as an unpublished song June 30, 1944.

REFRAIN

When the wagon starts,
Put the tailgate down.
Watch the band parade
All around the town.
Give the trombone man
Room to move his slide.
Wasn't long ago
I was in my teens,
And we played that way
Down to New Orleans.

DREAM

Music by Mercer. Published. Copyrighted January 22, 1945. Previously registered for copyright as an unpublished song June 30, 1944.

Mercer always thought that it was "easy to write rhythm songs—such as 'Old Cowhand' or 'Something's Gotta Give'—but a ballad is tough." He also believed that a songwriter doesn't always know just what he's written—and "Dream" was a case in point: "I discovered later on, after I'd written it and played it a long time, that you can play it with 'Whispering'—it's a kind of 'Whispering' sideways."

In a 1960s interview Mercer recalled the song's evolution: "I was just fooling around at the piano and I got a series of chords that attracted me. I played it for Paul Weston. He had the band and we were doing the *Chesterfield Supper Club* show on radio—and I was on it for six months. And he said—'Why don't we use it for the theme song on the show?' " And, indeed, it did end up closing every show. Alive to the commercial implications of a program sponsored by a tobacco manufac-

turer, he "put in the line about smoke rings. Otherwise it wouldn't have been in there."

Weston remembered that "Johnny seemed dissatisfied with the sixth note [of the refrain], the one that falls on the word 'blue,' but I think that almost 'makes' the song and I convinced him to let it stay."

"Dream" was a number-one record for the Pied Pipers (Capitol). Other successful recordings were made by Frank Sinatra (Columbia) and, a decade later, the Four Aces (Decca).

VERSE

Get in touch with that sundown fellow
As he tiptoes across the sand.
He's got a million kinds of stardust;
Pick your favorite brand,
And—

REFRAIN

Dream
When you're feelin' blue,
Dream,
That's the thing to do.
Just watch the smoke rings
Rise in the air;
You'll find your share
Of memories there.

So
Dream
When the day is through,
Dream,
And they might come true.
Things never are as bad as they seem,
So
Dream,
Dream,
Dream.

YOU CAN SAY THAT AGAIN

Music by Freddie Slack and Carl Sigman. Published. Copyrighted August 24, 1944.

VERSE

Maybe I have just been dreaming,
Maybe I've been hearing things.
I suppose it's strange,
But I could swear I heard the sound
Of angel wings.
Just to prove that I'm not dreaming,

Just to prove that I'm awake,
Say I understood
'Cause if you really said it,
Then for goodness sake:

REFRAIN

You can say that again,
Though I shouldn't believe a word.
If I hear what I thought I heard,
Then can't I hear it again?
Only three little words,
They've been kicking around for years,
But it's music to these old ears.
And you can say that again.
Yes, you can say that again.

DURATION BLUES

Music by Mercer. Published. Copyrighted October 26, 1944. Previously registered for copyright as an unpublished song September 29, 1944. This lyric is derived from Mercer's Christmas card of 1942. All four verses are spoken ad lib.

VERSE 1

This modern age we're goin' through
Has got me in a spin.
I ain't too bright to start with—
Now here's the state I'm in.

REFRAIN 1

For anything and everything
There's stamps you got to use;
The D's and G's are groceries,
And I think the T's are shoes.
You have to be an FBI man
To figure out all the clues—
And that's the situation
When you got the Duration Blues.

VERSE 2

The Army and the draft board
Keeps me kind of mixed up, too,
You is in if you is 1-A, but
If you ain't, then "Who are you?"

REFRAIN 2

The 3-A's is essential
And the 4-F's all have asthma,

2-B gents are in defense,
Or else they're givin' plasma,
Or else, man, you ain't got nothin'
That the armed forces can use—
That is the unfortunate situation
When you get the Duration Blues.

VERSE 3

Food will win the war, they say,
And that's okay with me,
But when I go to the corner store,
What do I see?

REFRAIN 3

There's Spam and Wham and Deviled Ham
And something new called Zoom—
Just take it home and heat it
To the temp'rature of the room.
And you can bake it, flake it,
Cake it, make it, take it any way you choose—
Jack, that's the situation
When you get the Duration Blues.

VERSE 4

Then on top of everything,
The taxes roll around.
I went to see the income man,
And this is what I found.

REFRAIN 4

You multiplies the profits
And incorporates the loss,
Deductin' all expenditures
And anything else you come across.
Then if you satisfy the government,
It's ten to one the little woman sues—
And that's my situation;
I've got the Duration Blues.

TO HAVE AND HAVE NOT (1944)

Produced by Jack L. Warner for Warner Bros. Released October 1944. Copyright January 20, 1945. Directed by Howard Hawks. Screenplay by Jules Furthman and William Faulkner. Starring Humphrey Bogart, with Walter Brennan, Lauren Bacall, Dolores Moran, Hoagy Carmichael, Sheldon Leonard, Walter Molnar, Marcel Dalio, Walter Sande, Dan Seymour, and Aldo Nadi.

The songs for this film are by Grant Clarke and Stanley Adams (lyrics) and Harry Akst and Hoagy Carmichael (music), except for "How Little We Know," lyrics by Johnny Mercer and music by Hoagy Carmichael.

HOW LITTLE WE KNOW

Music by Hoagy Carmichael. Published. Copyrighted October 19, 1944. Introduced by Hoagy Carmichael and Lauren Bacall.

Carmichael not only composed the song; he also played it in the film in his role as Cricket, the hotel piano player, accompanying Bacall "singing" with the dubbed voice of the young Andy Williams.

At one point there was a separate song called "Over and Over Again," that was later incorporated into this song.

Maybe it happens this way,
Maybe we really belong together—
But after all,
How little we know.
Maybe it's just for a day;
Love is as changeable as the weather—
And after all,
How little we know.
Who knows why an April breeze
Never remains?
Why stars in the trees
Hide when it rains?
Love comes along
Casting a spell—
Will it sing you a song?
Will it say a farewell?
Who can tell!
Maybe you're meant to be mine;
Maybe I'm only supposed to stay
In your arms awhile,
As others have done.
Is that what I've waited for?
Am I the one?
Oh, I hope in my heart that it's so,
In spite of how little we know.

Alternative lyrics

Who knows why the thrill of you
Always is mine?
Who knows why the feel of you
Fades out in time?
Maybe I'm meant to be yours;
Maybe you're only supposed to

Hold me a little while
And leave me behind.
But something keeps telling me
Fate will be kind.

Additional lyrics

You think that it's fine and free,
Something that sings;
It turns out to be
One of those things.

"Over and Over Again"

Over and over again
Through every moment of every minute of every
    day
I think about you;
Over and over again: should I stay away?
But what do I do?
I run to the telephone
Whenever it rings;
I can't be alone—
It's one of those things.
I tell a star my little woes,
Hang around in a bar
Till it's ready to close—
So it goes . . .

HERE COME THE WAVES (1944)

Produced by Mark Sandrich for Paramount Pictures. Released December 1944. Copyright December 15, 1944. Directed by Mark Sandrich. Screenplay by Allan Scott, Ken Englund, and Zion Myers. Sketch by Milt Gross. Lyrics by Johnny Mercer. Music by Harold Arlen. Ensembles staged by Danny Dare. Musical director: Robert Emmett Dolan. Starring Bing Crosby, Betty Hutton, and Sonny Tufts, with Ann Doran, Gwen Crawford, Noel Neill, Catherine Craig, and Marjorie Henshaw.

A sailor falls for twin Waves in a typical recruiting movie of the period. (WAVES, incidentally, was an acronym for "Women Accepted for Volunteer Emergency Service," a component of the Navy formed during World War II.)

THE NAVY SONG

Unpublished. Not registered for copyright until February 17, 1989. Introduced by Betty Hutton, who plays twin sisters, and female ensemble. Alternate title: "Join the Navy."

REFRAIN 1

ALL: Join the Navy,
That's the place to be.
Join the Navy,
You Double-U-A-V-E.
Do your doot—do your doot—do your duty,
do!
Join the Waves!
Join the Waves!
Be a boot or a cute little lieut.
In your suit of blue.
Join the boyfriend
Who's across the foam.
Help to bring him back home.
Join the Waves!
Uncle Sam needs ya, ma'am,
And he sent us out to say,
Join the Navy band when they play.
Do ya doot—do ya doot—do ya doot—
Do your duty today!

REFRAIN 2

BETTY
HUTTON
(AS ROSEMARY): Join the Navy,
Do your part today!

HUTTON
(AS SUSIE): Join the Navy,
Get hep to the U.S.A.!

HUTTON
(AS ROSEMARY): Snap your cap for a chap who will
say to you—

HUTTON
(AS SUSIE): "Well, all root, you're a beaut, I
salute
Your cute suit of blue!"

HUTTON
(AS ROSEMARY): Join the boyfriend
On the starboard side.
BOTH: He's already applied.
Uncle Sam needs your gam in a
uniform today—
Join the Navy band when they
play!

LET'S TAKE THE LONG WAY HOME

Published. Copyrighted December 1, 1944. Introduced and recorded by Bing Crosby (Decca). Leading recordings by Jo Stafford (Capitol) and Cab Calloway (Columbia).

Let's take the long way home,
Let's look for the long way home,
And on the way, let's pretend
That this wonderful night won't end.
Through Asia would be much too soon—
We'll circle once around the moon,
Our dream boat will carry us across the foam.
We'll take the long way,
Make sure it's the wrong way—
Let's take the long way home.

Shall we fly through the night?
Shall we dream as we go?
See the star on your right?
See the farm down below?
The whole trip, it appears,
Only takes a million years—
If you're in the mood to roam,
Then let's take the long way home.

AC-CENT-TCHU-ATE THE POSITIVE

Published. Copyrighted December 1, 1944. Introduced by Bing Crosby, Sonny Tufts, and ensemble.

Number-one record by Johnny Mercer (Capitol); Number-two seller by Bing Crosby and the Andrews Sisters (Decca). Nominated for an Academy Award but lost to "It Might as Well Be Spring" from *State Fair*, by Richard Rodgers and Oscar Hammerstein II.

Mercer recalled:

When I was working with Benny Goodman back in '39 I had a publicity guy who told me he had been to hear Father Divine, and that was the subject of his sermon: "Accentuate the positive and eliminate the negative." Well, that amused me so, and it sounds so Southern and so funny, that I wrote it down on a piece of paper.

And this was, what, five years later? Harold Arlen and I were riding home from the studio after a conference about writing a song for the sailors. The sailors wanted to put on a show on a big destroyer and Bing Crosby and Sonny Tufts were going to sing a duet. And could we come up

with something? And then Harold was singing me this offbeat little rhythm tune he had sung me before. Now, that's a strange thing about your subconscious, because here's a song that's been lying dormant in my subconscious for five years, and the minute he sang that tune, it jumped into my mind as if he'd dialed a phone number.

I remembered that sermon. With a beginning like that it practically wrote itself . . . It was like getting an elusive crossword. By the time we finished our drive, the song was more or less complete.

VERSE

[*Slowly, sermonlike.*]

Gather round me,
Ev'rybody,
Gather round me
While I preach some.
Feel a sermon
Comin' on me—
The topic will be sin,
And that's what I'm again'.
If you wanna
Hear my story,
Then settle back
And just sit tight
While I start reviewin'
The attitude of doin' right.

REFRAIN

[*Rhythmic.*]

You've got to
Ac-cent-tchu-ate the positive,
E-lim-mi-nate the negative,
Latch on to the affirmative—
Don't mess with Mister In-Between!
You've got to spread joy
Up to the maximum,
Bring gloom down to the minimum,
Have faith, or pandemonium
Li'ble to walk upon the scene!
To illustrate my last remark,
Jonah in the whale,
Noah in the ark,
What did they do
Just when ev'rything looked so dark?
"Man," they said,
"You better
Ac-cent-tchu-ate the positive,
E-lim-mi-nate the negative,
Latch on
To the affirmative,
Don't mess with Mister In-Between—
No, don't mess with Mister In-Between!"

THERE'S A FELLA WAITIN' IN POUGHKEEPSIE

Published. Copyrighted December 29, 1944. Introduced by Betty Hutton, Bing Crosby, Sonny Tufts, and female ensemble. Recorded by Bing Crosby (Decca).

VERSE

Sailor boy, don't believe
All the stripes you behold on my sleeve.
Just forget my rank, you beautiful Yank!
Let's pretend tonight we're both on leave.

Film version

REFRAIN 1

There's a fella waitin' in Poughkeepsie,
And he's just as sweet as sweet can be.
He hasn't even been tipsy
Since I left him and took to the sea.
There's another waitin' in Pomona
With the cutest dimple in his chin.
And there's a guy in Daytona
Who just waits for my ship to come in.
I miss 'em, honor bright!
I write 'em every night.
But if you held my hand,
I suppose they would all understand.
Oh, you mustn't think I'm just a gypsy,
But I really ought to set you right—
There's a fella waitin' in Poughkeepsie,
But I'm strictly on my own tonight!

REFRAIN 2

BETTY HUTTON: There's a Seabee waitin' in
Milwaukee,
One of my more gentlemanly
beaus;
Sometimes he goes to a talkie,
But I know that's as far as he goes.
There's another waitin' in Decatur,
And I often sat upon his knee;
I'm gonna look him up later—
He made quite an impression on
me.
Topeka, Kankakee,
Eureka, Tennessee—
I got 'em here and there.
What the heck, love is love
anywhere!
What's the difference if you have
lumbago
And your hair is gettin' kinda
white?

There's a fella back in San Diego,
But I'm strictly on my own
tonight!
TWO GIRLS: When a beachhead's gotta be
established,
The Marines are first in any fight.
BING CROSBY
& SONNY TUFTS: There are Waves awaiting at the
jetty,
But we're strictly on our own
tonight.
HUTTON: Got a guy in Hackensack,
In Pontiac,
Daytona,
Pomona,
In Mexico,
In Guam,
Palm Beach,
Idaho,
Colorado,
Indio?,
So far I'm doing all right!
But I wish someone would fall,
I'm so all alone,
Strictly on my own tonight,
Yes, I'm strictly on my own
tonight.

REFRAIN 3 (NOT USED IN FILM)

CROSBY: There's a Wave who's waitin' in Biloxi,
And she's gonna marry me or bust.
We're bein' married by proxy
When I find me a wolf I can trust.
There's a SPAR who's waitin' in
Waukegan,
Who is really different from the rest.
I think her last name is Reagan—
That's the name that's tattooed on my
chest.
WAC: A WAC in Hackensack.
WAAF: A WAAF in Pontiac.
CROSBY: I got 'em here and there—
What the heck, chicks is chicks anywhere!
Some of them are kind of bobby-soxy,
But it may be quite a lengthy fight—
There's a Wave who's waitin' in Biloxi,
But I'm strictly on my own tonight!*

Alternate lyrics not used in film

Oh, it isn't good for her libido
When a lady's love is out of sight—
There's a paratrooper in Toledo,
But I'm strictly on my own tonight!

---

* *Alternate line:*
  But I'm strictly on the prowl tonight.

I PROMISE YOU

Published. Copyrighted December 1, 1944. Introduced by Bing Crosby, Betty Hutton, and ensemble. Recorded by Bing Crosby (Decca).

VERSE

Hate to be pedantic
Or too darned romantic,
But gee,
These goodbyes
Do things to my eyes!
So I hope
That the same old phrase
Still applies.

REFRAIN

I promise you a faithful heart,
One that has always been free.
At night there's a handful of stars
That I pretend belong to me.
I promise you that, rich or poor,
I would be happy to share
The arms you have taken possession of.
The sun on the meadows,
A fire in the shadows,
And I promise you I'll be there.
A faithful heart,
A star or two,
And I'll be there,
I promise you.

HERE COME THE WAVES

Published. Copyrighted December 29, 1944. Introduced by female ensemble.

Here come the Waves,
Marching row on row—
Clear the way as they pass in review.
Any time there's a job to be done,
You'll find the gal behind the guy
Behind the gun.

Here come the Waves,
So the world will know
That the Yankees can do what they say.
If you have to be shown,
Ask the bunch who are known
As the Waves of the U.S.A.

When the bugle blows
And the chips are down,
And when we really need to go to town,
When GI Joe
Needs a helping hand,
Say the word,
Say the word
To the Navy and—

Here come the Waves,
So the world will know
That the Yankees can do what they say.
If you have to be shown,
Ask the bunch who are known
As the Waves of the U.S.A.

MY MAMA THINKS I'M A STAR

Published. Copyrighted December 31, 1944. Not used in film.

VERSE

I come from a vaudeville family,
Which right away makes me a bum.
I ate all my meals with performing seals,
And they rocked me to sleep in a drum.
If you've heard of Mullins and Mullins,
You've heard of my dad and his wife.
They headed the bill that killed vaudeville,
Now they want me to bring it to life.
So, ever since I've been three,
I've had my fate cut out for me.

REFRAIN 1

My mama thinks I'm a star,
And if it's up to Mama, I'll go far.
On the day I was born, she could see I was cute,
So she got me a suit and a vaudeville route.
I've laid an egg in Winnipeg
And laid an omelet in Butte,
But Mama thinks I'm a star.
I play the slide trombone and steel guitar;
I've appeared off and on in the classiest pubs,
Where I made with the eyes and the Indian
  clubs—
And when I couldn't get a booking,
I would pitch for the Cubs.

Though I can sing "Irish Eyes"
While hangin' down from a chandelier,

Mama just sighs,
"Your father did the same—and drank a bottle of
  beer."
From concert stage to the circus ring,
My mama is prepared for ev'rything.
For a time I was known as the Queen of
  Burlesque,
I would run through a strip while they played
  "Humoresque."
I got my training running, running round a
  manager's desk.
But I ain't upset,
I may get there yet,
'Cause according to my mama I'm a star.

REFRAIN 2

She makes me wear kiddie clothes in hope I'll
  catch a producer's eye—
Ev'ryone knows that I'm the only mother in
  Hollywood High.*
I'm not complaining, and that's a fact,
But take the time I did that magic act:
I would lie in a box while they sawed me in half,
If the knife ever slipped, it was my epitaph!
But Mama didn't care—
She only hollered, "Wait for your laugh!"
I may lay a bomb,
But if you ask Mom,
Twenty-five will get you fifty that I'm a star.
She makes me a star.

Alternative lyrics

My mama is prepared for ev'rything.
We'd apply for a job when the circus appeared,
And because Mama knew that I had to be weird,
She bought a jar of shaving cream and had me
  grow a beard.
But I ain't upset,
I may get there yet
'Cause according to my mama, why, I'm a star!

I may lay a bomb,
But if you ask Mom,
I'm at perfect ease
On the high trapeze.
I've swallowed swords
And sung trio chords;
I've had my name in lights
And my legs in tights.
I was shot from a gun
For a one-day run;
I was quite the rage
in the lion's cage

_____
* _Alternate line:_
    That I've got a daughter in Hollywood High.

(Incidentally, folks, I was underage)—
If you don't believe it I can show you the scar!
I missed many a prom,
But if you ask Mom
Twenty-five will get you fifty that I'm a star!

GOT TO WEAR YOU OFF MY WEARY MIND

Not used in film.

I've got to wear you off my weary mind;
I've got to leave those memories behind.
But the truth is that's it's hard to do,
Specially when my mind keeps runnin',
Runnin' back to you.
This love, love, love
Is strong, strong, strong;
It lingers in your heart
So long, long, long.
Guess I'll have to use
Whatever means a man can find
To wear you off
My weary, weary mind.

A WOMAN'S WORK IS NEVER DONE

Not used in film. Verse listed as missing; perhaps one never was written. Music for refrain dated March 28, 1944.

REFRAIN 1

A woman's work is never done.
She hits the deck at six-oh-one.
With soap in her eye
She ties her tie
And greets the morning sun.
Oh, a woman's work is never done!
She goes and gets in line for chow,
Because she's in the Navy now.
She gobbles her hash
And makes a dash
To do what must be done.
Oh, a woman's work is not much fun!
She runs a machine
Or keeps the barracks clean,

Whatever's the job of the day.
She does them all to a T—
And very frequently.
She'll say,
"Anchors aweigh!"
She puts on an old middy blouse
And does what she did round the house.
Whatever you choose
The gal can use—
A girdle or a gun.
Oh, a woman's work is never done,
No, a woman's work is never done!

REFRAIN 2

A woman's work is never done,
For there's a war that must be won.
Her beautiful knees
In dungarees,
She takes it on the run.
Oh, a woman's work is never done!
She puts her makeup on, and then
She takes her makeup off again;
In utter despair
She combs her hair
And ties it in a bun.
Oh, a woman's work is not much fun!
With grease on her face
She tidies up the place—
There's nothin' too good for her "uns,"
And when the last bugle calls,
Exhausted she falls—
Kerplunk!—
Back in her bunk.
She lies there more dead than alive
And dreams of Chanel Number Five,
And that's how it goes:
The bugle blows;
Another day's begun.
Oh, a woman's work is never done,
No, a woman's work is never done.

REFRAIN 3

A woman's work is never done.
They held the line at Lexington.
They wouldn't withdraw,
Until they saw the redcoat on the run—
Oh, a woman's work is never done!
In history you'll come across
A lady known as Betsy Ross.
With all of her might
She fought the fight
Until the fight was won—
Oh, a woman's work is never done!
And who held the reins
Across the open plains,

And who helped the menfolk* break ground?
Who built the house on the hill?
And who is it who'll still be found
Rallying round?
They've traded their gingham for braid,
But, mister, they're still unafraid.
They're filling the bill,
And will until they hear the final gun—
Oh, a woman's work is never done,
No, a woman's work is never done!

I OWE IT ALL TO YOU

Not used in film.

I was lonesome and I know it.
Now I'm happy and I show it.
Needn't tell you
That I owe it
All to you.
I was one of seven brothers,
No one's baby
But my mother's.
Then I met you—
Now, I'll never be another's,
Even if I live to be a million.
I'll never see how you ever fell
For someone like me.
If I'm talking like a poet,
Only hope I don't outgrow it.
What I mean is, ev'ry dream I had came true
And angel [baby],
I owe it all to you.

AW, COME ON NOW

Music by Mercer.
    Lyric missing.

---

* *Or:* And who helped the husbands

MEMORY SONG

Music by Paul Weston.
    Lyric missing.

PARTING SONG

Music by Nat Shilkret.
    Lyric missing.

WINTER IN MY HEART

Music by Nat Shilkret.
    Lyric missing.

YOU'VE GOT ME WHERE YOU WANT ME

Music by Harry Warren. Published. Copyrighted August 10, 1944.

VERSE

I don't know if it's glum or grand,
This feeling I can't understand.
I'm like a ship that's in a calm—
I mean you've got me in your palm,
I'm in the hollow of your hand.

REFRAIN

You've got me where you want me,
And I hope you're satisfied,
You've got me where you want me,
And you hardly even tried.
A single look was all I took,
And starry-eyed I watched my poor old heart
Go on that roller-coaster ride.
I say I won't surrender,
But I know darn well I will;
My hopes are pretty slender
And my chances almost nil.
Why should I try to alibi

When anyone can see
You've got me where you want me,
And it's where I want to be?

LAURA

Music by David Raksin. Published. Copyrighted March 6, 1945. Mercer wrote his lyric to Raksin's music after the release (in October 1944) of Otto Preminger's film *Laura*.

Otto Preminger initially wanted to use Duke Ellington's "Sophisticated Lady" as *Laura*'s theme, but David Raksin, who scored the film, objected. When Raksin's melody proved to be so popular with the public, Oscar Hammerstein II was asked to write a lyric for it, but the producers couldn't agree to let Hammerstein's company publish it. Then Irving Caesar was asked, but when he, too, failed to work out, Raksin suggested Mercer, and the studio wired him that there had been "tremendous calls for this tune from all over the country . . . hop on it right away." Mercer wanted to use the title "Footsteps in the Dark." He hadn't even seen the movie—"I simply absorbed the tune and let it create an atmosphere for me." Raksin said, "I thought Johnny's achievement was amazing, that he should get that feeling into a lyric. And I know he worked hard, sweated blood sometimes, but you would never have known it. He would show up without a hair out of place—with this thing he had written on the tip of his little finger."

Mercer didn't deny the effort:

If a fellow plays me a melody that sounds like something, well, I try and fit the words to the sound of the melody. It has a mood and if I can capture that mood, that's the way we go about it. *Laura* was that kind of picture. It was pre-designed, because Laura was a mystery. So I had to write "Laura" with kind of a *misterioso* theme.

That's hard, because there are so few notes. And because the intervals are tough, the key changes are strange. And at the time it came out, it was most strange. But since it has become so popular, it's easier now. But that kind of song is always difficult, because you have to write a lyric that's going to be a hit, and you don't have many notes to work with.

And, indeed, "Laura" was a hit: so far it has been recorded more than four hundred times. Cole Porter claimed that it was his favorite song—of those *he* didn't write himself.

VERSE

You know the feeling
Of something half-remembered,
Of something that never happened,
Yet you recall it well.

You know the feeling
Of recognizing someone
That you've never met,
As far as you could tell.
Well—

REFRAIN

Laura
Is the face in the misty light,
Footsteps
That you hear down the hall,
The laugh
That floats on a summer night
That you can never quite
Recall.
And you see Laura
On the train that is passing through,
Those eyes,
How familiar they seem!
She gave
Your very first kiss to you.
That was Laura,
But she's only a dream.

OUT OF THIS WORLD (1945)

Produced by Sam Coslow for Paramount Pictures. Released June 1945. Copyright June 4, 1945. Directed by Hal Walker. Screenplay by Walter DeLeon and Arthur Phillips, after stories by Elizabeth Meehan and Sam Coslow. Musical numbers staged by Sammy Lee. Specialty arrangements by Joseph J. Lilley and Harry Simeone. Musical director: Victor Young. Starring Eddie Bracken, Veronica Lake, and Diana Lynn, with Cass Daley, Harry "Parkyakarkus" Einstein, Donald MacBride, Florence Bates, Gary, Phillip, Dennis, and Lin Crosby, Olga San Juan, Nancy Porter, Audrey Young, Carol Deere, Carmen Cavallaro, Ted Fio Rito, Henry King, Ray Noble, and Joe Reichman.

The songs for this film were by Bernie Wayne, Ben Raleigh, Sam Coslow, Felix Bernard, and Eddie Cherkose, except for "Out of This World" and "June Comes Around Every Year," by Johnny Mercer (lyrics) and Harold Arlen (music).

In a parody of Frank Sinatra's popularity, a Western Union messenger becomes a hit crooner with the help of Bing Crosby's voice.

OUT OF THIS WORLD

Published. Copyrighted May 17, 1945. Introduced by Eddie Bracken (dubbed by Bing Crosby). Reprised by the "Piano Maestros": Carmen Cavallaro, Joe Reichman, Ray Noble, Henry King, and Ted Fio Rito, all playing themselves.

Leading recordings were made by Bing Crosby (Decca); Jo Stafford (Capitol); and Tommy Dorsey and His Orchestra, with vocals by Stuart Foster (Victor).

You're clear out of this world.
When I'm looking at you,
I hear out of this world
The music that no mortal ever knew.

You're right out of a book,
The fairy tale I read when I was so high.
No armored knight out of a book
Was more enchanted by a Lorelei
Than I.

After waiting so long for the right time,
After reaching so long for a star,
All at once, from the long and lonely nighttime,
And despite time,
Here you are.

I'd cry out of this world
If you said we were through,
So, let me fly out of this world
And spend the next eternity or two
With you.

JUNE COMES AROUND EVERY YEAR

Published. Copyrighted June 17, 1945. Introduced by Eddie Bracken (dubbed by Bing Crosby), Olga San Juan, Nancy Porter, Audrey Young, and Carol Deere.

REFRAIN

EDDIE
BRACKEN: June comes around every year;
June comes around every springtime.
Just when your poor old heart
Can't go on, it seems,
June brings a basketful of dreams.
And before you know it,
You see the moon wink his eye.
Two hearts are waltzing in swing time,
So, wear a great big smile,
'Cause after all
She'll never fall
For last year's style
And June comes around every year.

COUNTERMELODY

[*Sung against refrain.*]

Paper says "Cloudy with showers,
Cloudy and rainy for hours,"
Never a word about flowers.
Well, sump'in' must be wrong,
'Cause June comes around ev'ry
     springtime—
Just when your poor old heart
Can't go on, it seems,
June brings a basketful of dreams,
And before you know it
You see the moon wink its eye.

FEMALE
QUARTET: When there's a change in the weather,
People are gettin' together—
Talk about walkin' in heather,
The countryside is bloomin'.
BRACKEN: Two hearts are waltzing in swing time,
So, wear a great big smile.
FEMALE
QUARTET: 'Cause after all
She'll never fall
For last year's style.
BRACKEN: And June comes around every year.
FEMALE
QUARTET: Calendar's certainly funny,
Suddenly ev'rything's sunny,
Brother, you're right on the money—
ALL: 'Cause jolly old June is here.

CONVERSATION WHILE DANCING

Music by Paul Weston. Published. Copyrighted August 12, 1945.

REFRAIN

Do ya know what's groovy?
Have ya seen the latest movie?
Should I try and tip ya?
May I hip ya?
Yes, I know.
Do ya know what's playin'?
Have ya heard what folks are sayin'?
Should I try and sell ya?
May I tell ya?
Yes, I know.
I can see, baby,
You're the kind of chick
That's sharp on top,
Yessiree, baby,
(But) why are we talkin' this shop?
Mop! Mop!
You're a solid sender,
And the band is some ear bender—
We could both jump steady,
Are you ready?
Yes, I know.

I HEAR A SONG IN MY HEART

Music by Paul Weston.
     Lyric missing.

PARTING IS SUCH SWEET SORROW

Music by Joseph Meyer. Published. Copyrighted April 28, 1949. Previously registered for copyright as an unpublished song September 28, 1945.

VERSE

Even though you're leaving my arms,
Even though I'm leaving your kiss,

This night should be one of ecstasy,
To last until
You are back with me.

REFRAIN

Parting is such sweet sorrow,
Because I know we'll meet again.
Soon, dear, some bright tomorrow,
My lonely heart will beat again.
Hold me closer
And let us borrow
This moment's thrill to cherish till then.
Parting is such sweet sorrow,
Because I know we'll meet again.

CAMPTOWN RACES

Music by Stephen Foster. Mercer wrote new lyrics to the famous old song to perform with the Starlighters. Registered for copyright as an unpublished song October 13, 1945.

MERCER: Camptown lady sing this song,
Doo dah, doo dah.
Camptown racetrack five miles
     long,
Oh, doo dah day.
Came down here with my hat
     caved in,
Doo dah, doo dah.
Can't go back with a pocketful of
     gin,
Oh, doo dah day.
STARLIGHTERS: Oh, the long-tailed filly and the
     big black horse,
Doo dah, doo dah,
Fly the track and they cut across,
Oh, doo dah day.
Blind horse stickin' in a big
     mudhole,
Doo dah, doo dah,
Can't touch bottom with a ten-foot
     pole,
Oh, doo dah day.
MERCER: Whyn't they run all night?
Whyn't they run all day?
Bet my money on a bobtailed
     nag,
Somebody bet on de bay.
STARLIGHTERS: Oh, doo dah day.
MERCER: Grandstand's filled with a happy
     crowd—

149

Clothes ain't stylish but dey sure
    is loud.
Every highborn lady wears a fancy
    lid,
Sports all hollerin', "Oh, you
    kid!"
And if you ain't made a wager,
    time you did.

STARLIGHTERS: They're at the post,
They goes the gun,
They're off!
Oh, doo dah . . .

MERCER: Eee. Bobtail leading at the quarter-
    mile,
But look at the bay, got a lot of
    style.
Yes, now they're startin' on the
    homeward trek,
Looks like everybody's gonna
    collect,
It's a photograph finish—neck and
    neck.

STARLIGHTERS: Oh, those Camptown Races!
Oh, those happy faces!
Sure had a wonderful time.

I CAN'T BELIEVE MY EYES

Music by Harold Arlen. Intended for *Blues in the Night* (1941). Not used in film.

In 1941 Harold Arlen played Mercer one of those unconventionally long tunes—this one was sixty bars instead of the conventional thirty-two. Mercer thought of it as "a jazz tune like 'I've Got the World on a String' or something like it . . . rhythmical." For some reason neither the tune nor the lyric was ever used.

"I don't even know what picture it was for," Mercer would later claim.

He wasn't entirely happy with the way things turned out. In 1954 Arlen was collaborating with Ira Gershwin on the score for the film *A Star Is Born*. He had written a new tune and was playing it for Ira at the Gershwin home in Beverly Hills when Ira's outspoken wife, Leonore, remarked that it "sounds like Gershwin to me." Sensitive to the comparison, Arlen immediately abandoned the melody and somehow found himself playing the old tune he and Mercer had worked on a decade before. Ira listened to it and produced the lyric for "The Man That Got Away."

The ultimate irony was that the star of the film—making a major comeback—was Judy Garland, the girl who got away from Mercer. She was nominated that year for the Best Actress Oscar and the song for Best Song. Neither won. (The song that did win was "Three Coins in the Fountain," from the movie of the same name, with music by Jule Styne and lyrics by Sammy Cahn.)

I've seen Sequoia,
It's really very pretty,
The art of Goya
And Rockefeller City,
But since I saw you
I can't believe my eyes.
You've got that ooh-la-la,
That old je ne sais quoi.
I feel like shoutin', "Ma! Just my size!"
I've seen the table
That held the Declaration,
And Betty Grable
In my imagination,
But you're a fable
That's hard to realize.
You're one of them there things
That comes equipped with wings—
It walks—it talks—it sings—and it flies.
Fate didn't give me any warning,
I'm getting glasses in the morning.
I've heaved a sigh over
Famous Roman fountains
And in Ohio
The Appalachian Mountains rise.
I've seen a thing or two,
But there ain't no view like you—
Believe me, baby,
I simply can't believe my eyes.

THE HARVEY GIRLS | 1945

THE HARVEY GIRLS (1945)

Produced by Arthur Freed and Roger Edens for Metro-Goldwyn-Mayer. Released January 1946. Directed by George Sidney. Copyright December 28, 1945. Screenplay by Edmund Beloin, Nathaniel Curtis, Harry Crane, James O'Hanlon, Samson Raphaelson, and Kay Van Riper, based on the novel *The Harvey Girls* by Samuel Hopkins Adams and the original story by Eleanore Griffin and William Rankin. Lyrics by Johnny Mercer. Music by Harry Warren. Musical numbers staged by Robert Alton. Orchestrations by Conrad Salinger. Vocal arrangements by Kay Thompson. Musical director: Lennie Hayton. Starring Judy Garland, with John Hodiak, Ray Bolger, Angela Lansbury, Preston Foster, Virginia O'Brien, Kenny Baker, Marjorie Main, Chill Wills, Selena Royle, and Cyd Charisse.

A nineteenth-century restaurateur hires a group of young ladies to go out west as waitresses.

IN THE VALLEY (WHERE THE EVENIN' SUN GOES DOWN)

Published. Copyrighted June 19, 1945. Previously registered for copyright as an unpublished song September 8, 1943. Introduced and recorded by Judy Garland. (Decca).

When white clouds come sailin'
To make my wedding gown,
Then we'll go trailin' to the valley
Where the evenin' sun goes down.
And hidden away in the gloamin'
When leaves are turnin' brown,
We'll end our roamin' in the valley
Where the evenin' sun goes down.
We'll build a home in our valley there
And watch it grow into a town,
And you can sit in your rockin' chair
And watch the evenin' sun go down.
The evenin' sun go down.

WAIT AND SEE

Published. Copyrighted July 10, 1945. Previously registered for copyright as an unpublished song January 4, 1944. Introduced by Angela Lansbury (dubbed by Virginia Rees); reprised by Kenny Baker and Cyd Charisse (dubbed by Marion Doenges). Recorded by Kenny Baker (Decca) and Johnny Johnston (Capitol).

VERSE

This heart of mine is in your keeping;
I've known it ever since we met.
It will be yours awake or sleeping,
But just in case you ever should forget—

REFRAIN

I shall be loving you all through eternity,
But if you don't believe me,
Wait and see.
My heart will still be true
When stars on high have flickered out
Like little candles in the sky,
And when the evergreen has withered on the
    bough,
I still will feel the same
As I do now.
These little words, I know,
Can never show how true I'll be,
But if you don't believe me,
Just you wait and see.

ON THE ATCHISON, TOPEKA, AND THE SANTA FE

Lyric by Johnny Mercer. Additional lyrics credited in film to Ralph Blane, Kay Thompson, and Roger Edens. Published. Copyrighted June 19, 1945. Previously registered for copyright as an unpublished song October 13, 1943. Introduced by Judy Garland, Marjorie Main, Ray Bolger, Ben Carter, Virginia O'Brien, and ensemble. Number-one recording by Johnny Mercer and the Pied Pipers (Capitol). Other leading recordings by Bing Crosby with Six Hits and a Miss (Decca); Judy Garland with the Merry Macs and Lyn Murray's Orchestra (Decca) and Judy Garland with Lennie Hayton and His Orchestra (Decca); and Tommy Dorsey and His Orchestra, with vocal by the Sentimentalists (Victor).

Mercer recalled that he once noticed a railroad box-car with the legend "The Atchison, Topeka and the Santa Fe" and "thought it had a nice lyrical quality to it . . . [the song] was an easy one to write. As I recall, it took me about an hour."

When producers and director George Sidney decided the song needed extra verses—and knowing how slowly Mercer and Warren usually worked—they asked vocal arranger Kay Thompson and composer-lyricist Ralph Blane to contribute. Another Mercer train song made up for losing the Oscar for "Blues in the Night": this one gave him his first Academy Award.

Film version

BEN CARTER: Do you hear that whistle down the
    line?
    I figure that it's engine number
    forty-nine;
    She's the only one that'll sound that
    way
    On the Atchison, Topeka, and the
    Santa Fe.
    See the ol' smoke rising round the
    bend?
    I reckon that she knows she's gonna
    meet a friend.
    Folks around these parts get the
    time o' day
    From the Atchison, Topeka, and the
    Santa Fe.
MAN: Here she comes.
CROWD: Wooh, ooh, ooh, ooh-ooh-ooh!
ANOTHER
MAN: Hey, Jim, you better get the rig.
CROWD: Wooh, ooh, ooh, ooh-ooh-ooh!
TICKET MAN: She's got a list of passengers that's
    pretty big.
BOYS: And they'll all want lifts to Brown's
    Hotel,
    'Cause lots of them been travelin'
    for quite a spell.
    On the way to Californ-i-ay,
    On the Atchison, Topeka,
GIRLS: Choo-choo-choo,
BOYS: On the Atchison, Topeka,
GIRLS: Choo-choo-choo,
CROWD: On the Atchison, Topeka, and the
    Santa Fe.
    Atchison, Topeka, and the Santa Fe
    Atchison, Topeka—
ENGINEER: Oh, the roads back east are mighty
    swell,
    The Chesapeake, Ohio, and the ASL.
FIREMAN: But I make my run and I make my
    pay
FIREMAN &
ENGINEER: On the Atchison, Topeka and the
    Santa Fe.

MARJORIE
MAIN: Goin' back and forth along these
aisles,
My lands, you must have walked
about a million miles!

CONDUCTOR: It's a treat to be on your feet all day

MAIN &
CONDUCTOR: On the Atchison, Topeka, and the
Santa Fe!

VIRGINIA
O'BRIEN,
RAY BOLGER
& GIRLS: Here we come! Roaduraa, duraa,
duraa, durraa-raa
She's really racing down the line . . .
Looky, looky, looky, looky, look-
look!
Oh boy, we're huffin' an' a-puffin'
on the forty-nine!

GIRLS: In this day and age, girls don't leave
home,
But if ya get a hankerin' you wanna
roam,
Our advice to you is run away
On the Atchison, Topeka, and the
Santa Fe!

BOYS: Faith and didja ever see such purty
femininity
Arrivin' all at once in this here
town?
In this here town?
Never seen the likes of this for miles
around.

GIRLS: Round and round our heads are
spinning,
New adventures are beginning,

BOYS: What length a gal'll go with taffety
'n calico
To really put a cowboy on the bosh!
Cowboy!

GIRLS: Cowboy!

BOYS: Ki-bosh!

GIRLS: Ki-bosh!

BOYS: It's enough to make a feller want to
wash.

1ST GIRL: Wash your face and hands, we hope
You'll never be afraid of soap.

1ST BOY: Buttoned shoes and powdered
chalk
An' fancy smells and baby talk,
Hit's awful what a gal'll stoop to do!

2ND BOY: Even so, we aim to say,
We love to honor and, oh, baby!
Are there any more at home like
you?

CROWD: Wah-hoo!

BOYS: Hand me my hair comb and my
stickem,

Gonna get spruced up and out-trick
'em,
Put up on the dog and out–city
slickem
Mr. Harvey!
Mr. Harvey!!
Fred Harvey knows exactly how to
pick 'em.

THREE
GIRLS: We come from Debuque, Ioway,
That's where the tall, tall, tall corn
grows.

TWO GIRLS: We come from Louisiana,
Where the Miss-iss-iss-iss-ippi flows.

2ND GIRL: I was the Lillian Russell of
Cherryville, Kansas,
But they never gave me a chance.

CYD
CHARISSE: I finished high school in Providence,
Rhode Island,
And Providence, Rhode Island, is
where I learned to dance.

O'BRIEN: Oh, I'm from Chilicothee,

MEN: Ohio!

O'BRIEN: My middle name's Hi-a-wathee,

MEN: Ohio!

O'BRIEN: I'm gonna git the gold in them thar
hills
So I said, "Goodbye-o, Ohio!"

TWO GIRLS: We were schoolma'arms from Grand
Rapids, Mich.
But reading, writing, 'rithmatic
Were not our dish.

3RD GIRL: I was born in Paris,
I was raised in Paris,
Went to school in Paris, where I met
a boy.
I was married in Paris,
Almost buried in Paris,
But I finally left Paris,

FOUR GIRLS: Paris, Illinois!

RAY BOLGER: So, this is the wild and woolly west!
Give me my chaps and my
checkered vest!
Give me a gun and a holster for my
hip—
Bang, bang.
Yip-yip.

JUDY
GARLAND: What a lovely trip,
I'm feeling so fresh and alive
And I'm so glad to arrive.
It's all so grand!
It's easy to see you don't need a
palace
To feel like Alice in Wonderland.
Back in Ohio,
Where I come from,

I've done a lot of dreamin',
And I've travell'd some,
But I never thought I'd see the day
When I ever took a ride on the Santa
Fe—

CROWD: Wanna take a ride on the Santa Fe?

GARLAND: I would lean across my window
sill,
And hear the whistle echoin' across
the hill.
Then I'd watch the lights till they'd
fade away
On the Atchison, Topeka, and the
Santa Fe!
What a thrill!

CROWD: What a great big wonderful thrill!

GARLAND: With the wheels a-singin',
"Westward Ho!"
Right from the day I heard them
start,
'Cross the Kansas plains through
New Mexico,
I guess I got a little Gypsy in my
heart.
When I'm old and grey and settle
down,
If I ever get a chance to sneak away
from town,
Then I'll spend my busman's
holiday
On the Atchison, Topeka, and the
Santa Fe.
All aboard!

CROWD: They came across the country
lickety-split
Rollin' ninety miles an hour fit to be
tied.

GARLAND: I can't believe we're here at last!
Oo-oo!

CROWD: When you go travelin' it's natch for
you
To take the Atchison, Topeka, and
the Santa Fe.

GARLAND: I can't believe that anything would
go so fast!
Then you pull that throttle, the
whistle blows,
A-huffin' and a-puffin' and away she
goes,
All aboard for Californ-i-ay!
On the Atchison!

CROWD: On the Atchison!

GARLAND: On the Atchison, Topeka . . .

CROWD: On the Atchison, Topeka . . .

GARLAND: On the Atchison, Topeka, and . . .

CROWD: On the Atchison, Topeka, and . . .

ALL: On the Atchison, Topeka, and the
Santa Fe!

Additional lyrics not used in film

3RD GIRL: I was the Lillian Russell of Cherryville,
Kansas,
But they gave my acting the pitch.

4TH GIRL: I was a seamstress in Gary, Indiana,
I'd rather play p-i-an-o,
And never sew a stitch.

5TH GIRL: Can you imagine a blue-blood, a
Boston blue-blood,
Wanting a red-blooded man?

Additional lyrics (from Mercer's recording)

All aboard! All aboard!
Chug-a, chug-a, chug-a oo-oo,
Chug-a, chug-a, chug-a oo-oo,
Let her rip, let her rip, Mister Engineer,
Gotta go, gotta go far away from here.
While the man at the fire shovels in the coal,
Stick your head out the cab, watch the drivin' roll.
See the towns and the roads go a-whizzin' by,
Fare thee well, Laramie—Albuquerque, hi!
Yessirree, here we are goin' all the way,
Mustn't quit till we hit Californ-i-a.

OH, YOU KID

Published. Copyrighted July 20, 1945. Previously registered for copyright as an unpublished song January 27, 1945. Introduced by Angela Lansbury (dubbed by Virginia Rees) and female ensemble.

REFRAIN 1

Oh, you kid,
You lovey-dovey kid,
My heart is going ting-a-ling,
If you like chicken, grab a wing!
Oh, you kid,
Does wifey keep you hid?
I don't know if she does,
But she'd be wiser if she did!
I've been told round these parts
You could break a lot of little girlies' hearts.
I've been told when you wink
That a lot of girlies' cheeks get pink.

REFRAIN 2

I've been told if you'd try,
You would make a lot of girlies cry—
I've been told from the start,

So I guess that I'm not smart!
But oh, you kid,
You lovey-dovey kid,
My heart is going ting-a-ling,
If you like chicken, grab a wing!
Oh, you kid,
May I put in a bid?
I said I'd never fall again,
But oh, you kid!

IT'S A GREAT BIG WORLD

Published. Copyrighted July 10, 1945. Previously registered for copyright as an unpublished song September 22, 1943. Introduced by Judy Garland, Virginia O'Brien, and Cyd Charisse (dubbed by Marion Doenges). Recorded by Judy Garland, Virginia O'Brien, and Betty Russell (Decca).

REFRAIN 1

JUDY
GARLAND: I bought a bonnet to suit my face;
I had my petticoat trimmed with lace.
I looked at the mirror, around I twirled,
And then I went out in the wide, wide
world.
I dreamed of gentlemen I would meet;
I saw them all kneeling at my feet.
I can't understand it, my hair is all
curled,
But my goodness me, it's a great big
world!
And it's cold, cold, cold,
And we'll soon be old—
Alas and alack, it's a great big world!

REFRAIN 2

VIRGINIA
O'BRIEN: I learned to sew and I learned to bake;
I even frosted an angel cake.
On Saturday evening, when folks
dropped in,
My house was as neat as a brand-new pin.
I thought by learning each social grace,
Some likely chap might forget my face;
I can't understand it, I've knitted and
purled,
But my goodness me, it's a great big
world!
And it's cold, cold, cold,
And we'll soon be old—
Alas and alack, it's a great big world!

REFRAIN 3

CYD
CHARISSE: I had no petticoat trimmed with lace;
My angel cake was a pure disgrace.
My face was my fortune, my mother
said,
And my dancing slippers of bright,
bright red.
A million miles I have danced, or more,
In hopes Prince Charming would cross
the floor;
I can't understand it, I've waltzed and
I've whirled,
But my goodness me, it's a great big
world!
And it's cold, cold, cold,
And we'll soon be old—

O'BRIEN: But I'll keep on knitting and doing it
well.

CHARISSE: My slippers are one thing I never will
sell.

GARLAND: My petticoat's waiting, because who
can tell?
It's a great big world.

ALL: It's a great big world!

THE WILD, WILD WEST

Published. Copyrighted July 10, 1945. Previously registered for copyright as an unpublished song November 22, 1943. Introduced and recorded by Virginia O'Brien.

VERSE

Kindly check yore shootin' irons yonder at the door,
Please remove yore spurs before you come out on
the floor,
We'll have no gunplay here at this charade—
Nosirree, there's gotta be downright
respectability,
Where ev'rybody drinks pink lemonade.

REFRAIN 1

I was hopin' to be ropin' somepin' wild in the
wild, wild West,
I been settin' till I'm gettin' kinda riled at the
wild, wild West,
I read about them desperado guys,
As desperate as men can be;
I reckon it was just a pack o' lies—
The only one who's desperate is me.
I don't care if he's a sheriff or a real cattle-rustlin'
heel,

The property I've got ain't hard to steal, your
    deal!
Oh, they say they have hair on their chest;
The only thing I've seen is just a fancy vest.
Holy smackers, milk and crackers,
But it's wild in the wild, wild West!

REFRAIN 2

I was aimin' to be claimin' me a pard in the wild,
    wild West;
I was lookin' to be tooken off my guard in the
    wild, wild West.
They told me that the outlaws captured you
And never set a lady free;
I heard they held 'em all for ransom too,
But evidently ransom don't want me!
All that prattle 'bout the cattle bein' left on the
    range to graze,
Well, don't they ever have no roundup days, I
    raise!
Yeah, I heard about them western chaps;
I've only seen the kind you wear around your
    laps.
Sars'parilla, citronella, but it's wild in the wild,
    wild West.

SWING YOUR PARTNER ROUND AND ROUND

Published. Copyrighted July 10, 1945. Previously registered for copyright as an unpublished song October 13,
1943. Introduced by Judy Garland, Marjorie Main, Ray
Bolger, and ensemble. Recorded by Judy Garland with
Kay Thompson Chorus (Decca).

Published version

VERSE 1

When you go to a dance,
Do you know what to do?
Swing your partner,
Swing your partner,
Swing your partner to you.
Throw your partner way out,
Give your partner a spin,
Swing your partner,
Swing your partner,
Swing your partner back in.
Are you ready now?
Now steady now.
Are you ready now?
Begin!

REFRAIN

Round and round and round we go—
Will you waltz me once around the hall?
Did you know that you're the belle of the ball?
Round and round and round once more,
Oh, the music has such a wonderful sound!
Around, around, around.

VERSE 2

When they call the last waltz,
Do you know what to do?
Swing your partner,
Swing your partner,
Swing your partner to you.
While they play "Home, Sweet Home"
With the lights turned down low,
Kiss your partner,
Kiss your partner—
Not a person will know.
Are you ready now?
Now steady now.
Are you ready now?
Let's go!

REFRAIN 2

Round and round, how short it seems—
Why, we hardly danced around the floor!
May I see you safely home to your door?
You'll be dancing in your dreams,
And your head will spin to that wonderful
    sound—
Around, around, around.

Movie version

VERSE 1

GIRLS: When you go to a dance,
          Do you know what to do?
          Swing your partner,
          Swing your partner,
          Swing your partner to you.
          Throw your partner way out,
          Give your partner a spin,
          Swing your partner,
          Swing your partner,
          Swing your partner back in.
          Are you ready now?
          Now steady now.
          Are you ready now?
          Begin!

REFRAIN 1

Round and round and round we go.
Will you waltz her once around the hall,

Then you'll see that she's the belle of the ball!
Round and round and round once more,
Oh, the music has such a wonderful sound!
Around, around, around.

VERSE 2

MARJORIE
   MAIN: Take your girl in your arms,
          Then you point your right toe,
          Then you go right,
          Then you go left,
          And you rock to and fro.
          When you get the right swing,
          And you cain't find no faults,
          You'll be dancin', and a-prancin'
          Till the orchestra halts.
          Are you ready now?
          Get ready now.
          If you're ready now,
          Let's waltz!

REFRAIN 2

GIRLS: Round and round and round we go.
         If you waltz her once around the hall,
         Then you'll see that she's the belle of the
           ball.
         Round and round and round once more,
         Oh, the music has such a wonderful sound,
         Around, around, around.

[*Instrumental ballet.*]

REFRAIN 3

   GIRLS
  & BOYS: Round and round and round we go,
    MEN: If you waltz her once around the hall,
    ALL: Then you'll see that she's the belle of
          the ball.
         Round and round and round once
           more,
         Oh, the music has such a wonderful
           sound!

  GARLAND
 & CHORUS: Around and around and around and
           around
         And around and around and around
           and around;
         Round and around and around and
           around
         And around and around and around.

HAYRIDE

Registered for copyright as an unpublished song January 1, 1945. Intended for Ray Bolger and Judy Garland but not used in film.

VERSE

My oh my, there's a cloud in the sky
And it surely looks like rain;
But I know a secret, so I won't complain.
That young man with the freckle-face tan
And the great big load of hay—
He's our good luck, and he'll shoo the rain away.

REFRAIN

Most remarkable thing,
How it seems to be spring
On the gloomiest kind of day!
How your wishes come true,
Or it seems as they do,
When you wish on a load of hay!
First, you're joggin' along
And the weather's all wrong,
And the heavens above are gray;
Then a genie appears
And it suddenly clears
When you wish on a load of hay.
The farmer boy wavin' howdy-do
Has a wagonful of dreams for you.
Oh, it's perfectly fine
If you make the right sign
And you know the right things to say;
There's a wonderful thrill
That is waiting to come your way
Round a bed in the road
When you wish on a load of hay.

MARCH OF THE DOAGIES

Published. Copyrighted July 10, 1945. Previously registered for copyright as an unpublished song November 22, 1943. Intended for Judy Garland and ensemble but not used in film.

VERSE 1

Me for the sun comin' up in the sky,
Me for the rosy dawn.
Me for a panful o' bacon to fry
And I'll be moseyin' on.
Me for the land where the bluebonnets grow,
Me for a cowhand song,
Me for the gal in the new calico
And I'll be gettin' along.

REFRAIN

March on, little doagies,
March on, down the trail,
March on, little doagies,
Till we're past the last fence rail.
Out there lies the prairie,
Out there breaks the day,
Oh, we don't know where we're goin',
But we're on our way.

VERSE 2

Me for a campfire out on the trail,
Me and an old cayuse.
Me for the sound of the coyote's wail
And I'm all set to vamoose.
You for a pipe, when the evenin' is still,
You for your own backyard.
I'll be the first fella over the hill,
And I'll be seein' you, pard.

REPEAT REFRAIN

MY INTUITION

Published. Copyrighted July 10, 1945. Previously registered for copyright as an unpublished song November 22, 1943. Intended for Judy Garland and John Hodiak but not used in film. Recorded by Margaret Whiting (Capitol).

VERSE

I read your pretty speeches,
And I must admit they touched my heart.
I don't know where you borrowed them,
But most of them are works of art.
No schoolboy with his valentines
Was ever more sincere.
I've tried to read between the lines
To make the meaning clear,
But there's a little voice that whispers softly
As I fall asleep:
"You'd better look before you leap!"

REFRAIN 1

My intuition says to me,
"Don't ever give your heart away,"
And so I simply must obey
My intuition.
My intuition says to me,
"Those pretty words may not be true."
So, what am I supposed to do
In my position?
I'd like to trust my heart,
Believe in just my heart,
But it is much too young to know.
So, though it may be bad advice,
I guess I'll have to string along
Until you prove my intuition can be wrong.

REFRAIN 2

JOHN HODIAK: My intuition goes like this.
I'm playing poker with a bunch,
And all at once I get a hunch.
That's intuition.
I'm playing aces back to back,
And I can see a pair of kings;
But if there's one more of those things,
What's my position?

JUDY GARLAND: Well, if you get the cards,
Then you should bet the cards.
At least, that's what I've always heard.

HODIAK: You'll have your hunch,
And I'll have mine.

GARLAND: Suppose we both just string along.

BOTH: Until we prove our intuition can be wrong.

The cast of St. Louis Woman. *Inset: Pearl Bailey*

ST. LOUIS WOMAN | 1946

ST. LOUIS WOMAN (1946)

Tryout: Shubert Theatre, New Haven, February 14–16, 1946; Shubert Theatre, Boston, February 19–March 2, 1946; Shubert Theatre, Philadelphia, March 4–16, 1946. New York run: Martin Beck Theatre; opened March 30, 1946; closed July 6, 1946; 113 performances.

Music by Harold Arlen. Produced by Edward Gross. Book by Arna Bontemps and Countee Cullen, based on Bontemps's novel *God Sends Sunday.* Directed by Rouben Mamoulian. Choreography by Charles Walters (who replaced Antony Tudor). Settings and costumes by Lemuel Ayers. Orchestrations by Ted Royal, Allan Small, Walter Paul, and Menotti Salta. Orchestra directed by Leon Leonardi. Cast included Harold Nicholas (Little Augie), Fayard Nicholas (Barney), Pearl Bailey (Butterfly), Rex Ingram (Biglow Brown), Ruby Hill (Della Green), June Hawkins (Lila), Juanita Hall (Leah), Robert Pope (Badfoot), Louis Sharp (Slim), Milton J. Williams (Mississippi), Lorenzo Fuller (Josh), Milton Wood (Hopkins), and Herbert Coleman (Piggie).

Mercer recalled the show:

I was reluctant to leave California even for a smash story, which I didn't think this was . . . I was also promised Lena Horne, a promise which never was fulfilled.

I myself am immodest enough to think it is one of the best scores written for a colored musical . . . As we had already written "Blues in the Night," producers felt that Harold and I were the right choice for that kind of assignment. You must realize that the color barrier was still strong and for us to be chosen to do it was quite a compliment . . . We couldn't have asked for a better performance of our material.

The pre-Broadway version of the show had varied significantly: it had two acts instead of three, and included several songs that were subsequently cut. In act 1 Little Augie addressed his own shadow in "A Man's Gotta Fight." In act 2, Della and Ragsdale sang "High, Low, Jack and the Game"; Badfoot had a number, "It's One Thing You Gotta Find Out Yourself"; and Della introduced a song which was to become a cabaret favorite in later years—"I Wonder What Became of Me."

LI'L AUGIE IS A NATURAL MAN

Registered for copyright as an unpublished song February 27, 1946. Introduced and recorded by Robert Pope (Badfoot) (Capitol). Alternate title: "Augie Is a Natural Man."

BADFOOT: [*sitting on stool polishing bridle*]
They call me Badfoot,
'Cause I'm an old stable buck.
They call me Badfoot,
But I'm ridin' my luck,
Yes, I'm ridin' my luck.
Though I never had a education
I'm a-'sociated with a winnin'
    combination—
Come on, you rounders, and hear my
    song.

[*spoken*] I wanna tell you 'bout Li'l
    Augie. He's a jockey that's knee-high
    to a grasshopper, but when he
    rides—he's as big as all outdoors.

[*sung*] Since I was a li'l boy
I been 'round the tracks,
Seen a lot o' jockeys
Fast as mountain jacks.
But I know
What I know.
Heeeee-ooooooo-eeeeeeee!
Li'l Augie is a natural man—
He don't need a bridle,
He don't use his hand;
Augie talks a language
Hosses understand.
An' it's true
That he do—
Heeeee-ooooooo-eeeeeeee
Li'l Augie is a natural man.

I've seen plenty o' back-stretch ramblers,
But I'll tell you for fair,
Augie sits on a hoss's neck
Like most folks sits on a chair.
Though he's got a big heart,
You can get a bet
He don't weigh a hundred
Even soppin' wet.
He's as short
As his name—
Just the same,
Augie is the biggest little man.

[*spoken*] Country fairs and small towns
    wasn't big enough to hold Li'l Augie.
    Since the day he was born he was
    lookin' for he didn't know what.
    Maybe I ought to tell you what he's
    doin' now.

[*sung*] They couldn't hold him in his
    own backyard—
He's in St. Louis and he's ridin' hard.
And there ain't no tellin' what the end'll
    be—
We shall see, yes, we shall see . . . what
    we shall see . . .

Additional lyrics for an unproduced film version

He's as short
As his name.
Just the same,
Augie is the biggest little man.

A streak o' lightnin',
A streak o' lightnin',
That's what that lucky little jockey from the South is.
If you deny it
Or argufy it,
Than you can go an' put your money where your
    mouth is.

[*spoken*] Cause he win so many races most people
    think he's witchy, or haunted by spirits. Just so
    you get the straight of it, I'm goin' tell you
    'bout that, too . . .

[*sung*] Augie tol' the strok
What brought him through the air,
"Bet a half-a-dollar
I can beat you there."
And he did,
[*hum*]
Yes he did,
[*hum*]
Hee-oo-ee,
Li'l Augie is a travelin' man.
Daddy looked at Augie
Lyin' in the bed.
Augie looked at Daddy,
This is what he said:
"What a race."
[*hum*]
"Did I place?"
[*hum*]
Hee-oo-ee,
He spoke up like a natural man.
I ain't stoppin' to study

How come all this happen to be.
'Pears I'm lucky to Little Augie,
An' he's lucky to me.
Maybe 'cause his mammy
Borned him with a veil,
Maybe 'cause I totes a
Lucky cottontail.
Maybe yes,
Maybe no,
But it's so.
Augie is the biggest little man!

Maybe I ought to tell you
What he's doin' now.
I never will forget the time . . .

Packin' up a suitcase
Augie said to me,
"Goin' to St. Louis
See wha' we can see."
He was right.
[*hum*]
What a sight.
[*hum*]
Hee-oo-ee,
Li'l Augie is a gettin'-round man.

Gals is mighty stylish,
Mens is mighty bold,
Polish on their fingers,
Pockets full o' gold.
Millionaires
[*hum*]
Ev'rywheres.
[*hum*]
Hee-oo-ee,
Augie is a sociable man.
My boy's got him a string o' winners,
Got them other boys hexed,
Got his eye on a brownskin gal,
And Lord knows what happens next.
Augie's on the racetrack
Ridin' like the wind,
Badfoot's in the stable
Singin' Augie in!
Roll along,
Roll along,
That's my song,
Augie is the biggest little man

LIMERICKS

Registered for copyright as an unpublished song November 19, 1959. Introduced by Robert Pope (Badfoot),

Fayard Nicholas (Barney), Louis Sharp (Slim), Ruby Hill (Della), and male ensemble.

A MAN: Sweeten' Water's sweet as it can be.
ANOTHER MAN: Sweeten' Water is a sting-a-ree.
ANOTHER MAN: You take rock candy an' you pour
                 on gin—
SLIM: Give it the label o' Sweetenin'
                 Water and you bring it in.
BADFOOT: Sweeten' Water's—
ALL: Sweet as rock an' rye.
BARNEY: Sweeten' Water got me Butterfly.
BADFOOT: I bought her Scotch but she was
                 unimpressed—
BARNEY: So I just ordered her Sweetenin'
                 Water an'
                 She a'qui-esced.
ALL: Sweeten' Water's sweet as Della
                 Green.
A MAN: Like to put the squeeze on her, I
                 mean!
DELLA: A lady chooses
                 Who she's gonna squeeze—
                 Gonna be drinkin' my Sweeten'
                 Water any place I please.

ANY PLACE I HANG MY HAT IS HOME

Published. Copyrighted March 9, 1946. Previously registered for copyright as an unpublished song February 28, 1946. Introduced and recorded by Ruby Hill (Della) (Capitol).

Free an' easy, that's my style,
Howdy-do me, watch me smile,
Fare-thee-well me after a while,
'Cause I gotta roam
An' any place I hang my hat is home!

Sweet'nin' water, cherry wine,
Thank you kindly, suits me fine.
Kansas City, Caroline,
That's my honeycomb,
'Cause any place I hang my hat is home.

Birds roostin' in the tree
Pick up an' go,
An' the goin' proves
That's how it oughta be—
I pick up, too,
When the spirit moves me.

Cross the river, round the bend,
Howdy, stranger—so long, friend,
There's a voice in the lonesome wind
That keeps whisperin' "Roam!"
I'm goin' where a welcome mat is,
No matter where that is,
'Cause any place I hang my hat is home.

I FEEL MY LUCK COMIN' DOWN

Registered for copyright as an unpublished song November 19, 1959. Introduced by Harold Nicholas (Little Augie).

An introduction
Is now in order,
And you can call me
Baby.
The ladies love me,
And I don't blame 'em—
But do they get me?
Maybe.
Set 'em up, boy,
Lovin' cup, boy,
For the ladies and me.
Lucky horseshoe
Flew up and hit me,
New suit and dicty lid,
Call me the Candy Kid—
I feel my luck comin' down.

A four-leaf clover looked me in the eye
And jumped in my lapel,
A lucky seven rolled from out the sky
And rang that joyful bell.
The introductions
Have been accomplished
And you can call me
Honey.

[*Looking at* DELLA.]

My mornin' coffee
Was full of bubbles—
You know what that means?
Money.
Mercenary?
Not so very,
But I won't turn it down.
A lucky horseshoe
Flew up and hit me.
New suit and dicty lid,

Call me the Candy Kid—
I feel my luck comin' down.

I HAD MYSELF A TRUE LOVE

Published. Copyrighted May 10, 1946. Introduced and recorded by June Hawkins (Lila) (Capitol).

I had myself a true love,
A true love who was sumpin' to see.
I had myself a true love—
At least that's what I kept on tellin' me.
The first thing in the mornin'
I still try to think up a way
To be with him some part of the evenin'
And that's the way I live through the day.

"She had herself a true love,
But now he's gone and left her for good"—
The Lord knows I done heard
Those backyard whispers
Going round the neighborhood.
There may be a lot of things I miss,
A lot of things I don't know,
But I do know this—
Now I ain't got no love,
An' once upon a time
I had a true love.

In the evenin',
In the doorway,
While I stand there and wait for his comin',
With the house swept
And the clothes hung
And the pots on the stove there a-hummin',
Where is he while I watch the risin' moon?
With that gal in this damn ol' saloon!
No, that ain't the way it used to be.
No! An' everybody keeps tellin' me,
There may be a lot of things I miss,
A lot of things I don't know,
But I do know this—
Now I ain't got no love
And once upon a time
I had a true love.

LEGALIZE MY NAME

Published. Copyrighted May 2, 1946. Previously registered for copyright as an unpublished song April 1, 1946. Introduced and recorded by Pearl Bailey (Butterfly) (Capitol).

REFRAIN 1

Will I? Won't I?
Do I? Don't I?
All you wanna do is bill and coo—
But you're empty-handed when the bill is due.
If you really love me an' you love me true,
Legalize my name.

Will I kiss you?
Ain't the issue—
You've been sayin' ever since we met
That you want a sample of the way I pet.
You've had all the samples that you're gonna get—
Legalize my name.

'Fore we ever can dwell
Out of one valise,
You must learn how to spell
"Justice of the Peace"!
[spoken] And I spell that "peace" with an e-a!
[sung] My heart's glowin',
Sparks are showin'
If you want those little sparks
To burst into flame,
You got to
Legalize my name.

Even Adam
Called Eve madam,
And if I have read the Good Book right,
On the day the serpent made her take that bite
She was heard to murmur as she saw the light,
[spoken] "Come on, big boy, let's you and me build a little lean-to where we can raise Cain."
[sung] Don't eyeball me—
City Hall me.
Read your history and you will see
Cleopatra said the same to Antony.
What was good for her's good enough for me.
[spoken] So run up to Tiffany's and get me a silver band for this digit . . . Oh, honey, it's got such a lonesome look.
[sung] Wedding licenses cost
Just two dollars, no more.
I've seen times when you've tossed
Two away before.
[spoken] And that means just what you think it means

[sung] To get back to
Ipso factoo,
Lawyer I ain't, but I know my meaning's the same—
You got to
Legalize my name.

REFRAIN 2

Love words, sweet talk,
You-and-me talk—
You say just a glimpse of my allure
Is a glimpse of Paradise, I can be sure.
Brother, if you wanna take the dollar tour,
[spoken] I suggest you send out invitations to your nearest and dearest . . . I might even want to come myself.
[sung] Sparkin', spoonin',
Honeymoonin'—
That's the kinda talk I get from you,
And you often say you wish the whole world knew.
Just a pair of witnesses and a judge'll do.
[spoken] So bring a couple of aunts and cousins. Let's change this temporary expedient into a permanent state of affairs. Kindly affix your signature at the bottom of the document . . .
[sung] Don't care where I live at
Or what I live in,
House, apartment, or flat—
Any place but sin.
[spoken] And I might even live there—but not alone!
[sung] If you prize me,
Notarize me,
Gimme an old piece of parchment
That I can frame.
You got to
Legalize my name.

CAKEWALK YOUR LADY

Published. Copyrighted March 8, 1946. Introduced by Milton J. Williams (Mississippi) with J. Mardo Brown, Rhoda Boggs, Rosalie King and Robert Pope, and eight competing couples.

1. Betty Nichols and Smalls Boykins
2. Rita Garnett and Theodore Allen
3. Dorothea Greene and Milton Wood
4. Royce Wallace and Lonny Reech
5. Gwendolyn Hale and Norman DeJoie
6. Enid Williams and George Thomas

7. Pearl Bailey and Fayard Nicholas
8. Ruby Hill and Harold Nicholas

Recorded by Pope (Capitol).

VERSE

MISSISSIPPI: Howdy-do to you—
I has the honor to start this
function
And commenced the ball.
Grab a lady fair,
Pick out one anywhere—
Better have a partner
When you hear them call.
QUARTET: Better have a partner
When you hear them call.

REFRAIN

MISSISSIPPI: Cakewalk your lady,
Two-step your baby,
Cakewalk your lady
Left and right.
Trombone is talkin',
Best get to walkin'—
Don't you miss the boat!
Lift your petticoat,
Walk your gent'm'n
For de cake this night.

INTERLUDE

Missus Elvira Hayes,
Who's been cookin' it for days,
Won the cake-bakin' prize
At de county seat,
And she whispered to me,
"It's a secret recipe.
A full-o'-frolic, alcoholic*
Pastry treat—
Choc'lit filler,
Sugar frostin',
Pure vaniller,
Big enough to get lost in."

CODA

MISSISSIPPI: Cakewalk your lady,
Two-step your baby,
Cakewalk your lady
Left and right.
Dress up your proudest,
Sing out your loudest—
It don't have to rhyme,

_____
* *Alternate line:*
   A very, very 'fectionary

Have yourself a time,
Walk your gent'm'n
For the cake dis night!

Take your turn at the door
Till we calls you to the floor.
Ev'ryone in the hall
Has a place in line.
When the man starts to shout
And he calls your number out,
I na-tchul-ly expects to see you
Rise and shine.

[*Dance.*]

Howdy do to you.
I has the honor to
Start this function
And commence the ball.
It's my pleasure now to have 'em
Take a bow.
Toby Bayne accompanied
By Miss Lucy Small
ENSEMBLE: Toby Bane accompanied
By Miss Lucy Small.

MISSISSIPPI: Here we go again.
Ladies and gentlemen,
Next contestant that'll greet your eye
Are the happy pair.
Dashin' and debonair,
Known as Mister Givens
And Miss Alice Fry.
ENSEMBLE: Raggin' Mister Givens
And Miss Alice Fry.
MISSISSIPPI: Kindly clear the floor.
Here's what you waited for.
Those past masters of the heel and
toe,
Feature of the night,
Everyone's favorite,
Missus Johnson's Butterfly
And Barney Snow.
ENSEMBLE: Missus Johnson's Butterfly
And Barney Snow.
MISSISSIPPI: Pass the lovin' cup.
Contest is lookin' up.
Here comes dancin' like you never
seen.
Yes, you're gonna meet
The pride of Targee Street,
Mister Hi-Li'l Augie
And Miss Della Green.

COME RAIN OR COME SHINE

Published. Copyrighted March 9, 1946. Previously registered for copyright as an unpublished song February 27, 1946. Introduced and recorded by Ruby Hill (Della) and Harold Nicholas (Augie) (Capitol).

Major early recordings were made by Margaret Whiting with Paul Weston's orchestra (Capitol) and Helen Forrest and Dick Haymes with Earle Hagen's Orchestra (Decca). This was the only song Mercer wrote for a Broadway show that became a genuine hit.

When the melody came to Arlen, he played it for Mercer, who said immediately, "I'm gonna love you like nobody's loved you," but then couldn't think of how to take the lyric any farther. It was Arlen who offered facetiously, " 'Come hell or high water?' " "Why didn't I think of that?" Mercer replied. But it gave him the clue to what he *did* think of: "Come rain or come shine."

Once the song was finished, they asked Margaret Whiting to make a recording of it, to be released right after the show opened. Whiting, daughter of Richard Whiting, had just started recording as a solo artist, and she was nervous working with these two established talents, even though she had known them all her life. She admired the way their very different backgrounds somehow meshed. "Harold wrote songs with a marvelous blues-chord structure that was sensuous and sophisticated and also primitive. Johnny's lyrics blazed with originality and an American earthiness."

She had been schooled by her father to "sing the song the way the writers wrote it. They worked hard to get it just right." In the recording booth, however, "Something happened in my mind. I started thinking about Harold, the cantor's son. On that last note, I just let it wail: 'I'm gonna love you, come ra-in or sh-i-i-i-ne.' Well, Johnny burst through the door, mad as hell: 'What in God's name are you doing?' He was followed by Harold, who shouted, 'No, leave it, leave it! That's the way I *should* have written it.' "

RUBY

HILL: I'm gonna love you
Like nobody loved you,
Come rain or come shine,
High as a mountain
And deep as a river,
Come rain or come shine.
I guess when you met me
It was just one of those things,
But don't ever bet me,
'Cause I'm gonna be true if you let me.
You're gonna love me
Like nobody's loved me,
Come rain or come shine—

Happy together,
Unhappy together
And won't it be fine?
Days may be cloudy or sunny,
We're in or we're out of the money,
But I'm with you always, Augie,
I'm with you rain or shine!

[HAROLD NICHOLAS *repeats from "I guess when you met me."*]

EASY RIDER

Introduced by Ruby Hill (Della). Song fragment sung playfully by Della to Augie and his religious sister, Leah.

Easy rider went and said goodbye,
Easy rider left me high and dry.
I had some Macks that satisfied my soul,
But there ain't nobody else who can rock me with
     a steady roll.

WE SHALL MEET TO PART NO NEVER

Introduced by Herbert Coleman (Piggie).

We shall meet to part no never,
We shall meet upon the shore.
When this veil of tears is over
And they open wide the door,
We shall meet to part no more.

CHINQUAPIN BUSH

Registered for copyright as an unpublished song April 26, 1946 (as "Lullaby"). Introduced and recorded by Ruby Hill (Della) and children (Capitol).

Peekin' around the chinquapin bush,
Peekin' around the chinquapin bush,
Billy Goat came and gimme a push
In Aunt Sally's garden.

It seems like yesterday
I heard the grown-up laughter,
The clink of dishes,
And the sounds I loved the best,
And watched the kitchen lamp
Swing gently from the rafter,
As I lay half-asleep against my mother's breast,
There with my head on her apron.
The troubles of the world seemed far away.
A million years, a million miles
Have come between us,
An' yet it seems like only yesterday.

SLEEP PEACEFUL, MISTER USED-TO-BE

Registered for copyright as an unpublished song April 25, 1946. Introduced and recorded by June Hawkins (Lila) (Capitol).

Sleep peaceful, Mister Used-to-Be,
I'll see you to the door.
Too long you got the best o' me,
But you'll never in dis world
Git the best of me anymore—
You'll never find any feather bed as soft
As dat pinewood floor.
I ain't a-gonna fret my head,
I ain't a-gonna cry.
I'm gonna dress myself in red,
Gonna walk around da town wid my head
In the good Lord's sky.

Home was a big-town hotel
When he was courtin'—
You was a money-spendin', true-lovin' Mack,
And jus' as long as Lila
Did the supportin',
She was wid you when the train came rollin' down
     the track.
But you's alone on another train tonight,
One dat don't come back.
Sleep peaceful, Mister Used-to-Be,
I'll see you to the door—
You never in dis world goin' get the best
Of anybody anymore!

LEAVIN' TIME

Registered for copyright as an unpublished song April 26, 1946. Introduced and recorded by ensemble (Capitol).

A WOMAN: A baby's born, he starts to crawl—
He's just like a young saplin'
     growin' tall.
2ND WOMAN: And just as sure as he must climb,
Everybody has his own leavin' time.
ENSEMBLE: Everybody has his own leavin' time.
It ain't for you,
It ain't for me—
One of these days
It may have to be.
But there's the facts,
You can't deny 'm—
Everybody has his own leavin' time,
Everybody has his own leavin' time.
Sinner, sinner,
Take a helpin' hand
Reachin' out to you!
Raise up your head
An' seek the sky—
The sun an' moon,
Both is ridin' high.
But just as sure
As day must climb,
Everybody has his own leavin' time,
Everybody has his own leavin' time.
Sinner, sinner,
Take the helpin' hand
Reachin' out to you.
ENSEMBLE: Leav' time, leav' time,
Yes, indeed, I hear ya!
Leav' time, leav' time,
Yes, indeed, I know!
Leavin' time, leavin' time,
For the highest of the mighty
And for the lowest creature
Here below!
Yes, yes, you better be ready,
Yes, yes, the Gospel done said.
Yes, yes, you better be ready
When they fits that halo
Over your head!
A baby's born, he starts to crawl,
He's like a young saplin' growin' tall.
And just as sure as he must climb,
Everybody has his own leavin' time,
Everybody has his own leavin' time.
A MAN: Brother Biglow Brown
Gone to meet his Lord.
CHORUS: Brother Biglow Brown
Got his just reward—
Brother Biglow Brown

Gone to meet his Lord.
Everybody has his own leavin'
    time,
Leavin' time—
Fare thee well!

IT'S A WOMAN'S PREROGATIVE

Published. Copyrighted November 3, 1950. Previously registered for copyright as an unpublished song April 1, 1946. Introduced and recorded by Pearl Bailey (Butterfly) (Capitol).

I don't know who it was wrote it,
Or by whose pen it was signed,
Someone once said, and I quote it,
"It's a woman's prerogative to change her mind."
He may have you in a halter,
Harnessed before and behind,
But till you kneel at the altar,
It's a woman's prerogative to change her mind.

Promise anything,
Anything at all.
Promise everything,
Everything, honey—don't swerve,
Throw him a curve.
String 'em along
Till they show you what they've got in reserve.
Though his bank shows a big balance
And he seems heaven-designed,
If the boy's short on his talents,
It's a woman's prerogative to change her mind.

Any fruit, even a lemon,
Should have a beautiful rind,
But if that lemon's a lemon,
It's a woman's prerogative to change her mind.

If he won't bow from the center,
And you're politically inclined,
If he won't rise when you enter,
It's a woman's prerogative to change her mind.

They say precedent
Makes a thing a law.
Hooray, precedent!
I can say yes
When I mean no.

Hard to believe,
But they tell me that it's legally so.

So don't fret how much you kissed 'em,
If on their couch you're reclined,
Don't forget we've got a system—
It's a woman's prerogative to change her mind.

If he's tough or if he's tender
Or just the in-between kind,
Long as you're the feminine gender,
It's a woman's prerogative to change her mind.

He may be one of those vipers
Who has a cottage all signed—
Unless you like to change diapers,
I suggest that you cogitate and change your mind.
We're the weaker sex,
Everybody knows.
Stay the weaker sex,
Always be pure,
Shy and demure,
Tell him you don't, but remember,
Never tell him for sure!
He may have horses to curry,
Each with a hansom behind—
If there's no fringe on his surrey,
It's a woman's prerogative to change her mind.

RIDIN' ON THE MOON

Published. Copyrighted May 11, 1946. Introduced and recorded by Harold Nicholas (Augie) (Capitol).

VERSE

High luck or low luck
Or no luck at all,
I'll never care
If I rise or I fall.
I've learned a lesson
Since we've been apart—
I'll do all right
If I follow my heart.

REFRAIN

I walk under ladders,
Number thirteen doesn't scare me,
'Cause I'm dressed up in a rainbow
And I'm ridin' on the moon.
Old Jinx had me cornered,
But I found out when to shake it,
And my true love helped me break it—
Now I'm ridin' on the moon.
Ah, yes, you can preach it, sister,
While I shout for joy!

Ah, yes, say hello to Lady Love's baby boy!
You're my ring o' roses,
So I can't be heavy-hearted,
'Cause I'm right back where I started,
And I'm ridin' on the moon!

LEAST THAT'S MY OPINION

Registered for copyright as an unpublished song July 18, 1946. Introduced by Robert Pope (Badfoot), Lorenzo Fuller (Josh), Louis Sharp (Slim), and Milton Wood (Hopkins).

I say this and with impunity:
If you seize your opportunity
Least that's my opinion.
I bet you if you're bettable,
Idle hands are most regrettable,
Honest effort unforgettable—
Least that's my opinion.

JOSH,
SLIM &
HOPKINS: Oh yes, oh, ain't it a shame,
The hare could go
And the tortoise was slow,
But he got there just the same.
In conclusion I reiterate:
Educated or illiterate,
Work is what you can't obliterate
Rent is high.
HOPKINS: And time do fly—
At least that's my opinion.
SLIM: I'll try anything that's tryable
But my rule's the old reliable
Elbow grease is still appliable—
Least that's my opinion.

Birds who start their day out merrily
Get the worm but necessarily,
I say yes and I say verily—
Merely an opinion.
ALL: Oh yes, oh, ain't it the truth!
BADFOOT: You can't collect
Till you learn to correct
The mistakes you make in youth.
Take a philosophic attitude
And allow your smile some latitude—
Folks will smile right back in
    gratitude.
Ask me why—
ALL: And we'll reply—
At least that's my opinion!

RACIN' FORMS

Published. Copyrighted November 19, 1959. Introduced by Juanita Hall (Leah).

Racin' forms—
Sister Leah
Picks them all.
Get your green sheet—
Seven winners
Yesterday,
Every day!
Racin' forms,
Racin' forms,
Got everything a poor man needs but money.

Sister Leah's
Crystal ball—
One thin dime
Buys it all.
Seven winners
Yesterday,
Every day!
Racin' forms,
Racin' forms.

COME ON, LI'L AUGIE

Registered for copyright as an unpublished song February 27, 1946. Introduced by Ruby Hill (Della), Pearl Bailey (Butterfly), Herbert Coleman (Piggie), and ensemble.

ENSEMBLE: There they go, there they go,
Like a thunder crack—
There they go, there they go,
Burnin' up the track.
Every son-of-a-gun runnin' in a
row—
No two ways about it, there they
go!

1ST ONLOOKER: Hey, man, look at number
seventeen,
That boy carryin' the red and
green!

2ND ONLOOKER: He's some streak o' lightning,
what I mean!

ENSEMBLE: He's fast!

BUTTERFLY: There's old Barney goin' to the
rail!

1ST ONLOOKER: And there's Augie sittin' on his
tail!

ALL: And now where is number
seventeen?

ENSEMBLE: He's last!

DELLA: [praying]
Come on, Li'l Augie,
Throw dust in their eyes!
Come on, Li'l Augie,
And cut 'em down to your size!

AUGIE GROUP: Throw lucky dust in their eyes
And cut 'em down to your size!
Come on, Li'l Augie,
Ain't no time to fail!
We're all bettin' on you—
Come on and carry that mail
And keep us all out of jail!
Come on and carry that mail!

BARNEY GROUP: Hey, Augie, whatcha doin' now?
Hey, Augie, whatcha doin' now?
Hey, Augie, whatcha doin' now?

BUTTERFLY: He must have found that horse
behind a plow!

BARNEY GROUP: Hey, Augie, whatcha doin' now?
Hey, Augie, whatcha doin' now?
Hey, Augie, whatcha doin' now?

BUTTERFLY: That thoroughbred appears to be
a cow!

ONE GROUP: Here they come, here they
come,
In a cloud of dust!
Here they come, here they
come,
And it's win or bust!
If you can't hear the noise, then
you're deaf and dumb,
No two ways about it, here they
come!

OTHER GROUP: They're all comin' in a cloud of
dust—
They're all comin' and it's win or
bust!
There ain't any doubt about it,
here they come!

PIGGIE: [running over and climbing on
BADFOOT's shoulders]
Come on, Uncle Augie, today is
the day!
My heart's ridin' with you, I'm
with you all the way!

ENSEMBLE: We're with you all the way!
We're with you all the way.
Come on—come on—come
on—come on—come on—
come on—come on!
He walks under ladders,
Number thirteen doesn't scare
him,
'Cause he's dressed up in a
rainbow

And he's ridin' on the moon!
He's our ring o' roses
And he can't be heavy-
hearted
'Cause he's right back where he
started
And he's ridin'
Yes, he's ridin'!
[alternating]
Come on, Li'l Augie!
Come on, Danny!
Come on, Augie!
Come on, Danny!
Come on, Augie!
Danny!
Augie!
Danny!
Augie!

SLIM: [spoken] Augie's in the lead!

ENSEMBLE: There's the finish and Augie
wins!

HIGH, LOW, JACK, AND THE GAME

Registered for copyright as an unpublished song April 1, 1946. Introduced by Ruby Hill (Della) and Elwood Smith (Ragsdale) but dropped during pre-Broadway tryout.

DELLA: I'm a card-playin' woman,
An' I don't use a joker.
Sit me down in a nest of 'em,
I can play with the best of 'em
Scrape my feet on the rest of 'em
Playin' poker with me it's
High, low, jack, and the game.

RAGSDALE: Play your hand with me an' we can win
the game.

DELLA: I'm a high-livin' kind o' woman,
An' I don't fancy me no shanty.
Once I've really begun to play,
Any limit is fun to play,
But I never was one to play
Penny ante—
With me it's
High, low, jack, an' the game.

RAGSDALE: Livin'-high-style kind o' woman
Can't live fancy in a shanty.
No, with me ya won't play penny
ante!

RAGSDALE: Della, I can show ya things you've
never seen.

DELLA: He's crazy about me,
But I wonder, does he doubt me?
If he's better off without me,
Then I'll have to take the air,
Though I love him to a fare-thee-
well—
Oh, what the hell!
It's too much for a woman, lovin' that
way.
Better go like I came—
High, low, jack, and the game!

RAGSDALE: But his luck is goin' down,
I don't doubt ya—
You're the ring of roses round the
winner's neck.
I'm your good luck, can't you tell?
Let me keep you lookin' swell.
Can't live this way.

Encore

RAGSDALE: He's crazy about you.

DELLA: Rags, you're evil through and through!
I don't doubt him,
I ain't gonna listen to that evil talk.
Though I love him to a fare-thee-
well—
Oh, what the hell!
It's too much for a woman,
For a true kind o' woman,
Lovin' that way—
High, low, jack, an' the game!

RAGSDALE: But I wonder, does he doubt ya?
If he's better off without ya?
Then you'll have to take the air.
Let me keep you lookin' swell—
I'm your good luck,
Can't ya tell?
Livin'-high-style kind o' woman
Can't live fancy in a shanty this way.
Better go like I came

A MAN'S GOTTA FIGHT

Registered for copyright as an unpublished song November 19, 1959. Introduced by Harold Nicholas (Augie) but dropped during pre-Broadway tryout.

AUGIE: I ain't afraid o' nothin' my size—
I ain't afraid o' nothin' that walks.

SHADOW: [*mockingly*] A big man does what he says
he's gonna do,
But a little man only talks!

AUGIE: [*bravely*] I ain't afraid of nobody's
fists—
I ain't afraid of nobody's guns!

SHADOW: [*mockingly*] A big man does what he says
he's gonna do,
But a little man only runs.

AUGIE: You ain't so tall, you shadow on the
wall,
You ain't so tall at all!
When the light hits you right, you're
taller than me
But everybody knows I'm small,
Yes, everybody knows I'm small!
[*spoken*] Everywhere I go, it's "Hi there,
half pint!" Everyone I meet says,
"Hello, big shorty!" . . . Always
[*sung*] "Hey, whatcha say there, littler
than me?
How tall do you have to be, boy?
How tall do you have to be?"

SHADOW: You have to be as tall as you feel
inside—
You have to be as tall as me!

AUGIE: I'm gonna be as tall as I have to be,
That's what I'm gonna be!
A man's gotta fight for what he thinks is
right
And what he feels inside—
That's somethin' in his heart,
Nothin' to do with his pride.
He's gonna keep his woman in his arms
And keep the shelter over his heart.
A man's gotta fight for what he thinks is
right
Or else he's better off dead,
Or else he's better off dead.
I ain't afraid o' nothin' my size,
I ain't afraid o' nothin' that walks!

SHADOW: [*mockingly*] A big man does what he says
he's gonna do,
But a little man only talks.
You have to be as tall as you feel
inside—
You have to be as tall as me!

AUGIE: I'm gonna be as tall as I have to be,
That's what I'm gonna be,
That's what I'm gonna be!

[AUGIE *exits.*]

SHADOW: When the light hits him right,
He's taller than a tree,
And ev'rybody knows that's tall,
Yes, everybody knows that's tall.

SOW THE SEED AND REAP THE HARVEST

Registered for copyright as an unpublished song November 19, 1959. Introduced by Juanita Hall (Leah) but dropped during pre-Broadway tryout.

LEAH: [*with chorus humming underneath*]
Sow the seed and reap the harvest,
Sow the wind and reap the whirlwind.
I saw but I was blind
In the valley of the shadow.
Help me seek and I shall find!
Help this heart to know!
Help these ears to hear!
Help these eyes to see!
Take this sinner and help her to
understand—
Reach your helpin' hand out to me!

SOMETHIN' YOU GOTTA FIND OUT FOR YOURSELF

Introduced by Robert Pope (Badfoot) and Ruby Hill (Della) but dropped during pre-Broadway tryout.

BADFOOT: My boy, Li'l Augie an' me, dis ol' stable
buck,
Ol' hard time's got us, but we're ridin'
our luck,
Yes, we're ridin' our luck.
You start out learnin' 'bout your A B Cs,
Your papa tells you 'bout the birds and
bees,
And you picks up knowledge 'bout the
stars above—
But it's pow'ful different when it comes
to love,
Somethin' you gotta find out yourself.
You might know horses and you might
know tracks
And how much weight they carry on
their backs,
Figure when a colt is gonna make his
move—
But a bobtail filly is another groove,
Somethin' you gotta find out yourself.

Li'l Mister Augie,
Feelin' mighty doggy,

Thought he was a natural man.
Had the world in a jug,
Had the stopper in his han',
He lived too stylish and he lived too
     high,
And now we both is eatin' humble pie!

When you can't teach learnin' to a
     walleyed mule,
Then you got to take him to the hard-
     knocks school—
Somethin' you gotta find out yourself.
[*spoken*] Life is one damn thing after
     another, but love—love is two damn
     things after each other!
[*sung*] Seen some pickin's that was
     mighty lean,
But ain't seen hide nor hair of Della
     Green.
But I heard it rumored on the evenin'
     breeze
That she's gone to see if money grows
     on trees—
Somethin' you gotta find out yourself.

Ol' nags might dress her up in fancy
     clothes,
In rhinestone buckles and in feather
     boas,
But the day a better-lookin' brown
     comes on
Is the day that bank account is
     overdrawn—
Somethin' you gotta find out yourself.

Listen to me, Della—
Even Cinderella

Couldn't keep her dancing shoes!
Honey, when the clock strikes twelve,
Then you'll have to sing the blues.
DELLA: Lights are bright,
Piano makin' music all the night,
And they pour Champagne.
You left ol' Target an' you moved up
     North
While me an' Augie's scufflin' back an'
     forth,
An' there ain't no tellin' what the end'll
     be.
We shall see, yes, we shall see what we
     shall see—
Somethin' you gotta find out yourself.

TALKIN' GLORY

Intended for the funeral scene but not used.

Glory! Glory!
Room for everyone
In dat Promised Land!
Talkin' glory
Ain't go'n' git you dere
With dat angel band!
Sinner! Sinner!
Take de helpin' hand
Reachin' out to you.
Ahhhhh, ahhhhh,
You can walk it
Wearin' glory shoes—
You gotta live glory too.

I WONDER WHAT BECAME OF ME

Published. Copyrighted March 9, 1946. Introduced by Ruby Hill (Della) but dropped during pre-Broadway tryout.

Lights are bright,
Piano's making music all the night,
And they pour Champagne
Just like it was rain.
It's a sight to see,
But I wonder what became of me.

Crowds go by,
That merrymaking laughter in their eye,
And the laughter's fine,
But I wonder what became of mine.

Life's sweet as honey,
And yet it's funny,
I get a feeling that I can't analyze.
It's like, well, maybe,
Like when a baby
Sees a bubble burst before its eyes.

Oh, I've had my fling;
I've been around and seen most everything.*
But I can't be gay,
For along the way
Something went astray,
And I can't explain,
It's the same Champagne,
It's a sight to see,
But I wonder what became of me.

* *Alternative lines:*
     Oh, I've had my thrills;
     They've lit my cigarettes with dollar bills.

Top: *Mercer, Glenn Wallachs, and Buddy DeSylva, the founders of Capitol Records*
Bottom, left to right: *Mercer with Ella Mae Morse; alone at the microphone; and with Jo Stafford*

Songs of 1946–1949

CENTENNIAL SUMMER (1946)

Produced by Otto Preminger for Twentieth Century–Fox. Released July 1946. Copyright July 10, 1946. Directed by Otto Preminger. Screenplay by Michael Kanin, based on the novel *Centennial Summer* by Albert E. Idell. Lyrics by Leo Robin, Oscar Hammerstein II, Johnny Mercer, and E. Y. Harburg. Music by Jerome Kern. Dances staged by Dorothy Fox. Orchestrations by Maurice De Packh, Herbert Spencer, and Conrad Salinger. Vocal arrangements by Charles Henderson. Musical director: Alfred Newman. Featuring Jeanne Crain, Cornel Wilde, Linda Darnell, William Eythe, Walter Brennan, Constance Bennett, Dorothy Gish, with Barbara Whiting, Larry Stevens, Kathleen Howard, Buddy Swan, Charles Dingle, and Avon Long.

A Philadelphia family in the Great Exposition of 1876.

TWO HEARTS ARE BETTER THAN ONE

Published. Copyrighted April 26, 1946. Previously registered for copyright as an unpublished song January 10, 1946. Intended for Cornel Wilde and Jeanne Crain, but not used in film. Recorded by Louanne Hogan, who dubbed Crain's singing voice in the film.

VERSE 1

Being of the sex that's known as man,
Also being a Parisian,
I'm inclined to think whatever I do can't be
   beat—
Such is my conceit.
But I notice since you came along,
I've begun to sing a diff'rent song—
I'm inclined to think whatever I do
Might be wrong.

REFRAIN 1

Two hearts together
Are better than one.
In rainy or sunny weather
The outlook can't be a glum one
When there's someone who cares.
Just when you're sinking
Without a straw in sight,
Someone starts thinking
And ev'rything's all right!

Birds of a feather
Can never be shown
That living alone is fun
When two hearts are better than one.

VERSE 2

Being of the sex you can't refute,
And a Philadelphian to boot,
I'm inclined to think whatever I do can't be beat—
Such is my conceit.
But I notice since I work with you,
I've begun to change my point of view—
I'm inclined to think whatever you think,
I think too.

REFRAIN 2

Two heads together
Are better than one.
In rainy or sunny weather
The outlook can't be a glum one
When there's someone who cares.
Rain in the doorway
Can have its sunny side
When someone goes your way
And her umbrella's wide.
Birds of a feather
Can never be shown
That living alone is fun
When two hearts are better than one.

CINDY

Music and lyrics by Paul Weston, Anna Stafford, and Mercer. Published. Copyrighted July 24, 1946. Previously registered for copyright as an unpublished song April 19, 1946. Recorded by Jo Stafford (Capitol).

VERSE 1

Cindy has one blue eye;
She also has one brown.
One eye looks at the country,
And the other one looks in town.

REFRAIN 1

Get along home, Cindy,
Get along home, I say.

Get along home, Cindy,
One more night and day.

VERSE 2

Cindy's tall and skinny;
She has a real nice smile.
You can see her comin'—
Her teeth stick out a mile.

REFRAIN 2

Get along home, get along, little gal,
Get along home, get along, I say.
Get along home, get along, little gal,
One more night and day.

VERSE 3

Never marry Cindy—
I'll tell you the reason why:
She's so tall and skinny,
I'm scared she'll never die.

REFRAIN 3

Get along home, Cindy,
Hey, get along, I say.
Get along home, Cindy,
One more night and day.

VERSE 4

Wish I had a needle and thread,
Wish that I could sew,
I'd sew that gal to my coattails
And down the road we'd go.

REFRAIN 4

Fare thee well, Cindy,
Fare thee well.
Fare thee well, Cindy,
Fare thee well.

VERSE 5

I wish I was an apple
A-hangin' on a tree,
And every time't Cindy pass
She'd take a bite of me.

VERSE 6

She went down to the mailbox,
The one marked RFD,
Mailed herself a letter
Special delivery.

VERSE 7

She went up on the mountain
And hollered down the hill,
And every time she said "I won't"
The echo said "I will."

VERSE 8

She's gone back to the holler,
To all the folks she knew.
So goodbye to Cindy,
So long, farewell, adieu!

AND SO TO BED

Music by Robert Emmett Dolan. Published. Copyrighted November 4, 1946.

VERSE

Milkman whistles cheerily
As he goes his way.
Steeple bells are singing
A song to greet the day.

REFRAIN

The moon descends,
And so to bed.
The music ends,
And so to bed.
Should old acquaintance
Linger in your heart,
Then don't forget
We're just a dream apart.
Tomorrow night
Seems years away,
But after all
It's just a day,
And I'll remember
Ev'ry word you said.
I miss you so,
And so to bed.

(LOVE'S GOT ME IN A) LAZY MOOD

Music by Eddie Miller. Published. Copyrighted June 26, 1947. Previously registered for copyright as an unpub-

lished song February 7, 1947. After his stint with Benny Goodman, Mercer found himself missing his regular radio appearances, so he was particularly pleased to be signed on to do jazz-based shows with Bob Crosby's Dixieland Band. An instrumental piece ("Slow Mood") by tenor saxophonist Eddie Miller intrigued him, so he put words to it.

I'll tell you why
The days go by
Like caterpillars do,
And clouds are cotton blossoms
In a field of blue:
Love's got me in a lazy mood.

I'll tell you why
Stars in the sky
Pick ev'ry night to shine,
And why the moon is a watermelon on the vine:
Love's got me in a lazy mood.

When a bright and early sun
Begins to steam it up,
You'll find me underneath
The nearest tree
While I dream it up.
Pickin' petals off a daisy,
Just the absentminded kid,
That's me.

I'll tell you why,
I don't reply
To mail that's overdue.
And why I never answer
When I'm spoken to:
It isn't that I'm really rude—
Love's got me in a lazy mood.

DEAR RUTH (1947)

Produced by Paul Jones for Paramount Pictures. World premiere May 29, 1947. Copyright July 18, 1947. Directed by William D. Russell. Screenplay by Arthur Sheekman, based on the play *Dear Ruth* by Norman Krasna. Lyrics by Johnny Mercer. Musical score by Robert Emmett Dolan. Starring William Holden and Joan Caulfield, with Mona Freeman, Edward Arnold, Billy De Wolfe, Mary Philips, Virginia Welles, Kenny O'Morrison, Marietta Canty, and Irving Bacon.

A schoolgirl writes love letters to a soldier using her sister's photograph.

FINE THING!

Published. Copyrighted May 1, 1947. Not used in film.

VERSE

If you want to know
My reaction to
Anyone treating me this way,
If you want to know
What I think of you,
This is all that I have to say:

REFRAIN

Fine thing!
Waiting till you got me all alone.
Fine thing!
Turning on the glamour that way.
You must have known I was blue
And wanted someone who
Could teach me just what to do
And what to say.

Fine thing!
Knowing once you held me in your arms,
I'd cling just as long as you'd let me stay.
Just when I couldn't resist
And had to be kissed
By someone like you,
Fine thing!
Making all my dreams come true.

EVERY SO OFTEN

Music by Harry Warren. Published. Copyrighted June 12, 1947. Recorded by Martha Tilton (Capitol).

VERSE

You wouldn't think that I'd still be aware of
A half-forgotten phrase we used to know;
You wouldn't think I'd cling to my share of
A love affair that ended long ago.
But, darling—

REFRAIN

Ev'ry so often I still think of you,
And ev'ry so often the teardrops fall too.
How I wish that things could be
The same as they were then!
But you can't take a heart apart
And put it back again.

Somebody's hearing the same old sweet lies,
And new stars are shining in somebody's eyes.
You wouldn't think I wake at night
And cry, "How could you?"
You wouldn't, would you?
But ev'ry so often I still do.

YOUR HEART WILL TELL YOU SO

Music by Robert Emmett Dolan. Registered for copyright as an unpublished song October 22, 1947.
    Lyric missing.

FOREVER AMBER (1947)

Produced by Darryl F. Zanuck and William Perlberg for Twentieth Century–Fox. Released October 1947. Copyright October 22, 1947. Directed by Otto Preminger. Screenplay by Philip Dunne and Ring Lardner Jr., and adapted by Jerome Cady, based on the novel *Forever Amber* by Kathleen Winsor. Lyrics by Johnny Mercer. Music by David Raksin. Orchestrations by Maurice De Packh and Herbert Spencer. Musical director: Alfred Newman. With Linda Darnell, Cornel Wilde, George Sanders, Glenn Langan, Richard Haydn, Jessica Tandy, Anne Revere, John Russell, Jane Ball, Robert Coote, Leo G. Carroll, Natalie Draper, Margaret Wycherly, Alma Kruger, Edmond Breon, and Alan Napier.

The picaresque adventures of a beautiful young lady in the time of Charles II. Based on the novel by Kathleen Winsor that shocked contemporary audiences.

FOREVER AMBER

Published. Copyrighted November 10, 1947.

Forever Amber,
She gave a moment a name
To remember.
One glance from Amber,
Your heart within you became
As warm as candle flame.
Her smile was sweet
To ev'ry man she'd meet,
Innocent as April
But indiscreet.
If you desired her
Her lips were willing and warm,
Red as cherries;
But if you tired her,
She'd pass you by, true to form,
Swift as a summer storm.
Then you'd recall
A girl you used to know,
Forever Amber,
An afterglow.

THE CIRCUS IS COMING TO TOWN

Music by Bernie Hanighen.
    Lyric missing.

THERE'S NO BUSINESS LIKE SHOW BUSINESS

Music by Irving Berlin. Special lyrics by Johnny Mercer. Sung by Mercer and Frank Sinatra on Sinatra's CBS/Old Gold cigarette radio show, *Songs by Sinatra*. It was the first time they had performed together on radio—or as Sinatra put it, "rattled the speaker together."

JOHNNY MERCER
& FRANK SINATRA: There's no business like show business,
Like no business I know.

SINATRA: As a kid I'd take a song and croon it,
Till I made the neighbors' windows close.

MERCER: But you kept on practicing and soon it
Became a unit with Major Bowes.
You made money for your records
And sold—

SINATRA: Sold?

MERCER: May I ask a favor of a real nice guy?

SINATRA: You know I'll grant it,
But at least I'll try.

MERCER: Run out to the store and buy yourself a tie.

BOTH: Let's go on with the show.

BOTH: There's no business like show business,
Like no business I know.

SINATRA: With a wig and makeup they disguise you,
Pad your shoulders in the latest fash—

MERCER: Even your own mother if she spies you
Won't recognize you—

SINATRA: But you're a smash!

MERCER: A smash!

BOTH: No people like show people,
They smile when they are low.

SINATRA: If you mention certain jokes, your act is great.

MERCER: Like Crosby, you're always late.

SINATRA: Or a certain crooner who is underweight.

BOTH: Let's go on with the show.

MERCER: That Crosby!

SINATRA: That Mercer!

MERCER: That Sablon!

SINATRA: That Haymes!
It's gettin' pretty tough to make a buck.

MERCER: With youngsters like Jolson to add to the names—

SINATRA: Us older chaps are really outa luck!

MERCER: That's quite a lot of talent in a bunch.

SINATRA: They're good enough, but can they take a punch?

BOTH: There's no business like show business,

SINATRA: If your dancing isn't all you
planned on—
MERCER: Or if your vibrato is attacked—
SINATRA: (How dare they!)
Long as you have got a leg to
stand on—
MERCER: Well, then, you still can act.
BOTH: It's smart thinking to start
thinking
Of new ways to make dough.
MERCER: Vallee's a ventriloquist, I just
got word—
SINATRA: His dummy sings and he's
great, I've heard.
MERCER: Get yourself a Mortimer—and
I mean Snerd!
BOTH: Let's go on with the show.

MR. PEABODY AND THE MERMAID (1948)

Produced by Nunnally Johnson and Gene Fowler Jr. for
Inter-John, Inc., released by Universal-International.
Released August 1948. Copyright August 20, 1948. Di-
rected by Irving Pichel. Screenplay by Nunnally John-
son, based on the novel *Peabody's Mermaid* by Guy and
Constance Jones. Lyrics by Johnny Mercer. Music by
Robert Emmett Dolan. Starring William Powell and
Ann Blyth, with Irene Hervey, Andrea King, Clinton
Sundberg, Art Smith, Hugh French, Lumsden Hare, Fred
Clark, James Logan, Mary Field, Beatrice Roberts, Cyn-
thia Corley, Tom Stevenson, Mary Somerville, Richard
Ryan, Bobby Hyatt, and Ivan H. Browning.

A middle-aged husband imagines he has an affair
with a mermaid.

THE CARIBEES

Published. Copyrighted August 12, 1948. Previously
registered for copyright as an unpublished song
March 5, 1948. Introduced by Andrea King (dubbed by
Martha Mears).

The Caribees, the Caribees,
Where nothing goes by

But clouds in the sky above.
The tiny cays,
The rolling seas—
Their soft serenade
Just seems to be made for love.
I dream how heavenly the nights could be
With you with me in your arms.
Through lazy skies
The full moon's rise
From under a net
Of sleepy palmetto trees.
This dream come true
Needs only you
And the islands they call
The Caribees.

THE ANGELS CRIED

Music by Mercer. Registered for copyright as an unpublished song May 12, 1948.

The angels cried
And the rain came down
On a sad old town
The night you said goodbye.
The angels cried
For what might have been,
And the moon turned in
To hide a tearful eye.
I thought I could read your looks,
But I was a fool;
I'd better get all my books
And go back to school.
Our starry sky
Seemed to open wide,
And the angels cried—
But not as much as I.

HARLEM BUTTERFLY

Music by Mercer. Published. Copyrighted April 27,
1956. Previously registered for copyright as an unpublished song May 12, 1948.

The lyric's ending is a clear homage to poet Edna St.
Vincent Millay's famous "First Fig":

My candle burns at both ends;
It will not last the night;
But ah, my foes, and oh, my friends—
It gives a lovely light!

Harlem butterfly,
The moon got in your eye
The night you were born.
Harlem butterfly,
You listened to the cry
Of some lonely horn,
And that combination
Left you a mark
That you'll never, never lose.
While you chase some will-o'-the-wisp
In the dark
Your heart keeps on singin' the blues.

Oh, Harlem butterfly,
The writin's in the sky—
You'll come to no good.
But I'm not blamin' you.
I'm certain I would do
The same if I could,
For even though a candle
Burned at both ends
Can never last out the night,
Harlem butterfly,
It really makes a lovely light.

PINE TOP'S BOOGIE

Music by Mercer. Lyric transcribed from Mercer's own
recording.

In Chicago town very long ago,
Mr. Smith sat down at the piano
And he wrote a tune called his Pine Top strut,
And it's still a tune very few today can cut.
Boogie woogie,
Boogie woogie,
Was the tune that Pine Top played.
Boogie woogie,
Boogie woogie,
What did you see in the shade? [*unclear*]
Sounded like a locomotive coming down the
grade.

Well, the news went forth by word of mouth
And spread up north and spread down south.
The cats came round to hear old Pine Top's jive
'Cause he made that one piano sound like five.

Boogie woogie,
Boogie woogie,
[*Inaudible*],
Boogie woogie,
Boogie woogie,
Swept the countryside like rain,
Like a prairie fire sweeps across the plain.

Mr. Smith grew fat on his blues routine,
Bought a high silk hat and a limousine,
Walked the streets in patent leather shoes,
Just because his strut was the daddy of the blues.

Boogie woogie,
Boogie woogie,
Saw the years just slip away.
Boogie woogie,
Boogie woogie woogie,
Mr. Smith grew old and gray
And he looked around to find a protégée.

So the story ends.
Mr. Pine Top's gone,
But he left two friends who could carry on,
Who could play the things that only he had known
And could even add a few tricks of their own.
[*calling out*] Albert!
Albert Ammons plays like that.
[*Inaudible*] plays it when they clap
In a natural habitat.

So it first was played on a baby grand.
Well, it made the grade,
It was a twelve-piece band.
It was the same old tune that Pine Top used to
    play.
Only difference is, it's played the Goodman way.

GREAT GUNS

Music by Harry Warren. Published. Copyrighted January 11, 1949.

VERSE

Strike me bright vermillion
Or a close facsimile—
You're a babe in a billion,
Devastating to me.
Can't write words like some write
In a poem or a play,
So I reckon I'll come right
Out and say.

REFRAIN

Great guns,
Holy mack'rel,
And a couple of gollys, too!
Great guns,
Never thought these eyes
Would see anything like you.
First
Came talking pictures,
Then
Came television,
Now
They're makin' dreams come true.
Land sakes,
It's enough to make
A body get all perplexed.
By gosh,
Wonder what these modern
Fellers'll think of next!
You
Top anything of Thomas Edison's
With hot and cold running shivers
And superatomic charms,
And here you are in my arms—
Great guns!

LOVE WOKE ME UP THIS MORNING

Music by Harry Warren. A contract for this song found in the Harry Warren Archives is dated January 14, 1949.

VERSE

I yawned and rubbed my eyes,
And what a sweet surprise
Was there awaiting me:
The early morning sun
Had made the shadows run,
And all that I could see
Were sunbeams playing on the floor,
For even though I'd locked the door,
Someone had come along and found the key,
And—

REFRAIN

Love woke me up this morning;
This morning love tiptoed to my room.
Love went with me as I left my doorway,
Saying, "Do you mind if I go your way?"
What could I do for that old romancer?
How could I know what he had in view?

Then I saw your eyes and knew the answer:
Love woke me up
To lead me straight to you.

THIRTEENTH STREET RAG

Music by Wingy Manone. Published. Copyrighted May 15, 1950. Previously registered for copyright as an unpublished song March 13, 1949.

Just two blocks past Eleventh,
Or six streets after Seventh,
That's where the cats all used to meet.
They tell me
The passersby were breezy,
They took it slow and easy,
Downright artistic with their feet.
They tell me
Their attitude was regal,
Their shoes worn "spread-eagle,"
They'll pick 'em up and let 'em drag.
To see it was to love it,
They made a dance out of it,
That peachy-keen Thirteenth Street Rag.

Pardon me
If it's something you've never seen.
Go and get you a magazine
Like a *Metronome* or the *Downbeat*,
Yesiree!
Maybe on the *Police Gazette*
There's a picture you ain't seen yet
Or a photograph of that town.
They tell me,
Just two blocks past Eleventh
Or six streets after Seventh,
They stand around and chew the rag.
They tell me
To see it was to love it,
They made a dance out of it,
That peachy-keen Thirteenth Street Rag.

TRULY

Music by Antone Iavello. Published. Copyrighted December 21, 1949.

Truly the stars above me
Sent you to love me

As I love you.
Of ev'ryone I know
I'd choose you,
Cross my heart and hope to lose you.
Truly the old sweet story
In all its glory
Begins anew.
Let's start it with a kiss;
Then let me hear you whisper,
"Truly I love you, too."

WHEN SALLY WALKS ALONG PEACOCK ALLEY

Music by Harry Warren.

When Sally walks along Peacock Alley,
All the gentlemen tip their hats,
Fix their cravats,
And roll their eyes.
When Sally walks along Peacock Alley,
Do the old ladies stop and stare?
Well, I declare,
The fur just flies!
Tim O'Malley walks with Sally;
Danny Clancy buys her wine;
Joe O'Leary calls her "dearie";

And the flowers, well, they're mine.
When Sally walks along Peacock Alley,
Some Prince Charming will steal away
With her someday,
But till he's found,
I'll just hang around!

MAKE BELIEVE BALLROOM (1949)

Produced by Ted Richmond for Columbia Pictures. Released April 1949. Copyright May 26, 1949. Directed by Joseph Santley. Screenplay by Albert Duffy and Karen DeWolf. Story by Albert Duffy, based on the radio programs of Al Jarvis and Martin Block. Title song by Al Jarvis, Leon René, and Johnny Mercer. With Jerome Courtland, Ruth Warrick, Ron Randell, Virginia Welles, Al Jarvis, Frankie Laine, King Cole Trio, Toni Harper, Jack Smith, Kay Starr, The Sportsmen, Charlie Barnet, Jimmy Dorsey, Jan Garber, Pee Wee Hunt, Gene Krupa, Ray McKinley, and Adele Jergens.

Based on a radio series popular at the time. Two carhops—Gene and Josie—compete in the Q&A portion of a radio series. Although on-air competitors, they inevitably fall in love.

YOUR MAKE-BELIEVE BALLROOM

Music and lyrics by Al Jarvis, Leon Renee, and Johnny Mercer. Introduced by off-screen chorus behind credits.

Your make-believe ballroom—
All you have to do is close your eyes,
Wish upon a tune,
And pretty soon you'll be there.
Your make-believe ballroom
Has a canopy of starry skies,
Waitin' there especially for you
And you-know-who to share.
It isn't far,
Hop in your car,
Head for the starlight,
See!
Mister T.D.
Shows you the way,
Hey!
Don't sit in your hall room,
Bring the one you love along with you
To the free-for-all?
Make-believe dreams come true.

TEXAS, LI'L DARLIN' (1949)

Tryout: Westport Country Playhouse, Westport, Connecticut, August 29–September 3, 1949; Shubert Theatre, New Haven, Connecticut, October 25–29, 1949; Colonial Theatre, Boston, October 31–November 19, 1949. New York run: Mark Hellinger Theatre; opened November 25, 1949; vacation July 17–August 19, 1950; closed September 9, 1950; 293 performances. Music by Robert Emmett Dolan. Lyrics by Johnny Mercer. Produced by Studio Productions Ltd. and Anthony Brady Farrell. Book by John Whedon and Sam Moore. Directed by Paul Crabtree. Choreography by Al White Jr. Settings by Theodore Cooper. Costumes by Eleanor Goldsmith. Orchestrations by Robert Russell Bennett. Orchestra directed by Will Irwin. Cast included Loring Smith (Harvey Small), Fredd Wayne (Brewster Ames II), Kenny Delmar (Hominy Smith), Betty Lou Keim (Dogie Smith), Ray Long (Branch Pedley), Mary Hatcher (Dallas Smith),* Danny Scholl (Easy Jones), Jared Reed (Sam), and Kate Murtah (Melissa Tatum), the Texas Rhythm Boys (Eddy Smith, Bill Horan, and Joel McConkey, as the Three Coyotes), and ensemble.

Mercer recalled:

> One of my favorite shows was killed with loving kindness in my estimation . . . Lawrence Langner, who really called the shots, made it like a "Little Show" with that title and his casting. All the players were young, the director was young and we never had that big, brassy production that might have shoved it over, and that the book and score deserved. We really put down *Time* and *Life* and the political establishment severely! Perhaps that's another reason we weren't better known.
>
> You have to at least be adamant enough once the material is written to insist that it be done properly.

After the New York run the show was sent on tour. It did badly in Detroit, and in Chicago it closed before the end of its scheduled run. There was one last, muted hurrah a few months later, in Dallas at the State Fair, where it was hoped that the casting of film star Jack Carson as Hominy Smith might improve business—and, after all, wasn't the show *about* Texas? But in this case the Big D for Dallas also stood for show-business Death. The show, which had cost $100,000 to stage initially, ended up losing around $150,000. It has never been revived.

To be fair, it had considerable competition during the 1949–1950 Broadway season: *South Pacific* and *Kiss Me, Kate* were running at the same time.

---

* *In the Westport production the part of Dallas was played by Elaine Stritch.*

WHOOPIN' AND A-HOLLERIN'

Introduced by Betty Lou Keim (Dogie), Kenny Delmar (Hominy), and ensemble.

What's the matter with Hominy's kin?
What's the matter with Hominy's kin?
What's the matter with Hominy's kin?
There's enough of them to vote him in!

We're a-whoopin' and a-hollerin', hollerin',
Whoopin' and a-hollerin' night and day.
Whoopin' and a-hollerin',
Whoopin' and a-hollerin',
Whoopin' and a-hollerin' "He's okay!"

What's the matter with Hominy's smile?
What's the matter with Hominy's smile?
What's the matter with Hominy's smile?
You can see his gold tooth smilin' a mile!

We're a-whoopin' and a-hollerin',
Whoopin' and a-hollerin',
Whoopin' and a-hollerin' day and night.
Whoopin' and a-hollerin',
Whoopin' and a-hollerin',
Whoopin' and a-hollerin' "He's all right!"

TEXAS, LI'L DARLIN'

Registered for copyright as an unpublished song October 24, 1949. Introduced and recorded by Kenny Delmar (Hominy) and ensemble (Decca).

HOMINY: Where do you good folks expect to go
When this vale of tears is o'er?
CROWD: [*chants in response*] Texas!
HOMINY: What is the name of that magical,
mystical,
Sung-about distant shore?
CROWD: Texas!
HOMINY: Where will the Running- and Still-Water
Baptists
Sit down and clasp their hands?
CROWD: Texas!
HOMINY: Which is the only State of States
In the only land of lands?
CROWD: Texas, li'l darlin',
I'm plumb enraptured with you!
I been to Minnesota

And North 'n South Dakota,
But nary one o' them'll ever do.
Texas, li'l darlin',
I got ya deep in m'bones.
Can't find a thing agin' you,
Love everything that's in you—
Your famous names from Jesse James
Right up to Jesse Jones.
Your vast dominion
Makes all the others seem small.
In my opinion
You'd swallow Britain
'N' go on with your knittin'.
Texas, li'l darlin',
Here's what I'm tryin' to say:
I guess I'm only human,
I love a pretty woman,
I love a drink o' likker, yessirree,
But you hit me, Texas,
In my solar plexus.
Li'l darlin', you're the one for me!

Texas, li'l darlin',
You're like a mother to me!
I gaze across the prairie
From under my sombrery
And I'm in love with everything I see.
Texas, li'l darlin',
I know y'boundaries by heart.
Like Messrs Rand McNally
I know each hill and valley,
That is to say,
I know the ones they've had the time to
chart.
I'm writin' sonnets
'Bout how your bluebonnets grow.
Since Kostelanetz
Heard Texas fiddlin',
He's only fair to middlin'.
Texas, li'l darlin',
All states are jealous of you.
Some governor named Warren—
I guess he must be foreign—
Says California's the place to be.
Well, I'm shoutin', Texas,
They'll never annexe us!
Li'l darlin', you're the one for me!

THE YODEL BLUES

Published. Copyrighted December 1, 1949. Alternate title: "They Talk a Different Language." Introduced and recorded by Mary Hatcher (Dallas), Kenny Delmar (Hominy), and the Texas Rhythm Boys (the Three Coyotes) (Decca). Reprised by Hatcher and female ensemble. Also recorded by Jo Stafford and Johnny Mercer (Capitol).

DALLAS: [*spoken*] Well . . . I don't know. There's
       something about 'em . . .
       [*sung*] Way up in New York City
       They talk a different language,
       They talk a different style—
       So busy makin' money
       They ain't got time to smile.
       It was s'doggone crowded,
       I felt s'hemmed in there,
       I come back home to Texas
       To get a breath of air.

       O-dee-odle-o-dee-odle-o-dee got the
         blues
       Dee-odle-o-dee-odle-o-dee just for you
       Dee-odle-o-dee-odle-o-dee and the
         sweetest little home I ever knew.
       O-dee-odle-o-dee-odle-o-dee when I'm
         low
       Dee-odle-o-dee-odle-o-dee, don'tcha know
       Dee-odle-o-dee-odle-o-dee that I'll sing
       The Yodel-o-dee-odle Blues?!

       They talk a diff'rent language,
       They speak a diff'rent brand.
       Where we'd say "Plumb delighted!"
       They always say "How grand!"
       We say a thing's "real purty."
       They call the same thing "chic."
       You may as well be talkin'
       Eyetalian or Greek.

[DALLAS *repeats the yodel refrain as* HOMINY *sings.*]

HOMINY: I can understand how you felt
       With your worries and cares,
       Meetin' all o' them stuck-up strangers
       A-puttin' on all them airs.
       Why, enough of that la-de-da
       Can affect your morale—
       When you tell me home's best,
       You ain't just a-whistlin' Dixie, gal!
COYOTES: Down in the valley
       I'll meet you when the lights are low.
       Down in the valley
       You'll hear my yodel-o-dee-o!

[DALLAS *repeats the yodel refrain, the* COYOTES *repeat* "Down in the Valley," *and* HOMINY *sings.*]

HOMINY: They talk a different language,
       They talk a different style—
       So busy makin' money
       They ain't got time to smile.

       Listen to me, you rovers,
       When everything's bad news,
       Come back home to Texas
       And sing the Yodel Blues.

Reprise

DALLAS: Listen, you stage-struck maidens.
       Let me advise you, please.
       The stars up in Chicago
       Are thick as bumblebees.
       Be sure the world is ready
       To hear your pear-shaped tones,
       Or you know what'll happen?
GIRLS: What is dat, Mr. Bones?
DALLAS: O-dee-odle-o-dee-odle-o-dee got the
         blues
       Dee-odle-o-dee-odle-o-dee just for you
       Dee-odle-o-dee-odle-o-dee and the
         sweetest little home I ever knew.
       O-dee-odle-o-dee-odle-o-dee when I'm
         low
       Dee-odle-o-dee-odle-o-dee, don'tcha
         know
       Dee-odle-o-dee-odle-o-dee that I'll sing
       The Yodel-o-dee-odle Blues?!

       Lemme tell ya bout life, my friends
       On the wicked old stage.
       I was strictly a barnyard bluejay,
       A bird in a gilded cage.
       Never even saw one stage door,
       As a matter of fact,
       But for plenty of actors' agents
       I'd go into my act. Hey!

       O-dee-odle-o-dee-odle-o-dee got the
         blues
       Dee-odle-o-dee-odle-o-dee just for you
       Dee-odle-o-dee-odle-o-dee and the
         sweetest little home I ever knew.
       O-dee-odle-o-dee-odle-o-dee when I'm
         low
       Dee-odle-o-dee-odle-o-dee, don'tcha
         know?
       Dee-odle-o-dee-odle-o-dee that I'll sing
       The Yodel-o-dee-odle Blues?!

A MONTH OF SUNDAYS

Published. Copyrighted November 1, 1949. Introduced and recorded by Mary Hatcher (Dallas) and Danny Scholl (Easy) (Decca).

VERSE

DALLAS: First date you had with me you kissed me.
       Do you recall what you said then?
       One way to tell me how you've missed me
       Would be to say it once again.

REFRAIN

EASY: I'm glad I waited
       A month of Sundays
       To find somebody like you.
       I've seen more daybreaks
       Turn into lonely nights;
       Those signs on Broadway
       Should have that many lights.
       Have you tried waiting
       A month of Sundays
       For just one dream to come
         true?
       I'll have to own up
       That if you hadn't shown up
       There'd only be one thing to
         do—
       I'd wait for a million months of
       Sundays
       For you.

[DALLAS AND EASY *repeat refrain.*]

HOOTIN' OWL TRAIL

Published. Copyrighted November 1, 1949. Introduced by Danny Scholl (Easy), Betty Lou Keim (Dogie), and ensemble. Recorded by Scholl (Decca).

VERSE

EASY: When you hear my special kind o' whistle,
       Let me hear you whistle back an echo.
       If you do, then I'll know you can go;
       If you don't, then I'll go single-o.

REFRAIN

When it's just comin' grass on the old prairie,
With the trees greenin' up kinda pale,
That's the time of the year for my gal and me
To be ridin' down the Hootin' Owl Trail.
In the cool of the evenin' we burn the breeze
Where the stagecoaches once toted mail,
Or we amble along through the Joshua trees
When we're ridin' down the Hootin' Owl Trail.

It's a right nice sight
With the moon shinin' bright,
Spillin' silver on the hills of blue,
While a bald-faced bay
Starts to whinny away
When he hears that old whoo-oo-oo!

City folks, I suppose, find it mighty strange,
Same as I figure a town's like a jail,
But our heart's right at home on the old home
    range
When we're ridin' down that Hootin' Owl Trail!

INTERLUDE

1ST GUEST: I was moseyin' along in a dozy kind o'
    way,
Lackadaisyin' to homeward at the
    close of day,
When I seen the rosy embers of a
    cozy barbeque,
And because I'm kinda nosey—well,
    I just come, too!

2ND GUEST: I picked up the phone to call a friend
    of mine
And heard about the party on the
    party line,
I got my bib 'n' tucker and I took her
    on the run.
Hominy's politics is awful, but his
    hoedown's fun!

3RD GUEST: I got your invitation, which you
    didn't send,
So I thought I wouldn't answer it and
    bring a friend.
I got myself a partner and I'm feelin'
    kinda smug—
Incident'ly, can you point me at the
    cider jug?

4TH GUEST: We'll need a lot o' waiters and we'll
    need a lot of cooks,
We'll need a lot o' ladies who are long
    on looks.
So find yourself a partner who is
    starry-eyed,
'N' enumerate the beauties of the
    countryside!

[ENSEMBLE *repeats refrain*.]

THE BIG MOVIE SHOW IN THE SKY

Published. Copyrighted November 1, 1949. Introduced and recorded by Danny Scholl (Easy) and ensemble (Decca).

REFRAIN 1

EASY: A fella can get lonesome
ENSEMBLE: Fella can get lonely
EASY: When he is all alone
ENSEMBLE: Out there in the Pacific
EASY: Out there in the Pacific
    With no friends to call his own.
    A fella gits to thinkin'
    If he's gittin' anywhere,
    A fella gits to wond'rin
ENSEMBLE: Fella gits to wond'rin
EASY: How it's gonna be Up There
ENSEMBLE: If he will meet the Mayor
EASY: When your final chip is cashed
    And the Pearly Gates swing wide,
    And there is old Saint Peter
ENSEMBLE: There is old Saint Peter,
EASY: Askin' you to come inside.
ENSEMBLE: The Lord's official Greeter.
EASY: He whispers, "Son, go find a seat—
    I hope you like the show."
    And then you see a picture
    Of the life you led below!
EASY AND
ENSEMBLE: Bye and bye, bye and bye,
    Can you look yourself in the eye,
    When you come up on the screen up
      yonder,
    At the Big Movie Show in the Sky?

REFRAIN 2

EASY: Imagine you are one of
    That great celestial crowd,
    A-settin' back relaxin'
ENSEMBLE: Surely can't be taxin'
EASY: With your feet upon a cloud.
ENSEMBLE: A-settin' back relaxin'
EASY: You're pourin' buttered sunshine
    On your popcorn white as fleece
    And waitin' for the latest
ENSEMBLE: Hemispheric popcorn
EASY: Interhemisphere release
ENSEMBLE: Has got to be the topcorn.
EASY: The stars spell out the title
ENSEMBLE: Stars spell out the title,
EASY: And the cast before your eye;
ENSEMBLE: And ev'ry scene is vital.

EASY: The show commences on
    The silver screen they call the sky.
    The past begins unfoldin',
    And you see it takin' place—
    And pretty soon you're lookin'
    At your own big ugly face!
EASY AND
ENSEMBLE: Bye and bye, bye and bye,
    Can you look yourself in the eye,
    When you come on the screen up
      yonder,
    At the Big Movie Show in the Sky?
EASY: It must feel kinda funny
    To see Saint Peter smile
    And tell you that he's had
    A camera on you all the while.
    Yes, every little movement
    Has a meaning all its own;
    Your acting may be lousy
    Even when you're all alone.
    So, pardner, better mend y' fence
    And tend to your corral
    And don't go trespassin'
    With the other feller's gal.
    Be sure you do some actin'
    Of which later you'll be proud—
    'Cause that's one movin'-picture show
    Where retakes ain't allowed!
EASY AND
ENSEMBLE: Bye and bye, bye and bye,
    Can you look yourself in the eye
    When you come on the screen up
      yonder,
    At the Big Movie Show in the Sky?
EASY: Colossal and stupendous,
    Gigantic and immense—
    The cast is so enormous
    That it almost don't make sense!
ENSEMBLE: Cast is so colossal
    They even have a fossil!
EASY: There's hatin' and there's lovin'
    And there's sorrow and there's joy,
    There's thunder and there's lightnin'
    And it's all the real McCoy!
ENSEMBLE: Golly, but it's frightnin'
    To see the lightnin' light'nin'!
EASY: If you don't look pretty sharp,
    You won't see yourself at all;
    There's so much goin' on
    That everybody seems right small.
ENSEMBLE: Such a mighty topic,
    A man is microscopic!
EASY: It's quite a panorama
    And it must be quite a thrill
    And even big enough to please
    Cecil B. DeMille!
ENSEMBLE: Aaaaaahhh!

EASY AND
ENSEMBLE: Bye and bye, bye and bye,
Can you look yourself in the eye
When you come on the screen up
yonder,
At the Big Movie Show in the Sky?

HORSESHOES ARE LUCKY

Published. Copyrighted November 1, 1949. Introduced by Danny Scholl (Easy).

REFRAIN

Horseshoes are lucky,
Sun showers, too,
So is a wagon of hay.
If you see a pin
And you pick it up,
Fortune follows you
All through the day.
My four-leaf clover's
Gone out to lunch;
So have the horses of gray,
And my rabbit's foot
Must have lost its charm,
'Cause my girl
Turned me down
Today.

LOVE ME, LOVE MY DOG

Introduced by Kenny Delmar (Hominy), Danny Scholl (Easy), and ensemble.

VERSE

HOMINY: I bid you welcome, neighbors,
Let's have ourselves a time,
Ol' Hominy's campaignin',
So just get off the dime.
We're long on entertainment
But short on talk, you'll find.
Won't filibust,
But lemme just
Refresh your mind.

REFRAIN

Love me, you got to love my dog,
And love the hog that's rootin' in the
cedar bog,
Love the church I go to
And the mule I ride,
And my cross-eyed cousin on my
sister's side.
If I'm elected,
I'll tell you what—
You'll get the same damn treatment
that you always got.
You'll get some brand-new taxes
And the same old school,
You'll get the good old Golden Rule,
'Cause when it comes to lovin',
I'm a lovin' fool.
Love me, you got to love my mule!

EASY &
FOLLOWERS: And when I make a promise,
I'll do what I say
Before you all get old and gray.
To date I ain't done nothing,
But I surely might—
Love me, you gotta love me,
Love me, love what's right!

HOMINY &
FOLLOWERS: 'Cause when it comes to lovin'
Love me, you gotta love me,
Love me, love my mule!

TAKE A CRANK LETTER

Registered for copyright as an unpublished song November 29, 1949. Introduced by Jacqueline James, Ronnie Hartmann, Elyse Weber, Dorothy Mary Richards, Marion Lauer, and B. J. Keating (secretaries); reprised by them and Fredd Wayne (Brewster Ames II).

1ST SECRETARY: [with a shrug]
What does any secretary do?
SECRETARIES: We're the other women in your
husbands' lives,
Or perhaps you know us as the
nine-to-fives—
They're hirable, fireable, dumb
and desirable,
"Please take a wire"–able wives.
Any time he needs a boost in his
morale,
All he does is ring a buzzer for his
pal,

His cynical ninny, collected and
clinical,
Perched-on-a-pinnacle gal.
"Miss Jones! Miss Jones!"
I can hear the dear and dulcet
tones.
"Miss Jones! Miss Jones!
What the hell became of those
bank loans?"
Oh, we wish we were the ones to
light his pipe,
Or the ones whose lipstick he
forgets to wipe,
The sportable, courtable,
weekend-resortable,
Back-to-your-portable type!
But our husbands can't afford to
take the loss,
So we do his pen-and-inking,
We keep his shirt from shrinking,
We make his dates for drinking,
We keep his glasses clinking,
His joie de vivre from sinking,
Protect him when he's stinking—
But we don't do the thinking with
the boss!
Oh, he makes you feel as cozy as
he can—
"Never mind the chair, just sit on
that divan."
A "Please take a letter—no, take
off that sweater—now, isn't
that better?"–type man.
(Still and all, we're less a maid
and more machine,
With the extra work, if you know
what we mean.
That Saturday, Sunday, Oh, gee,
what a fun day,
"I don't know you Monday"
routine.)
And our pictures on those
Caribbean boats—
"Smart exec takes private sec
along for notes"—
We reach the Bahamas, unpack
our pajamas,
And wind up with commas and
quotes.
"Miss Jones! Miss Jones!"—
I can hear the dear and dulcet
tones.
"Miss Jones! Miss Jones!
Who's supposed to get the
goddamn phones?"
We're available, but never
overawed;

We appreciate, but never must
    applaud.
A capable, drapable, possibly
    rapable
Always escapable broad
Who is never called upon to come
    across.
So we do the first-of-Maying,
The "Pardon, you were saying?"
"He's all tied up today"–ing.
(We take the underpaying,
The after hours staying,
Of course, it means delaying,
But we don't do the okaying for
    the boss.)
"That cornerstone needs laying."
When bills require paying,
You'll even find us praying—
Ah, but never negligéeing with
    the boss!

Reprise

SECRETARIES: [*sung dolefully*] So we just go on
    P.S.-ing
And with conventions pressing
Observe his effervescing,
Attend his convalescing,
Perhaps apply a dressing,
For which we get his blessing—
But we get no real caressing from
    the boss!

POLITICS

Registered for copyright as an unpublished song January 10, 1950. Introduced and recorded by Kenny Delmar (Hominy) and Loring Smith (Harvey) (Decca).

HOMINY: If you can raise the flag and wave 'er,
    Never grant a favor,
    Smile and tell 'em maybe,
    Always kiss the baby,
    Give the kid a locket,
    Out of Daddy's pocket,
    Have him thank you for the crime—
HARVEY: My friend, the practice you're indulging
    in is politics!
HOMINY: Yes, it's politics!
BOTH: Simply politics!
HOMINY: You pay a fella seven dollars and he kicks
    back six!
BOTH: You're in politics every time!

HARVEY: If you can make a bold prediction,
    Brand it merely fiction.
    Scream to get the credit,
    Then deny you said it,
    Hand reporters wires,
    Call 'em lousy liars,
    When you see it in the press—
HOMINY: Son, you're a natural phenomenon at
    politics!
HARVEY: Sure, it's politics!
BOTH: Purely politics!
HARVEY: If you are loyal to a dozen different
    cliques or clicks—
BOTH: You're in politics—more or less!
HOMINY: If you can please the big employers
    And the workers' lawyers,
    Keep 'em busy fightin'
    While the fish are bitin',
    Don't improve conditions,
    'Cept for politicians,
    Then demand a little fee—
HARVEY: My boy, the papers have a name for it—
    it's politics!
HOMINY: Yes, it's politics!
BOTH: Filthy politics!
HOMINY: If you can treat the general public like a
    bunch of hicks—
BOTH: You're in politics, yessirree!
HARVEY: You must be either high and lofty—
HOMINY: Or a reg'lar softie.
HARVEY: Smart administrator—
HOMINY: Or a second-rater.
HARVEY: Stern and superhuman—
HOMINY: Or like Harry Truman.
BOTH: Then you'll really make it pay!
HARVEY: The occupation that's designed for you
    is politics!
HOMINY: Often called the fix!
HARVEY: But it's politics!
HOMINY: If you can mingle with the Dutchmen
    and the Irish micks—
BOTH: You're in politics, what the hey!
    You spell it P-O-L-I-T-I-C-S.
    You're in politics, what the hey!
HARVEY: If you can sit in Washington
    And be put upon,
    Get the Pentagon
    On the telephone,
    Cheer up Harry Vaughan
    Or John Marigon,
    Son, you've had a busy day!
HOMINY: You've had a busy day playing politics.
HARVEY: Is it business? Nix!
BOTH: Nix! It's politics.
HARVEY: If you create misunderstandings that
    are hard to fix—
BOTH: You're in politics! Hip hooray!

HOMINY: If you can calm an impolite House,
    Overhaul the White House,
    Play a mean piano,
    Raise a cute soprano,
    Render unto Caesar
    Only one deep freezer—
BOTH: You will be the people's choice!
HARVEY: Because the people choose a man who's
    good at politics!
HOMINY: Son, it's politics!
BOTH: Purely politics!
HOMINY: If you are stuck without a paddle up a
    zillion cricks—
BOTH: You're in politics! So rejoice!
    You spell it P-O-L-I-T-I-C-S.
    You're in politics! So rejoice!
HARVEY: But when you speak till you're
    perspiring—
HOMINY: And guests are tiring—
HARVEY: Older heads are leaving—
HOMINY: And the drunks are weaving—
HARVEY: Don't be bashful, lover—
HOMINY: Hit the road for cover—
HARVEY: 'Cause that's the time to say "Bon
    soir"!
    Of course, you know "bon soir" is really
    French for politics.
HOMINY: Fifty million hicks know it's politics!
BOTH: It's been delightful—it's been jolly—it's
    been solid kicks—
    It's been politics—au revoir!

RIDE 'EM, COWBOY

Introduced by Mary Hatcher (Dallas).

DALLAS: [*to* DOGIE] Ride 'em, cowboy!
    Stay in there and fight!
    Ride 'em, cowboy!
    Things will be all right!
    Love is like a wild mustang that's hard to
    break,
    But the happy ending's worth the pains
    you take.
    If he leaves you,
    He's not worth your tears—
    If he loves you,
    Watch how fast it clears!
    When the one you've counted on
    Has thrown your dreams sky-high,
    Ride 'em, cowboy!
    Don't cry!

Little orphan calf,
Dogie mine,
You don't know the half—
Only nine.
You think I'm oh so wise—
That's a bluff.
Don't you know life is hard,
Life is rough?
Big sis—that's a laugh—
Ain't so tough.

If he leaves you,
He's not worth your tears—
If he loves you,
Watch how fast it clears.
When the one you've counted on
Has thrown your dream sky-high,
Ride 'em, cowboy!
Don't cry!

AFFABLE, BALDING ME

Registered for copyright as an unpublished song January 10, 1950. Introduced and recorded by Mary Hatcher (Dallas) and Fredd Wayne (Brewster Ames II) (Decca). This was a favorite song of the dean of Broadway orchestras, Robert Russell Bennett.

VERSE

BREWSTER: Hardly a thought for older heads
But vital, you may be sure.
Fav'rite sport for average couple
At week's end remained amour!
Many a John and Mary
Neath many a leafy bough
Leaned on the dictionary
As I—to you—do now.

REFRAIN 1

BREWSTER: Consider the thing this way:
How wonderful it would be
If beautiful, ample-bosomed you
Loved affable, balding me.
My relatives all would say,
"A chip off the old block, he."
If fresh-as-a-daisy, windswept you
Loved socially top-drawer me.
Tradition states,
Although science disproves,
That opposites attract.
We're perfect mates,
So I think it behooves

Both you and me to act.
Don't think about just us two,
But think of our progeny—
The children all would have my IQ
And your physiognomy
If hourglass-figured, long-stemmed
you
Loved popular Back Bay me!

REFRAIN 2

DALLAS: Consider the thing this way:
How out of place I would be
If Gramercy Square, South Hampton
you*
Loved mail-order, outhouse me.
Your dowager aunts would say,
"No Stork Club balloon girl, she!"
If letterman, Yale man, ad man you
Loved Dallas from RFD!
A ma and pa,
Just suppose our wild oats
Came not as we rehearsed.
Said playwright Shaw
In some notable quotes,
Suppose it were reversed?
Then what should we ever do
To rescue our progeny
If all the children had my IQ
And your physiognomy?
If spindle-shanked, chestless, no-chinned
you
Loved ignorant, bird-brained me?

REFRAIN 3

BREWSTER: How long do I have to wait
That wonderful day to see
When country-fed, child-of-nature you
Loves Racquet Club, *Blue Book* me?
I toss in my sleep at night
And wonder when it will be,
When ripe-as-a-peach, curvaceous you
Loves eager, expectant me!
If I could read, "At a quarter to ten,
With scattered clouds above,
One night last week, as it must to all
men,
To Brewster Ames came love,"
In twenty-five million stalls
The magazine fans would see
A color plate of Niagara Falls,
And there in the foreground, we—
If every-day-more-enchanting you
Loved patient-but-panting me!

_____
* *Alternate line:*
If clothes-made-to-order, penthouse you

REFRAIN 4

DALLAS: It touches my tender heart,
That frustrated, frenzied plea,
That stuck-in-the-sticks-with-no-phone you
Loves nearby, adjacent me.
Besides being fond of you,
It flatters my vanity
That "What can I lose by trying?" you
Loves "Why should I give in?" me.
Should we indulge in the sport of amour,
Think well on who would win.
Your manly bulge is from Sulka's, I'm sure,
While mine are all built-in.
In twenty-five million stalls
Your magazine fans would view
A color plate of Niagara Falls,
And there at the bottom, you—
If vitamin-complex-minus you
Loved fully packed, stacked-up me.

REFRAIN 5

BREWSTER: The *Times* would say, "Fine old line
Weds new aristocracy!"
If apple-cheeked, apple-knocker you
Loved Beacon Hill, Back Bay me!
The *Herald Tribune* would read,
"Pair starting new dynasty!"
If deep-in-the-heart-of-Texas you
Loved steeped-in-tradition me!
Each Friday noon
We would lunch at the Stork,
Then hop into our plane,
Inspect the ranch,
Then be back in New York
For Sunday-night champagne.
Oh, rapture—oh, bliss—oh, joy!
Our life will be très jolie,
And we will be the same girl and boy
That now we are wont to be—
If socialite, graying, youngish you
Loved well-preserved, brainy me!

DALLAS: [spoken] That ain't the way I heered it.
[sung] Each Friday noon you would
lunch at the Stork,
Then, being conscience-struck,
Put in a call while you stayed in New
York
For Champagne with some cluck!
Oh, horrors—oh, woe—oh, strife!
Our life would be too chi-chi,
And we won't be the same girl and boy
That now we are wont to be—
If pot-bellied, rump-sprung, playboy
you
Loved wrinkled-up, dried-out me!

WHICH-A-WAY'D THEY GO?

Introduced by Mary Hatcher (Dallas), Jared Reed (Sam), Betty Lou Keim (Dogie), and ensemble.

VERSE

SAM: Our hero is in danger, fellas,
And we got to rescue him.
ENSEMBLE: And they won't do that to him.
SAM: Ev'ry single galoot
Better git a bathin' suit,
'Cause it's goin' to be sink or swim.
He might be on the railroad trestle
Or beneath the sawmill wheels—
Git your old shootin' iron,
'Cause we're goin' to keep a-firin'
Till we fill 'em full of oxygen, the heels!

REFRAIN

ALL: Which-a-way'd they go?
They was really burnin' gas.
Which-a-way'd they go?
Gotta catch 'em at the pass.
Giddyap! Giddyap!
ENSEMBLE: How I hate the sight o'blood.
Giddyup! Giddyup!
ALL: Or your name is mud.
Let the varmints know
That they cain't do that t'us.
Whichaway'd they go?
Hope they didn't catch a bus!
Ef you seen whar they been,
Won't you let a fella know?
This-a-way? That-a-way?
Which-a-way'd they go?

IT'S GREAT TO BE ALIVE

Published. Copyrighted January 23, 1950. Previously registered for copyright as an unpublished song December 12, 1949. Introduced by Danny Scholl (Easy) and ensemble. Recorded by Kenny Admar, Mary Hatcher, and ensemble (Decca).

The lyric came from a letter to Mercer's mother.

VERSE

EASY: Are we in trouble?
Yes, sir!
Is it a bubble?
No, sir!
What if a show'r is headin' our way?
Well, sir,
It's still the U.S.A.
My observation—
This is a nation—
Well, like I just now started to say,
It's still the U.S.A.

REFRAIN

It's great to be alive,
To work from nine to five,
To have a piece of land to farm.
It's great to be alive,
And have a car to drive
And have your baby on your arm.
In spite of bills
And other minor ills,
Somehow we manage to survive.
It's great to be in love,
To have a roof above,
To watch the little ones arrive,
Your own descendants—
Deductible dependents.
It's great to be alive.

LITTLE BIT O' COUNTRY

Introduced by Mary Hatcher (Dallas). Dropped from show before New York opening.

VERSE

You pushed my baby carriage,
You watched my growin' pains,
And you'll attend my marriage
If I've got any brains.
No secrets do I harbor
From you boys and my dad.
I ain't met Jake the Barber
But close shaves I have had.

REFRAIN 1

Packed my portmanteau, threw away my toys,
Headed for Chicago, Illinois.
Seen a lot o' sights, but I can tell you boys,
There's a little bit o' country left in me.
Bought some fancy gowns, had 'em cut real low,
In the proper spots they'd overflow.
You can rest assured, although it may not show,
There's a little bit o' country left in me.
Plenty o' rich folks—a lot o' fuss.
Plenty o' poor folks—the same as us.
Plenty o' wisecracks—'n' just as dumb.
A fella name o' Wrigley always says, "By gum!"
Care for some?
Straw was in my ears, hay was in my hair.
By the way, hay ain't the same up there.
Had a lot rubbed off, but I'm prepared to swear
There's a little bit o' country left in me.

REFRAIN 2

Oh, I seen some wolves and coyotes, too,
But the ones up there howl, "Yoo-hoo-hoo."
Though I got away, I had to hustle, too.
There's a little but o' country left in me.
Every single droop in Chicago's loop
Tried to build this prairie hen a coop,
But I won more fights right on my own front
stoop.
There's a little bit o' country left in me.
Gentlemen called me "*petite oiseau*,"
Gentlemen showed me *les grands chateaux*,
Gentlemen bought me *vin ordinaire*,
But when they made a pass I still could say, "Oh
yeah."
C'est la guerre!
I been kissed by cads, I been hugged by heels,
But they never once touched my ideals,
And my conscience saved me in the final reels.
There's a little bit o' country left in me.

OUR FAMILY TREE

Introduced by Mary Hatcher (Dallas). Dropped from show before New York opening.

VERSE

My mama told me, "Sister,
Yore papa's mighty dumb,
But still we love each other,
And that's where you come from.
If ever you should wander,
Which one fine day you might,
Remember yore relations
And you'll make out all right."

REFRAIN 1

M' great-grandpappy was married the day that m'
grandpa was christened—
We're mighty proud o' our family tree.
We know the weddin' was legal, 'cause Pappy was
there and he listened—

We're mighty proud o' our family tree.
Family tree!
Family tree!
I won't have nary a soul sayin' nary a word against
    thee!
You can have yourn
Sho as you born,
But we got ours, so we're all pretty sure blood is
    thicker than corn
(That's a likker, son!)
We stick together and that'un'll fight like a hound
    dog for this'un—
We're mighty proud o' our family tree!

REFRAIN 2

M'aunt Prunella was never a gal who'd approve of
    a prunin'.
It got right bushy, our family tree.
She'd kiss a fella and right away start settin' up
    honeymoonin'—
She done it so indiscriminately!
Mattie Mae Sue,
Florabelle, too—
Only th' good Lord is able to count all the
    branches they grew!
When the moon's bright,
Any old night,
You can bet somewhere there's some one of us
    who's a-doin' all right!
It's a-blossomin'!
If you ask anyone hereabouts what spot is dandy
    f'spoonin',
I bet they mention our family tree!

REFRAIN 3

Some trees are noted for shelter and shade,
Some f' fruit and f' flowers.
And then, of course, there's our family tree;
We find it mighty convenient when we are
    expectin' showers—
The kind they give for a mother-to-be.
Fearless and true,
Neighborly, too—
We have got good qualities that we ain't even
    counted up to!
Buildin' a nest
May we suggest
Effen you count every branch, we're the
    Montgomery Ward of the west!
Free delivery!
Y' ain't required to purchase—you're welcome to
    just come and "browers"—
We're mighty proud of our family tree!

REFRAIN 4

M' kissin' cousin Leviticus, loathsome and lanky
    and limber,
He done right good by our family tree—
He never looked at a lady without he would start
    yellin' "Timber!"
'Twas something glandular—sexually.
Charlie and Clem,
Luther and Lem,
Since they was travelin' men, why, there ain't no
    accountin' f' them.
Billy and Boyd,
Both unemployed,
Stayin' at home thataway,
Why, their wives took to readin'
Up Freud—
Enciente, they was!
But shucks, Aunt Minnie's got chillum she can't
    recollect or remember—
We're mighty proud of our family tree.

REFRAIN 5

If you want doctors or lawyers or injuns or even an
    Okie,
You'll find 'em all in our family tree.
And though there's also a couple o' boys spent a
    while in the pokey,
They got there kinda' impetuously!
Little acorns,
Little acorns,
'Fore they git growed into them mighty oaks,
    some is bound
T' have thorns.
Poker-faced Slim,
What about him?
Havin' them five of a kind, he was shore hangin'
    out on a limb—
Perpendicular!
We like our comical cousins, but that sort of
    thing's pretty hokey—
It don't look good on Our Family Tree!

JUST TO KEEP THE RECORD STRAIGHT

Introduced by Danny Scholl (Easy) and Mary Hatcher
(Dallas). Not used.

VERSE 1

EASY: Although it requires skill,
        Let those who will

Write the nation's laws,
Be the chairman of the board
Or Henry Ford—
Even Santa Claus.
Want no one messin'
Around with us—
Please call the press in
And quote me thus:

REFRAIN 1

Just to keep the record straight,
This is how I feel.
You're the girl I nominate,
My ideal.
Just to keep the record straight,
This is where I stand.
I am now a candidate
For your hand.
I'll tell the whole darn U.S.A.,
Except Vermont and Maine,
My heart's in the ring,
You're my big campaign.
If you'll be my running mate,
Tell you what you do.
Just keep the record straight,
Say that you
Love me too.

VERSE 2

DALLAS: Missus Martha Washington
        Was quite the one;
        So was Betsy Ross.
        I'd give up my claim to fame
        To bear your name.
        You can be the boss.
        I'll mix the salads
        To feed your face;
        I'll sing my ballads
        In your embrace.

REFRAIN 2

Just keep the record straight,
This is how I feel.
You're the boy I nominate,
My ideal.
Just keep the record straight,
This is where I stand:
There's no other candidate
For my hand
I'll tell the whole darn U.S.A.,
Except Vermont and Maine,
My heart's in the ring,
You're my big campaign.
If you need a running mate,
Maybe I will do.

Just to keep the record straight,
Say that you
Love me too.

HE THREW ME A CURVE

A pencil notation on the typed lyric sheet indicates Mercer probably had it in mind for this show.

My, he was cute,
Wore the zootest kind of a suit.
I went for the kid,
But soon as I did,
He threw me a curve.
Gee, he was grand,
Playin' slide trombone in a band!
I fell for it too,
But what did he do?
He threw me a curve.
Now my heart is filled with loathing,
Just because my honey lamb
Was a big bad wolf in cheap clothing
Who made me what I am.
I'll count to ten,
But if I should dig him again,
I'll go for his act,
In spite of the fact
That he threw me a curve.

THE WAY YOU FALL IN LOVE

In 1949 Mercer and Robert Emmet Dolan (music) worked on a musical titled *Free and Easy*, which had a book by Sid Herzig and Milton Lazarus. Never produced or even completed, the show was abandoned. Only one lyric, "The Way You Fall in Love," survives. At one time it was intended for *Texas Li'l Darlin'* but it was never used. No music is known to survive.

VERSE 1

Lord Tennyson and Milton
Might have known what to say.
Knowing what love is built on
They sat down, wrote a play.
There is a lot I miss of love,
But I can tell you this of love . . .

REFRAIN 1

Every time you see her,
You catch your breath.
Every time you're with her,
You're scared to death.
Soon you're passing
Every sleepless night
By tearing up
The poetry you write.
When you try to tell her,
You're like a boy.
She says you're her feller,
And, oh, the joy!
Then you kiss,
While angels sing above.
That's the way you fall in love.

VERSE 2

Lord Tennyson and Milton
Ogden Nash, E. B. White,
Just seem to put a lilt on
Every word that they write.
In junior high I read it all
And may I say you said it all.

REFRAIN 2

Every time you see him,
You catch your breath.
Every time you're with him,
You're scared to death.
Soon you're passing
Every night alone,
Just on the chance
That he might telephone.
How you long to tell him
That he's the boy.
Suddenly he tells you,

And, oh, the joy!
Then you kiss
While angels sing above,
That's the way you fall in love.

ISADORE SHAPIRO AND SONS

Another Mercer-Dolan collaboration, probably from the late 1940s.

We are employees
And our object is to please
Every single paying guest.
Everyone is a hero.
At Isadore Shapiro and Sons,
"We undersell the rest."
You will find us there
In milady's underwear
Or in madam's lingerie.
Everyone is a hero.
At Isadore and Sons,
"We make a friend a day."

Over here,
Silver, soup, soap, and sand in the rear,
Kitchenware and Kiddy Land,
You can buy anything in the store.
Every item goes, even Isadore.
So for down-right style
And for service with a smile,
Just pick up a phone and ring
Seven-two-seven zero.
For Isadore Shapiro and Sons,
"The customer is king."

THE PETTY GIRL,
THE KEYSTONE GIRL,
and Other Songs of 1950

THE PETTY GIRL (1950)

Produced by Nat Perrin for Columbia Pictures. Released August 1950. Copyright September 7, 1950. Directed by Henry Levin. Screenplay by Nat Perrin, based on a story by Mary McCarthy. Lyrics by Johnny Mercer. Music by Harold Arlen. Musical numbers staged by Eugene Loring. Music adapted by George Duning. Musical director: Morris Stoloff. Featuring Robert Cummings and Joan Caulfield, with Elsa Lanchester, Melville Cooper, Audrey Long, Mary Wickes, Frank Orth, John Ridgely, and Movita Castaneda.

A calendar artist uses an uptight college professor as a model and life becomes complicated for all concerned.

FANCY FREE

Published. Copyrighted June 5, 1950. Introduced by Joan Caulfield (dubbed by Carole Richards). Only the first refrain was sung in the film.

REFRAIN 1

Fancy free,
Fancy free,
Spring is here but it can't catch me.
I'm in love with them all—
The postman, the teller,
The violet seller!
Oh, life is gay,
Life is fun,
And there's safety in more than one,
So I like as many as I see!

Little glances on the stairs,
No one really cares.
No kiss, no embraces, and no tears—
So three cheers!

Fancy free,
Fancy free,
What a wonderful way to be!
Love is mysterious,

The Petty Girl: *left to right, Jany and Joey Pope (as the Toni Twins), Tippi Hedren (as Ice Box), Mona Knox (as Mazola), and Lois Hall (as Coca Cola), with Joan Caulfield on the sofa, performing the title song*

Gets you delirious,
Why take it seriously?
That is why I try to keep
My fancy free.

REFRAIN 2

Fancy free,
Fancy free,
Spring is here but it can't catch me.
I'm in love, but with whom?
The waiter who's shining
The glasses in the dining room?
My friend Gus
Drives a bus;
They're beginning to look at us—
Ev'ry day he blows a kiss to me.

They address me as Madame;
I'm their honey lamb.
They think I'm the Empress of Siam—
So I am!

Fancy free,
Fancy free,
I'm the sweetheart of NYC.
Out of this crowded
Chaotic confusion
There could come a charmer for me—
On the merest chance he may,
I'm fancy free!

REFRAIN 3

Fancy free,
Fancy free,
Singing songs in a major key.
Oh, what beaux smile my way—
The clerk and the doorman,
The labor-gang foreman,
They all salute,
Gee, it's cute!
And the boy with the paper route
Never breaks a single date with me.
Oh, what lovely summer nights
Under traffic lights,
Strolling with Patrolman Houlihan—
What a man!

Fancy free,
Fancy free,
I'm romantic numeric'ly.
Maybe some morn from this maze
Mister man will come
Moseyin' over to me—
On the merest chance he might,
I'm fancy free!

CALYPSO SONG

Published. Copyrighted June 5, 1950. Introduced by Movita Castaneda, Joan Caulfield (both dubbed by Carole Richards), and ensemble.

REFRAIN 1

All de men down in Trinidad
Sing calypso, it's the local fad,
But it's something I learn to do
So I learn it now to you.
Aye, aye,
I teach you my calypso song,
Directions short and sweet—
How can you go wrong
When you add a word or two that you
Make up as you go along?
Pick a word that occurs to you,
Any adjective or noun will do,
And before you can tell de time,
I will make you a rhyme.
Is handy for reporting news event
Or expressing sentimental sentiment
Or instructing audience to sing
Calypso song!

REFRAIN 2

Coconut is a funny fruit,
Hair is fuzzy like a union suit.
When you shake it down off de bough,
You can milk it like a cow.
Aye, aye,
I teach you my calypso song,
Directions short and sweet—
How can you go wrong
When you add a word or two that you
Make up as you go along?
Funny thing is a movie show,
Bran'-new picture ev'ry time you go,
Bran'-new star with a bran'-new name,
Story always just de same!
For advertising what you manufactured,
Or harmonizing when you're good and
   fractured,
Most heartily I recommend
Calypso song!

REFRAIN 3

Television is popular,
Children are de biggest fans by far.
Reason very plain to be seen—
Kiddies like de tiny screen.
Aye, aye,
I teach you my calypso song,

Directions short and sweet,
How can you go wrong,
Get a pretty girl to woo and to
Sing to as you go along?
Corner drug store de place to buy
Things from ham and eggs to shirt and tie—
You can find anything except
The apothecary dept!
Is handy for reporting news event
Or expressing sentimental sentiment
Or instructing audience to sing
Calypso song!

Extra verse

Soon calypso, de people say,
Is de big thing in de U.S.A.
Will it become de national song?
Man, you should calyp-so long!

Alternate version submitted to Production Code office

All de men down in Trinidad
Sing calypso, it's the local fad,
But it's something I learn to do
So I learn it now to you.
Aye, aye,
I teach you my calypso song,
Directions short and sweet,
How can you go wrong
When you add a word or two that you
Make up as you go along?
If you want to report de act,
First requirement to get de fact—
Put de fact in de song okay,
Everybody say "Hooray!"
Is handy for reporting news event
Or expressing sentimental sentiment
Or instructing audience to sing
Calypso song!

Take a word from the nearest book,
Daily paper is de place to look.
Pick an item and make up rhyme—
You can do it anytime!
Aye, aye,
I teach you my calypso song,
Directions short and sweet—
How can you go wrong
When you add a word or two that you
Make up as you go along?
Harry Truman, de President,
He is finding it convenient,
Helps de Good Neighbor Policy
When he's in de proper key!
Is good for entertaining after dinner,
Making announcement of de derby winner,

Or teaching audience to sing
Calypso song!

Trinidad not de only land
Where they make up songs to beat de band—
Recommended for having fun
At de Stork and "Twenty-One."
Aye, aye,
I teach you my calypso song,
Directions short and sweet,
How can you go wrong?
Get a pretty girl to woo and to
Sing as you go along.
It is quite popular with the
International society—
It is replacing "Alouette"
With the Riviera set.
So even Orson Welles and Elsa Maxwell
Who neither play piano nor a sax well
Get up at parties and perform
A calypso song!

Funny thing is a double Scotch:
You see double everything you watch!
Since you have twice as much to drink,
It gets pretty drunk, I theenk?!
Aye, aye,
I teach you my calypso song,
Directions short and sweet,
How can you go wrong?
Get a pretty girl to woo and to
Sing as you go along.
When a boy takes a girl to dine
And he fills her with de Champagne wine,
Best for girl use her common sense
And de art of self-defense!
Is good for having alcohol whirl
Or for propositioning a pretty girl
Or instructing audience to sing
Calypso song!

Quite a general is Eisenhower,
Changes parties like you take a shower—
Popular Democratic man
Also a Republican!
Coconut is a funny fruit,
Hair is fuzzy like a union suit;
When you shake it down off the bough,
You can milk it like a cow!
Aye, aye,
I teach you my calypso song,
Directions short and sweet,
How can you go wrong
When you add a word or two that you
Make up as you go along?
Daily paper de funny one—
In de *Mirror* you see nothing, son,
And the *Daily News*, strange to say,

Gives tomorrow's news today.
Comic section and photograph,
They are showing things to make you laugh—
Most difficult to find de fun
For de shooting of de gun!

Funny thing is a movie show,
Brand-new picture every time you go,
Brand-new star with a brand-new name—
Story always just the same!
Is good for singing on de telephone
Or getting attention when you all alone
Or instructing audience to sing
Calypso song!

Corner drug is de place to buy
Things from ham and eggs to shirt and tie—
You can find anything except
The apothecary department!
Aye, aye,
I teach you my calypso song,
Directions short and sweet,
How can you go wrong
When you add a word or two that you
Make up as you go along?
Great is Social Security:
Start to get it when you sixty-three—
Just when you feeling overjoyed,
Relatives get unemployed!

Soon calypso, de people say,
Is de big thing in de USA
Will it become de national song?
Maybe you should calyp-so long!
Is silly to indulge in parlor games, sir,
Or memorizing everybody's name, sir—
You can be the life of party
With calypso song.
Television is popular,
Children are de biggest fans by far.
Reason very plain to be seen—
Kiddies like de tiny screen.
For advertising what you manufactured
Or harmonizing when you good and fractured,
Most heartily I recommend
Calypso song.

Dis calypso won't pay de bill,
Make your wealthy uncle change his will,
Make your boss give you a raise in pay
Or your sweetie say okay—
But if you don't object to being jackass
Or possibility of starting fracas,
Most heartily I recommend
Calypso song!

AH LOVES YA!

Published. Copyrighted June 5, 1950. Introduced by anonymous group on radio, Robert Cummings (dubbed by Hal Derwin), and Joan Caulfield (dubbed by Carole Richards). The version sung in the film is essentially the same as the published version.

VERSE

HE: Dearest Professor, wouldn't I may
Sing thee a classic roundelay,
But, being a bathtub boy,
I'll sound my A.

SHE: I beg thee kindly do so,
I do not expect Caruso.
Commence it, Mister Como—
I'll step out and get a Bromo.

REFRAIN 1

HE: Ah loves ya,
Indeed I do—
Ah loves ya,
And that's for true.
Ah wants ya,
And that's a fact—
Why don't ya get in the act?
It must be your charm that gets me chiefly,
Baby, I don't know what it is, but briefly—
Ah loves ya,
I surely do.
Don't be a tease, ma'am,
Please, ma'am,
Won't you say, "Ah loves ya too"?
My voice is slightly porous—
Maybe you should take a chorus.

SHE: If you demand it, yes, sir,
Put me in the key, Professor.

REFRAIN 2

HE: Ah loves ya.
SHE: That's not my key.
HE: Ah loves ya.
SHE: Wrong harmony.
HE: Ah loves ya—
I think you're "presh."
SHE: Ah doubts ya—
Ah think you're fresh.
HE: You're cute and you're quaint
To the quintessence;
I could use longer phrases
But in essence—
BOTH: Ah loves ya,
I sho'ly do.

HE: Don't be a tease, ma'am,
Please, ma'am—
BOTH: Won't you say,
"Ah loves ya too"?

THE PETTY GIRL

Registered for copyright as an unpublished song April 20, 1950. Introduced by Joan Caulfield (dubbed by Carole Richards) and male quartet.

Film version

MEN: Over here, boys—over here, boys—
Meet the cutest little girl of the year, boys!
Take a look at the beauty on the billboard,
Take a look at the pretty Petty Girl!

JOAN
CAULFIELD: Show her drinking Coca-Cola
In the kitchen with a can of Mazola,
Looking sweet by a new electric icebox—
All at once it becomes a pretty nice box!

CAULFIELD
& MEN: Which twin has the Toni is not just baloney
When there's a pair of pretty girls underneath those curls!
Lend an ear, boys—over here, boys—
Meet the pinup and the gal of the year, boys
In the flesh they're the ladies who are known as the Petty Girls!

CAULFIELD: When wintry January storms occur,
With Jack Frost nippin' at our faces,
A lady should be covered up with fur—
At least in certain places!

Beware, beware the windy Ides of March,
When it just seems to blow in batches—
And don't wear any dress with too much starch,
'Cause when it blows it scratches!

There must be truth in what the poets say
About the origin of flowers—

You can't expect the ones that bloom in May
Without some April showers!

The June bride used to turn a telltale pink
When all those people started kissing.
Today the kissing is the same, I think,
Except the blush is missing!

Hark, hark, I seem to hear September call—
In fact I hear it fairly bawling.
The leaves start falling in the early fall—
And that ain't all that's falling!

The winter season isn't really born
Till old December comes a-knocking.
Suppose you rubbed your eyes on Christmas morn
And found *this* in your stocking?!

MEN: You have seen the girl for every month of the year—
Now we'll give you the girl for every day of the year.
Shapely, curvaceous,
And my goodness gracious,
In the flesh she's the lady who is
Known as the Petty Girl.

Additional lyrics not used in film

Over here, boys—over here, boys—
Meet the cutest little girl of the year, boys!
Take a look at the beauty on the billboard,
Take a look at the pretty Petty Girl!

Not with crayon, not with rayon,
Nor a leopard-covered sofa to lay on—
This is real, not a model or a dummy,
The McCoy—and she's positively yummy!
Shapely, curvaceous,
And my goodness gracious,
She's every little thing a sweet little thing should be!
Lend an ear, boys—over here, boys—
Meet the pinup and the gal of the year, boys—
In the flesh she's the lady who is known as the Petty Girl!

This June they're featuring the hankie suits—
The girls imported them from Paris.
They tell me over there they think they're beauts,
But here they just embarrass!

It's amazing and surprising
How a pretty face will boost advertising!

Step right up, get a pinup for your product.
Show her drinking Coca-Cola
In the kitchen with a can of Mazola,
Looking sweet by a new electric icebox—
All at once it becomes a pretty nice box!
Who has the Toni is not just baloney
When there's a pair of pretty girls underneath
    those curls!
Lend an ear, boys—over here, boys—
Meet the pinup and the gal of the year, boys—
In the flesh she's the lady who is known as the
    Petty Girl!

TRY YOUR LUCK

Not used in film.
    Lyric missing.

AT THE JAZZ BAND BALL

Music and original lyrics by D. J. (Nick) LaRocca and Larry Shields, and possibly by Edwin B. Edwards, Henry Ragas, and Tony Spago (1917/1918). New lyrics by Johnny Mercer: Published. Copyrighted April 12, 1950. The original writers were all members of the Original Dixieland Jazz Band and recorded the song in 1917 for Aeolian Vocalion and in 1918 for Victor.

VERSE

Back when a nickel would buy
One drink of respectable rye,
Piano players in the honky-tonks
Would have to work on the sly.
One tune was known to a few,
Some steady habitués too,
So the word of mouth
Spread around the South
Very entre-nous.

REFRAIN 1

Y' better
Dig that jazz-band ball,
'Cause it's the finest of them all.

Four or five musicians in a small saloon
Inventin' a ragtime tune—
They kinda make up their own brand
Without a note up on the stand,
And they call it D-I-X-I-E
Hyphen L-A-N-D.
And they call it D-I-X-I-E
Hyphen L-A-N-D Land.

VERSE 2

Well, sir, y'know it caught on;
What's more, it was strictly bon ton!
'Cause like a winner at the startin' gate,
The music got it and gone!
It moved from over the tracks
Into the society shacks.
It was wonderful—
And deductible
From the income tax.

REFRAIN 2

Y' better
Dig that jazz-band ball,
'Cause it's the finest of them all.
When the trumpet player takes a monologue,
The people shout, "Whew, hot dog!"
And if y'ask, "How come the yell?"
They kinda grin and then say, "Well,
When the band plays J-A-double-Z,
It's a B-A-double-L—
When the band plays J-A-double-Z,
It's a B-A-double-L!"

THE YEARS MAY COME

A poem by "little Johnny Mercer" dated June 8, 1950. Written for Johnny's wife, Ginger.

The years may come—but you don't show 'em.
They augur bad—and you don't know 'em.
They augur well—you never blow 'em.
And so I write this little poem
To you—who are unruffled, calm,
Who brings up children with aplomb
And lays her plans [?] but not a bomb.
To make this toast—We love you, Mom.
We love you even when you're cross
Or in the dumps or at a loss.
We love you when you're feeling bad,
Lulu, Brother Boy, and Dad,
Forgive your most ferocious fuss

In hopes that you will fo'give us.
We love our home because it's neat,
We love the food we get to eat,
We love the gray hairs in your wig,
We love you 'cause your feet's too big.
Despite my baldness and my bagginess,
My (shhh—it should be silent!) sagginess,
My tail has never lost its wagginess—
And nineteen years! My God, Miss Ag-g-nes!
In short, in toto and in essence,
As helpmates go, you're the quintessence!

AUTUMN LEAVES

Original French lyric ("Les Feuilles mortes") by Jacques Prévert. Music by Joseph Kosma. English lyric by Johnny Mercer: Published. Copyrighted July 7, 1950. One of Mercer's biggest hits: Roger Williams's instrumental version was a number-one recording (Kapp). Other major recordings by Jo Stafford (Capitol) and Steve Allen with George Cates's Orchestra (Coral).

    Capitol Records bought the English-language rights to Kosma's song and asked Mercer to write a lyric. Option time was running out, but under pressure Mercer wrote "the biggest-income song I ever had." He didn't speak French, but he knew that it was a rhyme-rich language—fifty-one rhymes for *amour*, while English has only five for love. Instead he used alliteration. There are only three rhymes in the song.

The falling leaves
Drift by the window,
The autumn leaves
Of red and gold.

I see your lips,
The summer kisses,
The sunburned hands
I used to hold.

Since you went away,
The days grow long,
And soon I'll hear
Old winter's song.

But I miss you most of all, my darling,
When autumn leaves start to fall.

HE DIDN'T HAVE THE KNOW-HOW NO HOW

Music by Robert Emmett Dolan. Published. Copyrighted October 25, 1950. Previously registered for copyright as an unpublished song September 1, 1950.

He informed me he could satisfy my ev'ry need,
That he had a way of lovin' which was guaranteed.
But I'll tell you right now
That he didn't have the know-how
No how.

He said the mean potential of a kiss should be
Consummated with industrial efficiency.
So I sighed "Holy cow!"
But he didn't have the know-how
No how.

My, my!
He gave me the eye
Like an engineer approves a grade.
Yes, I connected,
But not as I expected—
Boy, was I surveyed!

He approved the building site
And then got a short-term loan,
Then kept putting off the laying
Of the cornerstone.
So I'm forced to allow
That he didn't have the know-how
Somehow,
He didn't have the know-how
No how.

THE KEYSTONE GIRL (1950)

In the 1950 Paramount film *Sunset Blvd.*, studio producer Sheldrake (played by Fred Clark) tells screenwriter Joe Gillis (William Holden), "We're always looking for a Betty Hutton." Little wonder, considering that the exuberant Hutton was then the hottest female singing star on the lot.

In February 1949, Paramount announced its plans for *The Mack Sennett Story*, a movie based on the career of the innovative producer of silent-film comedy (1880–1960), with John Lund likely to play the part. Soon after, the studio acquired the rights to Gene Fowler's highly romanticized Sennett biography, *Father Goose*, which had been published in 1934. Betty Hutton would play Sennett's sometimes love interest and leading lady at the Keystone film company, Mabel Normand, who in the teens and 1920s was one of the screen's most beloved comediennes.

In retrospect, a musical film about the silent-movie era seems like a most peculiar enterprise for Paramount, considering that less than two years earlier, during the summer of 1947, the studio had released another musical film about the early days of Hollywood, the immensely popular *The Perils of Pauline*, co-starring the same two players, Betty Hutton (as serial queen Pearl White) and John Lund.

In December 1949, the press mentioned that Joseph Sistrom would produce the picture with Paul Douglas, not Lund, as Sennett, pending negotiations with Twentieth Century–Fox for the services of Douglas. George Marshall, who had helmed *The Perils of Pauline*, would direct the movie, now being called *Madcap Mabel*, the dramatic emphasis presumably having been shifted from Sennett to Normand to provide a suitable Hutton vehicle.

In March 1950, the title was changed to *The Keystone Girl*; and the following month Hoagy Carmichael and Johnny Mercer were signed to provide the songs. This would be their first collaboration since 1944, although separately each worked on Hutton pictures: Mercer on *Here Come the Waves* (1944) and Carmichael on *The Stork Club* (1945), both at Paramount.

The project came to a screeching halt late in April, when Paramount announced that *The Keystone Girl* was being "postponed indefinitely," because Betty Hutton objected to portions of the screenplay by George Oppenheimer, who had already left the lot. Paul Douglas returned to his home studio, Fox, to play the lead in *Fourteen Hours*.

With the brainless optimism so characteristic of Hollywood in those days, Paramount kept *The Keystone Girl* on life support by assigning Richard Breen to revise a script that would never be used, while Carmichael and Mercer continued to write a total of nine songs as late as August. Three of these found an afterlife in other movies, and one ("In the Cool, Cool, Cool of the Evening") even won an Academy Award. But *The Keystone Girl* was history.

In 1951, Mack Sennett, by now largely impoverished, donated much of his memorabilia to the library of the Academy of Motion Picture Arts and Sciences.

I GUESS IT WAS YOU ALL THE TIME

Published. Copyrighted June 29, 1953. Originally written for the unproduced *Keystone Girl* (1950). Later used in *Those Redheads from Seattle* (Paramount, 1953) where it was introduced by Guy Mitchell and Teresa Brewer. Recorded by Brewer (Coral).

I guess it was you all the time;
That's why I was blue all the time.
And no matter how many
I held in my arms,
The fires they started
Were only false alarms.
It must have been you all along,
Though I never knew all along.
But my heart knew, God bless it,
So I might as well confess it:
I guess it was you all the time.

HE'S DEAD BUT HE WON'T LIE DOWN

Published. Copyrighted December 20, 1954. Originally written for the unproduced *The Keystone Girl* (1950). Introduced in *Timberjack* (Republic, 1954) by Vera Ralston (dubbed by Virginia Rees), Hoagy Carmichael, and male ensemble.

VERSE 1

Harry the Mountie fought ten villains in the pass;
He was running out of cartridges, alas.
So he sent his palomino for aid,
Who galloped into town and neighed:

REFRAIN 1

He's dead but he won't lie down,
He's dead but he won't lie down!
They've shot more daylight in his vest
Than there is in the west—
He's dead but he won't lie down.

VERSE 2

When Jack Johnson and Jim Jeffries fought it out,
Tom O'Toole jumped in the ring to join the bout.
One punch later Tom lay flat on the floor,
And you could hear the people roar:

REFRAIN 2

He's dead but he won't lie down,
He's dead but he won't lie down!
Although his ribs are out of place,
There's a smile on his face—
He's dead but he won't lie down!

VERSE 3

Sawmill Frenchie, the Alaskan lumberjack,
Used to fell a tree with just a single whack,
But since he met the gorgeous Nugget Hall Nell,
You ought to hear the loggers yell:

REFRAIN 3

He's dead but he won't lie down,
He's dead but he won't lie down!
Although he's up and walking round,
He should be underground—
He's dead but he won't lie down!

VERSE 4

Old Mike Riley made a trip to the saloon,
Started drinking when the whistle blew at noon.
Late that night when Missus Riley came in,
The boys all shouted with a grin:

REFRAIN 4

He's dead but he won't lie down,
He's dead but he won't lie down!
He's had more whiskey, beer, and ale
Than Columbus could sail—
He's dead but he won't lie down!

Earlier version

Father O'Reilly was a family man;
Strolling on a Sunday afternoon,
Oftentimes he'd leave his little clan
For a seidel at the old saloon.
After we'd waited for an hour or so,
Mama would knock upon the door,
And as Mama looked in,
The men looked up with a grin,
And this is what they'd roar:

* * *

Hairbreadth Harry was a demon with the reins;
He would ride a buckin' bronco across the plains.
Six-guns blazin', he could stop any fray
Or split a dime a mile away.
One day he met some rustlers in the pass;
His revolver's out of cartridges, alas!
So he sent his palomino for aid,
Who galloped into town and neighed:

He's daid but he won't lie down,
He's daid but he won't lie down!
They let more daylight through his vest
Than there is in the west—
He's daid but he won't lie down.

* * *

When Jack Dempsey and Jess Willard did a show
Last September in T-O-L-E-D-O,

Needn't tell you that the verdict was bad;
You couldn't see for all that blood.
Wild an' primitive an' gory was the fray,
But it's nothing to what happened yesterday—
When Gilhooley battled Paddy McCoy,
The neighbors shouted out with joy:

He's dead but he won't lie down,
He's dead but he won't lie down!
Though all his ribs are out of place,
There's a smile on his face—
He's dead but he won't lie down!

ALL TIED UP

Song dated July 21, 1950.

REFRAIN 1

I'd love to be your cutie,
But I'm all tied up,
All tied up,
Ti-di-i-deed up.
I'd be your sweet patootie,
Yes, I would, kind sir!
But the dummy you see
On the ventriloquist's knee,
It seems that I've been spoken fer!
I'd be your peacherino,
But I'm all tied up.
Wish I could shake the vino
In your lovin' cup!
But like a box of bonbons
With a bow on the top,
I wish that I were open,
But I'm all tied up.

REFRAIN 2

I'd love to be y' dawlin',
But I'm all tied up,
All tied up,
Ti-di-i-deed up.
Ca'line, I hea'd you cawlin;
I know I've been paged,
But like a waiter or clerk
Who just quit lookin' for work,
It seems like I done been engaged!
I'd be your tootsy-wootsy
In your kiddie kar,
Might even play some footsy
Underneath the bar,
But like a conversation
'Tween the cat and pup,

I'd love to do some chasin',
But I'm all tied up!

ANY SIMILARITY (IS JUST COINCIDENTAL)

Any similarity is just coincidental.
If I sound like anybody
When I say "I love you,
Darling, darling, darling,
Adore you, 'dore you, 'dore you,"
That's the only, only, only thing to say.
There's no peculiarity in being sentimental
When the roly-poly moon
Begins to shine above you.
Hold me, hold me, hold me, hold me,
Kiss me, kiss me, kiss me, kiss me,
That's the only, only, only way.
Cross my heart, I love you,
Never old, always new.
They say familiarity can make a person hate you,
But like Christopher Columbus, that's a chance
    I'm takin'.
"Darling, darling, darling,
I adore you, 'dore you, 'dore you."
That's the only thing I long to hear you say—
Or any similarity to that will be okay.

BUT THEY BETTER NOT WAIT TOO LONG!

VERSE

With my hair in a bow
I must make a show
Like one of the social set.
Some delectable piece
That you saw in Nice
Or on the *Police Gazette*,
Well, I tell ya I ain't,
It's all mostly paint,
And now this complaint I make.
So I'm beautiful, but
I'm still in a rut.
It's time they were cuttin' the cake!

REFRAIN 1

Every day I swim
Or go to the gym,

Where I imitate a squirrel,
Or I permanent my poor old mop
At the beauty shop,
Till I haven't got a curl.
Evidentally they're savin' me for
Sumpin' special—
But they better not wait too long!

Boy, am I soignée!
My couturier
Says that I'm a hunk o' stuff.
Been continually shined and shined,
Like an apple rind,
Till there ain't no place to buff.
Incidentally, it may be just my intuition,
But I betcha that I'm not wrong,
Evidentally, they're saving me for
Sumpin' special—
But they better not wait too long!

My posture's very vital,
A big book on my head—
Do you know that the title
Is *How to Have Fun in Bed?*
And I'm there at eight,
Mustn't have a date,
Not a man within my reach.
Holy mackerel!
It ain't my type,
I'm as overripe
As a late October peach.
Yes indeedy, well, you must admit
The little lady
Has a moral in this here song.
Evidentally, they're saving me for
Sumpin' special
But they better not wait too long!

REFRAIN 2

I've a special course
How to ride a horse,
And another, how to dance.
And a physical instructor who
Knows a hold or two
In a sport they call romance.
Evidentally they're saving me for
Sumpin' special—
But they better not wait too long!

I've acquired poise
'N' I don't make noise.
Eatin' soup I hold my breath.
I'm so busy bein' real polite
When I'm out at night
That I'm darned near starved to death.
Now, if I can only stop
My poor old feet from runnin'

When they jingle the dinner gong,
Evidentally they're saving me for
Sumpin' special—
But they better not wait too long!

I tango and I'm Spanish,
I bullfight and I feint.
I'm practically mannish—
Which obviously I ain't!
No one has to hunt
For my charms in front;
They are not too hard to find.
If y'look a little lower down
In a certain gown,
There is even more behind.
If there is any part of me remaining undeveloped,
It'll never lie dormant long.
Evidentally they're savin' me for
Sumpin' special—
But they better not wait too long.

DON'T CARE

Song dated August 1, 1950. Alternate title: "Don't Care, for the Heck of It."

Don't care,
For the heck of it,
Found love,
Found a peck of it.
Don't care,
For the heck of it,
Now, now, now,
Nossirree, Bob!
Full moon,
Mighty white of it,
Sing songs
By the light of it;
Let's dance,
Make a night of it,
Now, now, now.
Yes, indeed,
I can hoot and holler,
Loosen up my collar,
Imitate a bobolink birdie,
Nothin' too wordy,
Sumpin' kinda purdy!
Bad luck,
Ain't a speck of it,
Good luck,
Cashed a check of it.
Love life is the cat's meow!
Don't mean maybe,

'Cause I found my baby!
Don't care,
For the heck of it now!

(IN THE BACK OF) MY LIDDLE OL' CADILL-OL-LAC

VERSE

Put your straw hat on
'Fore the moonlight's gone,
Tie it under your chin,
And we'll go for a bit of a spin.
First we'll ride, ride, ride
Through the countryside—
Though I'm slow as molasses
When somebody passes,
Just call me Speedy tonight.

REFRAIN 1

When I get you in the back
Of my Cadill-liddle-ol-lac,
Let the wind blow and bluster
Neath my linen duster—
My arms will surround you
Like General Custer.
A kiss is hard to steal
At the liddle steerin'-ol'-wheel,
So we'll park
In the dark
And we'll spark and we'll spoon,
Watching the rise of an isinglass moon,
And we won't be walkin' back
From the back
Of my liddle ol'
Cuddle-in-the-middle ol'
Cadill-ol-liddle-ol
Cadill-ol-liddle-ol-lac!

REFRAIN 2

When I get you in the back
Of my Cadill-liddle-ol-lac,
We will whiz by the dreamers
In their Stanley Steamers
And laugh as they read
All our banners and streamers
That say "Excuse our dust!"
Or perhaps "Niagara or bust!"
We'll continue till we don't know where we're
    at,
And just in case all the tires go flat,
I'll forget to bring a jack,

In the back
Of my liddle ol'
Warmer-tha-griddle ol'
Cadill-ol-liddle-ol-lac!

QUEENIE, THE QUICK-CHANGE ARTIST

Music by Hoagy Carmichael. Song dated July 26, 1950.

When I was workin' in the burlesque show,
I couldn't sell 'em my anatomy, so
I was Queenie, the quick-change artist,
Belle of the Baldhead Row.
I can't remember all the parts that I played,
I ran for sheriff and I ran the blockade.
I was Queenie, the quick-change artist,
Tops in the mezzanine trade.
I was the girl they tied upon the track;
Then I played the villain, beard long and black;
Then I became the handsome hero, Jack—
So I saved myself when I got back!

I often had to make the changes so fast,
I played the next one with the voice of the last.
I was Queenie, the quick-change artist,
Princess of present and past.
I acted Josephine in all of her gowns;
One night I even played the Saint Louis Browns.
I was Queenie, the quick-change artist,
Highness of hand-me-downs.
The Italian army was a mighty force,
Who'd they choose as general?—of course!
Funiculì, funiculà!

I didn't play Garibaldi, but I often played his
    horse!
While all the other girls were showin' their legs,
I was a down-and-outer, drinking the dregs—
I was Queenie, the quick-change artist,
Laying theatrical eggs.
While Flo and Maizie got their billing in lights,
Atomic Annie was cavorting in tights,
I was Queenie, the quick-change artist,
Scaling theatrical heights.
You have to play all kinds of parts to get to be a
    star.
The only Scotch I ever knew was served across a
    bar—
But Mr. Minsky whispered, "Lassie, give the act
    a try."
I pronounced my *t*'s and rolled my *r*'s
And they booked me into Rye.

Enormous talents on the stage there have been,
And others made it by revealing their skin.
But the cutest
And the smartest
Was Queenie, the quick-change artist.
Next week,
Coming attraction will be—
East Lynne!

HERE COMES THE GROOM (1951)

Produced and directed by Frank Capra for Paramount Pictures. Associate producer: Irving Asher. Released September 1951. Copyright September 2, 1951. Screenplay by Virginia Van Upp, Liam O'Brien, and Myles Connolly, based on a story by Robert Riskin and Liam O'Brien. New songs by Jay Livingston and Ray Evans, except for "In the Cool, Cool, Cool of the Evening": lyrics by Johnny Mercer, music by Hoagy Carmichael. Dances directed by Charles O'Curran. Orchestrations by Nathan Van Cleave. Musical director: Joseph J. Lilley. Starring Bing Crosby, Jane Wyman, Alexis Smith, Franchot Tone, and James Barton, with Robert Keith, Jacques Gencel, Beverly Washburn, Connie Gilchrist, Walter Catlett, Alan Reed, Minna Gombell, Howard Freeman, Maidel Turner, H. B. Wanner, Nicholas Joy, Ian Wolfe, Ellen Corby, James Burke, Irving Bacon, Ted Thorpe, Art Baker, Anna Maria Alberghetti, Adeline de Walt Reynolds, Dorothy Lamour, Phil Harris, Louis Armstrong, Cass Daley, Frank Fontaine, and the Four Hits and a Miss.

A journalist adopts war orphans and reforms his life.

IN THE COOL, COOL, COOL OF THE EVENING

Published. Copyrighted May 15, 1951. Introduced by Bing Crosby and Jane Wyman. Leading recordings were made by Crosby and Wyman (Decca) and Frankie Laine and Jo Stafford (Columbia).

The song won Mercer his second Academy Award for Best Song and Carmichael his first.

There was a small, if short-lived, problem, however: the song had not been written for *Here Comes the Groom* but had been intended for *The Keystone Girl*. Capra had heard it, liked it, and asked if he could use it. Since it had been neither published nor recorded before

its use in Capra's film, the award was allowed to stand. The Academy files contain additional material intended specifically for *Here Comes the Groom*.

Carmichael recalled the song's origin:

As I was driving down the highway, coming into Palm Springs, to join Johnny to write this score, I happened to think of an old, old joke, not a very funny joke. But it was about a jackass. And it seemed that the king of the jungle, the lion, sent an emissary to the jackass to say, "Jackass, are you coming to the king's big party?" And the jackass, sitting there with a pipe in his mouth and his legs crossed, said, "Tell the king in the cool, cool, cool of the evening, I'll be there." Well, I told this joke to Johnny Mercer and in two days we had the song, "In the Cool, Cool, Cool of the Evening."

Mercer and Carmichael went on working together intermittently, but it was Hoagy who later summed up what a lot of people felt—that as a regular team, they would have produced a body of work to rival Rodgers and Hart or the Gershwins:

We didn't get along so well [to begin with] . . . I guess the main trouble was that I considered him my helper . . . I got most of the credit because of my established name . . . I am sure now that my conception of property rights and values was unfortunate . . . It was a disappointment to me because, with the proper guidance and diligent work, Johnny and I could have flooded the market with hit songs. We were atune and I know he "knew" and he knew that I "knew." But the chips didn't fall right. Probably my fault, because I didn't handle him gently.

Mercer's own recollection? "[Hoagy,] with whom I had such a hard time writing words for in New York, was completely different in Hollywood. I had learned a lot but he had softened up, too."

VERSE 1

Sue wants a barbeque,
Sam wants to boil a ham,
Grace votes for bouillabaisse stew.
Jake wants a weenie bake,
Steak and a layer cake—
He'll get a tummy ache, too.
We'll rent a tent or teepee,
Let the town crier cry—
And if it's RSVP,
This'll be our reply:

REFRAIN 1

In the cool, cool, cool of the evenin',
Tell 'em we'll be there.
In the cool, cool, cool of the evenin',

Better save a chair.
When the party's gettin' a glow on,
'N' singin' fills the air,
In the shank o' the night,
When the doin's are right,
You can tell 'em we'll be there.

VERSE 2

"Whee!" said the bumblebee,
"Let's have a jubilee!"
"When?" said the prairie hen, "Soon?"
"Shore!" said the dinosaur.
"Where?" said the grizzly bear,
"Under the light of the moon?"
"How 'bout ya, Brother Jackass?"
Ev'ryone gaily cried,
"You comin' to the fracas?"
Over his specs he sighed:

REFRAIN 2

"In the cool, cool, cool of the evenin',
Tell 'em I'll be there.
In the cool, cool, cool of the evenin',
Slickum on my hair.
When the party's gettin' a glow on,
'N' singin' fills the air,
If I ain't in the clink,
And there's sumpin' to drink,
You can tell 'em I'll be there."

Film version

BING CROSBY &
JANE WYMAN: In the cool, cool, cool of the
                 evening
                 Tell 'em we'll be there
                 If you want a couple of deadheads
                 To fracture your affair.
    CROSBY: I can even sing Pagliacci.
    WYMAN: Spread out and give him air.
     BOTH: Everyone will relax
                 And we can have a few yaks
                 And you can tell 'em we'll be
                 there.
                 In the cool, cool, cool of the
                 evening
                 Tell 'em we'll be there.
                 In the cool, cool, cool of the
                 evening
    CROSBY: Slickum on my hair.
                 Now perhaps I may seem
                 unconscious,
                 But remember, *"C'est la guerre!"*
     BOTH: If we're still on our feet
                 And there's something to eat
                 You can tell 'em we'll be there.

CROSBY: [*spoken*] The natives are restless
              tonight.
WYMAN: In Boston?
CROSBY: No.
              [*sung*] Down in the Caribees
              Some aborigines
              Rowed out to pay me a call.
WYMAN: A-a e-e ah-ah.
CROSBY: You laka singo jingo?
WYMAN: Eh!
CROSBY: "We laka too," they cried.
WYMAN: O-o ya coo!
CROSBY: I didn't get their lingo.
WYMAN: Be-bop.
CROSBY: So here's what I replied:
              [*spoken*] Remember when we won
                 the Cup at Gloucester?
WYMAN: And you lost it in a crap game?
CROSBY: Well, they switched dice on me!
   BOTH: [*sung*] Oogaty, boogaty, boogaty,
                 boogaty, book, book!
                 Which means we like it rare.
                 When the tribe is getting' a glow on
                 An' tom-toms fill the air,
                 If the dinner is free and the
                 dinner ain't we,
                 You can tell 'em we'll be there.
CROSBY: If I can get out of bed
              And put a hat on my head
   BOTH: You can tell 'em I'll be there.
WYMAN: If you need a new face
              Or a broken down bass
   BOTH: You can tell 'em I'll be there.
CROSBY: Well, we had such a ball.
              Thanks for the use of the hall.
   BOTH: You can tell 'em I'll be there.

Finale

When the party's getting' a glow on,
'N' singin' fills the air,
Now if a wedding is nigh
Bring your own FBI,
You can tell 'em I'll be there.

Additional lyrics not used in film

In the cool, cool, cool of the evening,
Tell 'em I'll be there,
Even though Mother Q. Hubbard
Keeps her cupboard bare.
While the boys steal off in the garden
To woo their ladies fair,
While they roam in the gloam,
Though I shoulda stood home,
You can tell 'em I'll be there.

In the cool, cool, cool of the evening
Tell 'em we'll be there,

If they want a couple of deadheads*
To fracture the affair.
Oh, we both have tux and will travel
To almost anywhere,
For a thousand a night,
Or a turkey on white,
You can tell 'em we'll be there.

In the cool, cool, cool of the evening,
Tell 'em we'll be there.
We prefer to play before crowned heads
Or some poor millionaire.
We can even give 'em Pagliacci,
Chin up and debonair!
Watch the weeping, old gel,
It's a rented lapel.
You can tell 'em we'll be there.

[*spoken*] Any similarity to this material and an old
    joke is NOT merely coincidental . . . but the
    old wheeze has had its punch line removed and
    cleaned up for market openings, private
    functions, and itinerant passersby . . . All
    original stuff . . . She suggested it and I
    thought of it!

   BOTH: If perchance we look a bit peak-ed,
                 Remember, c'est la guerre.
                 Turn the faucet off, dear,
                 Or you'll water my beer—
                 You can tell 'em we'll be there.
CROSBY: If you need an old face
              Or a tenor or a bass
              You can tell 'em I'll be there.
WYMAN: If I still can play straight
              And get down to the weight
              You can tell 'em I'll be there.

Alternate couplets for chorus

If there's gas in my hack
And my laundry is back,
If you need a new face
Or a tenor or bass,
If I find the right sock
By eleven o'clock,
If I'm still on my feet
And there's sumpin' to eat,
In the shank o' the night,
When they're fixin' to fight,
If there's room for one more
And y' need me—why, shore!
If I can climb out of bed
And put a head on my head.

———————————
* *Or:* a couple of songbirds

Nursery verse

Old Simple Simon and
Alice in Wonderland,
Bo Peep and Little Boy Blue
Asked me to take a look
There in the story book,
Where people live in a shoe.
Having an Anniversary,
They planned a real big time,
Since it was in a nursery,
I sang this nursery rhyme:

In the cool, cool . . . etc.

Jackie Horner's my chum,
If he'll save me a plum,
You can tell 'em
Etc.
If the dinner is free and the dinner ain't we,
You can tell 'em we'll be there.

Comic strip version

Li'l Orphan Annie said,
"Gol-durn my punkin haid,
Life isn't fun anymore.
Here in the midst o' these
Space ships and mysteries
Sunday's a terrible bore.
I'm sick o' these here "Drummers,"
I tell ya what let's do,
Call up the Katzenjammers,
Jughead and Dagwood, too.

In the cool, cool, cool . . . etc.

Mercer with Donald O'Connor and Hoagy Carmichael
at the 1952 Oscar ceremony

CHIMNEY CORNER DREAM

Music by Robert Emmett Dolan. Published. Copyrighted January 12, 1951.

REFRAIN

Close your eyes with me
And see if you see what I see:
Those golden windows trimmed with lace,
A fireplace on winter nights.
We'd take the phone down off the hook
Or maybe curl up with a book,
Except on Saturdays, no doubt,
When we step out
To see the sights.
Evenings,
When we'd sung the kids their lullaby,
Maybe
Folks we really like, like Jane and Si,
Might drop by.
You will say, I bet:
"Oh, gee, how corny can you get!"
And yet I can't begin to tell
How really swell
It all would seem
If only you'd agree to share
My chimney corner dream.

LOCK THE BARN DOOR

Music by Mercer. Published. Copyrighted April 5, 1951. Previously registered for copyright as an unpublished song February 19, 1951.

VERSE

I'm just a little ol' country boy
And I ain't very smart.
More so especially when it comes
To dealin's of the heart.
Show me a plow, or an ol' red sow,
And I know right where I'm at,
But sell me a brick,
And you'll find right quick,
I'm a-reachin' for my hat.

REFRAIN

Better lock the barn door (Latch it, natch!)
'Fore the mule gets stolen (Old Satch).
Better lock your heart (With a catch)
'Fore I stroll along (Stroll, stroll).

Don't go rollin' those eyes (Take it slow)
Like you need consolin' ('T'ain't so),
Makin' people think (Max and Moe)
That I done you wrong (Seems to me I've heard that song).

I care for you, baby
Yes, indeed I do,
But just figure that maybe
There are bigger fish than you.

Better lock the barn door (Call the law)
'Fore the mule gets stolen (Hee-haw).
Better lock your heart (I'll tell Ma).
'Fore you lose my love—

Better lock the barn door (Toodle-oo and au rev-aw!)

HERE'S TO MY LADY

Music by Rube Bloom. Published. Copyrighted July 26, 1951. Dedicated to Ginger Mercer. Leading recording by Nat "King" Cole (Capitol).

VERSE

Although it lies outside of my dominion,
If you should ask me for my opinion,
When out with good companions
And voices ring,
There comes a time before the party's closing,
Perhaps the old ones have started dozing,
When one toast needs proposing,
I raise my glass and sing:

REFRAIN

Here's to my lady,
Here's a toast to my lady,
And all that my lady means to me.

Like a hearth in the winter,
A breeze in the summer,
A spring to remember
Is she.

Though the years may grow colder
As people grow older,
It's shoulder to shoulder
We'll be.

But be it sunshine or shady,
Here's my love to my lady.

I pray,
May she always love me.

WHEN THE WORLD WAS YOUNG (AH, THE APPLE TREES)

Music by M. Philippe-Gérard. Original French lyrics by Angèle Vannier: "Le Chevalier de Paris (Les Pommiers Doux)." English lyrics by Mercer. Alternate title "Ah, the Apple Trees." Published. Copyrighted August 17, 1951. Major recording by Peggy Lee (Capitol).

The surprising thing about this narrative lyric, adapted from a French chanson, is that Mercer never learned to speak French.

VERSE 1

It isn't by chance I happen to be
A *boulevardier*, the toast of Paris,
For over the noise, the talk and the smoke,
I'm good for a laugh, a drink or a joke.
I walk in a room, a party or ball,
"Come sit over here," somebody will call.
"A drink for m'sieur! A drink for us all!"
But how many times I stop and recall:

REFRAIN 1

Ah, the apple trees,
Blossoms in the breeze,
That we walked among!
Lying in the hay,
Games we used to play
While the rounds were sung—
Only yesterday,
When the world was young!

VERSE 2

Wherever I go they mention my name,
And that in itself is some sort of fame.
"Come by for a drink, we're having a game"—
Wherever I go, I'm glad that I came.
The talk is quite gay, the company fine,
There's laughter and lights and glamour and wine
And beautiful girls (and some of them mine),
But often my eyes see a diff'rent shine:

REFRAIN 2

Ah, the apple trees,
Sunlit memories,

Where the hammock swung!
On our backs we'd lie,
Looking at the sky
Till the stars were strung—
Only last July,
When the world was young.

VERSE 3

While sitting around we often recall
The laugh of the year, the night of them all.
The blonde who was so attractive that year,
Some opening night that made us all cheer.
Remember the time we all got so tight
And Jacques and Antoine got into a fight?

The gendarmes who came passed out like a light—
I laugh with the rest, it's all very bright.

REFRAIN 3

Ah, the apple trees
And the hive of bees
Where we once got stung!
Summers at Bordeaux,
Rowing the *bateau*,
Where the willow hung—
Just a dream ago,
When the world was young.

THE LITTLE BOATS OF BARCELONA

Music by Peter Tinturin. Registered for copyright as an unpublished song September 10, 1951.

VERSE

The story's old,
The setting, too,
But so the tale will always be
Whenever men put out to sea
And women's hearts are true.

REFRAIN

The little boats of Barcelona
Put out to sea at break of day,
And with the blessing of Saint Stephen
Return at even,
Across the bay.
She prays* the lights of Barcelona

* *Or:* I pray

Will guide him safely as before
And maybe soon will come the tide
When he'll decide to stay ashore.
And then one little boat of Barcelona
Will go to sea no more.

BLESS YOUR HEART

Music by Mercer. Registered for copyright as an unpublished song November 21, 1951.

Bless your heart
For being you,
Bless your heart
For coming true,
Looking just
The way you do,
Leaving heav'n above me,
Coming down to love me.
I was blue;
You understood,
Just the way
An angel would.
Now you say
Let's never part—
Darling,
Bless your heart.

ROCKY MOUNTAIN MOON

Music by Mercer. Registered for copyright as an unpublished song November 21, 1951.

Rock me to sleep again,
Old Rocky Mountain moon—
Someone is waiting in my dreams for me.
When shadows creep again,
Old Rocky Mountain moon,
Bring back the days that used to be.
We used to stroll on summer nights
To a trail up in the heights
Just to watch the twinkling lights
In the valley.
So, till that happy day
When we'll be meeting soon,
Rock me to sleep,
Old Rocky Mountain moon!

MY FAVORITE SPY (1951)

Produced by Paul Jones for Paramount Pictures. Released December 1951. Copyright December 25, 1951. Directed by Norman Z. McLeod. Screenplay by Edmund Hartmann and Jack Sher. Story and adaptation by Edmund Beloin and Lou Breslow. Additional dialogue by Hal Kanter. Lyrics by Johnny Mercer. Music by Robert Emmett Dolan. Musical score by Victor Young. Featuring Bob Hope and Hedy Lamarr, with Francis L. Sullivan, Arnold Moss, John Archer, Luis Van Rooten, Stephen Chase, Morris Ankrum, Angela Clarke, Iris Adrian, Frank Faylen, Mike Mazurki, Marc Lawrence, Tonio Selwart, Ralph Smiley, Joseph Vitale, and Nestor Paiva.

A burlesque comic is drafted by the government to pose as an international spy—who just happens to be his double.

I WIND UP TAKING A FALL

Music by Robert Emmett Dolan. Published. Copyrighted December 14, 1951. Introduced by Bob Hope.

VERSE

If you want to know a secret,
Then hark to an actor's fate.
An actor must play many parts

[*He takes a hat, grabs a tangerine from a fruit bowl, tosses it in the air, catches it in the hat, then spits tangerine out of his mouth.*]

And all of them are great!
Because you seem so interested
In a piece of fillum,
Listen to the parts I've played
And how I used to killum.

REFRAIN

Oh, I've learned to say, "How now, Brown Cow?"
Rehearsed a very fancy bow
That I plan on using for my curtain call,
But whenever that time does arrive
Tuppence ha'penny will get you five
That I wind up taking a fall.

[*Takes a comedy fall.*]

There is not a thing that I would lack
Playing Cyrano de Bergerac.
My nose, my sword, and I could play those scenes.

[*There are two long, silver candlesticks on the mantel, complete with long candles. He takes one of the candles out and fastens the end of it to his nose. He takes the candlestick, complete with candle, and brandishes it as a sword. He snatches a cigarette lighter from the table and ignites the candle on his nose.*]

[*spoken*] I duel in the dark, you know. So, you besmirch a lady's honor, huh? *En guard! Touché!* Ha! Ha! There you are! There you are! I poked you, didn't I? Band Aid, anybody? You fool, lay there and bleed, you amateur with your scalpknife.

[*He tries to blow out the lighted candle; blows from one side of his mouth, then another side, etc. No luck. Looks around, sees whiskey glass.* PEANUTS *goes to it, dips his head so that the end of the candle goes into the whiskey and the light is extinguished. Then he grabs the candle off his nose.*]

Thanks for the dip.
[*sung*] Well, I've worn the great big nose all right.
But the trouble was it had a light
And it spelled out, "EAT AT MAXINES."

I horsewhipped little chillun
As cruel Simon Legree
[*spoken as he whips*] Take that, take that, Liza, I'm gonna lash you good—I'm gonna give you the longest lashing you ever had! I was always known for my long lashes!

[*Into camera batting his eyes coquettishly.*]

[*sung*] Dr. Jekyll, yes, and Mr. Hyde—
One of whom indulged in homicide—
Those are parts that suit me right down to my socks.
[*spoken fiendishly as he pours*] Citric acid . . . hydrochloric sulphate . . . potassium nitrate . . . ice . . . one drink of this and I'll belong to the Monster's Anonymous . . .

[*By this time the mixture is smoking and bubbling.*]

It's finished!

[PEANUTS *takes a big drink. He pauses, waits for the effect. There is none.*]

Forgot the olive!

[*He drops the olive into the mixture, drinks again. He reacts horribly, laughs ghoulishly, turns his back to*

camera. When he turns back, his face is contorted, hair askew, and lemon-peel "fangs" stick out of his face.]

I like it!

[*He approaches* MONKARA, *making evil faces and gestures.* MONKARA *scowls at him, and* PEANUTS, *frightened, drops teeth, becomes himself again. He picks up a skull pen-holder from a desk, holds it in his hand, striking the accepted "Hamlet" pose.*]

Alas! Poor Yorrick!
To sleep, perchance to dream.
Have you been drinking peregoric?
Or could it be that new vanishing cream?
Aha! Blew your cork, huh?
Speak to me, speak to me,
Say something, you may be a straight man.
Won't talk, hey, you snob?

[*Puts skull down, pats the top of it.*]

Looks like a fellow I know who sings.
[*sung*] With my big low shoes and baggy pants
I went right into my song and dance
And I wound up taking a fall.

Production Code version

VERSE

Because you're a loyal fan club
And I cannot tell a lie,
Then list! to my adventures in
The happy days gone by.

REFRAIN

Oh, I've learned to say, "How now, Brown Cow?"
I've rehearsed a very fancy bow
That I plan on using for my curtain call,
But whenever that time does arrive
Tuppence ha'penny will get you five
That I wind up taking a fall.
There is not a thing that I would lack
Playing Cyrano de Bergerac
How my nose, my sword, and I would play those scenes.
Well, I've worn the great big nose, all right,
But the trouble was it had a light
And it spelled out, "EAT AT MAXINES."
Avast there! You lubbers!
I cried as Jean LaFitte.
And I got lots of hubba-hubbas
As Eloise in "Ain't She Sweet."
But no matter what role I portray
Or the character I'm cast to play,
To a cheering crowd with the Music Hall

There is not a scene that I can't steal
As I slip on some banana peel
And I wind up taking a fall!

Dr. Jekyll, yes, and Mr. Hyde—
One of whom indulged in homicide—
Those are parts that suit me right down to my socks.
Do you find me playing either guy?
No, sir, I'm the corpus de-lecti
And I wind up back in the box.
As Svengali I could save the day.
Giving Trilby my atomic ray
I could have her swooning all about the place,
But the chances are while so congealed
She would let one go from center field
And I'd wind up pie in the face.
Ah stole secret papers
For Marse Robert E. Lee.
I pulled one of the biggest capers
In San Francisco's history.
And in *Carmen* as the Toreador
I could play the part and the sing the score.
Even went and found myself a Spanish shawl,
But I played the bull . . . and here's the laugh:
Didn't even play the better half.
And I wound up taking a fall!

While in *Pinafore* I went to sea
And the ruler of the Queen's Navee,
But I soon incurred his Royal Highness' wrath,
For we got marooned and stayed so late
That they took to using me as bait
And I wound up taking a bath.
As the infamous Simon Lagree
What a deep, dark villain I could be
As I horsewhipped little children on the ice,
But the chances are I'd have to sneeze
And my pants would fall down past my knees
And I'd wind up back at half price.
Alas! Pooooor Yorick!
To sleep, perchance to dream.
You look a little prehistoric.
Must be that new vanishing cream.
Little Egypt was a role I chose,
And I held the veil up with my nose.
It was long and it was silk and that was all,
And with raised eyebrows they said, "Pourquoi?"
When they saw my large avoirdupois
And I wound up letting it fall.
With my big slap shoes and baggy pants,
I went right into my song and dance
And I wound up taking a fall!

Revised lyrics

Avast there! You lubbers!
I cried as Jean LaFitte

[*Looks up at an imaginary ship mast; yells angrily.*]

Avast! Avast! Avast!
[*spoken*] Avast'em three times.
Why don't they answer?

[*He puts the candles aside and goes into a minstrel shuffle.*]

[*sung*] Ah stole secret papers
For Marse Robert E. Lee.
I pulled one of the biggest capers
In West Virginny's history.
[*spoken dramatically*] Yankee bayonets were at the
    nawth of me! Yankee bayonets were at the west
    of me! Mo' bayonets flashed to the east of me!
    What happened, suhs? Ah was cut off!
[*sung*] There was not a scene that I can't steal
As I slip on some banana peel
And I wind up taking a fall!

[*He grabs a fez again, tears the tassle off of it, and
sticks it under his nose. Stroking it as a mustache, he
grabs a long-stemmed flower from a vase and whips a
low hassock with it as he continues song.*]

I horsewhipped little chillun
As cruel Simon Legree.

[*Spoken as he whips.*]

Take that, Little Eva! I'm gonna lash you good. I'm
    gonna give you the longest lashing you ever got!

[*Into camera batting his eyes coquettishly.*]

I was always known for my long lashes!

[*Evil laugh; strokes mustache.*]

[*sung*] There never was a villain
Half as villainous as me!

[*Snarling, he begins whipping another piece of
furniture.*]

So there you are, Uncle Tom! You old Uncle Tom,
    you!
Take that—and that!

[*He falls to the floor, plays Uncle Tom, cringing and
protesting.*]

[*spoken*] Cheese and crackers! Shtop already mit
    derv hip! Don't beat Uncle Tom. It giffs liver if
    the shtop beating Uncle Tom. Poor-r-r-r-r
    Uncle Tom!

[*Laughs.*]

Dutch uncle!

[*He gets up, replaces mustache, takes the flower and
ships it at an imaginary object. Sinister laugh.*]

Take that, you cur!

[*Barks like a dog.*]

We had bloodhounds, too!

[*Starts beating hassock again.*]

Soo, Little Eva, you thought you could get away
    from me! Take that, Little Eva!

[*Drops mustache and whip, grabs a bunch of grapes
from the fruit bowl. He places them on his head as a
wig, drops to his knees, clasps his hands under his chin,
and begs for mercy as Little Eva.*]

[*falsetto, pleading*] Oh, please, please have mercy
    on me Simon Legree! Mercy!

[*Throws off grapes, dons mustache again, picks up the
flower.*]

[*as Simon*] Mercy, eh? He, he, he—I'm gonna
    horsewhip you!

[*Reverts to Eva, cringing on the floor.*]

[*falsetto*] Oh, put down that horse! You shan't
    beat me anymore. You shan't! You shan't!

[*Reverts to Legree.*]

Oh, yes I shan!

[*"Whips" her again. Reverts to Eva.*]

Oh, save me Uncle Tom.

[*Takes off "wig" of grapes, becomes Uncle Tom.*]

Ah, cain't save you now, chile. Dat mean ole
    Simon Legree done beat me to death!

[*Replaces grapes.*]

[*falsetto*] Uncle Tom, if he beats me to death, will
    I go to heaven?
[*as Uncle Tom*] It's up to you little Eva—you git yo'
    choice. Either hebben or Texas!

[*PEANUTS gets up, snaps out of character, and bows.*]

What a performance. Next week—East Lynne.
[*sung*] As Svengali I could save the day
Giving Trilby my atomic ray.

[*He approaches EL SARIF and, with a wild gleam in his
eye, waves his fingers at EL SARIF in the manner of a
hypnotist.*]

[*spoken*] Oopadoop, sleep . . . Oopadoop, sleep . . .
    Oopadoop, sleep.

[*PEANUTS, asleep, falls back. EL SARIF catches him.
PEANUTS wakes up, alarmed.*]

[*spoken*] It works! My oopadoop fell asleep.

[*Shrugs his shoulders.*]

[*sung*] But the chances are, while so congealed,
Trilby'd let one go from center field
And I wind up pie in the face!
And in *Carmen* as the toreador
I could play the part and sing the score
Even went and found myself a Spanish shawl.

[*He yanks the shawl off the piano without disturbing
the flowers or lamps, etc. Wraps the shawl around him,
takes a rose from the flower vase, empties the candy
dish and uses it for a hat. He sniffs the rose passion-
ately, then tosses it to BRUBAKER.*]

[*spoken*] To the most beautiful señorita in all
    Barcelona, from the bravest, most fearless
    bullfighter in the world. Meet me later at the
    hospital!

[*He whirls the shawl around as though a bull were
attacking him, dances out of the way, grabs BEN ALI's
straw hat, tosses it on the floor, and does the "Hat
Dance" on it, ruining it.*]

[*sung*] But I played the bull . . . and here's the
    laugh.
Didn't even play the better half
And I wound up taking a fall!

And I got lots of hubba-hubbas
As Eloise in "Ain't She Sweet."
But no matter what role I portray
Or the character I'm cast to play
To a cheering crowd with the Music Hall
There is not a scene that I can't steal
As I slip on some banana peel
And I wind up taking a fall!

MESSER. MARCO POLO

Unproduced musical play. Music by Robert Emmett Dolan. Lyrics by Johnny Mercer. Book by Robert Nathan and Siegfried (Sig) Herzig, from the novel by Brian Oswald Donn-Byrne.

The story of how the young Venetian Marco Polo crossed the world to China, ruled by the powerful Kubla Khan, and met and married the beautiful Tao-Tuen ("Golden Bells").

THE BEST LOVE OF ALL

VERSE

Wherever you may be,
Listen close to what I have to say.
I tell the wind and sea
What I'll say to your face one day. . . .

REFRAIN

People have told me—
Love at first sight,
Sure, there is no other kind.
Old ones have told me—
Love at first kiss,
That's when you make up your mind.
How would I know,
When I have yet to hear you speak,
Yet to feel your lips
Brush against my cheek?
All I can say is
That if I love you,
Not having seen you at all,
Those other loves must be small—
This is the best love of all.

THE GENTLE ART OF MURDER

As professional assassins,
We have found the public fastens
Appellations quite appalling
To an old and noble calling.
It's become our observation

It's a thankless occupation,
And we've wasted years of study—
Incident'ly, rather bloody—
For we've roamed around the ghetto,
Wielding saber and stiletto,
With the blackjack and the billy,
Killing people willy-nilly.
We'd do in the Queen of Sheba
Or the lowliest amoeba,
But the wisdom of it we begin to doubt.
Every time we slit a gullet,
Now we sit around and mull it,
For we recently discovered
Every time a neck is severed,
Be the body thin or weighty,
If it takes a year or eighty,
That the Gentle Art of Murder
Will eventually OUT.

GOLDEN BELLS

VERSE

You can't expect a sailing man
To tell the tales a poet tells,
But I shall do the best I can
To make you see the lady Golden Bells.

REFRAIN 1

She's a silver moon on a clear blue lake;
She's the far-off tune that the wild birds make,
The tinkle of a crystal bowl
When everything is calm and still,
A ribbon in the breeze,
A vessel on the seas,
A row of poplar trees
Across a hill.
When you hold your ear
To the small seashells,
She's the sound you hear—
That is Golden Bells.

REFRAIN 2

Some more of Golden Bells:
She's a forest glade deep in unwalked snow,
Or a table made by the firelight glow.
Ah, she's the quick and merry laugh
Of someone passing on the street,
The summer rain that booms
On wooden-ceilinged rooms,
A field of clover blooms
Above your feet.

She's the magic place
Where the east wind dwells;
She's a small child's face—
That is Golden Bells.

THE HUMAN RACE IS HUMAN AFTER ALL

In my travels through the nations
And my daily observations,
I have gathered words of wisdom as they fall.
And in spite of some confusion,
I have come to the conclusion
That the human race is human after all.

Almost every single fellow,
Be he brown or red or yellow,
Or as multicolored as a Spanish shawl,
When he's first put up for shipment,
Each receives the same equipment,
So the human race is human after all.

We are blessed with knees
And personalities
And things like these
In varying degrees.
How odd
Of God
To take us from the sod
And make us all as similar as peas
In a pod.

Some are larger,
Some are smaller,
Some are shorter,
Some are taller,
Some are rounder than an India rubber ball.
But concave
Or rounder,
You'll discover
Deep down under
That the human race is human after all.

Extra verses

While the country of the Viking
Is divided to their liking,
In tres partes es divide omnes Gaul.
Though the boundaries be state lines
Or the International Date Lines,
The inhabitants are human after all.

We can name among our clients
Several nine-foot Gothic giants,

Which you must admit is really rather tall.
But except for growing higher,
Having started some years prior,
They are huge but they are human after all.

Some apes have shapes
That bother other apes,
Which leads to scrapes
Among these jackanapes.
Though in the pink,
They seldom stop to think
A woman is a woman, but a drink is a drink.
Towns in India have tenants
Who perpetually do penance,
Such as standing on one foot upon a wall.
But except they're well-developed
And the fact they won't be heluped,
Still, the human race is human after all.

COME UP AND SEE ME SOMETIME

Intended for the character of Augustine.

VERSE

I live in very private quarters
In this seraglio,
And there's a secret entrance
His Vileness doesn't know.
A tug upon the bell rope,
A pebble at the screen—
If anybody answers,
Just ask for Augustine!

REFRAIN

Come up and see me sometime,
Come up and see me,
Come up and see me sometime—
It's kind of dreamy.

[*incomplete*]

VENICE IN SPRING

Have you ever seen Venice in spring?
There's a sight to tug at your heart,
With the pigeons aloft on the wing.

The canals are all a shiny blue
And full of tiny craft
With the gayest flags of every hue
Bedecked both fore and aft.
'Tis a marvelous sight to behold,
So before you're another day old,
Make a wish on your wishing ring—
Make a wish to come
To Venice in spring.

Alternative version

Rosy roofs in the sun
Sparkle so that they dazzle your eyes,
But when night has begun
Gondoliers sing their faraway cries.

'Tis the talk of the world, so I'm told,
And they don't embroider a thing.
So before you're another day old,
Make a wish on your wishing ring—
Make a wish to come to Venice in spring.
Wait and see,
You'll agree,
There's nothing like Venice in spring . . .

A VERY IMPORTANT MAN

We've come to see His Highness Kubla Khan
And the throne he rests his royal seat upon.
Some foreigners pronounce it Kubla Kaan,
But Kubla Khan or Kubla Kaan,
His Highness is a wonderful sport;
He keeps a most celestial court—
In short, he is a very important man.

We saw the comet shooting through the sky,
And because we heard it came to earth nearby,
We thought we'd come to see what we could see.
Oh, yes, and incidentally,
It seems to be an order of his
And much the safest policy is
That we obey His Eminence's decree.
It's understood
That he is good,
As kind as kind can be,
But if you don't obey what's said,
It's very apt to mean your head
Or another part of your anatomy.
And so we call His Highness Kubla Khan
And the throne he rests his royal seat upon.
Some foreigners pronounce it Kubla Kaan,
(You note we don't)
But Kubla Khan or Kubla Kaan,

It really is a joy to report
That he's a most remarkable sort—
In short,
He is a very important man,
His Highness is A VERY IMPORTANT MAN.

THE WAY OF A MAID WITH A MAN

Many and mysterious are the ways
Of a maid with a man.
When she sees him first she will meet his gaze
Shyly across her fan;
She will maneuver him into a seat;
She will listen to him bray.
Just when her heart decides he's sort of sweet,
And perhaps she ought to stay,
She will run the other way!
Never be deceived that the game she plays
Isn't part of her plan.
Many and mysterious are the ways
Of a maid with a man.

Many and mysterious are the wiles
Of a girl with a boy.
She is not above using wide-eyed smiles
Babies would not employ.
She'll try abusing him, to make him think
That she really doesn't care,
But if she's losing him—quick as a wink,
She'll invent a new affair,
Or she'll rearrange her hair!
Military tactics could not devise
Half as complex a plan.
Many and mysterious are the ways
Of a maid with a man.

WE DO IT ON A HORSE

Other pastimes pall,
So we take a little ball
And we hit it with a stick.
And because we are human,
We have to make it harder,
Of course—
We do it on a horse.

Any fool can stand
With a mallet in his hand

While he gives his wrist a flick.
Seems a bit washy-wishy
And so,
To have sufficient force,
We do it on a horse.

We could sit akimbo
Like any bimbo
Imbibing bamboo tea,
Or lie on a pillow
Beneath a willow
And read a trilogy.
But a-mount our mounts
And all around the field we bounce,
Though it often makes us sick.
But we've no need of doses;
Our doctor diagnoses
The source—
We do it on a horse.

WILL-O'-THE-WISP

Will-o'-the-wisp.
Won't you let my heart be?
Why do you sigh,
"Follow me"?
Will-o'-the-wisp,
With your old siren song,
Always the same—
"Come along, come along."
Are you only the night wind's cry?
Or the brook on the stone?
Will-o'-the-wisp,
Find the love of my heart—
Or leave my heart alone.

YOU'RE MY LOVE

You're my love,
This much I know,
For a star in heaven told me so.
You're my love,
And you shall be
While the moonlight falls upon the sea.
For I have been bound to you
With tiny chains,
The dust from a falling star,
The quicksilver rains.
So take my heart
And make this vow—

Love me always as you love me now,
For heaven may be above
But you are my love.

THE SOUTHERN CROSS

VERSE

When far horizons wait across the sky,
Adventure calls,
And you reply,
"Who knows who has the true philosophy?"
I cannot speak for you,
But as for me:

REFRAIN

The Southern Cross is always calling,
The Southern Cross or Evening Star.
Winds come blowing
Across the islands
Called the Indies
Or Zanzibar.
Some sunny day you'll see me standing
Where canvas spreads and breakers toss.
And like the pelican or albatross,
You'll find me following
The Southern Cross.

KUBLA'S SOLILOQUY

Where is your Heaven now?
Where is your Almighty Deity?
See what he does to me
In my kingly halls.
I would shake a bough,
So he moves my little world round.
Down to the stony ground
The bright flower falls . . .

Is this the price I pay for these vast lands,
These human dolls who live beneath my hands?
One perfect rose plucked at its peak,
To grace his mantelpiece,
To press against his cheek,
To have eternally,
To be nearby
To keep him company
Within his lonely sky.
Or is it just a dream,

A wisp of smoke,
A superhuman jest,
A bitter joke?
[spoken] I think sometimes that's all it is . . .
[sung] The fools!
The waste!
The bloodshed!
Say it's so—
And yet the ordered universe says "No!"
Perhaps, Venetians, you can show me where?
I seek the path in books,
I knock upon the door in prayer
And yet no dusty answer says, "Who's there?"
Upon my bed at night sometimes I lie,
While stars cast down a cold and frosty eye;
And yet no window opens in the night,
No falling footsteps echo down the sky . . .

When I was young
My heart was unafraid;
When I was young
And lovely, like my maid,
My heart was anyone's who needed aid.
But perhaps because of place
Or lack of grace,
My reckless, young and true and eager heart
Was often tossed back in my face.
Now I am old,
So many years have passed,
So many roads have crossed
That I am old,
I'm old . . .
And I am lost.

Where is your Heaven now?
Where is your Almighty Deity?
See what he does to me
And see how I weep!
Where are my armies now,
Where the awful and the bloody sword?
Where is the just reward
For minding his sheep?
You laugh at us,
For calling Buddha divine.
You laugh at us,
But now the last laugh is mine!
Where is your Heaven now?
Can it bring my blossom back again?
You and your holy men!
You and your Hell!
Dear little Golden Bells,
Think about me in my loneliness,
Tell them of me in this lonely palace
Where I dwell.
Ah, dear little Golden Bells,
Farewell . . .

SAD LITTLE RAINS OF CHINA

The sad little rains of China fall
In my heart,
While in the dusk of the river haze
Fireflies dart.
Sometimes I hear the laughter—
That and the dreams live on.
But, oh, the sad little rains of China fall
In my heart
Since you're gone!

Three songs from *Messer. Marco Polo* appear to be missing: "Cock of the Walk," "It Seems a Long Time Ago," and "The World Today."

TONIGHT IS MINE

Music by Sammy Fain. Registered for copyright as an unpublished song October 29, 1951.

Tonight is mine,
Tomorrow come what may,
Tonight is mine,
I rule what I survey.
With you beside me in the afterglow,
Let lights and loveliness and laughter flow.
The breeze is mine,
I bid it kiss your cheek,
The stars that shine,
They sparkle when I speak.
Of course, it's only make believe.
But how divine!
Tonight is mine.

TOP BANANA | 1951

TOP BANANA (1951)

Tryout: Shubert Theatre, Philadelphia, October 9–27, 1951. New York run: Winter Garden Theatre; opened November 1, 1951; closed October 4, 1952; 350 performances. The show then toured until June 27, 1953. Music and lyrics by Johnny Mercer. Produced by Paula Stone and Mike Sloane. Book by Hy Kraft. Directed by Jack Donohue. Dances by Ron Fletcher. Settings by Jo Mielziner. Costumes by Alvin Colt. Orchestra directed by Harold Hastings. Orchestrations by Don Walker and Bill Finnigan. Vocal arrangements and direction by Hugh Martin. Cast starring Phil Silvers (Jerry Biffle) and Rose Marie (Betty Dillon), featured Jack Albertson (Vic Davis), Bob Scheerer (Tommy), Lindy Doherty (Cliff Lane), Herbie Faye (Moe), Joey Faye (Pinky), Judy Lynn (Sally Peters), Bradford Hatton (Mr. Parker), Ed Hanley (Denny), Zachary A. Charles (Russ), and Ted "Sport" Morgan.

Mercer wrote: "It started out as a story written around some old songs I had lying around . . . We sailed in to great notices in spite of a score that took a back seat to the comedy and maybe was just as undistinguished, because it remained unplayed!" But the notices weren't as great as Mercer remembered them.

The critics were virtually unanimous in their apathy and equally determined to show their own verbal dexterity. Brooks Atkinson in the *New York Times*: "Johnny Mercer's score is hackneyed. He has composed it as though he hoped it would not sound like music—successfully from this point of view."

George Jean Nathan in the *Journal American*: "Johnny Mercer's so-called songs . . . interrupt the proceedings . . . The music sounds like a juke box into which someone has poured a lot of coal."

And Richard Watts Jr. in the *Post*: "The brilliant Johnny Mercer, who has written some of the best lyrics and composed some of the most memorable songs in American popular music, has provided a curiously commonplace score that didn't sound worthy of him." Only Walter Kerr in the *Herald Tribune* seemed to spot a glimmer of daylight: "Johnny Mercer's tunes are brisk and showy. His lyrics lean a little too heavily on a somewhat picky verbal humor, and he comes a cropper with a second act song called 'A Word a Day.' But this is a minor qualification about a listenable score."

Top Banana: *Phil Silvers and company*

THE MAN OF THE YEAR THIS WEEK

Registered for copyright as an unpublished song December 10, 1951. Introduced and recorded by ensemble (Capitol).

He's the Man of the Year this week,
He's the man people cheer this week.
He's a dream, he's a doll,
And I'm telling you, Sol,
He's the Man of the Year this week.

He was found on a Catskill peak,
Where they booked him for one split week.
He became such a smash
Winchell gave him a flash—
But get hep to him fast,
'Cause his fame mightn't last.
He's a streak, so to speak, this week—
He's the Man of the Year this week.

You'll never find his photograph on *Life, Look*, or
    Pic—
This lover you'll discover on the cover of *Quick*.
His mentality and physique
Must be kept genuine antique,
So we keep him in trim
With canasta and gym—
He's the Man of the Year this week.
Back on the burlesque wheel, was he picturesque?
His star is one that's hard to dim.
Although they took the comic out of burlesque,
They can't get burlesque out of him.

When he hits you with his technique,
Might as well turn the other cheek.
He has jokes by the score
That you've all heard before—
He's the Man of the Year this week.

He's attended a dozen schools
Under Marquess of Queensberry rules.
He can read,
He can write,
But it's strictly a fight.
He doesn't wrestle with words, he drools!

There's nothing in the theater that he doesn't know,
He thinks the ancient verities was some kind of show!
He's the old and repulsive chic,
Not the body, nor the physique.
Not the prez, not the king,
Not Stalin, not the thing—
But the Man of the Year this week.

His routines are as old as time,
But he clicks no matter
How tired the patter.
His material's just a crime,
But he knows how to feel the show,
So he can steal the show.

INTERLUDE

Four stars is nothing with the newspaper crowd.
And you should count his curtain calls.
Last week the *Daily Forward* raved right out loud.
They gave him seven matzoh balls.

Wouldn't say he was in his prime,
But his ancient jokes
Kill the folks;
His kind of corn rakes in the green.
In Italian or Dutch or Greek,
Any language the locals speak,
For these one hundred and twenty hours he's
    grand—
He's the Man of the Year this week!
The man of whom we speak
Is the Man of the Year . . .
This week!

YOU'RE SO BEAUTIFUL THAT—

Registered for copyright as an unpublished song December 10, 1951. Introduced and recorded by Lindy Doherty (Cliff) (Capitol).

You're so beautiful that—
That Lana Turner turns green;
Liz, Ava, Greer, and Arlene
Run second to you.

You're so beautiful that—
Miss Rheingold switches to Coke,
The cigarette that you smoke
I gotta smoke too.

No Four Roses ad discloses
Lips like yours.
No baloney,
Messrs. Toni, Dreen, and Rayve
Must rave a lot
At that natural wave you've got.

You're so beautiful that—
When I write home to my folks,
Joe Miller doesn't make jokes

To picture the view,
Because you're just too beautiful to be true.

You're so beautiful that—
You put the "ooh" in "la la."
Without a Maidenform bra
I'd recognize you.

I'm simply carried away;
I'd drop my fiddle to say,
"Gee, babe, you're taboo!"
Jane Russell
Doesn't tussle
With such charm.
She's outstanding
While expanding,
But you've got the same thing, kid—
And better distribu-tid!

You're so beautiful that—
You're like a ten-to-one hunch,
I haven't got any punch,
So what'll I do
But say you're just too beautiful to be true!

TOP BANANA

Published. Copyrighted October 19, 1951. Previously registered for copyright as an unpublished song December 15, 1950. Introduced and recorded by Phil Silvers (Jerry), Jack Albertson (Vic), Lindy Doherty (Cliff), Herbie Faye (Moe), and Joey Faye (Pinky) (Capitol). Reprised in finale by entire company.

JERRY: Your big timers and small timers
Don't make it the easy way.*
The star comes first,
Then the leading man,
Then the actors in the play.
There are no comics like low comics
Who finally made the grade.
And recall, sweethearts,
All the phoney starts
And the lousy parts they played!

JERRY &
CHORUS: If you wanna be the top banana,
You gotta start at the bottom of the bunch,

---
* *Early version of opening lines:*
   There's no business like show business,
   A wise man was heard to say.

You gotta know the joke about the farmer's daughter,
Then take it in the kisser with the soda water.

VIC: If you wanna be a burlesque comic,
It's basic trainin' for you to take a punch.
You gotta roll your eyes and make a funny face,
Then do a take and holler, "Dis must be duh place!"

CLIFF: If you wanna be the top banana,
You gotta start from the bottom up.

ALL: If you wanna be the top banana,
You gotta start at the bottom of the bunch.

JERRY: Although the stage is always full of ripe tomatoes,
You simply murmur, "All that meat and no potatoes!"

MOE: Even if the broad is your own mother,
She's a straight man who oughta know her part.

PINKY: She raised you from an infant
And she's kind and sweet,
But does she know the way to get to Flugel Street?
If you wanna be the top banana,
You gotta start from the bottom up.

JERRY: A dancer wears a safety pin to keep her tights up—
Top banana's gotta wear a nose that lights up.

VIC: You may wanna imitate Noël Coward—
You'll get more laughs by saying, "What the hay!"
We hardly find a drawing room a source of mirth,
But put us in a bedroom or an upper berth . . .

ALL: If you wanna be the top banana,
You gotta start from the bottom up.

Additional lyrics from early version of script

If you wanna be the top banana,
You gotta start at the bottom of the bunch.
You gotta hit the trail and put the circus tents up.
You gotta tack a sign that's painted "Dames" and "Gents" up.
You complain because you sleep with leopards,
Then they bunk you with the orangutang.
You got an act that fits an English drawing room;
You're following the elephants without a broom.
If you wanna be the top banana,
You gotta start from the bottom up.

Finale chorus

ALL: If you wanna be the top banana,
You gotta start at the bottom of the bunch.
Your figure may be just as good as Gaylord Hauser's,
But who can see it underneath those baggy trousers?
Oh, you stand beside a door marked "Ladies"
Yellin', "Don't mind that—go in anyway!"
It doesn't matter if your voice is sharp or flat
If you know how to fall upon your P-R-A-T's.
The way to be the top banana,
You gotta start from the bottom up.

ELEVATOR SONG

Registered for copyright as an unpublished song December 10, 1951. Previously registered for copyright as an unpublished song December 15, 1950, under the title "Step to the Rear of the Car, Please." Introduced and recorded by ensemble (Capitol).

Going up—
Step to the rear of the car, please.
Going up—
Call out the name of your floor, please.
Going up—
Passengers, stay where they are, please.
Going up—
Kindly remove your cigar, please.

First floor—
Tea togs for tiny pets,
Bathrobes, baseballs, and bassinets.

Second floor—
Onyx and oysterettes,
Windows for two-dollar bets.

Third floor—
Rat traps and radios,
Cheesecloth, cupcakes, and cameos.

Fourth floor—
Peanuts and piccolos,
Leftover ushers from Loew's.

Going up—
Don't punch the operator, please.

Going up—
Just try to breathe through a pore, please.
Going up—
Sorry you have the wrong store, please.
Going up—
Step to the rear of the car, please.

We've got tassels and tiger skins,
Indian moccasins,
Jumpers and javelins,
Gold-plated safety pins—
Going up,
Going up,
Going up,
Going up!

Early version

First floor—
Tea togs for tiny pets,
Bathrobes, baseballs, and bassinettes,
Old prints, onyx, and oysterettes,
Windows for two-dollar bets.

Second floor—
Rat traps and radios,
Cheesecloth, cupcakes, and cameos,
Pie plates, peanuts, and piccolos,
Leftover ushers from Loew's.

Going up!
Mustn't stand in the door, please.
Going up!
No, sir, this isn't the bar, please.
Let's not
Jostle my *Harper's Bazaar*, please.
Going up!
Step to the rear of the car, please.

Third floor—
Bonnets for blushing brides,
Ice trays, ink, and insecticides,
Lampshades, lecture and lantern slides,
Handsome Tyrolean guides.

Fourth floor—
Cow-country catalogues,
Wholesome ham hocks from happy hogs,
Rare old MacArthur monologues,
Dogs that have gone to the dogs.

Going up!
Don't push the operator, please.
Going up!
Just try to breathe through a pore, please.
Going up!
Sorry, you have the wrong store, please.

Going up!
Step to the rear of the car, please.

Fifth floor—
Tassels and tiger skins,
Moose heads, Indian moccasins,
Jigsaws, jumpers, and javelins,
Odd lots of Siamese twins.

Sixth floor—
Quilts that are fit for queens,
Towels, thumbtacks, and tambourines,
Silk screens painted with sexy scenes,
And from our Boston branch—beans!

Going up!
Don't sever my jugular, please.
Going up!
Gentlemen, this isn't war, please.
Going up!
If you do not wish a scar, please.
Going up!
Step to the rear of the car, please.

Seventh floor –
Birdbaths for bobolinks,
Mink coats run up by local minks,
Kleenex, king-cut for curly kinks,
Egypt, its sand and its Sphinx!

Eighth floor—
Lorgnettes and landaulets,
Baguettes, barrettes, and bobbinets,
V-8, violets, and vinegarettes,
Clarinets and cigarettes and crystal sets and
    salmon croquettes
And alouettes—*gentille alouette*, etc.

Going up!
See that the takeoff is swift, please.
Going up!
Altitude, pressure, and drift, please.
Going up!
Four, seven, three, seven, shift, please!
Going up!
Step to the rear of the lift, please.

Going up!
Kindly leave something ajar, please.
Going up!
Now, men, per-pen-dic-u-lar, please.
Going up!
If you are vehicular, please.
Going up!
Step to the rear of the car, please.

HAIL TO MACCRACKEN'S

Introduced by ensemble.

ALL: Hail to MacCracken's,
The friendly store!
We work at MacCracken's
From nine until four,
And during the holidays
Even more.
BOYS: The salesgirls are nifty.
GIRLS: Our bargains are thrifty.
ALL: Pick up your phone and aim at Bryant—
GIRLS: Nine-two-three-four.
ALL: So, welcome to MacCracken's—
We aim to please.
Polite, industrious
Employees,
Whose only concern is your happiness,
And we spell it—
M-A-C-C-R-A-C-K-E-N-S—
Hoorah!

ONLY IF YOU'RE IN LOVE

Published. Copyrighted November 13, 1951. Introduced and recorded by Lindy Doherty (Cliff) and Judy Lynn (Sally) (Capitol).

SALLY: There are things you can say
In a certain sort of way.
CLIFF: Only if you're in love.
SALLY: There's a touch of the hand
That your heart can understand—
CLIFF: Only if you're in love.
There are times you simply long to sing,
You're so filled with melody.
SALLY: Times when winter changes into spring—
This is one of them for me.
CLIFF: There are some days you spend
That you wish would never end,
Sunny and bright above,
And in each other's eyes
There are looks you recognize,
Others know nothing of.
These are signs you can't miss
And it happens just like this—
BOTH: Only if you're in love.

MY HOME IS IN MY SHOES

Published. Copyrighted September 17, 1951. Introduced and recorded by Bob Scheerer (Tommy) and ensemble (Capitol).

Who cares if I'm a North Caribbean,
South European,
Central Chilean.
I figure I'm a Terpsichorean—
My home is in my shoes.

I know the dances back through the voodoo,
War steps the Sioux do,
Fox-trots that you do—
Show me a polka that very few do,
Then I can tell you who's
Got to dance, dance, dance
From Fort Wayne to France—
I'll assume the stance
Tout de suite.

I feel right at home
In Madrid or Rome,
When I'm roamin' with my feet.

Be patriotic,
Sing out your paeans,
Stick up for you-uns,
Fight back for we-uns,
Be one of them there Med-i-ter-ra-neans.
I harbor different views—
Old Terpsichore
Is the spot for me,
'Cause my home is in my shoes.

I FOUGHT EVERY STEP OF THE WAY

Registered for copyright as an unpublished song December 15, 1950. Introduced and recorded by Rose Marie (Betty) (Capitol).

It's hard to recall where I met him;
It's hard recollecting just where.
I seem to remember a garden,
And I think it was Madison Square.

Round one:
I knew that he outweighed me,
But I fought every step of the way.
From the first pretty speech he paid me,

Through the ride in the park
And the waltz in the dark
And the café au lait.
By the time the big night was over,*
I'd put in quite a working day.
When I tell you that he
Never laid a glove on me,
That's because he was wearing mittens,
But I fought every step of the way.

Round two:
I felt that I was losing,
But I fought every step of the way.
Don't know what method he was using;
I won't say the first blow was a haymaker, no,
But he really made hay.
A first date,
I thought he'd send me roses;
First date,
He sent a negligée.
Did I take the count? *Sí! Sí!*
And that's when the count took me.
Some day I'm going to write my memoirs,
Called *I Fought Every Step of the Way.*

Round three:
I figured he was gaining.
Round four:
I knew that he outclassed me—
But I fought every step of the way.
We kissed once, and I'm not complaining.
Like some jet-propelled plane he passed me;
While I played hard to make
For propriety's sake,
He was making his play.
All night he kept his motor running.
I won't say that his hands were busy,
Like he planned a quick getaway—
Let's just use the word "ricochet."
Couldn't itemize the theft,
But I know there ain't much left.
Oh, well, I'm covered by insurance.
Yes, dear, I know the facts of life now.
And I fought every step of the way.

I crouched and he crossed;
When he smiled I was lost.
Though I weaved and bobbed,
May I say I was robbed,
But I fought every step of the way.

Unused lyrics

Round one—
I knew that he outweighed me,
But I fought every step of the way.

---

* *Alternate line:*
    By the time we reached my doorstep,

From the first pretty speech he paid me,
Through the ride in the park
And the waltz in the dark
And the café au lait.
By the time we reached my doorstep
I'd put in quite a working day.
I put up a great fight, Mom,
But who dropped the atom bomb?
Meet the loser and last year's champion,
But I fought every step of the way.

Round two—
I knew that he outclassed me
But I fought every step of the way.

Round two—
I felt that I was losing,
But I fought every step of the way.
Like some jet-propelled plane he passed me;
While I played hard to make
For propriety's sake
He was makin' his play.
I won't say that his hands were busy—
Let's just use the word "ricochet."
He was pretty shifty, and
He could shift with either hand.
Yes, dear, I know the facts of life now,
But I fought every step of the way.

Round three—
I knew that he outgamed me,
But I fought every step of the way.
Don't know just who it was that framed me,
But the moment we met
I could see he was set
For a hit-and-run play.
First date—
I thought he'd send me roses.
First date—
He sent a negligée.
When I saw I couldn't win,
It was heaven giving in.
Someday I'm gonna write my memoirs
Called *I Fought Every Step of the Way.*
Did I take the count? Sí! Sí!
And that's when the count took me.
Someday I'm going to write my memoirs,
Called *I Fought Every Step of the Way.*

Round four—
They shoulda thrown in the towel,
But I fought every step of the way.
I won't say the first kiss was foul,
But I felt it, I know,
From my little chapeau
To my quadruple-A.
All night he kept his motor running,
Like he planned a quick getaway.

Couldn't itemize the theft,
But I know there ain't much left—
Oh well, I'm covered by insurance,
And I fought every step of the way.

Meet the loser and last year's champion
But I fought every step of the way.

O.K. FOR TV

Published. Copyrighted September 17, 1951. Previously registered for copyright as an unpublished song December 15, 1950. Introduced and recorded by Phil Silvers (Jerry), Jack Albertson (Vic), Judy Lynn (Sally), Herbie Faye (Moe), Joey Faye (Pinky), Eddie Hanley (Denny), and Zachary A. Charles (Russ) (Capitol).

ALL: Sally, Sally,
Don't be silly, Sally!
JERRY: Chin up and chest out, honey,
Don't let it get you down.
This thing called life is funny—
Just take it from a clown.
You've gotta grin and bear it,
No matter what you do.
Remember, though the world is full of
tedium,
That, like a steak, you've found your
proper medium.
[spoken] Wise guys! You thought I
couldn't rhyme "tedium," huh?
[sung] You're O.K. for TV,
That's easy to see.
You're O.K. for TV
And you're O.K. with me.
You're my fav'rite program,
My big song and dance,
The hour of charm,
The voice of romance.
ALL: Wah, wah, wah!
JERRY: I'd like to predict you're
The hit of my set,
The prettiest picture
That I'll ever get.
If I may T-L you,
I tell you it's L-U-V,
Which means that you're O.K. with me
On TV or in P-V-T.
SALLY: You're O.K. for TV,
That's easy to see.
You're O.K. for TV—
That's lucky for me.
You've made me so grateful,

My happy heart hums.
I think you're all dolls
And my little chums.
JERRY: [spoken; Ed Wynn imitation] This is very
embarrassing . . . Television is a
wonderful invention, you know. You
can reach millions of people—but they
can't reach you.
[sung; Maurice Chevalier imitation]
If I may T-L you,
I would tell you it's L-U-V,
Which means that you're O.K. with me,
Ma chérie.
[PINKY attempts a Charles Boyer imitation.]
BOYS: [spoken] Who's that, Charles Boyer?
JERRY: [spoken] Charles Boyer!?
[JERRY does a Jimmy Durante bit.]
JERRY: I may T-L you,
I tell you . . . it's L-U-V.
[spoken] Everybody wants to get in the act!
ALL: On TV or P-V-T.

Introductory verse from published version

I must be rather wary
When I start using words,
For my vocabulary
Is strictly for the birds.
But I'll be brave and risk it,
To try and make you see,
To me you are
An antonym for "tedium"
And like a steak you've found your proper
medium.

Early version of Sally's part

SALLY: You're O.K. for TV,
That's easy to see
You're O.K. for TV,
That's lucky for me.
Like Caesar and Coca,
Like Gracie and George,
You think I'm a doll
And I think you're "gorge."
Besides being funny
And sweet, may I say,
You're makin' me money
And money ain't hay.
If I may T-L you,
I tell you you're S-U-G,
Which means you're all O.K. with me
On TV or P-V-T.

SLOGAN SONG

Registered for copyright as an unpublished song December 10, 1951. Introduced and recorded by Phil Silvers (Jerry), Rose Marie (Betty), Jack Albertson (Vic), Lindy Doherty (Cliff), Eddie Hanley (Denny), and Zachary A. Charles (Russ) (Capitol).

JERRY: You gotta have a slogan you can sell.
ALL: S-E-double-L. Sell!
JERRY: You gotta have a slogan they can yell.
ALL: Y-E-double-L. Yell!
JERRY: For "sodium silicate" there wasn't a chirp,
But how the public yelled when they
changed it to "burp."
ALL: Yes!
If ya wanna ring the cash-register bell,
Get a slogan that'll sell.
CLIFF: You gotta have a jingle they can sing.
JERRY: S-I-N-G. Sing!
ALL: You gotta have a jingle they can swing,
Some reminiscent thing!
The jingle everybody sang for weeks,
you'll agree,
Was titled "My Abdominal Supporter and
Me."
Yes, if you want a catchy little toe-tapping
thing,
Get a jingle that'll sing.

MEET MISS BLENDO

Registered for copyright as an unpublished song December 15, 1950. Introduced and recorded by Phil Silvers (Jerry) and entire company (Capitol).

JERRY: You wanna meet a chick who's all washed
up?
Meet Miss Blendo!
Who sparkles like a snow-white china
cup?
ALL: Meet Miss Blendo!
JERRY: Love led her down the garden path
And then gave her a bubble bath.
Is this the face that you see everywhere?
ALL: Yes! Yes! Yes!
JERRY: Who's in your bathroom and your hair-
do?
Who does things Duz doesn't dare do?
Sweet and tendo,
Dear Miss Blendo—

Meet the press!

TOMMY: Whose photograph is in each magazine?
Meet Miss Blendo!

PARKER: Who's smiling from the television screen?
Meet Miss Blendo!

JERRY: There's not a single sink or john
That her facsimile ain't on.

VIC: Is this the face that launched a thousand
chips?

ALL: Yes! Yes! Yes!

RUSS: Who'll have a super-duper Hooper?

BETTY: Dates with Gable and with Cooper?

ALL: Big crescendo!
Dear Miss Blendo—
Meet the press!

ALL: Who's known to everyone from coast to
coast?
Meet Miss Blendo!
Who smiles at you above your morning
toast?
Sweet Miss Blendo!
Her advertising pull is great;
She's known in every single state.
And when the latest banners we've
dreamed up
Are unfurled
In Scotland, China, France, and Chile,
She will knock the people silly.
Elle Tremendo,
Fräulein Blendo,
Meet the world!

SANS SOUCI

Published. Copyrighted September 17, 1951. Introduced and recorded by Rose Marie (Betty) and ensemble (Capitol).

REFRAIN 1

You ought to be doing the Sans Souci,
Old New Orleans discovered it, *oui, oui, oui!*
You ought to be doing it, yes sirree!
It's gonna start a mild sensation
In every rhythm-speaking nation.
We should worry?—
That's the literal translation.
We ought to be finding a spot that's right,
Cool, comfy, and cozy and not too bright.
I ought to be holding you
Tight, tight, tight!
And shall we say we'll dance away
The night, night, night?
I don't care if the whole world should see me

Acting dreamy in your arms—
It only goes to prove
That romancing
While we're dancing
Still hath charms.

I'm gonna be calling you up some day
When somebody's giving a small soirée.
You'd better start practicing up for me—
And don't forget they call the dance
The Sans Souci.

DANCE

ALL: And shall we say we'll dance this way,
We'll dance until the break of day,
While all the jungle drummers play?
Let's do the Sans Souci!

Additional lyrics from early version of script

[*After Refrain 2*]

You take a beat that's fundamental,
Whose basic appeal is Oriental
With plenty o' push, but kinda gentle,
A hint of the intercontinental,
And you add a gourd, a brace o' bongas,
Those sticks that they use to spark the congas,
And you got a drive that tops the mambo
With all kinds o' jive from Uncle Sambo.
No matter if you like the combo
Or if it's the proper key,
It's gonna start a mild sensation
In every rhythm-speaking nation.
We should worry?—
That's the literal translation.
We'll find a spot that's sorta groovy,
A setting that even tops a movie,
'N' I'll put my cheek upon your shoulder
'N' we'll watch the moon begin t' smoulder
'N' what if the night gets cold and colder—
We'll linger until it's light
And shall we say we'll dance away the night, night,
night!

A DOG IS A MAN'S BEST FRIEND

Registered for copyright as an unpublished song under the title "Nobody Understands Me" December 15, 1950. Alternate title: "A Man's Best Friend." Introduced and

recorded by Phil Silvers (Jerry), Ted "Sport" Morgan, and the Three Grenadiers (Capitol).

JERRY: When I'm blue and lonesome, too,
Nobody understands me like my dog.
And when I'm low and teardrops flow,
Nobody understands me like my dog.
And when I'm with that gang of mine
And feeling fine
As rare old wine,
Who baritones my Old Lang Syne?
Nobody but my dog.
[*spoken*] Have you ever been lonely?
Have you ever been blue?
Have you ever needed a pal
That was true blue?
Don't depend on the two-legged kind.
When you're lonely at night and want a
friend,
As you travel alone along life's highways
And you want a true-blue friend,
Someone you can—
[*to dog*] Will you just wag your tail when
I'm talking, *please?*
[*to audience*] Do you ever want a true and
loyal friend
When you come home from a long day's
toil?
Someone you can trust—
[*to dog*] Buy a cat!

ALL: [*sung*] Who baritones my Old Lang
Syne?
Nobody but my dog.

THAT'S FOR SURE

Published. Copyrighted September 17, 1951. Introduced and recorded by Lindy Doherty (Cliff), Judy Lynn (Sally), and ensemble (Capitol). Cut during the New York run and replaced by "Be My Guest."

VERSE

CLIFF: I wish I could explain
A metrical refrain;
I don't believe my college had a course.
If I should pen an ode,
It might come out in code
As rhythmical as that of Mister Morse.

A noniambic fan,
My trochees do not scan;
I cannot rhyme to save my life,
And so I'll merely try

To ask you to be my
Idyllic, nondactylic wife.

REFRAIN

It's love
And that's for sure,
L'amour
Toujours, for sure.
Beside that fine old animal urge
This feeling is virgin pure.
You're mine and that's ideal,
I'm thine and that's for real.
Let's sing the sweetest words that we know
To Papa Mendelssohn's overture—
For keeps,
For rich or poor,
And that's for sure.

A WORD A DAY

Registered for copyright as an unpublished song December 10, 1951. Introduced and recorded by Phil Silvers (Jerry) and Rose Marie (Betty) (Capitol). Alternate title: "Ambiguous Means I Love You."

BETTY: "Assiduous."
JERRY: "Assiduous": Them's the things that live on sea or on land.
BETTY: "Amphibious."
JERRY: "Amphibious": That means someone who can use either hand.
BETTY: To "simulate."
JERRY: To "simulate": Take a Benzedrine and have a few yaks.
BETTY: "Escutcheons."
JERRY: "Escutcheons": A department store like Saks.
BETTY: "Appreciate."
JERRY: "Appreciate": That's like last year what you lost on your car.
BETTY: "Posterity."
JERRY: "Posterity": What you're sittin' on wherever you are.
BETTY: "Caricature."
JERRY: "Caricature": A caricature in China's a cab.
BETTY: To "disappear."
JERRY: To "disappear": When the waiter brings the tab.
BOTH: A word a day, a word a day,
  Like "résumé"—
  That's how you keep your fancy IQ.

A word a day, a word a day,
  Like "matinée"—*
BETTY: Or "cheese soufflé"—†
BOTH: Will keep you veddy Park Avenue!
BETTY: "Octagonal."
JERRY: That's a man who's over eighty years old.
BETTY: An "anagram."
JERRY: Always take it at the sign of a cold.
BETTY: "Premeditate."
JERRY: "Premeditate": That' a doctor who's still going to college. True?
BETTY: That's true!
JERRY: But "ambiguous"?
BOTH: "Ambiguous" means I love you.
BETTY: [*spoken*] Now try me.
JERRY: To "underrate."
BETTY: That's the word insurance salesmen use most.
JERRY: What's "tantamount"?
BETTY: What's "tantamount"? That's a picture company out on the Coast.
JERRY: A "lexicon."
BETTY: That's the big hotel the East Side of town.
JERRY: "Proverbial."
BETTY: Always takes a proper noun.
JERRY: Try "emphasize."
BETTY: "Try emphasize": When you try a suit to see if it fits.
JERRY: A "homily."
BETTY: In the South they eat a lot of it—grits.
JERRY: "Euphonious."
BETTY: "Euphonious": That's an instrument Hungarians pick.
JERRY: An "anecdote."
BETTY: If you're poisoned, take it quick.
JERRY: [*spoken*] You're pretty smart!
BETTY: A word a day, a word a day
  Like "résumé"—
JERRY: Or "récherché"—
BOTH: Will make you quite a hit at the bar.
BETTY: A word a day,
  Like "distingué"—
JERRY: Or "hit the hay"—
BOTH: Is like a breath of old caviar.
BETTY: "Colloquial."
JERRY: "Colloquial": You're "colloquial" if you talk all the time.
BETTY: A "labyrinth."
JERRY: A "labyrinth": You go down the stairs they charge you a dime . . .
BETTY: "Disseminate."
JERRY: "Disseminate": That's a fella with a feminine point of view.

* *Or:* "disarray."
† *Or:* "Chevrolet."

BOTH: Yoo-hoo!
  But "kaleidoscope"—
  "Kaleidoscope" means I love you!

Additional lyrics

To "correspond."
To "correspond": When you make two people get a divorce.
"Improvidence."
"Improvidence": That's a city in Rhode Island, of course.

A "monologue."
A "monologue": Up to Alexander's Band Monologue.

"Vernacular."
That's a great Italian song.

"Pantologist."
He's a tailor specializes in pants.

A word or two, a word or two,
Like "parvenu"—
Or "kangaroo"—
Will keep the cerebellum in trim.
A word or two, a word or two,
Like "derring-do"—
And "how are you?"—
Will keep you in society's swim.
To "ruminate."
That's when you sit alone in your room and stew.
Boo-hoo!
But "millennium"—
"Millennium" means I love you!

"Nativity."
"Nativity": That's a drink that all the Africans brew.
"Hypoteneuse."
"Hypoteneuse": Big fat animals they keep in a zoo.
"Familiarize."
"Familiarize": That's like when you're gettin' fresh with a chick.
A "subterfuge."
He goes in the game to kick.
"Prognosticate"
"Prognosticate": This is when you have a very big nose.

A "neophyte."
A "neophyte": That's a beef that never quite comes to blows.
And "counterfeit."
"Counterfeit": When you buy your clothes right there at the store.

To "venerate."
To "venerate": What they make a transom for.
And so it goes, and so it goes—
Be on your toes, be on your toes,
Be sure and let good grammar prevail.
Do not disclose, do not disclose
Our "dese" and "dose"—your "dese" and "dose"—
And you'll be veddy Harvard and Yale.

"Preoccupy."
"Preoccupy": Firstest with the mostest "preoccupy."
"Apochryphal."
"Apochryphal": Song of sixpence and
    apochryphal rye.
"Hallucinate."
"Hallucinate": Please "hallucinate" so I'll
    understand it, too.
Halloooo!
But "indubitably"—
"Indubitably" means I love you!

A "proselyte."
A "proselyte" has to give the madam all of the dough.
A "pedagogue."
A "pedagogue": Some big building where the
    generals go.
"Sagacity."
I think Hopalong Sagacity's swell.
And "revelry."
That's a bugle—like a bell.
A word a night, a word a night,
Like "satellite"—
Or "Fahrenheit"—
Will keep you very bravo and zounds.
A word a night, a word a night—
"Cosmopolite"—
Or "erudite"—
Will keep you really "riding to hounds."

What's "fabricate"?
To "fabricate": Weaving blankets—ask me
    sompin' else, chum!
What's "vagrancy"?
"Vagrancy": That's when you're out o' work, like a
    bum.
A "dinosaur."
"Dinosaur": She's that singer on the air and TV,
    too—you knew.
But "collateral"—
"Collateral" means I love you.

"Equivocate."
"Equivocate": That's the title of a Cole Porter show.
"Perfidious."
"Perfidious": That's a rumba—couple of seasons
    ago.
"Gregarious."
"Gregarious": Those are areas in occupied Greece.

A "paradox."
A "paradox": That has got to be a couple of geese.
A "sophomore."
A "sophomore": That's a flag the sailors use to
    send words.
A "semaphore."
A "semaphore": One of them there college birds.
"Commonplace."
"Commonplace": That's a place where all the
    common folks go.
"Corroborate."
When two fellows write a show.

"Anthology."
When you make a list of all your old aunts.

BE MY GUEST

Published. Copyrighted September 17, 1951. Previously registered for copyright as an unpublished song December 15, 1950. Introduced in the Philadelphia try-out by Lindy Doherty (Cliff) and Judy Lynn (Sally). Dropped before the New York opening and replaced by "Only If You're in Love." Later in the New York run it was reintroduced, replacing "That's for Sure." Recorded by Gordon MacRae (Capitol).

VERSE 1

CLIFF: The chance is one in eighty
    I'll be a big success;
    With taxes growing weighty,
    The chance is even less.
    But if I'm trustworthy, loyal, and helpful,
    Friendly, courteous,
    Kind, obedient,
    Cheerful, thrifty, brave,
    Clean and reverent, too,
    An Eagle Scout,
    I'll win, no doubt,
    The right to say to you—

REFRAIN

There's a place in my heart—
Be my guest.
It's been there from the start—
Be my guest.
Though I don't have a dime in reality,
Get a load of the old hospitality.
Though I can't buy you diamonds or furs,
Ev'rything will be marked His and Hers.
North or south, east or west,
Home in someone's arms is best.

Come and see,
Come and be
My guest.

VERSE 2

SALLY: If that's a proposition,
    Then I must, for a fact,
    Provide for some condition,
    Like the Atlantic Pact.
    If you will promise to love and cherish,
    Swear to, let us say,
    Honor and obey,
    Mend your erring ways
    Not too many days
    Hence,
    I shall not wait to duplicate
    Such tender sentiments.

REPEAT REFRAIN

GIRL OF ALL NATIONS

Registered for copyright as an unpublished song February 19, 1980. Not used in show. The refrain also survives under the title "Were Those the Days?"

VERSE

We just plugged in to say hello—
Hello—hello—hello—hello!
We just plugged in to let you know
We haven't got a thing on after the show.
So, if you've got a little time to spend,
We're looking for,
We'd just adore,
A gentleman friend.
So call us up and let us know.
Hello—hello—hello—
Hey, this must be the place!
What the hay!

REFRAIN

Girl of all nations,
You're tantalizing,
You're hypnotizing,
You're like a beautiful flower,
No matter what your locale.
Girl of all nations,
You're captivating,
You're fascinating,
There may be others as pretty
But you're international.
You're romance,

This is my theory,
In Spain or France,
Or on Lake Erie.
Girl of all nations,
Who could resist you
Once they have kissed you?
You're so divine!
Girl of the grange,
Of hill and range.
Beauty unfurled,
Girl of the World,
You're mine!

HAVIN' A BALL

Not used in show.

VERSE

Now that I think it over,
Why should I sit and mope?
Say to yourself, "Well, Rover,
Don't be a dope, you dope!"
Using your long medulla
Talk to yourself like this:
"What are the woods just full o'?
Girls who were made to kiss!"
So—

REFRAIN

Wouldn't it be silly o' me
Spillin' a tear into my beer
When I could be datin' 'em all,
Havin' a ball?
Wouldn't I seem kind of a creep
Losin' a dream, skippin' m' sleep
Rather extreme, just a bit steep, after all!
No, sir, not me, haven't you heard
Gonna be free, free as a bird
Wait'll you see, little ol' me come next fall
Leavin' a call,
Rentin' a hall,
Havin' a ball.

SEÑORITA DÍAZ

Registered for copyright as an unpublished song December 15, 1950. Not used in show.

REFRAIN 1

Aye, aye, aye, aye.
Señorita Diaz.
Aye, aye, aye, aye.
What an evening it was.
There is the dark,
So romantic and gay.
I loved it so,
But my name is not José.

REFRAIN 2

Use Blendo soap.
It's so fine for your hands.
Use Blendo soap
For your pots and your pans.
South of Juarez,
Down to old Vera Cruz,
They say the same:
Blendo soap's the soap to use.

WHAT A REVOLTIN' DEVELOPMENT THIS IS

Registered for copyright as an unpublished song December 15, 1950. Not used in show.

Used to dream of the day
He'd come waltzin' my way
With a glittering, glamorous grin,
When—jolt!
What a revoltin' development this is—
You walked in.
Used to climb into bed,
Curlers over my head,
Keepin' dreamy for I don't know who,
When—bam!
What a calamitous circumstance this is—
In came you.
Looks like I been caught with my arms down.
I reckon I'm fresh out of sighs.
Yes, you got me, you rat,
When I saw you bat
Those big blue eyes!
You're a fluke, you're a spook,
You're a monster, an ook
With that something that's hard to define,
What's more!
What an abhorrent predicament this is.
Suites me fine!

I KNOW YOUR KISS BY HEART

Not used in show.

I know your kiss by heart.
Sort of a second sight.
I memorize
The look in your eyes
At least every other night.
Maybe a hundred times
I've seen this moment start.
Somehow I knew
That you'd be like this.
I know your kiss by heart.

I've no wishing ring
And yet I can see
You are everything
That I hoped you'd be.

And here's the nicest part:
I know your kiss by heart.

BIFOCAL FRED

Registered for copyright as an unpublished song December 15, 1950. Not used in show.

They call me Bifocal Fred,
The kid with the Pyrex head.
A lot they care
About my looks—
With these things on,
I just keep books.
I'm known as Bifocal Jere,
The boy with the cut-glass stare.
I know I'd be a lover boy without my cheaters,
Except to find a girl I'd need some native beaters.
Bifocal Joe,
Where did everybody go?

They call me Bifocal Jim,
My outlook is always dim.
The horn-rimmed type
For open air,
The built-in kind
For formal wear.
I'm known as Bifocal Tom,
The romantic atom bomb.
With these appurtenances off, my stare's so glassy

I don't know if I'm out with Lana or with Lassie.
Bifocal Earl,
Has anybody seen my girl?

They call me Bifocal Jack,
I live off the beaten track.
In all my dreams
I'm Sigmund Freud,
But on a date
I'm Harold Lloyd.
I'm known as Bifocal Moe,
The myopic Romeo.
Because I've got a little old astigmatism,
That's practically as bad as liking communism.
Bifocal Max,
Take it off your income tax!

A bill of fare's
A cinch to read,
But when we dance
They have to lead.
I'm gonna have a pair
Equipped with windshield wipers
Preparing for the day
That I'm changing diapers.
Bifocal Pete,
Who wants to help me cross the street?

EVERYBODY IS YOUR PARTNER IN NEW YORK

Registered for copyright as an unpublished song December 15, 1950. Not used in show.

REFRAIN 1

Everybody is your partner in New York,
And it doesn't seem to matter who it is.
When the guy who drives a hack
Turns and says, "I'll tell ya, Mac,"
Needn't try to settle back—
You're in business!
You don't have to ask what anything's about;
They already have it figured out.
Y'wanna get to Flatbush by the Brooklyn tubes,
"What's a matter wit the Brooklyn Bridge—it's just f' rubes?"
You can come from Kankakee or County Cork,
Everybody is your partner in New York.

REFRAIN 2

Everybody is your partner in New York.
Grover Whalen ain't the only genial host.

When the waiter sidles up
Just as you're about to sup,
Though you want the stirrup cup,
"Take the roast beef!"
If you question his veracity or tact,
Then the manager gets in the act.
"For twenty years, my friend, I've been a restaurateur!
I ought to know the kind of food that you prefer!
And, incidentally, use the spoon and not the fork!"
Everybody is your partner in New York.

REFRAIN 3

Everybody is your partner in New York.
Like you're waitin' at the Capitol some night.
"How did you get up ahead?"
"Gee, you'd think this line's for bread!"
"How would you like droppin' dead!"
"Who's excited?"
Just suppose you're from the west or from a farm,
Or perhaps you use that southern charm—
You say, "Please, ma'am" or "Sonny, could you tell me, please?"
"Hey, fellas, get duh accent on duh Siamese!"
You can't tell me that those hoodlums came by stork—
Everybody is your partner in New York.

REFRAIN 4

Everybody is your partner in New York—
Almost any day it's likely to occur.
So you walk into a store,
Who knows what you came in for,
But the salesman's got to score—
"Fits yuh poifect!"
So you really get courageous and say "Noo!"
So he says, "I'll tell yuh what I'll do . . ."
If he don't have a suit that fits you limb for limb,
I guarantee you got a suit that might fit him!
It's enough to make a yokel flip his cork—
Everybody is your partner in New York.

CUCKOO

Possibly intended for *Top Banana* since the name "Rose Marie" is scribbled on the lyric sheet. Not used in show.

There they were—dig the scene—
At the stereo machine.
He was hippin' her about the ride-out:

"Didja dig that riff the cat blew?"
Cuckoo—cuckoo—cuckoo!

She was cool and aloof,
But she didn't wanna goof,
So she waited till he played the side out,
Then she whispered "Shooby-oo-doo"—
Cuckoo—cuckoo—cuckoo!

He did a flip and said, "I'm hip—
Let's make it to my pad."
Rollin' her orbs, she whispered, "Forbes,
Why don't you cool it, Dad?
Like I mean, this is it—
Skip the sentimental bit.
Shall we make it to a low-rent hideout
Where they don't start swingin' till two
And I can cha-cha with you?"
He replied, "My answer is ooooh!"
Cuckoo—cuckoo—cuckoo!

HAVE YOU WRITTEN ANY GOOD BOOKS LATELY?

Registered for copyright as an unpublished song December 15, 1950. Not used in show.

VERSE

My learned friend,
You may depend
We keep abreast of what is best,
Of what is new and what is going on.
Supposing he's had inquiries
To be on *Information Please*,
He's got to have a brain to sit upon.
Remember, though we're as frivolous as can be,
There's one thing we do take seriously.

REFRAIN 1

Have you written any good books lately?
You're passé without a novel to your name.
Everybody and his brother
Is outdoing one another
To get in the literary hall of fame.
If you can bake a chocolate cake,
If you can mix a drink
Or hatch an egg
Or shake a leg,
Or if your wife is pink,
Take advantage of your talent;
It is greater than you think.

"Fred'rick Hazlitt, are you nearly done?"
"Just beginning, Clarence Buddington!"

REFRAIN 2

Have you written any good books lately?
Have you started on another epic tome?
Is your little niece a charmer?
Have you learned to be a farmer?
Are you planning to redecorate your home?
If you're a cur,
A raconteur,
Or good at repartee,
A pot-and-pan or a diet man,
Or drink a quart a day,
Don't you dare to lose a weekend,
Tell us how to join AA!
"Don't you think so, Somerset, old bean?"
"Absolutely, Ellery, old Queen!"

REFRAIN 3

Have you written any good books lately?
Maybe you are not an author in your eyes.
But if Henry Seidel Canby
Says you can be, then you can be
A contestant for the million-dollar prize.
Do you love life
Or beat your wife
Or simply like to drift?
Then be a man,
Get off your can
And exercise your gift!
Find the highways to belles lettres
And start thumbing for a lift!
"Oh, I say, you are a card, Rudyard!"
"Well, I am delighted, George Bernard!"

Additional lyrics from early script

BEFORE REFRAIN 2

[Spoken or declaimed—over chords.]

Seven Ways to Cook a Wolf!
A Dozen Supper Snacks!
How to Reduce Your Figure While Reducing
    Your Income Tax!
I Married Adventure!
I Grew Another Head!
I Live Alone and Loathe It!
How to Make Friends in Bed!
I Was a Foreign Agent!
I Flew the Alps Alone!
I Was the General's Chauffeur!
I Was a Male Hormone!
I Was a Truman Booster!

I Hated Truman's Guts!
I Wasn't in Roosevelt's Cabinet!
I Told the Russians "Nuts"!

FOLLOWING REFRAIN 3

Have you written any good books lately?
Have you got a little five- or six-foot shelf?
Have you authorized Life with Mother?
Recollections of My Brother?
Have you had the courage to Expose Yourself?
Are you a dick?
Have you been sick?
Are you collecting stamps?
I knew them all!
Can you recall the silent-movie vamps?
Every kid I fought KO'd me,
And not one of them were champs!
"Samuel Hopkins, what exquisite prose!"
"Thanks a mywllion, but it's James Truslow's!"

Feeding and Care of Infants!
Children from One to Two!
Children from Six to Seven!
I Was a Child—Were You?!
Outfitting Jim for Boot Camp!
Mary's the Quiet Kind!
Is There a Teenage Dope Ring?!
Have You a Big Behind?!
I Worked My Way Through College Being a
    Dime-Store Clerk!
Sylvia Townsend Krutchfield: Teacher, Advisor,
    Jerk!
Call an Alumni Meeting!
Look Up That College Chum!
Children of Sixty-seven!
And so ad nauseam.

Have you written any good books lately?
Does your talent lean to flowers, games, or boats?
Men have made their reputations
By just holding conversations,
Making notes, and quoting other fellows' quotes.
As Lincoln said,
I've often read,
"Don't stop me if you've heard."
My latest book is called, I Took the Other Fellow's
    Word.
It's not hard to be original
When something has occurred.
"Richard Harding, I must say that's slick!"
"Rather clever of me, eh, Van Wyck?"

Fertilize Your Hydrangeas!
I Had Drooping Phlox!
Over the Vast Pacific We Sailed in a Cracker Box!

I Stood with Stonewall Jackson!
Lee Won the Civil War!
I Ran the German Blockade!
I Ran a Candy Store!
Are You a Rosicrucian?!
Secrets of Ancient Kings!
Swimming the English Channel!—
Are those things water wings?
Creatures of Air and Ocean:
Our Finny and Feathered Friends!
"By the way, do you read them?"
"No, but they fill bookends."

Have you written any good books lately?
Maybe just a little mystery, don't you know?
And perhaps it would be subtler
If you really had the butler
Do in dear Aunt Anastasia for her dough.
I went to spend a fortnight
With Lord Outclive, near Swineshead;
Four dozen sat at the table,
Forty-seven stayed in bed.
Didn't have to write a thank-you note—
By week's end all were dead.
"Oh, I say there! What a ghastly job!"
"Not at all—it didn't cost one bob!"

The Corpse on the Fourth-Floor Terrace!
The Corpse on the Garden Path!
The Corpse in the Bendix Washer!—
Boy, did he ever need a bath!
The Case of the Poisoned Birdseed!
The Skull of the Grinning Cat!
The Search for the Missing Body!—
Oh, body, where is you at?
The Tarantula at My Window!
The Dagger in Twomley's Back!
"It couldn't be . . . was it? . . . horrors!"
"It's solid murder, Jack!"
The Thin Man Kills the Fat Man!
The Falcon Slays the Saint!
"Quick, Watson, the spirits of ammonia—
I fear I'm going to faint."

"It isn't that I'm squeamish,
Or too sensitive to gore,
Or that I mind a friendly old cadaver on the floor,
But this book that I've been reading, Jeeves,
Is such a bloody bore!"
"Would you autograph this, Mignon G.?"
"I'd adore to, dear Honoré de!"
And now we bid you all good night,
But please remember when you write
That good books were meant to read!

THE BELLE OF NEW YORK
and Other Songs of 1952

THE BELLE OF NEW YORK (1952)

Produced by Arthur Freed for Metro-Goldwyn-Mayer. Released March 1952. Copyright February 12, 1952. Directed by Charles Walters. Screenplay by Robert O'Brien and Irving Elinson. Adapted for the screen by Chester Erskine, after the musical play *The Belle of New York* by Hugh Morton. Lyrics by Johnny Mercer. Music by Harry Warren. Musical numbers staged and directed by Robert Alton. Orchestrations by Conrad Salinger and Maurice De Packh. Musical director: Adolph Deutsch. Featuring Fred Astaire, Vera-Ellen, and Marjorie Main, with Keenan Wynn, Alice Pearce, Clinton Sundberg, Gale Robbins, Lisa Ferraday, Henry Slate, Carol Brewster, Meredith Leeds, Lyn Wilde, Roger Davis, Buddy Roosevelt, Dick Wessel, Percy Helton, and Tom Dugan.

 A playboy falls in love with a Salvation Army girl in the 1890s.

BABY DOLL

Published. Copyrighted September 24, 1951. Previously registered for copyright as an unpublished song June 2, 1945. Introduced and recorded by Fred Astaire (MGM). Danced by Astaire and Vera-Ellen. Reprised by Astaire and male trio.

VERSE

FRED
ASTAIRE: To say I'm fond of you
    Would merely be an attitude.
    To say you're wonderful
    Would be a platitude.
    And so to Santa Claus
    I owe eternal gratitude
    For leaving you beneath my Christmas
      tree.

REFRAIN 1

Baby doll,
You beautiful baby doll,
Let's go home and tell your mother
That you found a baby brother.

The Belle of New York: *Fred Astaire and Vera-Ellen*
Left: *In "A Bride's Wedding Day Song"*
Right: *Dancing to "Oops!"*

I'm takin' you off the shelf
And showin' you off myself.
Can't you see it now?
I'm takin' you walkin',
Holdin' your parasol;
Ah, honey, there's no use talkin'—
You're a beautiful baby doll.

REFRAIN 2

VERA-ELLEN: Baby doll,
    You beautiful baby doll,
    Let's go home and tell my mother
    That I found a baby brother.
    I'm takin' you off the shelf
    And showin' you off myself.
    Can't you see it now?
    You're takin' me walkin',
    Holding my parasol;
    Ah, honey, there's no use talkin'—
    You're a beautiful baby doll.

REFRAIN 3

ASTAIRE: Baby doll,
    You beautiful baby doll,
    I hope you're not bought and paid for,
    'Cause I'm the little boy you're made for.
    I'm takin' you off the shelf
    And showin' you off myself.
    Can't you see it now?
    I'm takin' you walkin',
    Holdin' your parasol.
    Ah, honey, there's no use talkin'—
    You're a beautiful baby doll.

REFRAIN 4

Baby doll,
You beautiful baby doll—
Not the kind for kids to play with
But to honor and obey with.
Just look at those big blue eyes
All full of those April skies!
Walkin' through the park—
You'll need a big brother,
Holdin' your parasol—
Run home and ask your mother,
You beautiful baby doll.

Additional lines

Surely Santa Claus designed you
And left you here for me to find you.
Please go home and ask your mother
If you don't need a baby brother.
I'm puttin' you on the shelf
And keeping you for myself.
I never was much for toys,
Not one of those mama's boys

Just look at that baby stare,
And look at those blue skies there.
Can't I have the job of takin' you walkin'?

WHEN I'M OUT WITH THE BELLE OF NEW YORK

Published. Copyrighted January 14, 1952. Previously registered for copyright as an unpublished song June 2, 1945. Introduced and recorded by male chorus (MGM). Reprised in the finale by the chorus; danced by Astaire and Vera-Ellen.

VERSE

Lillian Russell is fabulous fair;
So is the girl on that sign over there.
Ah, but to capture the maid of my heart
Challenges ev'ry photographer's art!
Charles Dana Gibson would even agree,
No Stage Door John holds a candle to me.

REFRAIN

When I'm out with the Belle of New York,
With the beautiful Belle of New York,
Ev'ry person we meet,
Like the cop on the beat,
Leaves whatever he's doing
And crosses the street.
It's a beautiful sight after dark
When we're strolling through Gramercy Park—
The stars in her eyes
And the stars up above
Just fill me with oceans
And oceans of love,
And my heart bobs around like a cork
When I'm out with the Belle of New York.

OOPS!

Published. Copyrighted September 24, 1951. Previously registered for copyright as an unpublished song June 2, 1945. Introduced and recorded by Fred Astaire (MGM). Danced by Astaire and Vera-Ellen.

"Oops!"
My heart went "Oops!"
The moment that we met
My heart went "Oops!"

I never will forget,
My heart turned hoops
The moment that I met you.
"Oops!"
My feet went "Oops!"
I nearly took a spill;
My knees went "Oops!"
They shook a bit until
My head went "Oops!"
You mustn't let it get you.

I was going for a very
What you'd call solitary
Sort of stroll,
Just a-twiddling my thumbs,
When I heard a lotta drums
Begin to pound and roll.
And "Oops!"
My heart went "Oops!"
It went into a spin of loop-the-loops;
You must have thought me kin to nincompoops,
The silly way I acted.
Of course, you couldn't know
That you were so aglow
And I was so attracted—
But, baby, take a bow,
My heart is going "Oops!"
Right now.

SEEING'S BELIEVING

Published. Copyrighted January 14, 1952. Previously registered for copyright as an unpublished song June 30, 1945. Introduced and recorded by Fred Astaire (MGM).

REFRAIN

Seeing's believing,
And when I see you
I realize what an angel I've found.
I never thought
I would see the day
When miracles occurred,
And though the best of authorities
May not believe a word,
Kissing's believing,
And when I kiss you,
I feel as though
We were miles off the ground.
Never knew that dreams came true,
But miraculously they do—
Seeing's believing with you.

A BRIDE'S WEDDING DAY SONG

Registered for copyright as an unpublished song July 27, 1945. Introduced by Vera-Ellen (dubbed by Anita Ellis) and danced by Vera-Ellen, Fred Astaire, and ensemble. Recorded by Ellis (MGM). Alternate title: "Thank You, Mister Currier—Thank You, Mister Ives."

We're posing for a picture by Currier and Ives,
And I can't wait till the great day arrives;
For he'll be so attractive and I'll be so in love
That years from now when I'm "Madame"
And ev'rybody calls him "Sir,"
We still can see the boy and girl we were.
For grooms turn into husbands
And brides turn into wives,
And there we'll be for the rest of our lives—
So, thank you, Mister Currier,
And thank you, Mister Ives!

BACHELOR DINNER SONG

Registered for copyright as an unpublished song July 27, 1945. Introduced and recorded by Fred Astaire and female ensemble (MGM).

The lyric hits a certain note of anticipation of Alfred P. Doolittle's "Get Me to the Church on Time" in *My Fair Lady* (1956).

Who wants to kiss the bridegroom
On his last night out?
Next time they bring Champagne on
I'll have the ball and chain on—
Yes, ladies, I must leave you,
I regret to say.
I've bought the ring;
This little fling
Will have to be our last soirée,
Because they're putting me away,
And tomorrow is the happy day.
Oh, I'll be a starry-eyed groom
By high noon, no doubt—
So who wants to kiss the bridegroom
On his last night out?

NAUGHTY BUT NICE

Published. Copyrighted January 14, 1952. Previously registered for copyright as an unpublished song April 16, 1951. Introduced by Vera-Ellen (dubbed by Anita Ellis) and Alice Pearce. Recorded by Ellis (MGM).

VERSE

As a mousy little hen
I will, nine times out of ten,
Being proper comes a cropper
When I operate with men.
As a maiden most demure,
I'm becoming, I am sure,
More discerning, full of learning,
With a yearning for l'amour.*

REFRAIN 1

Wanna be naughty,
Naughty but nice,
Disobey all my
Mama's advice.
One thing that sirens have all agreed to:
They all know what a bashfully lowered eye can
    lead to.
Wanna wear panties
Under my gown,
Shock the old aunties
All around town.
What's wrong with wining in a private dining
    room?
I wanna clink glasses and dodge a few passes
Before I dodge shoes and rice.
So I'll be naughty—
Not really naughty,
Just sorta naughty but nice!

REFRAIN 2

Wanna be naughty,
Naughty but nice,
See if I'm made of sugar and spice.
To all convention I call out "Gangway!"
I confess I wanna care less than Eva Tanguay.
Gladly I'd chance the
Stares of a few
If I could dance the
Bunny Hug, too.
Suppose a stranger should arrange a tête-à-tête—
While he becomes pleasant across hot pheasant,
I'll put the whole thing on ice.

* *Alternate lines:*
    A deceiver, bosom heaver,
    And believer in l'amour.

That's if I'm naughty—
Not really naughty,
Just sort o' naughty but nice!

Special material

VERSE 1

Now we'll open up the book on *What Every Girl
    Oughta Know.*
Read the paragraph entitled "How to Begin
    Catching Beaux."
Simply sit there looking saucer-eyed, sighing
    "Ah!," cooing "Oh!"
Men are silly enough to believe they have brains—
Don't discourage them, dear, in the thought.
Just give Willie enough rope to handle the reins,
Before he even knows it he'll be caught.
Sugared phrases have been luring fish long before
    rods and reels.
With clever statements flatter them
And devastate and scatter them
And leave them there to find out how it feels,
And let them cool their heels.

VERSE 2

First Instructions in the Art of Love—lesson one:
    how to flirt.
Never give a man an even break. Once begun, do
    him dirt;
Be a femme fatale in velvet gloves, acting prim,
    feeling pert!
If you wink it's divine, or just concentrate hard
With an innocent look in your orbs.
"Oh, I think it's divine!"—"Mister Smith, you're
    a card!"—
That's all a male intelligence absorbs.
Don't forget these little simple rules when an
    evening is o'er:
In small ways be delectable,
In hallways be respectable,
And only kiss him as you slam the door,
And he'll come back for more.

I WANNA BE A DANCIN' MAN

Published. Copyrighted January 14, 1952. Previously
registered for copyright as an unpublished song May 7,
1951. Introduced and recorded by Fred Astaire (MGM).

I wanna be a dancin' man, while I can,
Gonna leave my footsteps on the sands of time,
If I never leave a dime.
Never be a millionaire, I don't care,
I'll be rich as old King Midas might have been,
Least until the tide comes in.
Let other men build mighty nations
And buildings to the sky;
I'll leave a few creations
To show that I was dancin' by.
I wanna be free as any bird can be, yessirree!
Gonna leave my footsteps on the sands of time,
If I never leave a dime.
A dancin' man with footsteps on
The sands of rhythm and rhyme.

I LOVE TO BEAT THE BIG BASS DRUM

Registered for copyright as an unpublished song
July 26, 1951. Written for Fred Astaire but not used in
film.

REFRAIN 1

I love to beat the big bass drum,
A-rum-te-tum-te-tum-de-dum.
I'd be as happy as they come
If I could beat the big bass drum.
They tell me there are some who feel
A feeling for the glockenspiel;
I reckon that's all right for some—
I love to beat the big bass drum.

VERSE

If it's in the music store
Or a drum-and-bugle corps,
Marching forward as to war,
I repeat, it's the sweetest sound!
Would I rather play the fife?
Wouldn't try to save my life!
Would I rather beat my wife?*
No, not I!
I supply music by the pound.

REFRAIN 2

If I could only make the grade,
I wouldn't care how much it weighed;
I wouldn't care if I got paid,

---

* *Alternate line:*
    Would I harm my storm and strife?

Or if I had to promenade
Around the town in some parade—
It might be ninety in the shade.
A-rum-te-tum-te-tum-de-dum,
I love to beat the big bass drum!
Some can spot a sonata
Or plot a cantata,
But I gotta beat the drum!

INTERLUDE 1

Picture me on key,
In big-time company—
Gee!

TRIO

Not the fella with the big baton,
Even though he really carries on;
Not the squeaky little piccolo
Nor the trombones as they blow-ho-ho-ho-ho-ho-ho.
Holy mack'rel, see the cymbals fly!
Pretty soon I should be passin' by.
What, they had me hidden?
That was me, no kiddin'!
Holdin' up the big bass drum . . .

INTERLUDE 2

There's a part
When they start
Playin' a martial air,
When the brass
Shows real class,
Blowin' a bright fanfare.
For a moment all is quiet;
Then the rhythm starts a riot.

REFRAIN 3

Almost like a New Year's night
Or when a fella picks a fight
Or like a homer in the stands,
It makes you wanna clap your hands,
It makes you wanna tap your feet,
And that's the reason I repeat:
A-rum-te-tum-te-tum-de-dum,
I love to beat the big bass drum!
Some musicians are cuter
At tootin' a tooter,
But I love a big bass drum!

MEANT TO TELL YUH

Music by Al Rinker and Charles Dant. Registered for copyright as an unpublished song January 2, 1952.

REFRAIN 1

Meant to tell yuh,
Incident'ly,
Here of late
My heart's been acting sentiment'ly.
Just in passing,
Thought I'd mention
You have got its undivided rapt attention;
Merely making conversation,
I am in a state of helpless adoration.
Hate to seem to have a bill of goods to sell yuh,
But I simply meant to tell yuh,
"I'm in love."

REFRAIN 2

[*Repeat Refrain 1 for first four lines.*]

Should you ask for my opinion,
You outglow the rainbow seen by Mister Finian.

[*Continue with last five lines as before.*]

WHO'S EXCITED?

Music by Johnny Hodges. Published. Copyrighted March 31, 1952. Previously registered for copyright as an unpublished song January 30, 1952.

Because you
Fell off of a cloud
And picked me from out of a crowd,
A body would think
That I'd taken to drink.
Who's excited, excited,
For cryin' out loud?
Excited
Because my hand shakes?
Excited
Because the earth quakes?
A person would guess
That my nerves were a mess.
Who's excited, excited,
For criminy's sakes?
I'm collected and
As calm as a cucumber is cool.

I'd like to take you home to Mom—
Hope today ain't April Fool!
The birdies
Are singin' for me.
No church bells
Are in the right key,
And when you say I'm
Gonna hear 'em all chime,
Who's excited?
Delighted?
Nobody but me!

EVERYTHING I HAVE IS YOURS (1952)

Produced by George Wells for Metro-Goldwyn-Mayer. Released October 1952. Copyright September 23, 1952. Directed by Robert Z. Leonard. Screenplay by George Wells. Additional dialogue by Ruth Brooks Flippen. Musical numbers staged by Gower Champion and Nick Castle. Musical director: David Rose. Songs by Johnny Green, Clifford Grey, Rex Newman, Douglas Furber, Saul Chaplin, Walter Donaldson, Bob Wright, Chet Forrest, Gus Kahn, Richard Priborsky, Burton Lane, and Harold Adamson, except for "Derry Down Dilly," by Johnny Mercer (lyrics) and Johnny Green (music). Featuring Marge and Gower Champion and Dennis O'Keefe, with Monica Lewis, Dean Miller, Eduard Franz, John Gallaudet, Diane Cassidy, Elaine Stewart, Jonathan Cott, Robert Burton, Jean Fenwick, Mimi Gibson, and Wilson Wood.

A husband-and-wife song-and-dance team has to break up when the wife becomes pregnant.

DERRY DOWN DILLY

Music by Johnny Green. Published. Copyrighted October 8, 1952. Previously registered for copyright as an unpublished song February 13, 1952. Introduced and recorded by Marge Champion (MGM).

VERSE

I recall my first impression;
He was such a gentleman fine,
With his hair cut like a bow and arrow,
As he whispered, "Pretty little sparrow mine!"
Like the tales in *True Confession*,

I thought he'd surely give me a whirl;
Flowers and perfumes,
Meals in private rooms—
Wasn't I a giddy, headstrong girl?

REFRAIN

Heigh-ho, Derry Down Dilly,
Wasn't it silly of me?
When he kissed my ear
And he said, "My dear,
Shall we turn the parlor light low?"
Oh, I lost my head
Or I never would have said "No!"—
Just "Oh!"
Heigh-ho, Derry Down Dilly,
Wasn't it silly of me?
Ah, yes! *Mais oui!*
We played a game
Hide-and-go-seek by name,
And I, dumb kid,
When he said, "Hide," I hid!
Heigh-ho, Derry Down Dilly,
Life is remarkably grim!
For wasn't it silly of me?
And wasn't it silly of him?

GLOW WORM

("Glühwürmchen") Music by Paul Lincke. Original German lyrics by Heinz Bolten-Bäckers (1902). Original English lyrics by Lilla Cayley Robinson. New English lyrics by Johnny Mercer. Copyrighted. Published May 9, 1952.

The song has a long history. Its first English version had its U.S. premiere in New York when it was interpolated by May Naudain into the 1907 musical *The Girl Behind the Counter*. There were two hit recordings in 1908: one by the soprano Lucy Isabelle Marsh (Columbia), the other by the Victor Orchestra conducted by Walter B. Rogers (Victor). The Mills Brothers had a number-one hit in 1952 with Mercer's lyrics (Decca), and in 1953 Mercer himself had a successful recording (Capitol). In 1962 Mercer wrote a set of special lyrics for Bing Crosby to sing at Christmastime.

REFRAIN 1

Glow, little glow worm, fly of fire,
Glow like an incandescent wire,
Glow for the female of the specie,

Turn on the AC and the DC.
This night could use a little brightnin';
Light up, you li'l ol' bug of lightnin'.
When you gotta glow, you gotta glow—
Glow, little glow worm, glow.

REFRAIN 2

Glow, little glow worm, glow and glimmer,
Swim through the sea of night, little swimmer.
Thou aeronautical boll weevil,
Illuminate yon woods primeval;
See how the shadows deep and darken,
You and your chick should get to sparkin';
I got a gal that I love so—
Glow, little glow worm, glow.

REFRAIN 3

Glow, little glow worm, turn the key on,
You are equipped with taillight neon;
You got a cute vest-pocket Mazda
Which you can make both slow or "fazda."
I don't know who you took a shine to
Or who you're out to make a sign to;
I got a gal that I love so—
Glow, little glow worm, glow.

Christmas version for Bing Crosby

REFRAIN 1

Glow, little glow worm, light our tree up,
Show all the boys at old G.E. up.
Although the thought may still be ranklin',
You made the scene before Ben Franklin.
For years you've made the season merry
And never were incendiary;
Rev up your amps, and let 'er go—
Glow, little glow worm, glow.

REFRAIN 2

Dig all the up-to-date inventions;
Then add a few brand-new dimensions—
Sparkle and shine in Technicolor,
Red, white, and blue, cerise and yulluh.
Show us your product now has full worth,
Top everything at Grant's and Woolworth,
Make like a big department sto'—
Glow, little glow worm, glow.

REFRAIN 3

Glow, little glow worm, it's the season
For joy and love—and even reason.
So whether leaving or arriving,
Don't have a drink while you are driving.
Should you be forced to wet your whistle,

Be not an airborne flying missile,
Just nestle neath the mistletoe
'N' glow, little glow worm, glow.

REFRAIN 4

Be not an antique or a cast-off,
Hop on your pad, li'l chum, and blast off,
And when you hit that skyway freeway,
Fly it the nineteen sixty-three way.
Zooming between yon tall skyscrapers,
Make people holler, "Wow, what tapers!"
Turn on your private dynamo,
Glow, little glow worm, glow.

REFRAIN 5

Glow, little glow worm, small lamplighter,
Help us to make the darkness brighter,
Live up to your proud nomenclature
For Father Time and Mother Nature.
Through all the years that we have known you
Only one certain star's outshone you;
But you're a swinger, even so—
Glow, little glow worm, glow.

REFRAIN 6

Glow, little glow worm, and remember
Once, on a long-ago December,
There came to earth a tiny stranger
Who lit a dark and lonely manger.
Light up the sky from pole to isthmus
Spell out His blessing: MERRY CHRISTMAS!
(Then) come nestle neath the mistletoe,
Glow, little glow worm,
For us below, worm—
Glow, little glow worm, glow!

THE LIGHTS OF HOME

Music by Lew Quadling. Published. Copyrighted March 26, 1953. Previously registered for copyright as an unpublished song May 15, 1952.

You can see a million ports
Twinkle faintly through the gloom,
But you haven't seen a thing
Until you've seen the lights of home.

You can see the mountains rise,
Green and misty from the foam,
But the greatest sight you'll ever see
Will be the lights of home.

See all the world unfold,
Go and search ev'rywhere,
And wealth untold
May wait you there.

But believe me when I say
That no matter where you roam,
You have never seen a scene
Until you've seen the lights of home.

EARLY AUTUMN

Music by Ralph Burns and Woody Herman. Published. Copyrighted August 5, 1952.

The song was an outgrowth of Ralph Burns's instrumental *Summer Sequence*, written for Woody Herman's band. The first, pre-Mercer recording was an instrumental by Herman's band, featuring Stan Getz on tenor saxophone (Capitol), made in 1948. Leading recordings using Mercer's lyrics were made by Jo Stafford (Columbia) and Claude Thornhill and his orchestra, with vocal by Fran Warren (Columbia). Mercer remarked: "I think it's one of my best lyrics . . . Not a big hit, but you can't tell the public what they like—they usually pick the right ones."

When an early autumn walks the land
And chills the breeze
And touches with her hand
The summer trees,
Perhaps you'll understand
What memories I own.

There's a dance pavilion in the rain,
All shuttered down;
A winding country lane,
All russet brown;
A frosty window pane
Shows me a town grown lonely.

That spring of ours that started
So April-hearted
Seemed made for just a boy and girl.
I never dreamed, did you?
Any fall could come in view
So early, early.

Darling, if you care,
Please let me know;
I'll meet you anywhere,
I miss you so.
Let's never have to share
Another early autumn.

BONNE NUIT

Music by Mercer. Registered for copyright as an unpublished song September 24, 1952.

VERSE

Each morn she awakens and whispers to me,
"Sweet dreams you bring, cherie."
For here is the lullaby I sing each night
To her, for her, good night.

REFRAIN

Bonne nuit, good night dear, *bonne nuit*.
Come snuggle up close while I sing you to sleep.
Soft as a kitten,
Warm as a mitten,
Craddled in moonbeams,
The angels bring lovely dreams.
Close your eyes, *ma cherie, bonne nuit*.
Always I've told you
It's heaven to hold you
And always I'll love you
Beaucoup dear, *beaucoup, beaucoup*.
Oh, sleep and rest well.
Ev'ry night is noël.
Bonne nuit, goodnight dear,
Bonne nuit, bonne nuit.

THE MOONLIGHT WALTZ

Music by Al Rinker. Registered for copyright as an unpublished song October 24, 1952.

Please play the moonlight waltz
So we can fall in love.
While others glide,
We'll stroll outside
Beneath the moon above.

And while the moonbeams fall
Across the ivied wall,
I'll hold you near,
Our hearts will hear
The sweetest waltz of all.
The violins far away
La-da-da, la-da-da,
Hum the melody
While on the floor
Couples sway.
La-da-da, la-da-da,
You'll be close to me,
Tonight will always be
The night a dream came true—
The night you cared,
The night I shared
The moonlight waltz with you.
La-da-da, la-da-da,
Play the moonlight waltz.

HELLO OUT THERE, HELLO

Music by Wingy Manone. Published. Copyrighted December 2, 1952.

REFRAIN

Ev'rybody on yon twinkling star,
Doesn't matter on which one you are,
If you're diggin' me on your radar,
Hello out there, hello!
Though you are a strange and foreign race,
If you are equipped to fly through space,
Pay a little visit to our place,
Hello out there, hello!
If you've got nothing else to do,
Just rev up the rocket—
Tuh pucket, tuh pucket.
If you've a pair of wings
That you attach to a sprocket—
Fly on down!—

Don't you let appearances worry you.
We are pretty funny looking, too.
Anyway, in case I'm comin' through,
Hello out there, hello!

AREN'T YOU THE CHARMING ONE?

Music by Milton Samuels.

Aren't you the charming one, dear,
And disarming one?
Butter won't melt, as I've heard say,
Until you've gotten your way.

Aren't you the saucy one,
Bright-eyed and bossy one?
Oh, what a tune I'll have to dance
As long as you're wearing the pants.*

INTERLUDE

You're the contrariest,
Merriest, veriest,
Oh-I-don't-care-i-est
Girl I know.
I am the worriedest,
Harriedest, hurriedest,
As yet unmarriedest
Beau.

Dearie, but aren't you the clever one,
Now-and-forever one?
Surely I hope
You'll always be
The charming one
Only for me.

---

* *Alternate lines:*
  Oh, how I'll have to toe the mark
  When we pass the girls in the park!

Dangerous When Wet: *Esther Williams, with the help of Tom and Jerry, dreams about swimming across the English Channel.*

DANGEROUS WHEN WET
and Other Songs of 1953

DANGEROUS WHEN WET (1953)

Produced by George Wells for Metro-Goldwyn-Mayer. Released June 1953. Copyright May 11, 1953. Directed by Charles Walters. Screenplay by Dorothy Kingsley. "Tom and Jerry" cartoon sequence by Fred Quimby, William Hanna, and Joseph Barbera. Lyrics by Johnny Mercer. Music by Arthur Schwartz. Musical numbers staged by Charles Walters and Billy Daniel. Orchestrations by Skip Martin. Musical director: Georgie Stoll. Featuring Esther Williams, Fernando Lamas, Jack Carson, Charlotte Greenwood, and Denise Darcel, with William Demarest, Donna Corcoran, Barbara Whiting, Bunny Waters, Henri Letondal, Paul Bryar, Jack Raine, Richard Alexander, Tudor Owen, and Anne Codee.

An Arkansas family is sponsored to swim the English Channel.

FIFI

Registered for copyright as an unpublished song January 13, 1953. Introduced as a mumbled fragment by Fernando Lamas.

Très magnifique is Fifi—
The season's peak in chic is Fifi.
I merely look at her
And my heart has wings;
Hear how it sings:
"Do si la sol fa mi re do."
Beaucoup okay is Fifi—
Her kiss is, how you say?, terrifi!
A bigger hit than *South Pacifi!*
Oh, that Fifi—
I've gone crazee,
So has Paree,
Over *la belle* Fifi!

VERSE

In the center of the Paris whirl
Les hommes all wait for dates
From *la plus plus formidable* girl,
La femme who really rates
And, so to speak, United States!

REFRAIN 1

I get my yocks from Fifi—
My Champagne on the rocks is Fifi.

She's as Parisienne as the Fourth of July,
Ice cream and pie—
My heart starts singing "Ai yai-yai-yai-yai!"
She's in the groove
Is Fifi!
She should be in the Louvre,
Miss Fifi
In short, she's quite beyond-belief-y,
Oh, that Fifi!
Like Valley Forge
She's strictly George—
Gorgeous is my Fifi.

REFRAIN 2

FIFI: *Non, non, non, non!*
BOYS: But Fifi!
FIFI: You're too filet mignon.
BOYS: But Fifi!
FIFI: Please *ouvre la fenêtre* . . . don't you agree?
BOYS: *Oui, oui, oui, oui!*
FIFI: That's *je vous aime beaucoup* with me.
BOYS: All *chevaliers* love Fifi
FIFI: *Merci* and Charles Trenet.
BOYS: Ah, Fifi!
FIFI: How 'bout a small aperitifi?
BOYS: *Vive la Fifi!*
    Vous êtes jolie!
FIFI: *Ooh, probablee!*
BOYS: Thou swell,
    La belle Fifi!

I LIKE MEN

Registered for copyright as an unpublished song January 13, 1953. Introduced by Barbara Whiting and four male dancers.

REFRAIN 1

My ma asked me 'n' I told Ma,
I like men.
They don't have to look like Pa, but
I like men.
Since my birthday is comin' due,
I wouldn't dream of tellin' you
But in case you go shoppin' through
The Five-and-Ten,
Tell the lady at the counter
I like men.

REFRAIN 2

Though my marmalade takes the prize,
I like men.

Ain't no flies on my mince pies, but
I like men.
I told Pa when I graduates,
Don't want a bike or roller skates,
Told him to line me up some dates
Till half past ten.
'N' we ain't gonna duck for apples—
I like men.

INTERLUDE

For Cousin Ebenezer,
A funny-lookin' geezer,
I'm powderin' my beezer
When he comes to call.
My neighbor, name of Hiram,
A goat would not desire 'im,
I'm tryin' to inspire 'im with my folderol.
Must be tetched in the haid,
'Cause I'd really rather drop daid.
I can't explain it clearly,
I reckon that it's merely
Mother Nature . . .

REFRAIN 3

Some gals say they like fancy clothes.
I like men.
Nylon hose and great big bows, but
I like men.
At the crack o' dawn I'll be found
Milkin' the cows or tillin' ground,
But at night when I ain't around
The old pigpen,
I like to do the things I like to do, 'n'
I like men.

REFRAIN 4

Sittin' there in the pitcher show,
I like men.
Any Joe is my hero, 'cause
I like men.
Some dark foreigner sighs "*Chérie,*
Come to the Casbah now with me!"
Boy, don't I wish that I could be
The hero-enne.
Me in seven veils,
He in turban and in tails.
Oh, I like men!

REFRAIN 5

When they're callin' a do-si-do,
I like men.
Heel and toe and still no beau, but
I like men.
I can't read you a music score,

Can't tell you what a fiddle's for,
But if they wanna dance, why, shore!
Just tell me when.
Big 'n' ugly,
Small 'n' snuggly,
Round 'n' fat 'n',
Dark 'n' Latin,
Strong 'n' thrilling,
Weak 'n' willing,
Tough 'n' tender,
I surrender—
I
Like
Men!!

I GOT OUT OF BED ON THE RIGHT SIDE

Published. Copyrighted June 4, 1953. Previously registered for copyright as an unpublished song June 19, 1952. Introduced and reprised by William Demarest, Esther Williams, Charlotte Greenwood, Barbara Whiting, Donna Corcoran.

REFRAIN 1

I got out of bed on the right side,
On the bright side,
On the light side—
I got out of bed on the right side,
And I'm having a wonderful day.

I sang a duet with the rooster;
I'm a booster
Of the rooster,
But he doesn't crow like he use-ter—
Couldn't handle my yodel-dee-aye!

Who cares if the sun ain't shinin'?
The eggs are beamin' sunny side up.
And as for my silver linin',
The coffee's steamin' money side up.

When the day rolls around to the night side,
If I still seem on the bright side,
I don't want to sound on the trite side,
But I figure it happened this way:
I got out of bed on the right side,
And I'm havin' a wonderful day.

INTERLUDE

Well, I'll be switched—
Looks like old Goosey Gander's

Singin' as she meanders by.
The hay ain't pitched;
That's 'cause the man we hired
Feels downright uninspired—why,
Who the heck's gonna try
With the day goin' by
Like molasses?
N'ya, just wanna quit while ya sit
Where the grass is high.

REFRAIN 2

[First 10 lines as in Refrain 1.]

Poor guy, now he looks plumb jealous,
Can't even raise a speck of a note—
And that's, as the proverbs tell us,
In many ways a heck of a note!

[Lines 15–20 as before.]

I climbed up the dizziest height side,
Cosmic flight side,
Out-of-sight side—
I got out of bed on the right side,
And I'm havin' a wonderful day.

AIN'T NATURE GRAND?

Published. Copyrighted May 20, 1953. Previously registered for copyright as an unpublished song June 19, 1952. Introduced by Fernando Lamas and Esther Williams, then by Barbara Whiting, then by Denise Darcel and Jack Carson, then by Charlotte Greenwood and William Demarest.

REFRAIN 1

They made a girl and gave her charms—
Ain't Nature grand?
Ain't Nature grand?
They made a boy and gave him arms—
How grand can Nature be?
They made a great big moon above—
Ain't Nature grand?
The things she planned!
And then they gave me you to love—
Ain't Nature grand to me!

REFRAIN 2

They made a man with dreamy eyes—
Ain't Nature grand?
Ain't Nature grand?

A fellow almost twice my size—
How grand can Nature be?
A man who's sweet and tender, too—
Ain't Nature grand?
The things she planned!
And then they gave me all of you—
Ain't Nature grand to me!

REFRAIN 3

In spite of lines and double chins,
Ain't Nature grand?
Ain't Nature grand?
Down yonder where the west begins,
How grand can Nature be?
Although our hair is turning gray,
We understand—
Ain't Nature grand?
We're growing younger every day—
Ain't Nature grand to me!

C'EST LA GUERRE

Registered for copyright as an unpublished song June 19, 1952. Introduced by Fernando Lamas and Denise Darcel, but deleted prior to release.

VERSE 1

Why doesn't Cupid capture us, love?
You're clearly captivating,
I'm fairly fascinating;
It does seem a shame
We find us so tame.
We should be making rapturous love
Within a bower dewy,
But romance is sometimes screwy—
All our hormones say "Phooey!"

REFRAIN 1

We share a few toddies,
The old busybodies
Are eager to start an affair—
C'est la guerre, dear, *c'est la guerre.*
You don't love me;
I don't care—
When I see you smiling,
Bewitching, beguiling,
I'm filled with the old *mal de mer.*
What a love match not to share—
Shall we tango? *C'est la guerre!*

VERSE 2

You really mustn't mind it, my love,
If I at times grow huffy
Or find you rather stuffy,
No *je ne sais quoi*,
No ooh la la la.
Let's take it as we find it, my love,
And we have found it boring—
When one of us is adoring,
He finds the other snoring.

REFRAIN 2

When I'm most amusing,
You'd rather be snoozing
At home in a big easy chair—
C'est la guerre, dear, *c'est la guerre*.
Something missing,
Nothing there—
It's fun when we're drinking,
But I keep on thinking
Of you in your long underwear
Ah, the folly—not Bergère.
How revolting! *C'est la guerre?*

REFRAIN 3

When I am most active
At being attractive,
You order a chocolate éclair
C'est la guerre, dear, *c'est la guerre*.
I the tortoise,
Thou the hare—
No couple, I'll warrant,
Could be so abhorrent
And still seem so devil-may-care.
Put 'er there, pal, put 'er there—
We're repulsive—*c'est la guerre*.

CODA

C'est la guerre,
C'est la vie,
C'est l'amour,
C'est fini—
And y'know what?
C'est la, so what:
We should care—
C'est la guerre.

IN MY WILDEST DREAMS

Published. Copyrighted May 20, 1953. Previously registered for copyright as an unpublished song August 11,

1952. Introduced by Fernando Lamas and reprised in "Tom and Jerry" cartoon by Octopus (dubbed by Lamas).

In my wildest dreams
I never thought we'd meet.
I never knew how sweet
You'd be,
Believe me.
In my wildest dreams,
If I combined them all,
I never dreamed you'd fall
For me.
How could I know
That I could love someone so,
Someone so meant for me alone?
Oh, no—
My poor old heart
Never was more beguiled,
Never in all my wildest dreams.

LIQUAPEP

Registered for copyright as an unpublished song September 22, 1952. Introduced by group on recording; reprised by Jack Carson and group on recording (sung only partially).

If you are desiring
A new vitamin
To make you get fat
Or make you get thin,
To put the old energy
Back in your step,
You'll get your kicker quicker
Drinkin' Liquapep.

You spell it L-I-Q-
U-A-P-E-P.
You gota high IQ,
You buy it and see—
I bet you it like you,
I bet you agree.
You spell it
L-I-Q-U-A-P-E-P!

You're weepy and you're creepy,
Feelin' sleepy in your teepee,
You can get a quicker pickup
Drinkin' Liquapep.

SONG OF INDIA

Music by Nikolai Rimsky-Korsakov from his opera *Sadko*. Adaptation and English lyrics by Mercer. Published. Copyrighted July 8, 1953. Previously registered for copyright as an unpublished song June 29, 1953.

And still the snowy Himalayas rise
In ancient majesty before our eyes,
Beyond the plains.
Above the pines,
While through the ever never-changing land,
As silently as any native band
That moves at night
The Ganges shines.

Then I hear the song
That only India can sing,
Softer than the plumage on a black raven's wing;
High upon a minaret I stand
And gaze across the desert sand
Upon an old enchanted land,
There's the maharajah's caravan,
Unfolding like a painted fan,
How small the little race of man!

See them all parade across the ages,
Armies, kings and slaves from hist'ry's pages,
Played on one of Nature's vastest stages.

The turbaned Sikhs and fakirs line the streets
While holy men in shadowed calm retreats
Pray thru the night
And watch the stars,
A lonely plane flies off to meet the dawn,
While down below the busy life goes on,
And women crowd the old bazaars.

All are in the song that only India can sing,
Softer than the plumage on a black raven's wing,
Tune the ageless moon and stars were strung by,
Timeless song that only could be sung by
India, the jewel of the East!

SIGHS

Music by Laurindo Almeida and Nestor Amaral. Registered for copyright as an unpublished song July 13, 1953.

There are sighs, sighs, sighs
That tell lies, lies, lies,
Sighs that are sweet invitations,
Sighs that were meant to tease,
Sighs that from all indications
Make beautiful memories.
If you're wise, wise, wise,
You'll just close your eyes,
Close them and wait for those whispers
Ev'ryone longs to know—
They're the sighs that say, "I love you so."

COLLEGE NOVEMBER

Music by Lew Quadling. Registered for copyright as an unpublished song October 8, 1953.

I'll always remember
This college November:
The leaves that fell like drifting flames,
The dances following the games,
The gay campus laughter,
The kiss that came after,
Will live with me my whole life through
From those bright college years with you.

AUTUMN TWILIGHT

Music by Joe Dubin. Registered for copyright as an unpublished song November 16, 1953.

Autumn twilight, falling slow,
With a hint of early snow:
I see a winter's moon
Beginning to rise;
I hear the lonely tune
Our willow tree softly sighs.

Autumn twilight, frosty sky,
With the swallows flying high;
Then I remember all the moments we knew,
The starry nights, the days that flew—
How I wish I could be
Spending this blue
Autumn twilight
Close to you.

AROUND THE BEND

Music by Mercer.

The sun is shining
Around the bend,
Your silver lining's
Around the bend,
Across the river,
Beyond the hill,
Ol' Injun giver
That they call Fate'll pay his bill.
You'll hear that bluebird
Sing out once more;
You'll see that rainbow
End at your door,
With love and laughter
From hearth to rafter,
Forever after,
Around the bend.

DIG YOU MOST

No music is known to survive.

Talk about the cutest,
But the absolutest
Ain't no substitutest.
I don't wanna wig ya,
But I dig ya the most!

Talk about the "wildest,"
But the angel-childest
Strictly middle-aisledest
Mamma, I dig ya the most!

Besides the fact you're packaged in the craziest
    design,
You've got all your marbles and your I.Q.'s
    superfine.

Yes, Ma'am!, I've made my mind up.
You're the bitter wind up
Gotta get you signed up
So you can start burning my toast—
'Cause I dig ya . . . *the* most!

DON'T RUN AWAY FROM THE RAIN

Music by Mercer.

Don't run away from the rain,
We get the flowers in May from the rain,
We get the green fields of clover
And, after it's over,
The rainbow that shines down the lane.
Don't be afraid of the clouds,
The morning glories were made of the clouds,
So get your daily bouquet from
The sweet new-mown hay from,
But don't run away from the rain.

FOREMOST DAIRY COMMERCIAL

Music by Victor Schertzinger (based on "Tangerine").
    Lyric missing.

I PRAY

Music by Mercer.

I pray
To make the most of ev'ry day.
I pray
That love will lead me on my way.
I pray
To do the thing that's always right,
Although
It may seem wrong within my sight.
I pray
That should this song of mine be heard,
For joy
And consolation in each word.
I pray
The Lord hears everything I say
And grants the prayer
I pray.

OHIO

Music by Mercer.

O-hi-o, O-hi-o,
Your name is like a song,
A song of spring
The red birds sing
The lazy summer long.

O-hi-o, O-hi-o,
How pleasant to the eye!
Your rolling plains
Are gold with grains;
Your mountains reach the sky.

Ohio's where the residents
Go right on raising presidents.

O-hi-o, O-hi-o,
No matter where I roam,
The beautiful O-hi-o
Will be calling me
To my O-hi-o home.

THE POT AND PAN PARADE

Music by Howard Jackson.
    Lyric missing.

Seven Brides for Seven Brothers: *Matt Mattox leaps in the competitive dance between the brothers and the townsfolk in the barn-raising scene.*

SEVEN BRIDES FOR SEVEN BROTHERS
and Other Songs of 1954

SEVEN BRIDES FOR SEVEN BROTHERS (1954)

Produced by Jack Cummings for Metro-Goldwyn-Mayer. Released July 1954. Copyright June 15, 1954. Directed by Stanley Donen. Screenplay by Albert Hackett, Frances Goodrich, and Dorothy Kingsley, based on the story "The Sobbin' Women" by Stephen Vincent Benet. Lyrics by Johnny Mercer. Music by Gene de Paul. Dances and musical numbers staged by Michael Kidd. Musical supervision by Saul Chaplin. Orchestrations by Alexander Courage, Conrad Salinger, and Leo Arnaud. Musical director: Adolph Deutsch. Featuring Jane Powell, Howard Keel, Jeff Richards, Russ Tamblyn, Tommy Rall, Howard Petrie, Marc Platt, Virginia Gibson, Ian Wolfe, Matt Mattox, Jacques d'Amboise, Julie Newmar (as Julie Newmeyer), Nancy Kilgas, Betty Carr, Ruta Lee (as Ruta Kilmonis), Norma Doggett, Earl Barton, Dante DiPaolo, Kelly Brown, Matt Moore, Dick Rich, Marjorie Wood, and Russell Simpson.

Loosely based on the Roman legend of the Rape of the Sabine women, the story of seven brothers in the old West, who decide they need wives and carry off girls from the town nearby.

BLESS YORE BEAUTIFUL HIDE

Published. Copyrighted July 7, 1954. Previously registered for copyright as an unpublished song September 4, 1953. Introduced and recorded by Howard Keel (MGM).

Bless yore beautiful hide,
Wherever you may be—
We ain't met yet,
But I'm a-willin' to bet
You're the gal for me.

Bless yore beautiful hide—
You're just as good as lost.
I don't know your name,
But I'm a-stakin' my claim,
'Less your eyes is crossed.

Oh, I'd swap my gun
'N' I'd swap my mule,
Though whoever took it

Would be one big fool,
Or pay your way through cookin' school
If'n you
Would say "I do!"

Bless yore beautiful hide—
Prepare to bend your knee
And take that vow,
'Cause I'm a-tellin' you now,
You're the gal for me.

Pretty and trim but not too slim,
Heavenly eyes and just the right size—
Gotta be right
To be the bride for me.
Bless yore beautiful hide,
Wherever you may be.

Pretty and trim and kinda slim,
Bossy and bold but not too old,
Simple and sweet
Or sassy as can be.
Bless her beautiful hide,
Yes, she's the gal for me!

WONDERFUL, WONDERFUL DAY

Published. Copyrighted May 25, 1954. Previously registered for copyright as an unpublished song May 6, 1954. Introduced and recorded by Jane Powell (MGM).

Ding dong, ding-a-ling dong—
Were the steeple bells ever quite as gay?
Wonderful, wonderful day!
Bluebirds in the bluebells
Sing me a song to send me along my way—
Wonderful, wonderful day.

Though I've got to own up
I'm as grown up as can be,
Seems I've gone and flown up
To a bright, merry, airy fairyland.
And so you'll forgive me
If I simply throw out my chest and say:
Beautiful, glorious,
Heavenly, marvelous,
Wonderful, wonderful day!

Big clouds floatin' lazy,
Like a daisy in the sky,
Big things to be doin' bye and bye,
Goin' slow 'n' growin' things,

Big love for my darlin'
As we share whatever may come our way—
Beautiful, glorious,
Heavenly, marvelous,
Wonderful, wonderful day!

Earlier version

Big sun shinin' brightly
In a great big beautiful sky of blue—
Wonderful, wonderful world!

Big moon peepin' nightly
And that big moon's peepin' for me and you—
Wonderful, wonderful world!

Big clouds floatin' lazy,
Like a daisy in the sky,
Big things to be doin' bye and bye,
Goin' slow 'n' growin' things,
Big love for my darlin'
And a great big beautiful life for two.
Beautiful, glorious,
Heavenly, marvelous,
Wonderful, wonderful world!

WHEN YOU'RE IN LOVE

Published. Copyrighted May 25, 1954. Previously registered for copyright as an unpublished song October 26, 1953. Introduced by Jane Powell; reprised by Howard Keel. Recorded by Powell and Keel (MGM).

When you're in love,
When you're in love,
There is no way on earth to hide it.
When you're in love,
Really in love,
You simply let your heart decide it.
With ev'ry sigh,
With ev'ry glance,
With ev'ry heartbeat you confide it;
You'll want the world to know it, too,
When you're in love
As I am in love with you.

Reprise

When you're in love,
When you're in love,
There is no way on earth to hide it.
When you're in love,
Really in love,
You simply let your heart decide it.

How can you tell
What's in its spell?
How can you tell until you've tried it?
Wait for that kiss you're certain of
And let your heart decide
When you're in love.

Earlier version

When you're in love,
When you're in love,
There's no way on earth to hide your love.
For when . . .
When you're in love
As I'm in love,
You simply let your heart decide whom you will
   love.
Unless you dwell
Beneath its spell
How can you tell until [you've] tried it too?
Hold me till starlight fades above
And let your heart decide when you're in love.

GOIN' CO'TIN'

Published. Copyrighted July 2, 1954. Previously registered for copyright as an unpublished song October 26, 1953. Introduced and recorded by Jane Powell with Jeff Richards, Russ Tamblyn, Tommy Rall, Marc Platt, Matt Mattox, and Jacques d'Amboise (some of whom were dubbed) (MGM).

REFRAIN 1

JANE
POWELL: Goin' co'tin', goin' co'tin',
             Oh, it sets your senses in a whirl,
             Goin' co'tin', goin' co'tin',
             Dudin' up to go and see a girl.
             Oh, it's fun to hunt and shoot a gun
             Or to catch a rabbit on the run,
             But you'll find it's twice as spo'tin'
             Goin' co'tin'.

INTERLUDE

Now, there's lots o' things you gotta know:
Be sure the parlor light is low;
You sidle up and squeeze her hand—
Let me tell you, fellas, that it's grand.
You hem and haw a little while;
She gives you kinda half a smile.
You cuddle up, she moves away;
Then the strategy comes into play.

REFRAIN 2

Goin' co'tin', goin' co'tin',
If you find it hard to break the ice,
Goin' co'tin', goin' co'tin',
Here's a little feminine advice:
Roll your eyes and heave a little sigh;
Grunt and groan like you're about to die.
That is what's known as emotin',
Goin' co'tin'.

REFRAIN 3

MARC
PLATT: How about sparkin'?
POWELL: And you're longin' for her heart to
             break . . .
RUSS
TAMBLYN: What about pettin'
JACQUES
D'AMBOISE: And sofa settin'?
JEFF
RICHARDS: Suppose she ups and slaps your
             face?
POWELL: Just remember, blessed are the
             meek—
             Don't forget to turn the other
             cheek.
             Pretty soon you'll both be larkin',
             Goin' sparkin'.

REFRAIN 4

POWELL: Goin' dancin',
BROTHERS: [*spoken*] Goin' dancin'!
D'AMBOISE: You mean men are learnin' how to
             dance?
POWELL: It'll help with your romancin'.
TAMBLYN: Keep your dancin'
TOMMY
RALL: And huntin'
PLATT &
D'AMBOISE: And shootin'
BROTHERS: And trappin',
ALL: 'Cause we're goin' co'tin'!

Alternative refrain

Goin' co'tin', goin' co'tin',
You're a-settin' on the old settee,
Goin' co'tin', goin' co'tin',
She's as shy and prim as she can be.
So you pucker up and take good aim
And you bag the sweetest kind o' game,
But that ain't no bag you're totin',
Goin' co'tin'.

Demo recording version

Goin' co'tin', goin' co'tin',
Wear a shirt and collar when you call.
Goin' co'tin', goin' co'tin',
Scrape your boots before you reach the hall.
Never chew tobacco anymore—
If you do, don't miss the cuspidor.
That's a custom worth the notin',
Goin' co'tin'.

Goin' dinin', goin' winin',
Always use the proper knife and fork.
Goin' dinin', goin' winin',
Never ask if you can sniff the cork.
If you want a second helping—wait,
Wait until the hostess fills your plate.
Half the battle is declinin',
Goin' dinin'.

Goin' callin', goin' callin',
Never spill your ashes on the floor.
Goin' callin', though you're all in,
Rise when anyone comes through the door.
Always try to stay upon your feet,
'Till they ask you, "Won't you have a seat?"
Just to sit there is appallin',
Goin' callin'.

Goin' sparkin', parlor's dark 'n'
How you're wishin' for a fond embrace!
Goin' pettin', sofa settin',
All at once she ups and slaps your face.
Just remember, blessed are the meek—
Don't forget to turn the other cheek.
Pretty soon you'll both be larkin',
Goin' sparkin'.

Goin' co'tin', goin' co'tin',
Huggin' and a-kissin' in the hall,
Goin' co'tin', goin' co'tin',
You kin promise anything at all.
But I wanna warn you now, my friend,
That you always wind up in the end
With a wife that you're supportin',
Goin' co'tin'.

Goin' co'tin', goin' co'tin',
Beats canoein' through the underbrush.
Goin' co'tin', goin' co'tin',
Bet it takes the rag right off the bush.
Never had a chance to try it yet,
But I'd like to make a little bet—
That it outshines mountain-goatin',
Goin' co'tin'.

Goin' co'tin', goin' co'tin',
When you find you live too far away,

Goin' co'tin', goin' co'tin',
Write a letter to her every day.
Write whatever comes into your head;
You'll be proud of everything you've said—
Till she reads back what you've wrotin',
Goin' co'tin'!

Fight reprise

Goin' fightin', goin' fightin',
This beats any kind o' game I ever played.
Gettin' rough 'n' fisticuffin'—
Mama never would approve of this charade.
Hittin' someone with your left hand ain't polite,
You should always wait 'n' slug him with your
   right,
It ain't nice, but it's excitin',
Goin' fightin'!!!

Goin' bruisin', goin' brawlin',
There's so much to think about, it's a disgrace
Bustin' noses, holy Moses!
You must always bust 'em in the proper place.
If they want to have a second helpin', great!
Let 'em have another in the upper plate.
Ain't it messy, ain't it horrid,
Splittin' foreheads.

Ain't it awful, with a jawful,
I mean full o' pearly teeth that once were yourn,
Ain't it dreadful, with a headful
That resemble little grains of early corn.
Don't you know it never was polite to spit,
More especially when your pivot tooth is it.
Ain't it uncouth and appallin',
Goin' brawlin'!

Goin' bustin', uppercuttin',
Like you said, it takes the rag right off the bush,
Barin' pack 'n' knuckle-crackin',
Even though they say it isn't nice to push.
You must always try to stay upon your feet
Till they say, "I think you'd better have a seat!"
Oh, it shore beats sippin' highballs,
Blackin' eyeballs!

Goin' boxin', fellin' oxen,
Watch 'em topple over like a bowlin' pin.
Finger bustin', it's disgustin',
Less you bust the other fellas with your chin.
Darn! I just remembered, blessed are the meek,
So I guess I better turn the other cheek.

Ribs a-poppin', necks a-snappin',
Oh, such lovely things kin happen,
Goin' scrappin'!

LONESOME POLECAT

Published. Copyrighted June 18, 1954. Previously registered for copyright as an unpublished song October 26, 1953. Introduced and recorded by Matt Mattox (dubbed by Bill Lee), Marc Platt, Jeff Richards, Russ Tamblyn, Tommy Rall, and Jacques d'Amboise (some of whom were dubbed) (MGM). Alternate title: "Lament."

REFRAIN 1

I'm a lonesome polecat,
Lonesome, sad, and blue,
'Cause I ain't got no feminine polecat
Vowin' to be true.
Ooh, ooh, ooh . . .
Cain't make no vows
To a herd o' cows.
Ooh, ooh, ooh . . .

REFRAIN 2

I'm a mean old hound dog
Bayin' at the moon,
'Cause I ain't got no lady friend hound dog
Here to hear my tune.
Ooh, ooh, ooh . . .
A man cain't sleep
When he sleeps with sheep.
Ooh, ooh, ooh . . .

REFRAIN 3

I'm a little ol' hoot owl
Hootin' in the trees,
'Cause I ain't got no little gal owl fowl
Here to shoot the breeze.
Ooh, ooh, ooh . . .
Cain't shoot no breeze
With a bunch o' trees.
Ooh, ooh, ooh . . .

SOBBIN' WOMEN

Published. Copyrighted May 25, 1954. Previously registered for copyright as an unpublished song October 26, 1953. Introduced and recorded by Howard Keel with Jeff Richards, Russ Tamblyn, Tommy Rall, Marc Platt, Matt Mattox, and Jacques d'Amboise (some of whom were dubbed) (MGM).

VERSE 1

HOWARD
KEEL: Y'heard about them sobbin' women
Who lived in the Roman days?
It seems that they all went swimmin'
While their men was off to graze.
Well, a Roman troop was ridin' by
And saw them in their me-oh-my,
So they took 'em all back home to dry,
Least, that's what Plutarch says.
Oh, yes!

REFRAIN 1

Them a-women was sobbin', sobbin',
   sobbin',
Fit to be tied,
Ev'ry muscle was throbbin', throbbin',
From that riotous ride.
Seems they cried and kissed and kissed
   and cried
All over that Roman countryside,
So don't forget that
When you're takin' a bride,
Sobbin' fit to be tied
From that riotous ride.

VERSE 2

They never did return their plunder;
The victor gets all the loot.
They carried 'em home, by thunder,
To rotundas small but cute.
And you never seen, so they tell me,
Such downright domesticity.
With a Roman baby on each knee,
Named Claudius and Brute.
BROTHERS: Oh, yes!

REFRAIN 2

BROTHERS: Them women was sobbin', sobbin',
   sobbin',
KEEL: Passin' them nights,
While the Romans was goin' out
   hobnobbin',
Startin' up fights.
They kept occupied by sewin' lots
Of little old togas for them tots
And sayin', "Someday
Womenfolks'll have rights!"
BROTHERS: Passin' all o' their nights—
KEEL: Just sewin'—
BROTHERS: While them Romans had fights.

VERSE 3

MATT
MATTOX: Now, when their menfolk went to fetch
   'em,

Them women would not be fetched;

TOMMY
RALL: It seems when the Romans ketch 'em
That their lady friends stay ketched.
KEEL: Right, now, let this be, because it's true,
A lesson to the likes of you,
Treat 'em rough—
Rough 'em up
Like them Romans do,
Or else they'll think you're tetched!
BROTHERS: Oh, yes!

REFRAIN 3

BROTHERS: Them a-women was sobbin', sobbin',
sobbin'
Buckets o' tears
KEEL: Mighty sad!
BROTHERS: On account o' old dobbin, dobbin
Really rattled their ears.
KEEL: And that ain't all.
Oh, they acted angry and annoyed,
RUSS
TAMBLYN: But secretly they was overjoyed—
KEEL: You might recall that
When corrallin' your steers.
BROTHERS: Oh, them pore little dears,
Oh, yes.

REFRAIN 4

Them-a women was all sobbin',
sobbin', sobbin',
Weepin' a ton,
Just remember what Robin, Robin,
Robin
Hood woulda done.
We'll be just like them there Merry Men
And make 'em all merry once again,
KEEL: And though they'll be a-sobbin' for a
while,
ALL: We're gonna make them sobbin'
women smile!
BROTHERS: Oh, yes!

Additional lyrics on Mercer's demo

MERCER: They tell me when the Romans found
'em,
All clad in their birthday suits,
They each wrapped a toga round 'em
Just before they shot the chutes.
Didn't do no bareback ridin' there,
But Plutarch is prepared to swear
That a number of their backs was bare
And some of them was beauts!
Them women was sobbin', sobbin',
sobbin',
While the men grinned,

On account of their modesty and
clothes
Was gone with the wind.
Oh, they weren't embarrassed, shy, or
scared
To find their secrets all were bared,
But let's just say that
They was kinda chagrined,
Clothes all gone with the wind
While them Romans all grinned.
Let me ask you boys—
Are you mice or men?
MEN: [spoken] Masculine!
MERCER: [sung] What do all men do when they
gets a yen?
MEN: [spoken] Rise and shine!
MERCER: [sung] Well, I want you men to go out
and fight,
Although they're sob, sob, sobbin'
With all their might.
Will you hold 'em close?
MEN: [spoken] Close!
MERCER: [sung] Till their ribs is sore?
MEN: [spoken] Sure!
MERCER: [sung] Do we ride tonight?
MEN: [spoken] Right!
MERCER: [sung] Well, then, all right!
Hoot and holler,
'Cause I want you all to go out and ride,
Although they'll be sobbin', sobbin',
sobbin'
Fit to be tied.

JUNE BRIDE

Published. Copyrighted September 23, 1954. Previously registered for copyright as an unpublished song September 16, 1953. Introduced and recorded by Virginia Gibson, Julie Newmar (as Julie Newmeyer; dubbed by Betty Allen), Nancy Kilgas (possibly dubbed by Marie Vernon), Betty Carr (dubbed by Norma Zimmer), Ruta Lee (as Ruta Kilmonis; dubbed by Betty Noyes), Norma Doggett (dubbed by Barbara Ames), and Jane Powell (MGM).

Oh, they say when you marry in June,
You're a bride all your life;
And the bridegroom who marries in June
Gets a sweetheart for a wife.
Winter weddings can be gay,
Like a Christmas holiday,
But the June bride hears the song
Of a spring that lasts all summer long.
By the light of the silvery moon

Home you ride, side by side,
With the echo of Mendelssohn's tune
In your hearts as you ride.
For they say when you marry in June,
You will always be a bride.
The day a maiden marries
Is the day she carries
Through the years.
The church is full of flowers,
Bridal showers are passé.
The groom's waiting at the altar;
Here comes the bride—
They're each promising to love and obey.
Best man is celebrating;
Every bridesmaid's waiting
Just to see
Which one of them will catch
The wedding bouquet.
In November the snow starts to fly,
Piling up ankle-high;
In December it's up to your knees—
Still the bride's the bride-to-be.
January, higher still—
To the parlor windowsill.
February finds a drift
And the storm that seems never to lift.
March comes in like a lion—
What else?
Still the snow never melts.
April showers will come, so they say—
But they don't, and it's May.
You're about to forget the whole thing—
All at once
One day it's spring!

SPRING, SPRING, SPRING!

Published. Copyrighted July 7, 1954. Previously registered for copyright as an unpublished song October 26, 1953. Introduced and recorded by Matt Mattox, Jeff Richards, Julie Newmar (as Julie Newmeyer), Tommy Rall, Betty Carr, Jacques d'Amboise, Russ Tamblyn, Ruta Lee (as Ruta Kilmonis), Marc Platt, Norma Doggett, Virginia Gibson, and Nancy Kilgas (some of whom were dubbed) (MGM).

Like several other songs in the film, this one ran into censorship problems. On July 29, 1953, one Geo. G. Schneider in the MGM office wrote Johnny Mercer, Johnny Green, and Saul Chaplin:

We have been advised by the censor's office that the lyrics of the above song seem acceptable under the requirements of the Production Code with the following exceptions:

The lines "Nonetheless in the cactus/They indulge in the practice" are unacceptable, for obvious reasons.

The line "Is making his wagon fly" seems extremely questionable and should be changed.

The same applies to the line: " 'Cause Mrs. Katydid/Once did what her matey did."

When you have alternate lines, I will gladly submit them.

Subsequently, the censor's office decided to give their permission for all but the "cactus" couplet.

REFRAIN 1

MATT
MATTOX: Oh, the barnyard is busy,
In a regular tizzy,
And the obvious reason
Is because of the season.
Ma Nature's lyrical
With her yearly miracle—
Spring, spring, spring!

JEFF
RICHARDS: All the henfolk are hatchin'
While their menfolk are scratchin'
To insure the survival
Of each brand-new arrival.

JULIE
NEWMAR: Each nest is twittering,
They're all baby-sitting—
Spring, spring, spring!

TOMMY
RALL: It's a beehive of budding son-and-
daughter life—
Ev'ry family has plans in view.
Even down in the brook the
underwater life
Is forever blowing bubbles, too.

VIRGINIA
GIBSON: Ev'ry field wears a bonnet
With some spring daisies on it;
Even birds of a feather
Show their clothes off together.

JACQUES
D'AMBOISE: Sun's gettin' shinery
To spotlight the finery,
GIBSON: Spring, spring, spring!
RUSS
TAMBLYN: From his aerie, the eagle with his
eagle eye
Gazes down across his eagle beak
And, affixin' his lady with a legal eye,
Screams, "Suppose we set the date
this week?"
ALL: Yessirree, spring discloses
That it's all one supposes—
It's a real bed of roses.

Wagging tails, rubbin' noses,
Each day is Mother's Day,
The next is some other's day,
When love is king.

[*Song breaks off into dialogue.*]

Additional lyrics

REFRAIN 2

In his hole, though the gopher
Seems a bit of a loafer,
The industrious beaver
Puts it down to spring fever,
While there's no antelope
Who feels that he can't elope—
Spring, spring, spring!

Slow but surely the turtle,
Who's enormously fertile,
Lays her eggs by the dozens—
Maybe some are her cousins.
Even the catamount
Is nonplussed by that amount—
Spring, spring, spring!

Even out in Australia the kangaroos
Lay off butterfat and all French fries.
If their offspring are large, it might be dangerous—
They've just gotta keep 'em pocket-size.

Even though to each rabbit
Spring is more like a habit,
Nonetheless in the cactus
They indulge in the practice.*
Why, each day is Mother's Day,
The next day some other's day—
Spring, spring, spring!

REFRAIN 3

To itself each amoeba
Softly croons, *"Ach, du lieber,"*
While the proud little termite
Feels as large as a worm might.
Old Papa dragonfly
Is making his wagon fly—
Spring, spring, spring!

Ev'ry bug's snuggled snuggy
In its own baby buggy,
And in spite of policing
Seems the tribe is increasing,
'Cause Missus Katydid

---

* *Alternate for these 2 lines:*
Natural proclivity
They dig relativity

Once did what her matey did,
It's spring, spring, spring!

Daddy Long Legs is stretching out his creaking
joints,
And how busy can a bumble be?
Flitting hither and thither, she keeps seeking joints
With a spare room and a nursery.

Each cocoon has a tenant,
So they've hung out a pennant
"Don't disturb, please keep waiting.
We are evacuating
This home's my mama's, I'll
Soon have my own domicile."
Spring, spring, spring!

CODA

It's as old as forever,
But it's more fun than ever—
Spring, spring, spring!

REFRAIN 4

See the gay little finches
In connubial clinches,
As each fleet little swallow
Finds a swallow to follow.
Somehow the story old
Sounds best when orioled—
Spring, spring, spring!

Ev'ry male little mallard
Honks a heart-rending ballad
From the stream where he sloshes
In his web-foot galoshes.
He gurgles brimmingly,
"We'll get along swimmingly"—
Spring, spring, spring!

Little skylarks are larking,
See them all double-parking,
Cuddled up, playin' possum
There, behind ev'ry blossom.
Even the bobolink
Is merrily wobbelink—
Just hear them sing!
Shouldn't doubt such a chorus
Raised an old brontosaurus—
It's spring, spring, spring!

REFRAIN 5

In the treetops the squirrels
Whistle, "Gee, pipe the girruls,"
While at home, Mama Otter
Keeps an eye on her dotter:
"Dear, I'm a worrier,

Don't fall for some furrier"—
Spring, spring, spring!

Guinea pigs with no trouble
Make their families double,
And the minks go on minking
Seemingly without thinking.
Skunks do it breezily
And Mom! goes the weasely
Easily in spring.

Hear them sigh, those unhappy hippopotami—
What a weighty problem marks their joy!—
"From my top to my bottom my anatomy
Makes it hard to tell a girl from a boy."

Yessirree, spring discloses
That it's all one supposes—
Wagging tails, rubbin' noses,
But it's no bed of roses.
And if for the stork you pine,
Consider the porcupine,
Who longs to cling;
Keepin' comp'ny is tricky—
It can get pretty sticky
In the spring, spring, spring!

Oh, the trees will be buddin'
Buddin' all of a sudden,
And the limbs will be bloomin'
Full o' limbs that are human—
No petals clingin' there
Come spring, spring, spring!

In the soft balmy weather,
We'll go plantin' together,
But we won't plant potatoes
And we won't plant tomatoes—
No great amount of peas,
Jus' long rows o' Pontipees
Come spring, spring, spring!

When the meadows are sprinkled full o' crocuses,
Oh, how beautiful it all will seem,
Just a settin' and watchin' all the carcasses
Come a-floatin' down the old mill stream!

There'll be no time fer jawin'
And we won't call the law in
Wastin' time argufyin'
With a big jury tryin'!
No more palaverin',
Just lots of cadaverin'—
A sort o' community swing!
We'll be all harmonizing
At the big funeralizin'
In spring, spring, spring!

YOU TAKE AFTER YOUR MOTHER

Lyric for refrain dated August 26, 1953. Lyric for verse dated September 3, 1953. Not used in film.

VERSE

Reckon it's time we got to know
Somethin' about each other.
Reckon that you can help me out
In explaining things to your mother.
Maybe I'm clumsy, hotheaded too,
And lots o' times kinda dumb;
But it's easy to see
You're as cute as can be,
And instead of gettin' those traits from me,
You're as tender and gentle,
As pretty as she—
You're as beautiful as they come . . .

REFRAIN

You take after your mother,
I'm glad to say,
In many more ways than one.
So bright and gay,
Like wildflowers in the sun.
With that innocent look in your eyes,
Like you just had a great big surprise.
With that sly half a smile, half a tease,
You could charm the birds off the trees.
Someday we'll get you a brother
Who looks like me—
His mother might like that too,
But you take after your mother,
And wait and see,
The fellows'll all take after you!

QUEEN OF THE MAY

Registered for copyright as an unpublished song October 26, 1953. Not used in film.

Have a blossom from my bouquet!
I am monarch of all I survey!
Someone kissed me today,
And I am Queen of the May!
Footman, harness my coach and four;
Drive me up to the palace front door!
Have the trumpeters play—

"Make way for the Queen of the May!"
Have the bells rung in the towers;
Have the ballroom decked with flowers;
Have the Champagne poured in showers;
And we'll have a royal soirée!
As we roll along through the countryside,
Tell the peasants to please step aside,
And respectfully say:
"Hip hooray for the handsome young King of
    Bombay
And Her Highness the Queen of the May!"

SOME PLACE OF MY OWN

Registered for copyright as an unpublished song September 4, 1953. Not used in film.

REFRAIN

Dreams are funny things;
I dream mine alone,
And what I dream of
Is some place of my own.
Big place behind an ivy wall,
Just some place where friends can come to call,
That's all:
A tiny two-by-four near an apple grove,
A hearth where kittens purr, kettle on the
    stove,
And someone my heart has always known
Who will share that some place of my own.

VERSE

Evenings will find me sewing things,
You'll really point with pride,
Mornings you'll see me growing things outside.
Bees buzzin' round the flower beds,
Dog barking at the gate,
Kids coming home from Sunday school—
I can't wait
To have that place of my own.

DRAT 'EM

Not used in film.
    Lyric missing.

SHOTGUN WEDDING

Not used in film.
    Lyric missing.

STAR SONGS

Lyric dated August 26, 1953. Not used in film.

Star songs
Only come to lovers,
Star songs,
Softer than a sigh.
When your lips are clinging
And hearts are singing,
You'll hear them ringing
Star songs,
Softly,
From the blue horizon;
Star songs
Echo through the sky.
On the night you fall head over heels in love,
You'll hear star songs
The same as I.

THERE'LL COME A DAY

Lyric dated September 3, 1953. Not used in film.

There'll come a day,
Not so far away,
I'll say things that I could never say.
There'll come a night
When you'll understand
Time and love go hand in hand.
Wait and see,
When the fields are filled with bloom
And that tree
Makes this yard a shady room,
We'll be older,
But we will still be young,
Our best song still unsung.
Out of the years and the sun and rain,
Love will ripen like the golden grain,
And sure as the harvest is on its way,
Believe me,
There'll come a day.

BLOSSOM

Music and lyrics by Johnny Mercer, Duke Ellington, and Billy Strayhorn. Registered for copyright as an unpublished song February 5, 1954.

VERSE 1

Night
And white hibiscus glowing faintly in the dark
Of the moon,
That eerie light
When all the stars above
Are seeking the ghost of a tune—
From the darkness you came,
And I gave you a name,
Like a faraway flame in the night,
This was meant to be so,
My Blossom!

REFRAIN

Blossom,
You're the flower that blossoms in my heart.
Blossom,
You're as shy and as gossamer as moon glow.
My love for you
Grows and grows
Like a pale midnight rose.

Blossom,
Is it true you were once a falling star?
Falling
In my garden and watered by starlight?
Sent to me from above,
My blossom that grew to love.

VERSE 2

[Repeat lines 1–6 from Verse 1.]

When I hear it, I know
That a long time ago
This was meant to be so,
My Blossom.

HOPING

Music by Al Hansen. Registered for copyright as an unpublished song February 24, 1954.

VERSE

Walking with my mem'ries,
Who else can I trust?
Talking with my mem'ries
Is a lover must.

REFRAIN

Just hoping,
I'm always hoping
That someday, somewhere, somehow
You'll come back to me.
I don't know who it was,
But how untrue it was
When they said hearts are happy
When they're fancy free.
Gee, wishing,
I've heard by wishing
That you can make most anything
At all come true.
Perhaps it's so.
I wouldn't know,
But anything is worth a try,
And so I'm hoping
That you're hoping, too.

QUIÉREME Y VERÁS

Music by José Antonio Mendez. Registered for copyright as an unpublished song May 11, 1954.

"Quiéreme y verás."
I only heard her murmur, "Quiéreme y verás,"
Then something happened to my heart—
I felt it start
Pounding like the sea.
"Quiéreme y verás,"
I held her close and answered, "Quiéreme y verás,"
Not even knowing where it led
Or that I'd said,
"Love me and you'll see."
I'll never understand
How without knowing,
I could make the right replies.
When I held her hand
I spoke her language,
Just as she read my eyes.
Needless to remark,
I never will forget that whisper in the dark.
It brought another world to me,
Because, you see,
I loved her and I saw.
Or, as she would say, "Quiéreme y verás."

MIDNIGHT SUN

Music by Lionel Hampton and Sonny Burke. Published. Copyrighted May 24, 1954.

Mercer heard Lionel Hampton's instrumental "Midnight Sun" on a car radio in 1954:

So the title was already there. And the first thing I thought of . . . was "aurora borealis." So I heard it in the music. It fit the music. I thought, "What rhymes with 'aurora borealis'?" And I thought of "chalice" and "alabaster palace" and that kind of started the song . . . So then I called up to find out who published it and if they had a lyric, and would they be interested if they didn't? And they didn't and they were.

Your lips were like a red and ruby chalice,
Warmer than the summer night;
The clouds were like an alabaster palace
Rising to a snowy height;
Each star its own aurora borealis—
Suddenly you held me tight,
I could see the midnight sun.

I can't explain the silver rain that found me,
Or was that a moonlit veil?
The music of the universe around me,
Or was that a nightingale?
And then your arms miraculously found me—
Suddenly the sky turned pale,
I could see the midnight sun.

Was there such a night?
It's a thrill
I still don't quite believe.
But after you were gone,
There was still
Some stardust on my sleeve.

The flame of it may dwindle to an ember
And the stars forget to shine,
And we may see the meadow in December,
Icy white and crystalline,
But oh, my darling, always I'll remember
When your lips were close to mine
And I saw the midnight sun.

MUSICAL CHAIRS

Music by Mercer. Registered for copyright as an unpublished song October 1, 1954.

REFRAIN

Time to brighten, to brighten the corner,
Time to lighten, to lighten your cares,
Time to be like a Little Jack Horner.
Grab a chair anywhere,
Place 'em in a circle there.
Anybody can play who'll pitch in—
It's a cinch to eliminate cares.
Send the grown-ups to sit in the kitchen,
Gonna play Musical Chairs!

Round and round the circle you amble,
Singin' all the while as you go.
At a signal ev'ryone scramble,
Till all are seated,
But whaddaya know!
There is always a person too many—
Send the standee to sit with the squares.
Lose a chair till you haven't got any.
Whatcha say? Wanna play?
It was fun in Granny's day.
Man, you oughta dig Musical Chairs!

ANTONIA

Music by Howard Jackson. Published. Copyrighted October 25, 1954.

Antonia, does your heart remember
When we kissed beneath the olive trees?
Antonia, through this bleak December
Does it warm you with its memories?
When the wind is in the wheat field singing
Or some evening when the big stars shine,
I will hear the bells of San' Lucia ringing,
Antonia, Antonia mine.

JE T'AIME COMMERCIAL

Music by Mercer.
Lyric missing.

APACHE (1954)

Produced by Harold Hecht for Hecht-Lancaster, released by United Artists. Released July 1954. Copyright June 30, 1954. Directed by Robert Aldrich. Screenplay by James Webb, from the novel *Broncho Apache* by Paul I. Wellman. Lyrics by Johnny Mercer. Music by David Raksin. Orchestrations by Maurice De Packh and Ruby Raksin. Musical director: David Raksin. Starring Burt Lancaster and Jean Peters, with John McIntire, Charles Bronson (as Charles Buchinsky), John Dehner, Paul Guilfoyle, Ian MacDonald, Walter Sande, Morris Ankrum, and Monte Blue.

Geronimo has surrendered, but one Apache leader continues the fight.

LOVE SONG

Music by David Raksin. Copyright information missing. Not sung in film. Alternate title: "Apache Love Song."

The waterfall at eventide,
The echo calling down the mountainside—
So began the soft melody of our love song.
The sighing boughs against the sky,
The night bird's singing to his mate nearby—
They supplied the sweet harmony of our love
    song.
Night gave us the setting,
The crescent moon;
Now there's no forgetting
Our first tune.
And add to this two beating hearts
To swell the chorus as the music starts—
We've an evergreen memory of our love song.

BY THE WAY

Music by Vernon Duke.

By the way,
Did I happen to tell you I love you?
Nat'rally, who wouldn't love you?

One day in early spring
You taught my heart to sing.
By the way, just in passing, did anyone mention
That I have ev'ry intention
Of staying close to you
Until this dream comes true?

By the way,
If you've any castles to build in the air,
Any moments to spare,
For somebody to share,
I'll be there.
May I say that my life
Is becoming a love song?
So, if your heart needs a love song,
A lyrical bouquet,
I'll send it
By the way of love.

YOU TOOK THE WORDS RIGHT OUT OF MY HEART

Music by Mercer.

I don't know what I thought you'd say,
But when you said "I love you,"
You took the words right out of my heart.
I spent a lifetime ev'ry day,
A lifetime dreaming of you;
You took my dreams and gave them a start.
I longed so long to tell you so;
I had it all rehearsed.
You can't imagine what a glow I felt
To hear you say it first.
You read my eyes,
You read my lips,
And then you said "I love you."
Don't tell me you were playing a part—
You took the words right out of my heart.

Daddy Long Legs: *Fred Astaire and Leslie Caron in the
"Guardian Angel" ballet*

DADDY LONG LEGS
and Other Songs of 1955

DADDY LONG LEGS (1955)

Produced by Samuel G. Engel for Twentieth Century–Fox. World premiere May 4, 1955. Copyright May 5, 1955. Directed by Jean Negulesco. Screenplay by Phoebe and Henry Ephron, from the novel *Daddy Long Legs* by Jean Webster. Lyrics and music by Johnny Mercer. Dances staged by Fred Astaire and David Robel. Ballets by Roland Petit. Ballet music by Alex North. Orchestrations by Edward B. Powell, Skip Martin, Earle Hagen, Bernard Mayers, and Billy May. Music supervised and conducted by Alfred Newman. Starring Fred Astaire and Leslie Caron, featuring Terry Moore and Thelma Ritter, with Fred Clark, Charlotte Austin, Larry Keating, Kathryn Givney, Kelly Brown, and Ray Anthony and His Orchestra with the Skyliners.

An orphan grows up and falls in love with her unseen benefactor.

In addition to the songs Mercer wrote specially for the film, "Dream" (1944) is used intermittently as background music, with off-screen chorus, and at one point Astaire and Caron dance to it.

C-A-T SPELLS CAT

Published. Copyrighted March 1, 1955. Previously registered for copyright as an unpublished song November 8, 1954. Introduced by Leslie Caron and children.

C-A-T spells "cat."
R-A-T spells "rat."
Although the cat can catch the rat,
The rat can't catch the cat.

H-E-R spells "her."
F-U-R spells "fur."
Just pat her fur and listen to her
P-U-R-R, purr.

Mes petits chargés,
Just read after me.
To learn—how you say?—to *comprendre le speech
   anglais,*
We learn our ABC.

So . . . D-A-Y spells "day."
S-A-Y spells "say."
Now let me see if you can say
Your lesson for today.

D-O-G spells "dog."
L-O-G spells "log."
The dog sits on the log
To catch the F-R-O-G "frog."

R-A-M spells "ram."
L-A-M-B spells "lamb."
The big sheep is the R-A-M,
The little sheep the lamb.

Do you see the cow?
She is eating hay.
She is eating hay to give us milk—
M-I-L-K.

That was very good—
Now run out and play.
Go P-L-A-Y, play,
You've learned your lesson for today!

Additional lyrics*

I L-O-V-E
Y-O-U, *mais oui.*
L-O-V-E means "I love you,"
And now "Good night—*bonne nuit.*"

See the movie star
In the Jaguar.
The Jaguar is not a cat—
It is a foreign car.

See the Turhan Bey.
What is that you say?
You always spend your summers
On the beach at Turhan Bey.

S-P-A-M, "Spam."
T-U-M-S, "Tums."
Spam is what you eat
Before the T-U-M-S comes.

If you learn a lot,
I will tell you what:
If you study very good,
You go to Hollywood.

M-U-S-T, "must."
B-U-S-T, "bust."
You must wear a Maidenform
To have a great big bust.

B-R-A spells "Bra."
F-L-A spells "Fla."
When swimming at Miami, Fla.,
You have to wear a bra.

* *Clearly not intended for the film!*

DADDY LONG LEGS

Published. Copyrighted March 4, 1955. Previously registered for copyright as an unpublished song November 8, 1954. Introduced by off-screen girls' chorus.

Daddy Long Legs,
Daddy Long Legs,
Pretty please, make one little dream come true.
If Cinderella's godmama
Could make a coach and four,
I'm sure a real live godpapa
Could do a whole lot more.
Make me pretty, make me witty,
Make me just as nice as a girl can be.
Don't know how I'll find a way,
But I'll pay you back someday—*
Daddy Long Legs,
Wait and see!

Additional lines

All my love is right here
In this letter to dear
Daddy Long Legs . . .
Then I turn out the light
And wish
Dear Daddy Long Legs
Goodnight!

WELCOME, EGGHEAD

Published. Copyrighted March 10, 1955. Introduced by female ensemble. Alternate title: "The Freshman Song."

Welcome, egghead!
Wipe that smile off your face.
Never speak until you're spoken to.
You're in college
And Mama isn't here,
So she can't change your panties for you.
You're a birdbrain,
You're a mis'rable beast,
And the least you can be is unspoiled.
Welcome, egghead!
You're an egghead!
But you came, I presume,

* *Alternate lines:*
    If you help me just this once,
    I'll be good for months and months—

With a left-handed broom freshly oiled?
Welcome, egghead—
What an egghead!
You're an egghead,
But you're soon gonna be hard-boiled!

INTERLUDE

Blow your nose!
Dry your ears!
And get up 'n' salute when a senior appears!
Get your feet
Off the bed!
Put a hat on to cover the point in your head!
Tummy in,
Sweater out!
And eliminate that supercilious pout!
We think it most inopportune
To go to pot so soon!

REFRAIN 2

Welcome, egghead!
You just ain't upper set,
So we'll thank you to get off your tail!
You're a cell mate,
Like we told you before,
And we run a respectable jail!
Good behavior
And the proper concern
For your elders will help make the grade.
You're a pigeon
In a world full o' wolves,
And we don't want to see you waylaid.
Welcome, egghead!
You're an egghead,
But you're soon gonna be frappé'd!

SOMETHING'S GOTTA GIVE

Published. Copyrighted February 21, 1955. Previously registered for copyright as an unpublished song November 8, 1954. Introduced by Fred Astaire and danced by Astaire and Leslie Caron. Recorded by Fred Astaire (Victor) and The Skyliners with Ray Anthony and His Orchestra (Capitol). Other recordings by the McGuire Sisters (Coral) and Sammy Davis Jr. (Decca).

Fred Astaire and his producers had a problem. His leading ladies were increasingly younger than he. He was forty-nine when he starred opposite Judy Garland (twenty-six) in *Easter Parade* (1948); then there were *Royal Wedding* (1951) with Jane Powell (twenty-six) and *The Band Wagon* (1953) with Cyd Charisse (thirty-two). He was now fifty-five and Leslie Caron only twenty-two.

Mercer solved it by characterizing the romantic tension between the two. He had been puzzling over it for days; then, he recalled, "I don't know what woke me up but I woke up with an idea for a song. I went to the piano in the front room . . . and quietly picked it out with one finger. [The phrase] was a popular expression everybody used. And I wrote it down in the little hieroglyphics, which is my way of writing music . . . a kind of sketch of it. Like the bones but not the full structure . . . And then finished it the next day."

He played it for Astaire, who said, "Oh, that's wonderful!" "And I said, 'Why?' And he said, 'Well, don't you see? I'm forty or fifty years old and I'm in love with a girl who's about 18 or 20 . . . It makes the whole thing believable.' "

The song was nominated for an Academy Award as Best Song but lost to Sammy Fain and Paul Francis Webster's "Love Is a Many-Splendored Thing."

When an irresistible force
Such as you,
Meets an old immovable object
Like me,
You can bet as sure as you live,
Something's gotta give,
Something's gotta give,
Something's gotta give.

When an irrepressible smile
Such as yours
Warms an old implacable heart
Such as mine,
Don't say no, because I insist—
Somewhere,
Somehow,
Someone's gonna be kissed.

So *en garde*,
Who knows what the Fates have in store,
From their vast mysterious sky?
I'll try hard
Ignoring those lips I adore,
But how long can anyone try?

Fight, fight, fight, fight, fight it with all of our
    might,
Chances are some heavenly star-spangled night,
We'll find out as sure as we live,
Something's gotta give,
Something's gotta give,
Something's gotta give.

Alternate release

So *en garde*,
I'm warnin' you, sweet angel child,
Use your most mysterious charms.

I'll try hard
To capture those lips undefiled,
Try till you surrender your arms.

THE HISTORY OF THE BEAT

Introduced by Fred Astaire. On a demo recording Mercer introduces the number as "the opening song and patter for Twinkletoes Astaire" and calls it "That'll Get It (When It's Almost Gone)."

Because I hold you in affection and great esteem,
I shall now begin
To instruct you in
What the jazz élite
Call the modern beat,
A complete
Anthropology
(Well, all reet!)
And how I made the team . . .

You said it,
And yet it
Keeps wanting to run,
So let it,
But man, that'll get it
When it's almost gone.
You gotta feel it in your soul, soul, soul,
That roll, roll, roll
Beyond control.
'Cause when you feel it in your soul, soul, soul,
That rhythm's now at large,
It's really takin' charge.

Duet it,
Octet it,
Mazurka or minuet it,
I don't want to quit
Once it starts comin' on.
You've gotta feel it in your toes, toes, toes,
The way it is,
The way it flows.
Let that momentum take you
Where it goes.
Don't fuss it up or fret it,
Relax and you won't regret it.
You've got it and that'll get it
When it's almost gone.

You might recall, if mem'ry serves,
That we've come quite a way
Since Mama did the Charleston
And the old man said "Hey! Hey!,"

241

When things were "hotsy totsy"
And our feet were "happy feet"
And scholars professorial
Began to dig the beat.
They dug back in the archives
To when ragtime had its fling,
Through Sugarfoot and Dixieland,
When people shook that thing.
They tried to trace its progress
From the cotton fields away;
They analyzed it,
Categorized it
To the present day.
They used to holler "Ah, you dog!"
Then answer "Solid, Jack!"
Them cats are really comin' on—
They're so far gone, they're back!
The jitterbugs would cut a rug,
The joint would jump with jive,
They'd hit a lick
And blow a riff
When they were "takin' five."
You'd hear them holler "Well, all right!
We're really in the groove!"
It proved so many movements
There was nothing to improve.
They all came on like busted gang,
Until they blew their top;
They flipped their wig
From swing to bounce
And then bounced into bop.
And now it's [word(s) missing]
And "Crazy, man, crazy!"
And scholars professorial can "dig" in any key.
The beat is beaten but unbowed,
Though they still go, go, go.
Since my opinion wasn't asked,
I thought you'd like to know.

You said it,
And yet it
Keeps takin' off like a jet—it
Appears to be something you can't count upon.
But when you feel it in your toes, toes, toes,
The way it is.
The way it flows,
When that momentum takes you
Where it goes,
Don't la-di-da or lorgnette it,
Count Basie and Charles Barnett it,
I'm tellin' you
That'll get it
When it's almost gone.

SLUEFOOT

Published. Copyrighted February 14, 1955. Previously registered for copyright as an unpublished song November 8, 1954. Introduced by Marcie Miller and The Skyliners with Ray Anthony's Band. Danced by Fred Astaire, Leslie Caron, and dancers. Recorded by Fred Astaire (Victor) and The Skyliners with Ray Anthony and His Orchestra (Capitol).

SINGERS: Now hear this,
Now hear this,
Everybody,
Everybody,
Everybody,
Get ready for Sluefoot—
Go!

You want a dance that's easy to do,
Then dig the one I'm hippin' you to.
I'm gonna teach you to fall in
On what they're callin'
The Sluefoot!

You make your right foot point to the
north,
You make your left foot point to the south,
And then you stroll sort of westerly,
Slowly and siestally—
Sluefoot!

Don't be an oddball
And don't be a fig,
Try,
Why be shy?
After all, it's even better
If your feet's too big.

You put the old posterior out,
Then you manipulate it about.*
It is the most lackadaisiest,
I mean the craziest—
Sluefoot!

You gotta rock like a rocking chair.
The step is clocklike but slightly square.
You count to one, two, three, four,
Then you holler
"Sluefoot!"

You put your toe out,
You drag it back.
You really go out,

---

* Alternate lines:
    And if you learn to dance it just right,
    It shouldn't take but half of the night.

You ball the jack.
Do what you done, done, done before,
Then you holler
"Sluefoot!"

TEXAS ROMP AND SQUARE DANCE

Introduced by off-screen chorus and danced by Fred Astaire. Part of the "Day Dream" sequence.

BASSES: Bum! Bum! Bum! Bum!
MEN: Down in Texas where the stars are
        bright—
BASSES: Bum! Bum! Bum! Bum!
YODELER: Odle lay-ee hoo!
MEN: Down in Texas where they treat you
        right—
BASSES: Bum! Bum! Bum! Bum!
YODEL: Odle lay-ee hoo!
MEN: Everybody sings this little song.
BASSES: Bum! Bum! Bum!
MEN &
GIRLS: Daddy, Daddy, why's yo' legs so long?
    Love your figure 'cause it's so corn fed.
    [hand claps]
    Love each hair upon yore punkin head.
    [hand claps]
    Though you're richer than the
        Vanderbilts.
    [hand claps]
    Daddy, Daddy, where'd you get them
        stilts?

Square dance

Chicken in the bread pan pickin' up dough,
Pick out your hen an' pick out your rooster.
Number-one prize is a block o' stocks.
Second prize is Fort Knox.
Let me introduce that dancin' fool,
Long Leg Tex with the big fat wallet.
Wait'll he starts to walk the dog,
He'll bug out yo' eyes like a stomped-on frog!

Alouette left and alouette right,
Parley-vous and a Frère Jacques.
Big foot up an' the little foot down,
Both feet up, make a hol' in the groun'.
Hands up high and the gents go under,
Grab your gal and swing 'er like thunder.
Kiss her once and jump for joy.
Kiss her twice and promenade all!

DANCING THROUGH LIFE

Published. Copyrighted March 3, 1955. Previously registered for copyright as an unpublished song November 8, 1954. Not used in film.

I could go dancing through life with you,
On and on and on.
Watching the rainbow of years unfold,
Letting the laughter and the tears untold.
I wouldn't care what the piper played
On his merry old fife—
Gladly I'll pay for his sweet serenade
As we go dancing through life.

I NEVER KNEW

Published. Copyrighted May 1, 1956. Written for Fred Astaire but not used in film.

I never knew
That there were girls like you;
I never knew
They made them half as true—
So pretty, too,
So unassuming and so bright.
I've seen a few
On television screens
And one or two
In movie magazines,
But they weren't you.
And so the books I read were right,
So right to say,
"Keep looking everywhere
And wait that extra day
And pray that extra prayer."
I never knew
How much a heart could glow;
I never knew
How much I didn't know.
I only do
Because you came to show me how.
I never knew—
But I know now.

HARE PIECE

Not used in film.
    Lyric missing.

MINOR NURSERY

Not used in film.
    Lyric missing.

HOW I MADE THE TEAM

Not used in film.
    Lyric missing.

I'M WITH YOU

Music by Bobby Troup. Published. Copyrighted April 4, 1955.

REFRAIN 1

Ain't with the folks what has
The oil wells and all that jazz,
But, baby,
I'm with you.
Ain't with the upper crust;
The Stork Club is not a must,
But, baby,
I'm with you.
Gee!
Crazy mixed-up me.
I'm
Happy as can be.
They've got the old moola,
A big yacht.
Et cetera,
But, baby,
I'm with you.

REFRAIN 2

[*Repeat lines 1–8 of refrain 1, then:*]

Ooh!
Crazy mixed-up you.
You
Feel the same way too.
Who needs the Cadillacs,
The mink coats, the income tax?
So, baby,
I'm with you.

THE WORDS OR MUSIC— WHICH CAME FIRST?

In January 1955 the songwriter-performer Bobby Troup recorded an album *Bobby Troup Sings Johnny Mercer* (Bethlehem), which included a number of Mercer standards and one new song cowritten by Troup and Mercer. As a tribute to Troup, Mercer wrote a poem as a liner note for the album.

The words or music—which came first?
And was it pre- or un-rehearsed?
Which is your best, and which your worst?
I wish that I were better versed.
I might explain to all of us
The answers which are obvious.
I write because I love to write
And hope the words are not too trite.
A bigger gift, but seldom given,
Is music—probably from heaven.
I pass along what gifts it gave,
I do the best with what I have.
COME RAIN OR SHINE (twice used before,
By me, by others even more)
Was written for a simple play—
Said what I thought the tune should say.
DAY IN—DAY OUT—the tune preceded—
Seemed like the phrase the music needed.
If inspiration was the key,
The memory belongs to me.
The melody, both warm and gentle,
Of Eddie Miller's instrumental
Has pretty words, but they intrude—
I liked it best as LAZY MOOD;
While Mrs. Jones's boy, JAMBOREE
Was written for the great B.G.
The lyric lines not hard to trace, he
Seems a distant kin of Casey.
As in the case of LAZY MOOD,
May I express my gratitude

To all the tunes I mention next.
They were all hits before my text:
The melody entitled LAURA
Already had its special aura.
Two lyric writers turned it down
Before I wrote a verb or noun.
And MIDNIGHT SUN was two years old,
Both pre-recorded and pre-sold,
Before I heard it in my car,
Celestial and somnambular.
THAT OLD BLACK MAGIC is, of course,
The color of a different horse—
A winner when it started out—
The Arlen melody, no doubt.
ONE FOR MY BABY, Harold's too,
The foot within a different shoe.
Both jobs to us—both lots of fun,
Sincere, affectionately done.
The SKYLARK song, a sheer delight,
Took me about a year to write.
Carmichael's notes were all in place,
But they led me on a merry chase.
Then all at once, one afternoon,
They couldn't wait to find a tune—
I called up Hoagy on the phone;
He didn't change a single one.
You've heard the phrase, "songwriter's writer"
I give you two— and each the greater.
There is no way of choosing one
From Warren or from Donaldson.
The "naturals" they have to their credit
Make most guys wish "I hadn't said it."
To have my name on tunes they did
Was what I dreamed of as a kid.
Who could repay sufficiently
One tenth of what they taught to me?
And now the last song in the group,
The one I wrote with Massa Troup—
We wrote it, I hope I'm correct,
Out of our mutual respect.
I like the men with whom he works,
I like each crummy room he works,
I like the style with which they play,
Admire every stitch they play.
At any rate, I'm deeply thankful
I hope that Bobby makes a bankful.

THE ART OF CONVERSATION HAS DECLINED

Music by Alan Bergman. Registered for copyright as an unpublished song April 22, 1955. Written for the West Coast show *That's Life*.

The art of conversation has declined.
The time for talk is difficult to find.
With piano rolls and gramophones there's not
    much choice—
The Victor dog can't even hear His Master's Voice.
The art of conversation has diminished.
Polite society is nearly finished.
We used to get together and we'd talk about the
    weather
But with all the new inventions they've designed,
We glue a wary optic on the latest stereopticon—
The art of conversation has declined.

Conversing's getting tough.
The vaudeville's hot stuff.
Since crystal sets are all the rage,
We're entering the silent age.
Since talkies came to stay,
There's nothing left to say.
The traffic is terrific,
In fact, to be specific,
A quiet spot is pretty hard to find.
Why even in the rumble
You nary hear a mumble—
The art of conversation has declined.

Real gone.
Comes on.
Real square.
Nowhere.
Nervous George,
Gasser Jack.
Frantic wild.
Yak, yak, yak.
Dig this
You'll flip.
Real cool.
I'm hip.
The most like Custer.
To say the least, buster.
So far in front it's behind.
Dig this jive video.
Man, it's crazy, daddy-o.
We're progressing so terrific'ly,
We'll soon talk hieroglyphic'ly—
The art of conversation has declined.

I NEVER WANNA LOOK INTO THOSE EYES AGAIN

Music by Milton Raskin. Registered for copyright as an unpublished song May 27, 1955.

I never wanna look into those eyes again;
I never wanna see them shine.
I never wanna listen to those sighs again
Or feel your cheek so close to mine.
I never wanna dream about that kiss again,
Those huggable arms, so snuggable and so tight.
I never wanna ever feel like this again,
No! never until tomorrow night!

HIGGLEDY-PIGGLEDY

Music by Marshall Robbins. Registered for copyright as an unpublished song May 27, 1955.

Higgledy-piggledy, my old heart
Feels it's gonna burst wide apart—
What are you doin' to this old heart of mine?
Blinkety-blanket, these old eyes
Never saw so many starry skies—
Wonderful how you can make 'em rise and shine!
All you have to do is appear
Anywhere near
And, oh, what you do to me!
Heart begins to pumpety-pump,
Thumpety-thump,
I wonder what it can be?
Guess I love ya!
Just when I figure it's normal, oh!
I get a kiss and away we go—
Over the hills and the chimney tops it soars.
I know I knockety-knackety never knew
The blinkety-blanket likes of you.
Higgledy-piggledy,
My old heart is yours.

I CAN SPELL "BANANA" (BUT I NEVER KNOW WHEN TO STOP)

Music by Geoff Clarkson. Registered for copyright as an unpublished song August 9, 1955.

I can spell "banana,"
But I never know when to stop.
B-A-N-A-N-A-N-A—
I'm gonna blow my top!
I can spell "Mississippi,"
But I never know when to quit.
M-I-S-S-I-S-S-I . . .
"Antidisestablishmentarianism,"
That's just as easy as pie—
There's an A and an N
And a T and an I.
But ask me for "banana,"
Then go out for a drink of pop.
B-A-N-A-N-A-N-A-
N-A-N-A-N-A-N-A—
Please, won't somebody yell "Stop!"

THE DAYBREAK BLUES

Music by Walter Weschler. Registered for copyright as an unpublished song September 26, 1955.

VERSE

Between the dark and the daylight,
After the band's gone home,
In our nocturnal occupations
There comes a pause
When ev'rybody wraps his fun up,
Just before it's sunup.
As the first ray breaks,
You'll hear the daybreak blues.

REFRAIN

An old piano playin' down the street,
Policeman ridin' out a lonesome beat,
The buildings silhouetted in the sun,
The whisper of tomorrow just begun—
That's the big town
Singin' the daybreak blues.
That sound,
That eerie whistle walkin' on,

Is from a drunk whose carfare's gone.
His lonesome whistle seems to say,

[*spoken sadly*] "Mornin', day!
Come on, shoes,
Got a long way to walk
Till we lose the daybreak blues."

THE HEADLESS HORSEMAN

Music by David Raksin. Registered for copyright as an unpublished song December 16, 1955. Possibly intended for the film *Vera Cruz* but not used.

VERSE

Long ago a *vaquero*, while tending herd,
Was shot without a word
And left to die.
Now his ghost rides the valleys
And roams the plains
To guard the wagon trains
That go thundering by.

REFRAIN 1

In the still of the night
And dark of the moon,
When you hear a phantom rider
Sing a ghostly tune,
Then beware the Headless Horseman.
On a coal-black mount
With soft muffled hooves,
He is swift and silent
As a shadow
When he moves from his lair,
The Headless Horseman.
He was sworn to ride to the end of time
To avenge the innocent who died of crime.
So, I warn you bands of plundering men,
He'll be waiting for you when you hit the trail again.
He'll be there,
The Headless Horseman,
So beware!

REFRAIN 2

Oh, it matters not what trail you may ride,
You will turn and suddenly
He's riding at your side
Through the night,
The Headless Horseman.
And it matters not what marksmen you boast—
There is yet to live a gunman

Who can kill a ghost.
Who can fight a Headless Horseman?
Peons tell the tale round the fireside,
Steeds returning riderless and terrified,
And the only sign of those who have sinned
Are the cries of agony that echo down the wind.
Out of sight, the Headless Horseman,
The avenger.

I'LL CRY TOMORROW (1955)

Produced by Lawrence Weingarten for Metro-Goldwyn-Mayer. World premiere December 22, 1955. Copyright January 21, 1956. Directed by Daniel Mann. Screenplay by Helen Deutsch and Jay Richard Kennedy, based on the memoir *I'll Cry Tomorrow* by Lillian Roth, Mike Connolly, and Gerold Frank. Dramatic music score by Alex North. Miss Hayward's songs arranged and conducted by Charles Henderson. The songs for this film are by a wide variety of writers. Featuring Susan Hayward, Richard Conte, Eddie Albert, Jo Van Fleet, Don Taylor, and Ray Danton, with Margo, Virginia Gregg, Don Barry, and David Kasday.

Lillian Roth—a Broadway and movie star of the early 1930s—becomes an alcoholic.

I'LL CRY TOMORROW

Music by Alex North. Published. Copyrighted December 19, 1955. Not sung in film.

I'll cry tomorrow
When I know it's goodbye,
I'll cry tomorrow,
But tonight who could cry?
Who could say
To a heart that is full of spring,
They've written a blue song
For us to sing?
You brought the summer
And I thank you for this,
You'll warm the winter
With the thought of your kiss.
Let me hold to my heart
Ev'ry word you said,
Ev'ry laugh that I can borrow—

Tonight,
No sorrow!
I'll cry tomorrow,
I'll cry tomorrow.

LI'L ABNER
and Other Songs of 1956

LI'L ABNER (1956)

Tryout: National Theatre, Washington, D.C., September 17, 1956. Erlanger Theatre, Philadelphia, October 23–November 10, 1956. New York run: St. James Theatre; opened November 15, 1956; closed July 12, 1958; 693 performances. Music by Gene de Paul. Lyrics by Johnny Mercer. Produced by Norman Panama, Melvin Frank, and Michael Kidd. Book by Norman Panama and Melvin Frank, based on the comic-strip characters created by Al Capp. Directed and choreographed by Michael Kidd. Settings and lighting by William and Jean Eckart. Costumes by Alvin Colt. Orchestrations by Philip J. Lang. Orchestra directed by Lehman Engel.

Cast included: Peter Palmer (Li'l Abner), Edith Adams (Daisy Mae), Stubby Kaye (Marryin' Sam), Howard St. John (General Bullmoose), Charlotte Rae (Mammy Yokum), Tina Louise (Appassionata Von Climax), Joe E. Marks (Pappy Yokum), Bern Hoffman (Earthquake McGoon), Al Nesor (Evil Eye Fleagle), Ted Thurston (Senator Jack S. Phogbound), Julie Newmar (Stupefyin' Jones), William Lanteau (Available Jones), Stanley Simmonds (Dr. Rasmussen T. Finsdale), George Reeder (Dr. Smithborn), Ralph Linn (Dr. Krogmeyer), and Marc Breaux (Dr. Schleifitz).

A film version was produced by Paramount in 1959. Directed by Norman Panama and Melvin Frank. Most of the cast were repeating their Broadway roles, major exceptions being Leslie Parrish (Daisy Mae) (dubbed by Imogene Lynn), Billie Hayes (Mammy Yokum), and Stella Stevens (Appassionata Von Climax).

Tony Awards 1957: Edith Adams (Featured actress), Michael Kidd (Choreographer). Original cast album of Broadway show (Columbia). Soundtrack album of film (Columbia).

A TYPICAL DAY (IN DOGPATCH, U.S.A.)

Registered for copyright as an unpublished song July 11, 1956. Introduced and recorded by principals and ensemble (Columbia). Alternate title: "It's a Typical Day."

DOGPATCHERS: It's a typical day in Dogpatch,
  U.S.A.,
  Where typical folks
  Do things in a typical way.
  First we rub the sleep from our
  eyes,
  Git our grub 'n' shoo 'way the
  flies.
  We spend what's negotiable,
  Then we gets sociable,
  Sittin' around swappin' lies.
  And then we drops by to collect
  unemployment pay,
  Which leads us to say
  It's a typical day
  In Dogpatch, U.S.A.

LONESOME
POLECAT: Lonesome Polecat, Indian
  brave.

HAIRLESS JOE: Hairless Joe, me needum shave.

BOTH: We livin' and sleepin' in,
  Doin' housekeepin' in,
  Big subterranean cave,
  Where Kickapoo Joy Juice we
  makin' is heap grade-A.

THREE
SCRAGGS: Take us boys what's known as the
  Scraggs—
  Mama said she had us as gags.

CLEM
SCRAGG: Cain't get that depressin',
  'N' homely unless'n—

THREE
SCRAGGS: You comes from a long line of
  hags!
  There ain't any widders or
  orphans we won't betray.

MOONBEAM: Howdy, boys, I'm Moonbeam
  McSwine—
  Sleepin' out with pigs is my line.
  The fellas admire me,
  But they don't squire me,
  Unless the weather is fine.
  But I does all right when the wind
  blows the other way.

AVAILABLE
JONES: You take me, Available Jones—
  I don't bank
  And I don't make loans.
  Ain't got nothing saleable,
  But I's available,
  Just in case anyone phones.

DOGPATCHERS: Which leads us to say
  It's a typical day
  In Dogpatch, U.S.A.

MARRYIN' SAM: You're no friend to arryin' Sam
  If your name is Sir or Madame;
  But if you're a bachelor,
  Pack up your satchel or
  I'll have you pushin' a pram.
  For fifteen cents extra I furnish
  the bride's bouquet.

DOGPATCHERS: Which leads us to say
  It's a typical day
  In Dog—

EARTHQUAKE

MCGOON: Step aside for Earthquake
  McGoon,
  Bustin' out all over like June.
  I stands on the corner,
  Enormous and ornery,
  Makin' the fairer sex swoon.
  [spoken] My secret desire's to
  tangle with Daisy Mae!

DAISY MAE: Like he said, my name's Daisy Mae,
  'Cause my maw, she planned it
  that way.
  My one aim in life
  Is to be a good wife
  And marry Li'l Abner someday.

ALL: She's practicin' up
  Chasin' gophers and antelopes.
  She ain't never caught Li'l Abner,
  But she's got hopes!

PAPPY: Mammy here's sassiety's queen,
  And she heads the local machine.

MAMMY: I'se sweet but I'se mystical
  And pugilistical—
  Matter of fact, the champeen!

MAMMY
& PAPPY: Li'l Abner, we has both learned,
  Still don't know how money gets
  earned.

PAPPY: His heart is the tenderes'—

MAMMY: But neuter gender 's
  Far as young gals is concerned.

ABNER: I gets pretty tired o' runnin' from
  Daisy Mae.

DOGPATCHERS: Which leads us to say
  It's a typical day
  In Dogpatch, U.S.A.

IF I HAD MY DRUTHERS

Published. Copyrighted October 11, 1956. Previously registered for copyright as an unpublished song June 11, 1956. Introduced and recorded by Peter Palmer (Li'l Abner) and ensemble (Columbia). Reprised by Edith Adams (Daisy Mae).

ABNER: If I had my druthers,
  I'd druther have my druthers
  Than anything else I know.
  While you'd druther hustle,
  Accumulatin' muscle,
  I'd druther watch daisies grow.
  While they're growin' slow 'n'
  The summer breeze is blowin',
  My heart is overflowin', 'n' so,

If I had my druthers,
I'd rather have my druthers
Than anything else I know.
ALL: If I had my druthers,
I'd druther have my druthers
Than do any work at all.
ABNER: It ain't that I hates it,
I often contemplates it,
While watchin' the raindrops fall.
I sits there for hours,
Developin' my powers,
A-figurin' how flowers gits tall.
ALL: If I had my druthers,
I'd druther have my druthers
Than do any work at all.
ABNER: If I had my druthers,
T' choose from all the others,
I'd druther be like I am.
This thing called employment,
Detracts from my enjoyment
And tightens my diaphragm.
While I'm doin' nary
A thing that's necessary,
I'm happy as a cherrystone clam.
ALL: If I had my druthers,
T' choose from all the others,
I'd druther be like I am,
Yes, ma'am,
I'd druther be like I am!

Reprise

DAISY MAE: If I had my druthers,
I'd druther have some brothers
Who'd bash in his pumpkin head!
It ain't that I hates him—
I plumb idolerates him
And wishes that we wuz wed.
I turns on my smolder
In hopes that he'll get bolder,
But I keeps gettin' older instead.
If I had my druthers,
T' choose from all the others,
I'd druther that he'd—drop—

JUBILATION T. CORNPONE

Published. Copyrighted October 22, 1956. Previously registered for copyright as an unpublished song June 11, 1956. Introduced and recorded by Stubby Kaye (Marryin' Sam) and ensemble (Columbia). And reprised by them in finale.

VERSE 1

SAM: When we fought the Yankees and
Annihilation was near,
Who was there to lead the charge
That took us safe to the rear?

REFRAIN 1

Why, it was
Jubilation T. Cornpone,
Old Toot-Your-Own-Horn Pone,
Jubilation T. Cornpone,
A man who knew no fear!

VERSE 2

When we almost had 'em but
The issue still was in doubt,
Who suggested the retreat
That turned it into a rout?

REFRAIN 2

SAM: Why, it was
Jubilation T. Cornpone
Old Tattered-and-Torn Pone!
ALL: Jubilation T. Cornpone,
He kept us hidin' out!

VERSE 3

SAM: With our ammunition gone,
And faced with utter defeat—
ALL: Oh!
SAM: Who was it that burned the crops
And left us nothin' to eat?
ALL: Why, it was
Jubilation T. Cornpone!
SAM: Old September Morn' Pone!
ALL: Jubilation T. Cornpone!
SAM: The pants blown off his seat.
ALL: Hooray!
Doo-doo-doodle-oodle-oo-do
Doo-doo-doodle-oodle-oo-do!

Additional lyrics

VERSE

SAM: When it seemed like our brave boys
Might keep on fightin' for months,
Who took pity on them and
Capitulated at once?

REFRAIN

ALL: Why, it was
Jubilation T. Cornpone!

SAM: Unshaven and -Shorn Pone!
ALL: Jubilation T. Cornpone!
SAM: He weren't nobody's dunce!
ALL: Why, it was
Jubilation T. Cornpone,
Unshaven and -Shorn Pone,
Jubilation T. Cornpone,
He weren't nobody's dunce!

VERSE

SAM: Who went reconnoitering
To flank the enemy's rear,
Circled through the piney woods
And disappeared for a year?

REFRAIN

ALL: Why, it was
Jubilation T. Cornpone!
SAM: Old Treat 'Em with Scorn Pone!
ALL: Jubilation T. Cornpone,
The Missing Mountaineer!

VERSE

SAM: Who became so famous
With a reputation so great—
ALL: Who?
SAM: That he ran for President
And didn't carry a state?

REFRAIN

ALL: Don't have to tell us it was
Jubilation T. Cornpone!
SAM: Old Wouldn't Be Sworn Pone!
ALL: Jubilation T. Cornpone,
He made the country wait.

VERSE

SAM: Stonewall Jackson got his name
By standing firm in the fray.
Who was known to all his men
As good old Papier-Mâché?

REFRAIN

ALL: Why, it was
Jubilation T. Cornpone,
Jubilation T. Cornpone,
Completely Outworn Pone,
Jubilation T. Cornpone—
He really
Saved the day!

Encore

VERSE 1

SAM: Hist'ry says that Gen'ral Grant
Was pretty good with a jug.

ALL: Hic!

SAM: Who drank drink for drink with him
And wound up under the rug?

REFRAIN 1

ALL: Why, it was
Jubilation T. Cornpone!

SAM: Passed Out Until Morn Pone!

ALL: Jubilation T. Cornpone,
His whiskers in his mug.

VERSE 2

SAM: Hearing that a Northern spy
Had come to town for the night—

ALL: Shh!

SAM: Who gained entrance to her room
And lost a glorious fight?

REFRAIN 2

ALL: Why, it was
Jubilation T. Cornpone!

SAM: Old Weary and Worn Pone!

ALL: Jubilation T. Cornpone,
He fought all through the night!

VERSE 3

SAM: There at Appomattox,
Lee and Grant were present, of course;
As Lee swept a tear away,
Who swept up back of his horse?

REFRAIN 3

ALL: Why, it was
Jubilation T. Cornpone,
Footsore and Forlorn Pone,
Jubilation T. Cornpone,
The picture of remorse!
Why, it was
Jubilation T. Cornpone,
The man who really
Saved the day!

Finale

ALL: Though he's gone to his reward,
His mighty torch is still lit.

SAM: First in war and first in peace
And first to holler "I quit!"
Why, it was Jubilation T. Cornpone,

Unshaven and -Shorn Pone,
Jubilation T. Cornpone,
He really saved the day—
The man who really saved the day!

RAG OFFEN THE BUSH

Registered for copyright as an unpublished song under the title "Don't That Take the Rag Off'n the Bush" July 19, 1956. Introduced and recorded by ensemble (Columbia).

Don't that take the beard offen a goat!
Don't that take the nap offen the yarn!
Of all the very ordinary,
Most unloved, unnecessary
Places on this earth,
The fav'rite is ourn!

Don't that take the rag offen the bush!
Don't that take the tassel offen the corn!
Of all the very ordinary,
Most unloved, unnecessary
Places on this earth,
The fav'rite is ourn—
Dog! Patch!

NAMELY YOU

Published. Copyrighted October 11, 1956. Previously registered for copyright as an unpublished song August 3, 1956. Introduced and recorded by Peter Palmer (Abner) and Edith Adams (Daisy Mae) (Columbia). Reprised by Adams.

DAISY MAE: You deserve a gal who's willin',
Namely me.
One who'd love to raise yo' chillun,*
Namely me.
Standin' there in the doorway
Waitin',
At the close of day
With you all the way,
To love, honor, and obey.
You deserve two arms to hold you,
Namely mine.

---

* *Alternate version:*
One who'd love to have yo' chillun.

There to comfort and enfold you,
Rain or shine.
I deserve someone strong and
handsome,
Bashful and shy and true,
Sweet and tender,
And I know just the one who'll do,
Namely you.

ABNER: You deserve someone good-lookin',—
Namely me.
Someone who as yet ain't tooken,
Namely me.
That is how I'll remain unless you
Get me, shall we say,
In the fam'ly way
Come next Sadie Hawkins Day.
You crave arms to make you tingle,
Namely mine.
To a bachelor who's single,
That sounds fine.*
Comes the day I no longer batchel,
Natcher'ly
I'll be true—

ABNER &
DAISY MAE: And who could I be truest to?
Namely you.

Reprise

DAISY MAE: You deserve two arms to hold you,
Namely mine.
There to comfort and enfold you,
Rain or shine.
Say the word and I'll wait forever,
No matter what you do.

UNNECESSARY TOWN

Registered for copyright as an unpublished song June 11, 1956. Introduced and recorded by Peter Palmer (Li'l Abner), Edith Adams (Daisy Mae), and ensemble (Columbia).

ENSEMBLE: [*gaily sung*]Don't that take the rag
off'n the bush!
Sho' do!
Don't that take the tassel off'n the corn!
Yahoo!
Of all the very ordinary,

---

* *Alternate lines:*
As a bachelor who's single,
I decline.

Most unloved, unnecessary
Places on this earth,
The fav'rite is yourn!!!
Hoo-ray!
The fav'rite is yourn!!!
Great Day!
As sho' as you're born!!!
Why, natch!
The fav'rite is yourn!!!
Don't that tear the tar off'n the
    roof!
Don't that strip the gears off'n the
    bus!
Of all the places in the nation
That's in need of fumigation,
No one needs a fumigatin' like us!
Don't that singe the fat off'n the
    ham!
Don't that take the gravy off'n the
    roast!
Of all the extra-ordinary
Bona fide, fiduciary
Ways to blow you up,
We's costin' the most!

ABNER: [*spoken*] Just think what it'd mean in
    the fall evenin's—not to smell the
    smoke blowin' off the skunk
    works . . . not t' see the little pigs
    wallowin' on Main Street . . . never
    t' see the moon a-risin' over
    Unnecessary Mountain . . . while
    the couples at Kissin' Rock listen
    to the soft voices floatin' out over
    the water of Imaginary Dam . . .
    [*sung*] Oh, it's unnecessary,
    Just a speck on the map,
    Where the trail from the Smokies
    Reaches old Gopher Gap.

DAISY MAE: With the sheep in the meadow
    And the bees in the comb—

ABNER &
DAISY MAE: Oh, it's unnecessary,
    But it's home sweet home.

ABNER: With the twilight a-fallin'
    And the grass wringin' wet
    And the cows just a-mooin',
    'Cause we ain't milked 'em yet.
    And if I was a poet,
    I could write me a pome.

ABNER &
DAISY MAE: Oh, it's unnecessary,
    But it's home sweet home.

ALL: Oh, it's unnecessary,
    Just a small little town,
    With the stars in the willows
    And the moon peepin' down,
    It's almost like a postcard
    Done in pure Kodychrome—

Oh, it's unnecessary,
But it's home sweet home!

WHAT'S GOOD FOR GENERAL BULLMOOSE

Registered for copyright as an unpublished song July 17, 1956, under the title "General Bullmoose (What's Good For)." Introduced and recorded by ensemble (Columbia).

Three ringing rahs, a few huzzahs,
And a hip, hip, hip, hooray—
What's good for General Bullmoose
Is good for the U.S.A.!

He said the word, it's what you heard—
Don't question, just obey!
What's good for General Bullmoose
Is good for the U.S.A.!

He makes the rules and he intends
To keep it that-a-way.
What's good for General Bullmoose
Is good for the U.S.A.!

Those rights you'll get, on that we'll bet.
We'll make them shout "Hooray!"
'Cause what's good for General Bullmoose
Is good for the U.S.A.!

THE COUNTRY'S IN THE VERY BEST OF HANDS

Registered for copyright as an unpublished song July 19, 1956. Introduced and recorded by Peter Palmer (Abner), Stubby Kaye (Sam), and ensemble (Columbia).

ABNER: Them city folks and we 'uns
    Are pretty much alike.
SAM: Though they ain't used to livin' in the
    sticks.
ABNER: We don't like stone or cee-ment—
SAM: But we is in agreement—
ABNER
& SAM: When we gets down to talkin' politics.
    The country's in the very best of hands,
    The best of hands, the best of hands.
SAM: The treasury says the national debt

Is climbing to the sky.
ABNER: The government expenditures
    Have never been so high.
ABNER
& SAM: It makes a fella get a gleam of
    Pride within his eye
    To see how our economy expands.
    The country's in the very best of hands.
ALL: The country's in the very best of hands,
ABNER
& SAM: The best of hands.
ALL: The best of hands.
SAM: You oughta hear the Senate
    When they're drawing up a bill.
ABNER: "Whereas"es and "to wit"s are crowded
    In each codicil.
ABNER
& SAM: Such legal terminology
    Would give your heart a thrill.
    There's phrases there
    That no one understands.
ALL: The country's in the very best of hands.
SAM: The building boom, they say,
    Is getting bigger every day.
ABNER: And when I asked a feller,
    How can ev'rybody pay?—
ABNER
& SAM: He come up with an answer
    That makes ev'rything okay:
    Supplies are getting greater than
    demands.
ALL: The country's in the very best of hands.
SAM: Don't you believe them congressmen
    And senators are dumb—
ABNER: When they run into problems
    That is tough to overcome—
ABNER
& SAM: They just declares a thing
    They call a moratorium—
    The Upper and the Lower House disbands.
ALL: The country's in the very best of hands.
ABNER
& SAM: Us voters is connected to the nominee,
    The nominee's connected to the Treasury.
    When he ain't connected to the Treasury,
    He sits around on his thighbones.
    They sits around in this place they got,
    This big Congressional parking lot,
    Just sits around on their you know what—
    Up there they calls 'em their thighbones.
    Them bones, them bones gonna rise again,
    Gonna exercise a franchise again,
    Gonna tax us up to our eyes again,
    When they gets up off'n their
    thighbones.
ALL: The country's in the very best of hands,
    The best of hands,
    The best of hands.

SAM: The Farm Bill should be eighty-nine
 percent of parity.
ABNER: Another fellow recommends it should be
 ninety-three.
ABNER
& SAM: But eighty, ninety-five percent,
 Who cares about degree?
 It's parity that no one understands.
ALL: The country's in the very best of hands.

Encore

SAM: Them GOPs and Democrats
 Each hates the other one.
ABNER: They's always criticizin'
 How the country should be run.
ABNER
& SAM: But neither tells the public
 What the other's gone and done.
 As long as no one knows where no one
  stands—
ALL: The country's in the very best of hands.
ABNER
& SAM: They sits around in this place they're at,
 Where folks in Congress has always sat,
 Jes' sits around on their excess at—
 Up there they calls 'em their thighbones.
 They sits around till they start t' snore,
 Jumps up and hollers, "I has the floor!"
 Then sits right down where they sat
  before—
 Up there they calls 'em their thighbones.
 Them bones, them bones gonna rise again,
 So dignified and so wise again,
 While the budget doubles in size again,
 When they gits up off'n their
  thighbones.
ALL: The country's in the very best of hands,
 The best of hands,
 The best of hands.
SAM: The money that they taxes us
 Is known as revenues.
ABNER: They compounds the collaterals,
 Subtracts the residues.
ABNER
& SAM: Don't worry 'bout the principal
 And int'rest that accrues—
 They're shippin' all that stuff to foreign
  lands.
ALL: The country's in the very best of hands.

OH, HAPPY DAY

Registered for copyright as an unpublished song July 11, 1956. Introduced and recorded by Stanley Simmonds (Dr. Rasmussen T. Finsdale), George Reeder (Dr. Smithborn), Ralph Linn (Dr. Krogmeyer), and Marc Breaux (Dr. Schleifitz) (Columbia).

Oh, happy day, when miracles take place,
And scientists control the human race!
When we assume authority of human
 chromosomes,
And assembly-line women,
Conveyor-belt men
Settle down in push-button homes!

Oh, happy day, when all the cells conform,
And the exceptional becomes the norm!
When from a test tube we produce Gargantuas or
 gnomes
And assembly-line babies,
Conveyor-belt storks
Only come to push-button homes!

So much o' this, so much o' that,
For the ears and eyes!
So much o' that, so much o' this,
For the toes and thighs!
Pour in a pot, stir up the lot,
That's the basic plan.
What have we got? I'll tell you what—
We've got manmade man!

Oh, happy day, when we can choose their looks
From formulae in scientific books
And add their personalities from psychiatric tomes
And assembly-line husbands,
Conveyor-belt wives
Settle down in push-button homes!

Oh, happy day, when all the world can see
A healthy, hearty, hale humanity!
When even tired bus'nessmen have hair upon
 their domes,
Slenderella-type mothers
And muscle beach dads
Living in gymnasium homes!

Oh, happy day, when in collective brains
No individuality remains!
We'll be a race of busy bees in happy
 honeycombs,
With automaton couples
Getting gassed in self-service homes.

Chick after chick, chick after chick,
Rolling off the line.
Chick after chick, chick after chick,
In the same design.
Nobody thin, nobody fat, ev'rybody stacked—
We guarantee they're gonna be
Firm and fully packed!

Oh, happy day, when nothing need be fixed,
When everything we buy is ready-mixed!
We'll pour prepared martinis over shredded
 lemon peels
While caffeine-removed husbands
And sugar-free wives
Settle down to quick-frozen meals!

Oh, happy day, when we come home from work,
Drop a pill or two and watch it perk.
We'll even dream hypnotic dreams to soothe our
 weary heads,
Every rubber-foam husband
And Beautyrest wife
Trundlin' off to slow-motion beds!

Get out o' bed—to infrared,
Ultraviolet light.
Sit down to eat where filter heat
Warms the food just right.
No need t' fret—get in a jet—
Off to work you spin—
Or better yet, stay home and let
Wifey phone you in!

Oh, happy day, when trains are never late
And everyone's on time for every date.
We'll walk and talk and live like automatic
 metronomes
When assembly-line husbands,
Conveyor-belt wives
Go to bed in push-button homes.

Oh, happy day, when boys and girls on dates
Can tell electric'ly if they are mates!
If he goes for her kilowatts and she enjoys his ohms,
You can bet your magnetic,
Combustible shirt
They wind up in high-voltage homes!

I'M PAST MY PRIME

Registered for copyright as an unpublished song under the title "Past My Prime" November 19, 1956. Introduced and recorded by Edith Adams (Daisy Mae) and

Stubby Kaye (Sam) (Columbia). Written during the pre-Broadway tryout.

DAISY MAE: I'm past my prime—
SAM: [*spoken*] What a shame.
DAISY MAE: And I'm losin' time.
SAM: [*sung*] Guess the old clock's run down.
DAISY MAE: Seventeen last spring—
SAM: My, what a wasted life!
DAISY MAE: Still without a ring.
SAM: Would you become my wife?
DAISY MAE: I'm past my peak.
SAM: You's an early antique.
DAISY MAE: Look at this physique.
SAM: Just hear the old bones creak.
DAISY MAE: Where there was a glow—
SAM: Ain't there a glow no mo'?
DAISY MAE: Now the wrinkles show.
SAM: Where art thou, Romeo?
DAISY MAE: Who'd think of marryin'
An octogenarian, an—
BOTH: Eighty-seven-year-old hag?!
DAISY MAE: When you's in this position,
You lose yo' disposition.
BOTH: All the time it's nag! nag! nag!
DAISY MAE: Life's like a song—
SAM: And the happiest thing—
DAISY MAE: When you're young and strong.
SAM: Most ev'ry day is spring—
DAISY MAE: But it's just a crime—
SAM: You cain't git off the dime—
BOTH: When you're past yo' prime.
SAM: You's past your prime.
DAISY MAE: Gettin' grumpy and gray.
SAM: You's on overtime.
DAISY MAE: Ain't makin' take-home pay.
SAM: Ev'ry sun that sets—
DAISY MAE: All through the day I frets.
SAM: Brings you mo' regrets—
DAISY MAE: And larger silhouettes.
SAM: You's climbed the heights—
DAISY MAE: I is over the hill.
SAM: Of romantic nights.
DAISY MAE: My hand has lost its skill.
SAM: Comes the cruel dawn—
DAISY MAE: I's feelin' pale and drawn.
SAM: Lover boy has gone!
DAISY MAE: Doggone!
SAM: I ask you, who's elated
When you's Methuselated—
BOTH: Like a mummy underground?
DAISY MAE: When you is antiquated,
Boys ain't enchantiquated—
BOTH: They prefer you in the round.
DAISY MAE: Life's just like pie—
SAM: Huckleberry or peach?
DAISY MAE: When you're young and spry.

SAM: Heaven's within yo' reach!
DAISY MAE: But it's just a crime—
SAM: How can it be sublime?
BOTH: When you're past yo' prime!
When you're past yo' prime!
When you're past yo' prime!

LOVE IN A HOME

Published. Copyrighted October 11, 1956. Previously registered for copyright as an unpublished song June 11, 1956. Introduced and recorded by Peter Palmer (Abner) and Edith Adams (Daisy Mae) (Columbia). Alternate title: "(You Can Tell When There's) Love in a Home."

You can tell when you open the door,
You can tell if there's love in a home.
Ev'ry table and chair seems to smile,
"Do come in,
Come and stay for a while."
You almost feel you've been there once before
By the shine and the glow of the room.
And the clock seems to chime,
"Come again, any time,
You'll be welcome, wherever you roam."
You can tell when there's love in a home.

PROGRESS IS THE ROOT OF ALL EVIL

Registered for copyright as an unpublished song July 17, 1956. Music by Gene de Paul. Introduced, recorded, and reprised by Howard St. John (General Bullmoose) (Columbia).

Cast recording version

REFRAIN 1

Progress is the root of all evil.
Progress is the cause of it all.
Our living standard's now so good
I had to change my neighborhood.
Say, where is Levittown?
Billionaires are getting old-fashioned.
Labor is the new-fangled craze.
The crummy basic minimums are getting so high,
The workers at the plant are living better than I.
My lawyers all advise me that it's cheaper to die.
Bring back the good old days.

REFRAIN 2

Progress is the root of all evil.
Wall Street is the worst of the lot.
How can you break the market? How?
The SEC will not allow
One little penny.
Money nowadays is no problem,
Not with all these new giveaways.
I went to see a television quiz show today.
I thought at least I'd wind up with a Caddy coupé,
But damnit if they didn't try to give me away.
Bring back the good old days.

REFRAIN 3

Progress is the root of all evil.
Politics is breaking my heart.
Why, ever since the first New Deal,
A man who has no mass appeal
Is out of business.
If ya don't believe me, ask Dewey,
Go and see what Harriman says.
My friends say I could run for any office I seek,
But first I have to brush up on my TV technique.
I plan to get in touch with Bob Montgomery next
week.
Bring back the good old days.

REFRAIN 4

Progress is the root of all evil.
How's a busy man to relax?
I'd like to join a golf club where
They built a supermarket there—
And for the public!
Being wealthy seems to mean nothing.
Let me show you how the land lays:
I went to see the president; they asked me to wait;
And though I knew that he was swamped with
matters of state,
A fella named Ben Hogan walked right through
the front gate.
Bring back the good old days.

PUT 'EM BACK THE WAY THEY WUZ

Registered for copyright as an unpublished song July 11, 1956. Listed in program and vocal score as "Put 'Em Back." Introduced, recorded, and reprised by female ensemble (Columbia).

Put 'em back the way they wuz,
Oh, put 'em back the way they wuz!
They wuz dumb, they wuz heathen,
But at least they wuz breathin',
So whatever else you duz—
Put 'em back the way they wuz!

Put 'em back the way they wuz,
Oh, put 'em back the way they wuz!
They wuz plumb unattractive,
But, by gum, they wuz active!
So I beg you kindly, cuz,
Put 'em back the way they wuz!

Put 'em back
The way they wuz,
Oh, put 'em back the way they wuz!
They wuz not known for beauty,
But they sho' done their duty,
And they made the boudoir buzz—
Put 'em back the way they wuz!
They wuz long, lean, and lanky,
But they loved hanky panky,
They did things that outdone Duz—
Put 'em back the way they wuz!
They wuz vile-lookin' varmints,
Wearin' vile-lookin' garments,
But they knowed a hiz from huz—
Put 'em back the way they wuz!

Put 'em back, put 'em back,
Oh, put 'em back the way they wuz,
They wuz no shakes as lovers,
But they warmed up the covers,
Covered as they wuz with fuzz—
Put 'em back the way they wuz!

Reprise

Oh, they is back the way they wuz!
They's uncouth and unpleasant,
But at least they is present
Doin' things that we prefuhs—
[to HUSBANDS]
Welcome back the way you wuz!

THE MATRIMONIAL STOMP

Registered for copyright as an unpublished song July 19, 1956. Introduced and recorded by Stubby Kaye (Sam) and ensemble (Columbia).

SAM: You heard about Adam, who got
    married, and so began

That mizzuble race of creatures
    known as the married man.
He took an old rib of his he
    figured he'd never miss
And started that noble institution
    of wedded bliss.
Dearly beloved, we is gathered
    here today—
DOGPATCHERS: He's startin' to—
SAM: Dearly beloved—
To put an unfortunate, mizzurable
    critter away.
DOGPATCHERS: Better he wuz hung first!
SAM: Good people, I hopes that you'll
    forgive me if I digress,
Reviewin' the horrors of
    connubial blessedness!
You knows about Samson, who was
    Israel's strongest male
Till little Delilah went and gave
    him a pony tail!
King Nebuchadnezzar lost his
    marbles and lived on grass—
DOGPATCHERS: You know that some woman
    caused that mizzurable come-
    to-pass!
SAM: Now, Brother Earthquake,
    Does you take this little gal—
DOGPATCHERS: He's hollerin'!
SAM: Now, Brother Earthquake—
To shatter and scatter what's left o'
    yore shaky morale?
DOGPATCHERS: Think it over careful!
SAM: Don't let me influence you in
    saying those fatal words.
Just let me remind you—gittin'
    married is for the birds!
J. Caesar invited Cleopatra to
    share his tents—
Of course, his abrupt demise was
    mere coincidence!
Not being content with that, this
    breaker of royal hearts
Then married Mark Anthony, who
    suddenly left these parts!
State your objections
Or forever hold yo' peace!
DOGPATCHERS: He's yammerin'
    "State yo' objections."
SAM: You's signin' a genuwine, iron-
    clad, permanent lease.
DOGPATCHERS: Never no escape clause!
SAM: King Louis met Pompadour and
    whistled "Oh, boy—big deal!"
He whistled a different tune while
    touring the old Bastille.
Now and forever,
Till yo' earthly life is naught—

DOGPATCHERS: You promises,
    Now and forever!
SAM: Oh, horrible, terrible, pitiful,
    shudderful thought!
DOGPATCHERS: Wasn't he a good man!
SAM: As much as it pains me, I
    pronounces you man and—
You gets up at the crack of dawn—
DOGPATCHERS: That's right!
SAM: Slops the hogs, ya mows the lawn—
DOGPATCHERS: Poor soul!
SAM: Saws the wood and performs the
    chores—
DOGPATCHERS: Unnh-hunnh!
SAM: While it's rainy and wet outdoors!
DOGPATCHERS: A-choo!
SAM: You comes home to familiar
    scenes—
DOGPATCHERS: Ah, yes!
SAM: And a plate of familiar beans.
EARTHQUAKE: Oh, no!
SAM: There's twenty-two screamin' kids—
EARTHQUAKE: All mine?
SAM: Makin' both of you flip yo' lids.
DOGPATCHERS: What else?
SAM: You is jumpin' out of your skin—
DOGPATCHERS: Your nerves!
SAM: Then yo' mother-in-law moves in!
EARTHQUAKE: For good?
SAM: There's no place to rest yo' head—
DOGPATCHERS: No, sir!
SAM: 'Cause there's other folks in yo'
    bed!
DOGPATCHERS: Unknowns!
SAM: You has got to escape the noise—
EARTHQUAKE: Fat chance!
SAM: So you has a drink with the boys.
EARTHQUAKE: 'Bout time!
SAM: You proceeds to the old brass
    rail—
DOGPATCHERS: Your check!
SAM: The policeman throws you in jail!
DOGPATCHERS: No dough!
SAM: You can't get a cent from your
    wife—
They incarcerates you for life!
Now, if you still wants this little gal
As yo' lawful mate
By powers invested, I pronounces
    you man and—
ABNER: Wait! Stop the wedding!
I figgers to claim this little gal as
    my nach'l mate!
SAM: Li'l Abner, does you take Daisy
    Mae fuh yo' wife?
ABNER: I does!
SAM: And Daisy, is you agreed?
DAISY: I reckon ah always wuz.

SAM: Oh, beautiful, happy day—oh,
   lucky young gal and boy
   Together to walk the trail of
   heavenly wedded joy!
   Bless you, m' chillen!
   May yo' life be free from care.
DOGPATCHERS: We's echoin'—
   Bless you, m' chillen!
   Oh, frolicky, rollicky, joyful 'n'
   jovial pair!
   Happy ever after!
SAM: Now while you all clap yo' hands
   to mighty majestic chords,
   Let's think about marriage and the
   benefits it affords.
   You kin lie in yo' bed all day—
DOGPATCHERS: Yes, suh!
SAM: While the little wife slaves away.
   I mean, the aroma of pork-chop
   pie
DOGPATCHERS: Unh unh!
SAM: Will awaken you bye and bye.
DOGPATCHERS: Great day!
SAM: You admires her symmetry—
DOGPATCHERS: What's that?
SAM: While she's fixin' you trash bean
   tea!
DOGPATCHERS: Do tell!
SAM: When you's mizzuble, mean, and
   mad—
DOGPATCHERS: Doggone!
SAM: Or you's sufferin', sick and sad—
DOGPATCHERS: Pore soul!
SAM: She kin pet you until you's
DOGPATCHERS: That's true!
EARTHQUAKE: Got a feelin' that I been had!
DOGPATCHERS: Amen!
SAM: Has a passel o' kids tenfold—
DOGPATCHERS: Some gal!
SAM: To support you when you gits old.
DOGPATCHERS: Why, sho'!
SAM: Yes, you lives like a millionaire the
   rest o' yo' nach'l life—
   And so with my blessing, I
   pronounces you man and wife!!!
ALL: Oh, beautiful happy day—oh,
   lucky young man and wife!

THERE'S ROOM ENOUGH FOR US

Registered for copyright as an unpublished song September 28, 1956. Introduced by ensemble (Dogpatchers) during the pre-Broadway tryout but dropped before the New York opening. Recorded by the ensemble and released on a compact disc reissue of the original cast album.

If there's room for Oklahoma,
For Tucumcari, Tallahassee, and Tacoma,
And for South Chicago's beautiful aroma,
Then there's room enough for us!

If there's room for poor relations
And all the immigrants from all the foreign
 nations,
And the Indians on all the reservations,
Then there's room enough for us!

Oh, we'll admit
We're pretty funny,
And we'll admit
We're even freaks.
But you'll admit
We're worth some money
As genuine, American antiques!

If there's room—we're just assumin'—
For every type and every kind of bloomin' human,
And if there's still room for Landon and for
 Truman,
Then there's room enough for us!

If there's room for Santa Barbara
And for La Jolla and La Junta and La Habra
And for Liberace and his candelabra,
Then there's room enough for us!
If there's room for Ringling Bros. and Barnum
 Bailey,
For a revival of George Arliss in *Disraeli*,
And for Arthur Godfrey and his ukulele,
Then there's room enough for us!

Oh, I suppose we're just a hamlet
Or just a place to stop the bus,
But goodness knows, if Uncle Sam let them others
 in,
Perhaps he might let us!

If there's room for Ed and Wally, by golly!
For those mustachios of Salvadore Dali,
Or for anyone named Kukla, Fran, and Ollie,
Then there's room enough for us!

If there's room for Mantovani
And Gina Lollobrigida and Miss Magnani
And the folks who live way down upon the Swanee,
Then there's room enough for us!

If there're hills like Colorados,
And those maracas in a band like Pérez Prado's,
Or for Hollywood's enormous avocados,
Then there's room enough for us!

Yosemite is full of wonder,
Yellowstone is full of thrills,
But maybe we can steal their thunder,
'Cause there is more than gold in these hyar hills!

If there's room for Doowahdiddy,
Which, as you know, is awful small but awful
 pretty,*
If the U.S.A. has room for Jersey City,
Then there's room enough for us!

If there's room for Texas ranches
And yearly hurricanes, tornadoes, avalanches,
If there's room for Standard Oil and all its
 branches,
Then there's room enough for us!

If there's room on every station
For Dick and Dorothy's good-morning
 conversation
Or for Bridey Murphy's second incarnation,
Then there's room enough for us!

Oh, maybe we're a bunch of birdbrains,
Maybe we're a bunch of hicks,
But if it's clear we ain't preferred brains,
At least we might be good at layin' bricks!

If there's room for Groucho's stogie
And for a baseball player everyone calls Yogi
And a popular composer name o' Hoagy,
Then there's room enough for us!

If there's room for shows named *Fanny*
Or for a comic strip that's older than your
 granny—
We refers, of course, to "Little Orphan Annie"—
Then there's room enough for us!

We're hardly swells, we're hardly corkers,
Dressin' up like fancy sports,
But we're no worse than them New Yorkers
Who walks around in long Bermuda shorts!

If there's room for deep sea divers†
And room enough for several hundred million
 women drivers

---

* *Alternate lines:*
 If there's room for every ditty,
 Those crazy songs that rock-'n'-rollers think are
  pretty.
† *Alternate line:*
 If there's room for late arrivals

And a handful of pedestrian survivors,
Then there's room enough for us!

If there's room in field and furrow
For all them gophers and them prairie dogs to
    burrow,
And if every home has room for Edward Murrow,
Then there's room enough for us!

If there's a town called Doowahdiddy
And other villages both large and itty-bitty,
If there's room for Brooklyn and for Jersey City,
Then there's room enough for us!

Reprise (after Abner's trip to Washington).

He finished up like he begun it,
He went to Washington to win a fight and won it.
Abner Yokum seen his duty and he done it—
And there's room enough for us!

THE WAY TO A MAN'S HEART

Registered for copyright as an unpublished song June 11, 1956. Introduced and reprised by Charlotte Rae (Mammy Yokum) and female ensemble during the pre-Broadway tryout but dropped before the New York opening. Also reprised by Tina Louise (Appassionata Von Climax). Recorded by Percy Faith and His Orchestra (Columbia).

MAMMY: The way to a man's heart is through his
     stomach—
     It don't take you very long to find that
     out.
     It don't take you very long
     To know a woman cain't go wrong
     If she knows her suckling pig and
     sauerkraut.
     One whiff of hawg glacé
     Or a hot pork-chop soufflé
     Smells mo' beeootiful than any French
     perfume.
     By usin' smiles and sighs
     And a flutter of the eyes,
     You can get yo'self a groom—
     But you can't get him in yo' room!
WOMEN: Sez who?
MAMMY: Sez me!
     As any fool kin plainly see.
     The way to a man's heart is through his
     stomach,
     So you'd better learn your culinary art.

If you want him round the place,
Feed his ego and his face
And remember what I tell you from the
    start—
Fill his stomach and you'll always fill his
    heart.
WOMEN: The way to a man's heart is through our
     figures—
     That's an axiom which every young gal
     knows.
     Once you let a fella spot
     The equipment yo' has got
     He'll be tender as the bee is to the rose.
     Though we ain't got much sense,
     It's been our experience
     That when local beaux commence to
     entertain,
     They don't want no French dip
     Or a lemon-lime to sip,
     They just wants to sit and stare
     Like you was in your underwear!
MAMMY: Sez who?
WOMEN: Sez we!
     As any fool can plainly see,
     The way to a man's heart is through his
     feelin's.
     When he orders beer and pretzels, shore
     he beams,
     But he'll overlook the schnapps
     For two fallin' shoulder straps
     Or a shirtwaist that is bustin' at the
     seams—
     Fill a bathin' suit and you will fill his
     dreams!
MAMMY: The way to a man's heart is through his
     gizzard—
     Don't rely on your coquetries or your
     curves.
     He won't notice them at all,
     But he'll really git the call
     When you're whompin' up some turnip-
     green preserves!
     You might attract a man
     Lookin' shyly 'cross a fan,
     Or by any other plan that comes to you,
     But when the guests has gone,
     He'll be sure to linger on
     For a possum pie or two, served with
     some instant mountain dew.
WOMEN: Sez who?
MAMMY: Sez me!
     As any fool kin plainly see—
     The way to a man's heart is through his
     stomach.
     Don't forget, he's just a healthy growin'
     boy;
     Though he's gettin' on in years,
     He can still git young idears

'Cordin' to the recipes that you
    employ—
Fill his stomach and you'll fill his heart
    with joy!
WOMEN: The way to a man's heart is through our
     goodies—
     Show some cleavage and just watch 'em
     go to town!
     Maybe you don't recollect
     How their passions come unchecked!
MAMMY: Well, I must admit that Pappy has
     slowed down.
     You mean that when you cook
     From *Miz Godey's Lady's Book*
     And you're makin' fudge, they don't git
     shook atall?
WOMEN: No, ma'am, they don't one bit!
     But you really makes a hit
     When you're workin' round the house
     And lose a button off your blouse!
MAMMY: Sez who?
WOMEN: Sez we!
MAMMY: Well, I'm commencin' to agree.
ALL: The way to a man's heart is through his
     eyeballs—
     Let him see the merchandise, he'll take
     the hint!
     Let him gaze upon the glands
     That is almost in his hands,
     Git him contact lenses if he has a
     squint—
     He'll forgit the peanuts and the
     peppermint!

Reprise

MAMMY: The way to a man's heart is through his
     gullet,
     I reiterates, replies, and reaffirms!
     If you loosens up his belt,
     You kin outrun Roosevelt—
     You kin stay in office umpty-'leven
     terms!
WOMEN: Will we be lifelong chums
     When our golden wedding comes
     If bicarbonate and Tums are in the bin?
MAMMY: To hold the man you've got,
     Just keep fillin' up the pot—
     Not the pot you're cookin' in,
     I mean the pot beneath his chin!
WOMEN: Sez who?
MAMMY: Sez me!
     As any fool kin plainly see!
     The way to a man's heart is through his
     stomach.
WOMEN: Are the city fellers like the ones on
     farms?
MAMMY: If he's workin' in a sewer,

Or he's workin' in manure,
Wash him off and let a beef stew work
    its charms.
GIRLS: Fill his stummick and you'll always fill
    his arms!

Appassionata's reprise

APPASSIONATA: The way to a gal's heart is through
    a trust fund
    Or a well-filled little safe-deposit box.
    It don't matter what the size,
    Long as Mister Lincoln's eyes
    Keeps peekin' at her when the box
      unlocks.
    To make her love you more,
    Don't break down the lady's door—
    Put some Standard Oil New Jersey
      in her name.
    Then when you come to call
    And she sighs, "Come in, you all!"
    The returns that you collects
    Beats the returns that you expects!
WOMEN: Sez who?
APPASSIONATA: Sez me—
    And the U.S. treasury!
    The way to a gal's heart is through
    a sports car,
    A Ferrari or a Jaguar of chrome.
    When she gets it FOB
    And she says, "For li'l ol' me?"
    You can bet your petrol gauge
      she'll never roam—
    Keep her tank filled and you'll
      always keep her home!

IN SOCIETY

Registered for copyright as an unpublished song July 19, 1956. Introduced by ensemble (Guests and Dogpatchers) during the pre-Broadway tryout but dropped before the New York opening.

REFRAIN 1

In society,
High society,
There is hardly time to call your life your own.
"We're popping off to Zurich."
"Private plane?"
"No, doing it by ski lift."
"How insane!"
"Dine at sevenish?"
"Simply heavenish!"

"You can reach us via transatlantic phone."
"We'll motor back to London;
Pack a big lunch—
We're spending the night at Cannes."
"Anyone familiar?"
"Marvelous bunch!"
"Bring your riboflavin."
"Viola's a fan!"

In society,
High society,
It's essential you retain your joie de vivre,
"Sorry, darling, plane was late!
Adored your party! Bye!"
That's high society.

REFRAIN 2

In society,
High society,
Someone's always off to China or Ceylon.
"Remember Biff and Dodo?
Busy bees!
They bought a place in Chile.
Rubber trees!
Unexplorable?
How adorable!
Takes a half a day to reach the nearest john."
"Poor old Cornelius
Slipped playing squash!"
"And fractured his leg?"
"Much worse!
Compound of coccyx."
"Dreadfully posh!"
"Seven months in traction—
And with the nurse!"
In society,
High society,
You are with the most fantastic potpourri.
"Don't look now, but Consuelo's hair is to die!"
That's high society!

I WISH IT COULD BE OTHERWISE

Registered for copyright as an unpublished song June 1, 1959. Introduced by Peter Palmer (Abner) and Edith Adams (Daisy Mae) during the pre-Broadway tryout. Dropped before the New York opening and replaced by a reprise of "Namely You." Later used in the film version, introduced by Palmer and Leslie Parrish (Daisy Mae) (dubbed by Imogene Lynn). Alternate title: "Otherwise."

I wish it could be otherwise—
Otherwise, I'm sorry we met at all.
ABNER: I'm sorry I couldn't lend a hand on
    The sweet happy ending that you
      planned on.
    I wish I were two other guys;
    Other guys might have something on
      the ball.
    Just seems like fate put this heart of
      mine
    Under some In'jun sign,
    Or otherwise you'd still be mine.
DAISY MAE: I'm sorry we spoke of home and
    marriage;
    I'm sorry we planned a baby
    carriage.
    I wish you were two other guys—
    Other guys would never have made me
      fall.
    Just seems like fate put this heart of
      mine
    Under some In'jun sign,
    Or otherwise you'd still be mine.

I'M TOO DURN BASHFUL

Intended for Peter Palmer (Abner) and Edith Adams (Daisy Mae). Not used in show.

I'm too durn bashful
To tell you that I love you.
I get too breathless
To try and lovey-dove you.
But if you ever told me
You weren't my mate,
It would be too awful
To contemplate.
Though I'm too nervous
To be much of a lover,
I'm at your service
As soon as I recover.
So have a care how dramatic my end might be
When you say you love me!

I'm too durn homely—
No wonder you don't love me.
I get too lovesick
For you to lovey-dove me.
I get the same old feeling
Each time we meet
As you gaze intently
At your big feet.
I get all puckered

Whenever we go datin',But you're so tuckered
You never see me waitin'!
So have a care how ecstatic my end might be
If you say you love me!

SORRY

Registered for copyright as an unpublished song November 26, 1956. Intended for Peter Palmer (Abner) and Edith Adams (Daisy Mae). Not used in show.

Version prepared for publication

Sorry, gee, I'm sorry,
Really sorry ev'rything turned out this way.
Forgive me and forget me,
But remember ev'ry single thing I say.
I admire you and desire you,
That's what makes this farewell scene so hard to
    play;
And what makes it much harder to do
Is the fact I know you're sorry, too!

Show version

ABNER: Sorry,
    Gee, I'm sorry,
    Really sorry everything turned out
        this way.
    Forgive me
    And forget me,
    And forget about that dreamed-of
        wedding day.
    I admires you
    And desires you—
    That's what makes goodbye so
        doggone hard to say.
    But what makes it much harder
        to do
    Is the fact I knows you're sorry
        too.
DAISY MAE: Sorry,
    Gee, I'm sorry,
    Really sorry everything turned out
        this way.
    Forgive me
    And forget me,
    But remember I'll still love you come
        what may.
    I admires you
    And desires you—
    That's what makes this farewell scene
        so hard to play.

But what makes it much harder
    to do
Is the fact I knows you're sorry too.

I'M JUST A MAMMY'S BOY

Intended for Peter Palmer (Abner). Not used in show.

REFRAIN 1

ABNER: Talk about your long-faced critters
    Longin' for some homemade fritters!
    Guess I'm just a mammy's boy.
    And I'm powerful lonesome,
    I'm lonesome for the kinfolks I know.

    Talk about your sad hillbillies!
    Every night I get the willies,
    'Cause I'm just a mammy's boy.
    And I'm blue for the mountains,
    The mountains where the turnip greens
        grow.
    Whoo-ee-ooo-whoo-ooo-ooo-oooh!
    I still can hear the whistle
    A-whistlin' at the old depot,
    A-sayin' someone's waitin' at the station,
    Happier than all tarnation,
    'Cause I'm just a mammy's boy.
    And I'm powerful lonesome,
    I'm lonesome for the kinfolks I love.

REFRAIN 2

Washington is full of voters,
Politicians and promoters,
But I'm just a mammy's boy.
And I done been promoted,
I'm up to grammar school—seven B!
There is lots o' legislators,
Big, important operators,
But I'm just a mammy's boy
Who's still got his appendix.
I ain't been ailin' since I was three.
Hooo-ee-ooo-whoooo-eee-ooo-dee-oooh!
I'm lonesome as a hoot owl
A-hootin' by the light of the moon,
And as I stroll beside the ol' Potomac,
Everybody says "Hello, Mac,"
But I'm just a mammy's boy
And my name ain't McNothin'—
I'm Li'l Abner Yokum, that's me.

THERE'S SOMETHIN' MIGHTY PECULIAR GOIN' ON

Not used in show.

There's somethin' mighty peculiar goin' on,
There's somethin' mighty peculiar goin' on.
We love everybody, but they don't love us—
There's somethin' mighty peculiar goin' on.

There's somethin' mighty peculiar takin' place:
We been requested to leave the human race.
It's just like they packed us in a Greyhound bus
'N' told the driver t' head fer outer space.

Nooooooo—body wants us,
And it's a little on the lonesome side.

We thought of movin' to, say, Saskatchewan,
Or even further away—to Oregon.
We can't put a finger on what's wrong, and yet
We ain't so popular with the Pentagon—
There's somethin' mighty peculiar goin' on.
Life is really plumb peculiar;
It can educate and fool ya.
It's a mighty funny thing
How you cares to be cared for
When you ain't got nobody who cares!

Got the latest wind-up player,
Stacks o' records, layer on layer,
But they just don't seem t' swing
And it just don't seem fa-ir
When you ain't got nobody to love.

Reckon that ignorance is bliss—
For ages we been happy,
So happy we was puttin' on airs . . .

[*Lyric unfinished.*]

IT'S A NUISANCE HAVING YOU AROUND

Published. Copyrighted November 13, 1956. Previously registered for copyright as an unpublished song June 11, 1956. Intended for Peter Palmer (Abner) and Edith Adams (Daisy Mae). Not used in show. Recorded by Rosemary Clooney (Columbia).

REFRAIN 1

ABNER: It's a nuisance havin' you around,
But I finds that when you ain't
It's the usual complaint—
I'm as mizzrable as any man can be
Who ain't a gol-durned saint.
DAISY MAE: [*spoken*] Which you ain't.
ABNER: It's a nuisance havin' you so close,
But I finds that when you go,
I'm so ornery and low,
I don't pass the time t'folks who stop
T'pass the time and say hello.
DAISY MAE: [*spoken*] Well, whaddya know!
ABNER: Although you peeves me,
You changes the days t'spring,
And when you leaves me,
All joy you obliterates—
I reiterates,
It's a nuisance having you around,
But I feel I must repeat,
When you're comin' up the street,
I becomes my nach'ral self,
Which is, of course, most lovable and
sweet.
Have a seat!

REFRAIN 2

DAISY MAE: It's a nuisance having me around—
That's the picture you paint,
But you finds that when I ain't,
You're as miserable as any man can
be
Who ain't a goldurned saint.
ABNER: [*spoken*] Which I ain't.
DAISY MAE: It's a nuisance having me around,
But when I ain't on the scene,
You're so ornery and mean
That you feel like crawlin' underneath
The nearest atom-bomb machine.
ABNER: [*spoken*] I knows what you mean!
DAISY MAE: I aims to catch up
With you if it takes all year.
Folks say we match up;
We're both such illiterates—
I reiterates,
It's a nuisance having me around,
But I'm absent and you pines,
It's like working in the mines,
So, unless you does some thinkin'
And some signin' on the dotted lines,
I resigns!

REFRAIN 3 [*instrumental until release*]

ABNER: You spoke, I heard song
Descending from high above;

And as for birdsong,
The air fairly twitterates—
I reiterates,
It's a nuisance havin' you around,
But I finds when you're away,
It's a mighty gloomy day
And the moment you returns
I'm just as puffed up as a popinjay.
You kin' stay.

SOMEWHERE, SOMEPLACE, SOMEHOW

Not used in show.
Lyric missing.

EIGHT-DOLLAR WEDDING (WEDDING SONG)

Not used in show.
Lyric missing. Interestingly, in later versions of the book inflation had modified Marryin' Sam's rate from fifteen cents to "fo" dollars and his special Four Dollar Wedding was now eight.

MATADOR

Music by Howard Jackson. Published. Copyrighted February 7, 1956.

Just hear how they roar
To greet the entrance of the matador!
In cape of scarlet and of gold,
Black eyes as bold as his name,
The picture of grace,
Sardonic smile upon his handsome face,
A face that the ladies seem to love,
A mixture of ice and flame.
Today it's a rose

Some señorita throws;
Tomorrow, who knows?
Who cares?
Fight on, matador!
Only the brave deserve the fair's *amor.*
These golden moments that you spend
Too soon may end—
Such is fame.
More *vino* for El Matador!

NIGHT SONG

Music by Hal Borne. Registered for copyright as an unpublished song February 13, 1956.

Night song,
I seem to hear it yet.
Night song,
That came the night we met.
Bright song
That burned a silhouette
On the blue.

Out there
The breeze began it all.
Out there,
Where evening shadows fall.
Somewhere
A wild bird's lonely call
Joined it too.

These and the sound of the singing sea,
The music of the spheres,
The soft whispered words that you sighed to me
Still ring in my ears.

Life long
We'll keep the mem'ry of
Night song
That started high above.
Night song,
A symphony of love
Forevermore.

YOU CAN'T RUN AWAY FROM IT (1956)

Produced and directed by Dick Powell for Columbia Pictures. Released November 1956. Copyright November 1, 1956. Screenplay by Claude Binyon and Robert Riskin, based on the short story "Night Bus" by Samuel Hopkins Adams. Lyrics by Johnny Mercer. Music by Gene de Paul. Choreographed by Robert Sidney. Music arranged by George Duning. Orchestrations by Arthur Morton. Vocal arrangements by Norman Luboff. Musical director: Morris Stoloff. Starring June Allyson and Jack Lemmon, featuring Charles Bickford, with Paul Gilbert, Jim Backus, Stubby Kaye, Allyn Joslyn, Henny Youngman, Jacques Scott, Walter Baldwin, and the Four Aces.

A musical remake of *It Happened One Night* (1934): an heiress runs away from an arranged marriage and falls for a penniless reporter.

YOU CAN'T RUN AWAY FROM IT

Published. Copyrighted September 4, 1956. Previously registered for copyright as an unpublished song March 21, 1956. Introduced off-screen and recorded by the Four Aces (Decca).

You can't run away from it,
Better not even try—
Better just close your eyes and say your prayers.
I can't run away from it,
Not with those lips nearby.
Am I supposed to whisper, "Who cares?"
We could worry till we both got old and gray from it,
Trying our best to hide,
Trying our best to make believe
We never get starry-eyed.
The moment is right—
This is the night
That nearly was ours before,
And we can't run away from it anymore.

HOWDY, FRIENDS AND NEIGHBORS

Published. Copyrighted March 27, 1957. Previously registered for copyright as an unpublished song March 21, 1956. Introduced and recorded by June Allyson, Jack Lemmon, Stubby Kaye, and ensemble (Decca).

Howdy, howdy,
Howdy, friends and neighbors—
Won't you step up
And shake my hand?
I'm an old apple knocker,
And a pea picker, too,
And I need a bosom buddy,
So I reckon it's you.
Howdy, howdy,
Howdy, friends and neighbors—
You're the best folks
In this great land!
I'm a small-town doozie,
But I ain't been asleep,
So I'm downright choosy,
But I likes you a heap—
So!
Howdy, howdy,
Howdy, friends and neighbors—
Won't you step up
And shake my hand?

Howdy, howdy,
Howdy, friends and neighbors—
There's a whole lot of time to kill.
Got an old deck of playin' cards,
And just like I said,
I can even tell your fortune
By the bumps on your head!

Howdy, howdy,
Howdy, friends and neighbors—
There's a jug on the windowsill.

I know all the parlor tricks,
In case you get wild
We can play strip poker, friend,
With everything.

Howdy, howdy,
Howdy, friends and neighbors—
Won't you step up and give me five?
I'm a real city slicker
And a good-natured slob.
Right now it just so happens
That I'm out of a job.

Howdy, howdy,
Howdy, friends and neighbors—
I'm tickled to be alive.
I'm a full-fledged Mason
And an Elk and a Moose—
When I like folks,
I slap 'em on the caboose!
Howdy, howdy,
Howdy, friends and neighbors—
Won't you step up and give me five?

Howdy, howdy,
Howdy, friends and neighbors—
Won't you step up and shake my paw?

I'm an old bubble dancer
And a racketeer's moll,
But to folks who really know me
I'm a regular doll.

Howdy, howdy,
Howdy, friends and neighbors—
I'm a mean varmint on the draw,
I'm a two-gun terror
From Mournin Gopher Hall Gap
And back home I'm wanted
On a homicide rap.
So howdy, howdy,
Howdy, friends and neighbors—
Won't you step up and have a jaw?

Howdy, howdy,
Howdy, friends and neighbors—
Where this bus goes, I don't recall.
But with friends and relatives
Wherever it stops,
We'll go honky-tonkin'
Till they call out the cops!
So howdy, howdy,
Howdy, friends and neighbors—
We may never get home,
We may never get home,
We may never get home at all!

THUMBIN' A RIDE

Registered for copyright as an unpublished song March 21, 1956. Introduced and recorded by June Allyson and Jack Lemmon (Decca).

JACK
LEMMON: Didya ever play Kick the Can,
Sort of kick it as ya ran

On a vacant city lot?

JUNE
ALLYSON: Certainly not!
LEMMON: Gets your mind off the heat
And your aching feet.
ALLYSON: What about food?
LEMMON: Don't be rude.
Did you ever try bummin' rides?
Saves you money and, besides,
You can have yourself a ball.
ALLYSON: Not that I recall.
LEMMON: The professor will now
Show the little lady how.
ALLYSON: Do you mind if the "little lady" steps
aside?
LEMMON: Have a comfortable seat,
Take a load off your feet,
While I show you how to thumb a ride.
Now, you pay attention!
There's a special technique in thumbin'
a ride.
There's all kinds of ways—for example—
All in how you use your little old thumb.
Now, to illustrate, here's just a sample.
First, we have the confident, elegant
touch.
You know, the chap, I mean, is doing
them a favor.
The message that he uses is jerky and
short,
With a sort of to-heck-with-you flavor.
ALLYSON: Marvelous!
LEMMON: Now we have a full-of-personality kid.
He lands a ride or he entertains it.
Ever pick him up, I'm telling you,
You'll be sorry you did—
He tells the corniest jokes—and
explains 'em!
Then there's the schmo,
Sort of careful and slow—
He nearly has a passer-by crying.
Screech! They stop
And then they pick him up.
ALLYSON: Naturally, they figure he's dying!
The "little lady" will now
Tell the old "professor" how.
LEMMON: Please let me know when I applaud.
ALLYSON: Have a comfortable seat,
Take a load off your feet,
While I teach you what I learned at RADA.
Thumbin' a ride
Is really a universal sport.
Thumbin' a ride—
I'll give you a short rehearsal, sport.
Though the French and Swiss
Have a method that tops all this,
Though I never could dig their lingo,
Zingo!

Try it and you never ever miss.
LEMMON: Well, does it work?
ALLYSON: Start with, you have to be a girl.
LEMMON: Swell, but does it work?
ALLYSON: Let's give it a try and see.
Lift the petticoat high
And show 'em the thigh,
And, partner, we're on our way,
Thumbin' a ride
And seeing the U.S.A.!
Alabama!
LEMMON: Arizona!
ALLYSON: Carolina!
LEMMON: Oklahoma!
ALLYSON: This is the life, I'd say—
BOTH: Thumbin' a ride
And seeing the U.S.A.!

TEMPORARILY

Published. Copyrighted March 27, 1957. Previously registered for copyright as an unpublished song March 21, 1956. Introduced and recorded by June Allyson and Jack Lemmon (Decca).

VERSE

JACK
LEMMON: Behold the Walls of Jericho
To guard you through the night.
JUNE
ALLYSON: I guess you're going to tell me
That makes everything all right?
LEMMON: A mighty man was Joshua—
He split the walls in two.
But me, I have no trouble;
Now the question is, do you?
ALLYSON: Supposing something weakens
And our mighty fortress fails?
LEMMON: We'll simply have to face
The situation that prevails.

REFRAIN 1

LEMMON: This is your shack.
ALLYSON: Temporarily.
LEMMON: Your cul-de-sac.
ALLYSON: Temporarily.
LEMMON: So hit the sack—
ALLYSON: Temporarily.
LEMMON: While I unpack.
ALLYSON: Temporarily.
LEMMON: You can't be too darn particular—
I'm your vehicular,

Extracurricular spouse.
And even though you don't wanna play,
Looks like we're gonna play house.
ALLYSON: That's realistic and sensible,
But I am so indefensible,
Faced with so much masculinity.
I fear for my femininity,
So let's just skip the pajama bit,
Papa and Mama bit,
Hoping that neither one snores,
While I am involuntarily,
Necessarily—
LEMMON: Temporarily yours.

REFRAIN 2

LEMMON: But you are mine—
ALLYSON: Temporarily.
LEMMON: And I am thine—
ALLYSON: Temporarily.
LEMMON: We're man and wife—
ALLYSON: Temporarily.
LEMMON: To go through life—
ALLYSON: Temporarily.
Although I'm quite unassailable,
I'm so available;
These walls are scaleable, too—
How can a girl stay impeccable?
LEMMON: Rubberneckable you!
I've treated you like a brother would
And pulled you through like a mother
would.
ALLYSON: They call such great hospitality
In this here state "immorality."
LEMMON: Go right ahead, be a snob to me—
You're just a job to me
ALLYSON: Careful, you'll have to resign.
LEMMON: Don't worry,
You'll still be verily—
ALLYSON: Momentarily—
LEMMON: Temporarily mine.

REFRAIN 3

LEMMON: Well, let's not fret—
ALLYSON: Temporarily.
LEMMON: We ain't caught yet—
ALLYSON: Temporarily.
LEMMON: With half the long night already by,
It's time that we both went beddy-bye.
ALLYSON: While there's someone to say howdily,
Kinda crowdily,
What if it's cloudy, we'll shine.
LEMMON: We'll just dream on
Being merrily.
ALLYSON: I'll be.
BOTH: Temporarily mine.

WHATCHA-MA-CALL-IT

Registered for copyright as an unpublished song March 21, 1956. Not used in film.

REFRAIN

You put the whoosy
On the whatsy,
Attach the whatsy
To the whoosy,
Connect the thingamajig
To the thingamabob,
And that'll make the whatcha-ma-call-it go!
You hook the gidget
To the gadget,
Adjust the gadget
To the gidget,
Unhook the dingaly-dang
From the diddly-do—
That seems to settle the so-and-so
When the you-know
Doesn't almost
And the gizmo
Never quite.
Simply follow
These instructions,
Ev'rything'll turn out all right!
You put the whoosy
On the whatsy,
Attach the gidget
To the gadget,
Connect the diddly-dang
To the jigamabob,
And adjust 'em to the thingamajo and so,
Then sit back
And watch the whatchamacallit go!

OLD REPORTERS NEVER DIE

Registered for copyright as an unpublished song March 26, 1956. Not used in film.

REFRAIN 1

"Semper veritas," "sempter veritas," "semper
    veritas."
Old reporters never die,
They gradually decline.
That's because the copy desk
Blue pencils ev'ry line.
If we keep on covering
These cattlemen conventions,

How can we live long enough
To start our old-age pensions?
Old reporters never die,
They gradually decline.
"Semper veritas," "sempter veritas," "semper
    veritas."

REFRAIN 2

"Semper veritas," "sempter veritas," "semper
    veritas."
Old reporters never die,
They gradually decline.
That's because of what we eat
And where we have to dine.
We exhaust helpings
Of cold soup and hasenpfeffer
Just to find we've been assigned
As nursemaid to a heifer.
Old reporters never die,
They gradually decline.
"Semper veritas," "sempter veritas," "semper
    veritas."

IT HAPPENED ONE NIGHT

Registered for copyright as an unpublished song August 2, 1957.

It happened one night,
One wonderful night:
We parked the car
And found a star
To wish upon;
We both wished for love,
And far above
The summer night
Became a bright
Celestial phenomenon.
Your lips seemed to know
I wanted you so—
With ev'ry kiss another dream came true.
Supposing it does become a memory?
It happened one night
To you and me.

HILDA CRANE (1956)

Produced by Herbert B. Swope Jr. for Twentieth Century–Fox. Released May 1956. Copyright April 25, 1956. Directed by Philip Dunne. Screenplay by Philip Dunne, based on the play *Hilda Crane* by Samson Raphaelson. Music by David Raksin. Orchestrations by Edward B. Powell. Musical director: Lionel Newman. Featuring Jean Simmons, Guy Madison, and Jean-Pierre Aumont, with Judith Evelyn, Evelyn Varden, Peggy Knudsen, and Gregg Palmer.

An unhappy woman marries again, convinced it won't work.

RAINBOWS IN THE NIGHT

Music by David Raksin. Registered for copyright as an unpublished song September 19, 1957. Not used in film.

Once my lonely heart and I
Saw love passing by and followed far away,
Somewhere on the road to nowhere,
Chasing rainbows in the night.
But in the light
I always seem to find love's a dream
And just a star away.
Darling, where are you?
Are you searching, too,
Somewhere on the road to nowhere,
Chasing rainbows in the night?

SPRING REUNION (1957)

Produced by Jerry Bresler for Bryna Productions, released by United Artists. Released April 1957. Copyright March 15, 1957. Directed by Robert Pirosh. Screenplay by Robert Pirosh and Elick Moll. Story by Robert Alan Aurthur. Lyrics by Johnny Mercer. Music by Harry Warren. Choreography by Sylvia Lewis. Musical score composed and conducted by Herbert Spencer and Earle Hagen. Featuring Dana Andrews and Betty Hutton, with Jean Hagen, Robert Simon, Laura La Plante, Gordon Jones, Sara Berner, Irene Ryan, Herbert Anderson, Richard Shannon, Ken Curtis, Vivi Janiss,

Mimi Doyle, Florence Sundstrom, Richard Benedict, James Gleason, and the Mary Kaye Trio.

Two college classmates fall in love again at a fifteen-year reunion.

SPRING REUNION

Published. Copyrighted May 10, 1956. Introduced and recorded by the Mary Kaye Trio (Decca).

Ev'ry time spring holds her old reunion,
I remember you with all my heart.
When the daisies blossom in the rain again,
You and I go swinging down the lane again.
When the trees are filled with April music,
And I hear those moonlit whispers start,
Your lips and mine will always meet again
In sweet communion
At the spring reunion in my heart.

OVERLEAF   Merry Andrew: *Danny Kaye*

MERRY ANDREW
and Other Songs of 1957–1959

LITTLE OL' TUNE

Music by Johnny Mercer. Registered for copyright as an unpublished song February 8, 1957. This lyric is typical of Mercer's public self-deprecation of his craft ("I just rhyme a few words now and then").

VERSE

I know a friend of mine,
And his bizness is writing songs.
It's a kind of gift,
And I get a big lift
From his melodies and dipthongs.
We got to talkin' once—
I was curious as could be.
He explained what ya do—
Let me tell it to you
Just the way it was told to me.

REFRAIN

First you write a little ol' tune, real easy—
Not as hard to play as, we'll say, Parcheesi.
Real simple chords in the key of C,
A melody you can croon.
Next you add some little ol' words onto it,
Try to get some people who sing to do it;
Then if they say, "Boy! Have you got a hit!"
You act noncommittal and say,
"Just a little ol' tune."

Now record your little ol' tune—just hum it.
Should you try and fancy it up? Far from it!
Dub in some top tenor harmony,
Just "mi-mi-mi" as you croon;
Next you sing a baritone part from way back,
Add a zoom-zoom bass, and then start the
    playback.
Then when they say, "Man! He's singin' quartet!"
You act noncommittal and say,
"Just a little ol' tune."

BERNARDINE (1957)

Produced by Samuel G. Engel for Twentieth Century–Fox. Released June 1957. Copyright June 21, 1957. Directed by Henry Levin. Screenplay by Theodore Reeves, based on the play *Bernardine* by Mary Chase. Lyrics and music by Johnny Mercer. Song numbers staged by Bill Foster. Orchestrations by Pete King, Skip Martin, and Billy May. Vocal supervision by Ken Darby. Musical director: Lionel Newman. Featuring Pat Boone, Terry Moore, Janet Gaynor, and Dean Jagger, with Richard Sargent, James Drury, Ronnie Burns, and Walter Abel, Natalie Schafer, Isabel Jewell, Jack Costanzo and Orchestra, Tom Pittman, and Val Benedict.

A college student, busy with his exams, asks his older brother to look after his girlfriend.

TECHNIQUE

Music by Mercer. Published. Copyrighted May 21, 1957. Previously registered for copyright as an unpublished song March 13, 1957. Introduced and recorded by Pat Boone (Dot).

VAMP 1

Oh, de womenfolk,
Dey back is broad,
Dey brain is weak—
So, dey pigeon for
De bachelor technique!

REFRAIN 1

You love 'em,
You leave 'em,
Dat's what is known as
Technique, technique.
De mo' you deceive 'em,
De mo' dey like yo' technique.
Dey have de feminine mind,
Which is something like being color blind.
We keep 'em guessing
And dat is how you outmaneuver
Womankind!

REFRAIN 2

Strong-arm dem,
Caveman dem,
Dey unimpressed with de male physique.
De mo' you deadpan dem,
De more dey like yo' technique.
Some like de thrill of de chase,
Others never move away from home base.
De method varies
And accordingly
To de individual case!

VAMP 2

Oh, de womenfolk,
Dey face is fair,
Dey brain is weak—
So dey pigeon for
De bachelor technique!

REFRAIN 3

Protect 'em,
Respect 'em,
Dey mental process is quite unique.
De mo' you neglect 'em,
De mo' dey like yo' technique.
Some like the arrogant stare;
Others like de shy, retiring air—
While dere are others who like you
Best of all
When you ain't even dere!

REFRAIN 4

You warm 'em,
You cool 'em,
Known better as the approach oblique.
De longer you fool 'em,
De mo' dey like yo' technique.
She has a sensitive ear,
So you tell her what she's longing to hear.
It doesn't matter as long as you
Don't let the truth interfere.

VAMP 3

Oh, de womenfolk,
Dey shape is fine,
Dey brain is weak,
So, dey pigeon for
De bachelor technique!

REFRAIN 5

De less you
Caress dem,
De mo' dey turning
De other cheek.
De mo' you outguess dem,
De mo' dey like yo' technique.
Some like you tipping de hat,
Little civilized attentions like dat.
So keep in mind
When you kiss de hand,
You are also skinning the cat!

So just remember
What I have told you
And always keep it in mind.
We keep 'em guessing
And dat is how we outmaneuver
Womankind!

REFRAIN 6

You hug 'em,
You squeeze 'em,
And den you disappear for a week.
De harder you tease 'em,
De mo' dey like yo' technique.
To make 'em jump through de ring
Or to keep 'em dangling on a string,
You find out what dey want you to do,
And you do de opposite t'ing!
So just remember
What I have told you
And always keep it in mind,
We keep 'em guessing
And dat is how we outmaneuver
Womankind!

BERNARDINE

Published. Copyrighted May 21, 1957. Previously registered for copyright as an unpublished song March 13, 1957. Introduced and recorded by Pat Boone, with Richard Sargent, Ronnie Burns, Val Benedict, and Tom Pittman (all dubbed) (Dot).

REFRAIN 1

Oh, Bernardine!
Oh, oh, oh, Bernardine!
I can tell by the dimple on your chin
You're in beautiful shape for the shape you're in,
And I'm in shape for Bernardine!

Oh, Bernardine!
Oh, oh, oh, Bernardine!
When you wander into my dreams at night,
You're a vision in glorious pink and white,
I go, go, go for Bernardine!

Bernardine! Bernardine!
You're a little bit like ev'ry girl I've ever seen.
All your separate parts are not unknown
But the way you assemble 'em's all your own—
All yours and mine, dear Bernardine!

REFRAIN 2

Oh, Bernardine!
Oh, oh, oh, Bernardine!
Throw some stuff in a bag and leave us go
Where the natives ain't heard such a word as "no"
And I can love my Bernardine!

Oh, Bernardine!
Oh, oh, oh, Bernardine!
Say you'll wait for me out by the rocket base,
And we'll both blast off into outer space
At oh-oh-oh-oh Bernardine!

Bernardine! Bernardine!
Come away with me in my rocket-propelled
    machine.
We'll come home by the way of the drive-in spa,
Just a little bit this side of Shangri-la
And there I'll stay
With Bernardine!

ECHOES

Music by Mercer. Registered for copyright as an unpublished song May 16, 1957.

Echoes,
Echoes,
Echoes,
Echoes with shadows,
Couples dance under make-believe stars,
Stating thirty-two bars of dreams.
Whispers, heartaches, laughter,
Who knows what comes after?
All I hear down in Memory Lane
Are echoes,
Echoes,
Echoes.

SPEAK TO THE HEART

Music by Tex Satterwhite. Registered for copyright as an unpublished song June 10, 1957.

Speak to the heart
And listen well,
You might learn much,
For hearts recall it all,
The small and long-forgotten secret things
Only hearts can tell.
Only hearts can tell true love
From a magic spell.

Talk to the heart,
Ask all you may.
Your closest friend
Will whisper things to you
That stars and oracles and wise men, too,
Would not dare to say.
Speak to the heart,
And when it answers you—
Obey!

LOVE IN THE AFTERNOON (1957)

Produced and directed by Billy Wilder for Allied Artists. Released June 1957. Copyright May 23, 1957. Screenplay by Billy Wilder and I. A. L. Diamond, based on the novel *Ariane, jeune fille russe* by Claude Anet. Musical adaptation by Franz Waxman. Starring Gary Cooper, Audrey Hepburn, and Maurice Chevalier, with John McGiver, Van Doude, Lise Bourdin, Olga Valéry, and the Gypsies.

The songs in this film came from a wide variety of writers. "Love in the Afternoon" and "Ariane" were the work of Matt Malneck (music) and Johnny Mercer (lyrics), but, like the other songs, were heard only in instrumental versions.

The daughter of a Parisian private detective warns an American philanderer that a jealous husband is on his way to shoot him.

LOVE IN THE AFTERNOON

Published. Copyrighted June 11, 1957. Lyric not sung in film.

Love in the afternoon
Was as sly as a wink
And as gay as a pink balloon;
We walked along
In a kind of trance,
And the very streets
Began to dance.
To think that love nearly passed us by!
Then I happened to be
Where you happened to catch my eye,
And now
Both our lonely hearts are filled with June
Because of love in the afternoon.

ARIANE

Published. Copyrighted June 11, 1957. Lyric not sung in film.

Ariane, Ariane,
You are like your name,
Thistledown, on a breeze in spring.
Like a sunbeam playing
Hide and seek among the trees,
Or a moonbeam as it dances by
And disappears across the seas.
Oh, Ariane, Ariane,
Can I be the same,
Having once held you in my arms?
Tell me I've the right to shout it
To the stars above!
Ariane, Ariane!
You're a dream!
I'm a man!
Ariane! Ariane, my love!

THE MISSOURI TRAVELER (1958)

Produced by Patrick Ford for C. V. Whitney Pictures. Distributed by Buena Vista Distribution Company. Released May 1958. Copyright September 3, 1957. Directed by Jerry Hopper. Screenplay by Norman Shannon Hall, based on the novel *The Missouri Traveler* by John Burress. Musical score by Jack Marshall. Featuring Brandon De Wilde, Lee Marvin, Gary Merrill, Paul Ford, and Mary Hosford, with Ken Curtis, Cal Tinney, Frank Cady, Mary Field, Kathleen Freeman, Will Wright, Tom Tiner, Billy Bryant, Barry Curtis, Eddie Little Sky, Rodney Bell, Helen Brown, Billy Newell, and Roy Jensen.

A young orphan boy grows up in the pre–World War I Deep South.

A choral humming chorus is heard behind the opening credits and reoccurs throughout the picture, but there is no song of any kind in this movie.

THE PINEY WOODS

Published. Copyrighted February 20, 1958, as "(Theme from) *Missouri Traveler.*" Previously registered for copyright as an unpublished song July 18, 1957. Not sung in film. Alternate title: "Biarn's Song."

REFRAIN 1

The moon is big and shiny in
The Piney Woods;
The town is downright tiny in
The Piney Woods.
But I'd sure like to stroll agin
Out where the Ozarks roll agin,
And watch an oriole agin in
The Piney Woods.
I heerd of the Blue Ridge Mountains,
I heerd of the wide Missou'—
I ain't been there,
But they can't compare
To what I has reference to.

REFRAIN 2

The trees are tall and spiny in
The Piney Woods;
The roots go down to Chiny in
The Piney Woods.
If only I possessed agin
The comfort of their breast agin,
I'd lay me down to rest agin in
The Piney Woods.
I heerd of the old Grand Canyon,
I heerd of Niagara's roar,
I'd like to see
What was read t' me,
But it's like I said before.

REFRAIN 3

The air is cold and winey in
The Piney Woods,
So clean and turpentiney in
The Piney Woods.
I wish that I could lie agin
At the sky agin,
A-watchin' stars roll by agin in
The Piney Woods.
Oh, sometimes I git so lonesome,
So lonesome that I could cry—
I still dream dreams,
But they fade, it seems,
As the long, long nights go by.

REFRAIN 4

I git me such a yearnin' for
The Piney Woods,
The same old ache returnin' for
The Piney Woods.
When I think of the spring again,
The redbirds on the wing agin,
I ain't got a thing agin'
The Piney Woods.

RAINY NIGHT

Music by Mercer and Matt Malneck. Registered for copyright as an unpublished song December 13, 1957.

Rainy night,
So cold and friendless;
Rainy night,
The storm seemed endless.
Up above, no stars;
Down below, some slow-moving cars.
There I stood,
A lonely viewer;
Blue my mood,
And growing bluer.
Then I got your call
And all at once that rainy night,
Lonely night,
Was not a rainy night
At all.

YOURS FOR KEEPS

Music by Vernon Duke. Registered for copyright as an unpublished song December 13, 1957.

VERSE

This is no fly-by-night thing,
This is no mere affair,
No kiss-and-sigh-by-night thing
That will be gone in a day.
Let me put it this way:

REFRAIN

It's yours for keeps,
This heart ever true,
Yours for keeps,
The centuries through.

The ocean
May cease in its motion,
But not my devotion
To you.
The moon that creeps
Through heaven above,
Yours for keeps,
Wrapped up in my love
Forever.
Whatever your heart adores,
I'll see that it's yours
For keeps.

MERRY ANDREW (1958)

Produced by Sol C. Siegel for Metro-Goldwyn-Mayer. Released March 1958. Copyright January 15, 1958. Directed and choreographed by Michael Kidd. Screenplay by Isobel Lennart and I. A. L. Diamond, based on a story by Paul Gallico. Lyrics by Johnny Mercer. Music by Saul Chaplin. Music adapted and conducted by Nelson Riddle. Starring Danny Kaye, featuring Pier Angeli (dubbed by Betty Wand), Salvatore Baccaloni, Noel Purcell, and Robert Coote, with Patricia Cutts, Rex Evans, Walter Kingsford, Peter Mamakos, Rhys Williams, and Tommy Rall.

A teacher joins a traveling circus.

THE PIPES OF PAN

Registered for copyright as an unpublished song April 15, 1957. Introduced and recorded by Danny Kaye and boys (Capitol).

DANNY
KAYE: [*spoken*] When dryads played with
water sprites
And satyrs romped with trolls
In company of leprechauns and elves
[*sung*] Among the trees on moonlit
nights,
These merry little souls
Were often as inhuman as ourselves.
The *worst* of the *lot* was—
1ST BOY: Cupid!
KAYE: No!
2ND BOY: Psyche!

KAYE: No!
3RD BOY: Circe!
KAYE: No!
Who used to *lead* his little band of
thieves in—
4TH BOY: Orpheus!
KAYE: No!
5TH BOY: Morpheus!
KAYE: No!
Good heavens . . . Mercy!
I mean the astral alien,
The creature bacchanalian
No good Episcopalian
Believes in—

REFRAIN 1

KAYE: It's Pan!
BOYS: It's who?
KAYE: Why, Pan!
BOYS: Oh, Pan.
KAYE: He was half a quadruped and half a
man;
He was mischievous and naughty.
And your troubles all began
When you first heard the pipes of Pan!
Not Zeus
Nor Thor,
Though they made the lightning flash
and thunder roar.
If you journeyed all the way from
Madagascar to Japan,
You would not find the likes of Pan.
The goddess Aphrodite—
She seldom wore a nightie—
You may be high and mighty,
But that simply isn't done.
What made Medusa horrid?
BOY: The snakes upon her forehead.
KAYE: Her countenance grew florid
When they wriggled in the sun.
But Pan,
Ah, Pan!
He was sort of like a bad Samaritan,
With his cloven hooves and pointed
ears;
He simply had no time for tears—
He had to lead his gypsy caravan.
What a man—
Half a man—
Was Pan!!!

PATTER

KAYE: Achilles and Adonis and Apollo and
Aurora
Are a few that I might bring to your
attention.

Calypso and Cassandra and Pygmalion
and Pandora
Are among the ones too numerous to
mention.
There's Pegasus and Daedalus and
Icarus and Venus—
I'm sure that we could number quite a
few of them between us.
1ST BOY: Endymion.
2ND BOY: And Hercules.
3RD BOY: The Harpies.
KAYE: Ouch!
4TH BOY: The Furies.
KAYE: Enough to fill a regiment and several
hundred juries.
1ST BOY: Echo.
2ND BOY: Midas.
3RD BOY: Ceres.
4TH BOY: Vulcan.
KAYE: At his mighty forge!
5TH BOY: Galatea.
KAYE: So there was—
6TH BOY: Calliope.
KAYE: By George!
1ST BOY: Jupiter.
2ND BOY: His name was Zeus.
KAYE: Minerva was his daughter.
3RD BOY: And Gemini.
4TH BOY: And Pluto.
KAYE: He was famous for his water.
5TH BOY: And Neptune.
6TH BOY: And Ulysses.
1ST BOY: And the Titans and the rest.
KAYE: But who possessed the magic pipes that
no one else possessed?

REFRAIN 2

BOYS: His name—
KAYE: Yes, yes?
BOYS: Was Pan!
KAYE: Good guess!
He could neigh and he could whinny
when he ran,
And he played a sort of cross between a
Schottische and a pavane
When he played on the pipes of Pan.
Half goat, half lad—
BOYS: How sad!
KAYE: He was really very good at being bad.
BOYS: Quite mad!
KAYE: So his ways were most circuitous and
subterranean
When he led his nocturnal clan.
Fair Echo was the maiden
Whose charms were heavy laden—
He loved to serenade in hopes that
someday they would wed,

But she preferred Narcissus
And longed to be his missus
Till his analysissus found he loved
   himself instead!
BOYS: Oh, his analysissus found he loved
   himself instead!
KAYE: Dear Pan!
BOYS: Dear Pan!
KAYE: Sweet Pan!
BOYS: Sweet Pan!
KAYE: So we leave him in the fields
   Olympian,
And some April when he passes
We will see the waving grasses
Or a set of cloven hoofprints where he
   ran,
And we'll hear
Loud and clear
The pipes . . . of . . . Pan!!!!

CHIN UP, STOUT FELLOW

Registered for copyright as an unpublished song April 15, 1957. Introduced and recorded by Danny Kaye, Robert Coote, and Rex Evans (Capitol).

VERSE 1

BROTHERS: It's really now or never, son—
   Fair lady faint heart never won.
   We're with you all the way, old
      pot—
   Stiff upper lip and all that rot.

REFRAIN 1

Chin up, stout fellow—
By George, good show!
Chest out, and bellow!
Pip, pip! Eh, what? What ho!

VERSE 2

1ST BROTHER: I shan't forget the fateful day
   I collared him and had my say.
   I shook him by his blasted ears—
   It only took me twenty years!

REFRAIN 2

1ST BROTHER: Chin up—
2ND BROTHER: Chin up—
1ST BROTHER: Stout fellow!
2ND BROTHER: Stout fellow!

1ST BROTHER: By George—
2ND BROTHER: By George—
1ST BROTHER: Good show!
2ND BROTHER: Good show!
1ST BROTHER: Chest out—
2ND BROTHER: Chest out—
1ST BROTHER: And bellow—
   BOTH: Pip, pip! Eh, what? What ho!

VERSE 3

2ND BROTHER: For years I was a sniveling pup,
   But then I got my courage up;*
   I timidly began to shout—
   And thank the Lord, he threw me
      out!

REFRAIN 3

BROTHERS: Chin up—
DANNY
KAYE: Chin up—
BROTHERS: Stout fellow!
KAYE: Stout fellow!
BROTHERS: By George—
KAYE: By George—
BROTHERS: Good show!
KAYE: Good show!
BROTHERS: Chest out—
KAYE: Chest out—
BROTHERS: And bellow!

[DANNY *bellows*.]

   ALL: Pip, pip! Eh, what? What ho!

INTERLUDE

KAYE: What ho!
BROTHERS: Bravo!
KAYE: Bravo!
BROTHERS: All set?
KAYE: Not yet.
BROTHERS: Not yet?
KAYE: All set.
BROTHERS: Adjust your flaps.
KAYE: Ta ta, old chaps!
ALL THREE: Fling down the glove and take a
   chance!
   Summon up your nerve and thumb
      your nose at circumstance!
KAYE: I'll beard the lion in his lair,
   I'll pull his mane and give his tail a
      tweak.

————————
* *Alternate wording:*
  But then I got my dander up;

BROTHERS: Heah, heah!
KAYE: I'll make you fellows proud of me—
   I'll employ the tactics that I
      learned at Larabee!
ALL THREE: Larabee!
KAYE: Here goes for country and for
   school—
ALL THREE: Britannia rules the waves but never
   waives the rules!
KAYE: Watch me annihilate the Hun—
   Caution to the winds,
   I've got the rascal on the run—
BROTHERS: Dear boy, don't be a silly ass—
   You're speaking of
   The man we love,
   Our paterfamilias!

REFRAIN 4

KAYE: [*contrite*] Slipped out!
BROTHERS: Slipped out?
KAYE: So sorry!
BROTHERS: Indeed!
KAYE: Dear me!
BROTHERS: Dear me!
KAYE: Rum go!
BROTHERS: Rum go!
KAYE: And yet—
BROTHERS: And yet?
ALL THREE: Why worry? Push on! Eh, what?
   What ho!
   Chin up, stout fellow!
   By George, good show!
KAYE: Sing a capella
ALL THREE: Do re mi . . . etc. . . . .
BROTHERS: Chin up, stout fellow!
   By George, good show!
KAYE: I'll make you fellows proud of me!
   I'll employ the tactics that I
      learned at Larabee!
ALL THREE: Larabee!
KAYE: Here goes for country and for
   school—
BROTHERS: Chest out—and bellow!
ALL THREE: Britannia rules the waves,
   But never waives the rules!
   Pip, pip! Eh, what? What ho!

THE SQUARE OF THE HYPOTENUSE

Published. Copyrighted April 18, 1958. Previously registered for copyright as an unpublished song June 10, 1957. Introduced and recorded by Danny Kaye and boys (Capitol).

REFRAIN 1

The square of the hypotenuse of a right triangle
Is equal to the sum of the squares of the two
    adjacent sides.
You'd not tolerate letting your participle dangle,
So please effect the selfsame respect
For your geometric slides!
Old Einstein said it
When he was getting nowhere—
Give him credit,
He was heard to declare,
"Eureka!
The square of the hypotenuse of a right triangle
Is equal to the sum of the squares of the two
    adjacent sides!"

REFRAIN 2

Sure as shootin',
When problems get in your hair,
Be like Newton,
Who was heard to declare,
"Eureka!
The square of the hypotenuse of a right triangle
Is equal to the sum of the squares of the two
    adjacent sides!"

REFRAIN 3

The two Wright brothers,
Before they conquered the air,
Like those others,
Orville hollered,
"Lookee heah, Wilbur,
The square of the hypotenuse of a right triangle
Is equal to the sum of the squares of the two
    adjacent sides!"

YOU CAN'T ALWAYS HAVE WHAT YOU WANT

Published. Copyrighted April 18, 1958. Previously registered for copyright as an unpublished song May 20, 1957. Introduced and recorded by Danny Kaye, Pier Angeli (dubbed by Betty Ward), and boys (Capitol).

DANNY
KAYE: You can't always have what you want.
    I'm sorry to say that it's so,
    But we've all got to learn
    It's not always our turn,
    Oftentimes that's the way things go.
    I would if I could but I can't,
    I could say I should but I shan't,
    For it's high time we knew
    That the very wish we wish were true
    Is hardest of all to grant.
    If we try to do the things our elders say,
    We can have the things we want another
      day.
PIER: It's rather like putting your dreams
      away
    For a rainy and wet afternoon,
    Or reaching for stars in the Milky Way
    And getting a small toy balloon.
1ST BOY: And we are what my mater calls
    "All in the selfsame boat."
2ND BOY: We've drawn up what my pater calls
    A promissory note.
    He promises this and he promises that,
    Which he seldom is willing to pay—
    You daren't intrude till he's in a good
      mood
    And he's put a few whiskeys away.
KAYE: I see you have the idea, lads—
    I see you understand.
    And though you think us masters cads,
    We'll have the day we planned.
    Meanwhile, wish as hard as can be,
    And don't think harshly of me.
BOYS: You could say you should but you
    shan't.
KAYE: I would if I could but I can't.
PIER: For it's high time we knew
    That the very wish we wish were true
    Is hardest of all to grant.
BOYS: If we go to sleep and wish one right
    away—
KAYE: We will have the things we want
    another day.

EV'RYTHING IS TICKETTY-BOO

Published. Copyrighted April 18, 1958. Previously registered for copyright as an unpublished song April 25, 1957. Introduced and recorded by Danny Kaye and ensemble (Capitol).

REFRAIN 1

Ev'rything is ticketty-boo,
Ticketty-boo, ticketty-boo.
Ev'rything is ticketty-boo
On such a dreamy day-dle-dee-oo-dle-dee.
Who could be so persnickety poo,
Snicketty-poo, snicketty-poo
With the sky so blinketty blue?
It causes one to say,
Bless mankind,
Including my attackers!
I'm inclined
The feeling is so jolly well, oh,
It's absolutely crackers!
Incidentally, how about you?
Happier too?
How do you do!
Ev'rything is ticketty-boo
On such a dreamy, peaches and creamy day!

REFRAIN 2

Ev'rything is ticketty-boo,
Ticketty-boo, ticketty-boo.
Ev'rything is ticketty-boo
On such a dreamy day-dle-dee-oo-dle-dee.
Heart is going bucketty-buck,
Lor' love a duck, bucketty-buck,
Seems as there's a bit o' good luck
Awaitin' on the way.
Hi! Ho! Hey!
The breeze is in the trees-o!
Oh, I say,
The mornin' is quite a bit of all right,
I'm feelin' the very cheese-o!
Incident'ly, how about you?
Happier too?
Follow it through!
Ev'rything is ticketty-boo
On such a dreamy day—
Hi-ho-hip hooray,
On such a dreamy, peaches and creamy day!

SALUD (BUONA FORTUNA)

Registered for copyright as an unpublished song July 17, 1957. Introduced and recorded by Salvatore Baccaloni, Danny Kaye, Pier Angeli (dubbed by Betty Ward), and ensemble (Capitol). Alternate title: "Buona Fortuna."

Buona fortuna to ev'ryone,
Buona fortuna to me,
Buona fortuna to my *paesan*,
All-a de family.
Mamma to *babbo e bambinell'*,
Mio fratelli too,
Buona fortuna and down da hatch—
You couple for make-a de lovely match!
Somebody open another batch—
And all-a together we sing
Salud!
Vino asciutto pop ne prosciutto
Salud!
Bevere tutto!
You know when anyone come to Rome
They make-a dem feel at home—
Salud!
Buona fortuna to ev'ryone,
Buona fortuna to you,
Buona fortuna e parmigian',
Happy oregano too!
You wanna make-a me feel at home,
I wanna feel it too—
I'm-a don' know anything you say,
But *arrivederci*—is dat okay?
I'm-a so happy here anyway,
So I'm gonna sing-a with you!
Salud!
E Gorgonzola
Salud!
E Pepsi-Cola
Salud!
In your gondola—
You are the people I love the most,
So I'm-a propose a toast—
Salud!
Buona fortuna to ev'ryone,
Buona fortuna to me,
Buona fortuna to my *paesan*,
One o' de family.
He's-a to marry my little girl,
He's-a my son-in-law,
He's-a mo' handsome than Romeo,
And he's-a da bring home lots o' dough,
'N' I'm-a retire and take it slow,
So all-a together we sing
Salud!
With *troppo vino*

Salud!
Our *signorino*
They'll have a fat *bambino*
I'll feel so—what d'ya call it? proud!—
So everyone sing aloud,
Salud!

A CHARMED EXISTENCE

Not used in film.

VERSE

Step right up
And see the greatest show on earth!
Jungle beasts,
The strangest things that grow on earth!
Yessirree,
When Joe Public speaks of us
He gets two weeks of us,
Laughs at the freaks of us.
Well, he's right,
But we've our inhibitions too,
Hopes and dreams
And fears and superstitions too.
Danger's there
When we work the high trapeze,
Though you never know it from our knees.
There's one thing every one of us believes,
Although we never wear it on our sleeves:

REFRAIN

We lead a charmed existence,
No matter what we do.
We fear nothing mortal, not even fate,
And maybe because we believe in fate,
It comes to our assistance
And always sees us through.
Some guardian angel makes certain we're secure,
We lead a charmed existence, I'm sure!

THE CINDERELLA WALTZ

Music by Al Mack. Published. Copyrighted August 23, 1961. Previously registered for copyright as an unpublished song February 17, 1958.

It's time for Miss Matilda's dancing school
To hold its first recital.
There's yards of taffeta and miles of tulle
And ev'ry stitch is vital.
The day arrives at last;
Ev'ry heart beats fast.

There's Cinderella standing in the wings,
Her royal prince attending.
The wardrobe lady's busy sewing things;
A butterfly needs mending.

And now it's time to start,
And the curtains part.
See the white mice come twirling,
Go whirling across the stage;
Her coach she's ascending.
They prance
Off to the dance.
The clock chimes;
Our hero is near,
Overcome with rage—
But wait!
Happy ending!
A pause—
Wildest applause.

Backstage is like a happy free-for-all.
The snowy night grows colder.
In station wagons little goblins
Fall asleep on Mommy's shoulder.
Good night, sweet princess, to you—
May your dreams come true!

LONGING

Music by Don Borzage. Registered for copyright as an unpublished song February 17, 1958.

Longing,
Gee, but I'm longing,
Constantly longing
To be with you—
Longing
To have you hold me,

To even scold me
The way you do.
You'll never know how I miss
The tender thrill of your kiss.
This longing
Seems never-ending—
I hope you're spending
The long nights through
Just longing
As I long for you.

MAGIC ISLAND (FAR ACROSS THE SEA)

Music by Bernie Wayne. Registered for copyright as an unpublished song May 19, 1958. Alternate title: "My Magic Island."

Far across the sea
There is a tiny land,
A shiny land.
A star across the sea
Would often lead me there,
Precede me there.
In dreams I used to trail away;
I would sail away through the mist.
To greet my ev'ry landing there,
You'd be standing there to be kissed!
And when we'd stroll along the shore,
Where crystal fountains rose,
Green mountains rose,
The roll across the shore
Would whisper, "This is real,
Her kiss is real."
You came to guarantee it all;
I can see it all
Coming true—
Please share my magic island, too!

I'VE GOTTA BE ON MY WAY

Music by Eddie Miller, Nappy Lamare, and Matt Malneck. Registered for copyright as an unpublished song May 29, 1958.

Like the whistle of a train
Or the lights of a plane,

I've gotta be on my way.
Like a meadowlark in flight,
Or a trumpet at night,
I've got my own tune to play.
So whatever you do,
Be tender and true
And pillow your head on my breast.
Take the gossamer things
Life now and then brings
And love'll take care of the rest.
Yes, there's a whisper in the dawn
That keeps callin' me on,
As much as I'd like to stay.
So I thought you oughta know
I've got places to go,
So I'll be on my merry way.

OH, WHAT A MEMORY WE MADE

Music by Eddy Samuels. Registered for copyright as an unpublished song September 5, 1958.

Oh, what a memory we made tonight—
Oh, what a love scene we both played tonight!
No other arms ever held me as tight as yours,
No lips as right as yours,
As impolite as yours.
But, oh, I was sure each kiss was meant for life,
Though I said things I may repent for life—
You put a glow in my heart that will never fade,
Oh, what a memory we made!

I LOVE YOU (I THINK)

Music by Mercer. Registered for copyright as an unpublished song October 3, 1958.

I love you, I think.
I love you, I'm pretty sure.
Of course, I should hate to be headstrong
Or put it down in black-and-white,
But if this is arteriosclerosis,
I'm right.

You love me, I hope,
But I'm such an amateur,
I just know that lately
I can't sleep a wink,

And each time you happen to kiss me
I feel like I just had a drink.
So, I love you,
I love you,
I love you—I think.

I WISH I HAD SOMEONE LIKE YOU

Music by Al Hansen. Registered for copyright as an unpublished song October 30, 1958.

I wish I had someone like you;
I wish you had someone like me.
And I wish with all my heart
I had known you at the start—
How happy this old world would be!
I used to dream millions of dreams
That vanished like bubbles, it seems;
Made a lot of wishes, too,
But if one can still come true,
I wish I had someone like you!

SATIN DOLL

Music by Duke Ellington and Billy Strayhorn. Published. Copyrighted April 13, 1960. Previously registered for copyright as an unpublished song November 4, 1958. First recorded as an instrumental by Ellington and his orchestra in 1953 (Capitol). Mercer's lyrics were added in 1958.

Cigarette holder,
Which wigs me,
Over her shoulder,
She digs me—
Out cattin',
That satin doll.

Baby, shall we go
Out skippin'?
Careful, *amigo*,
You're flippin'.
Speaks Latin,
That satin doll.

She's nobody's fool,
So I'm playing it cool as can be.

I'll give it a whirl,
But I ain't for no girl
Catching me,
Switcherooney!

Telephone numbers,
Well, you know,
Doing my rumbas
With uno,
And that 'n'
My satin doll.

MY PIANO WON'T PLAY

Music by Lewis E. Gensler.
Lyric missing.

ON THE BRIDGE OF AVIGNON

Music by Lewis E. Gensler.
Lyric missing.

SLEEPYHEAD

Music by Lewis E. Gensler.

You go to parties 'most every night,
Trying your best to be grown-up.
When will you ever own up
That's not meant for you?
You're always tired yet you go on
Keeping the hours you're keeping.
Wake up and start in sleeping
As you ought to do.

Sleepyhead, why don't you go to bed?
You know this staying up late,
Having date after date,
Was never meant for you.
Sleepyhead, you're being so misled.
You go to dance after dance,
Never missing a chance
To find a thrill that's new.

Now I'll admit that nighttime is a gay time,
But a lot of things can happen in the daytime.
And you could use the morning as your playtime
    instead.
But go on, have your fun.
I'll wait until it's done.
Then when it's lost all its charms
There's a place in my arms
Just for your sleepy head.

BEAUTY FROM ASHES

Lyric missing. Composer unknown. Registered for copyright as an unpublished song June 13, 1958.

LOVE ME WITH YOUR HEART

Music by Gilbert Martinez.

I'm in love with you;
If you love me, too,
Love me with your heart—
That's the only way.
Say the things you mean,
Mean the things you say;
Love me with your heart,
If you love me.
Some make-believing
Can be sweet make-believing,
Like a gay Christmas Eve around a tree.
But some make-believing
Can be cruel and deceiving—
Promise you'll never make-believe with me!
Hold me close to you,
Ah, but when you do,
Swear to be as true as the stars above.
Thrill me with your kiss,
But remember this—
Love me with your heart, my love!

THE HAPPY BACHELOR, OR THE COURTSHIP OF MILES DAVIS

Music by Gene de Paul. Registered for copyright as an unpublished song March 31, 1959.

Trafalgar 3—
Hey, Rosalie,
How'dya like to tickle a few toes
With a fella such as me?
Must hit the pad?
I dig ya, Dad.
Call me for the Saturday-night hop,
When they let you have the Cad!
Axminster 4—
Say Eleanor,
How'dya like to chisel a few Cokes
At the soda-fountain store?
Must baby-sit?
I dig the bit.
Hit me with a jingle-dd-ring-ding
If the baby has a fit.
Fairhaven 2—
Hey, Mary Lou,
How'dya like to whistle a few bars
Of some shooby-dooby-doo?
Hop on your broom—
Here comes the groom.
I'll arrange a couple of good seats
In a groovy little room.
Can do? Faboo!
Livin'-Dollsville, that is you!
Me, too? Cuckoo!
One for all and two for two!
I'll call a cab;
You catch the tab.
Man, ya gotta listen to this group—
They are absolutely fab!
They're gonna blow in stereo—
And if you can yodel a few notes,
I can get you in the show.
Oh, promise me tonight
That you will fall in love with me
And really wail
Shooby-dooby-doo!
Oh, promise me that when
They hear us,
They'll turn eleven shades of pale.

Put a ring on that singer,
She's a real crazy swinger,
Runs those notes through a wringer.

We love her truly.
They'll promise us a steady job
If we guarantee to work for scale.
Shooby-dooby-doo!

We're really singing up a storm.
But must cut?
Daddy-o will pop his wig?
I'm hip; he'll flip!
Time for us to skip the gig!

Newmarket 8—
Oh, hiya, Kate!
How'dya like to cover a few spots
On an after-hours date?
It's only two,
The night is new,
We could really whistle it up fine
On some shooby-dooby-doo.
Can't make the scene?
I dig ya, Queen!
Hit me with a jingle-dee-ring-ding
If you're free for Halloween!
Longacre 9—
Hey, Caroline!
How'dya like to startle a few squares
Down at Hollywood and Vine?

SWING INTO SPRING

Music by Bob Swanson. Registered for copyright as an unpublished song May 18, 1959. Introduced on the CBS television show *Swing into Spring* (April 10, 1959) by Peggy Lee, Ella Fitzgerald, the Hi-Lo's, chorus, and Benny Goodman and His Orchestra.

REFRAIN 1

Swing into spring,
Let's swing into spring,
Like the larks that sing
Leave us wingin' to spring.
Like little squirrels,
Boys and girls,
Let's leap into May,
Knee deep into May,
On a big green carpet
Let's sweep into May—
Come on and swing into spring!

REFRAIN 2

Let's see how much fun
We can bring into spring.

Formation, hup!
Laugh it up
And stride into May,
With pride into May,
Nature's giving us a free ride into May—
Come on, let's swing into spring!

REFRAIN 3

Be like last year's hat,
Which you fling into spring!
Like said chapeau,
Off we go!
Let's hop into June,
Kerplop into June,
Shall we stroll and cha-cha
And bop into June?
Come on, let's swing into spring!

REFRAIN 4

Loyal cats,
Let's follow the king into spring.
You know the scale—
Shall we wail?
Let's lean into June
And preen into June
As we make that green,
Crazy scene into June—
Come on, let's swing into spring!

JOANNA

Music by Henry Mancini. Registered for copyright as an unpublished song June 1, 1959. Written for the NBC television series *Peter Gunn*. This was Mercer's first collaboration with Mancini. Recorded by Henry Mancini and His Orchestra (Victor) and Mike Clifford with Johnny Williams and His Orchestra (Columbia).

Joanna's like a day
With summer on the way,
All beautiful and gay
And bright.
One of Joanna's smiles
Lights up the sky for miles.
She walks in beauty
Through the night,
And when she does,
I stand there starry-eyed,
So proud
That I am by her side.
To think we even met,

I can't believe it yet.
She really has my heart,
And here's the wildest part—
Joanna says that she loves me.

THE AFTERBEAT

Music and lyrics by Fred Astaire and Mercer. Registered for copyright as an unpublished song June 8, 1959. Introduced by Fred Astaire on the NBC Television Special *Another Evening with Fred Astaire* (November 4, 1959) and recorded for the album *Now Fred Astaire* (Kapp).

VERSE

There's a lot of talk about the beat,
Ev'rybody knows about the beat,
Ev'rybody's dancing on the beat,
The downbeat beat!
There's a different angle which is new;
Another beat has always been there, too!
A new dance has hit—
This is it!

REFRAIN 1

The afterbeat
Is the next beat
After the downbeat—
Not the first beat
Or the "on" beat
But the offbeat,
Like a backbeat,
Or an echo beat,
That's the afterbeat.

REFRAIN 2

Not a three beat,
Or a four beat,
Or a three-four beat;
Not a square beat,
But a laughter beat,
And a swingin' beat,
And a dancing beat,
Is the afterbeat.

REFRAIN 3

Not a beat-up,
Or a beatnik beat,
But an afterbeat,
The em-pha-sis
Is on the last bit,

That's the afterbeat,
Not an oom-pah-pah,
Nor a cha-cha-cha,
But the afterbeat.

REFRAIN 4

It's a late beat,
And a great beat,
It's the afterbeat.
If you're looking
For a gay beat
And a fun beat,
Then the one beat
You are after
Is the afterbeat.

REFRAIN 5

The afterbeat
Is the next beat
After the downbeat—
Not the first beat
Or the "on" beat
But the offbeat,
Like a backbeat
Or an echo beat,
That's the afterbeat,
That's the afterbeat,
That's the afterbeat,
That's the afterbeat . . .

I WANNA BE AROUND (TO PICK UP THE PIECES WHEN SOMEBODY BREAKS YOUR HEART)

Music by Mercer. Lyrics by Mercer and Sadie Vimmerstedt. Copyrighted January 10, 1963. Previously registered for copyright as an unpublished song June 12, 1959. Leading recording by Tony Bennett (Columbia) in 1963.

The song was an accidental collaboration. Mercer received in the mail a suggestion for a song title from a lady in Youngstown, Ohio, who worked at a cosmetics counter. Her name was Sadie Vimmerstedt and the title was "I Wanna Be Around."

"That one was a natural," Mercer remembered.

She did the title and I did everything else, but I figure that's fifty-fifty. Because, as far as I'm concerned, that's a hit title. The guy who has it is a lucky guy, because he's got half the battle won if the general public already likes the title—which they did.

I told her we had a record by Tony Bennett and she was thrilled. She said, "You've changed my life, Mr. Mercer. People are coming in the store and asking for my autograph. Next week I have to go on the radio in Cleveland." Two weeks later she said, "I'm going to Cincinnati, I'm getting to be so famous." Finally, she came to New York and she was on *To Tell the Truth* and then she went to Europe. She said, "I'm tired, I'm going to get out of show business."

I wanna be around
To pick up the pieces
When somebody breaks your heart,
Somebody twice as smart
As I,
A somebody who
Will swear to be true,
Like you used to do
With me,
Who'll leave you to learn
That mis'ry loves company
Wait and see!

I wanna be around
To see how he does it
When he breaks your heart to bits;
Let's see if the puzzle fits
So fine.
And that's when I'll discover
That revenge is sweet,
As I sit there applauding
From a front-row seat,
When somebody breaks your heart
Like you broke mine.

THE STORM

Music by Milton Raskin. Registered for copyright as an unpublished song July 30, 1959.

Blue is the summer sky,
Soft is the breeze,
Sweet as a breath of spring
Stirring the trees.
Faint is the lightning flash
Off on the plain;
Then comes the thunderstorm,
Down comes the rain.
So is my love for you,
Such my desire,

Starting with just a kiss,
All ice and fire.
Loud beats my heart's refrain,
Wild, fierce, and true,
Till, with all passion spent,
I'm close to you,
At peace,
And the storm at last is through.

ECHO OF A DREAM

Music by Serge Walter. Published. Copyrighted June 23, 1961. Previously registered for copyright as an unpublished song August 18, 1959.

I still can hear
The echo of a dream—
How close at hand
The music used to seem!
But memories grow dimmer,
And soon they fade away,
And now there's just a glimmer
Of you and me and yesterday.

We tried to hold
The twinkle of a star,
To catch a gleam
Of moonlight in a jar.
Love vanished like the ripples
That float on a stream,
And you are just
The echo of a dream.

LOVERS IN THE DARK

Music by Gordon Jenkins. Registered for copyright as an unpublished song October 13, 1959.

Lovers in the dark,
Just you and I,
Underneath a dark
Enchanted sky,
Clinging close together
In the still of the night,
Losing ourselves
In the thrill of the night.
Lovers in the dark
With sweet desire,
Borrowing a spark

From love's old fire,
Finding that the oldest story
Always is new.
Lovers in the dark, we two.

YOU KNOW YOU DON'T WANT ME

Music by Mercer. Published. Copyrighted August 10, 1967. Previously registered for copyright as an unpublished song May 6, 1959, and again on October 21, 1963. Recorded by Jim Nabors.

You know you don't want me,
You know you don't love me,
So why don't you leave me alone?
You know if you string me along this way,
You'll end up by breaking my heart someday.
How seldom you see me,
And yet you won't free me
To look for a love of my own!
You know you don't want me,
You know you don't love me,
So why don't you leave me alone?

Saratoga: *Howard Keel and Carol Lawrence*

SARATOGA
and Other Songs of 1959

SARATOGA (1959)

Tryout: Shubert Theatre, Philadelphia, October 26–November 28, 1959. New York run: Winter Garden Theatre; opened December 7, 1959; 80 performances. Music by Harold Arlen. Lyrics (and additional music) by Johnny Mercer. Produced by Robert Fryer. Book dramatized and directed by Morton Da Costa ("with the assistance of Edna Ferber"), based on Ferber's novel *Saratoga Trunk*. Choreography by Ralph Beaumont. Settings and costumes by Cecil Beaton. Orchestrations by Philip J. Lang. Orchestra directed by Jerry Arlen. Cast included Howard Keel (Clint), Carol Lawrence (Clio), Odette Myrtil (Bella), Warde Donovan (Bart), Carol Brice (Kakou), Tun Tun (Cupide), James Millhollin (Mr. Bean), Richard Graham (M. Augustin Haussy), Truman Gaige (Mr. Gould, M. Begué, Editor), Isabella Hoopes (Clarissa), Edith King (Mrs. Sophie Bellop), Augie Rios (Shorty), Brenda Long (Maudey), Virginia Capers (Charwoman).

Mercer's musical contributions to *Saratoga* occurred because the composer was ill for part of the pre-Broadway tryout. Cast album (RCA Victor). Cecil Beaton, who was also nominated for a Tony for Best Scenic Design, won a Tony for Best Costume Design.

Mercer himself was doubtful about this project from the start. He told Harold Arlen, "If you're going to do *Show Boat*, you're thirty years too late." When asked later why he'd accepted it, he replied: "I'm always doing jobs I don't want. I thought my work the poorest I have ever done—even ruining one of Harold's tunes with a mediocre and unimaginative lyric."

New York critics certainly didn't want this one. *Women's Wear Daily* found the show "pretty as a picture but old-fashioned." Morton Da Costa bore most of the brunt for his top-heavy book, which John Chapman in the *Daily News* considered "the most complicated music-show plot since Richard Wagner wrote *Siegfried*." Walter Kerr in the *Herald Tribune* agreed: "The really distressing thing . . . was the quality of the book."

I'LL BE RESPECTABLE

Registered for copyright as an unpublished song October 19, 1959. Introduced and recorded by Carol Lawrence (Clio) (Victor).

VERSE

The time you've spent
In your discontent

Has taught me one thing well:
That lonely years
Full of lonely tears
Make life a living hell.
Since you've shown me the truth,
I'm not wasting my youth
As a shopworn lamb
Or faded *demoiselle*.

INTERLUDE 1

[*spoken*] I should turn gray at thirty like my mama—and let my mind go running away—to lose itself in a bottomless cavern of dark despair . . . Not I!

REFRAIN

I make a vow, now—
I'll be respectable—
I'll be a lady,
And I'll be rich.
Don't ask me how, now,
I'll be respectable—
I'll find the right way,
No matter which!
No matter what the social set there,
My rightful place I shall attain;
And I'll use any means to get there,
Even—if I have to—my brain!
I'll be perfection,
All that's perfectible—
The picture of re-spect-a-bil-it-y!

INTERLUDE 2

[*spoken*] I'll give my children a proper home—two parents beneath one roof, a name that rightfully will be theirs. They'll go to school with their heads held high—they'll have respect!

REFRAIN 2

I'll be the soul of
Well-bred propriety—
I won't be *nouveau*
But I'll be rich.
I'll get control of
And run society—
They'll want to have me
Burned as a witch.
I'll have the parson and the vicar
To Sunday tea upon the "po'ch";
I'll give the aldermen good liquor—
Then I'll send them home in my coach.
Who could reject one

So unrejectable?
The picture of re-spect-a-bil-it-y.

INTERLUDE 3

[*spoken*] I won't indulge, like Mama and you, in the dubious luxury of romance—or settle for favors. I'll have it all—money and power and men and love. I won't give up! I won't give up!

REFRAIN 3

I'll be austere, but
I'll be political,
For I'll agree with
Who wins the day.
I'll be sincere, but
Still hypocritical:
I'll find their weak spots—
I'll make them pay.
I'll be as regal as Du Barry,
Illegal as a courtesan,
Collecting all that I can carry,
After I've collected—a man.
I'll be the one thing
That's uncollectable,
The picture of re-spect-a-bil-it-y!

CODA

[*spoken*] And those who forced me to have no name, no other heritage than *une griffe*—I'll make them grovel and pay and pay and pay, till they themselves go mad, mad, mad—like poor Mama!

ONE STEP—TWO STEP

Registered for copyright as an unpublished song October 19, 1959. Introduced and recorded by Carol Lawrence (Clio), Augie Rios (Shorty), Brenda Long (Maudey), and ensemble (Victor).

One step—two step,
We make new step.
I step—you step soon.
After we cleans up ev'rything,
We gonna cut dat pigeon wing.
Ooh la la,
We *chantez là-bas*
And dance under de moon!

One step—two step,
Old bayou step
Makes dem blues step down.
I take my ol' bandana off,
Sport a fancy gown.
We do de one-step, two-step round de town!

GETTIN' A MAN

Music by Mercer. Introduced and recorded by Odette
Myrtil (Belle) and Carol Brice (Kakou) (Victor).

REFRAIN 1

KAKOU: Gettin' a man
And gettin' a husband
Is two different things.
Except for the lace on your corset,
They don't want to have any strings.
BELLE: Gettin' a man
And gettin' a husband
Is hard, goodness knows.
They listen to any proposal
As long as they needn't propose.
KAKOU: With eager stares
They buy your wares
As samples you unpack.
BELLE: They even pay,
Provided they
Can then send the merchandise back.
KAKOU: So keep him in doubt
Until he's committed
BELLE: To all marriage brings,
KAKOU: 'Cause gettin' a man
To kiss you with feeling,
BELLE: Gettin' a man
Who's actually kneeling,
I tell you
BOTH: Are two wonderfully opposite things.

REFRAIN 2

BELLE: Gettin' a man
And gettin' a husband
Demand some finesse.
KAKOU: It's something like catching a crim'nal
And making that crim'nal confess.
Gettin' a mate
And gettin' a helpmate
Is just like I said.
BELLE: They don't like to rush into marriage
The way that they rush into bed.
KAKOU: Their attitude,
While often rude,

Is best described as slow.
BELLE: They understand
The promised land,
But buying the property, no.
KAKOU: The minute you point
A man at the altar
Is when love takes wings.
'Cause gettin' a man
Who wants to be lovey,
BELLE: 'Cause gettin' a man
Who wants to be hubby,
BOTH: I tell you
Are two totally different things.

PETTICOAT HIGH

Registered for copyright as an unpublished song October 19, 1959. Introduced and recorded by Virginia Capers (Charwoman), Carol Lawrence (Clio), Odette Myrtil (Belle), Tun Tun (Cupide), and ensemble (Victor). Reprised by Lawrence and ensemble.

CLIO: [*spoken*] What music! What is it? It's
crazy!
COLORED
BOY: [*spoken*] Call ragtime, ma'm'selle.
NEGRO
MAN: When the leader man calls the tune,
Dat's the time we all do the coon!
BAND: You picks yo' partner like a do-si-do,
You starts to shuffle, den away you go!
MAUDEY: You parks yo' manners in the vestibule,
An' before you knows it, you is cuttin'
the fool!
NEGRO
WOMAN: Petticoat high, petticoat low—
Don't that slide trombone tickle yo'
toe?
Petticoat low, petticoat high—
Ain't the sounds they make sweeter
than pie?
When the leader man calls the tune,
Watch this gal jump over the moon!
Shoein' the mare,
Struttin' for fair,
And when I has caught every eye—
Dat's when I fly my petticoat high!

WHY FIGHT THIS?

Music by Mercer. Introduced and recorded by Carol
Lawrence (Clio) and Howard Keel (Clint) (Victor).

VERSE 1

CLIO: He's beautiful, you must agree.
And you'll admit that we're alone.
Wouldn't he make a good escort
Since we have none of our own?

I shouldn't get involved.
He isn't what I'm after.
I should really be discreet,
But I have a feeling he'll help me.
He really looks rather sweet.

REFRAIN 1

I can fight the fortunes of fate
And if I must I will.
So far I've gathered nothing at all
But empty years to fill.
And this may be the chance of a lifetime
No one wants to miss.
Yes, I can fight the devil's own luck
But why fight this?

VERSE 2

CLINT: She's pretty as a prairie rose
That someone else is sure to pick.
Maybe I should be that someone—
Or should I move along quick?

I shouldn't get involved.
I'm used to going solo.
Maybe I should play it smart,
But I have a feeling she needs me.
Something is ready to start.

REFRAIN 2

I can fight the fortunes of fate
And fight them till I drop.
I can fight a stacked deck of cards
And still come out on top.
But this may be the chance of a lifetime
No one wants to miss.
Yes, I can fight the devil's own luck
But why fight this?
BOTH: This may be the chance of a lifetime
No one wants to miss.
Yes, I can fight the devil's own luck
But why fight this?

A GAME OF POKER

Published. Copyrighted October 22, 1959. Introduced and recorded by Howard Keel (Clint) and Carol Lawrence (Clio) (Victor). Reprised by Lawrence, Keel, and Odette Myrtil (Belle).

REFRAIN 1

CLINT: Love
Is a game of poker—
Ev'rything's wild
And the chips are down.
One night
You may draw the joker;
Next night
You may own the town.
One look at the cards they've tossed you,
One look at her,
You decide to play.
You stay,
But they've double-crossed you,
And your hunch has cost you
More than you can pay.
You've won,
But oh,
You've lost your heart
Along the way!
So here goes
You and I,
Win or lose,
Do or die!
But it's sure
Worth a try
If it's love.

REFRAIN 2

CLIO: Love
Is a game of poker—
Anything goes,
And the stakes are high.
Guess wrong
And you go for broke, or
Guess right
And you own the sky!
One look at the cards they've tossed you,
One look at him,
You decide to play.
CLINT: One look at the cards they've tossed you,
One look at her,
You decide to play.
You stay.
But they've double-crossed you . . .

[*Lyric continues as in refrain 1.*]

LOVE HELD LIGHTLY

Published. Copyrighted November 16, 1959. Previously registered for copyright as an unpublished song October 19, 1959. Introduced and recorded by Odette Myrtil (Belle) (Victor). Reprised by Carol Lawrence (Clio).

VERSE

Two maidens in a railway carriage—
One, tearful and forlorn,
Tells her friend a saga of woe,
Wishes she'd not been born.
Poor victim of a faithless marriage!
Had she but sought reply,
Wept on my shoulder,
I could have told her why.

REFRAIN

Love held lightly,
Love held lightly,
All too often slips away.
So, welcome it in,
Like an angel caught in a storm;
Wherever it's been,
Make it safe and sheltered and warm.
And tend love nightly,
Brightly, brightly;
Make the most of ev'ry day.
Be gentle and true,
And forget the years that are past—
Whatever you do,
Do your best to keep holding it fast.
For love held lightly
Too frequently will fly away.
Hold it close to your breast,
Like a bird in its nest—
It will do all the rest,
If it's love!

SARATOGA

Published. Copyrighted October 22, 1959. Introduced and recorded by Howard Keel (Clint) and Carol Lawrence (Clio) (Victor). Reprised by the ensemble.

REFRAIN 1

Here we come, Saratoga,
And we're loaded for bear;
When we're through shootin' dice with you,

You'll wish the sidewalks were there!
Although we aim to play the game
According to Hoyle,
Our rabbit's foot
Is stayin' put—
And of course you
See the horseshoe!
Tell ol' Diamond Jim Brady
I'll arrive with my lady—
Her style, my style,
You guessed it—in high style!
Here we come, Saratoga,
We're out to break ya!
We're gonna take ya back home!

INTERLUDE

Can't you see them sports paradin',
Sunday-mornin' promenadin'?
Diamond Jim and Lilly Russell,
Feather boa and saucy bustle,
Noses up and mighty tony,
With their pony
Gallopin' home!

REFRAIN 2

Yessirree, bring the swells on—
We're arrivin' with bells on!
His style, my style,
You said it—in high style!
Here we come, Saratoga,
We're out to break ya!
We're gonna take ya back home!

HAVE YOU HEARD?

Registered for copyright as an unpublished song October 19, 1959. Introduced by Edith King (Mrs. Sophie Bellop), Isabella Hoopes (Clarissa Van Steed), and ensemble. Alternate title: "Gossip Song."

OTHERS: Have you heard?
Too absurd!
There they were—
Her masseur!—
Bold as brass
On the grass!
By the pool!
She's a fool!

Now, darling, don't quote me—
I know what I hear!

Abby Witherspoon wrote me—
She said it happened last year . . .

Have you heard?
Mum's the word—
Union Steel
Up a third!
Bulls and bears—
Million shares!
Left it all
To his heirs?
No broker would risk it!
Care to have a beaten biscuit—
Or iced tea?

Cissy Vanderbilt—
Missus Morgan—
The Commander built—
With an organ!
He's divorcing her—
She'll inherit—
Without forcing her—
Can you bear it?
She was willing!
Isn't it killing?
Without forcing her!
She'll inherit!
He's divorcing *her?*
Can you bear it?
Cissy Vanderbilt
With an organ?
The Commander built—
Missus Morgan!?
Forty-seven!
Isn't it heaven!!
Nobody told his wife!
They knew they shouldn't
And we thought they wouldn't
But they really couldn't
At their time of life!

Have you heard?
Mum's the word!
Her masseur!
Up a third!
Left it all!
By the pool!
Million shares?
She's a fool?
No broker would risk it! . . .
Care to have another biscuit?
Or iced tea?

Bart Van Steed—
Yes, indeed!
Rich as sin—
Zinc and tin!
Such a catch—

Perfect match!
No one yet—
Mama's pet!
They'd all like to get him—
Just look at them gawk!
But his mother won't let him—
She watches him like a hawk.
MRS. VAN STEED: Barty, dear,
Over here.
Not too near—
There's a dear.
Be polite—
Say good night.
OTHERS: That old hag,
She's a fright—
She'll keep him forever!
What would Mrs. Bellop ever
think of that?

[MRS. BELLOP *enters.*]

MRS. BELLOP: Good volley?
Oh, well up!
OTHERS: [*variously*] Best I ever saw!
Who is this Mrs. Bellop?
Her word is absolute law!
Which is she?
With the chest!
MRS. BELLOP: Mrs. Gould?
She's a pest!
OTHERS: Watch your scalp!
And my head!
MRS. BELLOP: Diamond Jim?
Great in bed!
OTHERS: [*variously*] It's law if she said it—
Gotta give the old girl credit!
More iced tea?
Countess So-and-So—
Convalescing—
MRS. BELLOP: Countess What's-Her-Name?
How depressing!
COMPANION: From Napoleon!
MRS. BELLOP: Not another!
Half Mongolian,
Like her mother!
OTHERS: Incognito!
MRS. BELLOP: Why, that mosquito!
OTHERS: [*variously*] Mrs. Bellop says,
"That mosquito!"
From Napoleon!
Incognito!
Mrs. Bellop says,
"Not another!
Half Mongolian,
Like her mother!"
MRS. BELLOP: European?
I say plebeian!
Some fake aristocrat!!

When she needs Bellop,
She will come to Bellopo!
OTHERS: That's what Sophie Bellop has to
say to that!

TAG TO SCENE

OTHERS: Fancy that!
I could swoon.
Bart Van Steed!
Clint Maroon!
Countess de—
So *intime!*
Pulled it off
Like a dream!
So charming and clever!
What will Mrs. Bellop *ever* say to
that?
MRS. BELLOP: I'll be damned!

COUNTIN' OUR CHICKENS

Introduced and recorded by Carol Lawrence (Clio) and
Howard Keel (Clint) (Victor).

REFRAIN 1

CLIO: I'll have pearls and a box at the races,
French châteaux and a castle in Spain,
Two or three dozen watering places,
And a yacht bounding over the main.
Liveried coachmen in constant
attendance,
Champagne suppers at seven each night
With the Sultan of Turkey upon my right.
CLINT: Your highness.
CLIO: Well, thank you.
I'd inspire a novel by Dickens
That the dealers would sell by the batch.
You'll forgive me for countin' my
chickens
Just before they hatch.

REFRAIN 2

CLINT: I'll be known as the boss of Montana,
Kissin' babies and robbin' the poor,
Smoking only imported Havana
On my yearly political tour.
Longhorn steers and a sunny *ranchero,*
Shot-up rustlers all over my yard
As I leave my opponents all battle-scarred.
CLIO: My hero!
CLINT: It's nothing

I'd pull it off with the easiest pickin's.
There'll be gold dust wherever I scratch.
You can't blame me for countin' my
    chickens
Just before they hatch.

REFRAIN 3

CLIO: We'll have dinners of seventeen courses.
    I'll give Kakou my yesterday's frocks.
CLINT: While Cupide drives a team of white
    horses
    From his perch on that gold-plated box.
CLIO: In New Orleans they'll build me a statue.
CLINT: In Montana they'll make me a chief.
BOTH: Won't we both look attractive in bas-relief
    By Renoir.
CLIO: Then I'll tell them to go to the dickens,
CLINT: Thumb my nose at the whole shootin'
    match,
BOTH: Millionaires who are countin' their
    chickens,
CLIO: The plot thickens,
CLINT: By Charles Dickens,
BOTH: Countin' chickens
    Just before they hatch.

YOU OR NO ONE

Introduced and recorded by Howard Keel (Clint)
(Victor).

You or no one,
You alone—
When I looked at you
I should have known.
From the moment
That you walked in
I've been guessing
How the wheel would spin.
Sure, I'm laying my heart on the line.
Sure, it's nothing or everything fine.
But I'll take my chances.
Rise or fall,
You or no one at all.

Sure, I'm laying my heart on the line.
Sure, it's nothing or everything fine.
But I'll take my chances.
Rise or fall,
You or no one at all.
You or no one at all.

THE CURE

Registered for copyright as an unpublished song October 19, 1959. Introduced and recorded by ensemble (Victor).

VERSE

[*with phony elegance*]

How do! How be you?
So nice to see you
All out this early,
Looking so pearly bright!
Oh, my poor brain!
Must be insane!
Too much Champagne last night.

GROUP 1: Oh, what a man can sink to!
GROUP 2: Shall we get in the pink to?
GROUP 3: Think about what we'll drink tonight!

REFRAIN 1

We're here to take the waters,
You may be sure—
High fashion's sons and daughters
Here for the cure.
Are you feeling a bit dyspeptic?
Have you plague?
Are you merely an epileptic
With the ag-ue?
Why throw a mild conniption?
Why be upset?
Try nature's own prescription,
Cold, clear, and wet,
For it's healthful
And natural
And mineral
And medical
And comes from a hearty artesian spring!

REFRAIN 2

We're here to take the waters,
You may be sure—
High fashion's sons and daughters
Here for the cure.
Get your picture in all the papers,
Take a dip—
It cures everything from the vapors
To la grippe!
Gadzooks and land-o'-Goshen,
Have you the gout?
Try nature's magic potion,
Inside or out,
For it's healthful
And natural
And mineral

And medical
And comes from a hearty artesian spring!

REFRAIN 3

Subject to mild dyspepsia?
Lost your allure?
We have the thing that helps ya
Here at the cure!
Why should anyone have to stoop to
Warm beef tea?
This cures everything from the croup to
Housemaid's knee—hee!
Have a case of colic?
Mayhap the bends?
Are you an alcoholic?
Come, join your friends!
For it's healthful
And natural
And mineral
And medical
And comes from a hearty artesian spring!

REFRAIN 4

We come with symptoms varied,
All set for bed—
End up getting married,
All set for bed!
Love is nothing but self-hypnosis;
So be sick
With arteriosclerosis,
Pulses quick—en!
Stroll through our spacious garden,
Discuss your glands,
Come, let your arteries harden
While holding hands.
For it's healthful
And restful
Natural
And sociable
And mineral—

MEN: Adorable!
ALL: And medical—
WOMEN: And eligible!
    And comes from a
ALL: Hearty artesian spring!

THE MEN WHO RUN THE COUNTRY

Music by Mercer. Introduced and recorded by ensemble (Robber Barons) (Victor).

We're the men who run the country,
We're the men who made it high.
Every time we crossed a meadow we would dig a
    little ditch,
Every time we crossed a river we would build a
    little bridge
Or we'd whittle down a mountain to a ridge.
We keep things humming, humming,
Tellin' folks prosperity is coming,
And while they're saving, and slaving,
We make a million dollars on the side!
Oh, we devastate the prairies
And we decimate the flocks
And we saturate the market
With some questionable stocks
While we populate the nursery with a lot of progeny
Who'll grow up to be more hideous than we!
It keeps us busy, busy,
Also keeps the ladies in a tizzy;
And while they're *that* way—the fat way—
We make a million dollars on the side!
Should there be a breath of scandal,
Should there rise a single doubt,
Should the population holler,
"Let us throw the rascals out!"
We erect a large museum or a public edifice
And the people think we're very, very nice!
That keeps them in their places
While we're at the Saratoga races
Or at some far oasis
To make a million dollars on the side!
We are predatory barons
But in rather hoary shape,
And the only crime we haven't tried
Is statutory rape.
Since the present-day constabulary couldn't catch
    a cat,
Eight or nine of us may get around to that!
Oh, we're the men who run the country
For a little private gain
As we desecrate the woodland
And we inundate the plain!
So before you go to bed tonight,
I beg of you to pray
For the men who run the good old U.S.A.,
The U.S.A.—
For the men who run the good old U.S.A.!

THE MAN IN MY LIFE

Published. Copyrighted October 22, 1959. Introduced and recorded by Carol Lawrence (Clio) and Howard Keel (Clint) (Victor).

REFRAIN 1

CLIO: The man in my life
        Will behave like a man,
        Not a spoiled boy
        Who refuses to play
        If he doesn't get his way.
        The man in my life
        Will be all that a man ought to be—
        Sweet and shy,
        But as brave and as bold
        As any hero of old.
        The day I find him, I swear,
        I'll be his then and there.
        By the heavens above him,
        I'll love him for fair!
        Then I'll lock the door
        To my heart evermore,
        For I plan to do all that I can
        To hold on to the man in my life.

REFRAIN 2

CLINT: The girl in my life
        Will behave like a girl,
        Not a tease, not a flirt,
        Who treats love as a thing
        That you dangle on a string
        The girl in my life
        Will be all that a girl ought to be—
        Good and kind,
        Always there by my side,
        No matter how rough the ride.
        The day that I find her, I swear,
        I'll be hers then and there.
        By the heavens above her,
        I'll love her for fair!
        Then I'll lock the door
        To my heart evermore—
        In a word, I would conquer the world
        To hold on to the girl in my life.

GOOSE NEVER BE A PEACOCK

Published. Copyrighted October 22, 1959. Introduced and recorded by Carol Brice (Kakou) (Victor).

VERSE

Takes a whole heap o' learnin'
For a person to know
Dis ol' world keep a-turnin',
But it turn mighty slow.
And it don't matter rightly
How you scheme and you plan;
Certain things gonna stay
The way they began.
Fo' instance—

REFRAIN 1

Goose never be a peacock,
Don't I know!
Crow try to be a jaybird,
He still crow.
Bust his cackle in two,
Still can't sing;
Got no feathers of blue
On his wing.
A hawk try to be a eagle,
Down he fall,
So don't walk around all biggety-like
Or squinchify up too small,
'Cause maybe you is
The very best you of all!

REFRAIN 2

Be proud of who you is
And what you do;
No matter where you is,
Act dat way too,
And everyone you see
Be proud of you!
Remember—
Hawk try to be a eagle,
Down he fall.
Dere ain't never been too many fine birds
A-settin' up on de wall,
And maybe you is
De prettiest of dem all!

DOG EAT DOG

Registered for copyright as an unpublished song October 19, 1959. Introduced and recorded by Howard Keel (Clint) and male ensemble (Victor).

Oh, the strong take the money from the weak,
And the smart take the money from the strong—
You can say what you want to,
But it's dog eat dog,
And there is no right or wrong.
It's the law of the jungle and the sea,
Every pond has a biggest little frog.
It's a race for survival,

It's a fight to the death—
And for all your flighty,
High-and-mighty, fancy talk,
It's dog eat dog!

Back in 'sixty-eight,
Things were goin' great,
And my daddy had a little spread.
He worked it all himself—
Then along came all them rustlers from New York.
Well, they passed us by,
Left us high and dry,
And they bought up all the congressmen,
The local sheriffs, too,
And our grazing land became a prairie fork.
I ain't about to let that happen,
Ain't about to fall in line.
No, I ain't gonna rob 'em
And I ain't gonna steal,
But I aims to try and get what's mine!

'Cause the slow lose the money to the swift,
And the swift lose the money to the shrewd—
You can say what you want to,
But it's dog eat dog,
And I hope that don't sound crude!
It's the law of the jungle and the sea,
Every pond has a biggest little frog.
It's a race for survival,
It's a fight to the death—
And for all your flighty,
High-and-mighty, fancy talk,
It's dog eat dog eat dog!

If you turn your back,
Crack the gate a crack,
The coyote's in the chicken coop,
The wolf is at the flock
And the mountain lion's prowlin' through the
     herd.
It's the same in life
With a man and wife:
If you turn your back a little bit,
Some fellow's in your bed,
And you can't afford to take the lady's word!
I ain't about to let that happen,
Ain't about to stay supine.
Gonna get me a fortune,
Gonna get me a wife,
And I aims to see that they stay mine!
It's the law of the jungle and the sea,
Every pond has a biggest little frog.
It's a race for survival,
It's a fight to the death—
And for all your flighty,
High-and-mighty, fancy talk,
It's dog eat dog eat dog!

I'M HEADED FOR BIG THINGS

Introduced by Howard Keel (Clint) during the Philadelphia tryout but dropped before the New York opening. Alternate title: "Headed for Good Things."

CLINT: I'm headed for big things,
    Fair ladies and fancy thoroughbreds,
    I'm off to the races.
    Who's coming along?
    My train pulls out tonight
    And the line forms on the right.
    We'll take some and we'll leave some.
    Who's coming along?
    With a ruby in my cravat
    Or maybe a diamond "shoe,"
    All I need is a stetson hat
    And a lady to tip it to.
    Yes! I'm headed for big things.
    Small change never did appeal to me.
    This year has a great feel to me.
    Who's coming along?
ENSEMBLE: He's headed for big things,
    Black horses and gold chariots.
    He's off to the races.
CLINT: Who's coming along?
ENSEMBLE: He'll be a sight to see,
    All the ladies'll follow him.
CLINT: So don't you try and stop me.
    Who's coming along?
    I'll put up at the best hotels
    Most rich people can't afford.
    Better come when the train man yells,
    Aaa-aaa-aaa-aaa-aaa-
    All aboard,
    'Cause I'm headed for big things.
    So you better start deciding.
    It's my wagon and I'm riding it.
    Who's coming along?
ALL: Who's coming along?

THE GAMBLERS

Introduced by Carol Lawrence (Clio), Howard Keel (Clint), and ensemble during the Philadelphia tryout. Dropped as a song before the New York opening, but danced in the New York production.
    Lyric missing.

LESSONS IN LOVE

Registered for copyright as an unpublished song October 19, 1959. Intended for Carol Lawrence (Clio) and Odette Myrtil (Belle) but dropped before the Philadelphia tryout.

VERSE 1

BELLE: Lessons in love,
    Lessons in love,
    Daily we learn our lessons in love.
CLIO: To the matter.
BELLE: First we have flattery.

REFRAIN 1

    Flattery will get you ev'rywhere.
CLIO: Eyes all aflutter—
BELLE: Words dripping butter—
    These will take you far.
CLIO: Snuggle up and whisper, "I declare!"
BELLE: "What, you ragout it?"
CLIO: "How do you do it?"
    "My, how smart you are!"
CLIO: "You really mean
    You paid fifteen
    And sold at ninety-three?
    You naughty lad,
    You must be mad!
    Perhaps you'll slip
    A little tip to me."
BELLE: Do you want a mouse
    Or a millionaire,
    Coachman and carriage,
    Offers of marriage?
BOTH: Flattery will get you to the royal ball—
    Anywhere at all!

VERSE 2

BELLE: Lessons in love,
    Lessons in men—
    Daily we learn them over again.
CLIO: There's no limit.
BELLE: Second comes symmetry.

REFRAIN 2

    Symmetry will get you ev'rywhere.
CLIO: Charms soft and rounded
    Leave them confounded.
BELLE: Ankles drive them mad.
CLIO: Plus the other things he *thinks* are there!
    Such as the muscles—
BELLE: Under our bustles.
CLIO: "Sir, you are a cad!"

BELLE: If he grows weak
 About your cheek,
 Your shoulders and arms—
CLIO: How he will bleed
 As you proceed—
BELLE: To let him eye more gratifying charms!
CLIO: Surely, if you mean my porte cochere . . .
BELLE: Don't let him pet it,
 Just silhouette it.
BOTH: Symmetry can make an empire rise or fall—
 Anything at all.

VERSE 3

BELLE: Lessons in style, lessons in chic—
 So we perfect our basic technique.
 I insist Her
 Highness learn mystery.

REFRAIN 3

BELLE: Mystery will get you ev'rywhere.
 You want a lover?
 Stay under cover—
 Wear those seven veils.
CLIO: Show a little here   and nothing there.
 You be exotic—
BELLE: He'll be erotic.
CLIO: Ambush seldom fails.
BELLE: The darkened room,
 The scented gloom,
 The silkened-curtained bed;
 And something sheer—
 Remember, dear,
 That fools rush in
 Where angels fear to tread.
CLIO: After you have lured him to your lair,
 Unmask your splendor—
 Total surrender!
BOTH: Once the battle's hopeless, let the castle fall—
 Anything at all!

VERSE 4

BELLE: Lessons in love, lessons in love,
 Wiles that a lady's capable of
 In the stretch her
 Weapon is treachery.

REFRAIN 4

BELLE: Treachery will get you ev'rywhere.
 Lie like a heathen;
 Start when you're teethin'—
 Flirting is a skill.
CLIO: Cultivate a wide-eyed baby stare.

BELLE: You just be ruthless—
 Have him make a will!
CLIO: Deceive, design,
 Contrive, combine
 To bring the stag to bay.
 With certain checks
 The weaker sex
 Can be a match for man, its natural prey.
BELLE: Institute a plan of laissez-faire.
 Get it in writing;
 Then be exciting.
BOTH: Treachery will get you omnes partes Gaul—
 Anything at all!

YOU FOR ME

Registered for copyright as an unpublished song October 19, 1959. Introduced by Howard Keel (Clint) during the Philadelphia tryout but replaced by "You or No One" before the New York opening.

I can see it's you for me,
That's the way it's got to be—
You and I and fate
Have a date.
Me for you,
I can feel you feel it, too.
What the stars would have us do
We cannot deny,
Though we try.
My heart is yours,
Your heart is mine,
So we start to play our part
In fate's great design.
Yes, it's time you knew
This is all I've wanted, too,
To live my whole life through
For you and only you for me!

PROMENADE

Registered for copyright as an unpublished song October 19, 1959. Intended for members of the ensemble but not used in the show. Alternate title: "Market Cries."

VEGETABLE
VENDOR: Dey just now brought the corn in—
 We picked it fresh this mornin'!
HAT
VENDOR: Come on and buy your lady
 A hat to keep her shady!
BASKET
VENDOR: In case the madame should ask it
 Fine palmetto leaf baskets for sale!
FABRICS
VENDOR: My spinnin' wheel is spinnin'
 To make the finest linen!
POULTRY
VENDOR: You doin' chicken buyin'?
 Got Rhode Island Reds for fryin'!
FRUIT
VENDOR: My grapes are somepin' to chew on—
 Lemme weigh you a few on the scale.
FISH
VENDOR: Mullet, croaker, pompano too,
 Cooked in a stew!

WORKMAN'S SONGS

Registered for copyright as an unpublished song October 19, 1959. Intended for members of the ensemble but not used in the show. This number segued into "One Step—Two Step."

CARPENTER: Heah come Mose de carpenter,
 He got tools he sharpener—
 Do de cho'es.
 Tools I got fuh hammerin'—
 All de folks is clamorin'
 Fuh ol' Mose!
GARDENER: Heah come Ned de gardener,
 I cleans up de yard'n ah
 Make it bright.
 You got weeds fuh hoein' up,
 I got seeds fuh growin' up
 Overnight!
DECORATOR: I hangs the curtain,
 You do the flirtin',
 Peepin' through the curtain
 Dra'pries!
MASON: Your walls tumblin' down
 Keeps me comin' to town—
 I'se your mason!
PICCANINNY: You want de best?
 You want de good work?
 I does de walls,
 I does de woodwork!
 Call fuh Shorty!

CHARWOMAN: What we does is sweepin' up,
Anse we's keepin' up—
Watch it shine!

CHIMNEY SWEEP: Chimneys is my specialty
And I does my specialty
Mighty fine!

COAL VENDOR: Coal, one dollar a ton,
Coal, one dollar a ton—
Coal man passin'!

MAUDEY: I helps to clean,
I helps t'tidy.
I change de bed,
I change de didy.
My name is Maudey!

BERRY WOMAN: Ah got berries, penny a pint,
Big as cherries,
Blackberries!

CLIO: Heah comes who is payin' you
But I sho' ain't payin' you till
you's done!
Sooner you stop frittin' time,
Sooner we has quittin' time,
Den has fun!
We gonna dance, we gonna sing
song—
We beat de drum, we play de
ding dong!

SHORTY: Lead me to it!

MAUDEY: We drop de mop, pick up de
trash, hey?

CLIO: An' then we stop an' do de
sashay!

MAUDEY
& SHORTY: How we do it?

CLIO: I teach you, Maudey,
Like Kakou teach me . . .

BON APPÉTIT

Registered for copyright as an unpublished song October 19, 1959. Intended for Carol Lawrence (Clio), Howard Keel (Clint), Truman Gaige (Begué), Odette Myrtil (Belle), and ensemble but not used in show. Alternate title: "Menu Song."

BEGUÉ: Perhaps the *dindonneau
breton?*

CLIO: I thought I'd try the
bourguignon.

1ST CUSTOMER: A plate of frog legs
provençal!

2ND CUSTOMER: *De ris de veau cardinale!*

3RD CUSTOMER: The *coq au vin* and bottle of
Chablis.

WAITER: Today we recommend the
fricassee.

2ND CUSTOMER: The *quiche lorraine!*

3RD CUSTOMER: *Potage du peigne!*

4TH CUSTOMER: The *saumon,* but *au
champagne!*

CLIO: *Boeuf à la reine* or *Saint-
Germain!*

1ST CUSTOMER: *Pâté à la napolitaine!*

CLINT: Hey, waiter, can a stranger
have this dance?
Or does a person have to be
a citizen of France?

2 WAITERS: *Bon!*

CLIO AND BELLE: *Mais non, mon Dieu,
Mon Dieu et sacrebleu!*

WAITER: There surely must be other foods
your palates would prefer?

CLINT: Ham hocks and beans,
A plate of collard greens?
A Spanish onion—
Chop it up
And mix it with sardines!

CLIO: *A Dieu de plaise,* and at M'sieur
Begué's!

WAITER: Have something *à la ravigotte* or
à la milanaise?
We'll ask the *chef,* the *maître d'.*

CLINT: I'm payin'—how 'bout askin'
me?

WAITERS: Pardon us, *m'sieur.*
Garçon!
We'll see.

2 WAITERS: *Bonjour, m'sieur,
Très beau, très bon,
A votre disposition!*
Some things you do not
comprehend—
Perhaps if we could recommend?
To help you more enjoy your
déjeuner,
We offer you the menu of the day.
We hope you like Begué's cuisine—
Say, something *à la Florentine?
Beef à la mode? Petite marmite?*

CLINT: Don't matter if it's fit to eat.

WAITER: But after all, it's you who must
decide.

CLINT: Well, how about some Irish stew
Or mountain oysters fried?

CHEF &
MAÎTRE D': *Bon appétit!*

CLIO &
PARTY: *Bon appétit!*

CHEF &
MAÎTRE D': *A votre santé, mes amis!*
Perhaps today *mousse aux choux-
fleurs?*

CLIO: *Très élégant, à la bonne heure!*

BELLE: Perhaps we'll have *potage du jour,*
and then
*Coquilles Saint-Jacques
parisienne?*

CLIO: *Filet croustade, une* green *salade*
Perhaps with dressing *anchoïade?*

MAÎTRE D': *Beef carbonade? Un grand
poulet?*
Or *omelette à la piperade?*

CHEF: *Chou rouge à la flamande* this
afternoon.

CLINT: A man who don't speak French
could starve to death in this
saloon!

CLIO: Ahhh, *bouillabaisse!* Or *shrimp à
la française!*
The *pain perdu,* perhaps, for two?
Or *lobster bordelaise?*

BELLE
(OR WAITER): *Bean cassoulet* or *omelette soufflée?*

CLINT: Believe you me, I'd settle for a hot
dog all the way!

BEGUÉ: *Coq franc-comtoise?
Potage du vichyssoise?*

CLINT: And while you're at it, bring a beer
and two or three long straws!

BEGUÉ OR
MAÎTRE D': *Au nom de Dieu!* Oh, pardon me—
It's here that we're supposed to be!!
Pardon us, *m'sieur! Garçon!*
We'll see.

BEGUÉ &
MAÎTRE D': [*like a Greek chorus*] *Les aubergines
la vaucauson—*

WAITERS &
BUSBOYS: *Et les chaussons aux champignons.
Gigue de chevreuil tourangelle,
Aussi une tarte demoiselle,
Les cailles sous la cendre et plus
tendre—*

CLINT: Say, ain't that Pelléas and
Mélisande?

WAITERS: *Oeufs en meurette* or *en brochette,*
Then for dessert some *crêpes
Suzette?
Farci en flamme?*
Or like madame,
*A la béarnaise,
A la bonne femme?*

Or *voulez-vous moules de Tours
 fourrés?*
CLINT: By God, I do believe they're gonna
 sing the Marseillaise!
WAITER: *Rognons de veau?*
CLINT: Well, I don't know.
WAITER: *Sauce aïoli?*
CLINT: Well, let me see.
WAITER: *Une brochette* of *escargots?*
CLINT: No, nothing from Chicago!
WAITER: A plate of tender scallions—
CLINT: And smother them with onions!
WAITER: Why not a *filet d'able?*
CLINT: *Le crayon sur la table.*
WAITER: *Chateaubriand,* et cetera.
CLINT: And *ouvray la fenetera!*
WAITER: *Courgettes aux choux!*
CLINT: *Gesundheit!* God bless *you!*
WAITER: A hot *pâté d'anguille?*
CLINT: And what might be that?
WAITER: Eel!
CLINT: Shore, bring it with the gizzard of
 some Arizona lizard!
WAITER: *En casserole or dijonnaise? Diable
 or dauphine?*
CLINT: Okay, okay! You win!
 Surprise me!

AL FRESCO

Registered for copyright as an unpublished song October 19, 1959. Intended for Carol Lawrence (Clio), Odette Myrtil (Belle), Edith King (Mrs. Bellop), and ensemble but not used in show.

CLIO: What could be better than you
 and I
 Letting this weary old world go by,
 Dining out under the open sky
 Al fresco?
BELLE: Sitting there under the lantern
 shine,
 Having the maître d' pour the wine,
 Showing the commoners how we
 dine
 Al fresco?
MRS. BELLOP: Stuffed shirts abhor it,
 You'll just adore it—
 Join our sorority!
 After we're squiffy on triple sec
 What does it matter who pays the
 check?
CLIO: So do dine—

MRS. BELLOP: Where few dine.
CLIO: You'll see how—
MRS. BELLOP: Who's who dine—
BOTH: When you dine al fresco with me.

LASSO

Intended for Howard Keel (Clint) and Tun Tun (Cupide) but not used in show.
 Lyric missing.

THE PARKS OF PARIS

Published in piano-vocal selections. Registered for copyright as an unpublished song October 19, 1959. Not used in show. Intended to follow "Al Fresco."

VERSE 1

Artists and models inhabit the attics of Paris;
Under the rooftops the starving bohemians dwell.
Not for the world do I wish to confuse or embarrass,
But there's another side as well.

REFRAIN 1

In the parks of Paris
You see ev'rything;
In the parks of Paris
It is always spring.
There gay young couples
Walking hand in hand.
No one pays them any attention;
They understand.

VERSE 2

Old people nap with their newspaper over their
 faces;
Nurses are rolling their eyes at the strolling
 gendarmes,
Letting the children discover the clandestine places
Where lovers share each other's arms.

REFRAIN 2

In the parks of Paris
You are always young.
In the parks of Paris
Lovers speak one tongue.

You may be a stranger
But it's in the air,
So, if you're in search of a lover,
You'll find one there,
In the park,
In the dark of the
Old Paris parks!

READING THE NEWS

Lyric missing.

HERE GOES NOTHING

Intended for Howard Keel (Clint). Early version of the song that became "You or No One." The music for the two songs is the same.

Here goes nothing.
Here I go,
All or nothing
On a single throw.
I had nothing
When I came in.
We can't lose
What wasn't ours to win.
Sure, I'm laying my heart on the line.
Sure, it's nothing or everything fine.
If we lose that something,
Just recall,
Here goes nothing at all.

FOLKS

Lyric missing.

TO MAKE A FINE LADY

Intended for Odette Myrtil (Belle), Carol Brice (Kakou), and Tun Tun (Cupide) but not used in show.

BELLE: To make a fine lady,
A truly fine lady,
Takes more than meets the eye.

KAKOU: When she's a wee stranger,
You bib her and change her—

CUPIDE: And hang things out to dry.

BELLE: There's etiquette and protocol
Permitting which beaux to call,
Deciding which ones to avoid.

KAKOU: You build her up, you trim her down—

CUPIDE: You tell her to simmer down
When she becomes overjoyed.
(Too loudly and you're unemployed.)

KAKOU: You wine her and dine her—

BELLE: And she becomes finer,
But you undergo change of life.

ALL: It really takes teamwork
To make every scheme work
And make a fine lady a wife!

BELLE: To make a fine lady,
A truly fine lady,
You'll have to be a thief.

KAKOU: With trips to the grocer—
"How much do we owe, sir?"
"And how much is the beef?"

CUPIDE: All frozen up and shivery
And dressed in red livery,
You sit in the carriage and drown.

BELLE: Outnumbered by your creditors,
You write to the editors,
Announcing that you're leaving town.

BABY

Music by Steve Allen. Registered for copyright as an unpublished song January 14, 1959.

Baby,
I guess I'll have to call you baby,
It may not be quite everything
That a nickname ought to be,
But it's you to a T.

Baby,
Can't find a better word than "baby,"
Though I confess that I have searched
Ev'ry dictionary through,
Not a one will do.

I've looked for phrases
To sing your praises,
Like ev'ry poet since time was new.
Whatever comes up,
Still nothing sums up
The very extraordinary you.

But, baby,
Who knows but some fine day
There may be
A little angel who will smile
And announce, "Well, here I am,
Baby's baby lamb."

Additional lyrics

I thought of "Honey"
And "Easter bunny"
And yet it's funny . . .

* * *

Yes, even "muffin"
And "turkey stuffin' "
Doesn't seem to catch
The real real you.
So maybe
It's like I tried to tell you, baby—
Let's name the day,
And in a year we can tell our friends that you
Call me baby, too.

BLUES OPERA/ FREE AND EASY (1959)

Blues Opera, or *Free and Easy*, as it was also titled, was an ambitious, misguided, and unsuccessful attempt to transform Harold Arlen and Johnny Mercer's magnificent *St. Louis Woman* (1946) into an opera, a sort of companion piece to George Gershwin, DuBose Heyward, and Ira Gershwin's great American folk opera, *Porgy and Bess*.

In his biography of Arlen, *Rhythm Rainbows & Blues*, Edward Jablonski gives a detailed account of the evolution of *Blues Opera*. The idea of making *St. Louis Woman* into an opera originated with Robert Breen, who had staged and toured *Porgy and Bess* in the early and mid-1950s. He approached Arlen in late 1953 or early 1954 after becoming familiar with some of the composer's songs and listening to the cast album of *St. Louis Woman* (at the suggestion of lyricist Betty Comden).

Arlen responded positively to Breen's enthusiasm,

and while he was at work with lyricist E. Y. Harburg on the score for the 1957 musical *Jamaica*, he began refashioning *St. Louis Woman* into what was to become *Blues Opera*. According to Jablonski, Arlen, with the help of conductor Samuel Matlowsky, first created a twenty-five-minute orchestral suite. André Kostelanetz premiered the piece in Minneapolis on August 28, 1957, and reprised it at New York's Carnegie Hall on November 2.

Jablonski notes that the suite from *Blues Opera* was in 17 sections and included "Any Place I Hang My Hat Is Home," "It's a Woman's Prerogative," "I Had Myself a True Love," "I Wonder What Became of Me," "Leavin' Time," and, of course, "Come Rain or Come Shine," all from *St. Louis Woman*, as well as "American Minuet," an instrumental Arlen wrote in 1939. At a post-Carnegie-concert party given by Gloria Vanderbilt in her New York apartment, André Kostelanetz, arriving late, told Arlen that his *Blues Opera* Suite would be recorded by Columbia Records.

Work on *Blues Opera* itself continued. The aim was to premiere it at the Brussels World's Fair in the spring of 1958; in fact, it didn't reach Brussels—for its "out-of-town tryout"—until November 1959. The title had been changed by then to *Free and Easy*. When the world premiere of *Free and Easy* took place at the Carré Theatre in Amsterdam on December 17, 1959, Stanley Chase was the producer, but Breen, caught up in a feud with Chase, had been replaced as director by Donald McKayle. On January 15, 1960, *Free and Easy* opened at the Alhambra in Paris, where it expired nine days later. The cast, which included Irene Williams, Harold Nicholas (repeating his role as Little Augie from *St. Louis Woman*), Moses La Marr, Martha Flowers, Irving Barnes, Paul Harris, Ruby Green, and Elijah Hodges, was stranded in Paris until two good Samaritans came to their rescue with money to get home. Quincy Jones, though, the show's conductor (and orchestrator), managed to put together a European tour with his band.

Reading the *Variety* review after *Free and Easy* opened in Amsterdam, Mercer, who had never really been involved with the project, was unhappy to learn that Arlen songs with lyrics by Ted Koehler as well as three new numbers with no lyricist credited—"Dis Little While," "Many Kinds of Love," and "Blow De Whistle"—had become part of the score. Jablonski also mentions two other additions: a song by Arlen and Ralph Blane and one new entry attributed to Mercer, "Won't Dat Be de Blessed Day."

Rumors abounded about the future of *Free and Easy*. It was even said, at one point, that Sammy Davis Jr. was set to replace Harold Nicholas. Despite some good reviews, investors lost $300,000. Chase, undaunted, announced an autumn 1960 Broadway production. It never happened.

CHAMPAGNE FO' DE LADY

Possibly written for *Blues Opera*. Registered for copyright as an unpublished song July 16, 1958.

Champagne fo' de lady,
Now what?
What about all dem fancy t'ings
Li'l Augie was getting for you?
How you mean?
Whatcha gonna do?
Warm clothes?
Scrub floors?
Sit fo' company?
Ya gotta have t'ings,
Ya gotta live easy,
Ya gotta have luck!
Augie mo' lovin',
His luck
Den you!
Luck done split Li'l Augie
And de mens done spoil me!

SNAKE EYES

Possibly written for *Blues Opera*.

Snake eyes, snake eyes
'Bout as welcome here as a adder.
You ghosty, you witchy,
You must o' climbed the old devil's ladder—
I'se itchy
To make yo' string o' bad luck badder!

Snake eyes,
Don't you try to evil-eye me,
Don't you try to conjurfy me,
'Cause my name is Count Two-Timey—
Can't no man alive outfly me,
And if you don't believes me, try me!

Snake eyes
(Dey's like a ferret),
Seen you comin' and I knew ya
(You evil sperrit).
Even though the devil grew ya
(So cold and beady),
Money says I'll out-hoodoo ya
(Oh, yes, indeed!)—
I can send yo' spell back to ya,
Yes, I can run my luck right through ya,
Hard luck—snake eyes!!!!

WON'T DAT BE DE BLESSED DAY

Possibly written for *Blues Opera*.

Oh, won't dat be de blessed day,
Dat seven-come-eleven day!
Lucky dust a-rollin' in,
Every race a race to win!
Deep river gotta flow some
Fo' dat day to shine,
An', sport, y' gotta go some
Till you makes it mine!
No denyin' dat it might be sweet
Ridin' dicty over Targee Street,
Highfalutin everyone we see
Scatterin' pearls and diamonds like dey made dem
    free—
Now, won't dat be de day!

OVERLEAF
Top: Breakfast at Tiffany's: *Audrey Hepburn singing "Moon River"*
Bottom: Days of Wine and Roses: *Jack Lemmon and Lee Remick*

"Moon River"
and Other Songs of 1960–1963

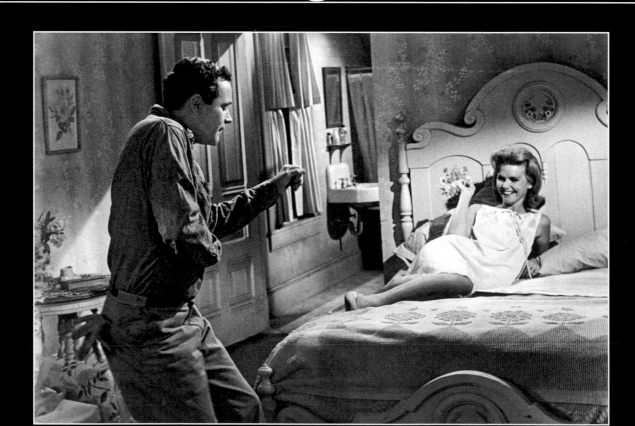

MY LOVE FOR YOU

Music by Stan Hoffman. Registered for copyright as an unpublished song June 3, 1960.

My love for you,
My love for you,
Sleeps in this heart of mine like slumbering
    thunder.
And when I see you, I see you through mist
Of golden sunlight and purple amethyst.
Your love for me,
Your love for me,
To even think about it fills me with wonder.
I won't believe it,
The longest day I live,
I don't deserve it,
For what have I to give?
Nothing, it's true,
Nothing except my love for you!

THE OLD BROWN THRUSH

Music by Alfred J. Thieme. Registered for copyright as an unpublished song July 5, 1960.

There's a redbird sittin' in the chinaberry tree,
Goin' "Tweedle-deedle-deedle,
Tweedle-deedle-dee."
Oh, he's just as happy as happy can be,
And he's thataway all day long.
There's a blue jay singin' on the sparkleberry tree,
Goin' "Husha-husha-husha,
Husha-husha-hush."
Old thrush, who ya foolin' with your sentimental
    mush?
Better git you a brand-new song!
When the sunset sky is blazin' red
And it's twilight on the hill,
If you wanna hear sumpin' that'll turn your head
And give your heart a thrill,
It's the redbird sittin' in the chinaberry tree
And the sparkleberry blue jay in a merrymakin'
    key,
Goin' "Husha-husha-husha,"
"Tweedle-deedle-dee."
So, even when things go wrong,
With their "Husha-husha-husha,"
"Tweedle-deedle-dee,"
They keep makin' life a song.

IF I DIDN'T LOVE YOU

Music by Lorelei Trepper. Registered for copyright as an unpublished song July 15, 1960.

If I didn't love you,
If I didn't care,
Would your name be whispered
In my every prayer?
Would I show the willow
How much a lonely heart can weep
Or talk to my pillow
And cry in my sleep?
If I didn't need you
As roses need rain,
Would I even bother
To try to explain?
Would I live a lifetime
Each night we're apart
If I didn't love you
With all my heart?

When somebody loves you,
When somebody cares,
When somebody whispers
Your name in his prayers,
When somebody needs you
The way the planets need the sky
And somebody wants you
So much he could die,
The least you can answer,
The least you can say,
Is "Now I don't love you,
But someday I may."
The least you can tell me
Is not tell a lie
When somebody loves you
As much as I.

THE FACTS OF LIFE (1960)

Produced by Norman Panama for Panama and Frank Productions. Released by United Artists. Released December 1960. Copyright December 15, 1960. Directed by Melvin Frank. Screenplay by Norman Panama and Melvin Frank. Lyrics and music by Johnny Mercer. Musical direction: Leigh Harline. Starring Bob Hope and Lucille Ball, featuring Ruth Hussey, Don DeFore, and Louis Nye, with Philip Ober, Marianne Stewart, Peter Leeds, Hollis Irving, William Lanteau, Robert F. Simon, Louise Beavers, Mike Mazurki, and Steve Lawrence and Eydie Gormé.

Middle-aged married suburbanites try to have an affair—without success.

THE FACTS OF LIFE

Music by Mercer. Registered for copyright as an unpublished song September 19, 1960. Introduced and recorded by Steve Lawrence and Eydie Gormé on the film soundtrack (United Artists). The song was nominated for an Academy Award but lost to "Never on a Sunday."

Such are the facts of life,
You wanna know the facts of life?
I'm gonna teach the facts of life to you.
Now, concerning the birds and bees
Inhabiting all those trees,
Establishing all those families,
Up with each daisy,
Singin' like crazy,
Storin' up honey,
Savin' their money—
Those are the facts of life,
The ordinary acts of life
That ev'ry livin' creature seems
To do.
So, stay after school tonight,
'Cause I wanna study with all my might,
The facts of life
With you.

TWO OF A KIND

Music by Bobby Darin. Registered for copyright as an unpublished song December 8, 1960. Written for the Darin-Mercer album *Two of a Kind*.

Two of a kind—
For your information,
We're two of a kind.
Two of a kind—
It's my observation
We're two of a kind.
Peas in a pod

And birds of a feather,
Alone or together,
You'll find
That we are two-oo-oo-oo-oo-oo-oo-oo-oo-oo-oo
Of a kind.
What's so wrong
Thinkin' life is a song,
And reachin' for a star?
Who's to say
If we'll go the whole way?
At least we got this far!
Sharing our lot,
Our victuals and viands,
We're two of an ilk.
What if we've got rare chateaubriands
Or crackers and milk?
Making it plain,
Explaining it fully,
We're sim-i-luh-luh-ly inclined,
Because we're two-oo-oo-oo-oo-oo-oo-oo-oo-oo-oo
Of a kind!

DON'T START CRYIN' NOW

Composer unknown. Registered for copyright as an unpublished song December 14, 1960.
  Lyric missing.

BOUQUET

Music by Percy Faith. Registered for copyright as an unpublished song January 4, 1961.

I still have the daisy
That we picked on the hill,
The one whose petals said to me,
"Just wait and see, it's love,
Really love."
What's more,
I remember that gardenia you wore—
You laughed and called it your bouquet,
It looked so gay on your glove.
The day you sent that forget-me-not
Became a day I never once forgot.
So many memories
Go drifting by,
October trees,
And if I could frame
That chrysanthemum you wore to the game—

Remember how we tied the score
With seconds more to play?
Little things, and yet,
These are memories I'll never forget,
For you are there in ev'ry scene
In my evergreen bouquet.

BRASILIA (SERENATA NEGRA)

Music and Spanish lyrics by Vico Pagano, Carlos Loti, and Tito Madinez. English lyrics by Mercer: registered for copyright as an unpublished song January 23, 1961.

Brazil, Brazil, Brazil,
Have you seen Brasilia?
Skyline of tomorrow,
Oh, what a sweep
Has the city on the plain!

You should see Brasilia—
In the midst of nowhere,
Shiny and bright
Like a jewel in the rain.

Knowing that a lover loves the moonlight
On the tree-covered plazas,
Architects have utilized the moonlight
Like latticework on the lawns.

Lovers in Brasilia
Fill the night with laughter;
So let your heart be a lover—
Come along.

INTERLUDE

Come with me for a flight there;
Let me show you its charms,
Come with me for a night there;
Spend the night in my arms.

CODA

Once you leave Brasilia,
You will not forget it.
It will remain in your vision
Like a spell.
Brazil, Brazil, Brasilia—
Farewell.

BREAKFAST AT TIFFANY'S (1961)

Produced by Martin Jurow and Richard Shepherd for Paramount Pictures. Released October 1961. Copyright October 5, 1961. Directed by Blake Edwards. Screenplay by George Axelrod, based on the novel by Truman Capote. Lyrics by Johnny Mercer. Music by Henry Mancini. Starring Audrey Hepburn and George Peppard, featuring Patricia Neal, Buddy Ebsen, Martin Balsam, and José Luis de Villalonga, with John McGiver, Alan Reed, Dorothy Whitney, Beverly Powers (as Miss Beverly Hills), Stanley Adams, Claude Stroud, Elvia Allman, Orangey (as Cat), and Mickey Rooney.

A New York writer has for a neighbor Holly Golightly, a young lady with a somewhat exotic lifestyle.

MOON RIVER

Published. Copyrighted August 31, 1961. Previously registered for copyright as an unpublished song January 31, 1961. Introduced by Audrey Hepburn. Leading recordings by Henry Mancini and His Orchestra (Victor), Jerry Butler (VeeJay), and Andy Williams (Columbia).

The song won the Academy Award for Best Song for its year as well as a Grammy Award for best song from N.A.R.A.S. (the National Academy of Recording Arts and Science).

Henry Mancini handed Mercer the melody and Mercer returned with three different sets of lyrics. Version three began . . .

  I'm Holly,
  Like I want to be,
  Like holly on a tree back home.
  Just plain Holly,
  With no dolly,
  No mama, no papa,
  Wherever I roam.

"I don't know about that one," Mercer said. "I'm calling it 'Blue River,' but it may change, because I went through the ASCAP archives and found that several of my friends—Joseph Meyer, for instance—have already written songs called 'Blue River.' 'Red River'—because all the rivers down there are so muddy? 'June River'?" Then he did what Stephen Foster had done when locating the Swanee—he consulted a map and found a river, this one north of Savannah in South Carolina. He returned to Mancini with "Moon River."

He sang the song as Mancini played, and Mancini recalled: "Every once in a while you hear something so right it gives you chills. When he sang that 'huckleberry friend' line, I got them. I don't know if he knew what effect those words had . . . but it was thrilling. It made you think of Mark Twain and Huckleberry Finn's trip down the Mississippi. It had such echoes of America." Irving Berlin was to predict that "Moon River" would achieve the stature of an American folk song.

"I don't know how I thought of that phrase," Mercer remarked. "Probably stems from the days of my childhood, when we'd go out in the fields and pick berries; they were everywhere. I was free associating for that song. The heroine, Holly Golightly, was from down there . . . I figured, it's springtime, she's in New York and thinking of her home down there when she was a child. And then I thought 'huckleberry.' I said, that's the right word. I know it's an odd word, but that's why it's so attractive."

Even so, the song nearly didn't happen. When the film was previewed, it was considered to be too long. At a meeting afterwards, producer Marty Rakin said, "I don't know what you guys are going to do, but I'll tell you one thing, that damn song can go!" Fortunately, wiser counsel prevailed—and Irving Berlin's prediction came to pass.

"Jeepers creepers," "something's gotta give," and "accentuate the positive" may have already been part of the English lexicon when Johnny Mercer wove those phrases into his songs; but today it is impossible to utter the words without thinking of the songs that ensconce them so comfortably. "My mamma done tol' me," "Lazybones, sleepin' in the sun," and "Hooray for Hollywood" are of Mercer's own conception, as is perhaps the most enigmatic of all, "my huckleberry friend."

Like nearly everyone in the civilized world, Miles Kreuger was beguiled in 1961 by lovely Audrey Hepburn when she sang "Moon River" in *Breakfast at Tiffany's*; but he always wondered about that "huckleberry friend." Why does a Moon River, whatever that is, suggest a huckleberry friend? So he asked Mercer.

He looked bemused and slightly embarrassed. He said, "You're the only one who has asked me about 'huckleberry friend.' Everybody loves that image, but it's really a terrible mistake." He went on to explain that the original lyric he had set to Mancini's tune was called "Blue River"; when suddenly he remembered a song with the same title by his friend and sometime collaborator Joseph Meyer, and if Mercer's own version became a hit, he did not want to hurt the feelings of a fellow songwriter. So, at the last minute, he altered the title to "Moon River."

But, in his haste, he neglected to alter the image "huckleberry friend," which would clearly describe a river that was blue. He added that every time he heard the song performed, he winced a little and regretted that he had forgotten to reconceive the image. The song that brought Mercer another Academy Award and tremendous acclaim and wealth made him cringe, because his work was less perfect than he might have made it.

Moon River,
Wider than a mile,
I'm crossin' you in style
Someday.
Old dream maker,
You heart breaker,
Wherever you're goin',
I'm goin' your way.
Two drifters
Off to see the world—
There's such a lot of world
To see.
We're after the same
Rainbow's end,
Waitin' round the bend,
My huckleberry friend,
Moon River
And me.

THE BILBAO SONG

Music by Kurt Weill. Original German lyrics by Bertolt Brecht. Free translation/adaptation by Johnny Mercer. Published. Copyrighted April 18, 1961. Originally written for *Happy End*, a three-act comedy with music first performed in Berlin on September 2, 1929, a collaboration between Weill and Brecht. Mercer's version was popularized by Andy Williams, accompanied by the Archie Bleyer Orchestra (Cadence).

REFRAIN 1

That old Bilbao moon,
I won't forget it soon,
That old Bilbao moon,
Just like a big balloon.
That old Bilbao moon
Would rise above the dune
While Tony's beach saloon
Rocked with an old-time tune.
We'd sing a song the whole night long
And I can still recall,
Those were the greatest,
Those were the greatest,
Those were the greatest nights of them all!

REFRAIN 2

No paint was on the door,
The grass grew through the floor,
Of Tony's two-by-four
On the Bilbao shore.
But there were friends galore
And there was beer to pour
And moonlight on the shore,
That old Bilbao shore.
We'd sing a song the whole night long,
And I can still recall
Those were the greatest,
Those were the greatest,
Those were the greatest nights of them all!

REFRAIN 3

Those old Bilbao guys,
They loved to harmonize—
Who stopped to realize
How fast the summer flies?
The moon was on the rise,
We'd catch the ladies' eyes
And whisper Spanish lies—
They never did get wise.
We'd sing a song the whole night long,
And I can still recall,
Those were the greatest,
Those were the greatest,
Those were the greatest days of them all!

MEXICAN MOON

Music by Walter Gross. Lyrics by Mercer and Charles Rinker. Registered for copyright as an unpublished song November 27, 1961.

See the view going through Acapulco—
The travel book said:
"Quite a sight by the light of the Mexican moon,"
Coming up big and bright on the water
And cherry-plum red.
So I stayed for the night and the Mexican moon;
Then you and your silhouette on the moonlit
    veranda
Took my mind off the view,
And I and my silhouette faded
Into the darkness with you.
Our shadows blended,
Our kiss never ended.
Time for saying goodbye, my beloved,
Comes always too soon;
So we just never said it,

And who gets all the credit?
That shy old, sly old rogue of a Mexican moon.

BAIIAO

Music by Les Baxter.

Baiiao, Baiiao,
The dance you may not know.
Baiiao, Baiiao,
From somewhere south of Mexico.
Is fast—but no,
Is sensuous and slow,
Baiiao, Baiiao, Baiiao.

Baiiao, Baiiao,
The music whispers low.
Baiiao, Baiiao,
Like very pianissimo.
I think I know
What makes me love it so—
It's you by me,
Baiiao.

Hold me—
I haven't heard a single word
You've told me.
Who listens while you hold me?
Hold me
While the cabasas and pandieros play.
Kiss me,
And make up lies about how much
You'll miss me.
Just look at me and kiss me,
Kiss me
And hold me closer
While I melt away.

Baiiao, Baiiao,
The rhythm may be slow,
But though it's slow,
My heart beats so fortissimo.
By now you know
A kiss is apropos
By you, by me,
Baiiao.

JACK-O'-LANTERN

Music by Hoagy Carmichael.

Jack-o'-lantern,
You old jack-o'-lantern moon,
Jack-o'-lantern,
What did you do to June?
She was really something to behold
When you dressed her up
In yellow gold.
We were lovers
In a starry-eyed embrace;
Then she vanished,
Like your ol' funny face.
Bring her back
And make the love light shine
In this jack-o'-lantern heart of mine!

MUSICA DI ROMA

Music by Gilbert Martinez.

Musica di Roma, echoing and rolling,
Rolling through the wide streets,
The little side streets where we were strolling.
Musica di Roma, where flower vendors
Sang a song among the splendors
Of that age-old town.
Ev'ry poster I see
Has a special meaning for me;
Ev'ry bit of old melody
Reminds me that we were so in love.
Even though I've lost you
And you're far across the sea,
Musica di Roma brings you back to me.

OASIS

Music by Donald Borzage. Lyrics by Mercer and Samuel Schwartz.
    Lyric missing.

THE YEARLY CONSULAR BALL

Music by Mercer.

We're havin' a do:
We want you here
At what we call the yearly consular ball.
The least political event of all,
We're plannin' to swing
At this thing
That we merely call the yearly consular ball,
So park your worry with your protocol.
Come make the scene
With Issa Serageldin,
That United Arab Republicat.
Like, what we need
Is for our guests to proceed upon the theory
It's the night of the year.
Remember to fall by—
It's black tie—
And dig the dignitaries
Here in the hall,
Because we're really gonna have a ball.
Man, a consular ball!

DRINKING AGAIN

Music by Doris Tauber. Published. Copyrighted January 10, 1962.

Drinking again
And thinking of when you loved me;
Having a few
And wishing that you were here.
Making the rounds
And buying the rounds for strangers,*
Being a fool,
Just hoping that you'll appear.
Sure I can borrow a smoke,
Maybe tell some joker a joke
But who's gonna laugh at a broken heart?
It's better
Drinking again
And thinking of when you left me,
Making it home with just a memory.

---

* *Alternate line:*
    Accepting a round from strangers,

HAV-ZIES

Music by Rube Bloom. Published. Copyrighted February 5, 1962.

Hav-zies—
Wanna go hav-zies with me?
Wanna go stingin' along
For the swinginest song and dance?

Through this old world we'll waltz,
Ignoring each other's faults,
And if we can't have wine with a bubble
We'll make it double malts,

Won't that be groovy?
Hav-zies—
Sharin' the things that are free;
Both of us livin' it up.
While we're divvyin' up the sky.
You get the gold that spills
Down over the daffodils,
And what do I get?
I get to be nearby.

I also get to press those lips,
Caress those lips,
And hold your hand;
This fifty-fifty bit,
What a nifty bit for me.

I'm glad I thought of hav-zies,
Seein' as how we agree.
Soon as I get me a raise
We'll be makin' that crazy scene,
The one with shoes and rice—
Two tickets to paradise.
The proposition's now up to you.
If'n you parlez-vous,
Fall in and say
You'll go hav-zies, too.

IF YOU COME THROUGH

Music by Rube Bloom. Published. Copyrighted February 5, 1962.

If you come through,
My life will be a summer song;
If you come through
And love me too.

One look at you,
I told myself, "Don't play this wrong,
She's all you've waited for so long."
Then all at once the skies were sunny,
'Cause something I said you thought was funny.
And then I knew
We both were standing hand in hand,
On the brink of a dream coming true;
Say yes,
And when you say it,
Say ev'ry word
As though you meant to pray it.
Dreams don't happen,
But they will
If you come through.

INDISCRETION

Music by Matt Malneck. Registered for copyright as an unpublished song February 7, 1962.

Indiscretion,
A slight indiscretion, was how it began,
That's true.
Secret glances
We couldn't resist,
Stolen dances,
And then we kissed!
That was foolish,
But love isn't foolish—
It told us what we should do.
Here's my confession:
May our indiscretion
Continue our whole life through!

I DON'T WANNA BE ALONE AGAIN

Music by Howard Smith. Manuscript is annotated "For Girl Singer." Registered for copyright as an unpublished song April 30, 1962.

I sang a love song
That came from the heart;
You took my love song
And tore it apart.
Now you're suggesting

We make a new start,
But I don't wanna be alone again.

We made the night spots
From pillar to post,
With beer and pretzels
We shared every toast.
To say the least
You were always the most,
But I don't wanna be alone again.

I guess it's happened ever since Adam
And I can see it happening now.*
You didn't want my arms when you had 'em,
I don't know why you should want 'em now.

Here's to you, baby,
Here's mud in your eye;
We're better off letting
Sleeping dogs lie.
I'm out of love
With a wonderful guy,
'Cause I don't wanna be alone again.

MR. HOBBS TAKES A VACATION (1962)

Produced by Jerry Wald for Twentieth Century–Fox. Released May 1962. Copyright May 25, 1962. Directed by Henry Koster. Screenplay by Nunnally Johnson, based on the novel *Mr. Hobbs' Vacation* by Edward Streeter. Lyrics by Johnny Mercer. Music and music score by Henry Mancini. Orchestrations by Leo Shuken and Jack Hayes. Starring James Stewart and Maureen O'Hara, featuring Fabian, John Saxon, Marie Wilson, Reginald Gardiner, Lauri Peters, and Valerie Varda, with Lili Gentle, John McGiver, Natalie Trundy, Josh Peine, Minerva Urecal, Michael Burns, and Richard Collier.

An urban family rents a seaside house for a family holiday—only to find that it is falling apart.

---

* *Alternate lines:*
    It must have happened to Adam—
    It always happens somehow.

CREAM PUFF

Music by Henry Mancini. Published. Copyrighted June 19, 1962. Previously registered for copyright as an unpublished song February 27, 1962. Introduced by Fabian and Lauri Peters.

REFRAIN

Cream puff, shortcake,
Sweet stuff, jelly roll,
Gumdrop, milk shake,
Curl up and be my baby doll.

VERSE

Woe is me,
My predicament is novel,
Can't chicken out and can't be brave;
Love your style,
But a fellow shouldn't grovel,
How does a guy behave?
When he simply can't let it go,
It's a crazy situation,
Feel like a feather in a gale;
Can't hold on—
It's a simple explanation,
I've got a tiger by the tail.

REPEAT REFRAIN

VERSE 2

Woe is me,
When I think of what I could be,
Master mechanic, engineer,
Ph.D.
Of the many things I should be,
I picked the wrong career,
'Cause I simply can't let go.
Could have been a picture framer,
Pitched for the Cubs,
Delivered mail.
Can't hold on—
Should have been a lion tamer,
I've got a tiger by the tail.

REPEAT REFRAIN

VERSE 3

Woe is me,
My solution isn't solvin';
Maybe the answer
Can't be found.
Looks like I'm gonna
Have to keep revolvin',
Just going round and round,

'Cause I simply can't let go.
It's a terrible confession,
I'm like a Jonah and the whale,
Can't hold on—
If you'll pardon the expression,
I've got a tiger by the tail.

BABY-O

Music by Johnny Rotella. Published. Copyrighted August 16, 1962. Previously registered for copyright as an unpublished song March 23, 1962.

Mercer clearly experimented with this format; the archive contains several variant lyrics.

REFRAIN 1

Baby-o,
You I dig,
Like the most,
Really big.
Love the shape
Of your brow,
Love your "Ooh,"
Love your "Aah,"
Love your "Wow!"*
Baby-o,
Tell me true,
Could you go
For me too?
Cross your heart
If it's so,
That you're my
Hope-to-die
Baby-o!

REFRAIN 2

Baby-o,
You won't quit,
Like, I mean,
This is it!

* *Alternate lines 5–9:*
   Love the style,
   Yessirree!
   Love your "Ooh,"
   Love your "Aah,"
   E-t-c.!

Love your mad
Swingin' pad.
You know what?
You're a nut
And I'm glad!
Baby-o,
May I fly
In a plane*
Through the sky,
Writing words
Just to show
That you're my
Ten-mile-high
Baby-o!

REFRAIN 3

Baby-o,
Sugar plum,
You are so
Yummy-yum—
Plus, to wit,
And whereas,
Très jolie,
E-t-c.,
All that jazz.
Baby-o,
There are laws,
So I wrote
Santa Claus:
Under my
Mistletoe,
Just for fun,
Please leave one
Baby-o!

REFRAIN 4

Baby-o,
Angel child,
Crazy-o,
This is wild!
May I yell,
Like "Huzzah"?
You are my
Two-for-tea
Cha-cha-cha!
Baby-o,
Say the word,

* *Alternate lines 12–18:*
   Through the blue
   Summer sky,
   Writing things
   So they'll know
   That you're my
   Two-mile-high
   Baby-o!

Take it slow,
Up a third,
Like the world
Ought to know
That you're my
Aye-aye-aye
Baby-o!

REFRAIN 5

Baby-o,
Who's one?
She's-a me,
Your *paisan*,
From-a same
Neighborhood.
Yours-a pop
He's-a wop,
That's-a good.
Baby-o,
Scusa, please,
I'm-a shout
To the breeze,
"Look-a here,
Whad'ya know!
She's-a my
Pizza pie,
Baby-o!"

HATARI (1962)

Produced and directed by Howard Hawks for Malabar Productions, released by Paramount Pictures. Released July 1962. Copyright December 31, 1961. Screenplay by Leigh Brackett, from a story by Harry Kurnitz. Lyrics by Johnny Mercer. Music by Hoagy Carmichael. Musical score by Henry Mancini. Featuring John Wayne, Hardy Kruger, Elsa Martinelli, Red Buttons, Gérard Blain, Bruce Cabot, Michèle Girardon, Valentin de Vargas, and Eduard Franz.

International hunters in Tanganyika hunt game to send to zoos.

JUST FOR TONIGHT

Published. Copyrighted July 3, 1962. Registered for copyright as an unpublished song April 16, 1962. This song became "A Perfect Paris Night." Not sung in film.

Original version

Did I hear you say *"Je vous adore"*?
Have you ever said those words before?
Do you really mean with all your might
All the pretty little things you've said
While holding me tight
This wonderful night?
If you wonder why I speak this way,
Not so long ago I was Fool for a Day.
Now hold me
If you want to kiss me—
Darling, make it all so right.
Promise it will never be
Just for tonight!

Revised version

Could we make it just for us tonight,
On the table only candlelight?*
Could we find some violins that say
All the little things we've thought and felt today?
Could we stop a while at old Maxim's
For a final round of absinthe and dreams?
Then, when the moment's right,
Take advantage of this mood,
Just for tonight?

A PERFECT PARIS NIGHT

Music and lyrics by Mercer and Hoagy Carmichael. Published. Copyrighted July 8, 1964.

Never has a night been quite so gay,
Never has the wine been so rosé,
Never has a Paris moon above
Made a hungry little heart like mine
So hungry for love.
How'd you like to go to old Maxim's
For a final round of espresso and dreams,
Darling, and then,
When the moment's right,
Take advantage of a perfect Paris night?

---

* *Alternate line:*
    At a corner table not too bright

THE CABINET OF CALIGARI (1962)

Produced and directed by Roger Kay for Robert L. Lippert Productions. Released by Twentieth Century–Fox. Released May 1962. Copyright May 23, 1962. Lyrics by Johnny Mercer. Music by Gerald Fried. Featuring Glynis Johns, Dan O'Herlihy, Richard Davalos, Lawrence Dobkin, Constance Ford, J. Pat O'Malley, Vicki Trickett, Estelle Winwood, Doreen Lang, Charles Fredericks, and Phyllis Teagarden.

A young woman appears to be held prisoner by the evil Dr. Caligari, but the story turns out to be all happening in her imagination.

THE SOUNDS OF THE NIGHT

Published. Copyrighted November 2, 1964. Previously registered for copyright as an unpublished song May 28, 1962, and again on March 21, 1963. Not sung in film.

The sounds of the night, drowsy and deep,
The sounds of the night lull me to sleep.
The touch of the wind stirring the leaves,
The murmur of birds under the eaves,
The sounds of the night steal through the sky
To sing me an old sweet lullaby.
I hear through the rain pattering down
The hum of a plane high over town.
Sometimes I awake with a feeling of danger;
The night is a dark and mysterious stranger.
My heart in its fright sounds like a drum to me,
But when you come to me in a dream,
Your lips kiss away my foolish fears,
The night is a friend I've known for years.
How lucky to be so close to you,
Listening to the sounds of the night!

MOON IN THE MULBERRY TREE

Music by George Motola. Published. Copyrighted August 28, 1962.

Moon in the mulberry tree,
Shine for me and my darlin' tonight,
Heavenly light of love.
Moon in the mulberry tree,
You can say with your silvery beams
All that I am dreaming of.
Peek down through the blossoms
And spot the shadows with gold;
An angel is really not easy to hold.
Love put the song in our hearts,
But nobody can keep them in tune
Like you, old mulberry moon.

ONCE UPON A SUMMERTIME (LA VALSE DES LILAS)

Music by Eddie Barclay and Michel Legrand. Original French lyric by Eddy Marnay. English version by Johnny Mercer: Published. Copyrighted October 1, 1962. Leading recordings by Blossom Dearie (Verve), Tony Bennett (Columbia), and Barbra Streisand (Columbia).

This was Mercer's first collaboration with French composer Michel Legrand, who was later to become a good friend with whom Mercer worked on several projects. In his unpublished autobiography Mercer refers to the possibility of their collaborating on a musical to be based on Rostand's *Cyrano de Bergerac*.

Once upon a summertime, if you recall,
We stopped beside a little flower stall.
A bunch of bright forget-me-nots was all
I'd let you buy me.

Once upon a summertime, just like today,
We laughed the happy afternoon away
And stole a kiss in ev'ry street café.

You were sweeter than the blossoms on the tree.
I was as proud as any girl could be,
As if the mayor had offered me the key
To Paris!

Now, another wintertime has come and gone;
The pigeons feeding in the square have flown;
But I remember when the vespers chime
You loved me once upon a summertime.

HOW THE WEST WAS WON (1962)

Produced by Bernard Smith for Metro-Goldwyn-Mayer and Cinerama. World premiere November 1, 1962. Copyright December 31, 1962. Directed by John Ford, George Marshall, and Henry Hathaway. Screenplay by James R. Webb, suggested by the 1959 *Life* magazine series "How the West Was Won." Lyrics by Johnny Mercer, Sammy Cahn, and Ken Darby. Music by Alfred Newman and traditional. Musical score by Alfred Newman. Musical coordination by Robert Emmett Dolan. Featuring Carroll Baker, Lee J. Cobb, Henry Fonda, Carolyn Jones, Karl Malden, Gregory Peck, George Peppard, Robert Preston, Debbie Reynolds, James Stewart, Eli Wallach, John Wayne, Richard Widmark, Brigid Bazlen, Walter Brennan, David Brian, Andy Devine, Raymond Massey, Agnes Moorehead, Henry (Harry) Morgan, Thelma Ritter, Mickey Shaughnessy, Russ Tamblyn, and Spencer Tracy, with Dave Guard and the Whiskeyhill Singers.

A saga following the story of the daughter of a pioneering family from youth to old age.

RAISE A RUCKUS TONIGHT

Traditional music arranged by Robert Emmett Dolan. Published. Copyrighted March 25, 1963. Previously registered for copyright as an unpublished song October 24, 1962. Introduced and recorded by Debbie Reynolds and ensemble (MGM).

Raise a ruckus tonight!
'Taint no time to sit and brood, tonight.
Time to strike a lively mood—
Raise a ruckus tonight!
Go and get that ole banjo—
Raise a ruckus tonight!
Pat your foot and tap your toe—
Raise a ruckus tonight!
Come on along, little children, come along,
While the moon is shining bright,

Come on along and raise your voice in song—
We gwine to raise a ruckus tonight!
We come quite a ways, I know, tonight—
Raise a ruckus tonight!
We got quite a ways to go, tonight;
Ain't you all done sat a spell?
Raise a ruckus tonight!
Now's the time to raise some—well!
Raise a ruckus, let's raise a ruckus tonight!

WHAT WAS YOUR NAME IN THE STATES?

Music adapted by Robert Emmett Dolan. Published. Copyrighted March 25, 1963. Previously registered for copyright as an unpublished song October 24, 1962. Introduced and recorded by Debbie Reynolds (MGM).

What was your name in the States?
Was it Thompson or Johnson or Bates?
Did you happen to draw on your mother-in-law?
Or sink the old lady with weights, my friend?
Oh, what was your name in the States?

What was your name in the States?
Was it Murphy, MacDonald, or Gates?
Did you hold up a bank as a juvenile prank
And pack up the money in crates, my friend?
Oh, what was your name in the States?

What was your name in the States?
Now, yuh must have had some honest traits.
Did you try to abscond with a beautiful blonde?
Such minor offenses we tolerates.
Oh, what was your name in the States?

What was your name in New York?
Was it Clancy, O'Toole, or O'Rourke?
Are you wanted for life 'cause you left your poor wife
When she caught you sniffing a cork, my friend?
Oh, what was your name in New York?

What was your name in the East?
And how recently was you released?
Are you ridin' the rails 'cause you held up the mails?
Or was it the females you held, you beast?!
Oh, what was your name in the East?

What was your name in the States?
Though you've suffered the cruelest of fates,
Way out there in the West ev'rybody's a guest,
So, line up and fill up your plates, my friend,
Whoever you was in the States!

WAIT FOR THE WAGON (WAIT FOR THE HOEDOWN)

Traditional music adapted by Robert Emmett Dolan. Registered for copyright as an unpublished song October 24, 1962. Introduced by Debbie Reynolds and ensemble.

REFRAIN 1

GIRLS: Wait for the hoedown,
Wait for the hoedown,
Wait for the hoedown,
And we'll all get a man!

VERSE 1

DEBBIE
REYNOLDS: The art of how to roll an eye,
You ladies may not know,
Or how to flounce a petticoat
And let the ankle show.
To show a dimpled shoulder,
Or to give a saucy glance,
It stirs 'em at a social,
But it shakes 'em at the dance!

REFRAIN 2

GIRLS: Wait for the shindig,
Wait for the shindig,
Wait for the shindig,
And we'll all get a man!

VERSE 2

REYNOLDS: In case you ain't familiar with
The ways of catchin' men,
It ain't so much the knowin' how,
It's more the knowin' when.
And here's a little sound advice—
Your ma may not approve—
It ain't the clothes that you put on,
It's them that you remove!

REFRAIN 3

GIRLS: Wait for the nighttime,
Soft-candlelight time,
Wait for the right time,
And we'll all catch a beau!

REFRAIN 4

REYNOLDS: Wait for the hoedown,
Redeye will flow down,
Wait for the hoedown,
And then let 'er rip!

REFRAIN 5

REYNOLDS
& GIRLS: Boys, hold your hosses!
MEN: We're still the bosses!
REYNOLDS
& GIRLS: Please hold your hosses—
ALL: Till we get to the dance.

I'M THE WORRYIN' KIND

Music and lyrics by Mercer and Pinky Tomlin. Registered for copyright as an unpublished song December 10, 1962.

I'm the worryin' kind,
Watching that old clock start to tick tock and chime,
Waitin' around to see who'll beat my time this time.
No wonder I'm the worryin' kind.
You just pay me no mind,
Takin' the watermelon, leavin' the rind;
Oh, what a great big eight-ball you'll wake up behind,
That day you find the worryin' kind ain't me.
It's you who'll be
The worryin' kind.

MA BELLE CHÉRIE

Music by Robert Emmett Dolan. Written for the NBC television special, *The World of Maurice Chevalier* (1963). Registered for copyright as an unpublished song December 10, 1962.

VERSE

In the course of either pleasure or of duty,
I have seen the girls of ev'ry race,
But my eyes have yet to witness any beauty
Like the timeless beauty of her face.

REFRAIN

Ma belle chérie,
The only girl for me,
Is quite a dozen girls in one.
One day she's sad,
The next a trifle mad,
Or then she's only out for fun.
Ma belle chérie
Is fickle as can be;
Each night she wears a diff'rent gown.
For years we share
This passionate affair,
Because, you see,
Ma belle chérie
Was always Paris town!

DAYS OF WINE AND ROSES (1962)

Produced by Martin Manulis for Warner Bros. Released December 1962. Copyright November 30, 1962. Directed by Blake Edwards. Screenplay by J. P. Miller, based on his *Playhouse 90* teleplay of the same name. Lyrics by Johnny Mercer. Music and music score by Henry Mancini. Starring Jack Lemmon and Lee Remick, featuring Charles Bickford and Jack Klugman, with Alan Hewitt, Tom Palmer, Debbie Megowan, Maxine Stuart, Jack Albertson, and Ken Lynch.

A man becomes an alcoholic. His wife gradually reaches the same stage, but while he recovers, she does not.

DAYS OF WINE AND ROSES

Published. Copyrighted December 28, 1962. Previously registered for copyright as an unpublished song December 4, 1962. Key recordings were made by Andy Williams (Columbia) and Henry Mancini and his orchestra (Victor). The song won the Academy Award for Best Song of 1962 and also, in Williams's rendition, a Grammy Award for Song of the Year for 1963.

A film about alcoholism didn't seem a likely context for a title song, but director Blake Edwards wanted one, and since he had enjoyed such success the previous year with *Breakfast at Tiffany's* and "Moon River," he naturally turned to the winning team of Mercer and Mancini. He even suggested the title, taken from a poem written in 1896 by Ernest Dowson, himself an alcoholic.

Mancini didn't want to write it. "It sounds like a French operetta or the War of the Roses, or Sigmund Romberg, or Hammerstein and Kern, and you go in and you see two kids getting stoned out of their heads and it's pretty depressing."

But clearly it was a song that was meant to be written, and Edwards had his way. "The title determined the melody," Mancini remembered. "I went to the piano [and] the first phrase fell right into place. The theme was written in about half an hour. It just came, it rolled out." Mercer taped it and took it home. He made himself a drink and leaned against the wall looking at the bar. Then an image came to him: days that "run away like a child at play." And from that point the lyric ran away with him.

"I think I wrote it in five minutes. I couldn't get it down fast enough. It was like taking dictation. It just poured out of me. I have no idea. I labored over it later, but the song came to me first, the words came to me . . . I can't take credit for that one, God wrote that lyric. All I did was take it down." (His "laboring" resulted in a single change: "golden face" became "golden smile.")

He and Mancini performed the finished song for Edwards and Jack Lemmon. Lemmon recalled: "[Mercer] started to sing this song and I have never been through anything like it in my life . . . I was wiped out, I was gone . . . It was one of the most thrilling moments I've ever had . . . in this business."

The days of wine and roses
Laugh and run away
Like a child at play
Through the meadowland
Towards a closing door,
A door marked "Nevermore"
That wasn't there before.
The lonely night discloses
Just a passing breeze
Filled with memories
Of the golden smile that introduced me to
The days of wine and roses
And you.

OLD VALPARAISO TOWN

Music by Matt Malneck.

Some steamer's loading supplies for old
    Valparaiso town,
On deck they're waving goodbyes for old
    Valparaiso town.
I have a feeling tonight that's where I ought
    to be,
Just standing there in the bow and gazing out to
    sea.
Where waves of aquamarine roll in on a green-
    fringed shore,
I'll find a sweet pair of arms to hold me
    forevermore.
But no, I'll put out the light and steer my dream
    boat down
Through lazy tropical skies to old Valparaiso
    town.

CHARADE (1963)

Produced and directed by Stanley Donen for Universal. Released December 1963. Copyright: none. Screenplay by Peter Stone, based on a story by Stone and Marc Behm and Stone's novel *The Unsuspecting Wife.* Lyrics by Johnny Mercer. Music by Henry Mancini. Starring Cary Grant and Audrey Hepburn, featuring Walter Matthau, with James Coburn, George Kennedy, Dominique Minot, Ned Glass, Jacques Marin (dubbed by Grégoire "Coco" Aslan), Paul Bonifas, and Thomas Chelimsky.

A young woman's husband is murdered and four threatening men are pursuing her. A handsome stranger comes to her aid—but is he friend or foe?

CHARADE

Published. Copyrighted August 26, 1963. Previously registered for copyright as an unpublished song June 13, 1963. Introduced by off-screen chorus. Leading recordings by Mancini and his orchestra (Victor), Sammy Kaye and his orchestra (Decca), and Andy Williams (Columbia).

Nominated for an Academy Award as Best Song of 1963 but lost to "Call Me Irresponsible" by Jimmy Van Heusen (music) and Sammy Cahn (lyrics) from *Papa's Delicate Condition.*

When we played our charade,
We were like children posing,
Playing at games,
Acting out names,
Guessing the parts we played.

Oh, what a hit we made!
We came on next to closing,
Best of the bill,
Lovers until
Love left the masquerade.

Fate seemed to pull the strings;
I turned and you were gone,
While from the darkened wings
The music box played on.

Sad little serenade,
Song of my heart's composing—
I hear it still,
I always will,
Best on the bill—
Charade.

ONE LONELY LIFE

Composer unknown. Registered for copyright as an unpublished song July 26, 1963.

    Lyric missing.

CLEOPATRA (1963)

Produced by Walter Wanger for Twentieth Century–Fox. World premiere June 12, 1963. Copyright June 19, 1963. Directed by Joseph L. Mankiewicz. Screenplay by Mankiewicz, Ranald MacDougall, and Sidney Buchman, based upon histories by Plutarch, Suetonius, Appian, other ancient sources, and *The Life and Times of Cleopatra* by C. M. Franzero. Lyrics by Johnny Mercer. Music composed and conducted by Alex North. Choreography by Hermes Pan. Starring Elizabeth Taylor, featuring Richard Burton, Rex Harrison, Pamela Brown, George Cole, Hume Cronyn, Cesare Danova, Kenneth Haigh, Andrew Keir, Martin Landau, Roddy McDowall, Robert Stephens, with Francesca Annis, Grégoire Aslan, Martin Benson, Herbert Berghof, John Caimey, Jacqui Chan, Isabel Cooley, John Doucette, Andrew Faulds, Michael Gwynn, Michael Hordern, John Hoyt, Marne Maitland, Carroll O'Connor, Richard O'Sullivan, Gwen Watford, and Douglas Wilmer.

The oft-told story of Caesar, Antony, and Cleopatra—at the time, the most expensive film ever made.

THE NILE (ANTONY AND CLEOPATRA THEME)

Published. Copyrighted November 18, 1963. Previously registered for copyright as an unpublished song July 29, 1963. Not sung in film.

The fury ends,
The sound of battle dies away,
And through the long, dusty day
There flows the Nile.
The sands that blow
Blow over kings as well as slaves,
And there is no diff'rence in their graves.
The barge where queen kept a lover's tryst
Is driftwood and broken spars.
What eyes know her lips or the lips she kissed?
No eyes except the frosty stars.
And life goes on;
New lovers walk along the shore,
And when they're gone as before,
There flows the Nile.
For we are here for just a little while;
Then we're gone.
But through the summers and the snows
Flows the Nile.

The fury flows
The silent Nile.

GUITAR COUNTRY

Music and lyrics by Johnny Mercer and Willard Robison. Registered for copyright as an unpublished song October 11, 1963.

REFRAIN 1

Every now and then
I get a Smoky Mountain yen
For my guitar country,
That big-star country
Back home.

Sittin' on the porch and lookin' at the hills,
Backin' up the singin' of the whip poor-wills,
When the friendly crickets
Started chirpin' in the thickets,
You could feel somethin',
That real, real somethin',
Take hold.

Since we never can go back to yesterday,
Now I close my eyes and let my heartstrings play,
And I still get a glow
From all the times I used to know
Back in that far country,
That moonlit, won't-quit guitar country
Back home.

REFRAIN 2

[*Repeat lines 1–12 from refrain 1; then:*]

Everybody's singin' songs in harmony;
Maybe things are better in your memory.
But what I'd give to be
That little genius that was me,
Back in that far country,
That moonlit, won't-quit guitar country
Back home!

LOVE WITH THE PROPER STRANGER (1963)

Produced by Alan J. Pakula for Paramount Pictures. Released December 1963. Copyright December 25, 1963. Directed by Robert Mulligan. Screenplay by Arnold Schulman. Lyrics by Johnny Mercer. Music, musical score, and musical direction by Elmer Bernstein. Starring Natalie Wood and Steve McQueen, featuring Edie Adams and Herschel Bernardi, with Anne Hegira, Harvey Lembeck, Marie Badolati, Penny Santon, Elena Karam, Virginia Vincent, Nina Varela, Nick Alexander, Marilyn Chris, Augusta Ciolli, Wolfe Barzell, Tom Bosley, and Jack Jones.

A musician tries to help a pregnant girl get an abortion, but they decide to get married instead.

LOVE WITH THE PROPER STRANGER

Published. Copyrighted December 31, 1963. Previously registered for copyright as an unpublished song November 21, 1963. Introduced by Jack Jones on the soundtrack and later recorded by him (Kapp).

Composer Elmer Bernstein was not the first to be impressed by Mercer's work habits. "He arrived with seven pages of lyrics and he said, 'Which one do you like?' He was an incredible writer."

I could fall in love with the proper stranger
If I heard the bells and the banjos ring,
If two certain eyes with a look of danger
Smiled a welcome warm as spring.
If the tom-tom in my heart
Sounded out a warning,
"Don't let her, don't let her walk through the
     door—
This is the one you've been waiting for,"
Oh, yes, I'd know.
However wild it seemed,
You know I'd know.
And I'd whisper,
"Come and take my hand, proper stranger.
Don't go through life as a stranger,
For I'm a proper stranger, too."

THE WINDOWS OF PARIS

Music by Tony Osborne. Registered for copyright as an unpublished song December 3, 1963.

Checkerboard of white
Lighting up the night,
Shining in the dark
High above the park—
What fifty million Frenchmen love are
The windows of Paris.
That constellation has a glow
Twice as bright as Polaris.
See the happy pair
Silhouetted there—
How could you forget
Such a silhouette?
Mon dieu! The view, if we could peek
Through the windows of Paris
Would even embarrass
The natives of Paris!
For we would find by looking
Behind the windows of Paris.
Ooh-la-la-la-la,
Ooh-la-la-la-la!!!

CAST YOUR BREAD UPON THE WATER

Music by Mercer.

Cast your bread upon the water,
Upon the water,
Upon the water—
From the most unexpected quarter
It comes back to you a thousandfold.
Give your love to everybody,
To everybody,
Yes, everybody—
In return,
And from everybody,
You'll get more than you can ever hold.

If there should ever come a time
They make you think that love's a crime,
If there should ever come a time,
No matter when,
Just keep your feelings in your heart,
Until such evil times depart,

And you can show them how to start
To love again.

Cast your bread upon the water,
Upon the water,
Upon the water,
'Cause I sure guarantee you, daughter,
It comes back to you a thousandfold.

JUST THE LETTER "Q"

Music by Mercer.
    Lyric missing.

THE MOMENT OF TRUTH

Music by Robert Emmett Dolan.

Time, go slow—
This, I know,
Is the moment of truth I've waited for;
Does it show,
Do I glow
With a bright inner light?
To think that ev'rything that I say and do
While you're with me
Could even decide what our
Two lives might be!
Never fear that it's merely a moment of youth
And nothing more;
This is true,
This is you,
This is ev'rything right!
My head is a mile in the clouds;
My heart is out of sight.
Whisper low
As we go
On our starry flight;
Whisper low—
It's the moment of truth tonight.

PINEAPPLE PETE

Music by Mercer.

VERSE

Pineapple Pete with the luau seat,
He loves to sit and he loves to eat;
The sweetest guy you could hope to meet,
But it seems that his dinner goes to his seat.
Pineapple Pete started out on poi,
And when he started, did he enjoy!
He isn't even a full-grown boy,
But he's one-quarter avoir- and half -dupois.

REFRAIN 1

He went to grapple
With Philadelphia scrapple
Like meatloaf and mustard
And cantaloupe and custard.
He ate so many starches
He flattened both his arches.
No one is able
To pry him from the table—
Pineapple Pete has become so fat,
He's got to stay seated where he's at.
He can't dig you, so hurry out and meet
This world-famous eater
With the enormous seater,
Pineapple Pete.

REFRAIN 2

While most folks are restin'
He's chompin' and digestin'.
He keeps so busy eatin',
He merely nods a greetin'.
A mouthful of papaya
Prevents him sayin' "Hiya";
He never says "Aloha"—
He signals for some moah.
Pineapple Pete.

[*Repeat last 6 lines of refrain 1.*]

SHAMELESS

Music by Mercer.

Shameless—aren't you the shameless one?
Shameless, the way you kiss and run;
Shameless, because I'm blameless.
You know I never so much as whispered "boo"
To anyone else but you.
But you, you're aimless,
Just like the weathervane.
But just you wait and see;

I'll still be there at the church
When you're left in the lurch,
To take you home with me.

SWINGIN' AT THE SUPERMART

Music by Mercer.

REFRAIN 1

We're gonna rock,
We're gonna roll,
We're gonna shop,
We're gonna stroll,
And here's the way we're gonna start,
Swingin' at the supermart.
Momma wants Ajax,
Poppa wants brandy,

Sister wants curlers,
Brother wants candy.
Ev'rything's there, ev'rything's handy,
Waitin' for you to take home.

REFRAIN 2

We're gonna rock,
We're gonna roll,
We're gonna shop,
We're gonna stroll,
And here's the way we're gonna start,
Swingin' at the supermart.
Sani-Flush, clothespins,
Sausage and potatoes,
Old Dutch Cleanser,
Little red tomatoes.
Toothpicks, Soil-Off, freezer tape, vodka,
Where is that odd-color cheese?

REFRAIN 3

We're gonna twist,
We're gonna turn,

We're gonna live,
We're gonna learn.
And here's the way we fill the cart,
Swingin' at the supermart.
Whisk brooms, pork chops,
Vinegar and mustard,
TV dinners, cream, 'n' frozen custard,
Beer 'n' napkins—whoa, I'm gettin' flustered!
What was it I forgot?
It wasn't milk, it wasn't lard,
It wasn't eggs—now, where's the card?
I turned around—now, where's the cart?
I had it swingin' at the supermart!
Here we go, up and down,
Back and forth, round and round,
Frozen food, instant mix,
Wait your turn, pick up sticks.
Please don't shove and don't grab—
Stand in line, pay the tab,
Swingin' at the supermart!

OVERLEAF   Foxy: *Bert Lahr, Larry Blyden, and Robert H. Harris (bottom)*

FOXY | 1962-1964

FOXY (1962–1964)

Strictly speaking, *Foxy* began in London in 1606, when Ben Jonson's *Volpone* (or *The Fox*) had its premiere. There were numerous revivals of the play over the next 350 years but none as unlikely as the one which took place in Dawson City, Yukon, Canada—a town of fewer than one thousand inhabitants, which had decided to inaugurate an annual Gold Rush Festival in 1962. This was to commemorate the part it had played in the Klondike Gold Rush of 1896, an event that seemed to replicate the theme of greed in Jonson's play. And while they were about it, why not make it into a musical?

1962 production: Palace Grand, Dawson City, Yukon, Canada; July 2–August 17, 1962. Music by Robert Emmett Dolan. Lyrics by Johnny Mercer. Book by Ian McLellan Hunter and Ring Lardner Jr., suggested by the play *Volpone* by Ben Jonson. Produced by Robert Whitehead and Stanley Gilkey. Directed by Robert Lewis. Orchestrations by Eddie Sauter and Bill Finnegan. Orchestra under the direction of Joseph Lewis. Cast included Bert Lahr (Foxy), Larry Blyden (Doc Mosk), Buzz Halliday (Brandy), Kit Smythe (Celia), Bill Hayes (Ben), Ralph Dunn (Bedrock), Edward Greenhalgh (Buzzard), Jack Bittner (Shortcut), and Scott Merrill (Inspector Stirling).

After the 1962 production closed in the Yukon, the show was revised.

1964 production: Tryouts: Hanna Theatre, Cleveland, Ohio, January 6–11, 1964; Fisher Theatre, Detroit, Michigan, January 13–February 8, 1964. New York run: Ziegfeld Theatre; opened February 16, 1964; closed April 18, 1964; 72 performances. Music by Robert Emmett Dolan. Lyrics by Johnny Mercer. Book by Ian McLellan Hunter and Ring Lardner Jr., suggested by the play *Volpone* by Ben Jonson. Produced by David Merrick. Directed by Robert Lewis. Choreography by Jack Cole. Scenic design by Robert Randolph. Costumes by Robert Fletcher. Orchestrations by Eddie Sauter and Hal Schaefer. Orchestra under the direction of Don Pippin. Cast included Bert Lahr (Foxy), Larry Blyden (Doc Mosk), Cathryn Damon (Brandy), Julienne Marie (Celia), John Davidson (Ben), Robert H. Harris (Bedrock), Edward Greenhalgh (Buzzard), and Gerald Hiken (Shortcut).

The critics were not happy. "The show as a show isn't ever firmly certain which side of the bed to get into," wrote Walter Kerr in the *Herald Tribune*. "[The Prologue] suggests at once an intimate, cozily styled, perhaps even literate entertainment (the suggestion of literacy stems not from Ben Jonson but from the articulate literacy of Johnny Mercer's lyrics). But lo and behold, no one knows how to follow through on that . . . Robert Emmett Dolan's score is on the whole conventionally pleasant." Only Howard Taubman in the *Times* showed a touch of enthusiasm: "The lyrics by Johnny Mercer are often bright, and Robert Emmett Dolan's tunes are bouncing and graceful in a way reminiscent of the self-assured twenties."

Mercer wrote: "*Foxy* I thought was salvageable . . . but I'm sorry I didn't save myself a year or two's worry by just saying 'no' Working with Bert Lahr was great fun, and I loved everybody in the show, but I just don't get any kick out of spending all that time and effort, getting into backstage politics, bitching and being bitched at, when one song can make me twice the money and never say an unkind word to me."

A Tony Award was won by Bert Lahr (actor). There was no original cast album.

PROLOGUE

Introduced by Larry Blyden (Doc).

Gold!
Women!
I have the honor to say
Our play,
Risqué and rowdy, concerns the problem of greed
And where its practice can lead.
My role is Doc,
A wily sort of rapscallion.
Around the clock,
I think by proxy for my friend Foxy,
A man whose limited mind,
Is kind but rather cloudy.
Our story starts to unfold
Where men are looking for gold,
And we should wax revelation upon occasion.
We do it not to offend you,
For all we're after is fun and laughter,
As is the custom today.
May we respectfully say,
We hope you're pleased with the play.

MANY, MANY WAYS TO SKIN A CAT

Registered for copyright as an unpublished song June 11, 1962. Introduced and reprised by Bert Lahr (Foxy) and Larry Blyden (Doc).

DOC: There are many, many ways to skin a cat.
FOXY: I see!
DOC: Especially a cat who's after a rat.
FOXY: Who, me?
DOC: The methods to accomplish this are various,
Both Machiavellian and multifarious,
Although it seems a shabby
Sort of trick to play on Tabby.
First we lure him,
Then we skewer him,
Like that!
FOXY: Like that!
DOC: There are many, many ways that this is done.
FOXY: How so?
DOC: For instance, I'll be glad to demonstrate one.
FOXY: Bravo!

REFRAIN 1

DOC: A normal cat prefers to have his tummy full,
And since a bit of fish or eggs are yummyful,
We just set out a plateful,
And our victim, being grateful,
Laps our cooking up
While looking up
A gun!
FOXY: What fun!
DOC: Some traps you bait with cheese
Or catnip, if you please;
Perhaps a silk chemise
Will do the trick.
Once we get him in the net, it's tit for tat!
FOXY: Tit for tat!
DOC: And so, you see, it's all as simple as that.
There are many, many, many, many, many, many, many, many ways
To skin a cat!
But promise me to keep it under your hat!

REFRAIN 2

DOC: There are many, many ways to skin a cat
And make his little heart go pitter-pat.
Because he has to operate illicitly—
You understand my language?
FOXY: Oh, implicitly!
DOC: —to find a plan to fit him
And eventually outwit him,
Though it's tiresome,
Requires some éclat!
FOXY: Oh, that!
DOC: There are many, many ways his goose is cooked.
FOXY: Perhaps you know a few that I overlooked.
DOC: Because he is a dealer in duplicity,
He's very surreptitious—
FOXY: Of nec*ciss*ity!

DOC: But once the trap is baited,
Tom is soon incarcerated,
Often plurally!

FOXY: Na*too*rally!
They're hooked!

DOC: No, cooked!
Just leave a juicy mouse
Somewhere around the house—

FOXY: Perhaps a ruffled grouse
Or wingèd bat?

DOC: They'll be squirming in the trap in
nothing flat!
And so you see it's just as simple as that—
There are many, many, many, many, many,
many, many, many ways
To skin a cat!
But promise me to keep it under your hat!

Reprise

DOC: There are many, many ways to skin a cat—
I told you it would be as simple as that!
Observe that our rewards are
multitudinous—
Already we are warm and have some food
in us.
The game is just beginning;
Now our cats are ripe for skinning.
While they're beady-eyed—

FOXY: And greedy-eyed—

DOC: We're fat!
There are many, many ways to make them
pay,
But we must never choose the obvious
way—
We have to be clandestine and nefarious.
Oh, Foxy boy, this ought to be hilarious—
We'll go upon our mission
Like a Spanish Inquisition,
Overpower them,
Devour them!

FOXY: Olé!

BOTH: Oh, what a joy to be
Such pleasant rogues as we!
What sweet conspiracy
Have we begun!

DOC: On their predatory souls *pax requiescat*!

FOXY: We'll have their hides before they know
where they're at!

BOTH: There are many, many, many, many, many,
many, many, many ways
To skin a cat!

DOC: (And you can bet your bottom dollar on
that!)

ROLLIN' IN GOLD

Registered for copyright as an unpublished song June 11,
1962. Introduced by Cathryn Damon (Brandy) and
ensemble.

PROSPECTORS: Glory be 'n' darned if we ain't
Rollin' in gold
Rollin', rollin', rollin',
Rollin' in gold!
Every day some bindlestiff is
joinin' the fold
'N' every livin' soul is rollin' in
gold!

BRANDY
& GIRLS: Ain't got to eat
No fancy meat,
Ain't got a decent pair o' boots
upon our feet.
No daily mail
Comes up the trail!
There ain't a single blessed
luxury for sale!

1ST PROSPECTOR: [*spoken*] Nothing to spend it on!

BRANDY: [*spoken*] Except whiskey and
women!

BRANDY &
ENSEMBLE: But—
Whoop-dee-doo and hallelu,
We're rollin' in gold—
Rollin', rollin', rollin', rollin',
Rollin' in gold!
River roarin', bringin' ore in
Out of the cold,
A-pourin' even more 'n
People can hold!
We live in shacks
Where we relax
By list'nin' to the blizzard
Howlin' through the cracks.
No feather beds
To rest our heads,
To sleep with centipedes and
other quadrupeds.
But—
Whoop-dee-doo 'n' glory be,
We're rollin' in gold—
Rollin', rollin', rollin', rollin',
Rollin' in gold!
Here we got a town that isn't
sixty days old*
'N' every livin' soul is rollin' in
gold!
Our chicken pen

---
* *Or:* two winters old

Could use a hen;
For every woman here there
must be forty men.
The old corral
Could use a gal;
It's pretty hard to snuggle up to
your morale!
Rich men, poor men,
Doctor, lawyer, clerk, and
doorman,
All are riding high.
Poor men, rich men,
Carnival and circus pitchmen,
Slicin' up the pie!
But—
Glory be 'n' darned if we ain't
Rollin' in gold—
Rollin', rollin', rollin, rollin',
Rollin' in gold!
Every day some bindlestiff is
joinin' the fold
'N' every livin' soul is rollin' in
gold!
Ain't got no cooks,
Ain't got no books—
There ain't a thing t' steal, so we
run out o' crooks!
Ain't got no nails
To build no jails,
So we just spend the evenin'
sittin' on our tails,
Rollin' in gold, rollin' in gold,
Rollin' in gold!

Additional lyrics

Ain't got to eat
No bread or meat,
Ain't got a decent pair o' boots upon our feet.
Ain't got no banks,
No water tanks—
Ain't got no nails t'build a buildin', and no
planks.
Ain't got no tools,
No Sunday schools—
Ain't got no deputies, 'cause we ain't got no rules.
No feather beds
To rest our heads;
Ain't got no shelter for the dogs that pull the
sleds.
But—
Whoop-dee-dee and glory be, we're
Rollin' in gold—
Rollin', rollin', rollin', rollin',
Rollin' in gold!
Our bonanza isn't even sixty days old
'N' every livin' soul is rollin' in gold!

Ain't got no clothes,
No girlie shows,
Ain't got no women here to listen to our woes,
Ain't got no squaws
Thank God, because
If we had them, we'd have to have their ma-in-
    laws!
Whoop-dee-doo and hallelu!
We're rollin' in gold,
Rollin', rollin', rollin', rollin',
Rollin' in gold!
Daffodils are out sproutin' brazen and bold,
'N' every livin' soul is rollin' in gold,
Rollin' in gold, rollin' in gold, rollin' in gold!

MY WEIGHT IN GOLD

Introduced by Julienne Marie (Celia) and female ensemble.
Alternate titles: "Worth My Weight in Gold" and "Celia's
Dilemma."

CELIA: What a blessing to be told
    That I'm worth my weight in gold!
    Seen in that light,
    It's really quite
    An honor to be sold!
    Wonder if he likes my size
    Or the color of my eyes?
    I'll have to wait and speculate
    Wherein my value lies.
    I'm certain my curves
    Are worth more than my nerves,
    But as I figure all around,
    Including my girth,
    That my overall worth
    Comes to roughly two-fifty a pound.
    So I look at things this way—
    Heaven sent me here today.
    How proud my dear papa would be
    If he could just be told
    That I'm worth my weight in gold!
GIRLS: What a beauty to behold—
    And she's worth her weight in gold!
CELIA: And ev'ry ounce
    By my account's
    Paid off a thousandfold.
GIRLS: That's an awful lot to pay
    For a single girl today!
CELIA: It's not the price
    That makes it nice—
    It's how I've been extolled.
GIRLS: He's brought in this case
    Not just some pretty face,

But a figure to enthrall!
CELIA: May I point with pride
    That the spiritual side
    Cost him practically nothing at all?
GIRLS: She's built for work or play—
    She's a bargain either way.
CELIA: And what a thrill
    To tell my children when I've gotten old
    That I was worth my weight in gold!
GIRLS: You were worth your weight in gold!

MONEY ISN'T EVERYTHING

Registered for copyright as an unpublished song June 11,
1962. Introduced by Bert Lahr (Foxy), Larry Blyden
(Doc), Robert H. Harris (Bedrock), Gerald Hiken (Shortcut), Edward Greenhalgh (Buzzard), and ensemble.

FOXY: When life's strong current is ebbing
        fast,
    And you're starting to breathe your
        last,
    A man can see his entire past
    Flash in front of his eyes.
    "Halloo—halloo!"
    The Reaper so grim
    Cries out "Halloo!"
    And what about Jim?
    He trusted you,
    But you welshed on him—
    Friends, it's then you grow wise.
    Money isn't everything—
    Die just once and you'll see.
    Money isn't everything—
    Fickle mistress is she!
    So say, "Money, money,
    Hey, money, money,
    Fa-la-la-lee!"
SHORTCUT,
BUZZARD &
BEDROCK: A friend in need is a friend indeed—
    Now old Foxy at last is treed.
    Will we desert him in time of need?
    No, a thousand times no!
    "Halloo—halloo!"
    I see you grow pale—
    It's time for you
    To hit the long trail.
    But when the register rings No Sale,
    Pal, we want you to know—
    Money isn't everything.
    Can it buy you a friend?
    We'll take care of everything,

Keep it safe to the end.
    So say, "Money, money,
    Hey, money, money,
    It's just to spend!"
DOC: The way poor mortals have got to
        go,
    Scalped by Injuns or frozen slow,
    We hate to think of the pals we know
    All struck down when they're young!
FOXY: "Halloo—halloo!"
    I see it so clear:
    You're stiff and stark,
    Shot down from the rear.
DOC: Snuffed out like that!
FOXY: And perhaps this year!
DOC: Knifed—or maybe just hung!
FOXY & DOC: Money isn't everything.
DOC: He's got millions to spare!
FOXY & DOC: Money isn't everything!
FOXY: Boys, I'll see you up there!
ALL: So say, "Money, money,
    Hey, money, money,"
    Take it from me and say, "Money,
    Hey, money, money,
    Fa-la-la-lee!!!"

LARCENY AND LOVE

Registered for copyright as an unpublished song June 11,
1962. Introduced by Cathryn Damon (Brandy) and
Larry Blyden (Doc).

DOC: Larceny and love are kissing cousins—
    Surely you agree with that, chérie?
    Every man alive will try to outsmart a
        dame—
    No one's to blame,
    It's a confidence game.
    Gals would take a schoolboy from his
        mother,
    Not to mention how they frisk each
        other!
    There is not a heist that you're incapable
        of—
    Larceny's a breeze compared to love.
BRANDY: Larceny and love are boon companions—
    I am in agreement, mon ami!
    Men will get a woman any way that they
        can,
    Whereas our plan
    Is to handcuff the man!
    Once you see a girl is easy pickin's,
    You begin to look for plumper chickens;

Flirting and forgetting seem to go hand
in glove—
Larceny's a pipe compared to love!
DOC: I call your hand and raise you a grand!
BRANDY: How do I know this isn't a trick?
DOC: You pays your money and takes your
pick!
BRANDY: Seven on the black!
DOC: Aces back to back!
BRANDY: Get a different pack!
DOC: Try your luck for only a buck!
BRANDY: You wouldn't deceive a babe in the wood?
DOC: I would if I could—I would if I could!
BOTH: All together now—
Larceny's a cinch compared to love—
Larceny and love are kissing cousins.
Maybe that is why we get along—
Just a pair of bunco artists
Born to deceive,
Adam and Eve
With an ace up our sleeve.
We're prepared for any situation,
Always have our baggage at the station.
Put your faith in honesty,
But, heavens above,
Be prepared for larceny and love!

THE S.S. COMMODORE EBENEZER MCAFEE THE THIRD

Registered for copyright as an unpublished song June 11, 1962. Introduced by ensemble. Alternate title: "Ebenezer McAfee III."

Thar she blows, she's a-puffin'—
Could it be the *Cyrus J. McGuffin*?
Bringin' cakes,
Hoes and rakes,
And a load o' Kansas City steaks?
Nosirree, don't you know,
Ain't you heard?
It's the boat we're waitin' for—
The S.S. *Commodore*
Ebenezer McAfee the Third!

See the smoke, she's a-burnin',
Look at all the water she's a-churnin',
Totin' eggs,
Whiskey kegs,
Pretty girls with pretty-lookin' legs!
Yessirree, spread the news,

Spread the word,
That we'll meet her on the shore,
The S.S. *Commodore*
Ebenezer McAfee the Third!

Jee-rus-a-lum,
That was some steerin'!
The cap'n got her here in jig time!
Shall we adjourn?
Why, ya durn tootin',
And pitch a highfalutin big time!

Is she glad she's arrivin'?
Listen to her paddle wheel a-drivin'!
If the rest haven't guessed what's occurred,
Read it on her semaphore:
The S.S. *Commodore*
Man, you hit it on the beezer!
That antiquated geezer!
Ebenezer McAfee the Third!

Corrected version—May 15, 1962

Reprise

What a great big bonanza,
Like a Broadway-show extravaganza!
Fancy hats and cravats,
Checkered vests and pearly-button spats!
Yessirree, can't you see what's occurred?
Wasn't she worth waitin' for?
The S.S. *Commodore*
Ebenezer McAfee the Third!

See the gowns made of satin
All the way from Boston and Manhattan,
Ostrich plumes and perfumes—
In the height of fashion, one assumes!
Guess it's true, feathers do make the bird—
Thanks to our department store,
The S.S. *Commodore*
Ebenezer McAfee the Third!

Our orchestree came from Se-attle,
And they can make a rattlesnake walk—
They play a hot turkey-trot ditty
Plus the Atlantic City cakewalk!

Yessirree, now you're talkin'!
Man, we plan to do some fancy walkin'
Once we're wined and we're dined and liquored,
And we'll do our walkin' for
The S.S. *Commodore*—
Yes, you hit it on the beezer!
That crowd and people pleaser—
Ebenezer McAfee the Third!!!!

TALK TO ME, BABY

Registered for copyright as an unpublished song November 26, 1963. One of the four songs published from the score. Introduced by Julienne Marie (Celia) and John Davidson (Ben).

VERSE 1

If you cannot toss your heart gaily in the ring,
Love me while the moment lingers.
If you cannot cross your heart that I'm ev'rything,
Try at least to cross your fingers.

REFRAIN 1

Talk to me, baby, tell me lies,
Tell me lies as sweet as apple pies,
And if your lips have never told a fib,
You might ad-lib with your eyes.
Say that we're helpless in the hands of fate;
Prevaricate if you must.
Just talk to me, baby, soft and low,
Then, if you do decide it's really so,
Swear you'll be mine forever.
Otherwise, just talk to me and tell me
Lies, lies, lies, lies,
Great big lies!

VERSE 2

Who shuts their umbrella up, or their
bumbershoot,
When it's absolutely pouring?
Who shuts any fella up when he's so darned cute
And his mind is busy soaring?

REFRAIN 2

Talk to me, baby, tell me lies,
Tell me lies as sweet as apple pies.
Whisper you tremble with a wild desire
To light the fire in my eyes.
Tell me I'm beautiful, exaggerate;
Prevaricate if you must.
Just talk to me, baby, soft and low,
Then, if you do decide it's really so,
Swear you'll be mine forever.
Otherwise, just talk to me and tell me
Lies, lies, lies, lies,
Great big lies!

THIS IS MY NIGHT TO HOWL

Registered for copyright under the title "My Night to Howl" November 26, 1963. One of the four songs published from the score. Introduced by Gerald Hiken (Shortcut) and John Davidson (Ben).

REFRAIN 1

Doo-di dee-dough dee-day doo dee-dle-dum—
Sun up this mornin', I began to hum.
I thought that five o'clock would never come.
This is my night to howl.

I warn you, Mary Lou and Daisy Nell,
You have begun to look adorable.
I am prepared to storm the citadel;
I'll be out on the prowl.
It's been a long, long, long, long day
To think about what I'm aimin' to do.
I spent a long, long time without a drink about—
Care to empty a few?

Doo-di dee-dough dee-day, I'm gonna sing,
For I propose to have myself a fling.
So, if you ladies hear the following,
T'ain't a wolf or an owl—
Aw-ooo aw-ooo aw-ooo—
I'm after you!
This is my night to howl!

REFRAIN 2

[Lines 1–4 as in refrain 1, then:]

I warn you, Jimmy Jo and Billy B.,
None of your lip—if you're too snippity,
I'll wrap you up and take you home with me,
'Cause I'm out on the prowl.
It's been a long, long, long, long day
To wait around with my motor in low.
I spent a long, long time without a date around,
And I'm rarin' to go!

[Lines 13–19 as in refrain 1.]

BON VIVANT

Registered for copyright as an unpublished song June 11, 1962. Introduced by Bert Lahr (Foxy) and ensemble.

Like every lyricist, Mercer learned to throw nothing away. Compare the use of British place names in "And Points Beyond" from *The Good Companions* (1974).

VERSE 1

Dear were the homes of Cheltenham;
Large were the hearts that dwelt in 'em.
I but a tad of a lad,
Mum and Dad
At the pub, just beltin' 'em away.
Now I've attained seniority
And come to my majority;
I've traveled far,
Tasted snails, caviar,
So with some authority
I say:

REFRAIN 1

If you want a bon vivant
To brighten up the scene
Or a jolly extra man
To give the party sheen,
Strolling on the Parthenon
Or bowling on the green,
I play mandolin and tambourine,
Will travel!
If you want a bon vivant
Who only aims to please,
Punting on the Hellespont
Or at milady's teas,
Tickling her fancy
And visibilities,
Just drop a note to me—
My services are free,
For I'm the bon vivant
You want!

VERSE 2

Now, for the life men dream about,
Days that a king might scheme about,
Once I have got
My palatial yacht,
I shall steam about the brine.
Fie on the word "economy"!
I'll live a life of bonhomie,
Sail into port
For a night *pour le sport*,
Full of rare gastronomy
And wine!

REFRAIN 2

Manchester and Dorchester
And Chichester and Perth,
Sailing on the Firth of Forth,
Or is it Forth of Firth?
Woppington-on-Battersea,
The shire of my birth,
In a thatchèd home
Of modest worth

(Unpaid for . . .),
Birmingham and Nottingham
And Sandringham and Crewe,
Shrewsbury and Tewkesbury
And Shaftesbury and Looe
(Lancashire and Lincolnshire
And Devonshire and—whew!),
Where I starred as Portia
In *The Taming of the Shrew*—
As we would say in school,
I've been around the pool,
So I'm the bon vivant you want!

REFRAIN 3

Of all the lads who drank the ale
And ate the buttered scones,
I remember Algernon St. Worthington
Smythe-Follansbee St. Johns.
Rainy days we'd gaze into our stereopticons—
Wonder why they dressed him in cretonnes
And lipstick?
Oh, the games we used to play
That got on Mummy's nerves,
Cycling through the Serpentine,
One-handed on the curves!
"Peter Piper picked a peck
Of prickly-pear preserves."
If she could see me now,
Dear Mater would allow
That I'm the bon vivant they want!

VERSE 3

I have a dear old guardian,
And he had ways Edwardian.
At tea every day
If he burped, he would say,
"Oh, I beg your pardon" to me.
Once in a while he'd skin a pear,
Sort of an after-dinner pear;
Then we would sing,
Maybe "God Save the King"
Or "A Partridge in a Pear Tree."

REFRAIN 4

All around the anteroom
The butler chased the maid,
Out the door and down the path
And through the leafy glade.
There is the gazebo—
It was ninety in the shade.
With the table set
And places laid
He made her
Stay with him and play with him
Until the mutton burned.

309

We were having trifle
When the two of them returned.
Later on, she taught me
Everything that she had learned.
So, if you have a maid
Who feels she's underpaid,
Then I'm the bon vivant you want!

VERSE 4

Back in the quoits-and-soccer room,
T-shirt-and-knickerbockers room,
Gay badinage
From the whole entourage
As around the locker room we sat.
Gad, what a game our kicker would
Play on the fields of Wickerwood!
They must have heard
Every unseemly word,
But the dear old vicar wouldn't tat!

REFRAIN 5

Biggleswade and Merthyr Tydfil,
Pontypridd and Poole,
They were on the playing schedule
Back in public school.
Although we were ridiculed
At rugby as a rule,
We outdressed them in the vestibule,
Rah-rah-rah!
Now we all are forty-odd
And grown to man's estate;
Some are in the government
And some have put on weight.
Still around the club
When fellows recapitulate,
Most everyone agrees
I'm absolutely cheese—
And I'm the bon vivant they want!

REFRAIN 6

Visiting my auntie Boo
In tiny Liechtenstein,
Strolling through ze meadowlands
Amongst ze lowing kine,
Flirting mit a milking maid
Mit cheeks of apple shine,
Strolling up above the timber line
Und sheeing . . .
Dueling the Hapsburgs—ach,
Ze carefree days zey vere!
Drinking beer at Heidelberg
Und making love mit her,
Yust before ze chancellor
Partitioned up ze Ruhr.
Ja, ever zince ze day

I rolled her in the hay,
I've been the bon vivant she wants!

FINALE ACT 1

Introduced by ensemble.
    Lyric missing.

IT'S EASY WHEN YOU KNOW HOW

Registered for copyright as an unpublished song January 22, 1964. Introduced by Larry Blyden (Doc) and ensemble.

Although I say it myself,
My mind is like a weasel.
But I'm not taking a bow—
It's easy when you know how.
Some small-town hick,
A chap named Benjamin Franklin, said,
"Son, to lick the hurlyburly,
Just get up early."
I simply follow my nose,
Get out my brush and easel,
Unveil a painting complete,
A masterpiece of deceit.
My words are smooth as vellum,
My cerebellum one jump ahead of the sheriff,
But, as I said, it
Does me no credit—
It's easy when you know how!

Take the average man—at best
He's just a puppet.
And how my happy heart sings
When I am pulling the strings!
To quote P.T.,
A sucker's born ev'ry minute.
You must agree,
Fate seems to make 'em
For me to take 'em!
Give any man enough rope,
The dope will climb right up it, and I,
The wily fakir, go "Poof,"
And they disappear for me.
To match friend or brother
Is just as normal as breathing.
Sounds complicated, attenuated,

But easy when you know how.
So, I repeat with all the sincerity
Modesty will allow,
Without the slightest touch of temerity—
It's easy when you know how.

RUN, RUN, RUN, CINDERELLA

Registered for copyright as an unpublished song November 26, 1963. One of the four published songs from the score. Introduced by Julienne Marie (Celia).

REFRAIN 1

Run, run, run, Cinderella—
The ball is through.
It's all done, Cinderella,
And so are you.
Gone, gone, gone, your three wishes—
Good night, sweet Prince,
And back to the dishes,
But no more dreams, Cinderella,
They won't come true.

INTERLUDE

Just to think he was there,
Right before my eyes,
The dream I had in my youth.
He said, "Talk to me, baby,
And tell me lies."
But all I told was the truth.
Now it's—

REFRAIN 2

Fly, fly, fly, Cinderella—
The dance is done.
Don't you cry, Cinderella—
You had your fun.
Gone, gone, footmen and carriage—
Good night, sweet Prince,
And all thoughts of marriage.
You won't recall Cinderella;
But if you do—

CODA

Just remember,
I'll think you're a wonderful fella
My whole life through!

I'M WAY AHEAD OF THE GAME

Registered for copyright as an unpublished song November 26, 1963. One of four published songs from the score. Introduced by Cathryn Damon (Brandy) and Larry Blyden (Doc).

VERSE

Lady luck,
It's goodbye—
Hate to see you go.
Fireworks
Filled the sky—
It was quite a show!
I just want to thank you for the free ride;
Out of all the others it was *the* ride.

REFRAIN

Whatever happens from here on in,
I'm way ahead of the game.
Whatever comes up, it's heads-I-win;
Your kiss was my claim to fame.
I rolled a seven
And locked up the store,
Walked into heaven
Right through the front door.
Whatever happens from here on out,
I won't be sorry I came.
I've had the kind of adventure I read of—
I'm way ahead of the game.

A CASE OF RAPE

Introduced by Julienne Marie (Celia) and John Davidson (Ben) and ensemble.

A recording of this song with inaudible lyrics exists.

IN LOVING MEMORY

Introduced by Bert Lahr (Foxy), Larry Blyden (Doc), Robert H. Harris (Bedrock), Gerald Hiken (Shortcut), Edward Greenhalgh (Buzzard), and ensemble.

BUZZARD: Old Foxy's gone to his just reward.
SHORTCUT: It's a loss we can ill afford.
BEDROCK: We rue the day, but we thank the Lord—
TRIO: That we knew him so well!
QUARTET: *L'envoi, l'envoi,* King Foxy the True
No, not *l'envoi,* but merely adieu!
Your wealth, compared to the loss of you,
Seems a mere bagatelle.
Money isn't everything
Once the spirit has fled.
Can it bring back anything
Once you're—shall we say—dead?
So say money, money,
Hey, money, money—
DOC: Please bare your head!
FOXY: [*As Lord Rottingham*] Though I hardly knew him, I feel like his next of kin
You might even say that I regard him as a twin!
True, he couldn't ascertain what creek the gold was in—
Still, he showed me where it might have been!
Stout fellow!
Witty and courageous, wise and generous and kind,
Not a mean nor petty thought would ever cross his mind!
So bring on the dancing girls, and let us all get blind,
For though he is kapished,
It's what he would have wished—
It's what a bon vivant would want!
TRIO: Though we did everything in our power—
BEDROCK: To save him and postpone this hour—
DOC: To fate's great sickle
The fairest flower
Seems no fairer than flax.
SHORTCUT: A weed indeed,
Cut down in its prime!
FOXY: Well, flax or phlox,
It does seem a crime!
BUZZARD: Farewell!
SHORTCUT: God bless you!
BEDROCK: Good luck!
FOXY: *L'chaim!*
TRIO: Now, let's open them sacks!
DOC: Money isn't everything
When you're under the grass.
FOXY: Money isn't everything,
You can bet your sweet . . . life.
TRIO: So say money, money,
Hey, money, money—
FOXY: Please fill my glass!
ALL: A—men!

FINALE

Introduced by Bert Lahr (Foxy), Larry Blyden (Doc), and ensemble.

And now, dear friends, the moral of this play is obvious,
Isn't it?
We simply proved that . . . that . . .
Doc?

Money isn't everything.
Die just once and you'll see.
Money isn't everything,
Fickle mistress is she.

So say money, money,
Hey money, money,
Fa la la li.

Gold!
New gold strike at Cape Nome!
Steamboat leaving for Alaska in three minutes!
Woo-hoo!
Yeah.

Tell them all from wall to wall
We're rollin' in gold—
Rollin', rollin', rollin', rollin',
Rollin' in gold!

Every day some ficklestick is joinin' the fold,
'N' every livin' soul is rollin' in gold!
Whoop-dee-do and hallelu,
We're rollin' in gold—
Rollin', rollin', rollin', rollin',
Rollin' in gold!

Hey little roar and bring that ore in out of the cold.
Rollin',
Rollin',
Rollin' in gold.
Gold!
Gold!
Gold!
Women and whisky and
Gold!

SHARE AND SHARE ALIKE

Registered for copyright as an unpublished song June 11, 1962. Introduced and reprised by Ralph Dunn (Bedrock), Edward Greenhalgh (Buzzard), and Jack Bittner (Shortcut) in the 1962 production.

The opening chorus. Not used in 1964 production.

Share and share alike,
Do and dare alike,
As we roam the creeks and bays—
It may be forty below
As over the snow we hike
But we ain't pullin' up stakes
Till one of us makes a strike!
And then, whatever we hit,
We promise to split
The take four equal ways,
Just the four of us
For the four of us
Over hill and dale and dyke!
To prove we're really agreed,
We got up a deed to sign,
Foolproof and legally drawn,
Our monikers on the line!
We hereby duly declare
And solemnly swear
To share and share alike!

Share and share alike,
Fare and fare alike—
We believe in equal rights,
Which may mean startin' the day
By chasin' away the mice
And later shakin' the spread
To empty the bed of lice,
Or sittin' makin' up bets
On which of us gets
The most mosquito bites!
Freeze and freeze alike,
Sneeze and sneeze alike—
When it's snowy on the pike,
We can't go sallyin' forth
To look at the Northern Lights,
Can't even scare up a moose
Or other exclusive sights,
So we just sit on our prats
And shoot at the rats
And share and share alike!

Reprise

Here we go again,
Single-o again,
As across the hills we climb.
When you've got nothin' to leave

But two or three beaver pelts,
It's fine to think of your chum,
To share 'em with someone else,
But if you're gonna be rich,
The son of a bitch
At least should be on time!
All alone again,
On our own again,
As we roll along the pike—
Although it's breakin' our heart
To split up the partnership,
This thing of sumpin' for free
We figger to be a gyp.
So there won't be any more
Dividin' by four.
If one should make a strike,
It isn't businesslike—
So we do solemnly swear
It wouldn't be fair
To share and share alike!

A CHILD OF THE WILD

Registered for copyright as an unpublished song June 11, 1962. Introduced by Bert Lahr (Foxy) in the 1962 production. Not used in 1964 production.

REFRAIN 1

A child of the wild am I,
Mushing along under this clear blue sky.
I love to make the huskies husk along
And live where I bivouac
Or stop awhile to catch a muskellunge
And stuff it in my knapsack.
The thing about a hermit
Is he doesn't need a permit
If he hankers to up and roam.
The beauty of the life here
Is you never need a wife here
Who will make of your house a home!
I sleep in a sheepskin bag,
Sharing a dell with a gazelle and stag,
The nights are often cold and driz-zi-ly,
And yet, they seem to pass quite busily
When one is sleeping with a griz-zi-ly.
And these are the reasons why
A child of the wild am I!

REFRAIN 2

A child of the wild am I,
Mushing along whether it's wet or dry.
Of course, a fellow has to divvy up

If there is a friend in need,
But he don't have to shut the privy up
When he has a book to read!
The pleasures of a recluse
Is he gets to let his neck loose
And to let his suspenders droop.
The joys of any nomad,
Is while city dwellers go mad,
By himself he's a Boy Scout troop!
I run through the sunlit glades
Gay as a lamb playing at ambuscades.
I always hope to trap a moose or two,
But I don't trap 'em like I use-ta do,
And so I settle for a goose or two,
Then homeward I fairly fly—
A child of the wild am I!

REFRAIN 3

A child of the wild am I,
Zooming ahead putting my sled in high.
I'm always looking for the mother lode,
But then with the rising moon
I'm home and I take on another load,
Or several, at some saloon!
The pleasures of a hobo
Is that no one plays the oboe
Or the pianoforte or drum.
A fellow can be busted,
But he don't get maladjusted,
'Cause he's always been just a bum!
Each grove is a rover's dream—
Onward I thrust, me and my trusty team.
Of course, the malamutes are hairy dogs,
But they're not really scary dogs—
In fact, a lot of them are fairy dogs,
Which may be the reason why
A child of the wild am I!

[spoken] I never thought of that! Hey, Rover—
here, Spot—here, Donder—here, Blitzen—
here, Mistinguett!

REFRAIN 4

A child of the wild am I,
Stalking the fawn under the dawn-drenched sky.
In reverie, I'm on the farm again,
Back hunting the tufted quail.
I sight a pheasant or a ptarmigan
And shoot 'em right in the ptail!
What's great in bein' single
Is you can't cointermingle
With nobody but Eskimos.
A few of them'll make it,
But you really have to fake it,
Or be born with a sexy nose.
I roar through the forest fens

With a "halloo" echoing through the glens.
A man don't have to do no showerin'
Or stop and give himself a scourin'
Until the smell gets overpowerin'
Or there is a crowd nearby—
A child of the wild am I!

REFRAIN 5

A child of the wild am I,
Letting out slack as in my shack I lie.
I like to walk around with no shoes on.
It's not that my feet need rest,
Up here we have to keep our snowshoes on—
Yes, even when she's undressed!
Sometimes you get the staggers
And your eyes are full of daggers
And you stumble toward your bunk—
There's no blindness like snow blindness!
For the fact is, my friend, you're drunk,
When lost in the frozen waste.
There on the scene I have a lean-to placed.
Some nights I have to turn and toss a lot,
When double-dating with an ocelot.
But ve don' bodder to discoss a lot.
Vat he says I don' deny—
A child of the wild am I!

REFRAIN 6

A child of the wild am I,
Eyeing the girls tossing their curls nearby.
I lead a life of single blessedness,
But ladies are not taboo.
They see my studied careless-ness-ed-ness,
And they get careless too!
We have a lot of reindeer,
But I find them pretty plain dear,
Rather drab when they might be gay.
There's fauna and there's flora,
And that goddamned aurora,
Always hanging the night to day.
By turns through the ferns and firs,
Some of them mine, some of them his and
    hers,
I must admit it often snows a lot.
And then, you have to blow your nose a lot.
When nature calls, you must expose a lot.
And then is it cold . . . ? . . . Oy . . . Oy!
A child of the wild am I,
A child . . . of the wild . . . am . . . I!

THE POWER OF LOVE

Registered for copyright as an unpublished song June 11, 1962. Introduced by Kit Smythe (Celia) and Bill Hayes (Ben) in the 1962 production; reprised by Hayes. Not used in 1964 production.

Oh, don't you know the power of love
And the things it's capable of?
It can make a person become compliant
Or a giant.
Oh, don't you know the whimsies of fate?
If you turn a corner too late,
You and your beloved might change directions,
Miss connections.
Star-crossed love is started in heaven
And it is given to few.
Gaze, my love, at visions undreamed of—
Don't be ashamed of the view!
Oh, don't you know whatever we are,
We have just to trust in our star that's rising
    above?
Oh, don't you know the power of love?

TAKE IT FROM A LADY

Registered for copyright as an unpublished song June 11, 1962. Introduced by Buzz Halliday (Brandy) and Kit Smythe (Celia) in the 1962 production. Not used in the 1964 production.

VERSE

BRANDY: Once you're married up
    And you're carried upstairs to bed—
CELIA: By a man?
BRANDY: [spoken] Naturally!
    [sung] If he fathers you
    And that bothers you,
    Use your head
CELIA: If I can.
BRANDY: Use all the tricks you know you have
    Although you have been wed.
CELIA: Use my head.
BRANDY: If he chases you
    And disgraces you,
    Don't see red—
    Just play dead!
CELIA: Don't see red—
    Just play dead!

REFRAIN 1

BRANDY: Take it from a lady,
    Use your wiles—
    Nothing really shady—
    Just coquetry and smiles.
CELIA: Take it from a lady,
    Use my wiles—
    Nothing really shady—
BRANDY: First . . .
    Lowering the lashes
    Starts the play.
CELIA: Lower go the lashes
    This okay?
BRANDY: Show him where the sash is—
CELIA: Melt his heart to ashes.
BRANDY: Upon your negligée.
    Now comes flattery—
    Charge up his battery.
    "Pretty please?"
CELIA: You're a tease!
BRANDY: He'll start to beg and plead,
    Cry out in need.
    Just let him bleed,
    Huff and puff and suffer.
    Be another Circe—
CELIA: Wasn't she a siren?
BRANDY: On the shore
CELIA: Here I am,
    Flustered and perspirin'.
BRANDY: When he begs for mercy,
    Just lock the bedroom door!
    Take it from a lady,
    He'll respect you, lady,
    And he'll come back for more!

REFRAIN 2

    Take it from a lady—
CELIA: Take it from a lady—
BRANDY: Lie a lot—
CELIA: Tell a fib—
BRANDY: But let him think you're not.
CELIA: "Sir, you're with a lady!"
BRANDY: Just cuddle up and snuggle.
CELIA: Snuggle up and cuddle.
BRANDY: Why refuse?
CELIA: Don't refuse.
BRANDY: Make it seem a struggle—
CELIA: Struggle in a huddle!
BRANDY: And then take off your shoes!
    Now the oldest trap—
CELIA: This is it.
BRANDY: Undo one shoulder-strap.
CELIA: Just a bit.
BRANDY: He'll start to pant, as a rule,
    And play it cool—
    Just let him drool.
    When he thinks he has you,

313

Change the conversation 'n'—

CELIA: "What is your vocation?"

BRANDY: Hold his hand.

CELIA: "My, that's grand!"

BRANDY: Now the situation—

CELIA: Ticklish situation!

BRANDY: Is more than he can stand,
But if he's really swooning,
Start the honeymooning—
Reveal the promised land!

ADDITIONAL REFRAIN

BRANDY: Take it from a lady—

CELIA: Take it from a lady—

BRANDY: Treat him rough.
If he wants a lady—

CELIA: Call his bluff.

BRANDY: He'll take a slight rebuff.

CELIA: "Watch it, Mister Brady!"

BRANDY: Yes, always keep him guessing.

CELIA: No-ing him and yessing

BRANDY: Tell a joke.

CELIA: Have you heard?

BRANDY: Don't begin undressing—

CELIA: Even acquiescing—

BRANDY: Until he has a stroke.
He's lascivious?

CELIA: He's a wolf.

BRANDY: Remain oblivious.

CELIA: And aloof.

BRANDY: Because, if he wants to cling,
Like anything he'll try to spring.
But to tame a tiger
Have a hoop of fire—

CELIA: Slacken his desire.

BRANDY: Burning bright—

CELIA: Mustn't bite!

BRANDY: Make him walk a wire—

CELIA: Till he starts to tire.

BRANDY: Then shove him out of sight!
Dearie, just deposit
Hubby in a closet
And let him spend the night!

LIFE'S DARKEST MOMENT

Registered for copyright as an unpublished song June 11, 1962. Introduced by Kit Smythe (Celia) and ensemble in the 1962 production. Not used in 1964 production.

All the things I prayed for,
All the plans I made for

This one day
Have turned and walked away.

All the things tonight meant
Now hold no excitement;
All the dreams I knew
Have left me too.
What a thing for dreams to do!

They say your wedding day
Should be the thrill of a lifetime,
A night of sheer delight
That happens once in a lifetime.
As far as I can see,
The promised joy and ecstasy
Have only turned out to be
Life's darkest moment for me!

TILL IT GOES OUTTA STYLE

Registered for copyright as an unpublished song June 11, 1962, under the title "Till It Goes Out of Style." Introduced by Buzz Halliday (Brandy) and Larry Blyden (Doc) in the 1962 production. Not used in 1964 production.

DOC: I am gonna ramble
And I'm gonna have fun
Till the ramblin' is done—
I am goin' roamin' for a while.

BRANDY: Your little while is many a long mile.

DOC: But then I'm comin' home 'n'
Love you till it goes outta style.

BRANDY: While you're away,
A lady could get gray.

DOC: Have gotta travel,
'Cause I wanna find out
What they told me about—
I am gonna miss you for a spell.

BRANDY: Fair Romeo is plannin' a road show?

DOC: But I'll be back to kiss you,
Kiss you to a fare-thee-well.

BRANDY: And I'm supposed to wait'll the show's closed?

DOC: So weep no more today, my lady love,
Your daddy's gone away, my lady love.

BRANDY: Try to bring me home a polar bear,
So baby doll can have a coat to wear!

DOC: I am gonna amble,
But I'm gonna be true
To the red, white, and you—
I am goin' roamin' for a while.

BRANDY: I'll keep a light a-flickerin' all night.

DOC: But then I'm comin' home 'n'
Love you till it goes—

BRANDY: (He's at the post.)
That's the way love goes!

DOC: (From coast to coast.)

BRANDY &
DOC: Love you, love you, love you
Till it goes outta style.

THE LETTER OF THE LAW

Registered for copyright as an unpublished song June 11, 1962. Introduced by Scott Merrill (Inspector Stirling) and ensemble in the 1962 production. Not used in 1964 production.

STIRLING: I suppose you wouldn't care if
I'm a bailiff or a sheriff,
And it's none of my affair if
You're aware if I'm a sheriff,
But a sheriff has an air if
There's a uniform to wear—if
He's a sheriff, he's a sheriff,
Anyone'll verify!

CHORUS: Yes, a sheriff has an air if
There's a uniform to wear—if
You're a sheriff, you're a sheriff,
We can truly verify!

STIRLING: I suppose I look contrary
To a clerk or actuary—
Say, a local dignitary
With a title honorary—
But for reasons necessary,
Most of which are monetary,
In the town constabulary
I'm a most important guy!

CHORUS: Oh, for reasons necessary,
Most of which are monetary,
In the town constabulary
You're the most important guy!

STIRLING: In fact, I am the only one
Who sees there's any law enforcement done.
If a stabbing or a shooting
Or a case of simple looting should arise,
I'm really rather wise:
I impose a fitting sentence
Till the culprit shows repentance for his crime!
He does a little time;
That usually corrects it—
But I have to make an exit

When a case of this complexity appears,
For no deputy or marshal
Can be truthfully impartial—
One's entitled to a trial by a jury of
    his peers!
It has now become the fashion
In a crime involving passion
One's entitled to a trial by a jury of
    his peers!
First juror for the Crown,
Swear in Nevada Brown!
Now, sir, do you agree
That you'll serve impartially
To the letter of the law—
To the letter of the law?

NEVADA: No, sir, I don't agree—
I b'lieve love should be free!
No gal looks twice at me
'Less I chase her up a tree—
I'm in favor of the crime,
And I do it all the time!

CHORUS: He's in favor of the crime
And he does it all the time!

STIRLING: Step down, Nevada Brown.
Who is next before the Crown?
Moosejaw Pittman!
Moosejaw, how do you feel about jury
    duty?

MOOSEJAW: Well, sir, there's just two things.
Back home in Mountain Springs,
I'm wanted on that charge—
Matter of fact, I'm still at large!
And I'm really kind o' proud
That I'm wanted by a crowd!

CHORUS: Anybody would be proud
To be wanted by a crowd.

STIRLING: Next man is Amos Gray.
Have you anything to say?

AMOS: Yes, sir, I've this to say:
All gals can run away—
There's no such thing as rape!
You say rape, I say red tape!
You can call it by a name
But the meanin' is the same.

CHORUS: Though the meaning is the same,
Hanky-panky is the name!

STIRLING: Next man is Skirts McGraw.
Will you observe the law
Doing the best you can
While you serve as juryman
And deliberate, McGraw,
To the letter of the law?

MCGRAW: No sir, not if I'm hung!
One time when I was young
I had a fi-an-cee,
But the one got raped was me—
And the reputation hurts
When y'moniker is Skirts!

CHORUS: You attract a lot o' flirts
When y'moniker is Skirts!

STIRLING: [addressing TESSIE] As the only lady
    juror,
Would you say a woman's purer than a
    man?
Speak briefly if you can.
Or if not exactly purer,
Would you say that she is surer of her
    ground
When there's a male around?
My question has a sequel:
Are the sexes really equal?
Ofttimes a woman's pique will turn to
    tears.
Being of a different gender,
Should you judge a male offender?
He's entitled to a trial by a jury of his
    peers.

CHORUS: Even very learned students
Who have studied jurisprudence
Say he ought to have a trial by a jury
    of his peers!

TESSIE: As the only lady witness,
If you're questioning my fitness as a
    judge,
I bear no man a grudge.
Men are stronger and profounder,
But we're softer and we're rounder—
    as a sex
We differ in respects.
But in case my contribution
Could be labeled persecution,
Then an obvious solution now
    appears.
Take him out and get him plastered
And string up the dirty bastard
'Cause he don't deserve a trial by a
    jury of his peers!

CHORUS: Her opinion's quite emphatic,
Though a trifle ungrammatic-al:
"He don't deserve a trial by a jury of
    his peers."

STIRLING: Though the plaintiff's allegation
That he harmed her reputation
May be just a fabrication
Of her own imagination,
In your sheriff's estimation
It's a big consideration
And a point the population
Seems completely to have missed.
Any further peroration
Would be merely affectation
And a recapitulation
Of a hopeless situation.
After due deliberation
In the interest of the nation,
It is my adjudication

That the jury be dismissed!

CHORUS: Hooray, we're all dismissed—
Our names are off the list!
Now we don't have to fear
Jury duty for a year,
And we needn't hem 'n' haw
To the letter of the law.
Hooray, we're on our own—
He'll try the case alone.
Stirling's an honest man,
And he'll do the best he can
To the letter of the law,
To the letter of the law!
Nolle contendere,
Whereas to wit,
He writes a writ,
That writ is it!
Corpus delicti,
If there's a fine,
He knows the line to draw!
Hooray and yessirree,
No culprit will go free—
We're mighty glad that we
Have a judge as fine as he!

CHORUS OR
STIRLING
OR BOTH: No cadet or
Baronet or
Learned legal etiquetter
Could upset a
Debtor
Better
To the letter of the law!

RESPECTABILITY

Registered for copyright as an unpublished song January 22, 1964. Introduced by Bert Lahr (Foxy), Robert H. Harris (Bedrock), Gerald Hiken (Shortcut), and Edward Greenhalgh (Buzzard). Dropped during 1964 tryout.

TRIO: Damned if we ain't struck it rich—
Wahee! Wahoo!
I'll be a ring-tailed sonofabitch,
Foxy come through!
He's gonna make us all millionaires!
That ain't the half:
After scroungin' all the way,
Cuttin' corners night and day, . . .
We gonna ride in sedan chairs*

* *Alternate line:*
  We're gonna be men of affairs—

FOXY: Ain't that a laugh!
When y' got it, then y' got it—
Respectability!
Reputation, admiration,
Respectability!
Nevermore no double-dealing
'Less the need arises;
Outright stealing
We call "enterprises"!
When you own a long Corona,
You got gentility.
What an aura a fedora brings!
We can even buy the one thing
Money can't buy
You spell it
With a dotted *i*-
T before the *y*
(Or is it *e*?).
It's called—
Respectability!

TRIO: Rich at last,
Cares all past—
Poor no more am I!
Lapis lazuli, where are you?
Jewels and pearls,
Harem girls—
We'll live free and fast,
Because we're rich at last!
It's called—
Respectability!

ALL: What a blessing, us possessing
Respectability!
Reputation, admiration—
Respectability!

FOXY: When you're poor, it ain't so funny,
You're out on your keester—
But the minute you get money,
You can pay next Easter!
When depleted,
You are treated
With cool civility.
If you got it,
You can get it—free!
You can have your wine and women, Happy
are we
'Cause we got—what's the word again
That you mentioned then?
Sing it to me!
Respectability!

TRIO: It's called—
Respectability!

FOXY: When y' got it,
Then y' got it—
Respectability
How'dja do, sir?
After you, sir!
Respectability!

Nevermore to view the good life
Through a veil of dreaming—
All at once, we find we've stood life
On its tail—I'm screaming!
Say it gently,
Eloquently,
And with humility—
Rich as Croesus,
Yes, bejeesus . . . me!
'T'aint so much a case of how much, but of
degree.
Remember,
If y'wanna get
In the upper set,
Lah-dee-dah-dee,
Get some—
Respectability

TRIO: Rich at last, . . .
Cares all past,
We'll live free and fast,
Because we're rich at last!
Get some—
Respectability!

CELIA'S FIRST ESSAY

Registered for copyright as an unpublished song January 22, 1964. Intended for Julienne Marie (Celia). Dropped during 1964 tryout.

She can cook a lot,
Make men look a lot,
Sew a fine silken seam,
Drive a plough or a team
Read the Book a lot—
Asininity!
Masculinity
Wants a girl to possess—
And will want it, I guess,
To infinity . . . and infinity—
That commodity rare
Which is not always there:
Her virginity!
With sanguinity
Masculinity
Puts us up on a star,
Wants us holier far
Than the Trinity.
Like the Trinity,
Femininity
Should be free from all sin
Or, at least, somewhere in
That vicinity.

We can save for them,
Be a slave for them,
And, if they have to leave,
Bolt the windows and even
Behave for them—
Asininity!
Masculinity
Wants a girl to possess—
And will want it, I guess
To infinity . . . and infinity—
What I just sold today,
And did not give away:
My virginity!

Alternative lyrics

Masculinity,
Femininity—
A dissimilar pair.
Yet they both seem to share
An affinity.
This affinity
By divinity
Seems to be preordained—
If the girl has retained
Her virginity.

SHIVAREE

Introduced by ensemble during 1964 tryout. Dropped before New York opening.
Lyric missing.

IF MOTHER COULD JUST SEE ME NOW

Registered for copyright as an unpublished song June 11, 1962. Introduced by Brandy and trio. Not used in show.

BRANDY: My dear old mother and daddy,
If they could just see me now!
It was my aim to seek fortune and fame,
So baby went out and learned how.
Now I've made good for the whole
neighborhood;
It just proves that honesty shows.
Daddy would say in his fatherly way,
"This child has a fortune right under her
nose."

I'm the most beautiful bird on the
    bough—
Oh, if Mother could just see me now!

TRIO: Your dear old mother and daddy,
If they could just see you now!

BRANDY: If they could see
What has happened to me—

TRIO: No wrinkles would furrow their brow!

BRANDY: "Workingman's pay for a workingman's
    day,"
They both said it time after time.
If they were right,
And the same goes for night,
I want you to know that I've earned ev'ry
    dime—
I've gone as far as the law would allow.
When you're in doubt, dearie, I'll teach
    you how—
Oh, if Mother could just see me now!

REVENGE IS SWEET (OPERA NUMBER)

Intended for Foxy and Doc. Not used in show.

FOXY: Revenge, revenge—
Ah, what a darling scheme it is!
To die, to die—
Ah, Doctor, how extreme it is!
To lie in state
And listen to 'em squabble
As the vultures try to gobble up my gold!
Hee-hee, ha-ha,
Oh, what a lovely joke it is!

DOC: Ha-ha, hoo-hoo,
A brilliant masterstroke it is!

FOXY: And then—like that!—
I'll jump up and I'll slaughter 'em,
Or maybe draw and quarter 'em—
I'll get my revenge, if it takes me nine
    hundred years!
I'll see them hung,
Strung by the tongue—or the ears!

DOC: I take it this is the night
You mean to fight?

FOXY: You're *Götterdämmerung* right!

DOC: Then, Prince, here are your horns!

FOXY: Am I a prince, or two unicorns?

DOC: *Der Meistersinger* calls you to battle,
Where you'll slaughter them all like cattle!

FOXY: *Nein, nein*, buddy of mine,
There is a way to deal *mit* swine—
I'll find a subterranean grotto

Where I'll kill 'em with my vibrato!
Ho-ho! I'll sing
An aria Wagnerian.

DOC: Aha, *The Ring*,
Dat melody Valkyrian?

FOXY: A simple thing
To please a Presbyterian—
Or maybe "Just A-Wearyin' "
By Carrie Jacobs Bond!

DOC: "Toreador"—now that would be a treat!
You want revenge?
That would be sweet!

FOXY: Which is sweeter, which the nobler art—
To stab them, or sing the part?
I'll save an arm or two for souvenirs—
But you can have the ears!
To think of the pal I've been!

DOC: What anguish you must be in!

FOXY: What anguish indeed—chagrin!
Vexation and pique!

DOC: To punish them slightly
Requires a method unsightly
And slightly oblique.

FOXY: Stabbing?

DOC: Bloody!

FOXY: Drowning?
Poison?

DOC: Chancy!

FOXY: Torture?

DOC: Fancy!

FOXY: Oh, what a lovely way to die,
Stung by the lowly tsetse fly!
Thrown to the ants
Or man-devouring plants!
Oh, what a rogue, what a conniving knave
    am I!
Oh, to bury them in a bank of snow—

DOC: That's revenge?

FOXY: In a bank of snow where the cold winds
    blow—

DOC: That's revenge?

FOXY: To the waist, or maybe a bit below—

DOC: That's revenge?

FOXY: Then pour a bowl of scalding soup on the
    parts that show!

DOC: So we bury them in a bank of snow—

FOXY: 'N' serve 'em simple little suppers
While their lower and their upper set
Begin to chatter and clatter—

DOC: In a bank of snow where the cold winds
    blow—

FOXY: A plate of dainty little dishes
Just to gratify their wishes
While they all are freezing and sneezing

BOTH: Pouring scalding soup on the parts that
    show,
So we'll be sure that their demise will be
    nice and slow!!!

And while they're shivering and quivering
    out there—

FOXY: We'll take some girls out to dinner and
    share—

BOTH: Tea for two and two for tea,
A belt or two, or maybe three!
Three or four, or maybe more, all having
    our private kicks
While they're stiff and stark and sailing
    down the River Styx!
And remember, dear old pals, that we'll
    still be around
While you jump the claim of that big gold
    mine in the ground!

FOXY: The jest is done,
Or begun—

DOC: You're a numbskull or a genius!

FOXY: Call them in
And we'll watch the fun!

DOC: You're a dreamer!

FOXY: Pulses failing—

DOC: Pulses . . .

FOXY: Forehead paling,
Elbows flailing—

DOC: Elbows!?

FOXY: Fever high!

DOC: It's just a sunburn!

FOXY: I'm going fast—

DOC: Make it faster!

FOXY: Fading fast—

DOC: Get a move on!

FOXY: Hold my hand
While I breathe my last!

DOC: What a hambone!

FOXY: Senses reeling—

DOC: Senses . . .

FOXY: Dizzy feeling—

DOC: Dizzy feeling?

FOXY: Heart contracting,
Holy smoke, what acting!
Now . . . I . . . die . . .

CHIEF INDIAN GIVER

Not used in show.

We make ceremony—
Take-um paleface out o' teepee,
Make him Injun same-um like we,
Give him special name.
Injun Giver, our friend,
Here with tribe all winter him spend.
Life with paleface he want-um end—

Now we all the same.
Treat him rough and grow him up tough,
Put rocks in his feet,
Think him do for Indian stew—
Him too tough to eat!
Woo-woo-woo, woo-woo-woo, woo-woo-woo!
Injun Giver learn how
Time is come for hold-um powwow.
He do dance and join-um up now—
We show what to do.
Put moose head on you,
Give-um bark canoe,
Also scalp or two,
We go woo-woo-woo,
You come in on cue—
Show what Injun chief can do!!!

Injun Giver, that me.
Once I paleface same-a like he.
You rescue, take pity on me,
Make me heap big brave!
Injun Giver my name,
I go down in crookedy fame.
Hunt for gold and strike-um big claim—
Much wampum I save!
You give me steam-heated teepee,
Antlers off of moose,
Give-um squaw and mother-in-law,
I give back papoose.
Injun Giver have ball,
Learn your ways and grow-um up tall,
Smoke-um peace pipe, thank-um you all.
Drum play Injun tune.
I give cry of loon,
Dance by light of moon,
Heap big Dan'l Boone,
Marry child bride soon
I name her Tang-Poon—
Injun Giver heap big brave!

Doc's reprise

They forsake agreement they make,
Leave old pal behind.
They take vote and cutt-um him throat—
We pay off in kind.
Injun Giver, big chief,
Get revenge and catch-um up thief—
Now their ha-ha turn-um to grief.
They take bait from me,
Soon they be up tree.
Plan work fine, now we
See what we shall see—
Injun Giver scalp-um three!

CELIA'S FIRST LAMENT

Not used in show. Alternate title: "Celia's Lament."

I couldn't speak Latin,
I couldn't speak Greek;
They never did teach 'em in school.
The moment he kissed me
I just couldn't speak;
I reckon I looked like a fool.
I wasn't even dressed up,
My hair was kinda messed up,
And though I pined away for romance,
For a girl who was brought up in Omaha,
     Nebraska,
I never had a Chinaman's chance!
The chance has flown
And wasn't it a rapid flight?
If I had known,
I would have gone to school at night.

He knew about painting,
He knew about art;
He had a terrific IQ.
I might have impressed him
If I had been smart
And spoken in calculus, too!
If I had whispered, "Howdy!
You're summa cum-a laude!"
He never would have looked so askance.
For a gal used to biscuits and buttermilk and
     bloomers,
I never had a Chinaman's chance!
Was he well bred!
And, boy, could he put on the dog!
But all I'd read
Was the Sears and Roebuck catalogue.

If I had been wearing
A mutton-chop sleeve,
A cute little bustle in back,
Or two gay deceivers
That really deceive,
They might have supplied what I lack.
With just a little urgin'
I wouldn't be a virgin,
'Cause I was really ripe for romance.
For a half Holy Roller and Running Water
     Baptist,
I never had a Chinaman's chance!

AS FAIR AS HER NAME

Registered for copyright as an unpublished song June 11, 1962. Not used in show.

DRUNK: There once was a lady who owned a
     saloon;
     She had a nice bar and a lovely spittoon.
     She wouldn't buy drinks on a man's
     honeymoon—
BRANDY: Unless maybe he was a ringtailed
     baboon.
DRUNK: Beautiful, beautiful Brandy,
     A lady as fair as her name.
     Old Buzzard and Shortcut she serves in a
     wink—
BRANDY: Old Buzzard and Shortcut can pay for
     their drink!
DRUNK: Her pal she won't offer so much as a
     beer.
BRANDY: You're drunk enough, buster, to last you
     a year!
DRUNK: Beautiful, beautiful Brandy,
     The lady as fair as her name.
     I knew if I sat here and played cat-and-
     mouse,
     Eventually, I'd get a drink on the
     house—
     But owning the joint, that's too good to
     be true!
BRANDY: Remember, you own all the hangovers
     too!
DRUNK: So give me a few little tips I could use.
BRANDY: First double the prices and water the
     booze.
DRUNK: Okay, and it won't be as bad as you
     think!
BRANDY: So when I stop in, you can buy me a
     drink!
DRUNK: Beautiful, beautiful Brandy,
     A beautiful, beautiful dame—
     Beautiful, beautiful Brandy,
     A lady as fair as her name! . . .

RABBIT'S FOOT

Not used in show.

Boy's version

Go hang a sign up
And send the wine up—

Here's your wandering boy.
I couldn't quit you;
Could I permit you
To throw away such joy?
I've been a bounder, a cad, a heel,
I've been a rounder, but now I feel
I've gotten mellow,
A different fellow,
Who nets a second try—
Why?
Rabbit's foot,
I figure you're my rabbit's foot—
When you're here I've got the whole thing made.
Queen of hearts,
When you became my Queen of hearts—
Lady Luck dealing every hand I played.
I am fat,
King of the world, my cup is full.
Add to that,
You are so downright lovable!
Rabbit's foot,
If you decide to throw me out,
I'm kaput,
I'll lose the luck I found.
Rabbit's foot,
Promise me to stick around!

Girl's version

Oh, what a con man!
How you come on, man,
And twist a lady's arm!
Though I may doubt you,
There is about you
A certain oily charm.
You know the saying that people say—
"It's hard to heat up an old soufflé."
But you can do it,
And nothing to it,

Except that I won't buy—
Why?
Rabbit's foot,
Who wants to be your rabbit's foot?
If it means playing a one-night stand.
Queen of hearts?
Sure, I can be your Queen of Hearts,
Long as I'm holding a diamond hand!
Life is good;
You'd like to carry me about—
Sure you would,
But does it help this rabbit out?
Rabbit's foot,
They're made to dangle on a string.
I'll stay put
Where there's a place to graze.
Rabbit's foot
Stays where the rabbit stays.

I'LL GET EVEN

Not used in show.

FOXY: We'll get even with them, but utterly.
DOC: Even with them, but subtly.
FOXY: Even, even if I should get the electric chair,
    I'll get even with them, the hypocrites.
    Just wait 'til I re-cip-o-crites,
    They'll wish they'd met up with a grizzly bear.
    I'll carve 'em up like pie,
    I'll watch 'em bleed and die.
DOC: Perhaps a tsetse fly could make them sick?

FOXY: I'll get those great big ants
    And drop 'em in their pants.
DOC: Or man-devouring plants might do the trick?
    I can tell you this confidentially,
    We'll get 'em all eventually,
    I'll stay on the case 'til the case is cracked.
    We'll get even, even if it's your dying act!

DOC: We'll get even with them parasites,
FOXY: Even with them, the blatherkeites,
    If it takes the rest of my natural days.
DOC: We'll get even with them, the bunch of 'em.
FOXY: Maybe I'll make a lunch of 'em,
    Serve 'em under glass with a sauce béarnaise.
    I'll have 'em boiled in oil,
    Perhaps a London broil.
DOC: Or let a cobra coil around their beds?
    Or pin 'em down, kerplop, beneath a faucet top
FOXY: And let the water drop upon their heads.
DOC: We may starve 'em to death or throttle 'em.
FOXY: Dip 'em in brine and bottle 'em,
    They'll be sorry they left me all alone.
BOTH: We'll get even
DOC: If it takes ev'ry cent you own!

FOXY

Not used in show.
    Lyric missing.

OVERLEAF
Top: The Americanization of Emily: *Julie Andrews, James Garner, and Joyce Grenfell*
Bottom: The Great Race: *Natalie Wood*

Songs of 1964 and 1965

LORNA

Music by Mort Lindsey. Registered for copyright as an unpublished song January 27, 1964. Theme of CBS Television's *The Judy Garland Show*, written in honor of Judy's daughter Lorna Luft. According to *Skylark*, Garland asked Mercer to write lyrics for the *preexisting* theme music written by Lindsey. The song was premiered on February 9, 1964, show by Garland, singing it to Lorna (as she had sung other "names" songs to Liza and Joey earlier in the show).

Lorna,
I can't believe what I see;
What I see astounds me!
Mirrors of love are your eyes to me;
Stars up above must delight to see them.
Lorna,
You won't believe what I say;
What I say I almost should pray—
Pray for the day
I can shout from the rooftops,
"Lorna loves me, too!"

MAN'S FAVORITE SPORT? (1964)

Produced and directed by Howard Hawks for Universal. Released February 1964. Copyright February 29, 1964. Screenplay by John Fenton Murray and Steve McNeil, based on the story "The Girl Who Almost Got Away" by Pat Frank. Lyrics by Johnny Mercer. Music and music score by Henry Mancini. Starring Rock Hudson and Paula Prentiss, with Maria Perschy, John McGiver, Charlene Holt, Roscoe Karns, James Westerfield, Norman Alden, Forrest Lewis, Regis Toomey, Tyler McVey, and Kathie Browne.

A salesman of fishing tackle finds himself in an embarrassing position when he is forced to enter a fishing competition.

MAN'S FAVORITE SPORT

Music by Henry Mancini. Registered for copyright as an unpublished song February 3, 1964. Introduced by off-screen chorus behind opening titles.

REFRAIN 1

Some men are good at hunting quail;
Some like to sail,
While others like to box.
Some men prefer to surf;
Still others like the turf
And lose a bit of money on the jocks.
Some men say judo is their dish,
While others fish where mountain water swirls.
But let a girl appear,
He'll pursue her
And run his fingers through her curls.
And that's the way it's been
Since the world began—
The fav'rite sport of man is girls!

REFRAIN 2

Some men like swimming in the sea;
Some water-ski,
While others like to fence.
Developing physique,
Some climb a mountain peak
And rough it in those little canvas tents.
To some, a parachute's the thing;
He pulls a string as down to earth he hurls.
But let a doll appear,
He'll pursue her,
And run his fingers through her curls.
And that's the way it's been
Since the world began—
The fav'rite sport of man is girls!

REFRAIN 3

Some men wear unattractive shorts
Around the courts
Or traipsing through the links.
Some think a game is nice
Called curling on the ice
Or even mumblety peg or tiddlywinks.
Some like the sports of yesterday
And even play the ancient game of scurls.
But let a maid appear,
They'll pursue her
And run their fingers through her curls.
And that's the way it's been
Since the world began—
The fav'rite sport of man is girls!

REFRAIN 4

One man is good at shooting skeet;
Another's treat
Is maybe throwing darts.
Some men go in for squash;
Some others, klabiash;
Still others love a lively game of hearts.

Some men put on an aqualung
And swim among
The barnacles and pearls.
But let a chick appear,
They'll pursue her,
And run their fingers through her curls.
And that's the way it's been
Since the world began —
The fav'rite sport of man is girls!

REFRAIN 5

Some like the arrow and the bow,
While others throw
A discus down the green.
Still others like to bowl
Or shooting for a hole,
Especially the one they call nineteen.
Some men go gliding through the sky
Or even try
To capture flying squirrels.
But let a lass appear,
They'll pursue her,
And run their fingers through her curls,
And that's the way it's been
Since the world began—
The fav'rite sport of man is girls!

THE PINK PANTHER (1964)

Produced by Martin Jurow for Mirisch-G-E Productions. Released by United Artists. Released March 1964. Copyright March 18, 1964. Directed by Blake Edwards. Screenplay by Maurice Richlin and Blake Edwards. Music by Henry Mancini. Starring David Niven, Peter Sellers, Robert Wagner, and Capucine, with Brenda de Banzie, Colin Gordon, John Le Mesurier, James Lanphier, Guy Thomajan, Michael Trubshawe, Riccardo Billi, Meri Welles, Martin Miller, Fran Jeffries, and Claudia Cardinale.

The first adventure of the incompetent French police inspector Clouseau, on the trail of the notorious jewel thief the Phantom.

IT HAD BETTER BE TONIGHT (MEGLIO STASERA)

English lyrics by Johnny Mercer. Italian lyric by Franco Migliacci. Published. Copyrighted March 20, 1964. Previously registered for copyright as an unpublished song June 26, 1963. Introduced in Italian only by Fran Jeffries. Mercer's lyrics not used in film. Recorded by Henry Mancini and His Orchestra (Victor) and, many years later, Fran Jeffries (in English) (Harbinger).

VERSE

Meglio stasera, baby,
Go! Go! Go!
Or as we natives say,
Fa subito!

REFRAIN 1

If you're ever gonna kiss me,
It had better be tonight,
While the mandolins are playing
And stars are bright.
If you've anything to tell me,
It had better be tonight,
Or someone else may tell me
And whisper the words just right.

REPEAT VERSE

REFRAIN 2

For this poor Americano
Who knows little of your speech,
Be a nice Italiano
And start to teach.
Show me how in old Milano
Lovers hold each other tight—
But I warn you, sweet *paisano*,
It had better be tonight!

REPEAT VERSE

TONIGHT MAY HAVE TO LAST ME ALL MY LIFE

Music by Don Borzage. Published. Copyrighted March 16, 1964.

Hold me close to you
And say you love me too;
Tonight may have to last me all my life.
Leave a memory
To keep me company;
Tonight may have to last me all my life.
Then when I'm alone without you,
I can always dream about you;
Ev'ry hour you stay
Will make a dream bouquet
That I'll see going past me all my life.
So have no regret,
For, darling, don't forget,
Tonight may have to last me all my life.

I DREAMED OF MY DARLING

Composer unknown. Registered for copyright as an unpublished song April 1, 1964.
    Lyric missing.

ROSA, I LOVE YOU

Composer unknown. Registered for copyright as an unpublished song April 1, 1964.
    Lyric missing.

BUSY LITTLE BUMBLE BEE

Music by Harry Warren. Registered for copyright as an unpublished song April 14, 1964.

Been a busy little bee,
Buzzin' all around from tree to tree;
Not a pretty flower gets by me.

Been a busy little bee,
Buzzin' all around from hill to hill,
Pollinatin' posies, that's my skill;
Makin' every little Jack and Jill
A Mister and Missus Daffodil.
Brother, when I rev up and start my takeoff,
Bz-z-z-z-z-z-z!
Ev'rybody hollers, "Here he comes!"
There ain't a flyin' insect I can't shake off,
Bz-z-z-z-z-z-z!
Other bumblebees are stumblebums!
At break of day
I'm on my way;
I'm makin' hay
Before the clock strikes five.
Before the sun
Is halfway done,
I've got a lot of honey in my hive.
I've got a reputation to uphold;
Even in the winter, when it's cold,
Plowin' through the snow drifts,
You'll see me,
Bein' a busy little bee!

LAKE SAINT MARY

Music by Louis Alter. Registered for copyright as an unpublished song June 17, 1964. Alternate title: "Moon over Lake Saint Mary."

When the moon is high,
High over Lake Saint Mary,
I ride alone through places we knew.
While the clouds roll by,
High over Lake Saint Mary,
They make a picture of you.
In the star-sprinkled pines
The whip-poor-will sings a blue note.
Sad are his words,
He wants to know
What made you go.
So I roam the hills,
Watching the moonlit prairie,
Counting the nights
Till you come in view
Down the silver trail
Leading to Lake Saint Mary,
Where we'll be waiting for you.

WAITING FOR JESUS

Composer unknown. Registered for copyright as an unpublished song June 22, 1964.
Lyric missing.

THE AMERICANIZATION OF EMILY (1964)

Produced by Martin Ransohoff for Metro-Goldwyn-Mayer. Released October 1964. Copyright July 17, 1964. Directed by Arthur Hiller. Screenplay by Paddy Chayefsky, based on the novel *The Americanization of Emily* by William Bradford Huie. Lyrics by Johnny Mercer. Music by Johnny Mandel. Musical director: Robert Armbruster. Starring James Garner, Julie Andrews, and Melvyn Douglas, featuring James Coburn, Joyce Grenfell, Edward Binns, and Liz Fraser, with William Windom, John Crawford, Douglas Henderson, Edmon Ryan, Steve Franken, Paul Newlan, and Keenan Wynn.

Just before the Normandy landing in World War II a war-widow driver falls for an American commander.

EMILY

Published. Copyrighted October 30, 1964. Previously registered for copyright as an unpublished song July 13, 1964. Major recording by Andy Williams (Columbia).

Warner Bros. was not happy with the song's ending and altered it for the sheet music to: "They see Emily,/ Emily too." Many singers recorded the song with this rewording, which never ceased to annoy Mercer. Not sung in film but can be heard on the soundtrack album (Reprise).

"Emily, Emily, Emily"
Has the murmuring sound of May,
Silver bells, coral shells, carousels
And the laughter of children at play.
Say,
"Emily, Emily, Emily"
And we fade to a marvelous view,
Two lovers alone and out of sight,
Seeing images in the firelight;
As my eyes visualize a family,

They see dreamingly
Emily too.

OLD GUITARON

Music by Laurindo Almeida. Registered for copyright as an unpublished song August 12, 1964.

REFRAIN 1

Old guitaron,
Speak low
And we'll sing her the prettiest song we know.
The pale moon is riding the sky;
The night is a kiss.
Time to whisper, "*Querida*, I love you so."
Show me how, guitaron,
Above,
How the angels would sing if they made love,
Or if you could only impart
The music she puts in my heart,
She'll hear me sigh and fly
To me like a dove.
That is what I'll be,
High in the jacaranda tree.
Am I not your oldest friend, *amigo*?
Am I not the one
Who taught you ev'rything I know?
And if you know,
And I think you do.
Oh, we could break her heart in two!
Teach me how to pray
Ev'ry word I say
Till she belongs to me alone!

REFRAIN 2

Old guitaron,
Don't lie
And we'll sing her a song that will make her cry.
The tears in her beautiful eyes
Will shine like the stars
When I whisper, "I'll love you until I die."
I know you, guitaron;
That tone
Has warmth that could melt a heart of stone.
So play in your prettiest way
And maybe she'll promise to stay
With me and love and you,
My old guitaron.

I WANNA BE IN LOVE AGAIN

Music by Mercer. Published. Copyrighted May 26, 1965. Previously registered for copyright as an unpublished song August 20, 1964. First recorded by Jackie Cain and Roy Kral (Roulette).

Mercer used the song again in the unproduced show *Mike* (1967), where the character Velda prefaced it with a verse.

I wanna be in love again,
I wanna be in love again.
I wanna try and beat the odds
Of the gracious gods
Up above again.
I wanna know the thrills again,
The fever and the chills again;
The quiver of the lightning fork,
And the million porcupine quills again.
I long to feel my temples pound
And pulses race again,
As helpless as a fox
Caught in a chase again;
Then feel that metamorphosis
Take place again,
The wild explosion of bliss
Politely known as a kiss.
I wanna know the fright again,
That panic in the night again,
When you're prepared to end it all,
Till a certain call
Comes through.
I wanna be alive again,
I wanna be in love again,
But only if the love again
I love again
Is you.

Verse from *Mike*

Poor old boss, can't you see
What's been going on?
Can't you see I'm *finis*,
G-O-N-E—gone?
I'm so deep in the throes,
It's a hopeless case;
That's as plain as the nose
On your boyish face!

I'VE WAITED FOR A WALTZ

Music by Johnny Rotella. Registered for copyright as an unpublished song August 20, 1964.

I've waited for a waltz
The whole night long;
I've waited for a slow and dreamy song.*
I've waited for the violins to play
The music to the words that I can't say.
My lips won't breathe a sigh,
Not a whisper or a word;
At times like this
Lips are felt and not heard.
But when you're in my arms
Where you belong,
My kisses will supply
A million reasons why
I've waited for a waltz
The whole night long.

EXERCISE YOUR PREROGATIVE

Music probably by Gene de Paul. Registered for copyright as an unpublished song October 19, 1964.

There's one way to be happy,
There's one way to be gay;
That goes for every woman and child
In the good old U.S.A.
Declare your independence—
Get in that voting booth.
Remember what Tom Jefferson said
When he struck a blow for truth:
Go out and exercise your prerogative—
Exercise your prerogative!
Your life's your own, so, brother, live!,
While you exercise your prerogative!

Created free and equal
And blessed with liberty—
If you intend to keep it thataway,
Take a little tip from me:

* Alternate lines 3–5:
    I've waited for the band to play our song.
    I've waited for the time when lights are low,
    The moment when you'll say, "I love you so."

Inspect the situation,
Discuss each pro and con,
And then go cast your ballot for the thing
That you set your heart upon.
Go out and exercise your prerogative—
Exercise your prerogative!
You get back double what you give
When you exercise your prerogative!

My gal and me went parkin'
Off Highway Ninety-three.
Like I told this here motorcycle cop
When he tried to spotlight me:
And that means, exercise your prerogative,
Exercise your prerogative!
You won't regret the time you give
If you exercise your prerogative!
Get out and exercise your prerogative,
Exercise your prerogative!
The time for action has arriv'—
Better exercise your prerogative!

Old man Sweetbody Goodpants
And Missus G., his frau,
You all know they's got twenty-seven kids—
Has I got to tell you how?
Right off they exercised their prerogative,
Exercised their prerogative—
They each knew something had to give,
So they exercised their prerogative!

SINGLE-O

Music by Donald Kahn. Registered for copyright as an unpublished song October 26, 1964.

Single-o, all the way,
Rain or shine, gonna stay
Single-o, till you're mine—
Like the peach at the top of the tree,
Gonna stay outta reach till it's me.
And though I don't know caresses
You expect to find,
I know my address is
Lonesomeville till you make up your mind!
When you do, and it's me you adore,
Then I'll be single-o no more!

A KISS FROM YOU

Music by Benny Carter. Published. Copyrighted December 21, 1964.

A kiss from you means more to me
Than any thrill there could ever be.
The very thought of your lips on my own
Opens the door to worlds I've never known.
A kiss from you
And there I stand,
Stars at my feet,
Tomorrow in my hand.
A glimpse of heaven is given to few;
But I've known more than this—
I've known a kiss from you.

CHEAT ON ME

Music by Gene DiNovi.

REFRAIN 1

Cheat on me
And I will skin your hide,
Have your teeth
Aerified—
I'll show you how rough a shook-up baby can feel!

Cheat on me
And I will wield my mace,
Change the shape
Of your face,
Slightly redesign your physiognomy!

If you're kind and gentle
And sentimental,
I'll be sweet as pie;
But to see the real me,
Double-deal me—
Watch the feathers fly!

Cheat on me
And I will drop a bomb.
Even worse,
Call up Mom—
You'll become the range that I shoot skeet on,
If you ever try to
Cheat on me.

REFRAIN 2

Cheat on me
But keep in mind, my love—
Iron hand, velvet glove.
They'll disclose I have a whim of ladylike steel.

Cheat on me
And I will blast your wig,
Snap your cap—
Do you dig?
You'll find out just how a brainwashed papa can
     feel!

If you wanna cool it
And golden-rule it,
I'll react the same.
Stroke my fur the right way,
The nice, polite way,
Tiger will be tame!

Cheat on me
And I will go the route,
Do you in,
Spread you out
Like the mat you wipe your big flat feet on,
If you ever try to
Cheat on me.

REFRAIN 3

Cheat on me
And you will get your lumps,
And it won't
Be the mumps.
I'll reveal to you my old Neanderthal side!

Cheat on me
And I will throw a fit,
Sprinkle pins
Where you sit—
Missus Jekyll
All at once will be Missus Hyde.

Be the constant lover
And you'll discover
I'm the constant wife.
Call another gal up,
I'll call a pal up—
Namely, Mack the Knife!

Cheat on me
And on your classic dome
I will play
"Home, Sweet Home."
It will be the bongo drum I beat up on
If you every try to
Cheat on me!

IF-FA

Music by Mercer.

Iffa, iffa, iffa don't count with me!
Iffa thatta ol' hound dog
Didn't sniffa that tree,
He'd a caught him a rabbit
Anybody could see!
Iffa I was a beauty
In a beautiful dress,
Iffa you was to ask me,
Maybe I'da say yes!
But iffa, iffa, iffa don't count with me—
Neither perhaps
Nor either maybe!

Don't say if I was different
And treated you real nice
That I could be your regular gal,
'Cause that don't cut no ice.*

Iffa thatta ol' rabbit
Hadda runna real fast,
Thenna thatta ol' turtle
Woulda come-a in last!

Iffa thatta ol' grizzly
Hadda laida low too,
He'd be in the mountains
Steada inna the zoo—
So iffa, iffa, iffa don't count with me—
Neither perhaps
Nor either maybe!

JUST LIKE TAKIN' CANDY FROM A BABY

Music by Robert Emmett Dolan. Song later rewritten with new music by Barry Manilow, page 387.

Just like takin' candy from a baby,
You're takin' me, baby,
You're robbin' me blind!

———————

* *Alternative lines for male singer:*
   Iffa I was a rich boy
   And I looka real fine,
   Iffa I was to ask you,
   Maybe you'd be mine!

The only heart I'll ever own
Just melts like an ice-cream cone—
Another kiss and I may lose my mind!

Just like takin' jelly beans from baby,
You're greedy, but maybe
You're generous, too!
For as we live, we learn,
And when it comes my turn,
Just like takin' candy from a baby, baby,
Watch me steal your heart from you!

ONE LITTLE EVENING

Music by Bob Corwin.

One little evening that was dull and unspectacular,
One little number on a calendar page,
Turned out to be, if you will pardon the
     vernacular,
The very most important night of our age!
One little evening that was headed for obscurity
Became a moment that was fit for the gods
When, just by lending it your innocence and purity,
We made it win against impossible odds!
I only played my part
By following my heart;
There was nothing I could do.
But thanks to luck and thanks to you,
Our little evening soon was beautiful and lyrical,
And though I must admit that love was there, too,
I hope you realize that we performed a miracle—
We made a dream come true.

SUMMER ON THE CAPE

Music by Al Dero.

Pick a night in June or July,
Indigo sky,
Stars are peeping down
Like jewels in a crown
As little Provincetown
Puts on a party gown
Of white.
Lights begin to twinkle in bars
Under the stars;
Couples disappear, and far away
You hear a radio that plays

The music for a lazy night.
Every year they come,
Don't know how or where from,
But oh, how the summer flies!
Things they want to say
As the train pulls away
Are hidden by gay goodbyes.
"Call me up when you get to town—
We'll run it down,
Have a lot of laughs,
Get out the photographs,
Or maybe play a tape
Of summer on the Cape!"

SWEET TIDINGS

Composer unknown.

Sweet tidings,
I hear sweet tidings,
Such sweet, sweet tidings hear I!
Birds sing them,
And church bells ring them,
And back I fling them to the sky.
You love me,
You do do love me!
What more could I be desirous of
Than those tender endearments,
Those whispered confidings
Sweet tidings of love!

A WIDE PLACE IN THE ROAD

Music by Mercer.

Oh, I wanna be back where I wanna be,
Where my home sweet home is a-callin' me,
Offa Highway Ninety-seven
At a wide place in the road.

Oh, you go ten miles by the county school
By a billboard sign readin' Chew Brown Mule,
Offa Highway Ninety-seven
In the place where I was growed.
There's a rusted Chevy chassis
And a pump of Red Chief gas
And the front yard ain't so grassy,

'Cause the sows and pigs keep a-rootin' up the
    grass.

Still, it beats your towns 'n' your neighborhoods
To be settin' there in the Piney Woods
In a Blue Ridge Mountain heaven,
Where your kinfolks all abide
Offa Highway Ninety-seven
At a wide place in the road.

Oh, I wanna be where I wanna be,
In a rubber tire swingin' from a tree
Offa Highway Ninety-seven
At a wide place in the road.

No, there ain't no hens in the chicken coop,
'Cause they're diggin' worms underneath the
    stoop
Offa Highway Ninety-seven
In the place where I was growed.
Rainy days there warn't much action;
Still, the young'uns made out fine,
And they got their satisfaction
Throwin' rocks and stones at the Nehi NuGrape
    sign.

On a Saturday night we could always go
Down the road apiece to the bus depot,
Hang around till about eleven,
Till we seen 'em all unload
Offa Highway Ninety-seven
At a wide place in the road.

HAVE A HEART

Music by Gene DiNovi. Published. Copyrighted March 1,
1965.

Have a heart,
Have a heart,
And when you do,
Have a heart
For a heart
That beats for you.

Have a dream,
Dreamed all alone,
No one has known,
No one has shared.
Lips,
Yours from the first,
Still unrehearsed,
Yet so prepared.

Glance at the stars
That shine above;
Take a chance on the stars
And fall in love.
When they all
Seem to be right,
There'll come a night
You can't decline.
If you do
Have a heart,
Have mine.

STAR SOUNDS

Music by Mercer. Published. Copyrighted May 26, 1965.
Previously registered for copyright as an unpublished
song March 10, 1965. Recorded by Jackie Cain and Roy
Kral (Roulette).

Star sounds,
Gossamer as spindrift,
Echo down the wind drift
When you're close to me;
Far sounds,
Like a siren calling,
Or guitar sounds
By a coral sea.
Star sounds—
Darling, can you hear them,
Or are you too near them
On your cloud of white?
Hold me,
Make those sweet bizarre sounds—
Keep the lovely star sounds
Floating through the night!
When we touch,
Your kisses take me straight to the moon.
You're too much,
That's all I need to say.
Listen to that wild celestial music
Coming from the crazy Milky Way!
Can't you see,
You really are the love of my life,
Which could be eternally sublime?
Sigh, love,
Like the stars and I, love—
Whisper you'll be my love
Till the end of time!

THE GREAT RACE (1965)

Produced by Martin Jurow for Patricia-Jalem-Reynard Co. Released by Warner Bros. Released July 1965. Copyright June 15, 1965. Directed by Blake Edwards. Screenplay by Arthur Ross. Original story by Blake Edwards and Arthur Ross. Lyrics by Johnny Mercer. Music by Henry Mancini. Choreography by Hermes Pan. Starring Jack Lemmon, Tony Curtis, and Natalie Wood, featuring Peter Falk, Keenan Wynn, Arthur O'Connell, Vivian Vance, Dorothy Provine, Larry Storch, and Ross Martin, with George Macready, Marvin Kaplan, Hal Smith, Denver Pyle, William Bryant, and Ken Wales.

In 1908, the Great Leslie and Professor Fate are bitter rivals in the first New York–Paris car race.

THE SWEETHEART TREE

Published. Copyrighted June 3, 1965. Introduced by Natalie Wood (dubbed by Jackie Ward). Leading recording by Johnny Mathis (Mercury). Recorded by Henry Mancini and His Orchestra (Victor). The song was nominated for an Academy Award but lost to "The Shadow of Your Smile," from *The Sandpiper*, by Johnny Mandel (music) and Paul Francis Webster (lyrics).

Ironically, Mandel's first choice to write the lyrics for his theme song was Johnny Mercer.

"I wrote it for the movie," Mercer recalled, "and it was turned down and [another] fellow wrote 'The Shadow of Your Smile,' which got to be one of the biggest hits ever.

"My song was kinda nice, it was poetic, it fit the picture":

> Today I saw a bird that broke its wing,
> Which isn't in itself a tragic thing.
> Yet I had the feeling start
> I had seen my counterpart,
> And love would come and break my heart
> Once again in spring.

As a songwriter who never disdained commercial success himself, there was a distinct tone of envy in Mercer's quip: "I figured with 'the shadow of your smile' he was in love with a lady with a mustache."

They say there's a tree in the forest,
A tree that will give you a sign.
Come along with me to the sweetheart tree,
Come and carve your name next to mine.

They say if you kiss the right sweetheart,
The one you've been waiting for,
Big blossoms of white will burst into sight
And your love will be true evermore.

HE SHOULDN'T-A, HADN'T-A, OUGHTN'T-A SWANG ON ME!

Registered for copyright as an unpublished song July 19, 1965. Introduced by Dorothy Provine and recorded by her with Henry Mancini and His Orchestra (Victor).

He sleeps out there, out where the coyotes wail.
The reason he ain't at the bar with the boys
Makes quite a dismal tale.

He shouldn't-a, hadn't-a, oughtn't-a swang on me,
He oughtn't-a, shouldn't-a, hadn't-a, nosirree!
You don't get many callers
Sleepin' on the lone prairie,
But he shouldn't-a, hadn't-a, oughtn't-a swang on me!

Way out West we're wild and woolly—
In order to explain it fully,
We're tall grown, all grown.
All the men are hairy-chested,
And all the women double-breasted—
We're ladylike until molested,
And then we're on our own!
He shouldn't-a, hadn't-a, oughtn't-a swang on me—
He oughtn't-a, shouldn't-a, hadn't-a felt so free.
His wife gets the insurance,
And I'm sorry as can be,
But he shouldn't-a, hadn't-a, oughtn't-a swang on me!

This here job is mighty trying,
Sometimes the room is fairly flying
With highballs, eyeballs.
One guy, till somebody got 'im,
Tore up the joint from top to bottom—
I think I was the one that shot him,
As near as I recall.
He shouldn't-a, hadn't-a, oughtn't-a swang on me.
He massacred eight or nine minutes, the lazy B.
He then took on the sheriff and the sheriff's deputy,
But he shouldn't-a, hadn't-a, oughtn't-a swang on me!

All you boys remember Harry,
The wrangler I was set to marry—
A long man, a strong man.
One night he yells, "I'm from Texas!"
And socks me in my solar plexus.
Well, having normal, good reflexes,
I knocked him on his can!
He shouldn't-a, hadn't-a, oughtn't-a blacked my eye!
I'm really a lovable, peaceable kind of guy.
I wouldn't scare a rabbit and I couldn't harm a flea,
But he shouldn't-a, hadn't-a, oughtn't-a swang on me!

If this story has a moral,
It's when you're lookin' for a quarrel or
Showdown—slow down.
If by now you haven't mastered
The gentle art of getting plastered,
You're just a low-down—
You ain't mastered
The motto of our town!
You shouldn't-a, hadn't-a, oughtn't-a start no fight.
Our burying grounds are a most impressive sight!
The message on them tombstones is as simple as can be:
He shouldn't-a, hadn't-a, oughtn't-a swang on me!

GET A HORSE

Registered for copyright as an unpublished song October 25, 1965. Not sung in film.

Crank her up and crank her up and give her the gas—
We're gonna put her into third and let her rip.
Spent about eleven hours polishing the brass
And got the carburetor purring for the trip.
Buckle up and snuggle up and stay in your seat,
'Cause we'll be leaning while careening round the bend.
We're goin' like sixty, so either get in
Or get a horse, get a horse, my friend!

We're goin' lickety, lickety, lickety, so everyone will know
We're gonna hit high speed or bust.
We put a rickety-rackety go-loogah on the front,
And on the back, excuse our dust!
We've got a son-of-a-gun of a run in the greatest place of all,

And we'll be in it till the end.
So put your grandmother's dough up and stay in
    your seat,
'Cause we'll be leaning while careening round the
    bend.
We're goin' like sixty, so either get in
Or get a horse, get a horse, my friend!

SUMMER WIND

Music by Henry Mayer. Original German words by Hans Bradtke. English lyrics by Mercer. Published. Copyrighted July 20, 1965. Mercer's version first recorded by Wayne Newton (Capitol); Frank Sinatra's recording (Reprise) reached *Billboard*'s number one in 1966. This song was Mercer's last major hit. Sinatra's recording played behind the opening credits of *The Pope of Greenwich Village*, United Artists, 1984.

The summer wind
Came blowing in
Across the sea;
It lingered there
To touch your hair
And walk with me.
All summer long
We sang a song
And strolled the golden sand,
Two sweethearts and
The summer wind.
Like painted kites,
The days and nights
Went flying by.
The world was new
Beneath a blue
Umbrella sky.
Then, softer than
A piper man,
One day it called to you—
I lost you to the summer wind.
The autumn wind,
The winter winds,
Have come and gone,
And still the days,
The lonely days,
Go on and on.
And guess who sighs
His lullabies

Through nights that never end?
My fickle friend
The summer wind,
The summer wind,
The summer wind.

Early version

[*Lines 1–17 as above; then:*]

And through it all
What made it all
A season touched with love?
The music of
The summer wind.
It filled the sails,
The mountain trails,
With melodies;
It whispered words
To charm the birds
Right off the trees.
And softer than
A piper man,
One day it called to you—
I lost you to
The summer wind.
Now I'm alone;
I might have known.
But who could guess
I'd hear a sound
And turn around
To emptiness?
I run to see
Who it can be,
That laughter on the stair,
But who is there?
The summer wind.
The autumn wind,
The winter wind,
Have come and gone.
I turn the lock
And watch the clock
Go ticking on.
And guess who sighs
His lullabies
Through nights that never end?
My fickle friend
The summer wind,
The summer wind,
The summer wind.

CALIFORNIA'S MELODYLAND

Music by Mercer. Registered for copyright as an unpublished song August 12, 1965.

REFRAIN 1

California's Melodyland—
Big surf booming over the sand,
Orange groves where mockingbirds sing
Summer, winter, autumn, and spring,
Starry nights all filled with the sound
Of those starlit shows in the round.
There is no place under the sun
That's half as much fun to be—
Come with me to Melody Land
Beside the sea!

REFRAIN 2

California's Melodyland—
Once you see it you'll understand.
Mountain peaks all covered with snow
Rise above the deserts below.
Sapphire pools neath shimmering stars,
Freeways jammed with millions of cars—
That blue heaven yet to be found
Keeps waiting around the bend.
Come with me to Melody Land,
Where rainbows end!

BEAUTIFUL FOREVER

Music by Frederic Spielman. Registered for copyright as an unpublished song October 18, 1965.

Beautiful forever,
That is what this moment will be,
Like a star that falls through the sky
Or the moonbeams that lie on the sea.

Beautiful forever,
Like the sudden look of surprise
That a photograph never shows
When your heart really glows in your eyes.

Let me memorize every turn of your head,
Every word that you say,
So I'll have this dream to remember,
When all other dreams fade away.

Speaking of forever,
As so very few mortals do,
You will be the star summer song
For my heartstrings the long ages through,
Beautiful forever,
Like my love for you.

HANK (1965–1966)

Produced by William T. Orr, Hugh Benson, and James Comack for Warner Bros. NBC series debut September 17, 1965, for twenty-six episodes. Directed by Allen Baron and Leslie H. Martinson. Teleplays by Tom Adair, James B. Allardice, and others. Music by Frank Perkins. Featuring Dick Kallman, Linda Foster, Howard St. John, Lloyd Corrigan, Katie Sweet, and Dabbs Greer.

In an era of college drop-outs, Hank is determined to become a college drop-in to help his career and that of his orphaned sister.

HANK

Introduced by off-screen chorus behind opening titles.

He's up with the sun,
And he's got the college winging,
As he goes off
On another swinging day.
There's jobs to be done
Or errands to run.
He's A—number one—OK!
He'll drive, clean your clothes,
Be your butler or a porter,
If it means another quarter
In the bank.
He'll get his degree,
His Phi Beta key,
And get 'em both for free!
That's Hank.

A SONG OF LOVE FOR YOU

Music by Bob Corwin. Song is dated 1965.

I took a little walk into the starry summer night,
I said a little private prayer or two,
And then I asked the angels if they'd help me write
A song of love for you.
The melody to fit you wasn't even in the scale,
And my vocabulary wouldn't do,
And so I asked a favor of the nightingale,
A song of love just for you.
He stood quite still
And waited till he saw you smile,
Then trilled a trill
As if he thought that songs were going out of style.
So here's my contribution, and if you'll supply the key,
By whispering that you could love me, too,
I'll promise ev'ry moment of my life will be
A song of love for you.

OVERLEAF *Mercer with Bing Crosby and Rosemary Clooney*

Songs of 1966–1969

MOMENT TO MOMENT (1966)

Produced and directed by Mervyn LeRoy for Universal Pictures. Released February 1966. Copyright February 5, 1966. Screenplay by John Lee Mahin and Alec Coppel, based on the story "Laughs with a Stranger" by Alec Coppel. Lyrics by Johnny Mercer. Music by Henry Mancini. Starring Jean Seberg and Honor Blackman, featuring Arthur Hill, Grégoire Aslan, and Sean Garrison, with Peter Robbins, Donald Woods, Walter Reed, Albert Carrier, Lomax Study, Richard Angarola, and Georgette Anys.

A housewife finds herself with a body on her hands.

MOMENT TO MOMENT

Published. Copyrighted November 9, 1965. Introduced by off-screen chorus behind opening titles.

From moment to moment,
Ev'ry moment that I live
I live for ev'ry moment with you.
To see you, to touch you,
To imagine this will be
The moment when a dream comes true.
Just an ordinary day becomes an adventure,
Such sweet adventure
I never knew,
And life will be rainbows
As I learn the secret of
The miracle that love can do
From moment to moment with you.

JOHNNY TIGER (1966)

Produced by John Hugh for Nova-Hugh Productions. Released by Universal Pictures. World premiere April 21, 1966. Copyright May 7, 1966. Directed by Paul Wendkos. Screenplay by Paul Crabtree and John Hugh, based on the original story "The Tiger on the Outside" by John Hugh. Lyrics by Johnny Mercer. Music by Johnny Green. Starring Robert Taylor and Geraldine Brooks, featuring Chad Everett, Brenda Scott, and Marc Lawrence, with Ford Rainey, Carol Seflinger, Stephen Wheeler, and Deanna Lund.

A shy schoolteacher finds himself while working on an Indian reservation and teaching a rebellious young Seminole how to study.

THE WORLD OF THE HEART

Registered for copyright as an unpublished song April 9, 1965. Sung by off-screen chorus behind opening titles.

The world that we really should chart
Isn't mountains or rivers,
It's the world of the heart.
We'd all see our own counterpart
In the faces of others
In the world of the heart.
If we were brave, yet forgave
Others as wrong as we,
If you and I only try,
What a world this could be!
And now comes the wonderful part,
Love is there at the floodgates,
Only waiting to start
When we open the door
To the world of the heart,
The door to the world of the heart!

TENDER LOVING CARE

Music by Ronnell L. Bright. Published. Copyrighted March 7, 1966.

The love I bring you, so April new,
Is like a flower breaking through.
It only needs to blossom
A little tender loving care.
With no instructions and no demands
I place my heart within your hands
And only ask that while it's there,
You give it tender loving care.
From the glow of a whispered "I love you"
Love can grow till it touches the sky above you,
And we can make life a love affair,
As long as you and I spare
A little kiss, a little pray'r,
And lots of tender loving care.

FOUNTAIN IN THE RAIN

Music by Milton Samuels and Charles Hale. Published. Copyrighted March 28, 1966. Previously registered for copyright as an unpublished song March 8, 1966.

Such a gloomy, rainy day,
Thought I'd walk another way;
And what did I see,
Just as merry as merry could be?
Saw a fountain in a square,
Splashin' water everywhere,
And singin' a song to me—
Whee!
If the birdies in the tree
Could be as full of *Joie de vie**
As I,
They'd have a serenade to hum-de-hum
And thumb their noses at the sky.

Small inverted waterfall,
Nothing dampens you at all,
Not even the pouring rain—
Whee!
Since you're makin' it the style to smile,
Guess I'll accompany your refrain.
So I started with a grin,
Soakin' wet to the skin,
Singin' like the fountain in the rain!

BITTERSWEET

Music by Mike Corda. Registered for copyright as an unpublished song May 11, 1966.

Bittersweet,
Our love is so bittersweet—
You're half an angel
And half a cheat.
Bittersweet,
You flirt with each girl you meet.
First you're indifferent,
Then indiscreet.
Though I love the spell I'm under
Each time you hold me tight,
My heart can't help but wonder
Whose heart you broke last night.
Wish I knew

---

* *Alternate line:*
    Could be as full of melody

Just what I'm supposed to do—
Because I love you,
And really do love you,
I'll just have to take
The bitter with the sweet.

MERRY-GO-ROUND IN THE RAIN

Music by Johnny Green. Published. Copyrighted May 27, 1966.

Merry-go-round going around
Under the cloudy skies,
Sad little horses with raindrops
Like tears in their painted eyes.
They keep asking me when
You'll come again—
How can my heart explain?
You left us all,
Even the small
Merry-go-round in the rain.
It seems to say,
"No show today"—
No you, no me,
No used-to-be.
As the old-fashioned beat
Floats down the street,
Who joins the brave refrain?
No one at all,
Only the small
Merry-go-round in the rain.

TIME TO SMILE

Music by Les Brown, J. Hill, and Geoff Clarkson. Registered for copyright as an unpublished song May 31, 1966.

Time to smile and laugh it up a while—
You start off and I'll be next in line.
I bet we'll find to our satisfaction
That we both have started a chain reaction.
When you grin,
You let the sunshine in,
And when the sun shines in,
It's all worthwhile.

Any time's the time to smile—
Don't ask me what the time of day is,
No matter if it's Standard
Or if it's Daylight Saving,
Or Rocky Mountain Central
Or Western South Pacific
Or International Date Line,
By satellite or rocket
Or Timex under water,
Any time's the time to smile.

A BIG HAND FOR THE LITTLE LADY (1966)

Produced and directed by Fielder Cook for Eden Productions. Released by Warner Bros. Released May 1966. Copyright February 7, 1966. Screenplay by Sidney Carroll, based on his teleplay "Big Deal in Laredo" for *The DuPont Show of the Week*. Music composed and conducted by David Raksin. Starring Henry Fonda, Joanne Woodward, and Jason Robards, featuring Charles Bickford, Burgess Meredith, Kevin McCarthy, and Robert Middleton, with John Qualen, James Kenny, Allen Collins, Jim Boles, Gerald Michenaud, Virginia Gregg, Noah Keen, Milton Selzer, Ned Glass, and Paul Ford.

A comedy-western in which a traveler bets more money than he can afford in a poker game.

MIRROR, MIRROR, MIRROR

Published. Copyrighted June 1, 1966. Not sung in film.

Mirror, mirror, mirror,
Fortune teller, crystal ball,
I beg of you to tell me, mirror, tell me,
Does he love me best of all?
Is the feeling I'm feeling showing?
Can you tell how my heartbeats pound?
Am I all starry eyes and glowing,
As I know I glow ev'ry time he's around?
If he catches by reflection
The affection in my eyes,
He will shine like the sun above me
And he'll love me to the skies,

For I'm certain that love's a mirror,
And a mirror never lies!

GEORGIA, GEORGIA

Music by Mercer. Registered for copyright as an unpublished song June 15, 1966. Mercer drew clear inspiration—and occasional exact wording—from passages in Stephen Vincent Benet's *John Brown's Body*.

VERSE 1

Georgia, Georgia,
Where do I start?
Words can sing,
But not like the heart—
There's no land in all this earth
Like the land of my birth!

REFRAIN 1

Georgia, Georgia,
Careless yield;
Watermelons ripe in the field;
Pine trees full of redbird song;
River rollin' along.

VERSE 2

Georgia nights,
When twilight is done,
Smell of peaches
Long in the sun;
Breeze comes blowin' through the shade
Like a cool lemonade.

REFRAIN 2

Georgia, Georgia,
Slow and deep,
Grown-up voices sing you to sleep;
Summer lightning in the sky,
River rollin' on by.

VERSE 3

Red clay hills
And late-standing corn
Sparkle in

The bright, frosty morn;
Pine-cone smoke curls on the breeze,
Through the mockingbird trees.

REFRAIN 3

Georgia, Georgia,
Crisp and clear,
Sweet and bitter time of the year;
Hound dogs bayin' through the cold,
River shinin' like gold.

VERSE 4

Row the old flat-
Bottom bateaux
To the lazy
Caw of a crow;
See the marsh hens as we pass,
Whirrin' up through the grass.

REFRAIN 4

Georgia, Georgia,
Land of dreams,
Where the moss hangs over the streams,
And the turtles, possum-toed,
Cross the oyster-shell road.

VERSE 5

Tomochichi,
Indian brave,
English settler, African slave—
Like the cotton fields they ginned,
All are gone with the wind.

REFRAIN 5

Georgia, Georgia,
From your coasts,
Come the sound of whispering ghosts;
Hear their hoofbeats riding by
Where the cannonballs lie.

VERSE 6

Old cotillions,
Parties and balls,
Linger in
The plantation halls,
Cars ride off where coaches drove,
Down the road through the grove.

REFRAIN 6

Georgia, Georgia,
Christmas cheer,
"Y'all stop by and see us, y'hear?"

Voices singing
Out of sight,
"Good night, ladies, good night."

VERSE 7

Doctors, lawyers,
Men of affairs,
Walk along the big
Shady squares,
Pause and pass the time of day,
"Hey there, boy, whatcha say?!"

REFRAIN 7

Georgia, Georgia,
Lush and green,
Old Man Summer
Painting the scene;
Old folks doze while children play
In the heat of the day.

VERSE 8

Georgia, Georgia,
How do I end?
Thank you as companion and friend?
Childhood close or worlds apart,
You will stay in my heart!

REFRAIN 8

Georgia, Georgia,
Sweet and wild,
Barefoot paradise for a child,
Arbors fat with scuppernong,
River rollin' along.

REFRAIN 9

Georgia, Georgia,
Careless yield;
Watermelons ripe in the field—
I will live my long life through
With these mem'ries of you!

DEIRDRE

Music by Michael Masser. Registered for copyright as an unpublished song July 25, 1966.

If only once she looked at you,
You'd fall in love with Deirdre, too.
Her eyes are shamrocks shining through
Lashes of night.

If only once you heard her sigh
You'd swear a dream were passing by
And leaving music in the sky,
And you'd be right.

You'll find
She's shy as spring,
She's bold as sin,
She's everything.
You'll find
A wistful child
Who'll leave your heart bewitched,
Bedazzled and beguiled.

Then you'll see frost turn into flame,
A face that never stays the same.
This dream has Deirdre for a name,
And oh, she drives me wild.

SHOOBY-DOOIN'

Music by Jerry Gray. Registered for copyright as an unpublished song July 28, 1966.

Shooby-dooin', making the scene,
Shooby-dooin', know what I mean?
Ev'rything is peachy and keen
When I'm around you.
Shooby-dooin', never go wrong,
Doodle-dooin', goin' along.
There'll be a short commercial
After the song,
But now the weather report:
Early bluebirds followed by rain.
Dig the two birds feelin' no pain,
Shooby-doo birds never complain—
They laugh ha-ha, ho-ho, hee-hee!
Buddy baby, never you'll care,
Baby Buddy's hangin' right in there,
Shooby-dooin', havin' a ball and a half!

NOT WITH MY WIFE, YOU DON'T! (1966)

Produced and directed by Norman Panama for Warner Bros. Released November 1966. Copyright November 19,

1966. Lyrics by Johnny Mercer. Music, musical score, musical direction by Johnny Williams. Choreography by Shelah Hackett. Starring Tony Curtis, Virna Lisi, and George C. Scott, featuring Carroll O'Connor, Richard Eastham, Eddie Ryder, and George Tyne, with Ann Doran, Donna Danton, and Natalie Core.

During the Korean War, Italian nurse (Virna Lisi) falls in love with two American fliers.

A BIG BEAUTIFUL BALL

Published. Copyrighted September 30, 1966. Introduced by off-screen chorus behind opening titles.

Hey, look at me, Ma! Mama, I'm dancin',
And I might somersault right over the wall.
This isn't a girl but a whole world I'm romancin'
And we're havin' a big beautiful ball.
It's like I went and got high on a wee toddy—
Yessirree, matey, I feel eighty feet tall!
My heavens above,
Everyone loves everybody,
And we're havin' a big beautiful ball.
Funny old world, I just adore you—
Fondly I implore you,
You old troubadour, you,
Please, when you get ready,
I'd like to go steady,
And gee, take it from me, it'll be groovy,
'Cause there's somebody up there diggin' us all,
Old chappie, it ends happy, just like in a movie,
And we're havin' us one fabulous,
Fantabulous beautiful ball!

MY INAMORATA

Published. Copyrighted September 30, 1966. Introduced by off-screen chorus.

Be my star on high,
Say I'll live or die—
In a word, be my inamorata.
Be the one for me
That I pray you'll be,
My affinity from the start;
Say it's all the way,
Say it ev'ry day,
Though you be only playing a part,
For I swear and I vow,

As of here and now
You are all I love,
Sweet inamorata of my heart,
Be my heart.

NOT WITH MY WIFE, YOU DON'T!

Introduced by off-screen chorus.

Listen, Daddy baby,
You can have my bread and gravy,
Crazy, baby, crazy,
My shades, my suedes,
But, man—
Not with my wife, you don't!
At the surfing show, Dad,
You can show the chicks
You're a ho-dad—
Take my board and go, Dad!
My comb? Okay.
My home?
Not with my wife, you don't.

WAIT NO MORE

Music by Elizabeth Firestone (Willis). Registered for copyright as an unpublished song November 6, 1966.

Version 1

Wait no more, my beloved,
Weep no more—
Wait no more for that knock upon your door.
My intuition
Is strong and true;
It says to me
My life is you.
Sigh no more, my beloved,
But for me;
Cry no more for the moonbeams on the sea.
You're the love of my life,
And now I know
I can't blame it on fate, no,
You can't say it's too late, so

Wait no more, darling,
Wait no more.

Version 2

Wait no more,
You have waited long for me.
Wait no more
For a love that's meant to be.
My intuition
Is strong and true;
It says to me
My world is you.
Sigh no more;
You have sighed enough for me.

[*Last seven lines as in version 1.*]

ALVAREZ KELLY (1966)

Produced by Sol C. Siegel for Ray David Productions. Released by Columbia Pictures. Released October 1966. Copyright October 10, 1966. Directed by Edward Dmytryk. Screenplay by Franklin Coen. Lyrics by Johnny Mercer. Music by Johnny Green. Starring William Holden and Richard Widmark, featuring Janice Rule, Patrick O'Neal, Victoria Shaw, and Roger C. Carmel, with Richard Rust, Donald Barry, Harry Carey, Jr., Mauritz Hugo, Robert Morgan, Stephanie Hill, Arthur Franz, Duke Hobbie, Howard Caine, G. B. Atwater, Paul Lukather, Indus Arthur, Clint Ritchie, and The Brothers Four.

Cattle owner Alvarez Kelly tries to drive a herd to the Union forces during the Civil War but is captured by the Confederates.

THE BALLAD OF ALVAREZ KELLY

Published. Copyrighted December 21, 1966. Introduced by The Brothers Four behind opening chorus.

REFRAIN 1

Alvarez Kelly
Rode over the rise
With a heartful of blarney
And a gleam in his eyes!

And wherever he'd stop
The gals kept dropping like flies—
Till a lady from Richmond cut him down to size!
War is hell, without a doubt,
But Kelly never found that out,
Or iff'n he did, he seldom gave a damn,
For when he met a pretty gal
In Texas, Tennessee, or Alabam',
He'd kiss 'em 'n' wink 'n' whisper, "Thank you,
    ma'am!"

REFRAIN 2

Alvarez Kelly,
The Irish señor,
Kept pursuin' his hobbies
While pursuin' the war!
Give him rum in a glass
And some fair lass to adore,
And he couldn't care less
What they were fightin' for!
Kelly fought a dozen foes
And came up smelling like a rose—
A gentleman drover needs his exercise!
And even when the Richmond belle
Betrayed him with her story-tellin' eyes,
For Kelly it proved a blessing in disguise.

REFRAIN 3

Alvarez Kelly,
The stylish señor,
Found the Yankees a nuisance
And the Rebels a bore!
So his major engagements
All were fought at the bar,
And the luck of the Irish
Got him through the war!

CODA

Alvarez Kelly,
I'll say it once more—
Alvarez Kelly,
The ay-yi-yi-Irish señor!

TOO GOOD TO BE TRUE

Music by George Shearing. Registered for copyright as an unpublished song March 10, 1967. This lyric is a reincarnation of one he wrote while he was still "John Mercer" in the 1930s, to music by Florence Leftwich. The idea got another refurbishing in the 1970s.

You're an angel, you're a devil,
And you're simply too good to be true.
You're the one girl with the right kiss
From the best dream that I ever knew.
Though they warn me
And they've warned me
I'll be sorry before I get through,
When I hold you like this in my arms
And you do what you do what you do,
I don't care how bad you may be,
You're too good to be true!

1970s version

That beautiful grin
That brings the sun in—
You're simply too good to be true.
That look in your eyes
Of constant surprise—
It's simply too marvelous, too.
The moment we met
I'll never forget;
My heart began pounding,
And it hasn't stopped yet.
You say "I love you,"
And oh, the way that you do,
You're simply too good to be true!

BAREFOOT IN THE PARK (1967)

Produced by Hal B. Wallis for Paramount Pictures. Released May 1967. Copyright May 25, 1967. Directed by Gene Saks. Screenplay by Neil Simon, based on his play of the same name. Lyrics by Johnny Mercer. Music by Neal Hefti. Starring Robert Redford, Jane Fonda, Charles Boyer, and Mildred Natwick, with Herbert Edelman, Mabel Albertson, and Fritz Feld.

Newlyweds adjust to married life in a tiny Greenwich Village apartment.

BAREFOOT IN THE PARK

Published. Copyrighted May 18, 1967. Previously registered for copyright as an unpublished song April 19, 1967. Introduced by off-screen chorus behind opening titles. Recorded by Neal Hefti (Dot).

VERSE

Going barefoot in the park
Where it says Keep Off the Grass
Isn't recommended for the very old,
But when you're young and you're in love,
The world is beautiful
And I'm not a bit afraid of you catching cold.

Running barefoot through the park,
Strolling bare-headed in the rain,
Just to look for a daisy
Seems kinda crazy to do.
But come along, my barefoot love,
To the fields that shine with spring—
Let me laugh and play all the way,
Knee deep in daisies with you.

Second ending

Come along, my barefoot love—
Let's go barefoot in the park.

ROSIE! (1967)

Produced by Jacque Mapes for Universal and Ross Hunter Productions. Released November 1967. Copyright December 2, 1967. Directed by David Lowell Rich. Screenplay by Samuel Taylor, based on the play *A Very Rich Woman* by Ruth Gordon, adapted from the play *Les Joies de la Famille* by Philippe Hériat. Lyrics by Johnny Mercer. Music by Harry Warren. Musical score by Lyn Murray. Starring Rosalind Russell, featuring Sandra Dee, Brian Aherne, Audrey Meadows, James Farentino, Vanessa Brown, and Leslie Nielsen, with Margaret Hamilton, Reginald Owen, Juanita Moore, Virginia Grey, Dean Harens, Richard Derr, Harry Hickox, Hal Lynch, Eddie Ness, Ann Doran, Than Wyenn, Walter Woolf King, Ronald Chisholm, Doris Lloyd, Ron Stokes, Eugene Roth, Kathleen O'Malley, Doodles Weaver, and the Boyfriends.

Rosie is a gentle and generous lady and her daughters are worried she will spend their inheritance. But her granddaughter saves the day.

ROSIE

Published. Copyrighted October 21, 1967. Previously registered for copyright as an unpublished song March 30, 1967. This was Harry Warren's final film song, reworked from "Me and My Baby" with lyrics by Sammy Cahn, unused in the 1958 Jerry Lewis vehicle *Rock-a-Bye, Baby.* Introduced by The Boyfriends behind opening titles and final credits.

How d'ya like our Rosie?
Is that a fabulous doll?
Throw her a great big posey,
Watch Rosie scintillate—
That lady radiates class!
She drives the men crazy;
They flip en masse
For all that individuality,
Entitled personality!
Mabel or Maude or Josie
Seen on the beauty-queen shows
Can't hold a candle to Rosie
Walkin' campy 'n'
Actin' vampy 'n'
Wearin' beautiful clothes!
Boys, the winner is,
Chicken dinner is,
It's unanimous—that's our Rosie!
All-American Rose!

HOW DO YOU SAY "AUF WIEDERSEHEN"?

Music by Tony Scibetta. Registered for copyright as an unpublished song May 22, 1967.

How do you say, "Auf Wiedersehen"
To things you'll never see again?
The Wilhelmstrasse in the rain,
The day we ran to catch the train
That puffed along the river Seine?
Remember Paris?
And, best of all, the Pyrenees?
Who could forget such memories?
That crazy trip—how typical of us
To miss the bus, the plane, too!
How do you say, "Auf Wiedersehen" to these?
The wild times, the small things,

That popular waltz of the day.
It ended, as all things,
But when does the music go away?
Say "au revoir" but not "goodbye."
I've said it until I want to cry.
Perhaps the French could tell us what to do—
I wish I knew.
Ah, Liebchen,
How do I say, "Auf Wiedersehen"
To you?

PAPA GOOD TIMES

Music by Les McCann. Registered for copyright as an unpublished song May 22, 1967.

Look at what love done, done—
Threw away all my fun.
Papa Good Times
Took a mind to walk on by
When you walked through that door.
Guess who walked in once more?
Papa Hard Times,
Givin' me the salty eye.
What was June and July,
Steak and cherry pie,
And ev'rything we had then,
Now it's rooms without heat,
Snowdrifts in the street,
And summer's comin' in Lord knows when!
Baby, come home to me,
So that we both can see
Papa Good Times
Smilin' through the window again!

BABY, DON'T YOU QUIT NOW

Music by Jimmy Rowles. Published. Copyrighted April 18, 1968. Previously registered for copyright as an unpublished song October 2, 1967.

What you do to me
You get through to me
With a beautiful vibration
That is new to me.
Instead of "No!"
What comes out is "Oh!"—
Oh, baby, baby, don't you quit now!

When two moral lips
Meet two coral lips,
Then they're kiss-me-now-and-later-
We-can-quarrel lips.
I should turn you off,
But you turn me on,
So, baby, don't you quit now!

Ev'ry kiss I take
Is a piece o' cake,
And to give me a sample
Was your first mistake,
'Cause I know when a little tastes like more,
And now I want the whole darn bakery store!
Take my pay from me,
Christmas Day from me,
And go anywhere you want
Except away from me!
Quit tomorrow noon
Or at nine o'clock the fifth of June,
But baby, don't quit now!

CIMARRON STRIP

CBS TV series.

TOMORROW NEVER COMES

Music by Morton Stevens. Published. Copyrighted December 22, 1967.

Tomorrow never comes,
Never ever comes.
All we have is us right now.
As the wonder starts
In our heart of hearts,
We'll try our very best to hold
This touch of love's quicksilver gold.
But should we come to know
Wishing makes it so
And we get the things we dream,
We can thank our stars
All of this is ours—
All of this for true,
And tomorrow too.
If it never comes,
Ever comes,
Never comes.

A COMET IN THE SKY

Music by Ronnell L. Bright.

A comet in the sky
Comes along only once in a lifetime,
And when you came blazing in sight,
I knew,
I knew that you and I
Were a thing that could light up a lifetime,
If I could be part of the glow
Of you!
Like the moth and the flame,
I was oblivious to danger;
I saw a fascinating stranger
So near.
Someone mentioned your name,
It seemed an ordinary meeting,
But I could hear my heart repeating,
"He's here, he's here."
So, comet in the sky,
Maybe I won't be able to catch you,
But I plan to give it
A real good try!

LOTUS LAND

Music by Ted Grouya.

Waves singing on the shore,
Calling me once more,
As they did before,
To the golden sand
Off in Lotus Land.
Waves underneath the moon
Whispering their tune
Of a blue lagoon
Where the palm trees stand
Off in Lotus Land.
Oh, is there anywhere still
Where the cockatoo's shrill
In the lonely velvet stillness?
Waves seem to say it's so,
So perhaps I'll go
Where the lotus grow
And the palm trees stand
By the golden sand,
Off in Lotus Land.

VELVET NIGHT

Music by Michel Legrand (adapted from Mozart). Published. Copyrighted May 7, 1968. Previously registered for copyright as an unpublished song February 19, 1968, and again on April 18, 1968.

Velvet is the night,
Drowsy is the hour,
Stars burning bright
To light our flower place.
Come, love, and lie with me
While high above
That swan that sails the summer sky
Will light the shadows where we lie,
And I, and I
Will linger with sweet desire
And hold you
As we borrow a spark
From the everlasting fire of love.
Velvet is the night,
Like a mother sighing,
Holding us tight
Away from prying eyes.
Come, love, and promise me
You'll be my own,
We'll climb way up to the Pléiades together,
Through an ocean of time,
Like leaves on a summer breeze take flight,
Floating back to earth together
On the velvet wings of night.

JUST ACROSS THE MOUNTAINS

Music by Arthur Kent. Registered for copyright as an unpublished song October 25, 1968.

Just across the mountains
There is somethin' callin' me,
Callin', "Come and see
Where you ought to be."
A valley full of buttercups
Is singin' me a song:
"Come and see the place
Where you belong."
I hear it's on the way
To a town called Home to Stay,
Right near a little village called Someday.
It's just across the mountains
Where the big airliners fly,

And I am gonna find it
By and by!

THE SONG OF LONG AGO

Music by Hoagy Carmichael. Registered for copyright as an unpublished song January 22, 1969.

Original version

No lullaby can make me gay
Like the song of long ago.
I can still see our spooning tree
And the girl I used to know.
I should forget,
But time has let
Little mem'ries overflow.
Show me the tears
And misty years,
Back to stardust days I go;
I think of how she loved me then
And how she told me so
In words unsung
When we were young,
Like the song of long ago.
But where's the end?
There is no end
To the song of long ago.
It makes me glad,
It makes me sad,
And it seems to grow and grow.

Revised version

No lullaby
Can make me cry
Like the song of long ago.
I still can see
Our high-school tree
And the girl I used to know.
I park the car
And watch a star
As I play the radio;
Then through the tears
And misty years
Down old memory lane I go.
I think of when
She loved me then
And of how she told me so
To words unsung
When we were young,
Like the song of long ago.
And where's the end?
There is no end,

Just an endless afterglow
To make you glad
And make you sad—
It's the song of long ago!

PHONE CALL TO THE PAST

Music by Henry Mancini. Registered for copyright as an unpublished song February 3, 1969.

Right over there there's a tired old phone booth—
I've got a dime to spend,
Plenty of time to spend,
And I could put an end to my misery
If I could make a phone call to the past.
Long about now everybody is swingin',
Cars begin rollin' in,
Couples come strollin' in,
And I could make the scene with the rest of them
If I could only make a phone call to the past.
This is the way it was and where it was:
I'm back at the bar
Where I'm a star.
It's like I say, there's nothin' much new,
Only I—I haven't got you.
But I got a friend and my friend's got a bottle,
'Cept there's no genie there,
Just a martini there.
We sit alone,
My own little wishing well,
Till we forget to make a phone call
To the love gone past—
This is the past.

MORNING STAR

Music by Jimmy Rowles. Registered for copyright as an unpublished song March 6, 1969.

REFRAIN 1

The voice of the bedroom clock—
Tick, tick, tock, tick, tick, tock—
Tries keeping me company
To pass the hours away.
I lie in the shadows deep,
Counting sheep, just counting sheep.
I know as the sky starts graying,
I'll be saying,

"Morning star,
Another lonely night of waiting
Finds us both alone.
You in your great big heaven above me,
Me in my small world,
Still here with no one to love me."

REFRAIN 2

[*Repeat first 8 lines of Refrain 1.*]

Travel far,
Until your starlight finds the pillow
That she dreams upon.
You in your great big heaven above me.
Me in my small world
Still here with no one to love me.

CODA

Give her a kiss when you find her,
And while she sleeps remind her
That dreams come true,
And ours will, too—
It's up to you,
Morning star.

MIRACLE OF CHRISTMAS

Music by Gilbert Martinez. Registered for copyright as an unpublished song April 7, 1969.

The miracle of Christmas
Is the greatest one of all.
Small noses pressed to windowpanes
As snow begins to fall;
Then overnight the roofs are white,
And far off in the sky
A drowsy ear can almost hear
Old Santa passing by.
The miracle of Christmas
Is a door that opens wide,
A family around a tree inside.
And wise men, too, like me and you,
Still thank that star above—
The miracle of Christmas
Is the miracle of love.

TREES (WITH SYMPATHY FOR JOYCE KILMER)

Four unusual little trees . . . produced from a tiny plug of unspecialized non-sexual tree cells, began their existence in a laboratory dish at the Institute of Paper Chemistry in Appleton, Wisconsin, today.
—*New York Times*, April 18, 1969

I think that never shall I see
A poem loveless as a tree.

A tree whose hungry mouth is prest
Against some scientific breast;

A tree from which no acorn springs
But comes from Mother's barkless rings;

A tree that looks to vitamin A
And lifts her leafless arms to pray;

A tree whose beauty, life and soul,
Starts in some laboratory bowl;

A tree who may at birth be found
With nests of nutrients all around;

Who must, as one nonsexual cell,
In niacin and thiamin dwell;

A tree who may in winter wear
No rain nor snowflakes in her hair;

Whose thirst is slaked—if slaked at all—
When auxins and cytokinins fall;

Who'll feel no sunshine kiss of love,
Just an electric light above;

A tree whose very birth may have
Joyce Kilmer whirling in his grave,

While God (if he's alive, of course)
Accepts retirement pay by force;

A tree improved in every way
For each undappled summer's day;

A tree that's neither he nor she,
Who'll know no dog, who'll know no bee.

Poems are made by fools in love
But only Dr. Linus Winton, biologist of the
    Institute of Paper Chemistry out there in

Appleton, Wisconsin, can make an entire
nonsexual aspen grove!

LOVE LIKE YOURS

Music and lyrics by Mercer and Luiz Bonfa. Registered
for copyright as an unpublished song April 22, 1969.
Written for the television movie *River of Mystery*,
which aired on NBC on October 1, 1971.

Love like yours
Can come only from the gods.
Love like yours
Will win over any odds.
Here in the drowsy delight,
The storm's a million miles away.
Should it come
Like some big drum,
Let it come.
We'll ride the foam
Safely home.
Love like mine
Could guide me to heaven's shores.
Love like mine
Could save a love like yours.

SMALL PETRUSHKA

Music by Louis Alter. Published. Copyrighted September 23, 1969. Previously registered for copyright as an
unpublished song June 24, 1969.

Small Petrushka,
You they call Petrushka,
Smiling as you window-shop in the rain.
Small Petrushka,
Are you yearning for things you can't explain,
Jewels and gowns
Made in far-off towns
Across the far-off seas?
Movie stars
Driving foreign cars—
Do you long to be one of these?
No, Petrushka,
With your gay babushka
And your apple cheeks,
You're fairer by far.
Child at heart,
Stay the work of art

You are,
You they call Petrushka!

I'LL NEVER FORGIVE MYSELF

Music by Al Kaufman. Published. Copyrighted July 7,
1969.

I'll never forgive myself
For giving myself a hangup over you,
Uh-uh.
I'll never forgive myself
For letting you put me down the way you do.
Uh-uh.
I'll never forgive the night that we met,
Never forgive the moon up above;
Their magical spell
Made everything jell
And managed to sell
My Simple Simon heart—
It was love!

I'll never forgive your eyes
For hitting me with that Theda Bara stare,*
Uh-uh.
I'll never forgive your lips
For—whaddaya think?—for just being there!
A loser in either direction—
You'll probably break my heart if you stay,
But I'll never forgive myself
For letting you get away!

FLOATING LEI

Music by Mercer.

REFRAIN 1

I send a floating lei
Across the ocean blue,
A floating lei to say
I'm coming back to you.
And when my ring of love
Comes drifting to the shore,

_____
* *Alternate wording:*
  . . . that Valentino stare,

Please keep it in your heart
Till I am there once more.

REFRAIN 2

Please send a floating lei
Across the silver sea,
A floating lei to say
You're coming back to me.
And when your ring of love
Comes drifting in to the shore,
I'll hold it in my arms
Till I hold you once more.

THE LAND WHERE THE OLD DREAMS GO

Music by Matt Malneck.

There's a land where the old dreams go,
On the road to a place known as Might-Have-Been,
Where the world's greatest losers,
Who can't be choosers,
Got lost and just wandered in.
Chasing rainbows across the sky,
Living life in the bubbles they blow—
Who can say they're wrong;
How do we know?
This dream we call life
Is as crazy as can be—
I'd swear I caught a glimpse of me
In the land where the old dreams go.

MY HANGUP IS YOU

Music by Wally Ridley.

My brand-new bag is not really new—
It's such a drag my hangup is you.
Night when I don't call the gang up,
They say, "Oh, him—he's got this hangup."
And should I miss your incoming call,
I tell you this—I'm climbing the wall.
Please, baby, get in my key
And end this hangup for me!

OLD SUMMERTIME

Music by Gene de Paul.

Let's go and meet the nicest guy I know—
He's kinda lazy, sweet, and slow,
This friend o' mine
Old Summertime.
We'll lie beneath a deep blue, fleecy sky
And let the world go drifting by;
He'll treat you fine,
Old Summertime.
Don't know how the bourgeoisie will go,
But we will go first class—
See the cloud that we'll be flyin' on?
Just dandelion on the grass!
Guess who will give the whole wide world to you
If you are good for nothing, too?
He did it to me—wait'll he gets a load of you,
That old apple-shine, lemon-lime Summertime,
That's who!

Mercer in rehearsal

MIKE (1967)

An unproduced musical written in 1967 about Mickey Spillane's hard-boiled detective Mike Hammer. The music, probably by Mercer, does not appear to have survived.

BALLAD OF A PRIVATE EYE

Opening number.

Today you cannot have a show without a group—
We are the group,
And here's the scoop:
We'll introduce some private eyes you may recall.
First, here's the dad-dad-dad-dad-daddy of them
    all!

Sherlock Holmes was this cat's name;
Doctor Watson dug his game,
Even though he always dug it late.
"Element'ry, my dear Watts—
Call the Yard and hip some Scots.
While I get this crazy hat on straight!"

Then from the paperback
Nick Carter made the scene
From nineteen twelve
To 'seventeen,
And he was such a daring, deft detective man,
We soon had Hercule Poirot and Charlie Chan!

In succession, rapidly,
Messrs Hammett and Charteris
Brought to life the Saint and Sam'l Spade.
Men from U.N.C.L.E., Jimmy Bond
Sprang from out the great beyond,
Came to join the mighty cavalcade.

For money made,
For ladies laid,
For copies sold,
Who takes the cake?
Who stops 'em cold?
Who casts the most gigantic shadow on the wall?
Who is, in fact, the dad-dad-daddy of them all?

Chapter one . . . and we shall see
Who this mighty man can be
And what great adventures lie in store.
Once upon a time, my son,

When the world had just begun,
Someone heard a knocking . . . on . . . the door!

ANY WAY THE WIND BLOWS

I tilts my nose
Any way the wind blows—
Any way the wind blows
Nice and free,
And off I goes.
Any way the wind blows
Through the canyons of Manhattan
You'll find me.

Where all the good guys go
In those old movies on TV,
That is where I'll be,
In fast company,
Beside a well-stacked dolly
Or a tall and frosty glass,
Just headin' off those varmints at the pass.

Because I knows
Any way the wind blows,
Anywhere the gang goes,
There I'll be.
This dogie shows
For the main attraction—
Anywhere you find the action
You'll find me.

I get my eggs at Toot's
Or at Dinty Moore's or Stark's;
Off to P. J. Clarke's
Droppin' bright remarks;
Then I walk west of Broadway
Through the chaparral and sage
Where Jack E. Leonard's holding up the Stage.

'Cause that's my beat,
Any way the wind blows.
Any time the bars close,
After three,
I points my feet
Straight as little arrows
To the old low-rise where I keep my teepee.
And so it goes
From the time the cock crows
Till the last saloons close—
Any way the wind blows,
Any way the wind blows.

THE BULLY BOYS

The pimp is two-timey
And out-'n'-out slimy
And schooled in the ways of deceit—
But the bully boys, the bully boys,
The bully boys, them's my meat!

The faggot is flabby
And soft like a tabby
Who usually lands on his feet—
But the bully boys, the bully boys,
The bully boys, them I eat!

They bust in a room
With a chip on their shoulder
All out for the blood
Of some handsome young stud.
I tickles their back
Like a pig in a sack
And I fattens 'em—
Then I flattens 'em!

The drunkard I pity;
The shark from the city
I generally manage to beat.
But the bully boys, the bully boys—
I couldn't hate you more fully, boys—
I has me a feast with the bully boys,
Those muley boys, unruly boys,
A marvelous feast with the bully boys,
'Cause them's my meat!

A CAT WITH NINE LIVES

Settle down and have a seat—
It isn't ev'ry day you meet
A cat with nine lives.

Thank my lucky rabbit's foot,
I'm livin' and I'm stayin' put,
A cat with nine lives.

Twilight, Daddy begins his day
Up tight, chasin' a tom away.
Each night some pussycat'll say,
"Better call a baby-sitter,
Sumpin' tells me it's a litter!"

Maybe I'm a lucky cat,
But you can bet your Sunday hat

With all o' those wives
A cat with nine lives ain't so free!

If I meet a lion,
Baby, I'll be in there tryin'
To be monarch of the turf I see.
But lose a tooth or risk a shiner,
Guarantee you number niner,
This life belongs to me!
That life belongs to you!

GERFRUNKT!

Registered for copyright as an unpublished song
May 14, 1979.

STANZA 1

DR. K: Mit zer human zocial strata
Rising from zer terra cotta
Zer medulla oblongata, don't conjunct!
MIKE: Doesn't it?
DR. K: Nein. . . .
Zo . . . zer logical conclusion
Due to all uf zat confusion
Iss . . . gerfrunkt!
MIKE: Gerfrunkt?
DR. K: Gerfrunkt!
Mit zer mental cycloramic
Running parallelogrammic,
Vell, zer brain iss zo dynamic—you
admits?
MIKE: I do?
DR. K: Ja!
Now, you zee vot's bound to happen,
Qvoting Doctor Karl Von Pappen,
You're . . . gerfritz!
MIKE: Gerfritz?
DR. K: Gerfritz!
Ven Freud vas young und Jung naïve,
Naïve was Havelock Ellis
You zee, zer brain iss a trellis!
You hang up zer clothes
Und efforting shows!
Zo, don't effer kiss your mudder,
For zer breast iss like a udder
Und too close to vun anudder shouldn't be!
MIKE: We shouldn't?
DR. K: Nein!
For if you don't vind up neuter,
You could efen be a fruiter,
All gerfrunkt!
MIKE: All gerfrunkt?
DR. K: Like me!

STANZA 2

MIKE: Do you mean to tell me, Doctor,
That my mind is all verkakte
'Cause my mom and Doctor Spock
spanked my behind?
DR. K: Your bohunkus?
MIKE: Right.
DR. K: Did you kiss your mudder's booby?
MIKE: Yes, indeed.
DR. K: Vell, scooby-dooby,
You're gershrined!
MIKE: Gershrined?
DR. K: Gershrined!
MIKE: Do you mean it's incorrective
And I've grown so introspective
That I'm sexually defective evermore?
DR. K: Mentally!
Vell, I vouldn't say it's fatal,
But zer longing iss prenatal—
You're gerschnorr!
MIKE: Gerschnorr?
DR. K: Gerschnorr!
You yearn one day
For Turhan Bey,
Zer next for Anna Q. Nilsson.
Vot luck, zese feelings you feel, son—
I'm happy to say
You sving eider vay!
MIKE: Well, I'm happy you explained it—
I thought nature had ordained it.
DR. K: Nein, mein, brain has ascertained it, I can
zee!
You're a male man, yet a missus,
Half Rapunzel, half Narcissus,
All gerfrunkt!
MIKE: All gerfrunkt?
DR. K: Like me!

STANZA 3

DR. K: From zer time you left zer tummy
Uf your overzealous mummy
Und zhe smecked you on zer bummy, a
kerplunkt—
MIKE: Yes?
DR. K: You've been fighting world conditions
Und acquivring inhibitions
Und you're zunked!
MIKE: I'm zunked?
DR. K: Gerfrunkt!
Brudder had a phallic zymbol,
Sister had a liddle thimble,
Vun iss Macy, Vun iss Gimbel, ven you're
young!
MIKE: And that means?
DR. K: Means you zuffer from depressions.
Vas you reading *True Confessions*?

You're gershprung!
MIKE: Gershprung?
DR. K: Gershprung!
Mit sex, vun necks, den genuflects,
Vich wrecks zer yout'ful complexion!
Discomfort leads to dejection;
You're dressing in drag—
Your bag iss a fag!
Hence zer law uf compensation
On a close examination
Shows your present occupation shouldn't
be—
Zo you choose a new objective
Und become a great detective—
You're gerfrunkt!
MIKE: I'm gerfrunkt?
DR. K: Like me!

THE EQUIVALENT OF A HAA-VUD EDUCATION

MIKE: The stuff I've seen on men's room walls
And, even worse, inside the stalls
Is equal to a Haa-vud education.
The sights I've seen in hotel halls
Outdoes the words on men's room walls—
It's better than a Haa-vud education.
The nights I spend with courtesan and
jester
Is why I sequester
Another semester.
When you can figure who digs who
And where and how, it's equal to
A brain as wise as any in the nation.
A Ph.D.
From MIT,
A doctor of
Philosophy,
The equivalent of a Haa-vud education!
JIMMY: Perhaps you'll let me tag along
And write the lyrics to your song?
I'd like to get a Haa-vud education.
I'd even pay a modest sum
To study your curriculum—
I'd most enjoy a Haa-vud education.
To dig firsthand the true Americana
At Julie's Nirvana,
The Copacabana
So sing me not a paean of praise
For ivy walls nor rah-rah days
With all their smug, attendant
information—
I'll take for me the Kappa key

You pick up at the Chez Paris—
The equivalent of a Haa-vud education!

HE NEVER EVEN KNEW WHAT HIT HIM

1

I suppose you knew my pa?
He was wanted by the law,
So the papers often showed his photograph.
Since his friends are on the lam,
And the rest don't give a damn,
I would like to say some words on his behalf.

Oh, he never even knowed what hit him!
He went out to do a job he liked a lot,
But he never seen Mike Hammer opposite him,
And I don't suppose he even heard the shot.

For a timid-lookin' dude
He was mean and he was rude,
Though he showed an attitude as sweet as pie,
He was friendly with a jug,
Beat my mama like a rug,
So it ain't no wonder that our eyes are dry!

No, he never even knowed what hit him!
He walked out all bushy-tailed and starry-eyed.
It was just as though a serpent up and bit him,
And he curled them crooked toes up and he died!

2

We was overcome with grief,
But the interlude was brief,
When we thought about the awful things he
    done.
Now we're livin' with our loss,
Since he left us both Blue Cross
And we got a little extra for his gun!

When the undertaker came to git him,
Though I felt so bad I nearly bawled out loud,
It was real artistic-like the way they hit him,
So I wasn't even sorry—I was proud!

Though we lived it up in style,
We moved every little while;
Our valises and our trunks was always packed.
And the Kansas City mob
Could have blasted off his knob,
So we get some consolation from the fact

That he never even knew what hit him!
And where he's a-goin' he won't ever write,
And he'll never wear them woolen socks I knit
    him,
'Cause he'll never know a Christmas that is white.

Everything considered, Mama feels right perky,
So you needn't send no notes of sympathy—
She would rather have a leg o' lamb or turkey,
'Cause he never knowed what hit him, nosirree!!!

KISS AND TELL

REFRAIN 1

VELDA: You'll know
When the butterflies start,
You'll know
By the wings on your heart,
You'll know
You won't have to be smart—
Kiss and tell,
Kiss and tell.

One day
You'll be walking on air,
Next day
In the depths of despair,
Some day
When you think you don't care—
Kiss and tell,
Might as well.

You'll see,
And you won't need any letter
From Dear Abby
To show you why.
Then when
You are really aware
Of the wind in the air above,
Kiss him,
Kiss him right then and there,
And tell the world you're in love!

REFRAIN 2

You'll know
When your head starts to whirl,
You'll know
When your toes start to curl,
He's there
And you feel like a girl—
You can tell,
And it's swell.

You'll know
When your Mister Right shows,
You'll know
By the shine on your nose,
You'll know
By the run in your hose—
You can tell,
And it's hell.

You'll know,
And no horoscope or analyst
Or tea leaves
Can change your mind.
You'll know
By the feeling of bliss
And the way the stars shine above—
And oh,
That's the time you should kiss
And tell the world you're in love.

REFRAIN 3

TRUDI: I'll know,
But it won't be that way.
I'll know
What'll happen that day.
He'll show
As my girdle gives way—
I can tell,
I'll be swell!

I'll know
By the look of my clothes,
I'll know
By the run in my hose,
I'll know
By the shine on my nose—
I foretell
Holy hell!

I'm sure
That no matter how I plan it,
I'll be melting
or have a cold.
And then
As I croak or I kiss,
He will whisper "My turtle dove,"
Right then—
That's when he'll want to kiss
And tell the world we're in love!

THE MAMA TORPEDO CHA-CHA-CHA

In my cell
I wait for the dinner bell
I say to me, "What th' hell!"
Poor Mama Torpedo,
You bad man!
You hold up a candy store,
Move in on a dozen more,
But somebody fink
And now it's Clinksville!
You think, Ma,
There's action in Omaha
They're doin' the cha-cha-cha
And casin' the broads!
All that while
I sit on my butt and smile
They're livin' it up in style,
Those miserable frauds!

My tango is sufferin'
My rumba is cooked;
I use so much Bufferin
I figure I'm hooked!
If Madame La Zonga
Saw me do the conga
She'd say, "He's a reglah Fred Astaire—I don't
    think!"
They give the Watusi cue,
I'd still do the Suzie-Q—
The chicks would be sayin', "Who's the old-
    fashioned gink?"

All year, Mac,
My old lady's at the track
Investin' my hard-stole jack!
Poor Mama Torpedo
In that pad—
It's Murder Incorpo, Dad,
Just thinkin' of babes I've had
And how they could cling,
I get the shingles!
Nosirree, no more life of crime for me—
I like to be fancy free
In body and mind.
So I'll stay
Legitimate, as they say,
Just goin' my normal way
And robbin' 'em blind!

From Cannes to the Lido
Ladies sigh, "Ooh-la-la!"
Does Mama Torpedo do a neat cha-cha-cha!
His frug's even greater

Than his mashed pertater,
But nobody tops his cha-cha-cha—olé!!!

MY CRAZY OLD SUBCONSCIOUS

JIMMY: If a blush suffuses my cheek
    And the old emotions emerge,
    If my knees grow suddenly weak
    With a wild primordial urge,
    Your psychiatrist will tell you that the
        fault's not my own,
    But my crazy old subconscious won't
        leave you alone.

    If I long to tousle your hair
    Or to kiss the nape of your neck,
    I can tell my lips to beware,
    I can hold my fingers in check,
    Even sit there like a statue with a heart
        made of stone,
    But my crazy old subconscious won't
        leave you alone.

    So, don't get shook if I give you a look
    Like a Pleistocene an-a-thropoid.
    Don't blame me or my family tree—
    Blame a wig name o' Sig-a-mund Freud!

    When you start exploring the brain,
    It's a vast mysterious place—
    Might as well be taking a plane
    To the outer reaches of space.
    But for sweet romance, let's take a
        chance and face the unknown,
    Synchronize our hearts and get 'em in
        tune
    As we launch ourselves like out to the
        moon!

OUR MAN IN PARADISE

SYNDICATE
FOUR: Our man in Paradise
    Knows just what to do—
    When you leave this world
    You're so powdered and curled
    You don't recognize you.

Our man in Paradise,
He lulls you to sleep;
And they know the ropes
Out at Slumbering Slopes—
They bury you cheap.

The fact that they try harder
Is the reason they're ahead—
Their valley's small but greener
Than the more expensive spread.

Who'll see that you get yours,
Your true money's worth?
Not our man in Budapest,
Not our man in Marrakesh,
But our man in Paradise—on
    earth!

Our man in Paradise,
He does things in style—
He'll bid you good day
In a dignified way,
And yet with a smile!

Our man in Paradise
Will welcome you in—
He'll throw the Gates wide,
Underscoring your ride
With a soft violin.

They add a new dimension;
That is why they're number one—
Because it's their contention
That a funeral can be fun!

Who'll see that you're well dressed
Whatever your girth?
Not our man in Samarkand,
Not our man in Beulah Land,
But our man in Paradise—on
    earth!

THANKS, BUT NO THANKS!

To a proposition, my position is cool;
My reasoning is like my bank's—
I have found it safer, as a general rule,
To simply say, "Thanks, but no thanks!"

When I see a tiger full of masculine charm
Who's up to his schoolboy pranks,
Although this aging pussycat will do me no harm,
My answer is "Thanks, but no thanks!"

345

Yes, "Thanks, but no thanks, my angel,"
Soft and controlled—
That's how I hold 'em down to size.
That little phrase has saved more virgins, I'm told
Than "Don't shoot till you see the whites of their
    eyes!"

Maybe I'm conceited, but my own citadel,
My summit, is like Mont Blanc's—
Open to the very few who really excel,
Not a motel.
Dammit to hell,
I am not a madame, I'm a mademoiselle—
In other words,
Thanks, but no thanks!

WHY DIDN'T I TELL HIM?

Alternate title: "Why Didn't She Tell Me?"

VELDA: Why didn't I tell him he loves me?
        Why didn't I tell him he's mine?
        Why didn't I show him how happy he'd
            be
        Married to me?
        Couldn't he see?
        If I were an Eskimo maiden,
        I'd bring him my dowry in pelts—
        Why didn't I tell him he loves me?
        I'll never love anyone . . . Gee!

        For a cat as hip, it should be a snap—
        Does he need a hint? Must I draw a
            map?
        For a guy who knows what it's all about,
        Any harebrained boss could have figured
            out—
        A schoolboy could see that he loves me, he
            needs me—
        The way I adore him, he's just gotta love.
        Why didn't I tell him he loves me?
        For now he may never find out!

MIKE: Why didn't she tell me I love her?
        A man's not supposed to read minds.
        Why didn't she tell me with glances and
            smiles,
        Notes in the files,
        Feminine wiles?
        Why didn't she leave me an inkling
        How cold this old city can be?
        Why didn't she tell me I love her
        Before fate turned sour on me? . . . Gee!

Working side by side every single day,
You would think just once one of us
    would say . . .
What a knucklehead, what a Maxwell
    Smart,
Being deaf and dumb from the very start!
Why didn't she tell me I want her, I need
    her?
No broad from the Copa could ever
    succeed her!
Why didn't she tell me I love her
And love her with all of my heart!

BETSY AND ME

It was love at the start with sweet Betsy and me,
It was love at the beautiful start.
She's as close to a man as a lady can be,
For I carry her next to my heart.
I depend upon her like my vitamin A,
Like my razor or my Listerine,
And wherever I go,
You'll be happy to know,
Betsy makes the scene!
She's as quiet and shy
As a nun passing by,
But her eyes can be spitfire blue;
But whatever she's like,
If you want to take Mike,
Then you've gotta take Betsy too!!!

THE MEDIUM (COULDN'T GET THROUGH)

Music possibly by Bernie Hanighen.

Yeah, yeah, yeah . . .
Yeah, yeah, yeah . . .
Yeah, yeah, yeah, yeah!

Man, the medium couldn't get through
To the chick he wanted to woo—
Like he blew his mind for Prudence Clive,
Who had split the scene in eighteen-o-five,
And she did not dig his wiggy jive—
Every fuse that he lit, she blew!
It was tedium
'Cause the medium couldn't get through!

Man, the medium started to flip
On his intercelestial trip,
For no matter what he came on as
With his Ouija board or his ectoplaz,
Like his spirit self and all that jazz,
She would not come in on cue—
It was tedium
'Cause the medium couldn't get through!
He couldn't get through to you know who.
He was so high-up on his way-out call,
He was lucky he got back at all!

No, he never, ever got through
To his prim though passionate Pru.
He was much too bright, or way too dim—
Maybe Zeus himself found her ankle trim,
But someone up there did not like him,
So they said, "Twenty-three skidoo!"
It was tedium,
Yes indeedy-um,
Man, the medium couldn't get through!

YOU CAN'T LOSE

Baby, if at first you don't make it,
Life is just as good as you make it—
Take that old equipment and shake it,*
And if you can't shake it, then fake it—try!
Homer said, "It's all how you take it,"
Or as old Confucius said, "Fake it."
Life's all in the way that you take it—
Take it easy, baby, and make it,
And if you can't make it, then fake it—try!

There's a tide in the affairs of mundane men
Which, taken at the flood,
Leads to greatness, nobility, fortune, and fame—
Or corpses, cadavers, and blood.
Was it Homer I read about—over the hemlock,
As he was about to drink it—
Was it Norman, or Vincent, or maybe John Peel
Who said, "Life is what you think it"?
At any rate . . .
You can't lose.
You wanna know who can't lose?
You can't lose.
You wanna know why?
When you feel your confidence sinking,
Use the power of positive thinking,
Do a little sociable drinking—

_____
* *Alternate line:*
    Take what nature gave you and shake it,

Lie!
You can't fail—
You've only begun to wail—
Wag that tail,
And wag it up high!
Tune in, baby—listen, 'cause maybe I've got news!
One and two, they're playin' your music cue—
Go get 'em, 'cause you can't lose!!!

Alternative version

Wag that tail
And lift it on high—
You're the king,
Or you can be anything you choose.
Think it through,
But pack a machine gun too,
And Bubbeleh,
You can't lose!

You can't lose!
You wanna know who can't lose?
You can't lose!
You wanna know why?
Don't be like a sour old gherkin;
If you find your humor ain't perkin',
Be like Johnny Ray when he's workin'—
Cry!
Have no qualms—
So what if your big step bombs!
Wave the flag or unzip your fly.
Yes, Miss Jenny,
No bad penny—
You can be anything you choose.
There's the vamp—
They're meetin' a brand-new champ—
Remember that you can't lose!

You can't lose!
You wanna know who can't lose?
You can't lose!
You wanna know why?
Although my philosophy varies
After four or five Bloody Marys
Boys and girls and quite a few fairies
Really fly!
Simply tap
Your positive-thinking cap—
Any sap
Can be a big guy!
Say "I'm great!"
Get into those elevator shoes.
There's the vamp—
They're meetin' a brand-new champ—
Go get 'em, 'cause you can't lose!

BUBBLES: You can't lose!
        I'm tellin' you who can't lose—

You can't lose!
I'm tellin' you why—
This new thing called positive thinking
Even stops a violet shrinking—
Do a little sociable drinking—
Try!
You can't fail.
I'm showin' you who can't fail!
Lift that tail
And wag it on high!
Say again, "I, too, can do anything I
        choose!"
See it through—
But pack a machine gun too—
I guarantee, you can't lose!

CHINK: They can't lose—
Like Hymie and Jay can't lose—
They can't lose.
But what about *me*?
You know how I stutter and stammer,
Specially when I think o' Mike
        Hammer—
I begin to, pardon the grammar,
Pee!
You can't fail—
The other broads too can't fail,
Playin' gin and sippin' your tea,
But great snakes,
A thirty-eight makes a nasty bruise!
I just pray
Our Thompsons all work okay—
I figure that *they* can't lose!

JAY: We can't lose!
You, Hymie, and me can't lose—
We can't lose!
It's like Bubbles said,
If we think good thoughts 'n' keep
        tryin',
And the Crab remains in Orion,
We'll be rich while Hammer is lyin'
Dead!
We can't blow—
The Tarrytown Three can't blow
Even though we've always been shy.
In this hat and lucky cravat I always
        use,
Yessirree!
Self-confidence, that's the key—
I'm positive we can't lose!

BUBBLES
& BOYS: Like I said,
It's positive thinking, Fred—
Use your head and how can you lose?
What one word has so many uses?
Summons up the natural juices?
Covers up a million excuses?
Booze!
Buy a pint

And be the Jolly Green Gi'nt
Get behint
The leader you choose!
Okay, sport,
Let's have a short snort for Howard
        Hughes!
Leave us drink—
Get in there and think, think, think,
And gentlemen, you can't lose!!!
[*spoken*] At least, I don't *think* you can!
[*sung*] You can't lose!
You wanna know who can't lose?
You can't lose,
Whatever you do!
When you feel your little world rockin',
That's just opportunity knockin'—
Look what Santa left in your stockin'—
You!
Ain't life grand?
Although it's a one-night stand,
Dig that brand-new star in the sky!
What a sight!
It's opening night,
And you know whose?
One and two,
They're playin' your music cue—
Go get 'em!
'Cause you . . . can't . . . lose!

Reprise

BUBBLES: [*to* DAUGHTER]
You can't lose!
You wanna know who can't lose?
You can't lose!
You wanna know why?
When you feel your little world rockin',
That's just opportunity knockin'—
Look what Santa left in your stockin'—
Pie!
Who can't fail?
The red, white, and blue can't fail—
You can't fail—
Just look at 'em fly!
What a sight!
It's opening night,
And you know whose?
One and two,
They're playin' your music cue—
Go get 'em!
'Cause you can't lose!
And Mama don't lie—
You know I don't lie.
So don't even try
So mustn't be shy
So give it a try
And neither can I
Go give 'em the eye

You're seven miles high
Go out there and fly—
There's a brand-new star in the sky!

(NO WONDER IT'S) BANNED IN BOSTON

Always heard that love is grand;
Since last night I understand—
Boy oh boy, no wonder it's banned in Boston!

There we were, parked all alone;
I learned things I'd never known—
Boy oh boy, and I only own an Austin!

Don't know where Boston has been,
Why they think love is a sin,
But that's why the Red Sox are in last place
What a treat they have in store
When they both finally score—
Boy oh boy, I wanna see Boston's face!

Darling Lili: *Julie Andrews in the opening number,*
"Whistling Away the Dark"

DARLING LILI | 1970

DARLING LILI (1970)

Produced and directed by Blake Edwards for Geoffrey Productions. Released by Paramount Pictures. World premiere June 23, 1970. Copyright December 31, 1969. Screenplay by Blake Edwards and William Peter Blatty. Music score by Henry Mancini. Musical numbers staged by Hermes Pan. Choral supervision by Alan Copeland. The score features many World War I standards. New songs by Johnny Mercer (lyrics) and Henry Mancini (music). Starring Julie Andrews and Rock Hudson, featuring Jeremy Kemp, Lance Percival, Michael Witney, Gloria Paul, Jacques Marin, and André Maranne, with Bernard Kay, Doreen Keogh, Carl Duering, Vernon Dobtcheff, Laurie Main, Louis Mercier, and A. E. Gould-Porter.

In World War I, an American air ace falls for a German lady spy.

WHISTLING AWAY THE DARK

Published individually and as part of the vocal selections. Previously registered for copyright as an unpublished song in 1969, 1970, and on January 5, 1971. Introduced and reprised by Julie Andrews. Nominated for an Academy Award as Best Song of 1970 but lost to "For All We Know" by Fred Karlin (music) and Arthur James and Robb Wilson (lyrics) from *Lovers and Other Strangers*. Recorded by Julie Andrews with Henry Mancini and His Orchestra (Victor).

Often I think
This sad old world
Is whistling in the dark,
Just like a child
Who, late from school,
Walks bravely home through the park.
To keep their spirits soaring
And keep the night at bay,
Neither quite knowing
Which way they are going,
They sing the shadows away.

Often I think
My poor old heart
Has given up for good.
And then I see
A brand-new face,
I glimpse some new neighborhood.
So walk me back home, my darling,
Tell me dreams really come true,
Whistling,
Whistling,
Here in the dark with you.

THE LITTLE BIRDS (LES P'TITS OISEAUX)

Published in the vocal selections. Registered for copyright in 1969 and 1970. Introduced by children and Julie Andrews. Recorded by Le Lycée Française de Los Angeles Children's Choir with Henry Mancini and His Orchestra (Victor).

REFRAIN 1

Hi-li-hi-li-lo,
Chantons* comme les p'tits oiseaux!
"Oui, oui," trills the tiny chickadee,
("Oui," dit the tiny bobolee)
"It's my turn now."
"Who, who, who are you?"
Hoots the wise old owl, too.
"Mi, mi," sings the sparrow in the tree,
"I teach you how."
China or Peru,
The thing to do
Is have a picnic ev'ry spring
Where you can listen to the birds,
Who need no words
To teach you how to sing!
Low, high, high and low,
Chantons* comme les p'tits oiseaux.
One, two,
All together, here we go—
It's our turn now!

REFRAIN 2

"Whir, whir, thank you, sir,"
Goes the scarlet tanager.
"Tweet, tweet," chirps the cheery parakeet,
"It's my turn now."
"Hear, hear, lend an ear,"
Limn the linnets loud and clear.
Hark, hark, look who's singing like a lark—
And he knows how.
This is how we pass
Our music class—†
We learn a little more each day.
And oftentimes we parlez-vous

---

* *Alternate wording:*
    Chantez . . .
† *Alternate wording:*
    Our nature class—

A language, too,
As now we speak Anglais!
"Coo, coo, broodle-oo,"
Goes the em'rald cockatoo.
"Bob white!" coos the partridge in the night—
It's our turn now!

REFRAIN 3

Old gray guinea hen
And the rosy-breasted wren
Trio with the yellow vireo;
They sound quite sweet.
But it's too absurd;
(Really, it's absurd)
Listen to the mockingbird—
Oui, he outsings ev'ryone he's heard
Oui, he outsings ev'ryone he's heard,
But what conceit!
Usually the bass
Is stern of face;
The tenor has a high-pitched sound.
Of course, the hardest part that's known
Is baritone—
It wanders all around!

REFRAIN 4

"Hi-lo-hi-lo-li,"
Goes the titmouse to the towhee.
"Mush, mush,"
Sings the dignified old thrush—
So take your bow.
Roosters join in too
With a cock-a-doodle-doo.
"Coo, coo," loudly singeth yon cuckoo,
Enough—enow!
If we practice well,
Why, who can tell?
The opera house we'll occupy!
And if we harmonize just so,
Next thing you know,
We might learn how to fly!
And so, off we go,
Chantons* comme les p'tits oiseaux,
Small birds
Hum the music and the words—
It's our turn now!

Alternative lines

"Once or twice a year
They're so nice to hear,"
Our choirmaster said to me.
"We may not sing the notes as well,

---

* *Alternate wording:*
    Chantez . . .

But who can tell?—
They might keep us on key!"
Someday we'll be great,
Like the birds we imitate.
Wait, wait while we tintinnabulate—
It's our turn now!

THE GIRL IN NO-MAN'S-LAND

Published in the vocal selections. Registered for copyright in 1969 and 1970. Introduced by Julie Andrews. Recorded by Julie Andrews with Henry Mancini and His Orchestra and Chorus (Victor).

VERSE

They tell a story back in London Town
That when you hear taps sound,
Then all you soldiers have a sweetheart
Who always comes around.

REFRAIN 1

When night is falling,
She comes calling,
The girl in no-man's-land.
She comes to cheer them
And be near them,
A dream they understand.
Doughboys, weary, cold and lonely,
Know her as their one and only,
The angel who at close of day
Comes round to kiss their cares away.
When this is over,
You'll discover
The love you've always planned.
Until that time
Pretend that I'm
The girl in no-man's-land.

REFRAIN 2

She holds them tightly
Almost nightly,
The girl who walks out there.
To some a mother,
Some the other
Girl he lost somewhere—
Each one
Has a special daydream,
Grown men
With a children's play dream.
To Jim his lady at their club,

To Tom a waitress at some pub—
But she's their dearie;
When they're weary,
She comes to hold their hand.
Though I'm not her,
I wish I were
Your girl in no-man's-land.

I'LL GIVE YOU THREE GUESSES

Published in the vocal selections. Registered for copyright in 1969 and 1970. Introduced by Julie Andrews and four chorus boys. Recorded by Julie Andrews with Henry Mancini and His Orchestra and Chorus (Victor). The lyric sounds distinct echoes of "Three Guesses" from *The Pajama Lady* (1930).

VERSE

If you're good at riddle solving,
If you make the claim
That no puzzle ever puzzles you,
Here is one that needs evolving—
Here's a guessing game
That should be a snap for you to do.

REFRAIN

I'll give you three guesses
Who loves you,
Who's loved you
Right from the start.
Not your mother,
Who likes to baby you so;
And not the girl back home
You used to know.
Oh, no!
There's somebody special who needs you,
Together or apart.
Bet you don't need three guesses,
And not even two,
To know that I'm the one,
Sweetheart!

DARLING LILI

Published individually and as part of the vocal selections. Registered for copyright in 1969 and 1970. Introduced by off-screen chorus during overture, cut prior to

release. Recorded by Henry Mancini and His Orchestra and Chorus (Victor).

Published version

Darling Lili
Is an angel
From heaven come to see us
A little while.
Stage-door Johnnies wait for her;
Our boys encore her—
They just adore her style.
Darling Lili
Doesn't dream of
The hearts she keeps on breaking
With just a smile,
But you'd better
Just forget her,
Toddle off
And let her be—
Leave that darling,
Darling Lili
To me.

Film version

Darling Lili,
Put a light in the window
And keep wearing
That bonny smile.
On those cold railway benches
Or in the trenches
Warm up our hearts awhile.
Darling Lili,
Blow a kiss to us, dearie,
As we travel each weary mile.
Not for mother
Or each other
Are we off
To end this war—
You're the darling
We'll be winning
It for.

SMILE AWAY EACH RAINY DAY

Published individually and as part of the vocal selections. Previously registered for copyright as an unpublished song January 5, 1971. Introduced by Julie Andrews. Recorded by Julie Andrews with Henry Mancini and His Orchestra and Chorus (Victor).

Smile away each rainy day
And laugh* away your blues.
Be like Old Mister Noah
When it starts to pour—
Make fun at trouble,
Although you're seein' double,
Keep in mind they're silver-lined,
Those gloomy clouds of gray!
Let love light the sky up;
Tell those clouds to dry up,
And smile away each rainy day!

SKÅL (LET'S HAVE ANOTHER ON ME)

Published in the vocal selections. Previously registered for copyright in 1969 and 1970. Introduced by off-screen male chorus. Recorded by Henry Mancini and His Orchestra and Chorus (Victor).

REFRAIN 1

Skål,
Jawohl,
A wee deoch an doris,
L'chaim,
Here's mud in your eye!
Cheers, mynheers,
Let's all sing a chorus
For this lovely night going by.
Eins und zwei,
Make drei
The martinis,
À votre
And bon appetit!

Let's drink to your mother,
Your sister and brother,
My uncle, your aunt—
May they each like the other!
But we'll drink it all by ourselves
If you'd druther—
So let's have another on me!

REFRAIN 2

Skål,
Jawohl,
Let's drink and be merry—
Tomorrow the barrel runs dry.

* *Alternate wording:*
  And sing . . .

Down the hatch,
And after we're down,
Bottoms up—
That's the best way to fly.
Proost, salud,
However you say it,
There's all kinds of ways to get high!

Let's drink to your mother,

[*Lyric continues as in refrain 1.*]

Alternate ending (film version)

Let's drink to the Kaiser,
Who's sadder but wiser
Since we put a howitzer
Right up his visor!
We'll make the old bastard
A French sympathizer,
So let's have another on me!

YOUR GOOD-WILL AMBASSADOR

Published as an individual song and as part of the vocal score. Copyrighted July 26, 1971. Previously registered for copyright in 1969 and 1970. Introduced by Gloria Paul. Recorded by Gloria Paul with Henry Mancini and His Orchestra (Victor).

VERSE

Your good-will ambassador
Would like to know,
Are you doin' okay?
Your good-will ambassador
Would like to feel
You're enjoying your stay.

REFRAIN 1

If you're calm and placid or
If you've got a red-hot desire to roam,
I want to get you all to know Paree,
For there's a fast Paree
And there's a slow Paree—
We'll do the whole big sexy potpourri,
'Cause, buddy, I'm gonna make you at home!
On the Left Bank
I'm gonna make you at home,
Or on the Right Bank
I'm gonna make you at home,
And that's official—
I'm gonna make you at home.

REFRAIN 2 (NOT SUNG IN FILM)

If you're from Lake Placid or
From Kankakee or from London or Rome,
The object is to get to know Paree,
For there's a fast Paree
And there's a slow Paree—
We'll do the whole big sexy potpourri,
'Cause, buddy, I'm gonna make you at home!
In my apartment
I'm gonna make you at home;
You'll meet my cousin—
I'm gonna make you at home;
We call her madam—
I'm gonna make you at home.

PICCADILLY CIRCUS

Not used in film.

Published version

REFRAIN 1

Why do they call it Piccadilly Circus?
There ain't a bloomin' elephant around!
'Undreds o' buses crowdin' up the pavements—
No wonder all the trains are under ground!
Somebody built a smashin' semicircle,
So wouldn't you know it's called Trafalgar Square?
It ain't to save the world that we're off t'war;
Ev'ry Cockney lad knows what he's fightin' for—
With the sound of Bow Bells ringin' out above,
'E's fightin' for this abysmal,
Dear old dismal
London Town we love!

REFRAIN 2

Why do they call it Piccadilly Circus
When never one orangutang appears?
Buckin'ham Palace always 'as the Guards out,
But they've not 'ad a robbery in years!
Look at the ruddy way they put the streets down—
You're meetin' yourself arrivin' as you leave.
Marylebone t' Hoxford,
Chelsea to the Strand,
You can 'ardly find a blinkin' place to stand!
Still, with all the drawbacks we're complainin' of,
It's seventeen-'undred-year-old,
Run-down, dear old
London Town we love!

REFRAIN 3

Makin' a bit o' fun of 'er as Blighty,
The pictures that they paint o' Johnny Bull—
Namin' ourselves the Tightest Little Island,
Hit don't mean us in'abitants is full!
We didn't get to be the British Empire
By standin' around 'n' sittin' on our hands,
And so if Fritzy boy wants 'is little war,
Ev'ry Cockney lad knows what 'e's fightin' for—
With the sound of Bow Bells ringin' out above,
'E's fightin' for this abysmal,
Fogged-in, dismal
London Town we love!

STEAL TWO EGGS

Not used in film.

Steal two eggs,
Some pepper and salt to taste.
Borrow a pan—
Anyone can—
Why should it go to waste?

And if you need some milk,
The cow supplies it free.
Maybe the Gypsies never dine like royalty,
But neither do we go hungery
In Hungary!

To be a great chef of France,
Par excellence,
Mais oui,
Matters not how hot your pot
Nor what you've got for tea!
The most important thing is
Can you give gendarmes the slip,
And with a Gypsy's skill?
Can you spot a pie
With a naked eye
While cooling on an open windowsill?
Or can you steal two eggs
To go with a parsley sprig?
Maybe a duck,
If you're in luck,
Even a suckling pig—
For if it strays off,
It's common property!
Maybe the Gypsies never serve a real high tea,
But neither do we go hungery
In Hungary!

OVERLEAF
Top: *Mercer with Richard A. Whiting, 1937*
Bottom: *With Whiting's daughter, Margaret, in 1973*

MARY ELLEN

Music by Billy Vaughn. Registered for copyright as an unpublished song January 19, 1970.

Mary Ellen,
I've kissed Helen,
Dated Daisy,
Danced with Sue,
But there's no one
That I yearn for
Through the long and sleepless nights
As I do
Over you.
Mary Ellen,
There's no tellin',
If you'd let me,
What I'd do.
Out of pure curiosity
Just try me out and see how I
Love you.

LITTLE ACORNS

Music by Arthur Kent. Registered for copyright as an unpublished song February 16, 1970.

Give my mama credit;
She's the one who said,
"Sow your little acorns made of love.
If that's how you sow 'em,
And with kindness grow 'em,
They'll turn into great big oaks above."
As I grow older
I can see it's true,
And Mama, that's what I intend to do—
This good life is made of restin'
In the shade of little acorns
That grew up with love.

HONOLULU

Music by Mercer. Registered for copyright as an unpublished song May 25, 1970.

Honolulu,
Thanks to you,

To the diamond stars that spread
High above old Diamond Head—
Ev'ry night
New dreams come true,
Honolulu,
Thanks to you!

MISGUIDED FAITH (SANCTIFYING GRACE)

Music by Brian Minard.

Faith took a bus to the city,
She didn't like it at home.*
Diggin' the scenes in those trash magazines,
She thought she could make it alone.

Faith got a job in a dime store,
Rented an East Village flat.
Money and fame was the name of her game;
Faith knew just where she was at.

She gave a banker the business
One night in his sleek Cadillac;
With one fleeting stare at her home of despair,
She knew there was no turning back.

From the crash pad in the Village
She moved to Fifth Avenue;†
Her friends were poets with brown paper bags,
Hoodlums and millionaires, too.

Last week they sent for her mother,
The person who'd loved her the most;
Faith left this earth on the eve of her birthday,
Effects of a small overdose.

Mother's alone in the lamplight,
Reading last week's *Daily News;*
Drinks whiskey and water and thinks of her daughter
But doesn't give out interviews.

Should she have called the child Janis?
Would it have done any good?
Scolded and spanked her or spoiled her and
   thanked her
And moved to a new neighborhood?

* *Alternate line:*
   She was unhappy at home.
† *Alternate line:*
   Faith moved to Park Avenue;

BLUES IMPROVISATION

Performed by Mercer at "An Evening with Johnny Mercer" at the 92nd Street Y, New York City, March 14, 1971, as part of the *Lyrics & Lyricists* series.

There's E. Y. Harburg
Sittin' unobtrusively in the seventeenth row,
And Mister Harold Arlen,
With whom I wrote a very unsuccessful show.
And what are old Episcopalian choirboys
Doin' up here?
I do not know.
In conclusion, ladies and gentlemen,
I would like to thank you all,
And including those guests
Whose names are up there on the wall—
And thank the Men's Hebrew Association
For the use of the hall.

RED SKY AT MORNING (1971)

Produced by Hal B. Wallis for Universal. Released May 1971. Copyright May 13, 1971. Directed by James Goldstone. Screenplay by Marguerite Roberts, based on the novel *Red Sky at Morning* by Richard Bradford. Original music composed and conducted by Billy Goldenberg. Featuring Richard Thomas, Catherine Burns, Desi Arnaz Jr., Richard Crenna, Claire Bloom, John Colicos, Harry Guardino, Strother Martin, Nehemiah Persoff, with Pepe Serna, Mario Aniov, Victoria Racimo, Gregory Sierra, Lynne Marta, Christina Hart, Elizabeth Knowles, Linda Burton, Alma Beltran, Jerome Guardino, Joy Bang, Claudio Miranda, Joaquin Garay, and Karen Klett.

During World War II an Army family finds life in New Mexico problematic.

RED SKY AT MORNING

Registered for copyright as an unpublished song May 21, 1973. Not sung in film.

Red sky at morning,
Sailor, take warning,
Expect a stormy sea before the night.

Old superstitions have a way of coming true,
Just as intuitions do,
And they may be right.
In any weather we're here together,
One little planet Earth, adrift in space.
Take warning, celestial sailor,
Look hard at the morning sky
And pray for luck as you fly.

BETTER DAYS

Music by Gilbert Martinez. Lyrics by Mercer and Martinez. Registered for copyright as an unpublished song May 17, 1971.

When your troubles seem to bury you,
Six feet below the ground you lay,
It is time to reevaluate
The things that made your life that way.
It didn't happen overnight
Or through some fancy quirk of fate,
But I wager it just crept on you,
'Cause life is funny that way.

I know 'cause I've seen better days,
I've seen better days,
Better days, better days.

So pick up your patching kit and see
If you can mend them one by one,
And before long you will see, I'm sure,
The side of life lit by the sun;
And I'll bet you that your luck will change
In anything you do.
Just remember an important thing—
That you can twist life your way.

I know 'cause I've seen better days,
We'll see better days,
Better days, better days.

Guess I'll call my gal and let her know
I'll be around to get her kiss.
If she asks why I have been away
So long from her I'll tell her this—
There's a trip each man must take alone
In every walk of life,
So believe me if you can, my love,
And hold me close like a wife.

Better days, we'll see better days,
Yes, we'll see better days,
Better days, better days,
Better days.

KOTCH (1971)

Produced by Richard Carter for ABC Pictures Corp. Released by Cinerama. World premiere September 30, 1971. Copyright September 3, 1971. Directed by Jack Lemmon. Screenplay by John Paxton, based on the novel *Kotch* by Katherine Topkins. Lyrics by Johnny Mercer. Music by Marvin Hamlisch. Orchestrations by Leo Shuken and Jack Hayes. Starring Walter Matthau, featuring Deborah Winters, Felicia Farr, Charles Aidman, and Ellen Geer, with James E. Brodhead, Jane Connell, Biff Elliot, Dean and Donald Kowalski, Darrell Larson, Larry Linville, Paul Picerni, Jessica Rains, and Penny Santon.

A crotchety old widower doesn't get on with his family and helps a pregnant babysitter.

LIFE IS WHAT YOU MAKE IT (THEME FROM KOTCH)

Published. Copyrighted March 15, 1972. Previously registered for copyright as an unpublished song September 15, 1971. Introduced by off-screen chorus behind opening titles. Nominated for an Academy Award as Best Song of 1971 but lost to "Theme from *Shaft*" by Isaac Hayes. Mercer's last Academy Award nomination.

Life is what you make it—
If you can make it,
It's worth a try.
Smile, the world is sunny,
Your Easter bunny,
Where even sad turns to funny.
Fame may run to catch you
Or look right at you
And pass you by;
Somewhere out there
Love waits to see you through—
Life is what you make it,
And what you make it
Is up to you.

SHAKE IT, BUT DON'T BREAK IT

Music by Erroll Garner. Published. Copyrighted July 26, 1977. Previously registered for copyright as an unpublished song October 12, 1971.

HE: Maybelle and me, we took a stroll
For some old-time jelly roll,
A cherry bun as sweet as honey in the comb.
She let me tote the box awhile;
Then she hollered with a great big smile,
"Yes, you can shake it, Daddy,
But don't break it till we got it home!
I got some high society
Fallin' by at ha' past three;
Then we will pour, you and me,
A jeroboam.
But till we toddle through that door,
Please don't tremble anymore—
Oh, you can shake it, Daddy,
But don't break it till we got it home!

SHE: Sweet Stuff and me, we took a stroll
For some old-time jelly roll,
A cherry bun as sweet as honey in the comb.
He let me tote the box awhile;
Then he hollered with a great big smile,
"Yes, you can shake it, baby,
But don't break it till we got it home!
We'll climb the stairs and turn the key
And get the Dodgers on TV;
Then we'll divide, you and me,
That jeroboam.
After we pass around the Certs,
You will get your just deserts—
Ah, you can shake it, baby,
But don't break it till we got it home!"

TWILIGHT WORLD

Music by Marian McPartland. Registered for copyright as an unpublished song December 3, 1971.

Twilight world
Over the China Sea,
Sing me a melody from ages ago.
In a twilight world,
Watching the sampans pass,

I fill a frosty glass
As lanterns burn low.
Life is a changing panorama;
Love is a dancing butterfly.
Catch them both while we may—
Come to Spain or Cathay,
I don't want to miss
That will-of-the-wisp passing by.
Life is holding out a twilight world;
Don't let it slip away—
Come take it while we may,
And let it begin.
Let's find our twilight world
Before the night sets in.

FLEUR DE LYS

Music by Hoagy Carmichael.

Pale flower of the night,
Star blossom cool and white,
Sleepwalker from antiquity,
Do they call you fleur de lys?

Sweet siren here at last,
An echo from the past,
When knighthood rose in chivalry
For their lady fleur de lys.

Dream on, my fair somnambulist,
Like some Dali work of art;
But when at last
Those Sleeping Beauty lips are kissed,
Perhaps I'll awaken your secret heart.

So, wild bird, fold your wings,
Come, let me whisper things.
Discover the captivity
Of my garden and be free,
Free to love me,
Fleur de lys.

HAPPY EVER AFTER

Music by Dick Hyman. Hyman says the song has different versions and was never finished. The differences between the two following versions are indicative of the way a lyricist's mind works. (In Version 2, the italicized passages show the variations from Version 1.)

Version 1

Second-mortgage man
Showed me a plan
Easy to swing
With a single little down payment.
So I'm savin' up,
Found an old cup,
Makin' it clang
With a gang o' nickels 'n' dimes.

Happy ever after—
Are ya gettin' the picture, same as me?
Kids on every rafter,
Runnin' over the nice clean floors,
All mine and yours.
A tiny station wagon,
Automatic disposal in the sink.
When I bring you home a dragon,
You'll fix us both a drink!

Mondays, I'll be off and slavin',
Stashin' stuff in the bank.
You'll be shoppin', blue-chip savin',
Puttin' gas in the tank.
Ajax, Brillo, instant Bourbon,
TV dinners at night;
Kids all bussin', interurban,
Too darn busy to fight.

Sunshine, flowers, laughter—
What a beautiful lifetime, wait and see!
Happy ever after,
After you say you'll marry me!

Second-mortgage man,
Coppin' your plan,
Buyin' a ring with a single little down payment.
For it to succeed
Whadda I need?
A little more greed
And a "Yes indeedy!" from you!

Version 2

Second-mortgage man,
I thought of a plan
Easy to swing
With a single little down payment.

Happy ever after—
Are you gettin' the picture *in my mind?*
Kids on every rafter,
Rollin' over the nice clean floors,
All mine and yours.
A *shiny* station wagon
And a little old garden out in back—

When I bring you home a dragon,
You'll fix us both a *snack!*

Mondays, I'll be off and slavin',
Sockin' stuff in the bank.
You'll be shoppin', blue-chip savin',
Puttin' gas in the tank;
Ajax, *Baggies, instant Brillo—*
After dinner at night,
We'll both hit that foam rest pillow,
Too darn weary to fight.

Sunshine, flowers, laughter—
What a beautiful *ending there will be!*
Happy ever after,
After you say you'll marry me!

Second-mortgage man,
I thought of a plan
Easy to swing
With a single little down payment . . .

[*Fade.*]

MY MOTHER'S LOVE

Music by Jimmy Rowles.

Why do I appreciate the beauty that I see,
The wind song in a willow, or a star caught in a
    tree?
My life is like another's,
Except it had my mother's love.
She taught me to have a smile for every passer-by,
Especially the people not as fortunate as I.
I guess I'm like my father,
Who also had my mother's love.
It was her sense of humor she gave me;
It never lets anger enslave me—
It comes to the rescue to save me
Ev'ry time, ev'ry time.
So, I thank the Lord for every gift with which I'm
    blessed,
For maybe being luckier or different from the rest,
But more than all the others
I thank him for
My mother's love!

PLEASE, WORLD, STAY OPEN ALL NIGHT

Music by Stan Hoffman.

VERSE 1

Ooh! Wow! Hey! What a night it's been so far—
I could touch the nearest star!
What a far out girl with me—
What a lot there is to see!
In this town I feel like shouting.

REFRAIN 1

Please, world, stay open all night!
Don't be so casual hearted.
Please, world, don't lower a light—
My life is just getting started!
What a scene!
I really mean
It's out of sight—
I know we'll be all right.
Please, world, stay open all night—
Please, world, stay open all night!

VERSE 2

Love! Man can love, put on a show.
What a groovy way to go!
I would hate to see it end.
If you wanna be a friend,
To me, world, don't keep me hanging!

REFRAIN 2

Please, world, stay open all night—
Don't close up shop without warning!
Hey, world, don't lower a light—
You'll hate yourself in the morning.
Help us out—
Without a doubt we'll be all right.
Please, world, stay open all night.

MY NAME IS LOVE, FLY ME

Music by David Raksin. Registered for copyright as an unpublished song January 20, 1972.

Fly me to Paris!
My name is love.
Fly me to Rio de Janeiro!

Won't somebody
Fly me to somewhere
I'm dreaming of?
Start the enchantment of
Mysterious stars above
What's out there in the night?
Pagan moments of untamed delight!
Down we go through the stars
Where the jet set adorn tropical bars
So off to Majorca—
Don't tell me how.
Fly me to anywhere,
But fly me now!

EL CAMINO

Music by Michael Shanklin. Registered for copyright as an unpublished song February 11, 1972.

Since I was a small vaquero
Underneath a big sombrero,
Every sunset on the highway
Whispered, "Are you going my way?"

El camino,
Where are you taking your amigo?
El camino,
Do you know the way back home?
Do you know the way back home?

Under the twilight skies
Sleep treasures untold.
Out there El Dorado lies
With streets paved of gold.

So I'll tread one more mile beside you,
Like the other fools who ride you.
But I wonder, eh, amigo,
Do you know the way back home?
Do you know the way back home?

Maybe some pale moonrise
You'll turn and I'll see
A stranger with laughing eyes
Just waiting for me.

So, I'll travel one more mile beside you,
Hoping that the gods will guide you.
But you tell me, eh, amigo,
Don't you know the way back home?
Can we find the way back home?

OCTOBER TWILIGHT

Music by Joseph Myrow. Registered for copyright as an unpublished song February 14, 1972. Written for the film *Those Days Before the War*, which was never made.

Red leaves were falling through
The dusky blue
October twilight
To hide tomorrow from sight,
Those days before the war.
And drinking to a song
All through the long
October twilight,
How could a pair of kids believe
What fortune had in store,
What fortune had in store?
For just a start
Was the world we kept within our heart.
Beauty and truth,
Sweet dream of youth,
All fell apart.
But now we're back again
As we were then
That long-ago October twilight,
To make it all work out once more
The way it was before,
Before we knew of war.
But that's how lovers are
And that's what love is for.

HANGIN' LOOSE

Music by Sammy Nestico. Registered for copyright as an unpublished song April 10, 1972.

What a day!
I mean to say,
I could handle Toulouse
Hangin' loose.
Mother nature 'n' me,
Good for nuthin's are we,
Couldn't spring for a dime,
But squanderin' time—
I gotcha covered. Me?
I'm ridin' free
As a little papoose.
"Rubberneckin',"
Hangin' loose.
What a world, what a life, what a feelin'
Like on the juice.

And that only goes to prove
Old Dad's in a mellow groove.
I'm in there a-swangin',
Just sort o' hangin' loose.
Gotcha covered. Whee!
I feel as free as a little papoose.
Window shoppin',
Hangin' loose.
If you can't find a seat in the diner,
Grab our caboose!
We're off to another town,
Out there where the sun goes down.
Both in there a-swangin'
Both kinds o' hangin' loose.

Or as they like to say in Australia
Of kangaroos,
Not only the ride is free,
But mom's takin' care of me.
She does all the swangin'
I do the hangin' loose.

ROCK IN A WEARY LAND

Music by Mercer. Registered for copyright as an unpublished song May 3, 1972.

Let me be a rock in a weary land,
Let me be a rock in a weary land,
Let me be a rock in a weary land,
Spreading out my shade on the burning sand,
Sheltering the flock, like the shadow of a rock
In a weary land.

Let me be a well in a barren waste,
Let me be a well in a barren waste,
Let me be a well in a barren waste,
So the heavy laden can have a taste,
Resting for a spell by the water in the well
In a weary land.

You can use me, Lord,
Till I shake and quake,
But I'm beggin' you, Lord,
Not to let me break!

Let me be a star in the deep blue sky,
Let me be a star shinin' way up high,
Let me be a star in the deep blue sky,
Shining like a lamp for the passers-by,
Burning like a light in the middle of the night
In a weary land.

Let me be an oak in a tractless plain,
Let me be an oak in a tractless plain,
Let me be an oak in a tractless plain,
Sheltering the sheep from the sun and rain,
Throwin' out a cloak like a mighty, mighty oak
In a weary land.

Let me be a spring in a desert place,
Let me be a spring in a desert place,
Let me be a spring in a desert place,
Where the weary wanderer can dip his face,
Healing ev'rything in the water of the spring
In a weary land.

You can work me, Lord,
Till my old bones ache,
But I'm beggin' of you, Lord,
Don'tcha let me break!

Let me be a rock in a weary land,
Let me be a rock in a weary land,
Let me be a rock in a weary land,
So the little children can take my hand,
Right aroun' the clock, just as steady as a rock
In a weary land.

PAESAN

Music by Ray Sinatra. Registered for copyright as an unpublished song May 8, 1972.

Paesan, we've seen a lot of years,
Paesan, a lot of laughs and tears.
Paesan, I'm glad to have a friend like you,
It's true.
Recall the happy times when we were small—
We're lucky we're both here at all,
The crazy things we used to do!
If you believe in fate,
You know it shows up late—
Perhaps this little talk just had to wait
Somehow till now, old friend,
We're close enough not to pretend
And wise enough to comprehend
The tiny threads two people's lives can hang upon.
So, as the years go by,
I hope you feel the same as I,
So lucky and so thankful
You are my paesano.

MY JEKYLL ISLAND

Music and lyrics by Isa Thomas. Lyrics edited by Mercer. Registered for copyright as an unpublished song May 8, 1972.

VERSE

"Millionaires' Island,"
This isle of history,
"Millionaires' Island"—
Giants of industry,
They made a dream land
Where magic fills the air,
A golden dream land
With beauty rare.
I'll always love you so.

REFRAIN

My Jekyll Island,
My island by the sea—
This Georgia island
Belongs to you and me.*
I dream of Jekyll
When I am far away;
I dream of Jekyll,
Where hearts are gay.
My sunlit island,
Where sunbeams fill the air,†
My starlit island,
No other could compare.
My golden island,
Where silver moonbeams glow,
My Jekyll Island,
I'll always love you so!

FRAZIER (THE SENSUOUS LION)

Music by Jimmy Rowles. Registered for copyright as an unpublished song May 12, 1972.

This lyric is complicated by the fact that there are

* *Alternate lines:*
  No other island
  Could mean so much to me.
† *Alternate line:*
  The sunbeams linger there,

many variances between the sheet music (where the lion is called "Frasier") and the lyric published in the liner notes to Mercer's recording *My Huckleberry Friend* (1982).

VERSE 1

Frazier was an aging lion
Living in a cage of iron
In a circus out of Tia Juana.
Frazier was their main attraction,
And he gave them satisfaction,
Doing it with talent and with honor.
Growling for his daily dinner,
Frazier kept on getting thinner
On a measly can of Spam and tuna.
So one night in Pasadena
Through the bars he split for South Laguna.

REFRAIN 1

"Oh cruel is fate, but it's never too late," said
    Frazier.
"I'm ninety-one and I haven't a son," thought
    Frazier.
"The blue-eyed truth is I'm ready for
    euthanasia."
Although matted and tarry, a local safari
Rescued poor old Frazier.

VERSE 2

First they combed his tangled tresses,
Housed him with the lionesses,
Thinking him a harmless old grandpapa;
Fed him niocin and chloride,
B-one, -two, -six, -twelve and fluoride,
Clams, cod liver oil, cobalt, and copper.
Younger studs brought in for breeding
Wound up beaten, bruised, and bleeding.
Ev'ry day the same thing kept occurring:
Stretched out on an old serape,
There lay Frazier tired and [but] happy,
All his ladies on the list and purring.

REFRAIN 2

"Oh cruel is fate, but it's never too late," said
    Frazier.
"Announce the feast—I'm king of the beasts,"
    grinned [yawned] Frazier,
"But king or not, I am certainly hot!" yawned
    [grinned] Frazier.
Well, when you're hot and you're hitting the
    spot,
[And when you are hot, boys, and hitting the
    spot, boys,]
The action might [will] amaze ya!

VERSE 3

Children by his wives eleven
Added up to sixty-seven [fifty-seven]—
What [Such] nocturnal bliss he must have tasted!
For no matter what the night time,
Any night time seemed the right time.
Daytime found him fast asleep, just wasted.
When the circus owner found him,
Brought a lawsuit to impound him,
Claiming, "You cats have to go where we go."
Frazier roared, "*Hasta la vista!*
You think [theenk] all these chicks [girls] my sista
    [seesta]?
I'm in business for myself, amigo!"

REFRAIN 3

"Oh, cruel is fate, but it's never too late," said
    [crowed] Frazier.
"I thank my stars I'm not behind bars," said
    [thought] Frazier.
"They pay to see what comes naturally in Asia—
No African cat ever had it like that,
And that goes for Malaysia!
No one olés ya,
Elephant outweighs ya,
Giant sloth outstays ya!"

He's up above, dear Frazier,
Raising cubs, oh, Frazier . . .
Bless his heart, happy Frazier!
So hang in there, King Frazier!
Olé!

ROBIN HOOD (1973)

Produced and directed by Wolfgang Reitherman for Walt Disney Productions. World premiere November 8, 1973. Copyright October 25, 1973. Story by Larry Clemmons, based on character and story conceptions by Ken Anderson. Music score by George Bruns. Orchestrations by Walter Sheets. The songs for this film are by Roger Miller, Floyd Huddleston, and George Bruns, except for "The Phony King of England" by Johnny Mercer. Featuring the voices of Roger Miller, Peter Ustinov, Terry-Thomas, Brian Bedford, Monica Evans, Phil Harris, Andy Devine, Carole Shelley, Pat Buttram, George Lindsey, Ken Curtis, and Nancy Adams.

THE PHONY KING OF ENGLAND

Traditional music. Published. Copyrighted November 7, 1973. Previously registered for copyright as an unpublished song December 8, 1972. Introduced by Phil Harris (voice of Little John), Pat Buttram (voice of the Sheriff of Nottingham), and Terry-Thomas (voice of Sir Hiss). Recorded by Harris (Disneyland).

REFRAIN 1

Oh, the world will sing of an English king a
    thousand years from now,
And not because he passed some laws or had that
    lofty brow.
While bonny good King Richard leads the great
    Crusade he's on,
We'll all have to slave away for good-for-nothing
    John.
Incredible as he is inept,
Whenever the hist'ry books are kept,
They'll call him the Phony King of England—
A pox on the Phony King of England!

REFRAIN 2

He sits alone on a giant throne pretending he's the
    king,
A little tyke who's rather like a puppet on a string,
And throws an angry tantrum if he cannot have
    his way,
And then calls for Mum while sucking his thumb,
    because he doesn't want to play.
Too late to be known as John the First,
He's sure to be known as John the Worst—
A pox on the Phony King of England!

REFRAIN 3

While he taxes us to pieces and he robs us of our
    bread,
King Richard's crown keeps slipping down around
    that pointed head.
Ah, but while there is a Merry Man in Robin's wily
    pack,
We'll find a way to make him pay and steal our
    money back.
A minute before he knows we're there,
Old Rob'll snatch his underwear,
The breezy and uneasy King of England—
The sniveling, groveling, blubbering, blabbering,
Measly, weasly, jibbering, jabbering,
Plundering, plotting, wheeling, dealing Prince John
That phony King of England.

A LITTLE BOY'S RAINY DAY

Music by David Saxon.

I'm gettin' tired o' all o' this sunshine—
How I'd love to spend a little boy's rainy day!
Coat around my shoulder,
Wind a-blowin' colder,
Swirlin' all the leaves in a kind of whirly way;
Ol' tin-roof attic drummin' above me—
Got a great big book,
An apple, 'n' games to play.
When it starts to thunder,
Let the grown-ups wonder
What I'm up to under
A bed or in the hay.
Hey, I'm eatin' stuff 'n' gettin' fatter,
'N' feelin' warm as pancake batter,
'N' watchin' puddle jumpers scatterin' on their
	way.
Seein' all the raindrops patterin',
Hearin' thunder rat-tat-tatterin',
Scared to bits but that don't matter, 'n'
I'm okay.
Let the raindrops pitter-patter,
Let the lightnin' play,
Let the thunder boom and roll away!
Say, I'm havin' me a windowpaney,
Hurricaney, weathervaney,
Take-a-look-I-betcha-couldn't-find-me
Little boy's rainy day!

THE LONG GOODBYE

Music by John Williams. Published. Copyrighted April 23, 1973. Introduced throughout the film by the Dave Grusin Trio, Jack Sheldon, Clydie King, Jack Riley, Morgan Ames' Aluminum Band, and the Tepoztlan Municipal Band.

There's a long goodbye,
And it happens ev'ry day
When some passer-by
Invites your eye
To come her way.
Even as she smiles a quick hello,
You've let her go,
You've let the moment fly.
Too late you turn your head;
You know that you've said
The long goodbye.

Can you recognize the theme?
On some other street
Two people meet
As in a dream,
Running for a plane
Through the rain—
If the heart is quicker than the eye,
They could be lovers until they die.
It's too late to try
When a missed hello
Becomes the long goodbye.

And what a happy time
Filled a Sunday afternoon,
And the minstrel orchestra
Gave us a street parade.
They used to start
Down at City Hall
And march to Cedar Point,
And if a kid
Couldn't hear them play,
His summer was thrown out of joint.
For they would no sooner get there
Than they had to march back—
Man, you knew they were all pretty tired.
But what really made it the best parade
Was the fact a shot would never get fired.

Squeeze up to me, oh, my honey,
Let's do the Cedar Point Glide;
We'll do the fox-trot and bunny,
Like Daddy did until he was ossified!
Cuddle up back in the rumble seat,
Cuddle up until the end of intermission;
Then we'll go back and do the hoochamacooch
Or we can stay outside.

Squeeze up to me, oh, my honey,
Let's do the Cedar Point Glide;
Squeeze up to me like a bunny,
Like Daddy did until he was satisfied!
How'd you like to be that young again,
Doing all the things we all did then,
And fall asleep on someone's shoulder
As the gramophone played the Cedar Point Parade?

THE LONG GOODBYE (1973)

Produced by Elliott Kastner and Jerry Bick for Lion's Gate Films. Released by United Artists. Released March 1973. Copyright February 23, 1973. Directed by Robert Altman. Screenplay by Leigh Brackett, based on the novel *The Long Goodbye* by Raymond Chandler. Lyrics by Johnny Mercer. Music by John Williams. Starring Elliott Gould, featuring Nina Van Pallandt, Sterling Hayden, Mark Rydell, and Henry Gibson, with David Arkin, Warren Berlinger, Jo Ann Brody, Jim Bouton, the Dave Grusin Trio, Jack Sheldon, Clydie King, Jack Riley, Morgan Ames' Aluminum Band, and the Tepoztlan Municipal Band.

Philip Marlowe helps an eccentric friend suspected of murdering his wife.

CEDAR POINT PARADE

Music by Robert G. Friedman. Registered for copyright as an unpublished song April 30, 1973.

Back yonder ev'ry little town would have its own
	Cedar Point,
On the lake where people went to have picnics and
	stuff,
Where boys and girls would park
In the friendly summer dark,
And the price was beautiful—
It was all on the cuff.
There was a dance pavilion that was open on
	Saturdays,
On Sunday afternoons we'd have an outing with
	pink lemonade,

I'M SHADOWING YOU

Music by Blossom Dearie. Recorded by Dearie (Verve). Registered for copyright as an unpublished song July 20, 1973.

It's interesting to note that this was written shortly before the Watergate scandal reached its peak.

Everywhere you go
I think you ought to know
I'm shadowing you.
Turn around 'n' find
I'm half a step behind—
I'm shadowing you.
You lug, you,
I wouldn't bug you
Except whenever I can—
You see, love,
You are to me, love,

The indispensable man.
After you decide
You want me for a bride,
The deed'll be done.
Both of us'll be
So independent we
Will live on the run,
Picketing for every cause,
Fighting all the unjust laws,
Happy as can be,
Just you, J. Edgar Hoover, and me.
I'm shadowing you.

Like I said before,
I'm campin' at your door—
I'm shadowing you
How can you escape?
I'm getting out a tape
And video too.
In Venice
I'll be a menace
In your Italian motel.
In Paris
I shall embarrass
You on the Rue de Chappelle.
After you decide
You wanna be my bride,
The deed'll be done.
Both of us'll be
So independent we
Will live on the run,
Picketing for every cause,
Fighting all the unjust laws,
Happy as can be,
Just you, the Secret Service, and me.
I'm shadowing you.

YOU GO YOUR WAY

Music by Mercer. Recorded by Margaret Whiting and later by Polly Podewell (both on Audiophile).

You go your way,
I'll go my way,
But let's walk this mile together
While we may,
Merrymaking
For the taking
Through the watermelon weather
Of this bountiful day.
All too soon the road will turn;
Our pathways may part.
All I have to offer is

The love in my heart.
So let each hour*
Come full flower,
And Godspeed them with a toast
To auld lang syne.
Then you go your way
Through your golden doorway,
And wish me well as I go mine.

EMPTY TABLES

Music by Jimmy Van Heusen. Published. Copyrighted February 5, 1976. Previously registered for copyright as an unpublished song March 21, 1974. Recorded by Frank Sinatra (Reprise).

It's like singing to empty tables
Or a gallery that's full of ghosts,
Or like giving a great big party
Where nobody shows but the host.

That's what it's been like, baby;
That's what it's been like, all right—
Without you around to applaud me,
Ev'ry night is like closing night.

And I'm doing the same old numbers,
Yes, and I'm telling the same stale jokes;
But there's nothing out front but memories
And a lot of transparent folks.

Please call for a reservation
Our favorite spot for two,
'Cause I'm singing to empty tables
Without you,
Without you,
Without you.

_____

* *Alternative ending:*
    So you sing your song,
    I'll sing my song;
    We may even share a touch
    Of auld lang syne.
    Then you go your way
    Through your golden doorway,
    And wish me luck as I go mine.

THAT'S MANCINI

Music by Harry Warren ("That's Amore"). In early 1974 Ginny Mancini was planning a party to celebrate her husband's fiftieth birthday, on April 16, and asked Mercer to write some parody lyrics for the occasion. Unable to attend because he was in London with composer André Previn preparing their show *The Good Companions* for rehearsal (it opened later that year), Mercer obliged by penning special lyrics to "That's Amore" (original lyrics by Jack Brooks), the hit tune first sung by Dean Martin in the Martin and Lewis film *The Caddy* in 1953 and closely identified with Martin ever since.

If you're hearing a band
Full of wops on the stand,
That's Mancini!
There's Giuseppe and Dom,
Giovanni and Mama
Cabrini!
If you're throwing a ball
For Eye-talians, that's all,
Call the man in—
You will find when you pay the bills
You have had the Beverly Hills
Lester Lanin!
He'll play on until eight
If you give him a plate
Of linguini
Like Don Costa
He'll take josta big bowl of pasta fagiol'
For a score wall to wall
Call the Zachary ALL Toscanini . . .
S'cusa me,
Who'sa he?
Anybody can see
That's Mancini!

If he's laughing like Frank
All the way to the bank,
That's Mancini!
Though he's too shy to sing
Until after a single
Martini!
Talking back on the mike
Pianissimo-like. A capella,
He's-a yell "Wha' da fuckin' hell!
"Wha' you learn in school,
Some fongool
Tarantella?"
He's-a scream and let fly
With a big pizza pie
At the drummer.
He's-a hire each man
With an offer they cannot refuse!
Then he says, "Now you play

Or we just gonna stay here all summer!"
That's our pal
And our friend
And our Godfather . . . Henry Mancini!

Victor Herbert, when small,
He's composing it all
On the cello;
Hank is starting in drab
Little movies for Abbott, Costello.
He's begin to get rich
By arranging, like Mitch,
For Glenn Miller,
Where his flute has a funny tone
Rather like a flat valve trombone
By Godzilla.
On the stage he's-a strike
Many poses just like
Mussolini,
'Cause up there he's-a name,
But he can't do the same
Thing at home!
There, he has to ask Monica,
Chris and Felicia
And Geeny!
S'cusa me,
Who's-a she?
She's our godmother, Geeny Mancini!

Happy birthday, dear Hank—
Save your money and bank spaghettini!
May we be ninety-three
And be dancing to Lawrence Mancini!

LITTLE INGÉNUE

Music by Jimmy Rowles. Registered for copyright as an
unpublished song December 20, 1974.

Little ingénue,
They're applauding you
For the way you make your entrance at the proper
    cue.
As you turn and pose
In your pretty clothes,
The people seem to know you're a star.
Little ingénue,
I'm applauding you,
Quite impressed with ev'ry gesture you're about to
    do.
Your dramatic flair
And your savoir-faire
Confirm the super-siren you are.
Has that talent scout
Never come about?
Did that newspaper contest leave your picture out?
Are you still longing for that chance at fame?
Or will you let the preacher change your name?
Little ingénue,
There are fellows who
Would be proud to play a leading role supporting
    you.
Either life you choose,
Promise Daddy he will never lose
His little ingénue!

THE GOOD COMPANIONS | 1974
and Other Songs with André Previn

THE GOOD COMPANIONS (1974)

Tryout: Palace Theatre, Manchester, England, June 7–22, 1974. London run: Her Majesty's Theatre; opened July 11, 1974; 252 performances. Music by André Previn. Lyrics by Johnny Mercer. Produced under the management of Bernard Delfont, Richard Mills, and Richard Pilbrow. Book by Ronald Harwood, based on J. B. Priestley's novel *The Good Companions*. Directed by Braham Murray. Choreography by Jonathan Taylor. Designed by Malcolm Pride. Orchestrations by Herbert W. Spencer and Angela Morley. Orchestra directed by Denys Rawson. Musical supervision by Marcus Dods. Cast included John Mills (Jess Oakroyd), Judi Dench (Miss Trant), Christopher Gable (Inigo Jollifant), Marti Webb (Susie Dean; the part was played on tour by Celia Bannerman), Ray C. Davis (Jerry Jerningham), Hope Jackman (Mrs. Joe Brundit), Malcolm Rennie (Morton Mitcham), Roy Sampson (Jimmy Nunn), Jeannie Harris (Elsie Longstaff), Bernard Martin (Mr. Joe Brundit), Ann Way (Miss Thong), and Richard Denning (Ted and Felton).

In 1969 a conversation began between Mercer and composer/conductor André Previn about the possibility of writing a show together. When they were looking at likely subjects, Mercer suggested *Little Women* and wrote to Previn: "You may think this is a crazy idea . . . but I want to do it before somebody else fucks it up."

As an alternative Previn suggested J. B. Priestley's *The Good Companions*, to which Mercer replied: "I can't believe you really said that. When I was a young man that was my single favorite book of the twentieth century. I would much rather do *The Good Companions*. Let's do it."

So they did. Mercer bought a two-year option on the rights for $2,000, and as soon as he went to work, he felt that he had so absorbed the spirit of the book that "lyrics kept bursting out of me."

His colleagues were to experience that old Mercer professional black magic.

Previn recalled: "Johnny was mind-boggling, the facility and the depth of his writing. I would send tapes to his flat near Grosvenor Square, and he would send me things and then we'd meet . . . I would give him a tune and he would sit and have the lyric finished in half an hour. Then he would polish it for days and days, but basically it was done . . . 'Ta, Luv' was done in about ten minutes."

When the number "Camaraderie" was added in rehearsal for the London opening, Ronald Harwood said, he "went off into the gentlemen's lavatory at Her Majesty's, scribbled something, and came back with a pretty well complete lyric. He must have been gone about twenty minutes. But I think he must have been thinking about it because it was too terrific to do it just like that. But that was the impression he gave—that he just thought of it."

The London critics were divided. The *Times* concluded: "Competence is not lacking—only dramatic vitality," whereas the *Financial Times* critic "came out glowing all over with sentimental pleasure." The *Sunday Times* felt that "Mercer's lyrics have, as you would expect, zip and dexterity. He manages English English at all levels well, and the rhymes chime away like bells."

"The Good Companions," a concert party touring England in the early 1930s:

Act I

In which a touring concert party named "The Dinky-Doos," stranded in Rawsley, a midland town, are joined by Mr. Jess Oakroyd from Bruddersford, Miss Elizabeth Trant from Hitherton-on-the-Wole, Mr. Inigo Jollifant from East Anglia, and all become "Good Companions."

Act II

In which the "Good Companions" go on tour, encounter setbacks by the seaside, survive to play the Sandybay Pavilion where they have a mixed reception on Susie Dean's birthday benefit, Mr. Jollifant visits Wonderland, Miss Trant is reunited with an old friend, and Mr. Oakroyd sets off again.

Alternative wordings in brackets or footnotes are taken from Mercer's demo tape of songs from the show but do not appear in the show's vocal score. The demo is an undated audition tape for the show.

Before the London opening, "Camaraderie" had replaced the original opening song ("Extravaganza!"), and another song, "Little Lost Dream," had also been dropped. Mercer's own files indicate several other numbers written with the show in mind but, in the event, never used: "Balls," "A Wanted Man," "The Fair Sex," "Fate Moves in Mysterious Ways," "My Alter Ego and Me," and "Carnival Stall Song."

GOODBYE

Introduced by John Mills (Jess Oakroyd), Judi Dench (Miss Trant), Christopher Gable (Inigo Jollifant), Marti Webb (Susie Dean), Ray C. Davis (Jerry Jerningham), Hope Jackman (Mrs. Joe Brundit), Malcolm Rennie (Morton Mitcham), Roy Sampson (Jimmy Nunn), Jeannie Harris (Elsie Longstaff), Bernard Martin (Mr. Joe Brundit), and Ann Way (Miss Thong), and ensemble, and reprised by the company.

G'bye, g'bye,
We 'ate to say g'bye.
We like it 'ere a lot, as you can see.
The old g'bye, the new g'bye,
Pip-pip and toodle-oo g'bye,
And if you parley-voo g'bye,
"Arriverdercheree!"
It's been a lot of fun,
We've 'ad a week o' smiles,
A beautiful engagement 'ere in Rawsley British Isles!
So off we go to tour our little show.
And though it brings a teardrop to our eye,
We leave you with a hundredfold
Good wishes and a jolly old
Goodbye,
Goodbye,
Goodbye!

CAMARADERIE

Published. Copyrighted September 1, 1974. Introduced and recorded by Ray C. Davis (Jerry), Marti Webb (Susie), Bernard Martin (Joe), Hope Jackman (Mrs. Joe), Roy Sampson (Nunn), Jeannie Harris (Elsie), and ensemble (EMI-UK, Stet-USA).

JERRY &
SUSIE: We 'aven't got a threepenny piece
To buy a cup of tea,
But we've got—
OTHERS: They've got—
ALL: Camaraderie!
PRINCIPALS: Our act is in a little valise
That hasn't got a key,
But we've got
OTHERS: They've got—
JERRY &
SUSIE: Camaraderie!
Fat or thin,
Doesn't matter what shape we're
in—
If you give us an aspirin,
We'll do a little dance!
Thin or fat,
Anybody can pass around the hat
And practice high finance!
MR. &
MRS. JOE: We haven't got the bonny physiques
We had at twenty-three,
But we've got
Camaraderie!
The roses people see in our cheeks
Aren't what they used to be—

PRINCIPALS: But we've got—
We've got—
Camaraderie!
If we fail to sufficiently rag the scale
Or if Salomé's veil fails to save the
day,
Then they get in a coloratura-bass
duet—
MRS. JOE: "The Road to Mandalay"!
MR. JOE: By the old Molmain Pagoda!
BOTH: By the old Molmain Pagoda!
BOTH: We haven't got the uppity jokes for
high society,
But we've got—
PRINCIPALS: We've got—
JERRY &
SUSIE: Camaraderie!
You're looking at a couple of blokes
Whose secret seems to be
Compatibility!
Give us these,
Bread and cheese,
Stars above,
Lots of love,
Our future is as plain as A-B-C—
It's A-B-C-A-M-A-R-A-D-E-R-I-E—
And that spells—
ALL: That spells—
JERRY &
SUSIE: With bells—
Camaraderie!
MR. &
MRS. JOE: We may not have the patter and song
In perfect harmony,
But we've got—
PRINCIPALS: We've got—
MR. &
MRS. JOE: Camaraderie!
And that'll keep us rolling along
When people come to see
Old buskers such as we!
Baggy pants,
Floppy shoes,
But do we
Sing the blues?
Nosiree!
It's plain as A-B-C—
It's A-B-C-A-M-A-R-A-D-E-R-I-E—
And that spells—
With bells—
Camaraderie!
NUNN &
ELSIE: The circus has a covey of clowns,
A huge menagerie,
And they've got
Camaraderie!
They're stuck in indiscriminate
towns

The very same as we,
But they've got
Camaraderie!
Here they come,
Para-diddle-dee,
Yum-de-dum—
See the elephant beat the drum
To scare the kangaroo!
Watch 'em stare
At the comical Russian dancing bear,
Who somersaults on cue!
The thing about theatrical folk
That people come to see
Is constant,
ALL: Instant
NUNN &
ELSIE: Camaraderie!
We may not have the price of a
smoke,
But let us hear a D
On our calliope—
CHORUS: Lions roar,
Monkeys squeal,
Tigers growl
At the seal!
What they hear is plain as A-B-C—
NUNN &
ELSIE: It's A-B-C-A-M-A-R-A-D-E-R-I-E—
And that spells—
With bells—
Camaraderie!

BRUDDERSFORD SEQUENCE, including ALL MUCKED UP and THE POOLS and AYE, LAD.

All Mucked Up

Part one of the Bruddersford sequence. Introduced and recorded by John Mills (Jess) and male chorus (EMI-UK, Stet-USA).

JESS &
MALE CHORUS: All mucked up,
It's all mucked up.
The more you live,
The more you learn
It's all mucked up.
It takes a lot of bloody skill
T'play like bloody Jane and Jill,
'N'wind up nil t'bloody nil—
It's all mucked up!
JESS: A bit cheesed off,
You're a bit cheesed off.
I reckon like as not that you're a
lot cheesed off.
But I am wise enough to say
Tomorrow is another day,
And anyway it doesn't pay
To be cheesed off!
[spoken] Definitely not! Just look
at it this way . . .

The Pools

Part two of the Bruddersford sequence. Introduced and recorded by John Mills (Jess) and male chorus. Reprised late in the first act by Mills (EMI-UK, Stet-USA).

One of these days the wheel'll spin
And make us each a mandarin,
'Cos one of these days we're gonna win the pools!
One of these days a bulletin
Will say someone has stuck a pin
And landed on a number in the pools!

One of these days we're gonna be
As filthy rich as royalty,
As high as the nobility it rules!
Aye, one of these mornings I expect
I'll thank the Lord and genuflect,
Then call a cab and go collect the football pools!

One of these days I'll live, no doubt,
On nightingale wings and pickled trout,
That fortunate day I've sorted out the pools!

Maybe I'll call Menuhin in,
And get 'im to play 'is violin,
That ever-so-lucky day I win the pools!

One of these evenings diamond pins
Will sparkle beneath my missus' chins.
She'll dawdle about in crinolines and tulles!

Guineas'll flow a golden flood
For everyone here in Bruddersford
The minute I've gone and won the bloody football
pools!

Reprise: The Pools

JESS: Son of a double-barreled gun,
Just look what Lady Luck has done!
I feel like a bloke who's gone and won the
pools!
Out of the Easter Sunday blue
Old Jess has become a Dinky-Doo,

A travelin' man—owes it to his tools!
Breakfast in bed at nine or two,
Then order the whole thing up again—
The vicar'd say it's all against the rules.
None o' the lads at Mucky Duck
Would ever believe my bit o' luck—
It's better than even having struck
The football pools!

Aye, Lad

Part three of the Bruddersford sequence. Introduced and recorded by John Mills (Jess), Laurie Webb (Sam), and Richard Denning (Ted) (EMI-UK, Stet-USA).

JESS,
SAM & TED: I tried to 'elp a chap today
Who suddenly got cross—
'E runs off to t' foreman to complain.
The foreman calls the manager,
'Oo takes me to the boss,
'Oo paid me off and left me in the
rain!
SAM & TED: So twenty years of workin' 'ard
Is simply gone for nowt?
JESS: I'm sacked,
I'm on the dole—
A lot to take!
It makes a fellow wonder
What in 'ell it's all about—
Aye, lad,
Pie in the sky, lad,
Aye, lad, and no mistake!

Demo version

Mercer's demo tape contains a version that combines "All Mucked Up" and "Aye, Lad."

Was that a bloody soccer match we had ourselves
today?
Aye, lad—and no mistake!
A bunch of ruddy lasses knowing nowt about
t'play—
Aye, lad, they took the cake!
They finally play a game at home we wait two
weeks to see;
We had to scrimp and save to foot the bill.
They must have had a strategy as canny as can be
To have it wind up nil to bloody nil!
The one thing you can count on
Is you cannot count on life—
It never gives the working bloke a break.
Oh, I don't know,
It takes us home to greet a nagging wife—
Aye, lad,

Pie in the sky, lad,
Aye, lad,
And no mistake—
It's all mucked up,
It's all mucked up!
The more you live,
The more you learn
It's all mucked up!
When there are two or three about
To kick society about,
The one thing they agree about—
It's all mucked up!

Bad enough to have a wife who nags me night and
day.
Aye, lad—and no mistake!
But then I have a son who thinks I'm only in the
way—
Aye, lad, tha' needs a break!
A break?
I tried to help a chap today
Who suddenly got cross—
'E runs off to the foreman to complain.
The foreman calls the manager,
'Oo takes me to the boss,
'Oo pays me off and leaves me in the rain!
So twenty years of workin' 'ard
Is simply gone for nowt!
I'm sacked,
I'm on the dole,
I'm busted flat.
It makes a fellow wonder
What in 'ell it's all about—
Aye, lad,
Tha needn't sigh, lad—
Why, lad,
We'll pass the hat!
Here, lad,
Another beer, lad—
Aye, lad,
I'll drink to that!
Still—
It's all mucked up,
It's all mucked up!
The clergy and the Communists,
They're all mucked up!
The leader of our union,
He advocates the looney 'un.
We organized communion—
It's all mucked up . . . !

[*Mercer on track says, "Then they trail off."*]

FOOTLOOSE SEQUENCE, including THE GREAT NORTH ROAD and FANCY FREE and POOR SCHOOLMASTERS and ON MY WAY

Mercer's files contain what appear to be introductory verses to the first three songs in the Footloose Sequence. Recorded in variant form by John Mills (Jess), Judi Dench (Miss Trant), and Christopher Gable (Inigo) (EMI-UK, Stet-USA).

Miss Trant verse

When you are Cotswold born and bred
And thirty-five and still unwed,
And no one shares your board and bed,
You long for something else instead.
You long to break the old routine
Of having tea at four-fifteen.
The slightest glimpse of other things
Can make the heart take wings!

Jess Oakroyd verse

Yer meet a lad from Bruddersford
'Oose football team 'as been outscored.
Wi' not t' do an' na reward
Yer see a lad oo's bloody bored.
If 'e can change t' old routine
O' gettin' 'ome at four-fifteen,
'E's like an actor openin' night,
A mole 'oo sees t' light!

Inigo Jollifant verse

When you have had a run of jobs
Of teaching little British snobs,
But dream of writing gobs and gobs
Of books that sell to cheering mobs,
You thank whatever gods there be
That see your plight and set you free—
The very thought of greener scenes,
Your little world careens!

The Great North Road

Part one of the Footloose Sequence. Introduced by John Mills (Jess).

JESS: When you've been 'ad and the world seems
agin' you,

When good old Bruddersford looks grimy
    and grey—
That's when a lad loses heart t' continue;
That's when a fellow feels like runnin' away.

Job gone and wife mad and son acting barmy,
Even my good old salt is bitter to taste.
If I were young, I'd be off to t'army—
Now's when a fellow feels his life is a waste.

Keep on talkin'—
I'll be off walkin'
On t' Great North Road.
Just sit there naggin'
I'll pack my bag and be gone for good.
Where traffic's zoomin',
Big lorries boomin',
I'm summat,
I'm human!
Head high, lad,
Aye, lad,
Nobbut'll say you're a nobbut, I'll be blowed—
You're off on t' Great North Road!

Fancy Free

Part two of the Footloose Sequence. Introduced by Judi
Dench (Miss Trant).

MISS TRANT: When you've been left an estate
    that's a bother,
    Home loses even its Cotswoldian
    charm.
    Deeply bereft of a bedridden father,
    Oh, how you long to be in
    somebody's arms!
    Nagged by a house and the chores
    of a household,
    Chained to a drab routine and feeling
    her age,
    Meek as a mouse who is properly
    mouseholed,
    Think what it means to be let out of
    your cage!
    Not quite a spinster, nor much of a
    mixer,
    More like a butterfly with wings yet
    unfurled,
    I feel like Alice who drank the elixir—
    All of a sudden it's a storybook world!
    Fancy being finally footloose and
    fancy free!

    Just fancy seeing stodgy old
    nobody—fancy me!
    I'm floating, flying, laughing, and
    crying,

And if I'm not dying,
I'm living, giving some great adventure
A chance to dance with me!
At last I'm fancy free!

Poor Schoolmasters

Part three of the Footloose Sequence. Music for the first
three lines of the lyric is the same as the music to "Good
Companions." Music for the last six lines of the lyric is
the same as the music to "Slippin' Around the Corner."
Introduced by Christopher Gable (Inigo).

INIGO: Poor schoolmasters stick together,
    Like old donkeys on a tether,
    Eating steaks as tough as leather, once a
    week.

    Slippin' around the corner to the Tarvin
    flat
    To give her bum a pat—
    Oh, wouldn't she love that!
    Slippin' around the corner for an
    interlude
    Of romping in the nude,
    And if she's good, I'll show her my
    ribcage . . .

On My Way

Part four of the Footloose Sequence. Introduced by
Christopher Gable (Inigo), Judi Dench (Miss Trant),
and John Mills (Jess).

INIGO: "In partes tres omnes Gallia est
    divisa"—
    I have the little fellows bleating like
    sheep.
    When did da Vinci complete the
    Mona Lisa?*
    I'm sure that I could say it all in my
    sleep!
    Chaps, do your Greek and your Latin
    declensions.
    Write twenty times "amo," "amas,"
    and "amat."
    There, comb your hair, straighten
    up, pay attention—
    Hail and farewell, oh, professorial lot!

    Right this minute,
    Free as a linnet,
    I'm on my way,
    So, save your laughter
    Heaven looks after

---

* *Alternate line:*
    Who was the woman they called Mona Lisa?

All drunks, they say.
We falter, fumble, stagger, and stumble,
But just as we tumble,
She smiles benignly
And quite divinely
Steps in to save the day—
At last I'm on my way!
MISS TRANT: Fancy being finally footloose and
    fancy free!
INIGO: Forgive my laughter,
    Heaven looks after
    All rogues like me.
MISS TRANT: Unwashed, unwed, un-
INIGO: -kempt and unbedded—
JESS: Lord knows where I'm headed!
ALL THREE: Broad highway faring,
    Not even caring
    Tomorrow where I'll be.
MISS TRANT: By heavens!
INIGO: By Jove!
JESS: By gum!
ALL THREE: At last I'm free!

(MAY I HAVE THE) PLEASURE OF YOUR COMPANY

Published. Copyrighted under the title "The Pleasure
of Your Company" July 9, 1974. Introduced by Malcolm
Rennie (Mitcham) and Christopher Gable (Inigo).
Reprised by them with Judi Dench (Miss Trant), John
Mills (Jess), and ensemble, and later reprised by Gable
and company. Recorded by Malcolm Rennie (Mitcham)
and Christopher Gable (Inigo) (EMI-UK, Stet-USA).

MITCHAM: May I have the pleasure of your
    company
    On this crazy-quilt adventure we call
    life?
    If I may have the pleasure of your
    company,
    I'll guide you through the pitfalls like a
    wife.
    Old boy, old bean, by that I mean
    You have a pal on whom to lean—
    A buddy in your hour of need,
    A friend indeed.
    So may I have the pleasure of your
    company
    To tag along wherever fate may lead?
INIGO: May I have the pleasure of your
    company,
    As we trip the light fantastic we call life?

If I may have the pleasure of your
    company,
I'll be a Robbie Burns to your Will
    Fyffe!
Old sport, old bean, by that I mean
Let's find a bar on which to lean,
Becoming at increasing speed
Fast friends indeed!

BOTH: So let us share the pleasure of our
    company
And tag along wherever fate may lead!

Reprise

MITCHAM: Will you bestow the pleasure of your
    company
Upon two weary travelers in distress?

INIGO: May we share the pleasure of your
    company
To discover what this journey has in
    store?

MISS TRANT: [*to* JESS] Can we afford the pleasure of
    their company?

JESS: Well, room for one means room for
    three or four.

MISS TRANT: I cannot guarantee the car,
But, judging how it's been so far,
It's safe to say we may proceed at any
    speed!

ALL FOUR: So let us share the pleasure of your
    company
To Rawsley or wherever fate may lead!

MISS TRANT: May I have the pleasure of your
    company
As we journey where the gods may
    ascertain?
If I can have the pleasure of your
    company,
We'll celebrate the future with
    Champagne!
By that I mean I'm rather keen
To sample Rawsley's best cuisine,
Then gallop on our trusty steed
To Runnymede!

ALL: So may we have the pleasure of your
    company
To tag along wherever fate may lead?

Mercer/Crosby duet version

Mercer's demo tape also includes a fully orchestrated adapted version performed by Mercer and Bing Crosby. Record producer Ken Barnes explained how it came about. He was recording an album for United Artists with Crosby (*That's What Life Is All About*) and played him the score of *The Good Companions*. Crosby liked "Pleasure" in particular but pointed out that it was a duet. Who should be the "other half"? Barnes imme-

diately suggested Mercer, with whom he had recently worked. The recording was made in Mercer's own studio in Burbank in October 1974 with a rhythm section, and the orchestral backing was added later in London. It was to be Mercer's last recording session.

When asked what he wanted for a fee, Mercer thought for a moment, then said: "You can pay me the same as I got for my first professional singing engagement—twenty dollars." When the record was released commercially, it sold 250,000 units, so he ended up with a little more than that!

CROSBY: May I have the pleasure of your
    company—

MERCER: [*spoken*] Sure! Where we goin'?

CROSBY: As we trip the light fantastic we call life?

MERCER: If I can have the pleasure of your
    company,
I'll be a Robbie Burns to your Will
    Fyffe.

CROSBY: [*spoken*] I want to be Harry Lauder.

MERCER: You got it.

CROSBY: [*sung*] Old boy, old bean, by which I
    mean
We'll find a bar on which to lean.

MERCER: Becoming at increasing speed
Fast friends indeed.

CROSBY: [*spoken*] Permanent!
[*sung*] So may I have the pleasure of
    your company

BOTH: To tag along wherever fate may lead?

MERCER: May I have the pleasure of your
    company.

CROSBY: [*spoken*] I'm with you all the way.

MERCER: [*sung*] On this crazy-quilt adventure we
    call life?

CROSBY: If we can have the pleasure of their
    company,
We'll treat the bonny lassies like a wife.

MERCER: [*spoken*] The little darlin's!
[*sung*] Old boy, old bean, by which I
    mean
You have a pal on whom to lean.

CROSBY: A buddy in your hour of need,
A friend indeed.

BOTH: So, may I have the pleasure of your
    company
To tag along wherever fate may lead?

CROSBY: May I have the pleasure of your
    company
On this crazy misadventure we call life?

MERCER: [*spoken*] Oh, don't call it that, Bing!
[*sung*] If I can have the pleasure of your
    company,
I'll still be Robbie Burns to your Will
    Fyffe.

CROSBY: Old boy, old bean, by that you mean

We'll find a bar on which to lean,

MERCER: Becoming at increasing speed
Old drunks indeed.

CROSBY: So may I have the pleasure of your
    company

BOTH: To tag along wherever fate may lead,
To tag along wherever fate may lead!

While the Scots poet Robert Burns (1759–1796) needs no further explanation, Will Fyffe (1885–1947) was a popular Scots music hall entertainer. Sir Harry Lauder (1870–1950) was another and writer of "Roamin' in the Gloamin.' "

STAGE STRUCK

Published. Copyrighted October 20, 1975. Introduced and recorded by Marti Webb (Susie) (EMI-UK, Stet-USA).

In my crib I was stage struck;
Behind a bib I was stage struck.
The very first time I spoke,
Unrehearsed I told a funny joke!

Most adolescents of teen age
Go daft about the machine age,
But never me—
Variety's toy,
On one knee,
"Sonny Boy"*
School was an error,
A holy terror,
But I loved the pantomimes!
Cast as a fairy,
All pink and airy,
I quoted the Bard
Or palmed a card
As I segued to "Tipperary."
Had no sister or brother
But, boy, did I have a mother!
She dressed me up, calmed me down,
Hauled me all over town.
There's not a manager in the land
She hadn't planned to see!
Instantaneous tears of sorrow,
Extemporaneous glee!
Phone available stage-struck me!

I was born with a mission,
A mission just to audition.

* *Alternate:*
  "Danny Boy"

A draughty hall,
Barren room—
All they meant to me was
"Love in Bloom"!
Monday I would play Duse,
On Tuesday, John Philip Sousa.
When we said grace at our meals,
We all meant Gracie Fields!
Armed with a trumpet,
A toasted crumpet,
I made every casting call.
Sitting and waiting,
Gesticulating
With my mandolin, I'd Charleston in
For ten minutes of imitating!

When in heaven I wake up
I bet I wake up in makeup,
Emotions high for the scene,
Doing my tap routine.
And as the angels play *Lohengrin*,
If it is in my key,
Stand aside,
For I'm starry-eyed
And as petrified as can be.
[*shouts*] Hey, Saint Peter,
It's stage-struck me!

THE DANCE OF LIFE

Published. Copyrighted July 9, 1974. Introduced and recorded by Judi Dench (Miss Trant) (EMI-UK, Stet-USA). Judi Dench remembers the director had little faith in the song and advised her: "Sing it and get off fast—in case they don't applaud."

The Dance of Life begins;
A thousand violins
Play softly in our ears
The music of the spheres.

The Dance of Life says "Now"—
Come, hold me in the shadows;
We'll find a way somehow
To save the wasted years.

Our crystal ball on high
Goes spinning through the sky;
Each twinkling spot of light uncovers
Lonely strangers, laughing lovers.

Let fortune call the tune,*

---

* *Alternate line from demo tape:*
    Immortal or immune,

We have our love to gamble on,
Turn on our friend the moon,
Come dance with me,
Come dance with me,
Our music ends too soon!

GOOD COMPANIONS

Published. Copyrighted August 28, 1974. Introduced and recorded by Christopher Gable (Inigo), Malcolm Rennie (Mitcham), and company, and reprised by the company as part of the act 2 finale (EMI-UK, Stet-USA).

INIGO: When voyagers are cast away on
    strange exotic lands,
        Much precious time is passed away in
        wringing of the hands.
        Far better to fall in with one another,
        Find something else to eat besides
        each other!
MITCHAM: Kind fate sees fit to stake us all to
    brandy and cigars,
        The vehicles to take us all towards the
        distant stars.
INIGO: Good companions stick together,
        Sunny skies or stormy weather,
        Birdies of uncommon feather,
        Come what may.
MITCHAM: Even when the raindrops tumble,
        Good companions never grumble.
        "Them's the breaks,"
        As William [Mister] Shakespeare used
        to say.
INIGO: Through the highways
        And the byways
        Of our native land,
        Playing both the big time
        And the one-night stand,
        Hand in hand.
BOTH: Good companions, that's the ticket—
        This old life's a game of cricket;
        Sitting duck or sticky wicket,
        Work or play,
        We're Good Companions all
        And we are on our way!

Mercer/Crosby duet version

The demo tape also contains an orchestrated version for Crosby and Mercer, which incorporates adapted elements of "And Points Beyond."

MERCER: When voyagers are cast away on strange
    exotic lands,
        Much precious time is passed away in
        wringing of the hands.
CROSBY: Far better to fall in with one another.
MERCER: Find something else to eat besides each
        other.
CROSBY: Kind fate sees fit to stake us all to
        brandy and cigars,
        The vehicle to take us all towards the
        distant stars.
MERCER: [*spoken*] Hear! Hear!
BOTH: Good companions stick together,
        Sunny skies or stormy weather,
        Birdies of uncommon feather,
        Come what may.
MERCER: Even when the raindrops tumble,
        Good companions never grumble,
        "Them's the breaks,"
        As Willie Shakespeare used to say.
CROSBY: [*spoken*] Oh yes, he's widely quoted.
MERCER: [*spoken*] He said it all!
CROSBY: [*sung*] Through the highways
        And the byways
        Of our native land,
        Playing both the big time
        And the one-night stand,
        Hand in hand.
MERCER: Good companions, that's the ticket,
        Sitting duck or sticky wicket
CROSBY: This old life's a game of cricket
BOTH: Each must play,
        For we're the Good Companions
        And we're on our way.
CROSBY: [*to the tune of "And Points Beyond"*]
        Kankakee.
MERCER: And Tennessee.
CROSBY: To Omaha
        And Wichita,
        We'll travel through the good old USA.
MERCER: [*spoken*] Like Lewis and Clark!
MERCER: [*sung*] Washington.
CROSBY: And Oregon.
MERCER: Saskatoon, Saskatchewan.
CROSBY: And back to San Francisco by the
        bay.
        Off to old Bavaria
        Aboard the *Berengaria*.
MERCER: We'll skitter our way across the pond.
CROSBY: Then the Wembley Stadium.
MERCER: Off to the Palladium
BOTH: And points beyond.
        This old life's a game of cricket
        Each must play,
        For we're the Good Companions
        And we're on our way,
        On our way.

SLIPPIN' AROUND THE CORNER

Published. Copyrighted August 28, 1974. Introduced and recorded by Ray C. Davis (Jerry) (EMI-UK, Stet-USA). This is the opening of act 2.

Slippin' around the corner to the Rose and Crown,
The very best in Town,
The bloomin' Rose and Crown,
Slippin' around the corner for an 'alf and 'alf,
We'll have ourselves a laugh,
And if you care to tickle me fancy,
Tickle me fancy while we're in the vestibule,
A jolly custom, you'll agree!
Then 'arf a mo,
And in we go,
'Allo, 'allo,
Who's 'ere we know?
Plan your holiday, dearie,
Slippin' around the corner with me!

Good old Harry
There at the end,
He's brought a friend.
Les and Larry,
Bernie and Lew,
Havin' a few!
Should I tarry
Over me head in the foam?
Rescue me, Guv,
Give me a shove!
Point me back 'ome!

Slippin' around the corner to the local pub,
A ruddy country club.
I mean the local pub.
Doin' the Jackie 'Orner with a bob or three,
We'll 'ave the treat on me,
So, if you have to squander me fortune,
Squander me fortune, dearie, with a royal flair,
As if the king were there to see.
Then 'arf a mo,
And off we go
On tippy-toe,
Vo-do-do-de-o,
Peel a bleedin' banana,
Slippin' around the corner.
Skippin' around the corner,
Nippin' around the corner,
Tippin' around the corner,
Whippin' around the corner,
Zippin' around the corner,
Slippin' around the corner with me!

A LITTLE TRAVELLING MUSIC

Published. Copyrighted August 28, 1974. Introduced and recorded by Malcolm Rennie (Mitcham), Christopher Gable (Inigo), Ray C. Davis (Jerry), Jeannie Harris (Elsie), and ensemble (EMI-UK, Stet-USA).

MITCHAM: A little travellin' music, Professor, if
you please—
Sca-ra-tat-tat-tat!
I left a farewell note [tickets] on the
dresser
And the keys are under the mat!
Our season is full from Brighton to
Hull;
We haven't got a lull that I recall.
A nice little bill, booked solid until
We lay 'em in the aisles at Royal Albert
Hall!
So with your kind indulgence,
Professor, on my knees!
A little high-class, low-down music
made for travellin', please!
The key of B-flat!
A little travellin' music, Professor, if
you please,
Sca-ra-tat-tat-tat!

INIGO: To photograph a real spiffy dresser, I'll
say "Cheese!"

ALL: I hope you got that!

JERRY: "A nice little turn, with talent to
burn,"
Is what the local *Morning Bugle*
says.

ELSIE: 'Sa matter of fact, a smasheroo act.
We wow 'em in the villages* and
provinces.

ALL: So agitate your tempo, Professor, and
let's breeze!
A little high-class, low-down music
made for travellin', please!
I'll go get my hat.

CHORUS: So with your kind indulgence,
Professor, on our knees—

MEN: A little high-class, low-down music
made for travellin', please!

ALL: A little travellin' music, Professor, if
you please.
Sca-rat-tat-tat.
We follow all attractions except
performing fleas!

---
* *Alternate:*
We wow 'em in the big towns . . .

They dance on our cat!

GIRLS: Whenever they need somebody to
lead
A *potpourri* of speed and expertise.

MEN: You're gazing upon a rare paragon
diminuendo.

ALL: On the drum, Professor, please!
We play for kings or primitive
aborigines!
A little high-class, low-down music
made for travellin', please!

1ST MAN: No time for a chat.
2ND MAN: We're off like a bat
1ST GIRL: To fortune and fat
2ND GIRL: You're looking right at
ALL: *Les Aristocrats
Éclat* and *Éclat*,
We tap in top hat,
A bargain at that,
Sca-rat-tat-tat!

1ST MAN: [*spoken*] Your patter is flat!
ALL: So agitate your tempo, Professor,
I taught the score to your predecessor.
A little high-class, low-down music
made for travellin', please!

BLACK WEEK MEDLEY

Introduced by Malcolm Rennie (Mitcham), Christopher Gable (Inigo), Judi Dench (Miss Trant), and John Mills (Jess).

MITCHAM: Sca-ra-tat-tat.
"Dear pal of mine, I'm here at the
seaside at my ease—
And plenty of that!
I'm here with a show—a little bit
slow,
But business ought to grow from
week to week,
The bookings are great, but as for
this date,
I hate to tell you, mate, we're really
up the creek—
They don't exactly queue up for
tickets on their knees!
Your old chum Morton Mitchum—
Answer with a bob or two, please!"
[*spoken*] We just ate the cat!

INIGO: "Greetings, Fauntley, no one needs
me;
But I'm free and fortune leads me,
And the golden fleece precedes me

MISS TRANT: [spoken] "Hilda, my dear, in reply to
  your letter,
  [sung] This week is awful,
  Eggs would fry in the street!
  [spoken] Bus'ness is slow, but it's
  bound to get better
  [sung] Give Hugh Macfarlane my
  regards, if you meet."
JESS: [spoken] "Mother dear, a glass of
  beer,
  A Woodbine and a match;
  A fourpenny-halfpenny walking
  stick
  To go to the football match,
  See old Grady score a goal—
  Knock old Fulham up the pole,
  Go it, the boys in blue!

  The ball was in the center;
  The ref, 'is whistle blew.
  Old Grady got excited
  And nearly shot it through!
  He passed it out to Austin,
  But Austin wouldn't do;
  He passed it back to Grady,
  And Grady shot it through!
  Goal!"

AND POINTS BEYOND

Published in a professional copy. No copyright informa-
tion. Introduced and recorded by John Mills (Jess),
Marti Webb (Susie), Malcolm Rennie (Mitcham),
Christopher Gable (Inigo), Ray C. Davis (Jerry), Judi
Dench (Miss Trant), Ann Way (Miss Thong), Hope Jack-
man (Mrs. Joe), and emsemble (EMI-UK, Stet-USA).

JESS: [spoken] Eh, but you are ungrateful,
  that's what you are . . . I mean,
  we're seein' England, week
  after week. Just think of all the
  places we've been to, and all
  the places we're goin' to!
  [sung] Manchester 'n' Chichester 'n'
  Colchester 'n' Winchester,
  Dorchester 'n' Rochester 'n'
  Leeds!
SUSIE: [spoken] Don't you adore it?
JESS: [sung] Birmingham 'n' Beckenham
  'n'
  Badlingham 'n' Buckingham
  'n'

Gillingham 'n' Thornaby-on-Tees!
SUSIE: [spoken] I'd love a cuppa!
MITCHAM: Tottenham 'n' Twickenham 'n'
  Nottingham 'n' Wokingham—
MISS TRANT: And others which refuse to
  correspond.
INIGO: Change trains for—
  Cheltenham 'n'
JESS: Chippenham 'n' Caterham 'n'
  Billingham
ALL: And points be . . . yond!
JESS: Aberdeen 'n' Gretna Green 'n'
  Abingdon 'n'
ELSIE: Hoddlesdon 'n'
  Wimbledon, for tennis with the
  swells!
JERRY: [spoken] Look at me blazer!
JESS: Atherton 'n' Ashington 'n'
  Bedlington 'n'
SUSIE: Bridlington 'n'
INIGO: Reynoldstown 'n' Royal Tunbridge
  Wells.
MRS. JOE: [spoken] A poor relation!
JESS: [sung] Annanford 'n'
MISS TRANT: Barrowford 'n'
JESS: Bruddersford 'n'
MITCHAM: Wallingford 'n' coves you wouldn't
  even take a blonde!
JESS: [spoken] Perhaps her mother!
  [sung] Paddington 'n' Tiverton—
  'n'
MISS TRANT: Warrington 'n' Wellington*
ALL: And points be . . . yond!
MITCHAM: Higham Cold 'n'
INIGO: Higham Hot 'n'
MRS. JOE: Higham Cross 'n'
JERRY: Higham not 'n'
MRS. JOE: Higham Green
MISS TRANT: And other Higham Gems
JESS: [spoken] Meet at the bus stop!
MISS THONG: Dewsbury 'n'
INIGO: Washbury 'n'
ELSIE: Shaftesbury 'n'
MITCHAM: Tewkesbury 'n'
MRS. JOE: Salisbury
MISS THONG: And Sudbury-on-Thames.
JESS: Don't touch me sunburn!
  Do I see a cuppa tea,
  Or, better still, a WC?
  How lovely it would be to have a—
MISS TRANT: Lull!
  Press on to—
MITCHAM: Tingley Town 'n'
MRS. JOE: Tingley Green 'n'
MISS THONG: Inishcog 'n'

---

* The cast album has "Hitherton."

JERRY: Inishkeen
ALL: And good old Hull!

  Oxfordshire 'n' Monmouthshire
  Montgomeryshire,
  Northamptonshire 'n'
  Cardiganshire to play another
  week.
JESS: [spoken] Held over!
ALL: Effingham 'n' Folkingham 'n'
  Tillingham 'n' Billingham 'n'
  Forth'ringham 'n' Frisby-on-the-
  Reek.
JESS: [spoken] Gor blimey!
ALL: Dancing Ledge 'n' Maidenhead 'n'
  Mincing Lane 'n' Dripping Well
  'n' Flinty Fell 'n' Fannyville
  It's right here on the map!
  We're off to Fairly Lodge 'n' Fairly
  Small
  And Fairly Hard to Find at All—
  And points be . . . yond!
JESS: [alone now] Winnipeg and Montreal
  and Calgary and Ottawa,
  Out Canada is where I long to be.*
  Ketchican, Saskatchewan,
  I'll find my way to hell and gone,
  Or any place where someone cares
  for me.
  If I could see my daughter there,
  I'd even walk on water there,
  And t'ocean would be nothing but a
  pond.
  I'd travel to Bombay and back
  Or to the Milky Way and back,
  And points be . . . yond.
  And points be . . . yond.

DARKEST BEFORE THE DAWN

Published. Copyrighted August 28, 1974. Introduced
and recorded by Judi Dench (Miss Trant) (EMI-UK,
Stet-USA).

I'm no philosopher, nor do I wish to be,
But when my little world has toppled in the sea,
Instead of moaning that all hope has taken wings
I find it helpful to remember certain things.

---

* Alternate lyric:
  That's where I ought to be.

One is a nurs'ry rhyme I've often put to use,
Along with other girls, including Mother Goose.

Alternative verse

I'm no philosopher, nor do I wish to be,
But when you've talked it out above a cup of tea
And realise your final hope has taken wings,
It may be helpful to remember certain things.
One is a saying I've been told all my life,
Along with other girls—including Aesop's wife . . .

REFRAIN

When things are too appalling,
It's worthwhile recalling
It's always darkest just before the [it's] dawn.
That scarecrow at your window,
Making faces in the night,*
Turns out to be a rose bush on your lawn!
This optimistic saying
Old maids keep crocheting
Makes quite a useful motto one can pawn.
So, when you've sunk so low
That even down resembles up,
The biscuit-tin itself is overdrawn,
Remember the prediction
Of the tea leaves in your cup:
It's always darkest just before the [it's] dawn.

SUSIE FOR EVERYBODY

Published. Copyrighted August 28, 1974. Introduced and recorded by Christopher Gable (Inigo) and Marti Webb (Susie) (EMI-UK, Stet-USA).

VERSE

INIGO: Strictly off the record, would you say after
         being together, Susie,
         Strictly off the record, would you say after
         thinking it through,
         Could you ever settle for a wee little
         house† in the heather, Susie?
         Would you ever settle for a beau who is
         steady and true?
         Though you clam up like a shellfish
         When the talk gets round to us,
         At the risk of sounding selfish,
         May I put it to you thus?

---

* *Or:* Making faces through the night
† *Alternate wording:*
     wee little home

REFRAIN

         Susie for me,
         Sweet as a cherry tree—
         Which is it gonna be?
SUSIE: Susie the screen vampire,
         Queen of the movie shows!
         Susie Sit-by-the-Fire,
         Knitting for those ten little toes?
INIGO: Don't be a spoilsport, Susie, don't be a
         tease,*
         Make some decision, please!
SUSIE: I'll have my fill of bright lights, dancing
         on air
INIGO: Those small suburbanite lights still will be
         there.
         Then, darling Susie for everybody,
         Promise you'll be
         Susie for only me!
SUSIE: We do have fun together,
         Lord knows you're sweet,
         And maybe someday
         When I'm swept off my feet,
         You'll see your Susie for everybody
         blossom into
SUSIE: Susie for only you!
INIGO: Susie for only me!

TA, LUV

Published. Copyrighted July 9, 1974. Introduced and recorded by John Mills (Jess). Reprised by Marti Webb (Susie) and Mills (EMI-UK, Stet-USA).

JESS: Ta, luv,
        Ta, luv,
        A great big hurrah, luv,†
        Ta, luv, for you.
        Carry on, luv,
        The stars are not gone, luv,
        Just out of view.
        Aye, lass,

---

* *Alternative lines from demo:*
   Give us an inkling, Susie, give us a clue,
   Which means the most to you?
   Go have your fill of bright lights, dancing on air,
   Those small suburban night lights still will be there.
   Then, darling Susie for everybody,
   Promise you'll be
   Susie for only me!
† *Alternate line from demo:*
   Go tell your mamà, luv,

        Cry, lass,
        Raindrops fill the sky, lass,
        Smile and the sun shines through.
        But ah, luv,
        Pshaw, luv,
        Snowy, blowy, or braw, luv,*
        Ta, luv, for you!

Draft version

Ta, luv,
Ta, luv,
How 'bout your old da, luv,
Dancing for you?
Oom-pah-pah, luv,
When I *entrechat*, luv,
You *pas de deux*!
One, two, three, lass,
Just you follow me, lass,
I'll bring you in on cue!
And then—tada, luv,
A great big hurrah, luv,
Ta, luv,
For you!

Another alternative

When I *pas de deux*, luv,
You *pas de* too!
First we *entrechat*, luv,
Then *pas de deux*!
Heel and toe, lass,
Down the stairs we go, lass,
Wait for the proper cue.
(Climb through the window, too!)
(Circle the table, too!)

Reprise

SUSIE: Ta, luv,
         Although it's tarra, luv,
         Keep smilin' through.
JESS: Aye. God bless, lass,
         Remember old Jess, lass,
         When you feel blue.
         I guarantee you,
         I'll show up to see you
         Here or in Timbuctoo!
         For aw, luv,
         Pshaw, luv,
         You're my favorite star, luv,
         Ta, luv, for you!

---

* *Alternate line from demo:*
   Be it blowy or braw, luv,

I'LL TELL THE WORLD

Published. Copyrighted August 28, 1974. Introduced and recorded by Ray C. Davis (Jerry), Marti Webb (Susie), Christopher Gable (Inigo), and ensemble (EMI-UK, Stet-USA).

I'll tell the world that it's a wonderful day,*
And what a wonderful day* I see!
I'll tell the world that things are going my way,
And that's exactly the way they turn out to be.
I get some grumbles and some gloomy remarks,
But I get beautiful smiles
From people happy as larks.
So I'll tell the world that I'm top of the world
And that is just what the world tells me!

STAGE DOOR JOHN

Introduced and recorded by Marti Webb (Susie) (EMI-UK, Stet-USA).

Stage Door John,
Stage Door John,
Won't you ever be here
With your topper and cane
And insane boutonniere?
Stage Door John,
Do come on,
Aren't you dreaming of me?
Are you lost,
Where on earth can you be?
If the hero doesn't come to save her,
He may find his leading lady gone.
Pretty soon comes the dawn,
Please get a move on,
Stage Door John!

LITTLE LOST DREAM

Introduced during the pre-London tryout by Christopher Gable (Inigo) but dropped before the London opening.

———————
* Mercer demo tape has "an elegant day."

VERSE

Wishy-washy—granted.
Namby-pamby—granted.
Searching for the rainbow's end?
Could be.
Lost my job—accepted.
Prospects poor—admitted.
What I want is unattainable,
Maybe even unexplainable;
I suppose I'll have to wait and see.

REFRAIN

I'm looking for a dream that got away,
Like a runaway sheep that I couldn't quite keep in
    sight.*
I'm sure I'll come across it any day,
For I know it's somewhere out there in the night.
She took me in her arms and kissed me sweetly,
Most indiscreetly,
And then it disappeared completely.
I only need the girl—I wonder who?—
To turn my little lost dream
Into a dream come true!

EXTRAVAGANZA!

Lyric dated June 1, 1973. The original opening number of the show. Intended for the ensemble. Replaced by "Camaraderie."

Stop all the presses and change all the plans—
Introducing the Extravaganza!
Here is the greatest attraction of man's,
Our sensational Extravaganza!
Girls fifty,
And all nifty,
Their toes tapping
And things flapping,
The sky lighting
And men fighting for Nubian slaves!
Rome burning,
The sea churning,
A fat hero
They call Nero.
The smoke curling
And all whirling
Around in their graves!
Titanic, thrilling,

———————
* Alternative line from demo tape:
    Like a little lost sheep you can never quite keep in
    sight.

And all for a shilling,
We bring you a real live bonanza!
Wild horses,
The czar's forces—
The true story
Of man's glory,
Bathsheba to Dan.
Extravaganza!!!

Paste up the billboards and publish the banns—
We're performing an Extravaganza!
Send for the Irish and call out the clans—
We will give them an Extravaganza!
Tap dancing
And group singing
And Swiss yodels
And bell ringing—
Trapeze flyers!
By toes swinging
Out over the crowd!
Fire eaters
And old mummies
And full bosoms
And bare tummies,
Just all sorts
Of good yum-yummies,
For crying out loud—
All in a vast panorama of drama
Contained in a gold-strike bonanza!
Battalions of wild stallions
With live lions and Hawaiians
In gigantic vans—
Extravaganza!

THE FAIR SEX

Intended for John Mills (Jess). Not used in show.

When everything has gone to pot,
We've always got
The fair sex!
A man's a fool t' curse his lot
While he's still got
The fair sex!
There's fat and tall
And wee and small;
There's sweethearts, wives, and mothers.
There's some who'd drive
You up the wall
And some what's more like brothers.
So when the world is all uphill
And when the score is nil t' nil
Or times you feel you canna even bear sex,

Besides a lager at t' bar
The two things we can count on are
The high cost of living
And the fair sex!

When nowt in life is goin' right,
There's one delight—
The fair sex!
Alone upon a wintry night
We still can fight
The fair sex!
Life ain't no bed of roses, mind,
But wouldn't it be horrid
T' stagger int' bed and find
A fullback or a forrard?
So anything you say about
They summat we could do wi'out
Or even consider them a spare sex,
Poor darlin's, they cannot be blamed
I give you in

[*Lyrics illegible.*]

CARNIVAL STALL SONG

Not used.

Lemme tell ya, Mister,
What I'm gonna do.
I'm gonna give you five
An' for the price o' two.

Hurry, hurry, hurry,
Get your fortunes told.
The knowledge in the stars
Cannot be bought or sold.

Go 'n' get your sister,
Tell 'er what you seen,
And say it can't be shown
In any magazine.

Hurry, hurry, hurry,
'Fore y' get too old.
The lines across the hand
Are worth their weight in gold.

These 'ere little dollies
Wi' the kewpie smiles
Is all imported stuff
Made in t' British Isles

Hurry, hurry, hurry,
Let 'er feel yer head.

She will reveal the past
An' who you're gonna wed.
Lemme tell ya, Mister,
You're a lucky man,

Things the ancient pyramids cannot disclose
Only Madame Sonia knows!

Y' better buy a dozen
While you can!

Over here . . . a prize in every letter,
Worth a bob or better,
Merely as an introductory gift.
That's 'ow the company advertises—
You get all the prizes,
We take all the risk.
I'm tellin' ya.

A WANTED MAN

Intended for John Mills (Jess). Lyric dated June 6, 1973.
Not used. No music is known to survive.

I never even stole a nap when I were on t' job;
The most I even borrowed was a comb.
But now they think that I am worth perhaps two
      hundred bob—
'Tis more than I were ever worth at home.
It goes t' show, a proper Boy Scout
Ain't good enough t' figure it out.
Once you incur the finger of doubt,
There's nowt 'ere but strife—
No hope t' be
All footloose and free
From naggin' wife—
You're labeled for life
A wanted man!

HAPPY ENDINGS

Composer unknown, but possibly André Previn. Lyric
dated June 6, 1973, the same date as "A Wanted Man,"
which was definitely intended for *The Good Companions*. No music is known to survive.

Happy endings,
I have learned,
Happy endings

Must all be earned.
The glummest situation
With care and application
Becomes a celebration
For all concerned.
Give your laughter—
If you do,
You'll live ever so happily after, too!
A truly happy ending,
There's no use pretending,
Makes everyone's dreams come true!

IN THE HANDS OF FATE

Composer unknown, but possibly André Previn. No
music is known to survive. Lyric dated June 6, 1973, the
same date as "A Wanted Man," which was definitely intended for *The Good Companions*.

We're in the hands of fate,
Both you and I,
Caught in the strands of fate
Until we die.
Each one a puppet
Pulled by a string—
When it says "Dance!" to us we dance
Or "Sing!" we sing!
Life took the longest time
To start the play;
It seemed the wrongest time
Until today.
But with the kindly hands of fate
Directly above,
Sweet skies of blue are here,
All dreams come true are here,
At long last you are here to love!

BALLS

Intended for John Mills (Jess) and Madeleine Newberry
(Mrs. Oakroyd). Not used in show. No music is known to
survive.

JESS: Despite the fact we played a draw—
          the score was nil and all—
       Suppose we had a world withaht t'
          ordinary ball.
       I mean the kind y' throw about
          and bounce against the wall,

The ordinary tuppenny-'apenny
   India rubber ball?
There wouldn't be no rugby, nor a
   single soccer match,
And boys and girls would 'ave t'
   do withaht a game o' catch.
All practicin' piano or crochetin'
   up a shawl,
If no one had invented up the
   regulation ball?
The saving grace of the 'uman race,
The backbone of the nation,
The favorite toy of each girl and
   boy,
The grown man's relaxation—
The boon of civilization!

Withaht a ball, no cricket and no
   tennis would be seen,
No barroom game o' skittles and
   no bowlin' on t' green,
We'd 'ave t' sit and sing "God
   Save Our Gracious King"—or
   "Queen"!
Or even worse, "I Dwelt in Marble
   'alls."
A real rich dowager loves to pour
   and stir;
What we ordinary blokes prefer is
   balls!

On Saturdays 'n' Sundays all us
   men 'd sit about
Just thinkin' up excuses for our
   wives to let us out
While whittlin' a stick or throwin'
   darts against the wall—
I mean wifout the ordinary penny-
   farthing ball.
A bunch o' noisy childer runnin'
   up and down t' hall
Wi' nowt t' do but muck about,
   get underfoot 'n' all,
Their little noses runnin' while
   their voices caterwaul—
I mean, withaht t' tuppenny,
   'apenny, India rubber ball.

The one bright spot
In a dreary lot
For all the working classes—
A holiday
And the perfect way
Of escaping from the masses
While sitting on our asses.

There wouldn't be no niblicks and
   no leather shoes wi' spikes,

No chains wi' roller bearin's on
   the scooters 'n' t' bikes.
Conveyor belts and factories
   would slow down to a crawl;
The banks would all go bust and
   big monopolies would fall.
No balls of steel for the auto
   wheel—
We'd use the rubber band still.
No Brighton trains and no
   aeroplanes;
The boats would be on land still,
The world would come to a
   standstill!

In paradise, there'll be a few
   surprises, I am sure,
Although, as yet I'm not in any
   rush to make the tour—
I mean, what fun is anything
   where everything is pure!
So 'til I get behind them pearly
   walls,
Let well-bred gentlemen 'ave their
   gun and spur,
What we ordinary blokes prefer is
   balls!

The world is gettin' better every
   hour, so I'm told,
And who knows in the future all
   the wonders we'll behold?
Someday they may send movies
   through the air and through
   the sky
And come into our sittin' rooms
   made for the naked eye.
But 'til we go to heaven with Saint
   Peter and Saint Paul,
And 'til I get to play me harp
   behind them pearly walls,
What we ordinary blokes prefer is
   balls!

Consider now t' huge related
   industries and all
Connected wi' t' rubber, gutta-
   percha, leather ball.
The banks would all go bust and
   big monopolies would fall
Withaht t' simple tuppenny-
   'apenny India rubber ball.
There wouldn't be no niblicks and
   no leather shoes wi' spikes
No chains wi' roller bearings and
   no noisy motor bikes;
Conveyor belts and factories
   would slow down to a crawl,

If summat hadn't come up with t'
   ordinary ball.
No gloves and bats,
No sporty hats—no uniforms
And no metal hats
To protect the driver's forehead.
When they got all flushed and
   florid.
No stadiums on Sundays full o'
   spectators 'n' players;
No newsreels of the matches
   done by Metro-Goldwyn-
   Mayer—
And that would mean no movies
   wi' the lovely Agnes Ayres.

I shudder whin I think about it
   all!
From King to commoner in his
   overalls,
Don't gi' me money or
   frankincense 'n' myrrh,
What we ordinary chaps prefer is
   balls!

MRS. OAKROYD: D'ja ever stop t' think of 'ow it
   mighta been and all,
If we lived in a world wi' out t'
   ordinary ball?
No dirty boots and sweaty shirts
   all piled up in the hall,
When they come home from
   playin' with an India rubber
   ball.
The mud is always clingin' to the
   golf clubs and the bats.
No sooner do you get the weekend
   grass stains off the mats,
The curtains and the pillow slips,
   the linen coverall
Are soiled beyond repairing by a
   penny-farthing ball.
Aye, it were more excitin' and a
   nicer place and all
When we lived in a world wi'out t'
   ordinary ball.
They'd take us out t' pitchers or a-
   strollin' on the mall,
Before they all went daffy o'er t'
   ordinary ball.
We'd maybe 'ave a picnic on a
   Sunday afternoon
Or share a choc'lat' soda or a bit
   o' macaroon.
But now we sits about like bloody
   'orses in a stall,
Because they're off their 'eads
   about the blinkin' game of
   ball!

The greatest curse in the universe
Is a little sphere of leather.
For, lost or won, when t' game is
     done,
Then they drink and sing together
Till they all float like leather!*
And seldom do they wander in 'til
     summat after nine—
And who's t' say how many bells
     they rang preceding mine?
Along the way, there's many, as
     you might say, ports of call—
I shudder when I think about it
     all!
But even when t' beddy-bye 'e
     crawls,
'E still keeps mutterin' 'ow he'd
     luv t' score!
It's no wonder what we wives
     abhor is balls!

JESS: She'll nag me and she'll nag me
     'til I'm down on me all fours!

MRS. OAKROYD: I'll nag him and I'll nag him 'til I
     get him out of doors
And then throw out the paper
     with the latest soccer scores!

PICCADILLY CIRCUS

The number "Piccadilly Circus" was originally written
for the film *Darling Lili* (1970). Mercer now wrote both
a Cockney version and one for Jess. Intended for John
Mills (Jess). Not used in show.

JESS: I took a trip to Piccadilly Circus,
     But there weren't a bloomin' elephant
          about!
     Nothin' at all but double-decker buses,
     A fearful lot o' noise and sound,
     Wi' trains that rumble underground!
     Somebody built a smashin' semicircle,
     So wouldn't y' know it's called Trafalgar
          Square!
     Nevertheless 'n' all,
     You can drop a Yorkshireman in Timbuktu,
     But 'is 'eart's right there in Piccadilly—
     Aye, 'is 'eart's right there!

---

* *Alternate lines:*
     They prepare against the weather
     Getting pissy-arsed together!

FATE MOVES IN MYSTERIOUS WAYS

Intended for Malcolm Rennie (Mitcham) and Christopher Gable (Inigo). In alternative versions Miss Trant,
Jess, and Susie are also involved in the song. Not used in
show.

Printed version

MITCHAM: Fate moves in mysterious ways
     Its wonders to perform.
     Fate chooses the oddest of days
     To turn from cold to warm.
     Just when you are down in the dumps,
     Your porridge is nothing but lumps,
     Up suddenly lady luck jumps,
     Like a sunbeam through the storm.

INIGO: Absolutely!

MITCHAM: Fate moves in mysterious ways
     Enchantments to pursue—
     For instance, our happenstance
          rendezvous!
     Here's me with my trusty banjo,
     There's you writing tunes like a pro,
     And this is our opening show
     As if on cue
     All together now!

BOTH: Fate moves in mysterious ways
     To see you through!

Demo tape version

INIGO: [*Presumably singing about* SUSIE] Fate
          moves in mysterious ways
     Her wonders to perform;
     Fate chooses remarkable days
     To circumvent the norm.
     One morning you're taking your place
     Back in the old chariot race
     When there is that mythical face
     And your heart beats up a storm.

MITCHAM: Absolutely.

INIGO: Love uses pure legerdemain,
     Her marvels to pursue,
     Like, out of a hat she invented you!*
     Nocturnally I was in flight,
     When in a great dazzle of light,
     You entered from paradise right,
     As if on cue.
     I reiterate:
     Fate moves in mysterious ways

BOTH: To see you through!

---

* *Alternate line:*
     Like, abracadabra! she dreamed up you!

Alternate version

MISS TRANT: Fate moves in mysterious ways
     Its wonders to perform.

INIGO: She gives you a ladylike gaze
     And strolls into your dorm.

MISS TRANT: Life seems to be utter despair;
     Nobody could possibly care,
     Then all at once somebody's there
     And the world is nice and warm.

INIGO: Absolutely!
     She picks the unlikeliest days
     To take you by the hand—

MISS TRANT: And lead you like Alice in
          Wonderland!

JESS: One day on a Bruddersford street
     Four fivers are there at my feet,
     And now, like a Santa Claus treat,
     I'm here with you!
     I'll never in all of my days,
     See through all the tricks that it
          plays.
     Here's me, by some intricate maze
     A Dinky-Doo—
     It's a miracle!
     Fate moves in mysterious ways
     T'see you through!

MISS TRANT: It's a miracle!

ALL: Fate moves in mysterious ways
     T'see you through!

Inigo solo draft version

Love chooses the funniest days
Her marvels to pursue—
Like, baby, the way she kept hiding you!
I nearly had given up hope
When, right at the end of my rope,
In glorious CinemaScope
You came in view!
Like Orpheus, I was in flight,
No hope and no future in sight,
When, like a big star in the night,
You came in view!

We see, we hear, smell, taste, and feel—
These five primary senses
We have as life commences
With which to cut expenses.
But as we grow to manhood we'll
Develop yet another—
Like when to run to Mother
Or how to bash each other.*
It tells us when to bet a ten
Or when there may be showers;

---

* *Or:* big brother.

Sense number six is full of tricks
And supernatural powers.

You're sloshing around in the rain,
Somebody turns into your lane—
It's suddenly raining Champagne . . .

Just when you are wondering why
Dame Fortune keeps passing you by,
Somebody will look you in the eye . . .

Fate chooses mysterious days
To weave her magic spell;
But if you will do as she tells you to,
As if she were making amends,
She gathers up all the loose ends—
Two strangers are suddenly friends.
You'll find that's true
And skies are blue . . .

MY ALTER EGO AND ME

Intended for Inigo (Christopher Gable) to sing to a poster of Susie (Marti Webb). Not used in show.

My alter ego and me,
We've got each other for company.
We talk it over, we two,
When either one of us is feeling blue;
We cheer each other up,
And other folks as well.
But when the party's over,
[*aside*]—And everybody's happy—
When something breaks the spell,
[*aside*]—As far as we can tell—
And gee, it's then,
Then who is just as lonesome as can be?
My poor old alter ego . . . and me!

OTHER SONGS WITH ANDRÉ PREVIN

In André Previn's Mercer file were several other lyrics, some of them clearly first jottings and many unfinished.
    At least one—"Taste"—can with reasonable certainty be considered to be intended for *Little Women*, a

project Mercer and Previn briefly contemplated before settling on *The Good Companions*.

TASTE

Taste is what you don't say;
Tact is how you say it;
Breeding is intuitively knowing
What a lady and a gentleman
Would never, ever do!

Crass is being pushy;
Gauche, a country bumpkin;
Manners are the password
To the bosom of society—
The language of the really chosen few.

If you must inquire
What it takes to make a lady,
You will never make a lady, I'm afraid.
For taste is what you don't say,
The quintessence of politeness;
It's a sense the Good Lord gave you
That will ultimately save you
From mistakes before mistakes are even made!

THE DAY THAT I'LL FIND YOU

VERSE

I'll never see eighteen again;
I won't see twenty-eight or -nine.
My first long dress won't be seen again
But something tells me I'll be fine.

REFRAIN

Don't let them say I've missed the boat!
Just as sure as the sea is blue,
There'll come a day when the anchors float
And the seagulls whistle "Tea for Two"—
And that's the day that I'll find you.

CUTLERY (WHERE DO WE GO FROM HERE?)

1.

You're wondering how
To make the first move.
I'll tell you right now
I won't disapprove,
Nor will I disappear.
So—
Where do we go from here?

2.

I'm bound to confess
Resistance is low.
If you want to say yes,
I wouldn't say no.
I might just raise a cheer!
But—
Where do we go from here?

This way, that way, up or down,
We could go both ways.
Forward, backward, round and round,
What do I care so long as when we get together
    and you're

3.

Restless again
And losing your grip
And needing a friend
To help with the zip,
You have a volunteer?
So—
Where do we go?
When do we go?
Darling, I'm so ready to go!
So—
Why don't we go from here?

PADDLING YOUR OWN CANOE

Oh, the Injuns say,
And I guess it's true,
Single runner makes
Half the noise of two,
Travel twice as fast

Keepum balance, too,*
If you paddle your own canoe.

And the Bible says,
Unto others do
Just as you'd have them
Doing unto you.
So I guess that means
You're a Christian, too,
When you paddle your own canoe.

Heap big lesson to learn, all right,
Much easier said than done,
But two mouths have to have twice the food,
Make twice as much talk as one.

So until I know,
As the old folk do,
How to say, "My child,
My advice to you . . ."
I will go along
And I'll take my cue
From an adage they say is true,
Like the wise old chiefs
In the powwows do
Or the ministers say
In the pulpits, too:
I'd be safer alone
And as dry as a bone
If I paddle my own canoe!

---

* *Alternate line:*
   And your spills are few

THE LONG WAY ROUND

VERSE

We're working girls on 'oliday
And we say "Vive la France!"
We're little chickens, 'ow you say,
Les petites poules sur leurs vacances,
So 'appy that we're homeward bound,
The long way round.

REFRAIN

The long way round.
First we went to Venice,
Going by Ben Nevis,*
The long way round.
And then Tashkent
By way of Ghent†
And learned to play deck tennis
The long way round.

Monsieur and Madame'll
Turn into enamel—
May they never!
If they ever
Find a map, we're sunk!

---

* *Alternate lyric:*
   Then we climbed
† *Alternate lyrics:*
   We sailed to Spain
   By way of Maine

CASABLANCA

REFRAIN 1

My mother, she always would say
There's places a girl shouldn't stray.
Do disembark
In Guernsey or Sark,
And you're perfectly safe in Torbay.
I've heard Mandalay is sort of okay;
I like what they say about Tiger Bay.
But never drop anchor
In Casablanca—
And especially not on market day!

REFRAIN 2

My mother, she always would say
There's visits a girl shouldn't pay.
Ramming the dock
In Vladivostok
Would be generally reckoned okay.
I hear that Bombay's no worse than L.A.;
I'm almost blasé about Galway Bay.
But never drop anchor
In Casablanca—
And especially not on market day!

REFRAIN 3

My mother, she always would say
There's places a yacht shouldn't stay.
You can get off
At Fisherman's Wharf;
Not a lot happens in Monterey.
I hear Saint Tropez is out of the way;
The company's gay around Hudson Bay.
But never drop anchor
In Casablanca—
And especially not on market day!

Songs of 1975-1989

In late 1974 or early 1975 Mercer and Rod McKuen began writing songs together and planned a tour during which they would perform. Mercer's illness prevented the tour from taking place. McKuen sent the editors the two lyrics that were completed.

DRINKIN' DOUBLES IN A SINGLES BAR

Words and music by Mercer and Rod McKuen.

VERSE

You know me. I used to be
The Man in the Moon's best friend.
I was the one who won all the bets
While living it up in Let's Pretend.
That was some distant yesterday
Before that Moon Man
Picked up his toys
And finally went on his way.

CHORUS

Wish I may, wish I might
Find a face to face tonight,
A bit par-boiled and far from par,
Drinkin' doubles in a singles bar.

Wish I might, wish I may
Find a light to light my way.
Nothin's cookin' in the cookie jar
Drinkin' doubles in a singles bar.

If I sit here long enough hopin'
I know the door will open.
She'll come through it. Watch her do it.
Guess you know I always knew it.

Wishes may, wishes might
Right whatever isn't right,
But wherever you go, here you are,
Drinkin' doubles in a singles bar.

Mercer in Savannah

DON'T BE AFRAID OF AUTUMN

Words and music by Mercer and Rod McKuen.

VERSE

I'm a seasoned citizen.
I've been around awhile.
When people rave and rage at age,
I summon my sweetest smile.

CHORUS

Don't be afraid of autumn.
Autumn is everything.
The song of the summer,
Sigh of the winter,
The promise of every spring.

Don't be afraid of autumn,
That tip-of-the-old-hat time,
When loosing your heart means
Winning at wisdom,
As passion gives way to prime.

Every September morning
Makes you more aware
That after a lifetime
Of hither and yon you've
Gotten from here to there.

Don't be afraid of autumn,
With all its false alarms.
You've arrived and survived
Aware and alive.
Greet autumn with open arms.

A TRIBUTE TO IRA GERSHWIN

Written by Mercer for the *Salute to Ira Gershwin* held for the benefit of the Reiss-Davis Child Study Center's 25 Years of Service to Emotionally Disturbed Children on July 27, 1975, at the Dorothy Chandler Pavilion in Los Angeles.

There was an old woman
Who lived in a shoe.
She had so many children,
She didn't know what to do.

She said "Take a hegira
To see your Uncle Ira,
He'll have a good solution
For such lay-abouts as you."
(We checked with our attorney.
"Hegira" means a journey.)
When Ira received them,
The wily physisch,
He made them swear off liquor,
Lib'ral politics,
And fish.
This modern-day Hippocrates,
Our California Socrates,
Advised a generous portion
Of his sunny disposish.
And now from dawn 'til late at night,
'S wonderful to see them write,
And skies from here to Omaha
Are blue instead of being blah.

IF SOMEDAY COMES EVER AGAIN

Music by Alec Wilder. Published. Copyrighted September 23, 1976.

One day we promised that someday,
When we grew to be women and men,
We'd take off in June
And fly to the moon—
When we were both seven and ten.

One day we promised that someday
We would follow the road to romance,
But only to learn
The straightest roads turn
And life is run mostly by chance.

Mystified and saucer-eyed,
We never knew at all
Our Humpty Dumpty world
Could ever take a fall,
Never knew that very few,
No matter who they are,
Ever fly to reach a shiny star.

Today I would pray a lot harder
And I'd end with a stronger "Amen"—
And if I have you,
We'll make it come true,
If someday comes ever again.

THE SOUNDS AROUND THE HOUSE

Music by Alec Wilder. Published. Copyrighted September 23, 1976.

The sounds around the house
Are all the sounds I love the best:
Footsteps, singing, wind in the leaves,
Swallows nesting under the eaves.
The sounds around the house
Can break your heart with what they say.
I lie awake
And search the dark
And whisper, "Small boy, small boy,
Why aren't you there
In the sounds around the house?"

HAVE A NICE DAY

Music by Sammy Nestico. Registered for copyright as an unpublished song November 22, 1976.

Old rooster's crowin',
Time to get goin';
The sun is up
Showin' the way.

Last one out of bed
Is a lazy old sleepyhead;
Shower and dress
And heat up some Nescafé.

Now the toast is burnin',
Your tum is churnin',
But who comes near earnin' your pay?

Doctor, lawyer, Injun chief,
And everybody else is on relief.
Cheer up and have a nice day.

The freeway is leapin',
Rev up your heatin'
And gone all those horns beepin' away

Any cat who can sign in next
Is pickin' up his unemployment checks.
But who's complainin'?
What's more it's rainin'.
Punch in and have,
Have a nice day.

BLUEBIRD

Composer unknown. No music is known to survive. Registered for copyright as an unpublished song June 22, 1977.

REFRAIN 1

Don't turn your back on a bluebird,
You might get a crow in its place.
A crow is the kind
Who'll pilfer you blind,
Then sit there and "caw" in your face!
You might get a minah
From far Indo-China
Whose language will deafen your ear,
Or even a head-hiding ostrich
Who sits there exposing his rear!

REFRAIN 2

Don't turn your back on a bluebird,
You might get a small parakeet.
You could get a wren
Or an enceinte hen
Or even a rooster in heat!
You might get an eagle
Or even a seagull
(They're Jewish, of course, but they're nice!)
So don't turn your back on a bluebird,
You might get a penguin on ice.

REFRAIN 3

You might get a buzzard instead.
Be grateful to find
The sweet-singing kind
Who's partial to using his—head!
All pigeons are stuffy:
Ask poor Father Duffy
Who stands there attending his flock.
Instead of a pretty young pullet
You could get a very old cock!*

RECITATION

B is for the brilliant blue that glistens on his
    wings.
L is for the love contained in every note he sings.
U is for unflappable—I threw that in for laughs.
E is for his ears—which do not show in
    photographs.
B is for the bobolink—his friend a tree away.
I is for the insects they fight over every day.

---

* *Alternate lyric:*
    You could get an old extinct Roc!

R is for his rippling voice, which floats above our
    bed.
D is what a bunch of people wishes he were . . .
    dead!

MY NEW CELEBRITY IS YOU

Music by Blossom Dearie. Registered for copyright as an unpublished song July 18, 1977.

I dig Modigliani,
Jolson doing "Swanee";
Several maharanees are my intimates too.
I played with Mantovani,
And that's a lot of strings to get through.
But anyone can see
My new celebrity is you.

I've sung with Ethel Merman,
Swung with Woody Herman,
Played a gig in Germany with Ogerman too.
I nodded at a sermon
Billy Graham barely got through.
But anyone can see
My new celebrity is you.

I'm not a bit
Ashamed of it—
My rapier wit
Kept Serge Koussevitzky in line.
I'd reprimand
The Dorsey band
And right on the stand,
'Cause Annie's cousin Fanny was a sweetie of
    mine.

I've golfed with Lee Trevino,
Won at the casino,
Danced the Piccolino,
When the movie was new.
Spent the night with Dino—
Had to sleep with Jerry Lewis too.
But anyone can see
My new celebrity is you.

I've swooned at Mia Farrow,
Angular and narrow,
Drove her Pierce-Arrow
To a *Gatsby* preview—
Though frozen to the marrow,
Who would dream of leaving that queue?
But anyone can see
My new celebrity is you.

Her husband, André Previn—
Absolutely heaven.
Even Herman Levin
Wants to hire him too.
And as for Lady Bevan,
We were both in labor, that's true.
But anyone can see
My new celebrity is you.

I played the uke
With Vernon Duke
So well in Dubuque
That Vladimir Dukelsky
Said "Gee!"
My fingering
A certain string
Was such a big thing
That Fanny's cousin Annie's taking lessons from
    me.

I'm quite a fan of Lena,
Close to Caterina,
Very fond of Gina
Lollobrigida too;
And as for Pasadena,
Everybody there's an old shoe.
But anyone can see
My new celebrity is you.

I've drunk with Willie Harbach,
Also Roger Staubach,
Wiggled pretty far back,
When you start to pursue.
And talk about your star back,
Tarkenton can scramble some too.
But anyone can see
My new celebrity is you.

I see Muhammad Ali,
Clanking goes my trolley;
Starred in *Hello, Dolly!*
When it ran out of glue;
And Salvador Dali
Did a little sketch of me too.
But anyone can see
My new celebrity is you.

You need a pair
To give an air
Of fashion and flair,
Have Bob and Danny Zarem fly down.
The older set
Will need a pet,
So who do you get?
Well, Danny
Has a granny
Who's the talk of the town.

The incidents are many;
Jack and Mary Benny,
Nick and Sister Kenny
Made the scene for me too.
And little Lotte Lenya
Helped to entertain at chez nous,
Where everyone could see
My new celebrity is you.

NOMA

Composer unknown. Registered for copyright as an unpublished song August 16, 1977.
    Lyric missing.

GIRL, IT'S YOU

Composer unknown. Registered for copyright as an unpublished song September 28, 1977.
    Lyric missing.

TO BE FREE

Composer unknown. Registered for copyright as an unpublished song September 28, 1977.
    Lyric missing but this is possibly the same song as "And Ain't It Fun to Be Free."

I CAME HOME TODAY

Composer unknown. Registered for copyright as an unpublished song October 7, 1977.
    Lyric missing.

(BACK TO THE) HARD TIMES

Composer unknown. Registered for copyright as an unpublished song January 3, 1979.
    Lyric missing.

LONELY SHADE OF BLUE

Composer unknown. Registered for copyright as an unpublished song March 23, 1979.
    Lyric missing.

YOUNG AND FREE

Music by Johnny Rotella. Registered for copyright as an unpublished song December 8, 1981.

All the world's a bubble
When you're young and free.
Like an eagle, you can swoop and fly.
Fools can borrow trouble,
But not you and me,
As we sail our bubble through the sky.
Summers we can surf until the sun goes down;
Winters we can dance until the dawn,
Even though our actions make the old ones frown—
"Goodness, how the young ones carry on!"
So hold me closer, baby,
Say there's a chance that maybe
We'll make it last for years.
I thank the stars above me
They sent you here to love me.
Life's really groovy,
Just like a movie.
Dig the things you want to
If you're havin' fun;
Dance with any handsome guy* you see.
But when all the diggin'
And the dancin's done,
Promise you'll stay young and free with me.
Promise you'll stay young and free with me—
    whee!—
Just as I'll stay young and free with you!

MISTLETOE MANSION

Music by Vern Hansen. Lyric by Mercer and Hansen. Registered for copyright as an unpublished song November 22, 1982. Hansen believed that this was one of the last lyrics Mercer worked on.

* *Or:* "pretty girl"

There's a garland of lights in a window,
Of a house with a snowy white crown;
It's a cottage called Mistletoe Mansion,
With a chimney where Santa comes down.

Now it may not be much of a palace,
And it may look a little bit old;
But you'll find in my Mistletoe Mansion,
All the good things your two arms can hold.

Christmas is a seasoning
As well as a season,
For love is so evergreen,
And love is the reason
That Saint Nick is there,
If there is love in the air,
For where love is,
That's where he'll be found.

It's a lowly white house on the highway,
Small and humble and all tumble-down;
But the love in my Mistletoe Mansion
Makes it Christmas the whole year around.

Alternate ending

There's a cottage called Mistletoe Mansion,
Where an angel is sure to be found;
For you're living in Mistletoe Mansion
If your love dwells there all the year round.

WHEN OCTOBER GOES

Music by Barry Manilow. Registered for copyright as an unpublished song June 6, 1984. Leading recordings by Manilow (Arista), Nancy Wilson (Columbia), and Monica Mancini (Concord Jazz).

    After Mercer's death his estate gave composer/performer Manilow access to a number of unpublished and, in a few cases, previously published lyrics, which he set to music.

And when October goes*
The snow begins to fly;
Above the smoky roofs
I watch the planes go by.
The children running home

---
* *Alternate line:*
    And when the summer goes,

Beneath a twilight* sky—
Oh, for the fun of them
When I was one of them.
And when October goes,
The same old dream appears,
And you are in my arms†
To share the happy years.
I turn my head away
To hide the helpless tears—
Oh, how I hate to see October go!

I should be over it now, I know;
It doesn't matter much
How old I grow—
I hate to see October go!

MY VALENTINE LETTER

Music by Mercer. Registered for copyright as an unpublished song May 3, 1985.

VERSE 1

This letter I write is my valentine;
You'll find an "I love you" in ev'ry line.
And, darling, between ev'ry "I love you"
Is hidden an "honest and true."

REFRAIN

So, read, read, read ev'ry line,
Read, read the name that I sign;
A heart and an arrow are woven through
My valentine letter to you.

VERSE 2

The o's are all heart-shaped; the a's are, too;
The x and s are kisses—of course you knew.
But what you don't see, and might not appear,
I've dotted each i with a tear.

REPEAT REFRAIN

FIRST, LAST, AND ALWAYS

Music by Barry Manilow. Registered for copyright as an unpublished song March 10, 1986.

---
* *Or:* "wintry" and "frosty"
† *Alternate line:*
    You're in my arms again

First, last, and always,
I'll always love you.
First, last, and always,
I'll tell you I do.
I knew it from the first time,
It just has to be;
And there'll never be a last time—
Just wait and you'll always see.
What does it matter
If time hurries by?
What does it matter?
You're here—so am I.
Now dreams are worth the dreaming;
I know they'll come true,
First, last, and always with you.

DAY AFTER DAY AFTER DAY

Music by Barry Manilow. Registered for copyright as an unpublished song March 10, 1986.

I love you more every single minute,
Day after day after day.
Knowing the day even has you in it
Carries me most of the way.
I'm like a lamb in a field of clover,
Day after day after day.
And then to prove that my cup really runneth
    over,
There's still the night time.
Oh, promise now that you'll always linger
Down through the swift-running years—
I've got a ring for your marriage finger,
Woven of laughter and tears.
I promise you that if I'm your lover,
I'll be your lover to stay,
Day after beautiful day after beautiful day!

(THEY'RE) PAVIN' CALIFORNIA

Music by Jimmy Rowles. Registered for copyright as an unpublished song March 21, 1988. Alternate title: "Pavin' California."

A panic-stricken gopher
Hollered, "Mama, hip the chauffeur—
We are splittin',

Really quittin',
'Cause they are pavin' California!

We're pilin' in the Pinto,
Circumventin' San Jacinto—
Pack the kids in,
'Cause the bid's in—
Man, they're pavin' California!"

A bunch o' tractors
Backed us out of the cactus,
Right off the Lazy T,
And if the builders want to,
They're goin' on to
Indochina,
Pavin' like crazy,
With an eye on Asia Minor!

They blacktopped Watts and Garvey
And they're headed for Mojave;
Cucamonga and Tujunga
Have been surfaced wall to wall.
Yes, they're pavin' California,
And I think I oughta warn ya,
They are out to readorn ya—
They are out to get us all!

The lizards and coyotes
All are off to the Dakoties,
While the rattler's
A Seattler,
'Cause they're pavin' California!

The orange is no safer;
It is flatter than a wafer.
Tang is better
And it's wetter—
Man, they're pavin' California!

They're pourin' concrete faster than alabaster,
Like in a plaster caster;
And if you really wanna,
I betcha on a
Clear day, madam,
You can see like a prairie of macadam!

The vineyards owned by Gallo
Are, by golly, lyin' fallow,
Vegetatin',
Simply waitin'
For the old bulldozer's call.
Yes, I guess I better warn ya
Dinosaurs and unicorn, ya,
All the creatures from the tar pits,
They are layin' cement carpets—
They are pavin' California,
And they're gonna pave us all!

AT LAST

Music by Barry Manilow with revised lyric. Registered for copyright as an unpublished song April 11, 1988. Recorded by Nancy Wilson (Columbia) and Monica Mancini (Concord Jazz).

Mercer lyric

Here you are.
I've pinched myself and I'm not crazy—
Here you are
At last.
My guardian angel sent you to find me,
Kiss and remind me
I've left the heartaches behind me.
Here you are,
But, oh, the times I've asked a daisy
When you'd hold me fast!
In this big world full of losers,
Though beggars can't be choosers,
I saw my chance,
Wished on my star,
And here you are
At last!

Revised lyric

I wandered near and far,
I wished upon a star,
And, darlin', here you are
At last.
My guardian angel must have sent you
To find me;
Now I've left the headaches
Behind me.
Although the road was long
My heart and I were strong
And now the saddest song
Is past.
In this big world of losers,
Tho' beggars can't be choosers,
I wished on my star
And here you are at last.

FINDERS ARE KEEPERS

Music by Barry Manilow. Registered for copyright as an unpublished song April 11, 1988. For an earlier song with the same title but with different music and lyrics, see page 14.

Finders are keepers,
And dreams do come true;
Finders are keepers—
At last I've found you.
Somebody overlooked you
And left you for me,
But I couldn't know the love
You called my big discovery.
What does it matter
How lonesome I've been?
What does it matter
Since you wandered in?
You better make your mind up
That we'll never part,
For finders are keepers, sweetheart!

HEART OF MINE, CRY ON

Music by Barry Manilow. Registered for copyright as an unpublished song April 11, 1988. Recorded by Nancy Wilson (Columbia).

You say we're pretending—
Heart of mine, did you hear?
You mean it's the ending—
Heart of mine, why the tear?
How calmly you tell me
To part with a smile;
How calmly you tell me
It's just for a while!
But something in your eye
Says it's really goodbye.
Dear Lord above,
Why does this have to be?
Dear Lord above,
Must it happen to me?
We'll end like we started—
Tell her [him], heart, make her [him] stay!—
Both gay and lighthearted—
Heart of mine, are you gay?
You don't want to hold me
When love has passed by;
I'm so glad you told me,
And now, dear, goodbye!
Oh, heart of mine, cry on—
She's [He's] gone.

IF IT CAN'T BE YOU

Music by Bernie Hanighen not known to survive. Later version of song with music by Barry Manilow using only the refrain. Registered for copyright as an unpublished song April 11, 1988.

VERSE

There may be lots of pebbles on the beach
And millions of fish in the sea,
But, darling, as far as I'm concerned,
There's only one you and there's only one me.

REFRAIN

If it can't be you,
If it can't be you,
Then it can't be anyone,
If it can't be you.
I've thrilled to your kisses,
Your tender embrace;
Who else could ever take your place?
If it can't be me
In your arms tonight,
If it must be someone else,
Then it can't be right.
I've got a funny little dream I'm dreaming,
But you've got to dream it too,
'Cause it can't come true
If it can't be you.

THE LAST DREAM HOME

Music by Barry Manilow. Registered for copyright as an unpublished song April 11, 1988. Recorded by Nancy Wilson (Columbia).

Make a date right now,
Somewhere, somehow,
To catch the last dream home.
Save a place for me—
That's where I'll be,
Aboard the last dream home.

My darling love,
When dawn first streaks the sky,
Our lips will say goodbye.
Ah, but not our hearts—
We've traded hearts for keeps,
You and I!

But in case we lose our way,
Somehow, someday,
You'll know, wherever we roam,
I'll meet you on the last dream home.

LOOK AT YOU

Music by Barry Manilow. Registered for copyright as an unpublished song April 11, 1988. Recorded by Nancy Wilson (Columbia).

Look at you,
Just look at you,
I can't believe my eyes.
Look at you,
Just look at you,
So shy and worldly wise.
Out of place,
That angel face,
This fire in your kiss.
All life through
I'm hoping to
Just look at you like this.

WHEN THE MEADOW WAS BLOOMIN'

Music by Barry Manilow. Registered for copyright as an unpublished song April 11, 1988. Recorded by Nancy Wilson (Columbia) and Monica Mancini (Concord Jazz).

In April weather,
When the meadow was bloomin',
We walked together
To the top of the hill.

Among the clover,
When the meadow was bloomin',
We dreamed together,
Just as true lovers will.

But summer flies on
Far across the horizon,
And winter lies on
Over the valley and the hill.

Do you remember
When the meadow was bloomin'?

In bleak December
Do you think of me still?
Do you remember
Just as I always will?

WITH MY LOVER BESIDE ME

Music by Barry Manilow with small lyric revisions. Registered for copyright as an unpublished song April 11, 1988. Recorded by Nancy Wilson (Columbia) and Monica Mancini (Concord Jazz).

I sit here dreaming
With my lover beside me,
The firelight gleaming
And the room all aglow.

I sit here dreaming
With my lover beside me;
My eyes are beaming
With the mem'ries they know:

The meadow blooming
And the golden grain waving,
Two sweethearts kissing
In the long, long ago.

I sit here dreaming
With my lover beside me,
The firelight gleaming
And the room all aglow.

I GUESS THERE AIN'T NO SANTA CLAUS

Music by Barry Manilow and Eddie Arkin. There was an earlier version of this song called "I Guess There Ain't No Santy Claus," with music by Joseph Meyer and lyrics by "John" Mercer, which would date it to 1930–32. Meyer's music is not known to survive. The Manilow-Arkin version incorporates all of the earlier lyrics.

I got evenings to spare
That nobody will share,
I guess there ain't no Santa Claus.
I don't flirt, I don't dance,
'Cause I don't get a chance,
I guess there ain't no Santa Claus.

Jingle bells, wedding bells,
Ring so merrily,
But jingle bells and wedding bells
Never ring for me.
Like the clock on the shelf
I hold hands with myself.
I guess there ain't no Santa Claus.

I got wine, I got cheer,
I got nobody here,
I guess there ain't no Santa Claus.
Well, they sure got it right,
When they sing "Silent Night."
I guess there ain't no Santa Claus.

Lovers walk, holding hands,
Everywhere I go.
Ready, set, here I stand
'Neath the mistletoe;
Sugarplums in my head,
Only me in my bed.
I guess there ain't no Santa Claus.

My dad and mother
Told one another
They saw a future for me.
But since I've grown up
I got to own up,
It's not like they said it would be.

Lovers walk, holding hands,
Everywhere I go.
Ready, set, here I stand
'Neath the mistletoe;
Sugarplums in my head,
Only me in my bed.

I guess there ain't no Santa Claus,
I guess there ain't no Santa Claus,
I guess,
Guess there ain't no Santa Claus.

BYE AND BYE

Composer unknown. Music not known to survive.

Bye and bye
When you and I
Have known each other more,
Bye and bye
I'll tell you why*
You're all that I adore.
When I do,
I'll prove to you
That it was love at sight.
Let me try to,
Bye and bye—
Like bye and bye
Tonight.

JUST LIKE TAKING CANDY FROM A BABY

Music by Barry Manilow. See earlier version with music by Robert Emmett Dolan, p. 325.

VERSE

Pa sent me to college,
First off, to get rich,
Then, guard against,
Work hard against,
Losing every stitch.
They filled me with knowledge;
I tried to get wise.
They put me right;
You cut me right
Down to my own size
With those two baby blue,
Sweet pickpocket eyes.

REFRAIN

Just like takin' candy from a baby,
You're takin' me, baby,
You're robbin' me blind!
The only heart I'll ever own
Just melted like an ice cream cone,
And now I'm just about to lose my mind.

---

* *Alternate line:*
    I'll whisper why

Just like takin' lollipops from baby,
You're naughty, but maybe
You're nice to me, too.
For as we live and learn,
And when it comes my turn,
Just like takin' candy from a baby, baby,
Watch me steal your heart from you!

SOMETHING TELLS ME (I'M FALLING IN LOVE)

Music by Barry Manilow. Published. Copyrighted April 11, 1988. Recorded by Nancy Wilson (Columbia) and Monica Mancini (Concord Jazz). Manilow used the refrain of the 1938 Mercer–Harry Warren version of this song, and wrote new music for it. See page 69 for the Mercer-Warren original.

Something tells me
I'm falling in love;
Something tells me
You're sent from above.

Not the stars or
The man in the moon,
Though I'm certain
They set the stage
And opened the curtain.

Something tells me
My waiting is through;
I hope something
Is telling you, too.

Something whispers
That we'll never part;
Something tells me
It's my heart.

Other Mercer lyrics set to music by Barry Manilow can be found in earlier chapters under the titles "Just Remember" (refrain only), "South Wind (refrain only)," "Love Is Where You Find It" (the version not previously set to music) and "Can't Teach My Old Heart New Tricks" (the alternate lyrics).

OVERLEAF *Mercer with Louis Armstrong and Maxine Sullivan*

Miscellaneous Songs | Undated

This chapter contains mostly undated Mercer lyrics arranged alphabetically. Although we were able eventually to determine dates in some cases, it was too late in the production process to move those lyrics into their chronological places. And a few last-minute additions are included at the end of this chapter.

AGE OF INNOCENCE

Composer unknown. No music is known to survive.

Version 1

We were in an age of innocence,
And we were such innocents for our years.
Back when the world
Was once upon a time,
We never had the time
For tears.
We were in an age of make-believe
And so we made believe life away,
And seen through the mild,
Sweet eyes of a child,
The world is the same today.
And where love has gone,
The children go on
Believing the games they play,
Livin' in an age of innocence
That we had to leave one day.

Version 2

We were in an age of innocence,
But we were innocents for any age.
Life was so much like a story book
That we would both forget
To turn the page.
It was a lovely, dreamy age of make-believing,
And so we made believe our lives away.

Those lovely days we strolled beneath the cliffs of
    Dover,
The same as German children played along the
    Rhine;
We never saw the storm that sent the breakers over
The little castles we built with such great love
    upon the sand.

Yes, we were in an age of make-believe;
We made believe the time away.
Now, when I see children in the country,
Never knowing as they play,
They'll leave an age of innocence one day.

ALL THE STALLS GO DARK

Composer unknown. No music is known to survive.

Version 1

Lights, opening nights,
Parties where all are gay.
Ah, life on the stage must be a lark;
More often than not
We see a different play,
When the curtain falls
And all the stalls go dark . . .
You think of the times
Pretty bouquets are passed.
You think of the nights
Flowers are thrown,
More likely than not
It is a different cast
When the curtain falls
Who walks the malls alone.
Here is where Lawrence and Lillie
Had a great triumphal tour.
Here is where Kean knocked them silly.
Faced like a painting,
He had the girls fainting.
Stage Johnnys galore . . .
Flowers and sparkling wine,
Ah, but when the wine loses its spark?
Then out of the flies . . .
One hears a ghostly whine
When the curtain falls
And all the stalls—go dark.

Version 2

More likely than not
We're in a different cast
When the curtain falls
Who walks the malls alone.
Here is where Garrick and Power
Had their great triumphal tours.
Lauder sang here for an hour.*
Charmed and cajoled them,
What stories he told them.
Sure, life is a lark . . .
Flowers and sparkling wine,
Ah, but when the wine loses its spark?
Then, back in the wings . . .
One sees a ghostly shine
As the curtain falls
And all the stalls go dark . . .
And they walk the halls
As all the stalls go dark!

---
*Alternate line:
    Bernhardt held forth for an hour.

ALL THE WORLD KNOWS WE'RE IN LOVE

Composer unknown. No music is known to survive.

All the world knows we're in love.
You can feel it all around:
In the twinkling eye
Of the passerby
And the willow's softly whispered sound.
All the world thinks you're a dream.
They can see how much I care,
So they all conspire
That my heart's desire
Be the fairest of fair.
The snowy swan,
The lake of blue,
Are but a background to the loveliness of you.
The fleecy clouds
That frame your face
Just seem to try to be as gossamer as lace.
All the world knows we're in love.
Shall we tell the stars above?
The singing boughs
Bow as you go.
They say you're beautiful, as if I didn't know.

"ALMOST" DON'T COUNT

Composer unknown. No music is known to survive.

"Almost" don't count in anything.
"Nearly" ain't it.
"Missed by an inch," you say to me.
I say—"Tough tit."
Then again, some days you spin the wheel,
Luck has a wonderful smile.
When you miss that old banana peel,
A miss is as good as a mile.
So, don't you brag, "I almost did";
"I almost won," "darned near."
Second don't pay you very much.
Fourth don't pay none at all.
Get in there and buy your underwear,
Go for the whole amount,
'Cause in life, like in a love affair,
"Almost" don't count.

ALOHA

Composer unknown. No music is known to survive.

The blue and lazy days,
The scent of flower leis
Are in the simple phrase "Aloha."
The sweetest sounding bird
The islands ever heard
Could never match the word "Aloha."
That's what the waves are always saying
Beneath a big Pacific moon.
Sometimes it rains a while,
But then the rainbows smile
And send a kiss across the sea.
That's what "Aloha" means to me.

THE AMERICANA

Composer unknown. No music is known to survive.

REFRAIN 1

Here's the new Americana,
It's the true Americana—
It's the thing that we created,
The highly underrated,
The widely imitated dance.

Uncle Sam, I wanna warn ya,
From New York to California,
They'll be dancing it in ballrooms,
Rehearsing it in hallrooms,
The great Americana dance.

REFRAIN 2

It's the new Americana,
From Seattle to Savannah,
From Missouri to Montana,
They're hollerin' hosanna
For that American dance.

Little shavers and old codgers,
Fred Astaire and Ginger Rogers,
Everybody and his brother
Is teaching one another
The great Americana dance.

AND AIN'T IT FUN TO BE FREE

Composer unknown. No music is known to survive.

This is really our night to howl;
Four jazz babies out on the prowl.
We're out pettin'
And suffragettin',
And ain't it fun to be free.

We can dress any way we please:
Rolled down stockings below the knees,
Bobbed hair blowin',
And bosoms showin',
It's really fun to be free.

Men—who needs 'em?
We've got everything that's his'n.
Who succeeds 'em?
Ladies who've been let out of prison.

We're all set with our tap shoes on;
We'll be dancin' until the dawn,
Drinkin' whiskey
And feelin' frisky,
And ain't it fun to be free.

Each one's wearin' a new chemise:
That's a French word for B.V.D.s.
French and frilly
And downright chilly,
But ain't it fun to be free?

John J. Pershing and Marshall Foch
Had no weapon to touch the cloche.
And what's bolder,
We show our shoulder,
And ain't it fun to be free?

Irene Castle—
Here's to you and here's to drinkin'.
Margaret Sanger—
You're the feminine Abe Lincoln.

Dressed for driving or *pour le sport*,
See you out on the tennis court.
Step up, lassie
And use your brassie,
'Cause ain't it fun to be free?

What do we love?
Speak up, ladies, please don't mumble.
He and she love
Most especially in the rumble.

Fill your flask full of hooch tonight
And we'll shimmy 'til broad daylight,
Liberated,
Emancipated,
And ain't it fun to be free!

AND THERE SHE SITS

Composer unknown. No music is known to survive.

And there she sits—regal—serene in her glory
Unloosing a torrent of feminine story
With gay little gestures—delectable movements,
A beautiful woman, with all the improvements.
Head tilted, eyes flashing, absorbed in her duty
Of telling a tale—unconcerned with her beauty.
Now sitting as straight as a queen on a throne,
Now forward, allowing her breasts to be shown,
Lips curving in laughter—so beautifully dressed
Aware—but aloof—that the room is impressed.
Now giving a look to the man at her side
And making the poor fellow humble with pride;
Now glancing across at a man that walks by,
Thus making her date want to wither and die.
Her fingers aflutter and shining with rings,
She whispers of intimate, personal things,
Then suddenly thinking of what happened after,
She throws back her head, her voice pealing with
    laughter.
Has ever there been a more joyous delight?
A beautiful, ravishing, glorious sight.
A blush on her cheek—just the hint of perfume,
The center of each pair of eyes in the room.
She skips over words—like a bee over flowers,
Unconscious of all her remarkable powers.
The millions of errands she has yet to do
Can certainly wait till this luncheon is through.
Brows arching—mouth open—her lips in a curl
She gestures, she giggles, she squeals—she's a
    girl!

And then with a sigh—there's a pause in her glee
With eyes big as saucers—she listens to *me!*
She turns her head this way—inclines her chin
    that,
Quite sure of her coiffure—quite proud of her
    hat.
The cigarette smoke makes a frame for her face,
The queen of a long-ago, far-away race.
Her eyes seem to say—if impressed by my charms
She might let me spend a few nights in her arms.
Ah, rapturous thought—and the heart in me
    swells

For the nights would be twice what the promise
    fortells.
Don't ask how I know such a thrill could be so,
I sense it—I feel it—I'm certain—I *know!*

My beautiful darling—adorable kook,
I don't want to spoil things—I just want to look!
Go on with the story we still haven't heard,
I fall more in love—with each scatterbrained
    word.
The way you manipulate napkin and knife
Are things I'll remember the rest of my life.
The way you manoeuvre the guests into glee
Is nothing to how you manipulate me.
Be shy with your glances—be bold in your touch.
I love your performance—I love *you* so much.

Dear God—take your lightning—and take back
    your thunder*
And all of your vast and incredible wonders.
The moon and the stars—and I never shall miss
    one,
But never take woman—and least of all this one!

ANGEL FACE

Composer unknown. No music is known to survive.

Angel face,
Oh, angel face,
It's heaven when you smile.
When you kiss
It's like a kiss
Were going out of style.
When you go
It's just as though
The sun forgot to shine.
Evermore
Let me adore
That angel face of mine.

I know my heart,
I know my heart,
I know what it's about to say.
I know my lips,
I know my arms,
They'll never let you get away.
They've felt your kiss,
They've held you as close as this.
Could either of them dismiss or let you go? No.

---
* *Alternate line:*
    take your gifts back—your lightnings and thunders

To make it clear,
If you come near,
I won't be blamed for what they do.
I know my heart,
I know my heart
And I know you.

ANY BLESSING HEAVEN SENDS MY WAY

Composer unknown. No music is known to survive.

REFRAIN 1

Even though I don't understand it all,
I suppose the Lord must have planned it all.
And so, for goodness' sake,
I'm prepared to take
Any blessing heaven sends my way.

Under this façade of a Bible man
Beats the savage heart of a tribal man . . .
And little Laughing Boy
Might as well enjoy
Any blessing heaven sends my way.

Here are one, two, and three
Souls entrusted to me.
If I save your souls from hell,
I must save the rest as well!

So it looks a bit Saturnalian
To a proper E-piscopalian
But who am I to say
Definitely "nay"
To the little blessings that heaven sends my
    way!

REFRAIN 2

Though my better self says to fight it off,
Call you an expense to write it off,
A feeling in my shoes
Tells me not to lose
Any blessing heaven sends my way.

Pleasures of the flesh can be wearyin'
To a Quaker or Presbyterian.
I, being more naïve,
Gratefully receive
Any blessing heaven sends my way.

Girls, I hope you agree,
Bread that's cast on the sea

Will come back ten-thousand-fold,
More than one man's arms can hold.

Better far to give than receive, you know,
What I have in mind—I believe you know.
You'll find me most adept,
Eager to accept
Any little blessing that heaven sends my way.

ANY OLD DAY

Music by Mercer.

Any old day,
I'm happy to say,
I can forget
We ever met.
Just like I said
I'd do.

I'll bet you any old night,
I'll turn off the light,
Knowing the tears
Won't fall.
And that ought to be,
Just you wait and see;
Any old day,
At all!

AROUND THE FIREPLACE

Composer unknown. No music is known to survive.

Many years ago,
As a little boy
At my mother's knee
In the wintertime
Beside the fireplace
She would read to me.
In imagination I would sail away
On a stormy sea.
Now that I am grown
And the night is cold
When the wind blows free
In the wintertime
Around the fireplace
With my family,
I can tell you

That around the fireplace
Is the place to be.

Oh, the happy times
In the olden days.
Saucer-eyed were we
When the cantor sat
Beside the fireplace,
Wise as he could be,
As he listened to the smaller ones
Say their A B C.

Those were happy days,
Happy children, too,
Happy as could be,
In the wintertime
Around the fireplace
With the family.
I still like to be
Around the fireplace
In my memory.

AUTUMN AFTERNOONS

Composer unknown. No music is known to survive.

Autumn afternoons,
Smiling through a tear—
Brightly painted,
Unacquainted
With the time of year.

Autumn afternoons,
Courtesans of joy—
Flirting madly,
Rather sadly
Looking for a boy.

See the old *coquettes*,
Rouged—and getting on . . .
Pirouetting,
Still coquetting
With their best days gone.

Lovers of the spring,
Underneath your moons
You will learn, too,
Summers turn to*
Autumn afternoons.

---

* *Alternate lyric:*
    Youth will turn to

See them toss their auburn tresses,
Done up in October dresses,
Organdies of yellow, pink and gold.

See the way they swirl and billow.
Can't they feel the winter chill? Oh,
Don't they know they'll catch their death of cold?

While the piper wind
Plays his dancing tunes,
Pick a fast one;
It's the last one,
Autumn afternoons.

THE BAR-MAID

Music possibly by Mercer but is not known to survive.
Song dated April 1, 1938.

When I met her that day
I was well on my way
Down the road that leads straight to the gutter.
All my money I'd use
To buy myself booze
Instead of some bread and some butter.
In the city alone
With no way to get home
The old folks had nothing to send her.
At the end of her rope
But not giving up hope
Poor girl—she became a bartender.
A bum wandered in
And demanded free gin.
She said, "Sir, there is none in the place."
But this ignorant vulture
Disregarding her culture,
Called her a name to her face.
The only thing near
Was my bottle of beer,
And though I hated to waste it,
It was he or the beer.
So I broke it right here.
It was my crucial test and I faced it.
They sent me to jail
But she furnished the bail
With money she stole from the joint.
You've got to take off your hat
To a girl who'll do that.
As for me, it was my turning point.
Well, we're wed, she and I,
And I'm high and dry
In a cottage instead of a cell.
And to my dying day

I'll never betray
That bar-maid who saved me from—.

BIG DADDY

Music by Mercer.

REFRAIN 1

BOY: Doll baby,
        Come to your big daddy.
        Big Daddy
        Wants to baby you
        With rings and things
        Like twenty-one strings
        Of sapphire blue,
        A Coke machine,
        And S&H Green Stamps, too.

        Doll baby,
        Make a wish and maybe
        Big daddy,
        He can bull it through.
        Let's greet the dawn au natural
        On some tiny atoll.*
        Big daddy loves his baby doll.

REFRAIN 2

SHE: Big daddy,
        Come to your doll baby.
        Doll baby
        Wants to baby you.
        Untie that tie;
        I'll get you a dry
        Martini to sip;
        At times I'm hip
        That even big daddies flip.

        Big daddy,
        Don't you be a baddie.
        Doll baby
        Hates to see you blue;
        Take off those slacks,
        Lie back and relax
        Those sweet double chins.
HE: Big daddy loves his baby doll.

---

* *Alternate lines:*
    Let's greet the dawn together upon
    Some tropic atoll.

BIG TIME IN A SMALL TOWN

Composer unknown. No music is known to survive.

Strong whiskey and weak women
Are what sourdoughs like.
A big time in a small town
Is a bear ridin' a bike.
Eight bells we fold up,
Come rain or shine.
There's seldom even a flight.
The streets are rolled up
At half past nine
And tucked away for the night.
Disgustin'—
We're just bustin'
To get goin' and dance.
A big time in a small town
Is a real kick in the pants.
Our boilermakers'll mow you down,
Come on and see how it feels.
A big time in a small town
Is a hellbender on wheels.

BY JOVE

Music by Robert Emmett Dolan.

By Jove!
How'd ja do?
Aren't you new here?
Jove . . .
Fancy meeting you here.
Gad . . .
Shall we pass the time of day?
Nice spot . . .
But the traffic's a menace.
What? . . .
Anyone here for tennis?
Rot! . . .
What's a chap supposed to say?
Clumsy of me—
My monocle's fallen in my cup.
Beastly bad luck, old girl,
May I stir it up?
Pip, pip . . . pardon me,
I'll be popping.
Eh? . . . where'd ja say
You were stopping?

Say! . . .
That's a pleasant sort of cove.
I fear . . .
That my heart's rather skittish.
Dear! . . .
Though it's not very British,
I'm in love . . .
By Jove!

CALL HIM DAD

Music by Mercer. Alternate title: "The Old Man."

VERSE

The paternal side of your family,
The old boy who squired the brood,
You should take the bother
To address as your father,
Or else he might think you rude.
They react most frightfully hammily
To a friendly pat on the back.
Besides, it's the custom
—That's unless you adjust 'em—
To come when you yell, "Hey, Mac!"

Call him Dad or call him Daddy,
Daddykins or Daddio,
He's your father and he loves you just the same.
Call him Pop or call him Poppa,
You can even say *Mon Père*,
Call him a silly ass,
Paterfamilias,
He won't care.
Call him Chief or call him Cuddles,
Or the Guy Who Pays the Bills,
That familiar appellation . . . the Old Man!
Call him Toots or perhaps the Old Gink,
Call him late for his six o'clock drink,
Call him up whenever you can.

Call him Fatso, call him Baldy,
Call him Shorty, call him Slim,
He's the head man of the house—except for Mom.
Call him Grumpy, call him Happy,
The Old War Horse, the Old Gent,
Call him Old Mister Pickle-puss,
Even Popsicle-puss,
He's content.
Call him Charlie, call him Irving,
Call him Pappy, call him Boss.
If he's British,
Call him Governor . . . or "Guv."

When you don't get the check you expect,
Call him person-to-person collect.
But no matter what you call him,
Call him up and give him your love.

Call him Dreamboat, call him Sweetstuff,
Call him Lover, call him Pet,
Majordomo of your daffy domicile.
Call him over to pick up the tab,
When he's loaded then call him a cab.
But no matter what you call him,
Call him up just once in a while.

VERSE

Well, I must admit that's an attitude
Which the French would treat as a joke.
With normal *Parisiennes*
It could lead to adhesions,
Accompanied by a stroke.
They expect obedient gratitude
Four-and-twenty hours by the clock,
But since you all say it,
And your parents okay it!
I'll learn how to yell, "Hey, Jacques!"

CECILIA

Composer unknown.

Does your mother know you're out, Cecilia?
Does she know that I'm about to steal you?
Oh, my, when I look in your eyes
Something tells me you and I should get
    together.
How about a little kiss, Cecilia?
Just a kiss you'll never miss, Cecilia.
Why do we keep on wasting time?
Oh, Cecilia, say that you'll be mine.

Doeth your mother know you're out, Cecilia?
Doeth thee know that I'm about to thteal "yuh"?
Oh, my, when I look in your eyth
I feel very, you-know, tho unneththary,
How about a little kith, Thethielyuh?
Jutht a kith you'll never mith, Thethielyuh.
Why do we two keep on wasting time?
Oh, Thethielyuh, thay that you'll be mine.

CLOSE YOUR EYES

Composer unknown. No music is known to survive.

Close your eyes
And tell me lies
Like "I'm in love with you."

Tell me this
With every kiss
And cross your heart, it's true.

If you know
It isn't so
Then cross your fingers, too.

But close your eyes
And tell me lies
Until you really do.

DEAREST DARLING

Composer unknown. No music is known to survive.

Dearest darling,
Dearest thing I know.
Darling of my heart,
May I tell you so.
Dearest darling,
That will be your name,
And my claim to fame . . . I love you.
Oh, my lover,
I could sing your praise
With so many words
In so many ways,
But I'll cover
Everything with these.
Dearest darling, please love me too.

DEEP IN THE MOON-COVERED MOUNTAINS

Composer unknown. No music is known to survive.

I went to look for the treasure of Sierra Madre,
Deep in the valleys and mountains,

For the treasure of Sierra Madre.
Only the lights of a small hacienda before me
Kept me from losing my way,
As the tempest broke o'er me lightning flashed.
Suddenly rain fell and the lightning flashed o'er me,
I saw a small bright hacienda before me,
Offered a bright light.

[*Lyric incomplete.*]

DISENCHANTED

Composer unknown. No music is known to survive.

I am one of the disenchanted,
Disenchanted
With the business of love.

I guess I took too much for granted
And the stars you planted
Turned to dust in my eyes.

You were the one who led me
Like a child into Disneyland.
Gone are the tales you read me,
Disappeared with a wave of your hand.

Gone, gone, gone is the sweet confusion.
Disillusion
Now inhabits my heart.
My companion-to-be
Where, oh, where are the dreams you planned
That I took for granted?

[*Lyric unfinished.*]

DON'T CROSS YOUR HEART WITH PROMISES

Composer unknown. No music is known to survive.

Don't cross your heart with promises,
If you don't mean what you say.
Don't even start with promises,
If you can't go all the way.
"No knife can cut our love in two"
Are the words we used to say.
I say them still,

I always will,
And I mean just what I say.
I beg of you
To love me true
In the same old honest way.
Don't cross your heart with promises,
If you don't mean what you say.

DON'T PLAY ME CUT-RATE

Music by Mercer.

People say with a smile
There's a change in your style,
You've forgotten the friends you knew.
But I hate to believe
You could be that naïve,
'Cause it sure doesn't sound like you.
Everything that goes up,
Well, it's bound to come down,
And it's always been true somehow.
I was a friend
When you really needed a friend,
So don't play me cut-rate now.

DON'T YOU RECOGNIZE ME?

Composer unknown. No music is known to survive.

Don't you recognize me?
I'm the fellow you see
Every seventy years or so.
Don't you recognize me
From the neighboring tree
Where I used to swing long ago?
I will never forget
How the two of us met
When there wasn't a soul in sight.
Don't you recognize me
From the Caspian Sea
When my tentacles held you tight?
I've lost a fin
And my fur is thin
But I'm in good shape for the shape I'm in.
I could tell it was you,
Just a glance and I knew.
Incident'ly my name is Bill.

See, I always show up and I reckon I always will.
Don't you recognize me?
I'm the fellow who loves you still.

DOWN IN THE DUMPS

Composer unknown. No music is known to survive.
    Note from Mercer on lyric sheet: "Mood of 'Winchester Cathedral' or 'The Trouble with Harry.' "

When you're given the sack

[*Whistle echo.*]

And you're gettin' your lumps,

[*Echo.*]

That's the moment for highjinks,
When you're down in the dumps!

When you're hittin' the dole

[*Echo.*]

With the rest of the chumps,

[*Echo.*]

Be the happiest cockroach,
When you're down in the dumps.

Stick out your chin,
Wear a grin,
Show the world you're a winner.
What's that in your lapel?

Walk down the street
While the beat
Of your feet keep repeatin'
"A scarlet pimpernel."
When they're givin' a dance

[*Whistle echo.*]

But you 'aven't no pumps,

[*Echo.*]

That's the time t'go dancin'.
In the depths of despair,
When the cupboard is bare,
And you're down in the dumps!

EAST OF THE ROCKIES

Composer unknown. Intended for Mercer and unnamed singer.

MERCER: I left my baby east of the Rockies,
North of the Rio Grande,
West of the 'Sip-pi,
South of Dakota land.
When you hit Texas
Take route thirty-three,
Turn right at Dreamy Valley,
Left at Lover's Alley,
Standin' 'neath the apple tree.
My boat is shovin' off
And I'm sailin',
But I'll return, I know,
And I'll remember
Just where I have to go:
East of the Rockies,
North of the Rio Grande,
West of the 'Sip-pi,
South of Dakota land.
Just think of Texas, route thirty-three,
Dreamy Valley, Lover's Alley,
Stop and see the apple tree.
I'll find my baby, waitin' there for me.
Stop and see the apple tree.
BOTH: I'll find my baby waitin'.
MERCER: That's why we're procrastinatin';
I'll find my baby waitin' there.

THE ECHO OF MY HEART

Composer unknown. No music is known to survive.

The words my lips keep whispering,
They're the echo of my heart.
The music too. They sing to you.
That's the echo of my heart.
I'd bring along
A newer song
If I knew just where to start,
But all I know
Is I love you so.
That's the echo of my heart.
If we should stray
A kiss away
Or a million miles apart,
I hope and pray

You can find your way
From the echo of my heart.

EVERYBODY LOVES YOU

Composer unknown. No music is known to survive.

Everybody loves you.
Everywhere you go it's the same.
There's a sudden lull in the room,
Then the room starts to boom with your name.

Everybody loves you
And they're all surprised as can be.
Looks of curiosity turn
To respect when they learn you're with me.

You should see the girls looking glum
As the fellows succumb to your charm.
You should see the smiles of delight
When you whisper goodnight on my arm.

Everybody loves you.
Everyone agrees you're a ball.
But in case you're ever in doubt,
Get the phone numbers out
And recall
Everybody loves you,
I the most of all.

EYES OF THE BELOVED

Music by Mercer.

Beauty is in the eyes of the beholder.
I behold you—and beauty is all I see.

Joy where you walk and music at your shoulder.
No one else to witness it but me.

Love fills the sky, and, oh, my heart grows bolder
As each day's new miracles meet my gaze.

I only pray the eyes of this beholder
May go on beholding you all his days.

[*Lyric unfinished.*]

FALLING STAR

Composer unknown. No music is known to survive.

Falling star,
Beautiful to see,
Are you telling me
Everything must die?
And love,
The old sweet story,
Ends in a blaze of glory?

Falling star,
Does your ageless flight
End in just a bright
Flicker of the eye?
I pray not so,
But if it has to be,
Just as you go,
Please grant this wish to me:
Will burn as bright
And travel just as far,
As pretty as a falling star.

FINDERS KEEPERS

Music by Virgilio Panzuti is dated 1966.

Finders keepers,
Losers weepers,
And I know
The tears will flow
Somewhere tonight.
Someone lost you
When I found you,
But he never should
Have let you
Out of sight.
Tell your friend
I'm just as sorry as can be,
But I'll never make
The same mistake as he.
Finders keepers,
Losers weepers,
And I'll live my life
To keep you loving me.

THE FLAME OF LIFE

Composer unknown. No music is known to survive.

Version 1

The flame of life
We all keep seeking,
The golden fleece—the magic key.
The flame of life
With all its secrets,
It holds no mystery for me.
I warm my heart
Beside the fire,
Dance in its glow
My whole life through,
Because the flame of life
Is love.
The flame of love
Is only you!

Version 2

That magic essence
Called the flame of life,
From the day it arrives
Seems to brighten our lives
With joy!

The sweet elixir
In the game of life
Is the laughter
Of each golden girl and boy.
Too long I hid my head
Beneath the covers,
Now my heart discovers
To catch the spark
You must be lovers.
The flame of life is love,
It must be true,
And, oh, the beautiful flame of love—
Its name is you!

THE FLYING CARPET

Music by Franz Steininger.

Fly with me,
Fly with my
Flying carpet across the sky,
Over the sand,
Over old Samarkand,

Till we leave tonight
On a flight
Where the beaches are diamond white,
Out there where the dolphins play
In the silvery, salty spray.
Land and we stand on the moon!
Soon we can be
By a drowsy coral sea
And the night meets the golden day.
Up-up-up-up-up-up-up-up-up!
Fly with me,
Fly away,
Flying carpets are here to stay.
You and I,
Riding high,
Fly, fly, fly!

FORGET-ME-NOT

Composer unknown. No music is known to survive.

While I am away,
Remember to forget-me-not.
Every time you pray,
Remember to forget-me-not.
Say it every day
And never let a day go by.
As we used to say,
"I cross my heart and hope to die."

For I'll be living through
Each moment we ever met,
As though I could forget,
As though I would forget.
As though I ever could
Or would forget you now.

Would you like to know
What moments I'll be thinking of?
Would you like to know
My one and only lifetime love?
How about the sight
Of lowered eyes one summer day?
Or the wild delight
The night we gave our hearts away?
Like fire in the sky,
The memory lingers yet.

As though I could forget,
As though I would forget,
As though I ever could
Or would forget you now.

FOR YOU'RE WORTH WAITING FOR

Composer unknown. No music is known to survive.

Hit or misses,
Here's what bliss is,
Certainly this is worth waiting for.
We missed some kisses.
No matter, this is
Worth those—and more.
No use pretending.
There was no ending
To years I kept spending.
But, oh, my darling,
I would be willing
To spend a dozen years,
For you're worth waiting for.

I'm poor at talking,
Better at walking
Or standing and gawking.
For I'd be willing
To wait a lifetime more,
For you're worth waiting for.

F'RINSTANCE

Music by Mercer.

F'rinstance—if I promised f'ralways
'N'always, f'rinstance, to be true,
'N' if like—on a stack of bibles I swear
Never to leave, ever to care.
F'rinstance—would you reconsider?
Do f'rothers
Half what others do for thee.

Would you take a chance for better or worse
F'rever, f'rinstance, with me?

[*Lyric probably incomplete.*]

GEE, BUT IT'S GOOD TO BE HOME AGAIN

Music by Robert Emmett Dolan.

Gee, but it's good to be home again,
Home in your own honeycomb again.
This poor little bee discovered
Just how wide this old world could be.
Oh, gee, but it's heaven to rest again
Close to the only one's breast again.
No foolin', I've had my schoolin',
It's good to be home in your arms.

GEE, IT'S GOOD TO HEAR IT AGAIN

Composer unknown. No music is known to survive.

Same old siren song,
The same old college spirit,
But gee, it's good to hear it again.
Same old jazzy line,
The networks wouldn't clear it,
But, gosh, it's nice to hear it again.
The same old song and dance
Called romance.
Mom and Dad went through it.
It still goes, I suppose,
All depends on how you do it.
So, turn the lights down low
And we'll atmosphere it,
'Cause, gee, it's nice to hear it again.

GHOST TOWN BLUES

Composer unknown. No music is known to survive.

Beggars can't be choosers—shake hands with
     some losers.

We are really down—we are really out,
Down to forty cans o' beans and out o' sauerkraut.

We are really out—we are really down,
God-forsaken people in a God-forsaken town.

Join me in a toast on your hungry host,
Join me in the ghost town blues.

If something doesn't happen tomorrow
I think we better head for the hills.
There isn't any gold in 'em,
Mighty, mighty cold in 'em,
But we can dodge a few bills.

Drink up, happy boozers, beggars can't be
     choosers.

Drink up and forget that we're all in debt.
Either it's the sheriff or the fellow with the net.

Either we're in jail sittin' on our tail
Or we better mush a little further up the trail.

With a little luck maybe make a buck,
Maybe lose the ghost town blues.

You couldn't find a mangier hamlet
If twenty million maps were unfurled.
It isn't just inferior—
This is the posterior,
I mean, the end, of the world!

Join me in a bender . . . join me while I render
The most—without a doubt—empty-handed,
     down-and-out
Place in all creation, rear end of the nation . . .
     BLUES!

GOD IS LOVE (AND LOVE IS GOD)

Music by Ida Thomas.

As long as we can see a tree,
A star above the mighty sea,
The lightning in the far-off sky,
And flowers when the storm goes by.
Just as long as someone's there,
There to answer every prayer,
And if clouds and trees and birds
Can speak in unseen words.
As long as there is shelter from the snows,
Long as we have rain and food that grows,
Then, why on earth does it seem odd
That God is love and love is God.

THE GOOD OLD DAYS

Composer unknown. No music is known to survive.

The good old days,
The good old days,
What became of them?
It's been only ten or fifteen years
Since we used to run from racketeers
And the speakeasies sold needled beers.
In the good old days,
When the two-a-day was all the rage
And an actor earned a living wage
When he laid eggs on the Palace stage.

When we all had crystal radios,
Played our ukes and sang our vod-eo-dos,
While we imitated two black crows.

Wonder what became of all those heels
Who accompanied performing seals,
Then would save the fish for their own meals,
In the good old days?

THE HANDS OF FATE

Composer unknown. No music is known to survive.

I feel as though
I'm in the hands of fate.
Insignificant pawn,
Irresistibly drawn to you.
A puppet dancing
To the strands of fate,
And there's a single thing
That I can do.
Alone at night,
I wonder why and whether
We're meant together,
Two birds of such uncommon feather.
But, since I have no charm
To break the spell,
I pray that
Maybe you're in the hands of fate
As well!

HAYSTACKS ON A HILL

Composer unknown. No music is known to survive.

Haystacks on a hill,
Summery day,
Same old cider mill
Creakin' away;
Far-off whippoorwill,
Clean out o' sight;
Late evenin' breeze
Kissin' the trees good night.

Haystacks on a hill,
Big yella moon,
Crickets hummin',
Harvest comin' soon.
I don't know;
It seems as though
It's made to go with you.
Won't you make it all come true?

You can plough and milk the cow
And don't you worry—I'll teach you how.
When we're hot as like as not,
We'll stop a minute to have a spot.
Real polite, he says goodnight.
I hope he's happy—it serves him right.

Right—the trees and breeze are takin' it easy.
Time to rest and feather nest.
And that's the moment I like the best.
Soon we'll spoon 'neath the silvery moon.

HERE WE ARE

Music by Robert Emmett Dolan.

I must have dreamed a million dreams of you or
    more,
And here you are,
And here you are.
It's just as if somebody opened up a door.
The scene it set
And you're the star.
I hope you say the lines that you're supposed to say,
I know I can't say mine in any other way.
The years until we met were long,
The miles were far.
But here we are,
Yes, here we are.

HIP LITTLE WORLD

Music by Mercer.

'N' we'll be Mommy 'n' Dad
In a mad little pad,
Where the art'll go Pop
From a top little shop.
We'll sip a nip in the kip
Till we flip in our hip
Little world.

[*Lyric unfinished.*]

Alternative

We'll have a crazy façade,
Which is odd 'n' quite mod,
Like a nod from the quad
Of the Harvard-y yard.

THE HONEYMOON IS OVER

Composer unknown. No music is known to survive.

For a month or so
There's a rosy glow,
You don't care what hours you keep.
But you know the honeymoon is over,
When you both begin to oversleep.

First he marries you,
Then he carries you
Up the stairs in your wedding gown.
But you feel the honeymoon is over,
When you have to carry him back down.

There may be indications
And little signs
That all is not as it was.

Take the oldest trap
Of a shoulder strap
Falling down nine inches or ten.
You can tell the honeymoon is over,
When he helps you put it up again.

Yes, the honeymoon is really over
And it happens to the best of men!
He may tire a bit
Or perspire a bit,

All without a word of complaint.
But you know the honeymoon is over,
When he falls down in a pale, grey faint.*

He may sigh a lot,
Even cry a lot—
Then again he may be too proud.
But you're sure the honeymoon is over,
When you hear him holler "help" out loud.

These are the little signals†
Along the way
That indicate a slight change.

When the hustle's off
And the bustle's off,
And you're getting ready for bed,
You can tell the honeymoon is over,
When he yawns and mutters, "Good night,
    Fred."
Yes, the honeymoon is really over
And your nightingale of love has fled‡

And your nights in paradise have fled!
Paradise of love,
Nightingale of love,
The bow-and-arrow boy,
Moments filled with bliss . . .
Etc.

I KNOW MY HEART

Music by Johnny Varro.

I know my heart,
I know my heart,
I know what it's about to say.
I know my lips, I know my arms,
They'll never let you get away.
They've felt your kiss,
They've held you as close as this.
Could either of them dismiss
Or let you go?
No.

---

* *Alternatives to final line:*
    When he throws a catatonic faint
    or
    falls down in a pole-axed faint
† *Or:* sign-posts
‡ *Alternate lines:*
    Yes, the honeymoon is really over
    And it happens just the way I said!

To make it clear,
If you came near,
I won't be blamed for what they do.
I know my heart,
I know my heart,
And I know you.

I LOVE YOU LIKE IT'S GOING OUT OF STYLE

Composer unknown. No music is known to survive.

I love you like it's going out of style, baby,
Love you like it's going out of style.
Whatever people do goes out of fashion, they say,
And so I'm gettin' all the love I can while I may.
Come on and
Kiss me like it's goin' out of vogue, baby,
Make believe we're on some desert isle.
The way this crazy world of ours is carryin' on,
We'll wake up one fine mornin' to discover it's gone.
Stay here and
Linger in my arms a little while, baby,
I love you like it's goin' out of style!

I NEVER HAD IT SO GOOD

Composer unknown. No music is known to survive.

I've had seven no-trump double
Made without a bit of trouble
But I guess I never had it so good.
I've had oysters Rockefeller,
Piper Heidsieck in the cellar,
But I know I never had it so good.
You're such a lamby
With your triple whammy;
From the day your two blues crackled
I was shackled.
Few remarks are worth the quoting
But as long as I'm repot-ing
Like the wolf remarked to Red Riding Hood:
You're so tasty
Leave us not be hasty
'Cause I never had it oh, so good!

I REALLY GET A MESSAGE FROM YOU

Composer unknown.

On my door there's a knocker that never knocks,
And the hinges are all rusty, too.
Never find any mail in my letter box,
But I really get a message from you.
Oh, the sound of the bell is a cheerful noise,
But it's something that I never knew.
I'm a stranger to all Western Union boys,
But I really get a message from you.
Don't know what you said,
When you said what you said,
But it gave me a terrific yen.
Don't know what you did
When you did what you did,
But I wish you'd do it again.
Not a soul ever sends me a valentine,
I don't waste any time guessin' who.
Never get any rings on my party line,
But I really get a message from you.

I REMEMBER WITH MY HEART

Composer unknown. No music is known to survive.

No photograph
Can show the laugh
I remember with my heart.
No bits of string
Nor anything
Can bring back the happy part.
And late at night,
When lights are bright
And the old-time love songs start,
No one can see
The memory
I remember with my heart.
Sometimes I rise
To hide my eyes
Quickly as the teardrops start,
So they can't see
The you and me
I remember with my heart!

I STRUCK IT LUCKY

Composer unknown for all versions. No music is known to survive.

Version 1

Heads I win,
Tails I win,
I struck it lucky
When you flashed that grin.

Could it be
You and me?
I struck it lucky
When you stayed to see . . .

I can't wait
Until fate
Calls the play ahead.
Even if I lose,
I'll be way ahead.

Love came through
Right on cue
And brought me every dream I ever knew.
I struck it lucky—with you!

Version 2

May I say
Come what may
I struck it lucky
When you came my way
Can't you see
Right or wrong
I struck it lucky
Knowing you this long.*

I'll just wait until fate
Calls the play ahead.
Even if I lose
I'll be way ahead.

Love came through
Right on cue
And made my most fantastic dream come true
And brought me every dream I ever knew.
I struck it lucky with you.

* *Alternate final four lines:*
  Rich or poor,
  Rise or fall,
  I struck it lucky
  Knowing you at all.

Version 3

Heads I win,
Tails I win,
I struck it lucky
When you first walked in.

Could it be
You'd like me?*
I struck it lucky
When you stayed to see.

Now I'll wait until fate
Calls the play ahead.
Even if I lose
I'll be way ahead.

Love came through
Right on cue
And made my most fantastic dream come true.
I struck it lucky—with you.

Version 4

Win or lose,
Right or wrong,
I struck it lucky
When you came along.

Rich or poor,
Can't you see
I struck it lucky
When I found you free.

Like some great wheel of fate,
Round and round life goes,
And where love comes up
Only heaven knows.

Fate came through
Right on cue.
I spun the wheel and saw it all come true.
I struck it lucky with you.

I THINK WE NEED A DRINK

Music by Mercer.

* *Alternate first two lines:*
  Can it be
  You like me/she likes me?

So whaddya think? I think*
We need a little drink.
A drink I think
'ill keep us in the pink,
'N' make us play,
'N' keep the cold away,
'N' warm our toes,
'N' redden up our nose.
So, whoops, down the hatch
To the tummy she goes.
So whaddya think? I think
My friend could use a drink.
He's Engelbert
And I'm Humperdinck.
His eyes are crossed,
His legs are on the blink.†
I tol' y' so.
He feels like new.
Now, let's have one
For the new man, too!
Oh, before we go,
Let's have a little drink—on you!

I WANT YOU

Composer unknown. No music is known to survive.

I want you,
I want you close,
I want you close to me—like this.
I want your lips,
I want your arms,
I want to explore
Those sweet here-to-fore
Unexplorable charms.
I want you,
I want you near,
I want you nearer than a kiss.

I love you,
I love you,
I want you,
I want you,

* *Alternate lyrics, probably to opening lines:*
  The night is cold
  And just as black as ink.
† *Alternate to lines 13–16:*
  Before we have
  To pour him down the sink,
  I think the fink
  Could use another drink.

But only
If you want me.

The reason is plain to see
What other could there be.
You mean the world to me.
I love you—I want you the whole night through—*
But only if you want me, too.

I want you,
I need you, too,
I need you to say—it's right.

IF PEANUTS WERE RUBIES

Composer unknown. No music is known to survive.

If peanuts were rubies,
Your own room
Would turn into a throne room
Tonight.
If popcorn were emeralds,
Your hall room
Would turn into a ballroom
Of white, where knights with bouquets of flowers
Would line up for hours
All hoping for just one dance,
One chance of willingly sharing
Some great deed of daring
Well knowing they'd either be wedded
Or they'd be beheaded!
Sure, I'm pretending,
But wouldn't I wish that kind of ending for you?
If daydreams were diamonds
And wishes could all come true!

If diamonds were wishes (peanuts) and wishes etc.

IF YOU CAN IMAGINE SUCH A THING

Composer unknown.

If you can imagine such a thing,
Imagine a place like this,

---

* *Alternate line:*
  I want you to love me the whole night through

Imagine a race like this,
Just hangin' in space like this.
Imagine a crazy population—over a billion souls
On one little ol' planet.
Bless whoever began it.
I'm so grateful that I'm here at all,
I'm so lucky I'm alive,
Gave up hoping you'd appear at all,
Sound of trumpets—you arrive.

If you can imagine such a thrill,
Imagine my soaring joy
When heavenly girl meets boy,
Like out of the blue,
And all of a sudden this old world becomes
Their private toy
And everything in life comes true.

Up, up, up you go,
And all at once you know
That there's no ceiling to the sky.
Down, down, down you swoop,
Your heart goes loop-the-loop,
And all that you can say is . . . "Bye"!

If you can imagine all that extra-sensory psychic
     jazz
Or what is referred to as
Subliminal powers,
The stars in the sky begin to sing
'Cause somebody wants to wear your ring—
If you can imagine such a thing—
It's ours!

I'LL HATE MYSELF TOMORROW

Music by Geoff Clarkson.

I'll hate myself tomorrow if I leave tonight,
Your lips are much too warm,
Your eyes are much too bright.
Darling,
You'll hate yourself tomorrow if you make me go,
Especially when I long to surrender so.
Nights like this come only once in a year of Junes.
Moons like this the poets tell us are lovers' moons.
That's why
We'll hate ourselves tomorrow and our whole lives
     through,
So love me tonight and all my tomorrows too.

I'M A MAN

A poem.

Ain't you proud of me? I'm a man,
I spoil everything that I can,
And I'll never be satisfied
Til I've ruined the countryside.
I catch all the fish in the seas,
Burn up forests and chop down trees,
Fill the rivers with sludge and oil,
Wash the minerals from the soil.
I kill tigers and leopards, too,
I put everything in the zoo.
(Those I haven't destroyed, I save
To remind me that I'm so brave!)
Soon not one of them will be here—
I make everything disappear:
Giant turtles and blue sperm whales
Now are rarer than nightingales.
I shoot eagles and bears from planes,
They're all gone with the whooping cranes.
I have mountaintops leveled down
For one ticky-tack high-rise town.
Soon the air will be black as ink
All the water unfit to drink.
I raise cattle and pigs for meat,
Ducks and chickens are good to eat.
As for hummingbirds, they're no loss—
They're delicious with bernaise sauce!
I kill sables and minks for furs—
Some are his 'n' and some arc hers.
I stuff everything else I can.
Ain't you proud of me? I'm a man!
When I've got 'em all on a shelf,
I may even destroy myself!

I have children my wife adores,
So I send 'em all off to wars,
Where they shoot someone else's sons;
Ain't that wonderful? That sells guns.
That ain't all. I been on the moon
Like a fly on a macaroon;
But them planets are no damn good,
Ain't no animals there for food.

Some damn dreamers—and I mean damn—
Think they're better than what I am,
Say by usin' the sense God gave
There's no species they couldn't save.
If we only killed one apiece
We might even make things increase!
Did you ever hear such damn rot?
They don't know of the plans I got.
Like the buffalo and the gnu,
Like the passenger pigeons, too,

I plan startin' in on the shrew;
Soon, ol' buddy, I'll start on you!
Then, imperious, I will stand
In a waterless, treeless land,
On a planet of sand and stone
Picked as clean as a chicken bone!

Well, I'd like to just stay and "jaw"
But in Africa I just saw . . .
Say! They tell me in Timbuktu
There's a panda or two in view.
And I know, 'cause I seen the map—
Oil lies under the polar cap;
So I'm takin' my blastin' rig,
That uranium's tough to dig!
Well, ol' buddy, I'll see you roun',
Don't take nothin' that ain't nailed down.
Some day when you instruct your son
Tell the little chap what I've done;
He'll be sort of impressed, I bet.
Hell, I haven't got started yet!
There ain't nothin' that man can't do.
Ain't you proud of us?
You're one too!

I'M GOING BACK TO THE FARM

Music by Mercer.

Reuben, Reuben, I've been thinking,
You were right and I was wrong.
Reuben, Reuben, I've been thinking,
Soon I'll be where I belong.

REFRAIN 1

I'm going back to the farm,
I want pastoral charm,
I need quiet, a long steady diet,
So, I'm going back to the farm.
Early to bed and to rise,
Rub the sleep from my eyes,
Roosters crowing, "Get up and get going,"
Oh, I'm going back to the farm.
All the noisy hustle-bustle
Can't compare with leaves that rustle
In a lovely woodland scene.
Underneath the willows' shelter
Brooks are running helter-skelter
And the grass is always green.
Back there the sunshine is free,
No more hallroom for me,

I'm through looking for old-fashioned cooking,
'Cause I'm going back to the farm.

REFRAIN 2

I'm going back to the farm
Where I'll keep out of harm;
Strange desires of out-o'-town buyers
Are sending me back to the farm.
When I arrived I was pure,
Now I'm not at all sure.
Those nice brokers were practical jokers
So, I'm going back to the farm.
I've forgotten what a blush is
Since I bought those Fuller brushes.
Gracious, I was so naive
When the landlord said, "Don't bother,
Just pretend that I'm your father,"
There was something up his sleeve.
I paid the piper a call,
And I paid with my all.
He got plenty . . . but I got a twenty,
So, I'm going back to the farm.

REFRAIN 3

I'm going back to the farm.
I've got cause for alarm.
I'm enlarging from too much massaging,
So I'm going back to the farm.
Milked in the old-fashioned way,
I'd give ten quarts a day.
This is grand style but give me the hand style.
Oh, I'm going back to the farm.
How's a cow to be contented
With a thing like this invented?
I can hardly chew my cud.
Really, it's quite aggravating
When I know my boyfriend's waiting
For our little game of stud.
I'm really getting the works.
This machinery jerks.
My poor udder is now giving butter,
So I'm going back to the farm.

I'M JUST ANOTHER DATE TO YOU

Composer unknown. No music is known to survive.

You're everything to me,
You're the only one I see,
But I'm just another date to you.

Whenever you're alone
Then you get me on the phone,
'Cause I'm just another date to you.

You want a partner for a dance,
It makes me think I've got a chance,
But when others come in view
It's "Twenty-three Skidoo!"

You think I'm kinda cute
Till you find a substitute.
Guess I'm just another date to you.

I'M ON TO YOU

Composer unknown. No music is known to survive.

Wherever they grow one,
It takes one to know one,
And I'm on to you!
A tiger may iron his spots out straight,
But he's gotta go some to fool his mate.
You may fool the yokels
And even the locals
By pulling a fast one or two,
But fast one or slow one
It takes one to know one,
And I'm on to you!
I've been there (Dear Countess)
I'm on to you!

The fox who is cagey and smart as sin
Has gotta rise early to fool his twin.
You may be bewitching
When you're in there pitching
And throwing a fast ball, it's true,
But high one or low one
It takes one to know one
And I'm on to you.

IN THE TWINKLING OF AN EYE

Composer unknown. No music is known to survive.

I got an inkling
In the twinkling of an eye
Of how wonderful life can be.
I saw it quicker

Than a flicker passing by.
It began when you smiled at me.
Angels were playing,
I was walking on air—
Then I turned around
And there was nobody there,
But I got an inkling
In the twinkling of an eye
And that's as good as a guarantee!

THE INVISIBLE SIDE OF LIFE

Composer unknown. No music is known to survive. The
lyric is clearly unfinished.

Sometimes we cannot see
How things are supposed to be
Until a lot later on.
I can't live without you.
Waiting, that's all I'm doing,
Waiting.
And I call this the invisible side of life.
There is a destiny that shapes our ends,
Rough hew or plan* them as we may.
Do good, be loyal to your friends
And, most of all, pray.
If luck is on your side,
And fate is your friendly guide,
You've got it practically made.

[*Handwritten lyric breaks off here.*]

IT'S OUT OF MY HANDS

Music by Mercer.

It's out of my hands,
It's simply too big for me,
Out of my hands,
How strong can a person be?
I feel like a leaf
That's caught in the tide,
Perhaps I'll go under but oh, what a wonderful ride.
I'd like to turn back,
But this is a one-way street,
So clear the track,
My heart's in the driver's seat.

---

* *Or:* shape

Wherever it goes
I've got to go, too,
It's out of my hands
And it's up to you.

JOHN HENRY

Composer unknown. No music is known to survive.

VERSE

Grandchildren, let me tell you a story,
Tell you 'bout the folks down in purgatory.
Grandchildren, let me tell you a story.

REFRAIN 1

John Henry was a travellin' man,
He travelled all around the earth.
John Henry used to do it in style,
You always found him in an upper berth.
He went to China, he went to Bombay,
He settled down in Savannah, GA.
John Henry was a travellin' man,
Lawd, have mercy on his soul.

REFRAIN 2

John Henry was a musical man,
He used to play the slide trombone;
My goodness, how he used to swing off,
The ladies wouldn't leave that man alone.
He played it pretty, as nice as you choose,
But he was king of the St. Louis Blues.
John Henry was a musical man,
Lawd, have mercy on his soul.

REFRAIN 3

John Henry was a triflin' man,
He had a gal in ev'ry town.
John Henry was a triflin' man
And that's the thing that turned his damper down.
He saw a brown skin he thought was the one,
She had a husband and he had a gun.
John Henry was a triflin' man,
Lawd, have mercy on his soul.

JUST ONCE

Composer unknown. No music is known to survive.

Just once
I mean to have my little fling.
Just once
I'll be as reckless as a king.
Just once
I'll shoot the works with everything
Even more on the side
Let it ride,
Let it ride!

Just once
I'll give this staid old world a thrill
And never even think about the bill.
Then, after that,
Why, after that,
Oh, well, I'll think of that tomorrow . . .

Just once I'll give the dice a roll
And risk my own immortal soul.
But why be gloomy?
This is no time.
Let's drink up;
Can't you see? It's
Show time!

One night,
To be as free as I can be.
One swingin' world,
The guest of honor
Me!
Then when the dawn discloses I'm the dunce
And life goes spinning by me,
Can anyone deny me
That I had it once, at least,
Just once?

JUST TO REMIND YOU

Music by Howard Jackson does not survive.

I thought our love affair was splendid,
So I let matters drift along;
Then one day it ended,
I was wrong.
And now you're sorry that you met me,
You're more than glad we said goodbye;
But dear, you never can forget me
No matter how you try.

The moon keeps shining
Just to remind you
That it was shining when we met.
And though that night is far behind you

It won't be easy to forget.
And spring keeps coming
Just to remind you
That once it came upon us, too.
The summer breeze will always find you,
Remind you of the love we knew.
No matter where you wander
My song will come to your ear
Though you are here, are yonder,
My face will never disappear.
So while you're trying
To put behind you
Each thought of days that used to be,
I'm saying this just to remind you
That there's no need reminding me.

KEEP YOUR PIGS OUT O' MY POTATOES

Music by Mercer, who noted: "This has a cute 'folk' melody." Written circa 1971 for *The Pig War*, an apparently unproduced show, script by Don Devendorf, based on an obscure 1859 conflict over the Pacific Northwest's San Juan Islands, claimed by both the United States and Britain. The so-called war began when a trespassing pig was killed by an American settler. "It was eating my potatoes," the settler reportedly said. "It is up to you to keep your potatoes out of my pig," the pig's British owner allegedly replied.

Good fences make good neighbors
And I believe that's true.
I never trespassed on your land
And now I'm tellin' you . . .

Keep your pig out o' my potatoes,
Keep your chickens out o' my tomatoes,
Keep your pig out o' my potatoes,
Else this means war!

[*Lyric unfinished.*]

THE LAFAYETTE ESCADRILLE

Composer unknown. No music is known to survive.

Have you seen
The Lafayette Escadrille

Zooming along
Seventy strong
Over the nearest hill?
I guarantee you'll see
A sight you won't forget.
They can accomplish things the eagles can't do yet.
Nothing can touch the Escadrille of Lafayette.

Oui, Lafayette, we are here,
Here to repay a debt.

THE LAND OF MY LOVE

Composer unknown. No music is known to survive.

I shall remember the oyster-shell roadway,
The cat-tails beside it,
The gray moss above,
The smell of the marshes, the boat at the landing,
The cherries that fell where my bare feet were standing,
The whurrr of the partridge,
The land of my love.

I shall remember the hills of Virginia,
The wheat bending to them,
The cold stars above.
The eyeshades at nighttime, the bell ending classes,
The Christmas train home that was slow as molasses,
And the frost on the glasses,
The Rapidan River,
The land of my love.

I shall remember the country club dances,
The taffeta dresses,
The blue lights above.
The old-fashioned shirt-studs, the telephone ringing,
The drinks in the car and the barbershop singing,
The lips in the darkness,
The land of my love.

LEAVE THE KEY IN THE MAILBOX

Music by Helmy Kresa.

Leave the key in the mailbox,
Leave the light in the hall,
I'll get in when the milkman makes his regular call.
When the party is over and the sun peeps through,
I'll be coming home to you.
If I have any trouble,
There's a cop on the beat,
He can give me directions,
He can show me the street.
I can open the door if I can find the house at all.
Leave the key in the mailbox,
Leave the light in the hall.

LESSON IN JAZZ

Music by Wingy Manone.

You say you wanna have a lot of fun?
Professor Jazz'll show you how it's done.
We now commence with lesson number one.
It goes, "A-re-bop, sha-be-bop, sha-bam, buh-lam."
The fellows love it and the ladies, too,
Because it's such a lot of fun to do.
Proceeding now to lesson number two,
We holler, "Rock it and sock it and thank you, ma'am!"
Gee. Lesson number three
Makes you want to go to four or five.
Six gets you the bricks,
Seven, eight, and nine are full of jive—
Jazz-a-roo-ti!
Now your curriculum is nearly done,
But all the merriment has just begun,
'Cause we are back to lesson number one,
Remember "Re-bop, sha-bebop, sha-bam-buh-lam."

LEST YOU FORGET

Composer unknown. No music is known to survive.

Hold me in your arms and kiss me
And say you'll miss me.
Say it again.
When the summer sky is burning,
I'll be returning,
But until then—

Lest you forget
How I love you here in my heart,

Lest you forget
How I'll miss you while we're apart,
There is the lane
Where I found you that night we met.
It will remain
When I leave you—lest you forget.
I'll have your arms
As a keepsake while I'm away,
I'll have your kiss
As a memory.
You'll have the moon to remind you
I'm coming back to find you.
Lest you forget
To remember me.

LET'S KNOCK ON WOOD

Composer unknown. No music is known to survive.

Let's knock on wood,
Let's cross our fingers
And thank our stars
We fell in love.

Let's knock on wood
And hope it lingers
Until the starlight fades above.

We're in a field of four-leaf clovers.
They must have blossomed where we stood.
That love will endure—
Then, to make sure—
Let's knock on wood.

LETTERS FROM MY MOTHER

Composer unknown. No music is known to survive.

Letters from my mother
Lighting up the lonely years.
Letters from my mother
Full of laughter and of tears,
Telling me the gossip,
Telling me the news from home,
Saying that she's for me,
Always will adore me,
Whatever I do, wherever I roam.
Letters from my mother
Making me a boy again.

Never was another
Who could mean what she did then.
Though she's not beside me
Still her love will guide me
Just as long as I have this.
Letters from my mother
Every one a good night kiss.

LIFE'S A PIECE OF PIE

One of three surviving lyrics apparently written for a musical about Cyrano de Bergerac, a project Mercer and Michel Legrand never got around to working on. No music is known to survive.

Life is not a bubble
Nor a lot of trouble,
Life's a piece of pie.

Just ask any baker
Who is not a faker.
He will tell you why.

Water, sugar, flour,
Make it sweet or sour,
Bake it wet or dry.

Any way you bake it,
Life is what you make it,
Like a piece of pie.

A powdery crust of sugary dust
You add to give it a tang.
A strawberry tart's a vision of art
With just a little meringue.
And living is nice when sugar and spice
Can change a tear to a sigh.

You come out a winner
And for after dinner
Life's a piece of pie!

If you ask a dancer
She perhaps will answer,
"Life's a *tour de tête!*"

If you ask a tailor
Or, perhaps, a sailor,
Who knows what they'll say.

But ask any artist
Who perhaps is smartest,
He'll say, "Watch your fly!"

But, upon my maker
As an honest baker,
Life's a piece of pie.

LIGHT OF MY LIFE

Composer unknown. No music is known to survive.

Light of my life,
It's time you knew,
You make it all worthwhile.
Light of my life,
Because of you,
The world is wearing a smile.
You fill the room with daisies,
You fill the air with song,
So sunny-hearted,
That once you get started,
The rest come tagging along.
Heart of my heart,
You give me wings,
I seldom touch the ground.
Marvellous part
Of planning things
Is knowing you'll be around;
For in the shining moments
And in the dark ones, too,
Truly, truly,
The light of my life is you.

A LITTLE CHURCH

Composer unknown. No music is known to survive.

A little church is close to you,
It seems to hug you tight
Because its prayers are really true
You pray with all your might.

The angel's wings are close at hand,
Not way up in the air,
And God is there to understand
You really feel His care.

By day or night in spring or fall
Its doors are open wide,
And anyone who comes to call
Is welcome there inside.

So from the days of Sunday school
Until the last long rest,
To really know God's great big love
A little church is best.

LITTLE MR. BOWLEGS

Composer unknown. No music is known to survive.

Who's that cowboy chasing that rustler?
Nothing scares him, sure is a hustler.
Who's that straight-shooting ranger
Riding smack into danger?
Little Mr. Bowlegs on his rocking horse.

Bucking bronco, rope and a six-gun,
Never gives up, not till his trick's done.
All those outlaws go hiding,
When that guy comes a-riding,
Little Mr. Bowlegs on his rocking horse.

Get along, little cowboy,
Get along, get along,
You've rode the range all day.
Put your horse in the closet,
Get along, say your prayers,
'S time you were hitting the hay.

Bad men fear you, I know you're playing.
Come now, cowhand, hear what I'm saying.
Pack your guns in your holster,
Climb into that four-poster.
Little Mr. Bowlegs on your rocking horse.

LIVING IN THE USED-TO-BE

Lyric by "John" Mercer. Music by Afred Opler does not survive.

You are far away.
Be that as it may,
I can feel you near my side.
Just a word or two,
Some old song we knew,
Takes me back again through time and tide.

Yesterday has ended, tomorrow is here,
But there's no tomorrow for me.
I keep finding mem'ries that won't disappear

Living in the used-to-be.
Climbing up the hillside that we used to climb,
Seeing things that we used to see,
Walking down the roadway where we spent our
    time,
Can't forget the promise that we swore by,
Set so much store by.
We meant it then.
And if I am still the one and only
You must be lonely
And want me back again.
Am I right in thinking that you're lonely too?
Is there just a chance left for me?
Say that you will come back and tell me I'm
    through
Living in the used-to-be.

LODGE SONG (I LOVE TO "SHEE")

Composer unknown. No music is known to survive.

Some like to ice skate,
But I like to ski.
Some like to bobsled,
But I like to ski.
Give me a *fraulein*
To sit next to me,
Cheeks red and rosy,
I'm comfy and I'm cozy.
Some like to sleigh ride
All wrapped up and warm.
Some like to snowshoe
Just after a storm.
Give me a fireplace,
A hot spot of tea
And let me ski, ski, ski.

Never believed it when the Swiss would say
S-K-I spells "shee."
It didn't matter what the Swiss would say,
S-K-I spelled "ski."
I wondered what a Swedish miss would say,
Seated close to me,
And I must agree,
For since she taught me what a kiss would say,
I love to "shee" . . .
Some like to polka
And some to gavotte.
Oscar Homolka,
He likes it a lot.
Some like to yodel
Alone on an alp.

That makes the days long,
But me, I like to *chaise longue*.
Give me a fireplace,
A schnapps, or a beer,
Give me a *fraulein*
To call me *Mynheer*,
I'll be as happy
As happy can be,
Because I love to "shee."

LONELYHEART

Music by Robert Emmett Dolan.

Back in the big town,
Back in Chicago,
The lights are brighter than day.
People are dancin'
And I should be there
But if I were there I'd just say:
Love is a smile
Love is moon mist and vapor
Guess maybe I'll put an ad in the paper:
Lonelyheart, do you need a friend?
Need a pal?
Have time to spend?
Where do you go,
That's if nobody sees you?
There's a new show playin' down at the Bijou.
Gee, it's tough when you're really blue
Finding someone who's a lonelyheart, too.

THE LONG-BURNING LIGHT OF THE PAST

Composer unknown. No music is known to survive.

May is all thunder, deception, and plunder,
A runaway going too fast,
And I turn with relief
From that arrogant thief
To the long-burning light of the past.
The men are all bluster,
The women lackluster,
Bit parts of a nondescript cast,
So I search for the truth
And the peace of my youth
In the slow-burning light of the past.

When the names and the colors,
The sights and the smells
Are only alive in the mind,
But there they live on
In the fact that they're gone,
Frozen in the patina of time.
There's comfort and solace
In knowing Cornwallis
And Herod are sleeping at last,
And there in a book
We can take a good look
At the long-burning light of the past.

THE LONG OF IT, THE SHORT OF IT

Composer unknown. No music is known to survive.

The long of it,
The short of it,
Let's compare them just
For the sport of it.
A giraffe is as tall as the loftiest tree,
But he runs from the most insignificant bee.
The big of it,
The small of it,
Rome was great but great
Was the fall of it.
Oh, the bigger they come,
Why, the harder they fall,
That's an adage we've always known.
Elephants, people say, are as big as a house,
But they tremble with fear at the tiniest mouse.
When you think about
The rest of us,
I suggest we both
Make the best of us.
It's a helluva life to live alone.

The short of it,
The long of it,
Someone really should
Write a song of it.
Take a great cobra snake who is limber and
    loose,
He gets tied up in knots by a little mongoose.
Or take a skunk,
The smell of it.
Yes, he does, and ain't
That the hell of it?
Better count up to ten
When you're pickin' a fight,
Just remember you might get thrown.

Yessirree, though you're THE biggest fish in the
    brook,
Keep your eye on the guy with the little old hook.
Nothing further to
Report of it.
That's about the long and
The short of it.
It's a helluva life to live alone.

LOST IN THE SUN

Lyrics by E. Y. Harburg and "John" Mercer. Music by Henry Souvaine does not survive. The song dates from 1932, when Mercer was working with Harburg and Souvaine on *J. P. McEvoy's New Americana*.

My voice was still,
It had no song to sing;
I felt it wrong to sing
Unless my heart sang, too.
I went along
With no one guiding me,
With darkness hiding me
That I could not break through.
There I was, searching for you where I was.
Here you are, all at once how near you are.

Now that I've found you,
I'm lost in the sun;
Each thing around you
Seems lost in the sun.
Blind with light, light that trembles in your eyes,
Blind with love, love I dare not realize.
How can I follow this light I have won?
I'm no Apolle—I'm lost in the sun.
Through the gloomy darkness you looked at me,
Then suddenly I seemed to be
Lost in the sun.

MADE FOR EACH OTHER

Composer unknown. No music is known to survive.

It's wonderful to be
Made for each other.
To be like you and me,
Made for each other.
To know that if I'm blue
You understand me,

And if I smile,
After a while
You're smiling too.
It's wonderful to know
You like what I like,
The way you tell me so,
So gentle and shy-like.
Our lips, our arms, our hearts
Go so hand-in-glove
Just made, it seems, for each other to love!

MERCI BEAUCOUP

Music by Ray Navarre is not known to survive.

Mademoiselle,
How can I tell
All the things that I want you to hear?
Can I reveal
Just how grateful I feel?
There's one phrase that may make it clear, dear.

Merci beaucoup,
I'm thanking you
For the love that you've brought to my heart.
Merci beaucoup,
I'm thanking you
For the thrill that I've felt from the start.
When you came to me smiling
And I kissed your hand,
Then I found in a moment
The lifetime I'd planned.
Merci beaucoup,
I'm thanking you
For the love that you've brought to my heart.

NE PLUS ULTRA

Composer unknown. No music is known to survive. Alternate title: "Baby o' Mine."

Baby o' mine,
You're nothin' but ultra to me.
You shine,
That's somethin' quite ultra to see.
You're simply a dream
Beyond the extreme. 'N' ya knows
That I merely quote.
That's what the man wrote

And he oughta know—shoah!
Mr. Noah Webster says that ultra
Means way out in space.
Surely he referred
To only your fabulous face,
Baby.
Just like a fine watch,
Or maybe a bottle of rare old Scotch,
You are *ne plus ultra*!

NEVER HAD IT SO GOOD

Composer unknown. No music is known to survive.

Never thought I'd have you,
But ever since I've had you,
I know I've never had it so good.
Old Joe Sophistication,
The cross patch of the nation
Is like a little babe in the wood.
Dreams I've waited for
Tied with string,
Roses round the door
And everything.
If the plans I'm laying
Get lady luck's okaying,
We're gonna leave the old neighborhood.
While we Mom and Dad it,
Aladdin can Alad it
And bring us lots of babes in the wood.
The world may treat us so-so
But we'll sing *amoroso*.
I never had it oh, so good.

NINETY-SEVEN CARS ON A MIDNIGHT TRAIN

Music by Archie Rosate.

Ninety-seven cars on a midnight train,
Count 'em as it rattles across your rainy
    windowpane,
Add 'em to the raindrops and think when you do
Of the tears I used to cry for you.

Now, count a million stars in the deep blue sky,
Add 'em to the tumblin' weeds as they go rollin'
    by,

Maybe that'll give you an idea or two
Of the dreams that never did come true.

I smiled the while you kissed me sad adieu,
Saying you'd come back some day . . . to stay,
But ninety-seven cars couldn't carry the heartaches
You left me when you went away.

NO WIKI WIKI

Music by Mercer.

The moon is low,
It's time to go,
But no wiki wiki.
The palm trees say
It's nearly day,
But no wiki wiki.
We haven't got a minute to lose,
We're both on a twenty-day cruise
With so many beautiful views to see . . .
Gee!
We'll take that tour
Tomorrow, sure,
But no wiki wiki.
Tonight's the night
We'll never quite recall,
There'll come a time we'll have to go home,
. . . and as our boat sails over the foam . . .
We'll sigh, "All right,"
Just not tonight,
There's no wiki wiki at all.

But with that great big moon up above,
If I may quote the language of love,
I whisper "Phooey,"
Aloha nui
There's no wiki wiki at all.

NOBODY ASKED ME

Composer unknown. No music is known to survive.

Nobody asked me, so I'll tell you anyway.
To me you're like the sparkle of an April day,
And when you smile,
It's like walking into a room where the sunlight
    pours.
My goodness gracious,

My heart's as spacious as all outdoors.
No, nobody asked me, so I thought you'd like to
    know.
Your image follows me no matter where I go.
At the risk
That I might bore you,
May I say I adore you?
No, nobody ever inquired
If I had a dream to come true,
But if anybody ever asks me now—it's you.

NOT FOR SALE

Music by Mercer.

The only heart I've got to give
Is not for sale.
The only life I've got to live
Is not for sale.
I wouldn't hesitate a minute if I thought you
    loved me too,
But my kisses aren't for sale to even you.

Not for sale.
Not for sale.
If you want a wedding ring or bridal veil,
You can buy it at the ten-cent store,
Or get it through the mail,
But my one and only heart is not for sale.

Not for sale.
Not for sale.
If you want a peck o' wheat or cotton bale,
You can go down to the marketplace and weigh it
    on a scale,
But my one and only heart is not for sale.

NOTHING UP MY SLEEVE

Music by Archie Bleyer.

VERSE

You're so afraid of me,
What can the reason be?
Just try to put yourself in my position.
I think you're simply swell,
Want to do right by Nell,
Now won't you clear your mind of all suspicion.

REFRAIN

Parlor tricks are something I could never do,
Wouldn't even try if I were able.
Don't you see why you think I've got designs on
     you,
When there's really nothing up my sleeve.
My intentions are the very best you'll find.
All my cards are placed upon the table.
I'll admit that there is something in my mind,
But there's really nothing up my sleeve.
Why the big resistance?
Think of all the magic that should be done.
Lend me your assistance,
I will soon begin making two hearts one.
And here's the way I'll go about it:
First I'll turn a penny into twenty grand,
Hit upon a little bit of land, and
Then when I say won't you please believe
That there's really nothing up my sleeve?

NOW

Composer unknown. No music is known to survive.

Now,
The moment is now
To share the wine of sweet desire.
Now,
With spring on the bough,
While both our hearts are full of fire.
Now,
While all the stars are right.
There's no tomorrow night,
That's when their far-off light
May fade and go.
Now, I want you to know
That you are all I've ever prayed for,
All
My heart can recall,
All that my lips were ever made for,
Do
Promise you'll love me, too.
Not in a year or two,
Say it can all come true
With you right now!

NOW IT'S A THING OF THE PAST

Music by Alexander Fogarty.

VERSE

Like a sudden song in the air,
I heard your voice and knew you were there,
Bringing the dream I'd hoped to find.
I had not begun to exist,
When all at once from out of the mist
I saw your face so well defined.
Just when I wondered where you were—
There you were.

REFRAIN

I saw you smile. I heard my heart sing.
Here is a real love at last.
Would we end it never,
Hold it forever.
Now it's a thing of the past.
Without a word some unknown feeling
Told me the die had been cast,
And before I knew love,
I had been through love.
Now it's a thing of the past.
I was too sure of that glory,
That wonder of you and I.
I saw no end to our story,
Thought love could never die. I was wrong.
Once I had hopes of your returning,
One foolish dream to hold fast,
And though it was splendid,
How soon it ended.
Now it's a thing of the past.

OH, BOY!

Composer unknown. No music is known to survive.

Oh, boy! Some fun! Oh, boy!
This'll really knock you out
Did you hear the one about
Oh, boy! What yells! Oh, boy!
Well, it seems this guy was passin' by
Laugh I thought I'd die!
He said—and looked at me
Get a load of this gag
I said—well, honestly,
Wait'll you hear the tag

Is this the real McCoy?
Say, did we have laughs the other day—oh, boy!

THE OLD BOY

Composer unknown. No music is known to survive.

I address him as the Old Boy,
For, you see, he's been here awhile,
Though he's never been in fashion,
Never once is he out of style.
He may woo you in an instant
Or pursue you for months and months,
But whatever be your station,
If it's any consolation,
Everybody meets the Old Boy,
Though they only meet him once.

Though the Old Boy is a stranger,
Many times we have almost met.
He could prove to be the worst friend
Or the best one that I've had yet.
If I wind up with the Old Nick
Or the holiest saints in Rome,
I'll be carefree, I'll be jolly,
Unembarrassed by my folly,
I'll go proudly, cursing loudly,
When the Old Boy walks me home.

When the Old Boy pays a visit
I will stand with my head held high.
Be it painful or exquisite,
He will find that my eyes are dry.
And I'll bellow, "Well, old fellow!
Do you mean this it how it ends?"
I'm not bragging that we're cronies,
But in countless ceremonies
Sharing battle after battle
We've become the best of friends.

Any dumbbell knows the Old Boy
Could appear any time of day.
Like your shadow, he is always
Just a step and a half away.
When you hear him, never fear him,
But resist him the best you can.
Don't be frightened or a coward
Though outweighed and overpowered,
For the Old Boy gives no quarter
But he loves a fighting man.

Everybody knows the Old Boy,
He's around from the day of birth,
And he's present in the background

Every day we are on this earth.
He can call you in the morning
Or perhaps in the dead of night,
But whenever, night or morning,
He's inclined to give you warning,
And the Old Boy must know something.
Got to hand it to the O.B.
For he's never lost a fight.

Though the Old Boy is a scarecrow
Maybe that's just a wise* disguise.
Many people find him ugly†
But there's kindness in his old eyes—
Full of mercy for the aged
And the hopelessly, helpless lame.
Only ruthless in a duel
With the reckless and the cruel.
Never bait him or underrate him
For the Old Boy is his name!

You may know him as "The Reaper,"
As "The Big Sleep" or "Old Man Bones."
He has names like "Uncle Bright Eyes,"
"The Convincer," and "Davey Jones."
And some evenin' when "Old Paleface"
Looks at me comin' through the gloam,
Then whatever I may call him,
I won't fool him nor outstall him;
I'll be smiling at the Old Boy
When the Old Boy walks me home!

ON OUR GOLDEN WEDDING DAY

Music by Carl Sigman.

On our golden wedding day,
When we both are old and grey,
You will hear me call you sweetheart,
Just the way I do today.
When the spring has turned to fall,
I will love you best of all.
We'll be side by side,
Just a groom and bride
On our golden wedding day.

* *Or:* good
† *Alternate line:*
   I've heard rumors that he's ugly

ONE FOR ALL

One of three surviving lyrics apparently written for a musical about Cyrano de Bergerac, a project Mercer and Michel Legrand never got around to working on. No music is known to survive.

One for all
And all for one,
We're friends to the end of the line.
We'll be as close as Romulus and Remus,
Together in absentia or extremis.
It's all for one
And one for all.
Whatever is yours will be mine,
The highest mountain or the deepest canyon,
Your bosom buddy and your boon companion,
Like Porthos and Aramis and d'Artagnan,
Will be with you.
One for all, all for one, rain or shine!

OOM-PAH-PAH

Composer unknown. No music is known to survive.

Oom-pah-pah,
Our musical pride and joy.
Cradled a bass
Up to his face
When he was just a boy
And blowin'
"Oom-pah-pah"
With everything he had.
Developed a tone that made the players shout, "Hurrah!"
There never will be a greater bass than Oom-pah-pah.

Oom-pah-pah
Goes merrily on his way.
Trumpet and flute,
Rootle-dee-toot.
Whaddya hear him say?
Y' hear him, Oom-pah-pah,
As happy as can be.
None of the fellows workin' in the or-chess-trah
Has half the talent or the fun of Oom-pah-pah.

Cornets go, "Doo-wacha-doo-wacha-doo" all day.
Fifes outsqueal the high-pitched peal the glockenspielers play

(A dog can hardly hear it).
Trombones go "glassanderoo,"
That's what the trombones say,
While ten piccolos on their tippy toes
Go "Yodel-eedle-eidle-odel-ay,"
Yay, yay, yay.

Oom-pah-pah
Goes staggering up the street.
Look at him play.
Boomity-ay!
Givin' the band the beat.
And as the crowd goes wild
And everybody cheers,
Mademoiselles are heard to whisper, "Ooo-la-la!"
We're waiting to get the autograph of Oom-pah-pah!

OUT THERE

Music by Mercer.

Out there a world is waiting,
A world we've never known,
With tea in Barcelona
And dinner in Cologne.
Out there they're sailing oceans
And flying to the moon.
Out there if you can hear me,
Come and get me soon!

THE PAINTED DESERT

Composer unknown. No music is known to survive.

Sundown on the painted desert
When the day is fading
And the night is new;
That's the time for dreaming with you.
Sundown on the painted desert
Where the sky of crimson
Meets the hills of blue;
What a perfect setting for a dream come true.
How I hurry from the round up,
Leave my pony there to graze.
He's in clover
'Cause the day's work's over
And he knows we'll linger in the haze.
Who cares if the day brings worries.

There is always sundown
When the day is through.
I'll linger till it turns to moonrise
On the painted desert with you.

PARIS

Composer unknown. No music is known to survive.

Paris is the biggest whore of all,
And every time the young men come to call
She smiles and calls her sisters in,
New York and London and Berlin,
But Paris is the oldest whore of all.
Enticing men, she rolls her painted eyes,
Lifts up her skirts, and lets them see her thighs;
Then, having taken them to bed,
Deserts them, leaving them for dead,
And plans another night, a new surprise.
She can't be true
To you, or you.
She is a wanton, faithless, and deceiving wretch.

PASSÉ

Composer unknown.

Our little song
That everybody sang all summer long—
Passé.

The silly hat
That you had everybody staring at—
Passé.

The chic *boutiques,*
The latest movie that we waited weeks to see,

Where are they?
*Démodé
Déclassé,
Finis!*

The friends we knew
As well as all the bands we partied to 'til dawn
Are paper caps—confetti on the lawn.

So with regrets,
Darling, let's simply steal away

Where we can be
Quite happily
Passé!

PICTURES IN AN ALBUM

Composer unknown. No music is known to survive.

Pictures in an album,
What memories they bring.
Here's the one we took, dear,
That day we bought the ring.

Gee, don't we look happy
In those old wedding clothes?
Pictures in an album,
With love in every pose.

Here's one of us at Niagara Falls,
My heart recalls it well.
And here we are at the river bend,
Remember when you fell?

Pictures trace our romance,
The happiness we knew.
Pictures in an album . . .
Pictures of a dream come true.

PLAYGIRL

Composer unknown. No music is known to survive.

Playgirl,
See the pretty playgirl,
Starlet-for-a-day girl
In a magazine.

Playgirl,
See the cabaret girl,
Live-it-up-today girl,
All of seventeen.

Baby,
Innocently playing with fire,
Don't you know you may be
Losing every dream you desire?

Playgirl,
Better make your mind up,

Or perhaps you'll wind up
A plaything with a broken heart.

THE PREACHER

Composer unknown. No music is known to survive.

They used to call him the preacher
And it was true,
For he would preach from his heart, the
Only way he knew.
He'd stand up there in the pulpit,
Horn* in his hand,
And let that melody take you
To the promised land.

He'd play one hymn for the ladies,
One for the men,
Then he would turn right around and
Play 'em both again.
And when they all got to singin'
And clappin' hands,
He had the swingin'est congregation
In the land.

And when the sermon was over,
He'd leave a town
And travel on the next to
Lay his gospel down.
So, bow your heads and we'll join in
One mighty chord
To say a prayer for the preacher,
Gone to his reward.
Yes, Lord!

THE PRETTIEST GIRL

Composer unknown. No music is known to survive.

I guess you're just about the prettiest girl I ever saw.
To even walk around like that ought to be against
    the law.
I used to have a dream, but never a dream like you.
How can you have a dream of something you
    never knew?
Not only could you cause the biggest traffic jam
    in—in time;

* *Or:* Cornet

That devastating face could lead one to a life of
crime.
I guess I'm just about the luckiest man alive
tonight,
I only hope and pray my guardian angel guides me
right.
So, darling, drink a toast to my luck—
Win, lose, or draw—
And another to the wittiest, dreamiest, prettiest
girl I ever saw.

PREVIOUS

Composer unknown. No music is known to survive.

VERSE 1

There's a word in the dictionary called "previous."
It means "little bit before."
Some folks don't know much about it,
But experience taught me a lot more.
One day I went to call on a gal—
She said her husband had gone to the war—
I had no sooner got there
When somebody stuck a key in the door.

REFRAIN 1

The door flew open and her husband walked in
And pulled a gun. I got right pale.
I left that woman's house so fast,
People thought I was carrying special delivery
mail.
I ran down the street, the man took the gun
And shot at me in ways most devious,
But whenever them bullets passed any place
whatever,
I had been there myself just "previous."

VERSE 2

A friend of mine that owned an automobile
Used to fill my head with pain.
Every day he'd go rushing to the railroad crossing,
And just barely get cross 'head the train.
I said to him: "Will you tell me how
You've got that train calculated down so fine?"
He said: "The train is due at three o'clock,
And I just crosses there two fifty-nine."

REFRAIN 2

Well, to make a long story shorter than what it is,
You can see this as plain as A B C.

Everybody living by the railroad crossing
Knew that the train usually crossed there at
three.
Yesterday, Sam was crossing the track
And his smile was most mischievous,
But today Sam's gone to his last resting place
The train arrived one minute "previous."

VERSE 3

I was down to a high-class entertainment
In the theatrical part o' town.
It was a minstrel show, with an interlocutor
Tryin' to put the end men down.
Them cats were so hilarious,
Everyone had a high old time.
They laughed at the jokes, they laughed at the
songs,
Even cried at the pantomime.

REFRAIN 3

When the show was through the crowd shoved so
hard
From the peanut gallery
That I found myself at the stage-door entrance
Where a rich fellow said to me:
"You were funny up there. Now get your makeup
off
Or your life ain't gonna be too longevious."
I laughed—as I ran—and yelled back to the man:
"Mister, this black face has been here somewhat
'previous.' "

I checked with Mister Webster
Not only Daniel but his brother Noah,
And they both said the word called "previous"
Means a little bit before.

QUE LE VAYA BIEN (MAY THINGS GO WELL)

Music by Fabian Andre.

Que le vaya bien, amigo,
My frien', may luck throw a kiss to you!
Que le vaya bien,
I say it again,
May the world offer this to you . . .
A meal and a bed,
A roof overhead,
When the snow flurry swirls at night.
A wink when you pass,

Some wine for your glass,
And the laughter of girls at night.
May manna bring health,
A small bit of wealth.
Although worn at the sleeve you are,
May you never grow old,
But if you grow old,
May you never believe you are.
May time as before
Bring you to my door,
Where we joke and we sing again.
One never knows when . . .
Till then—
Que le vaya bien.

REMIND ME TO DREAM OF THIS

Composer unknown. No music is known to survive.

When I'm alone and kinda gloomy
And want my own true love to hurry to me,
When everything goes amiss,
Remind me to dream of this.
When there are clouds on my horizon
And there's no angel face to lay my eyes on,
Whenever I want your kiss,
Remind me to dream of this.
Of the sky all aglow
And the breeze that stirs your hair.
They were made long ago,
Kept in trust for—just for—us to share.
When lady luck just kinda shoves me
And I begin to think nobody loves me,
Remind me to dream of this,
Remind me to dream of this.

ROXANNE

One of three surviving lyrics apparently written for a
musical about Cyrano de Bergerac, a project Mercer and
Michel Legrand never got around to working on. No
music is known to survive.

I love you,
I want you,
I need you,
Roxanne.

You're all I
Can think of
Or dream of,
Roxanne.

I can't live
Without you.
You're in
Every plan.

And I mean
To have you
Alone if I can.

Remember
As children
The pathways
We ran?

Remember
Your first gown,
Your first lady's fan?

Be gracious,
Be human,
Have mercy,
Roxanne.

Remember,
My darling,
That I am a man.

Awaken
And give me
The one gift
You can.

The love from
The lips of
My destiny love . . . Roxanne.

SALE ON DREAMS

Composer unknown. No music is known to survive.

Someday, they'll have a sale on dreams,
Someday, oh, wouldn't that be nice?
Sequins and pretty laces,
Airplanes to foreign places,
Going for less than half the price.

SAN DOMINGO

Composer unknown. No music is known to survive.

One night along the sands of San Domingo
I saw her silhouette against the moon.
"Hello?" I called in my best native lingo.
We rowed out to my ship past the lagoon.
She was so exciting. I had shore leave for the
    night.
What was a sailor boy to do?
With her lips inviting, was it wrong or was it right
When we pledged our love as lovers do?
But I had to quench my thirst for dat ol' debbil
    sea,
Though reluctantly I sailed away.
Through her tears she promised to forever wait for
    me,
I said I'd come back to her some day.
I sailed the seven seas since then, by jingo,
And may the Lord forgive us all our sins,
When I got back to her and San Domingo,
She introduced her husband and her twins,
For she was wed that day, by jingo,
The day I sailed from San Domingo.

SARA JANE

Composer unknown. No music is known to survive.

If she's sweet and shy
And her eyes say, "Hi,"
You have just met my
Sara Jane.

If she fractures you
With her wild I.Q.,
You've been talking to
Sara Jane.

And if, like me,
You're enchanted as can be
And plan on seeing her again,

You go ahead and try,
Break your heart—not I
After all—she's my
Sara Jane.

THE SEA OF LONG AGO

Music by David Saxon.

Spread the sail to canvas,
Hoist the anchor high,
Off to find blue water
Where the fishes fly.
Spices from Samoa
Fill the trade winds as they blow
And we will soon be sailing
Across the sea of long ago.
There's the Jolly Roger
Flying in the breeze.
Pirate ships will chase us
Through the seven seas.
Flower leis they welcome us
To their island homes once more.
Sitting in the office,
Birds are flying by.
Looking through the window
I follow them across the sky.
There's another freighter
Leaving me behind.
Ev'ry time it whistles
I know I'm gonna blow my lonely uncivilized
    mind.
Spread the sail to canvas,
Hoist the anchor high,
Off for buried treasure
'Neath a tropic sky,
Where the porpoise race you
And the blue whale sounds below.
There's got to be somewhere in this world
A sea of long ago.

SIMPATICO

Music by Joseph Meyer.

[*Bossa nova.*]

I guess you know
I find you so
Simpatico,
So very—oh!
Fortissimo
Simpatico.
You have a touch,
You have a feel,
You have a way with you;

413

Like how you say with you
That turns me on.
I cannot speak
A word of Greek
Or Portuguese;
But I know this,
A single kiss
Says more than these.
So, if we lie beneath the sigh-
Ing oleanders above,
Perhaps you'll grow
Simpatico to my love.

SINNER OR SAINT

Composer unknown. No music is known to survive.

Your lips are warm, your heart is cold,
The look in your eyes is a thousand years old,
But underneath it all you are charming and
    quaint,
Are you a sinner or a saint?

You make your kiss a work of art.
How am I to believe that it comes from your heart?
Am I supposed to rejoice or to voice a complaint?
Are you a sinner or saint?

When you are willing,
I'm yours to the end,
But when I'm willing,
You condescend.

You're like a Madonna
That only the devil could paint.
Are you a sinner or a saint?

SPELLED BACKWARDS I LOVE YOU

Music by Robert Emmett Dolan.

REFRAIN 1

U-O-Y E-V-O-L I
Isn't one of those samplers Grandma knits.
Spelled backwards it's
"I love you."
E-VO-BA SRATS LLA

Isn't anyone's radio from Mars.
It's "all stars above you."
It's not in bottles at the corner drug.
You aren't apt to trap it in Brazil.
LLIRHT GIB
Doesn't mean that I'd die for old Eli,
It means you're my big thrill.
You can praise me sideways, if it pleases you,
Long as you EVOL EM, too.

REFRAIN 2

UOY EVOL I
Isn't one of those Tin Pan Alley hits.
Spelled backwards it's
"He loves you." UOY EVOL I
May not resemble a *Tribune* anagram,
But truly, ma'am,
He loves you.
It's not a lot of Polish refugees.
It ain't them or L.S.M.F.T.
EEOOH DOUBLE U.
It isn't anything Malay natives shout.
Spelled inside out it's "whee."
Any terms from a worm's- or a bird's-eye-view,
Long as you EVOL EM UOY, too.

THE SPLENDOR OF YOU

Music by Mercer.

The splendor of you,
The way you hold your head,
It shows in all you do.
The things you leave unsaid,
The gracious way that you acknowledge a
    greeting,
Your gay, quicksilver laugh—so happy and so
    fleeting.
The splendor of you,
It shines within your eyes,
So humble and so warm,
So tender and so wise.
I've seen some splendid things
And I have admired the view.
The moon on the sea,
A star when it's new,
Perhaps someday I'll know the sweet surrender of
    you,
And really see the shining splendor of you,
The past-defining, shining splendor of you.

STARMAKER

Composer unknown. No music is known to survive.

Starmaker,
In your sky up there
If you can hear one tiny prayer
Send me an affirmation,
Some little indication
Of what my attitude should be.

Starmaker,
I am just a man
Who's following your master plan.
I do my best, I stumble,
And if I win, I'm humble.
I use my gifts the best I can.
Have I not made the most of my life
Without riches or even a wife?

Are there another thousand foes?
Or should I wear a larger nose?
I beg for small corrections,
Give me my stage directions
Before the final curtains close.

Dear Father, I appeal to you.
God in heaven, what am I to do?

STRICTLY THE REAL MCCOY

Composer unknown. No music is known to survive.

It's only a business
With Robert Montgomery
When he kisses Myrna Loy.
But you know darn well,
You can trust what I tell you,
It's strictly the real McCoy.
It's making a living with Gable and Garbo.
It's nothing that they enjoy.*
Perhaps I don't screen well,
But, darling, I mean well,
It's strictly the real McCoy.
Is it love
Or is it love
Or don't I make it plain?

---

* *Alternate lines:*
    It's just for a living
    When Garbo and Gable make love for the hoi polloi.

It's fourteen karat,
Solid sterling, wrapped in cellophane.
I'm no Gary Cooper,
You're not Norma Shearer,*
We're only a girl and boy.
But our happy ending
Is not just pretending,
It's strictly the real McCoy.

SWEET ESCAPADE

Composer unknown. No music is known to survive.

Love, your eyes are opening the door.
Is it to be forevermore?
Or is it just another escapade?

I know it's too late for me to go,
And the reason why I know
Is my heart keeps beating so
It sounds like muffled thunder.

Love, I've never felt this way before.
I'm on a green and coral shore
And you're the siren with a serenade.

Godspeed. Pity me who has to go where you lead,
To love,
Or to a stormy, indiscreet escapade,
Sweet escapade,
Sweet escapade.

TABOO

Composer unknown. No music is known to survive.

Taboo
Means "Don't do,"
"It's forbidden,"
Or untrue.
And you
Are taboo to me.
Some old superstition,
A strong premonition,
Says a kiss

* *Alternate lines:*
    You're no Bette Davis,
    I'm no Jimmy Cagney.

Such as this
Is not meant to be.
Taboo
Seems to say
"Mustn't touch,"
"Stay away."
Not even a gambler would play.
I must have your love,
Take the consequence of,
Whatever it costs, come what may.
So do
Say that you
Are really taboo.
If not—if you are—
I'll be lost either way.

TAKE THE MULE TRAIN

Composer unknown. No music is known to survive.

EEEE—OOOOOOO— hah!
Do you hear that ghostly clatter overhead?
EEEE—OOOOOOOO—hah!
It's that new recordin' gimmick, like I said.
It's about that time o' year
When the geese are flyin' high
And the swamp boy
And the wolf gal
Take the mule train through the sky.

EEEE—OOOOOO—hah!
From that great big echo chamber up above.
EEEE—OOOOOO—hah!
It's a symphony of unrequited love.
When you hear the thunder crack
Then the time is drawin' nigh
When the swamp boy
And the wolf gal
Take the mule train through the sky.

Clatter, clatter, pitter-patter,
Can't you hear them hoofs
Way above the roofs?
They'll be takin' off tonight
Unless somebody goofs.

EEEE—OOOOOOO—hah!
They will sell a million copies, wait and see.
EEEE—OOOOOOO—hah!
When he's forty-five and she is thirty-three,
Then they'll settle down and have
Little albums by and by,
When the swamp boy

And the wolf gal
Take the mule train through the sky.

TENDER AND TRUE LOVE

Music by Joe Dubin.

I want a tender and true love,
Not a love that lasts just for a day,
Not a "here for a moment or two" love.
I could never be happy that way.
I want the gentle gay love
I've been waiting a lifetime to find.
Not the "I love you only,"
Who's left to be lonely kind.
When we kiss, kiss, kiss,
And one of these nights we will,
I won't leave your arms until
There's that wonderful one big thrill. Still,
Please don't forget, when we do, love,
When the stars in our eyes start to shine,
That I long for a tender and true love
Who'll be mine, all mine!

THANK YOUR LUCKY STARS

Music by Robert Emmett Dolan.

For the wind in the willow,
Thank your lucky stars.
You won't find a lovelier sight
For the dream on your pillow.
Thank your lucky stars.
It's yours for the dreaming each night,
The sun on the ocean as it sparkles and
    shines,
A full lazy moon just comin' up through the
    pines.
And perhaps there's that big dream
Waiting to come true.
You'll meet for the first time
Your once in a lifetime.
So, just thank your lucky stars
You're you.

THAT'S THE WAY IT IS

Composer unknown. No music is known to survive.

I don't want to bore you, baby,
But that's the way it is.
You're the only thing
I've got on my mind.
Seems that I adore you, baby,
And that's the way it is.
Never thought
I'd be the marrying kind

[*Lyric incomplete.*]

THERE IS NOBODY JUST LIKE HIM

Composer unknown. No music is known to survive.

I've met men with an air,
Some sultry, some fair,
Divine, debonair,
The old savoir-faire.
But this man of mine,
He's so . . . he's so square!
There is nobody . . . just like him.

They all have a flair
Of just what to wear,
A mere boutonniere
Just cries, "I don't care!"
But this man of mine,
He's so . . . well, he's no-*where*!
There is nobody . . . just like him.

If I tried classifying his system,
I'd just have to say it was "gone!"
'Cause, oh, Sister Mary,
His methods may vary,
But his appeal is basic—right on!

I've had some doff their hat
Or flick their cravat
With downright élan
And outright éclat.
But this man of mine,
He's . . . a . . . a cat that is fat.
There is nobody . . . just like him.

When we met, he gave me a pat where I sat.
Don't do it like that!
There is nobody . . . just like him.

THIS IS THE NIGHT

Music by Mercer.

This is the night
When the heavens are right.
This is the night
Of our lives.
This is the hour
When the stars are in flower,
Slowly the moment arrives.
Stars in the sky
Know that love's passing by.
See how they glimmer and shine.
Never in time
Such a moment sublime.
This is the night
You're mine.

TOSS A SONG IN THE DEEP BLUE NIGHT

Composer unknown. No music is known to survive.

Toss a song in the deep blue night,
See the sounds ripple out to infinity.
As the small circles widen,
They ride the tide in
To where "some" someone may be.
So I'm hoping with all my might,
As I sing to that indigo sea,
Lucky star, oh please tell her tonight
Before echoes fade
And grow softer than a sigh,
As they go spinning through the sky.
Make her hear
And sing back to me!

TWILIGHT REFLECTIONS (MY REFLECTIONS)

Music by Joseph Meyer.

Like a weather vane they come and go,
They change from happiness to tears,
As I sit here in the after-glow,
With my reflections of the years.
In the twilight when the lights are low,
As I relive each memory,
My reflections tell me what I know;
That you mean all the world to me.

[*Lyric incomplete?*]

UNINVITED GHOST

Composer unknown. No music is known to survive.

When I am low,
I tell myself a ghost story,
A story of a ghost I used to know.
A sunny, happy, laughing girl
With spring in her smile
Who lives with me yet,
Who let me share some summer
I can never forget.
It kind of makes me happy being sad
As scenes we knew
Come into view.
I try and I try
To live again
As we did then,
Those summers gone by.
Then someone comes along
To end my ghost story
And that is when
The teardrops fill my eyes.

VALPARAISO BY THE SEA

Composer unknown. No music is known to survive.

On my way
And there's no holding me.

I want those sunny skies
In Valparaiso by the sea.
You can say
I'm leaving life behind,
But if you saw those eyes
In Valparaiso you would change your mind.
While you're up here
Learning all the latest tangoes,
I'll be there
Where the moon is shinning through the mangoes.
By the way
Just send my mail to me,
But don't expect replies
From Valparaiso
By the lazy sea.

WAKE ME WHEN YOU LEAVE

Composer unknown. No music is known to survive.

Wake me when you leave,
Tell me you're real,
Wake me when you leave,
That's how I feel.
Maybe I'm naive. What can I do?
Darling, you seem
Just like a dream come true.
Shake me when you fly
Back to the sky,
Gently brush the cobwebs from my eye.
Can't you see
Your kiss will be
The sweetest of alarms?
Wake me when you leave my arms.

WALL STREET

Composer unknown. No music is known to survive.

Wall Street, like the girls, has a very strong union,
You cannot belong 'til you've been to communion,
Also to Groton or Choate or Old Eli
And vote the right way about taxes and My Lai.
You might be the brightest like little Jack Horner,
But Wall Street is one pie which no one can corner.
If you get too big, they will buy you out pronto,
And if you won't sell, Merrill, Lynch and Monsanto

And all of the other names I can't recall
Will see that your company's squeezed to the wall.
The name of the street and the name of the game
And if you attempt it you'll find out the same.
How big you can get has no limit, provided
You do what the board of directors decided.
So when you get feeling like little Jack Horner
Take only a very small pie to your corner
And reach with your thumb for a very small plum
Or someone might steal it and leave you a crumb,
For they speak very shhhhh, but their sticks are
     much longer . . .
And they tell me that only the D.A.R.'s stronger!

WALTZ WITH ME

Composer unknown. No music is known to survive.

Waltz with me.
Leave the others and waltz with me.
Velvet shadows and mystery
Call to us from the floor, love.
Here we are
And, oh, how near we are.
The party's divine, the talk is gay and fleeting,
But my heart is wildly beating!
Come with me.
Leave the others and come with me
To the moonlit eternity
Waiting just through the door, love.
We'll dance on air
To those waiting stars out there,
A beautiful life of love beside a shining sea.
I know it all can be
If you will waltz with me!

WAY OUT WHERE

Composer unknown. No music is known to survive.

Way out where I come from,
Around the end of June,
The sunset has more colors
Than a Mickey Mouse cartoon.

Way out where I come from
The poker gits so hot,
That you gotta have five aces
'Fore you ever win a pot.

Way out where I come from,
They still have swingin' doors.
Oh, you might go in on two legs
But you come out on all fours.

Howdy, stranger—you look mighty fine.
Step right up and call me pard.
If you ever come out my way,
Say you're a friend of mine
And the whole darn West is your back yard.

Way out where I come from,
The hosses don't eat hay.
Naw, they won't even go near it
'Less it's got vitamin A.

Way out where I come from,
The cows are like a dream,
But they ain't much good for milkin',
Only thing they give is cream.

Way out where I come from,
The chickens is our pride.
They lay eggs the way you want 'em,
Some are scrambled, some are fried.

THE WAY YOU FALL IN LOVE

Music by Robert Emmett Dolan.

VERSE 1

Lord Tennyson and Milton
Might have known what to say.
Knowing what love is built on,
They sat down, wrote a play.
There is a lot I miss of love
But I can tell you this of love . . .

REFRAIN 1

Every time you see her,
You catch your breath.
Every time you're with her,
You're scared to death.
Soon you're passing
Every sleepless night
By tearing up
The poetry you write.
When you try to tell her,
You're like a boy.
She says you're her feller,
And oh, the joy.
Then you kiss,

While angels sing above—
That's the way you fall in love.

VERSE 2

Lord Tennyson and Milton
Ogden Nash, E. B. White,
Just seem to put a lilt on
Every word that they write.
In junior high I read it all,
And may I say you said it all.

REFRAIN 2

Every time you see him,
You catch your breath.
Every time you're with him,
You're scared to death.
Soon you're passing
Every night alone,
Just on the chance
That he might telephone.
How you long to tell him
That he's the boy,
Suddenly he tells you
And oh, the joy.
Then you kiss,
While angels sing above—
That's the way you fall in love.

WE ALL CAN MAKE MISTAKES

Music by Carl Sigman.

VERSE

I never knew when I left you
That I would feel this way.
I never dreamed the way things seemed
That I'd come back someday.
But now I find you're on my mind
Each moment we're apart.
I never knew when I left you,
I also left my heart.

REFRAIN

We fell in love. I wasn't true.
And now I'm begging you to let me start anew.
I've one excuse to offer—
We all can make mistakes.
If it were you instead of me,
And if you said that you were sorry as could be,

You know that I'd forgive you.
We all can make mistakes.
A road may bend but in the end
Will find a way of returning.
I lost my way. I'm back to stay.
Oh, what a lesson I've been learning.
I loved you then, I love you now,
Give me the chance and I will make it up
    somehow.
Let's put the past behind us.
We all can make mistakes.

WE CYCLE!

Composer unknown. No music is known to survive.

People tell us that the Croats
Exercise by chasing goats.
What do we do? We cycle!
While the silly Eskimos
Stalk a walrus through the snow,
What do we do? We cycle!

The Finns swim
To keep in trim
And cowboys like to rustle.
The Chinese
Remain at ease
But then they have no muscle.
While the Germans sit and cheer
Drinking Czechoslovak beer,
What do we do? We cycle!

While the natives in Ceylon
Go about with nothing on,
What do we do? We cycle.
While in Lapland many chaps
Climb on one another's Lapps,
What do we do? We cycle!
The Japs do the jiujitsu
In manner acrobatic;
They're quit wise to exercise
But why be so dramatic?
Such effort is beyond our ken,
After all, we're Englishmen!
What do we do? We cycle!

WHAT THE WELL-DRESSED WORLD WILL WEAR

Composer unknown. No music is known to survive.

What the well-dressed world will wear
When spring is in the air
Is a big green bonnet
With roses on it,
To make the neighbors stare.

And the well-dressed world will look
Just like a fashion book,
And the best designer
Could do no finer
With all the pains he took.

In a brand-new coat of clover
With a dash of marigold,
Why, she won't look one day over
A million years old.

If you want to have that air
Of careless *savoir faire*,
Take a tip from me,
Stick around and see
What the well-dressed world will wear.

WHEN I'M A BUST IN THE HALL OF FAME

Composer unknown. No music is known to survive.

When I'm a bust in the hall of fame,
Everybody's gonna know my name.
Like Michael Angelo, Da Vinci, and Marconi,
I'll be on more people's lips
Than a plate of macaroni.
When my nose is in the Louvre, have you'vre
Be sure to lock me up.
I'll tip my hat when you pass,
Provided they don't make it
Out of marble or brass.
I'll be as good as my agents claim,
When I'm a bust in the hall of fame.

When I'm a bust in the hall of fame,
I'll be the world's favorite flame.
I'll be the reason for a wife and hubby quarreling,
The old maid's dream boat,

And everybody's darling.
My emoting will leave 'em weak,
Everyone'll envy my technique.
When I send Little Nell (Eva) and Topsy over the
　　ice,
I'll be so good you'll wanna stay and see it through
　　twice.
I'm gonna sparkle just like my name,
When I'm a bust in the hall of fame.

WHEN SNOWFLAKES FALL

Music by Ted Fiorito. The composer wrote Mercer an
undated letter:

> The Embers Steak House and Motel
> Colorado Springs
>
> Hi Johnnie,
> 　　Will be here until Sept. 16th. My next engage-
> ment in Reno, Nev. Ponderosa Hotel for 3 weeks
> beginning October 16th.
>
> 　　I'll be trying to land a record. However, please
> give it a pitch thru your firm [Capitol]. Maybe
> we'll get lucky. I sure need a break.
> 　　If the boys see fit to handle the song, I have no
> objections.
>
> 　　　　　　Hoping that something breaks.
> 　　　　　　Sincerely,
> 　　　　　　Ted

When snowflakes fall
A lonely sadness
Steals over the night.

When snowflakes fall
And leave the sidewalk*
All silent and white.

They say each one
Is beautiful to see,
Just like the summer days
You spent with me.

Each one a flower,
A little different,
A true work of art.

Now ev'ry hour
Comes back to haunt me
And live in my heart.

---

* *Alternate line:*
　And leave the city

I count them all
And, darling, as I do,
Like the snowflakes that fall
The tears fall too.

WHO BUT YOU?

Music by Mercer.

Version A

Who but you
Could keep me feeling blue?
Who but you
Could make me happy, too?
Who else could treat me
Just like an old shoe,
The way that you do,
And even make me like it, too?
Who but me
Would act so timidly?
Darn it all,
That's how I've got to be
'Case I need someone
To make my dreams come true,
And who do I need,
Who indeed,
Who but you?

Version B

Who, but you
Would I take any horoscope for?
Who, but you
For me?
Who else can start me suddenly crying,
Can send me flying,
And feel like living—or dying?
If you knew
The dreams I've dared not even hope for
You have made come true.
In this big world of losers,
Though beggars can't be choosers,
It's plain to see
One has to be,
And who, for me, but you?

WHO CAN TELL?

Composer unknown. No music is known to survive.

1st version

Who can tell
When two people meet and fall in love?
Who can tell?

Who can tell
What they both are really dreaming of?
Love's a spell
Their two hearts create.

2nd version

Who can tell
What's to be?
Maybe you,
Maybe me.
Life has always been a mystery,
But your heart
Holds the key,
Both for you
And for me.
If you follow it,
Perhaps you'll see.
Believe in it,
You'll see.
Perhaps you'll see!

WHO KNOWS

Music by Mercer.

Who knows
If we will ever meet tomorrow?
Who knows
How many nights we have to borrow?
You're here
And I'm enchanted that you are.
I'm here
For which I thank my lucky star.
Who knows
What guiding angel may proceed him?
One goes
Wherever fate and fortune lead him.

WHO TAKES CARE OF THE CARETAKER'S DAUGHTER?

Composer unknown. No music is known to survive.

REFRAIN 1

[*Lyric missing.*]

REFRAIN 2

Who makes time with the timekeeper's daughter,
While the timekeeper's busy keepin' time?
Who makes every scene
While he's winding his Longine?
You know that the timekeeper must keep time,
And someone's gotta make her tick-tock chime.
So who makes time with the timekeeper's
    daughter
While the timekeeper's busy keepin' time?

REFRAIN 3

Who gets tense with the tent-maker's daughter,
While the tent-maker's busy makin' tents?
You talkin' 'bout Omar Khayyam?
Well, that's exactly who I am.
And you know, Papa Khayyam, he must make
    tents.
But while he's makin' tents,
Who is makin' sense?
Yes, who makes tents for the tent-maker's
    daughter,
While the tent-maker's busy makin' tents?

REFRAIN 4

Who plays house with the housekeeper's daughter,
While the housekeeper's busy keepin' house?
They can't afford a maid
Or to call up the Ladies Aid,
And you know that the housekeeper must keep
    house.
And that child ain't busy readin' Mickey Mouse.
So who keeps house with the housekeeper's
    daughter,
While the housekeeper's keepin' house?

REFRAIN 5

Who tends bar with the bartender's daughter
While the bartender's busy tendin' bar?
You know it ain't Jack Paar
Or Simon Bolivar.
You'll agree that the bartender must tend bar.
But she ain't a member of the D.A.R.

So, who tends bar with the bartender's daughter,
While the bartender's busy tendin' bar?

REFRAIN 6

Who buys stocks for the stockbroker's daughter
While the stockbroker's busy buyin' stocks?
She don't play with blocks,
Except maybe blocks of stocks,
Well, it's plain that the stockbroker must buy
    stocks,
But when he's buyin' stocks,
Who supplies her "yaks"?
Who buys stocks for the stockbroker's daughter,
While the stockbroker's busy buyin' stocks?

WHY DON'T MEN LEAVE WOMEN ALONE?

Music by Gene de Paul.

REFRAIN 1

Why don't men leave women alone?
I wish I knew.
We can't call a moment our own,
Our whole life through.
From the day our bassinet is done up in pink
They decide that we should get whatever they
    think.
We are wondrous creatures and strange, when first
    we're found.
Then it seems they can't wait to change us all
    around.
Some day they'll admit that they're outnumbered
    and outclassed,
Then maybe they'll leave women alone at last.

REFRAIN 2

Why do men leave women alone,
To sink or swim?
What good is a life of our own,
Without, well, him?
First he puts you on a perch with stars in your
    eyes.
Next, he leaves you at the church with two other
    guys.
Why do men run out on a gal? They're all the same.
There's no one to boost morale, no one to blame.
What good is the weaker sex without the one that's
    strong?
Oh, why do men leave women alone so long?

WHY HAVEN'T I MET YOU?

Composer unknown. No music is known to survive.

REFRAIN 1

I've met a Japanese or two from Yokohama,
And I remember meeting twins while in Siam.
I went to college with a German,
I knew an Eskimo named Herman,
My very dearest friends are down in Birmingham,
Yes, ma'am.

I've climbed the pyramids with all the best
    Egyptians,
I've seen their mummies, and I've seen their
    daddies, too.
I've met every single soul from hemisphere to
    hemisphere
And pole to pole,
So why in the world
In all the world
Why haven't I met you?

REFRAIN 2

I've sat upon the laps of many Lapps from
    Lapland.
I've met a lot of fakirs while in Hindustan.
I know the mayor of Honolulu, and ev'ry up-and-
    coming Zulu
And all the natives living in the French Sudan,
Yeah, ma'am.

I've had a drink with ev'ry Colonel in Kentucky.
I've had a bag of oats with ev'ry horsey, too.
I know all the living men from longitude to
    latitude
And back again,
So why in the world
In all of the world
Why haven't I met you?

WILDFIRE

Composer unknown. No music is known to survive.

When it hits you,
It hits you like wildfire.
There's no way to say who lights it,
But the slightest spark ignites it.
When it happens,

It happens like wildfire,
And just like wildfire,
Keeps burning for days.
What I'm feeling
Came to me like wildfire,
Runs through me like wildfire
In so many ways.
Listen well, my love, and hear me*
And please don't bring those lips too near me,
Or else I'll see my heart go up in the blaze.

WITHOUT BENEFIT OF CLERGY

No music is known to survive. Written circa 1971 for *The Pig War*, an apparently unproduced show, script by Don Devendorf, based on an obscure 1859 conflict over the Pacific Northwest's San Juan Islands, claimed by both the United States and Britain. The so-called war began when a trespassing "British" pig was killed by an American settler. President James Buchanan sent General Winfield Scott to defuse the situation, which threatened to escalate into a military confrontation between the two nations. Ultimately the only casualty was the pig. The typescript of this lyric indicates that it was to be sung by Scott to an "attractive British spy."

If I were free
To marry thee
I'd love thy wifely touch.
But without benefit of clergy
I'd love thee just as much.

If thou gave me
A family
Our offspring I'd adore.
But without the benefit of clergy
I'd love them even more.

So, hesitate not, dear damosel,
Illicitly with me to dwell.
Though we've no license, worry not,
Thou'll still be known as Mistress Scott.

If you agree,
I guarantee
The match will last for life.
For without benefit of clergy,
You'll be my second, secret, Western everloving
    wife!

---

* *Alternate line:*
    So, my darling, say you hear me

America is both broad and wide
And there the Lord is on my side,
For who will know or care what's done
In either place called Washington?

YOU CAME ALONG

Music by Robert Emmett Dolan.

BOY'S VERSE

As a little boy, I recognized a little girl
As someone whose swing you used,
A tomboy—that *thing* you used to date.
Since I learned to vote, I've analyzed a petticoat—
The greatest boon known to man.
This prom boy has grown to man's estate.
Who is to blame for this
Weird metamorphosis?

REFRAIN

You came along
When this topsy-turvy old world was all wrong.
Yes, you came along
To the place I'm hoping you'll say you belong.
You may pass me by,
But at least I'll give it that old college try,
For life's been a song
From the moment you came along.

GIRL'S VERSE

As a little girl, it seemed to me a little boy
Was sort of a new-type child,
A horror, a zoo-type child in pants.
Must have been a hex, for I can see the stronger
    sex
Is really not bad to take,
Begorrer! I'm glad to take a chance.
Who is to blame for this
Weird metamorphosis?

REPEAT REFRAIN

YOU DON'T KNOW THE HALF OF IT

Music by Mercer.

I wrapped the world up in a ribbon
And that wasn't easy to do,
But you don't know the half of it, baby,
I'd do it all over for you.

[*Lyric breaks off here.*]

YOU GOTTA BE A GRANDPARENT

Music by Mercer.

We've a darling new relation
Who's the wonder of creation,
And I needn't say I'm proud enough to burst.
But it really is apparent,
Before you are a parent,
You oughta be a grandparent first!

It's 3:30 in the morning,
And without a word of warning
There's a bellow that informs you of his thirst.
Never run to get their Jello.
Let 'em bellow—are you yellow?
You gotta be a grandparent first.

You gotta be the soul of kindness
And have the patience of a saint.
It helps to have a spot of blindness
Because a prodigy it ain't.

Sure, it's like I told my daughter.
She'll be seeing so much water,
Like Columbus, she'll be thinking she's
    accursed.
And she'll wish instead of diapers
They made little windshield wipers.
You gotta be a grandparent first!

Why should you go out and forage
For a bowl to mix his porridge
Or a formula you've never once rehearsed?
Watch your program and get plastered
And ignore the little darling.
You gotta be a grandparent first

When you're sittin' in some hovel
Trying hard to read a novel
Be prepared for anything—it's safety first!
Keep a bottle close at hand, Dad,
Like a bottle of Old Grandad.
Us older kids can also get a thirst!

The generation gap is shocking.
The kids that you once chaperoned
Have hired you to do the rocking
While they are nicely getting stoned!

While you're sitting there all burned out,
Think of how your kiddies turned out.
Fat and sloppy, independent—just the worst!
Get your grandson up and swat 'im
Several good ones on the bottom.
His mom'll say you dassen't, but you durst!
Because you've been a grandparent first!

Newlyweds are strangers to it
But we elders have been through it
So we know from all the babies that we've nursed,
Never give the kid a rattle
Give him nothing, give him battle!
Yes, you gotta be a grandparent first.

When they've got you nearly frantic,
Don't pull off your cutest antic
Even though at baby-talking you're well versed.
Don't out-chuckle or out-babble 'em.
Drop a Nytol in his pablum.
You gotta be a grandparent first

The way this modern world has gotten
Can really drive us grandmas wild.
What used to be a brat—spoiled rotten—
Is now a maladjusted child!

TAG

Comes the moment of decision
When you're watching television
And he hollers like he's just about to burst.
Spray his rump with itching powder,
Turn the TV set up louder,
Have another drink to quench your thirst.
Oh, you gotta be a grandmother first.

EXTRA TAG

Oh, yes, this motherhood's a glory.
It's life's oldest, sweetest story,
'Til about a million didies you've immersed.
Ah, then, motherhood I pity.
It's absolutely shitty,
A job for which you're never reimbursed.
You gotta be a grandparent first.

YOU INSPIRE ME

Composer unknown. No music is known to survive.

You inspire me,
And I am inspired to sing
A whimsical, musical thing
In praise of your eyes,
In praise of your passionate face,
Your almost ethereal grace,
Which happens to be, in your case,
Both wanton and wise.
You inspire me,
And I am inspired to do
Magnificent actions for you,
As heroes of old.
You inspire me
And fire me
To hold you ever so fast
And create a love that will last
When time grows old.
You inspire me,
And I am inspired to write
A beautiful ballad tonight
In praise of your eyes,
Eyes that Michelangelo perhaps might have
    painted
Had the angels and himself been better
    acquainted.

YOU KNOCK ME OUT

Composer unknown. No music is known to survive.

You knock me out,
You really do.
I never dreamed
That there'd be anything like you.
That lofty brow,
Those crazy looks,
They're even better
Than you read about in books.
You knock me out,
But O.U.T.
I never dreamed
Of such things happening to me.
That I have really fallen hard,
There is no doubt.
To quote the language of the bard—
You knock me out!

YOU NEVER HAD IT SO GOOD

Composer unknown. No music is known to survive.

You shootin' off your mouth about a new boy,
You gonna make a change.
You better think it over 'fore invitin' some
    stranger to your boudoir;
You never had it so good.

You got yourself a turkey in the deep freeze,
A television set,
Piano in the parlor and in case you forget, I kissed
    you Tuesday;
You never had it so good.

Don't you go complainin'
Because it's rainin',
Your top'll go up and down.*
I don't hear you snorin'
But if I'm borin',
This here's a pretty big town.
I loves you and I'm grateful to you, honey,
I loves to have you 'round,
But I can still recall the night when somebody
    crowned me with the soup spoon,
I never had it so bad,
It nearly made me mad.

I said it once and I'll reiterate,
What I have done reiterated,
If necessary I'll obliterate
Such memories from my mind.
So 'stead o' bein' busy makin' sheep's eyes
At everyone you meet,
I think it might be wiser if you tried to be sweeter
    to your Daddy;
You never had it so good.

M—A—M—A, mama;
Think it over, comma,
Cause you never had it so G—O—O—D!

YOU'RE IN SAVANNAH

Composer unknown. No music is known to survive.

_____

* Alternate line:
    Don't your top go up and down?

Hominy grits when you waken,
Peaches a breeze has just shaken,
Lyin' around for the takin'—
You're in Savannah.

You're in Savannah,
Where the Spanish moss hangs lazy on the trees,
Where they say "Thank you, ma'am"
Almost as much as "If you please."

Even though folks are old-fashioned,
Bourbon and smiles are unrationed.
They can get pretty impassioned
About Savannah.

So if you're walkin' through a tree-filled square,
Where they say, "Y'all come back, y'hear,"
Traveller, you're in Savannah—
My home town.

LATE ADDITIONS

A number of lyrics were discovered just as this book was going to press.

THE H. C. POTTERS BALL

Music possibly by Don Raye.

DON RAYE: [*spoken*] Hey, Johnny, what you all draped up in that banquet suit for?

JOHNNY: Man! I just got my invite this morning to the Potters fling-ding. Didn't you get one?

DON RAYE: No, let me see that thing. Hmm. What does that RSVP mean?

JOHNNY: I don't know, Don. I guess it just means BE THERE!
[*sung*] I never miss a soiree or tea
That the H. C. Potters throw,
So when I got my RSVP,
You know I had to go.

I had to drape up, drop in, and drip out
Just as soon as I got the call.
I had to tee up, take off, and trip out
To the H. C. Potters ball.
I had to broom down, breeze in, and brush up
To the jumpinest place of all.
I had to leg out, latch on, and lush up
At the H. C. Potters ball.
Don't know who might be there,
Who I'll see there gettin' his kicks.
That's why you will see there
Li'l ol' me there talk to the bricks.
I had to drape up, drop in, and drip out
To take the Lucy and Hank at all.
I had to tee up, take off, and trip out
To the H. C. Potters ball.

CODA

Don't know who might be there,
Who I'll see there gettin' his kicks.
That's why you will see there
Li'l ol' me there talk to the bricks.
I had to drape up, drop in, and drip out
To take the Lucy and Hank at all.
I had to tee up, take off, and trip out
To the H. C. Potters ball.
DON RAYE: Oh, tell them to send that keg up.
JOHNNY: John is gonna leg up.
BOTH: To the H. C. Potters ball.

NIGHT OVER SHANGHAI

Written for the movie *The Singing Marine* (page 54).
Sung by Doris Weston.

REFRAIN 2

Night over Shanghai
Under your veil,
Dressed like a siren,
With dreams for sale.
Pale hands that beckon,
Eyes that are bright,

These are the blossoms
That bloom in the night.
Old city of dreams,
If it were told,
How many heartaches
You could unfold;
And how many dreamers
Fade out of sight
In the darkness over Shanghai
In the night.

PALSY WALSY

Written for the movie *They Got Me Covered* (page 137).
Sung by Martha Mears.

REFRAIN 2

Palsy-walsy,
You old nifty.
I'm your pigeon,
Sharing your lot.
Palsy-walsy.
Fifty-fifty.
With a smidgen
Or with a yacht.
Come rain,
Come snow,
The icy winds may blow
And go to 45 below.
Who's excited?
Rooms and hallways
Wait for baby.
[*spoken*] Because you are my
[*sung*] Palsy-walsy, dear.

CODA

Through thick, through thin,
Or any "How've you been?"
We'll grin and take it on the chin.
Who's excited?
Plan your campaign,
You'll get my vote.
I'll take champagne or beer,
Because you are my
Palsy-walsy, dear.

OVERLEAF   *Ginger and Johnny*

Merry Christmas

Johnny Mercer's annual Christmas cards were eagerly awaited and highly appreciated by all who received them.

CHRISTMAS CARD 1939

Blessings on thee, everyone,
Every single mother's son;
Blessings, friends of ancient vintage,
Blessings, friends of recent mintage—
Whomsoever you may be,
Merry Christmas unto thee!
Old year's gone and we got through it—
Though I wouldn't own up to it.
Hope and pray the next one's better—
If it ain't, we'll make it wetter,
Drown our sorrows and our woes—
Barkeep, give me one of those!
Let's all drink a toast or toddy
Wishing well to everybody.
This is one day hearts have wings—
Hark the *Herald Tribune* sings!
There is peace in Sunday's chimes;
There is—quote—peace in our *Times*.
Brilliant is the *Evening Star*,
Brilliant and somnambular.
Let's repeat it once again—
Peace on earth, goodwill to men!
Gather neath the mistletoe,
AFL and CIO,
Wendell Willkie, Gerald Nye,
Messrs. ASCAP, BMI—
With the world hell-bent for leather,
Now's the time to stick together,
Drop the hatchet, stop the fuss,
Climb aboard and come with us.
Mr. Kringle drives the sleigh—
Don't you hear a reindeer neigh?
Here we go! He cracks his whip;
Our imaginary trip
Takes us through the snowy night—
Better wrap those blankets tight!
Time for all to go once more
Through the holly-covered door,
Down the candle-lighted hall—
Merry Christmas to you all!
Things are bad from pole to isthmus,
But we still believe in Christmas!

Choir, let these guests be caroled:
Annie Arlen, hatless Harold,
Johnny Arledge, Fred Astaire,
Jane and Squirrel, the Ashcroft pair,
Juney Adams (hiya, bub!),
Ager, Alter, Auto Club,
Square and Edith Anderson,
Henny Bacchus, Billy Blun,

Nora and the kids and Carleton,
All of 301 East Charleton,
Irving Berlin, Perry Bodkin—
What's the difference if you're not kin?
Get together, hug each other—
You may be somebody's mother!
Berkeley, Bargy, Bleyer, Bloom,
This way to the drinking room!
Morton Bernstein and his wife—
The first woman in my life:
Gladly did I let her munch on
My first kindergarten luncheon!
Johnny Burke, that wine should bubble!
Well, poor boy, he's seeing double!
I hear Bells—and all the way
From Savannah town, GA!
Greetings, darling Aunt Nell Blackie—
Bless you, and your boys in khaki!
Butlers, Burroughs, Mildred Bailey,
Try this on your ukulele,
Take this old one off the shelf:
"Love thy neighbor as thyself"!
Ronny Burla and his Una
And this summer in Laguna
Henri Blanke and Miss B,
Mr., Mrs. Broccoli,
All of A.S.C.A.P.,
Harry Barris, BVC,
Pink and Mary, hey nonny!
Susie, Belle, and killer Johnny,
Bing and Dixie and their clan,
Barefoot boys with Daddy's pan—
And if Daddy's wits are keen
He knows "pan" ain't what I mean!
Carol Carol, J. Colonna,
All the smudgepots in Pomona,
Hattie Clinton, daughter Ann,
And the lost Republican.
Greetings, Ducky, Bob Carmichael,
Hoag and Ruth complete the cycle.
Christmas gifts to Chan and Chaplin,
Leonard Ross and H*Y*M*A*N K*A*P*L*A*N.

Bless the Dolans, Mims and Bobby,
We the people, Hobby Lobby,
Bette Davis, Mary and Mary,
And the dwelling of McCarey.
Pour the port and fill the chalice
For the Dougalls, Bern and Alice,
Tommy Dugan, Buddy Dill,
And the folks upon the hill,
The DeSylvas (hello, chief!
When do I go on relief?)—
Pass the eggnog, pass the wines,
Fill the goblets, fill the steins!
William Dozier, Meta Reis,
Never let the pouring cease!
Drink a cheer to Mr. Dubin,
Dorsey Brothers, how have *you* been?
Walter Donaldson, drink hearty—

Barney Dean, it's your block party!
Jimmy Downey and his mummy,
Joseph Dubin and his tummy.
E's for Ellfeldt, Emerson,
Edelman, and everyone—
Harry Evans, Eberle,
Fill the house with harmony!
Skinnay Ennis, have a chair,
Everybody, everywhere!
Arthur Fishbein, Arthur Franklin,
Dwight and Mary, won't you ankl' in?
Shake my writin' hand, Coach Frawley—
You still rhyme with Dick MacCauley!
Leo Forbstein, start your band—
Play for Miss de Havilland!
Henry Fonda, Mrs. F,
Shout it till the crowd is deaf,
O'er the snowy countryside—
Happy, happy Xmastide!
To the friends too seldom seen,
Ira Gershwin, Johnny Green,
Close that window—look who blew in—
Jack Gordean and Jimmy Green!

Darling Peggy and their John,
Followed by the tribe of Kahn,
Benny Goodman, there's Mose Gumble—
Won't you help him from the rumble?
Goodwins, get up from the table,
Make your bow to Betty Grable!
Johnny Gallaudet and Connie,
Looking apple-cheeked and bonny,
Ring the bells in St. John's steeple
For the Hulls, our favorite people!
Here comes Hunter, Christmas calling;
Here comes Herzig, ashes falling;
Dr. Harris, Byron Harvey,
There's the turkey—feeling carvey?
Bob and Peg and Hanighen
All together once again,
Greetings coming, going back—
Are you kiddin'? Murder, Jack!
To the Houstons and the Hitches
And the Hendersons, like Skitch is,
Merry Yule and Noel too!
Lindsay Howard, Judyroo,
Taste the peaches, slice the mutton
For Ray Heindorf, Betty Hutton—
If the madam's glance is wayward
For that dream girl, Susan Hayward!
Bob Hope and his bride, Dolores,
May I pour a doch-an-dorris?
Footman! Do you hear those Klaxons?
Meet the Jenkins and the Jacksons!
Here comes Jarvis and his ballroom—
Open up that extra hall room.
Irving Kahal and Teddy Koehler,
Charlie Chan and Sidney Toler,
Hey, toy soldier, hit your cymbals
For Miss Karol down at Gimbels!

Hy and Reata, Missy Jill,
Holly on your windowsill—
I know all you people, but
Who is Wilhelmina Thutt?

Kaufman, Keys and Kuhl and Kress,
Everybody, more or less,
Even those whom I've forgotten—
Jim! My memory is rotten!
And if you think that's a curse,
Madam's list is even worse!
So if your name is omitted,
We both pray to be acquitted,
And we love you anyway,
If that meets with your okay!
Jimmy Kern, his bairn and marm,
Best of luck from madam's arm.
Jerry Kern, my circumspect eyes
Say. "Go on and wear those neckties!"
Who's that beauty over there?
Gentlemen, meet Annie Lehr!
Edgar Leslie, Eddie Lowe
With those cute LaMonts in tow,
Jolly, jumping Jerry Lester,
John and Mildred Malatester.
Lamp Miss Landis's apparel—
That's my kind of Christmas Carole!
And "Toujours Lamour" toujours
Is my favorite song, I'm sure.
Who's that in the living room?
Donald Livingston, I presume?
Footman! Bring Priscilla Lane
In out of the frozen rain.
Look! We have a pinecone fire
From the house of McIntire
And some frankincense and myrrh
From the house of Mehlinger
And some old imported vino—
Malneck, this is Mannerino,
Mayhew, this is Modisett—
Have you met the Mitchells yet?
Joseph Wingston (lawd!) Manone,
Jack, I do not dig your tone!
Miss MacLaughlin, Mr. Markey
Always tries that old malarkey!

Here they come, those sailing sharks
Buddy Morris, Albert Marx.
Have you met the Mercer tribe?
These cats really can imbibe!
Juliana and Miss Lily,
Uncle Robbie—he's a dilly—
Hugh and domicile of three,
Walter and his family,
Mercer, Nancy—best to them—
Joseph and Virginia M.
Chris and Liz and George and Bess,
Uncle Joe is in distress:
Cousin Mamie's hid the liquor—
That just makes a Scotsman sicker!

Uncle Lewis and Uncle Ed
Soiled Aunt Katherine's table spread!
Pray continue, eat your fill
While we call up Jacksonville—
Say hello to Mother there,
Ed and Deborah and Claire.
Goodness how the party grows!
Millers, Myers, Monacos
Freddie Martin and Tchaikowsky
Dagmar, I believe, Godowsky,
Ray and Eadie Mayer and Jeanie,
Count Oleg and Gene Cassini,
Harmon Nelson, how's the ham—
Baked and cured by Uncle Sam?
Mr. Noble sound your A,
Play a simple Christmas lay
To O'Brien, to O'Connell,
Out-of-meter John MacDonell,
The Orsattis and O'Neills—
Mrs. O's a dream on wheels—
To the Oxnards and the Oakies—
O'er the Rockies and the Smokies
Santa brings our heartfelt wish:
May your new year be delish!

I could count till I got weary
Playing one, two, three, O'Leary,
Once again, here comes that snowman
Fat and smiling-faced Phil Ohman.
Herb and Midge Polesie, howdy!
Just in time, we're getting rowdy!
Hello, Helen Paup and Merle—
Whatcha gettin', boy or girl?
Cheers to Miriam and Jeanette
(If *he* calls, I'm on the set).
Really, it's too hard to count
All the friends at Paramount,
So they'll simply be yclept.
Louis Lipstone's Music Dept
And that goes for Fox and Metro
Warner's, RKO, et cetro . . .
And the pious folk deserve a
Merry Christmas—hi, Minerva!
Hey, Miss Phillips, talk to Peer—
Call him Cuddles—that's a dear!
Nina Pape, no teacher's topped her,
And that goes for Miss Willhopter.
Love to Roy and Lucy Potter,
Love to all of John Scott Trotter,
Dick and Joan, the Powell twain,
Walter Rivers, his demesne—
We go back in memory
To the old LBBC.
Leo Robin, J. J. Robbins,
Park your dog sleds and your dobbins;
And that man whose name is spelt
Mr. Franklin Roosevelt,
We're 101 percent
With you, Mr. President!
Mickey Rooney, bring your jive in—

Greetings to my favorite drive-in!
Romanoff and Cave and Carl and
David Rose and Judy Garland,
Divest your coats and fill your glasses
Ere the jolly season passes!
(I suppose I'm in a rut—
Can't place Wilhelmina Thutt.)
Read and Rains and Smith and Shacker,
Jimmy Stewart—he's no slacker—
Swczcy, Schwartz, and Sherwood yet,
And the Navy Blues Sextette.
Henry Steif bring Artie Shaw in,
William Sexton and his squaw in,
Silvers, bring both Phil and Sid in—
Glad to zee you, we ain't kiddin'!
Footman, grab that horse's halter—
Here's Saroyan, also Salter—
Gentlemen, up on your feet
Find Ann Sheridan a seat!
(Ha ha, oh boy, that's a hot one—
Just as if she hasn't got one!)
Dave and Libby Shelly, hi!
You're the apple of our eye.
Tinturins and Temple too—
Gracious, what a varied crew!
Square and hip chick, saint and sinner,
Lana Turner—"chicken dinner"—
Friends and neighbors, love you all—
Sit thee doon and have a ball!
Mighty glad to call your name—
Only hope you feel the same!
Blessings on you where you are—
Glad those wise men saw that star;
Glad in spite of wars and weather
All of us can be together!

Rocco Vocco and his cutie,
J. Van Heusen, J. Venuti,
Jerry Vogel, Rudy Vallee,
Come back to our alley, Sally—
Come and sit around the tree
Lit without the aid of "tea"!
Gangway for the house of Whiting,
Still our sweethearts at this writing.
Bright red ribbons for Cobina—
I mean Juna—also Seena.
Brothers Warner, Brothers Barker,
Harry Wise and Connie Parker,
Sammy Weiss and Vernon Wood,
Harry Warren—feeling good—
Paul and Margaret Whiteman too,
You know what we wish for you!
Double that and add a very
To the "home folks" at Woodberry.
Slicker Warnell, Sambo White,
Allie Wrubel—have a bite!
Brother, you ain't tasted cakes
Till you've had those Mother bakes!
Choir, sing hello to Young
And your song is almost sung.

Now the last guests have been kissed,
Sam and Maggie Zimbalist—
Now the room is really humming,
And we thank you all for coming!
Eat the food you want to eat,
Meet the friends you want to meet!
This is Christmas—fill your plates—
These are these United States!
So we won't invent a new toast;
We'll propose the tried-and-true toast.
We love you and you're our friends,
And we hope it never ends!
So, good neighbors, here's a cheer
Same old
MERRY CHRISTMAS
And a . . . .

Johnny, Ginger, and Amanda

P.S. Combed the country over,
Under haystacks, deep in clover,
Highest snowcap, lowest cut—
Still no Wilhelmina Thutt!

CHRISTMAS CARD 1942

This modern age we're going through has got me
in a spin
I ain't too bright to start with—now here's the
shape I'm in
With everything and anything—there's stamps
you gotta use
The Bs and Cs are groceries—I think the Ts are
shoes
You have to be a F.B.I. man to figure out all the
clues
And that's the situation when you get the duration
blues
The Army and the draft board gets me kinda
mixed up too
You're in if you are 1A—but if you ain't then who
are you
The 2As are essential—and the 4Fs probably have
asthma
The 3B gents are in defense—or else they're
giving plasma
But if you ain't got nothin' then you are
somebody that nobody at all can use
And that's the situation—when you get those
duration blues
Now food will win the war they say, and that's
okay with me
But I went to the corner store—what did I see?
There's Spam and wham and deviled ham and
somepin new called zoom
Just take it home and cook it to the temperature of
the room

And you can bake it—cake it—flake it—make it—
take it anyway you choose
And that's the situation—when you got those
duration blues
And then on top of everything the taxes roll
around
I went to see the income man and this is what I
found
You multiplies the profits and incorporates the loss
Deducting all expenditures business fees you
come across
Then if you satisfy the government—it's ten to
one the little lady sues
And that's the situation when you get the duration
blues
Howdy do, Mr. Crosby, I would—like to say
Happy New Year to you in the—good old way
Well, thank you, Mr. Mercer, that is—mighty fine
And the same to you from me and mine
And while I'm passin' those—words your way
Let's extend 'em to the whole wide—U.S.A.
Every city and village and farm and town
And every front door from the—White House
down
To the boys in khaki—and the boys in blue
To the generals and the admirals and the company
and crew

Let the whistles whistle and the bells all ring
For General Marshall, General Arnold and
Cominch King
Red, white and blue confetti in a veritable shower
For Messrs. MacArthur and Eisenhower
To the fightin' Marines on Guadalcanal
Wherever you are, Happy New Year, pal
To the ship-yard workers and the swing-shift
crowd
We can't sing good but we sure sing loud
So we send our heartiest felicitations
To our allies—the United Nations
Get out the brightest-colored paper hats
For Nimitz and Hadley—Doolittle and Spaatz
Mr. Nelson, Mr. Jeffers, Mr. Morgenthau
Had the busiest year we ever saw
And an even busier one comin' in
Well, the harder we work—the quicker we win
Happy New Year, everybody, near and far
From John Q. Public to F.D.R.
To the New *New Jersey*, and all her crew
To Birmingham Bertha and Suzy Q.
That's our 1943 wish for you
And thanks for all you did in '42
Around this time in forty-four
We hope you'll be with us in person once more
But till that time be of good cheer
And to everybody—Happy New Year!

CHRISTMAS CARD 1949

Noel, Yule, and Christmastide
To everybody, every side—
Best of fortune, health, and cheer
In everybody's atmosphere.
Let foe kiss friend and friend kiss foe
Beneath a common mistletoe!
Republicans! Be Democratic—
Drag the tinsel from the attic,
Light the tree and fill the bowl
(You won the *Lit'ry Digest* poll)!
Step right up and love thy neighbor—
Capital! Shake hands with Labor!
Hurry and unlatch the door,
For Santa Claus is here once more.
Despite a million annual beatings
Here he is, dispensing greetings,
Bringing them from us to you,
From who knows, Lord, to Lord knows who,
To all the people on our list,
To everyone we may have missed,
To those who'll say to us, "I see—
You didn't send a card to me!"
To those who'll say, "Of all the gall!"
A merry Christmas to you all!
A happy Yule to all of you
Who should have sent us something too!
Season when the heart has wings—
Hark! The *Herald Tribune* sings!
Have a pretzel, have a beer,
Christmas comes but once a year.
Greetings Harold, Anya Arlen,
Buddy Morris, you too, Carlin,
Johnny Arledge, Fred Astaire,
Edith Anderson and "Square,"
Greetings, Ashcrofts, Jane and "Squirrel,"
Milton Ager and his girl,
Greetings Mr., Mrs. Alter,
Billy Blun and Lawrence Salter,
All the guys on Bull and Broughton,
Messrs. Arco and MacNaughton
Botkin, Borut, Brewster, Blum,
Come and make yourselves "to hum"!
Drink with Bacchus, ring up Bell,
Charles, Ed, Mac, and Muriel;
Mrs. Baldwin, bring your Earl in;
Where's a chair for Irving Berlin?
Mr. Bargy, Mr. Bloom,
Let's have music in the room!
Archie Bleyer, Johnny Burke,
Busby Berkeley, go to work—
Show the Burroughses and the Blowes
How the Anvil Chorus goes!
Merry Christmas—sing it gaily,
Ronny Burla, Mildred Bailey,
Bacon, Lloyd, and Aunt Nell Blackie,
Call time out on Nagasaki!

Sing a simple Christmas lay,
Barris, Harry, Bregman, J.!

So we go from B to C—
Greetings to Cochran, Charlie B.,
Prosit Pink and Mary Cavett,
'S only schnapps, but you can have it!
Philip Charig, prosit too,
Carol Carol—both of you!
Greetings Crosbys, Bing and Larry,
Dixie, Coop and Lin and Gary,
Philip, Dennis, Everett, Bob—
What do you Crosbys hear from the mob?
Happy New Year, fide bona,
Clinton, Clark, and chez Colonna,
May the Carmichaels be lucky,
Hoagy, Ruth, and Bob and Ducky,
Ken Carpenter, Sidney Clare,
Everybody, everywhere!
To the Davis clans, hey nonny,
Marvin, Mary, Bette, Johnny,
Tommy Dugan, Buddy Dill,
Buddy (now B.G.) DeSyl,
Dorsey, J., and Dorsey, T.,
Dubin, Al, and Douglas, P.,
Dubin, J., and A. Devine,
Hello, Oscar Hammerstein!
Here's a crimson wreath of holly
For Walter Donaldson and Wally,
P. De Rose, May Singhi Breen,
Jimmy Downey, how've *you* been?
And Margot de la Falaise,
You wear that name no matter what any says!
Ere the jolly season pass
Happy, happy Michaelmas!
Turkey stuffing, hot cross buns,
Edelmans and Emersons,
William Ellfeldt, Skinnay Ennis,
Johnny Faunce (and how's *your* tennis?),
Fishbeins, Franklins, how you all,
Dave, Dwight, Mary (née McCall)?
Wishes can't be Fonda, Hank,
Just like money in the bank.
Then there's F for families—
Christmas gif' to both of these.
Mother, Mother, Father too,
Walter, Big and Little Hugh,
Ed and Deborah and Claire,
Polish up the silverware,
Lay the snowy table spread,
Uncles Lewis and Rob and Ed,
Gather round and all get clubby,
Meet Elizabeth's new hubby—
George and Bess and George the third,
Cousin Mamie, cut the bird!
Mercer, Adeline, Aunt K.,
Polish off the egg frappé,
Dorothy and Mary Lou,
Joseph and Virginia too,
Every oldster, every sprout—

Mustn't leave a person out!
Uncle Joe will mix the toddy—
Happy headaches everybody!
Ira Gershwins, Johnny Greens,
Elliott Grennards, Jack Gordeans,
Here's a package tied in ribbons,
For the Gruens and the Gibbons,
While the Goffs and L. Wolfe Gilberts
Get a box of chocolate filberts,
And to Goldie, mon chouchou,
The remaining nuts to you!
Mr. Gumble, Mrs. Geary,
Hope your Xmas comes on cheery,
While B. Goodman's—Krupa's too—
Comes on like gangbusters do!
Farmer or sophisticate
Happy New Year to you, Gate,
Gallaudets and Crooner Frawley,
Allie Wrubel, Dick MacCauley,
Dr. Joe and Mrs. Harris,
Happy, happy plaster Paris!
Harry, Arthur—Harris, Jane—
Charlotte, Jack, long may you reign!
Blessings on your domiciles
Here and in the British Isles.
May a goodly batch of manna
Find the Hull home in Savannah;
Laughter in the Herzig den;
Love to Bernie Hanighen;
And may Joe and Mrs. Helbock
Open up a keg of swell bock!
To the Harveys, Bob and Peg,
Goes the biggest turkey leg,
And the Hawkins, Housons, Herts,
May they get their just deserts!
Greetings Bob, Dolores Hope,
Here's a present—do not ope!
Lindsay Howard and Seabiscuit,
Here's a fin—or should I risk it?
Sonny Hitch and Margery,
Willie Horowitz—how be?
Isaacs, Jarvis, how do *you* be?
And the Jolsons, Al and Ruby?
Babo Jackson, Poppa Bill,
Your socks would be hard to fill!
Gordon Jenkins, Georgie Joy,
Mrs. Johnston's little boy,
Irving Kahal, tap the barrel—
Miriam, sing a Christmas karol!
Blessings Margaret Keyes and Zipper,
Teddy Koehler—hiya, Dipper!
Hiram Kraft and daughter Jill,
You too, Reata—now be still!
I know all you people, but
Who *is* Wilhelmina Thutt?
Lots of Noels, lots of Yules
To the Cal and Mandy Kuhls;
Love to Grace and Gus (the Kahns)
"Kosty"-lanetz, Lily Pons,
C. and E. Kress—by the way,

Have you ever thought of writing a play?
Harry Kaufman wants to know—
Harry, we can't do that show!
Guy Lombardo, Harry Link,
Carmen, Leibert, have a drink!
Eddie Lowe and Bonnie Lake,
Have a slice of angel cake!
Hello, Fud, and hello, Don,
In the name of Livingston!
Mr. Leslic, Mrs. Lehr,
Here's a rather tough affair:
How's a guy to rhyme LaMont?
Maybe Nash can, but I cawn't!
Greetings, greetings, greetings all—
Hallelujah! Have a ball!
Have a party and we'll pay
If we get the bank's okay!
Put the taper to the fire
In the house of McIntire;
Bring the frankincense and myrrh
To the house of Mehlinger.
Ralph Malone and Una Merkel,
Gather round the family circle.
Jeeves, get out more firewater—
Toast McDonough's wife and daughter!
Jeeves, go fetch the *old* Bacardi
Comes the Malnecks and Mienardi,
Comes the Mitchells and Marcels
From the land where King George dwells,
Mrs. Mannerino (Mary)
Jno. Mayhew, Leo McCarey,
Modisetts and Monacos,
Have you tasted some of *those*?
Have you tried the seven-layer?
Have some, Ray and Edith Mayer!
Mr. Rothmere, have some too—
Really, there's enough for you!
I know all you people, but—
Who *is* Wilhelmina Thutt?
Greetings, Millers—Everett, Charlie—
Bless your hearts particularly!
Here, you minstrels! Tune your lyres,
Sing to Zi and Bett Myers!
Mr. Norvo, taste the jam!
Mr. Nelson, how's the Ham?
Nolan, Joe, and Noble, Ray,
Merry, merry Xmas day!
Mr. Gordon Oliver,
May you get what you prefer—
Though the censors find it shocking,
May a brunette fill your stocking!
Keep the sweets from Oakie, Jack,
Or the poundage may come back!
To the Tommy Oxnards, hey!
To the Bennys, whatcha say?
Greetings, Temple, Dot, not Shirley,
Just because her teeth are pearly,
Rocco Vocco and his Dolly,
Joe Venuti and his Sally,
Jerry Vogel's smiling pan,

Emmerita Vanneman!
Who's that singing in the alley?
Let him in—why, Rudy Vallee!
Hang the geese and stuff the pheasants—
Almost time to open presents.
Comes the late guest through the yard
To present his calling card,
Hang his off'ring on the bough—
Jeeves, there goes the doorbell now!
In the late arrivals float:
Mrs. Whiting, rest your coat!
Margaret, Barbara, and Blossom,
Cut yourself a slice o' possum!
Look who's here! It's Harry Wise,
Christmas spirit in his eyes
Here's the Warner music staffs
(Can I have your autographs?)—
Kenny, Hazel, Sandy, Sammy,
Polished up with soap and chamois,
Jack and Ruth and Norman Foley,
Harold, Mack, both roly-poly—
Love to *all* the Warner house—
Look out, ladies, there's a Mouse!
And his brother, Harry Warren,
Back with Jo from travels foreign.
Hal B. Wallis, J. L. Warner,
Sorry I ain't in your corner,
But it's nice to have a day off
Knowing that it's not a layoff!
Margaret Whiteman! Hello, Paul—
Still the daddy of them all!
Will you howdy-do for me
To the Big and Little T?
Vernon Wood, it's *time* you came!
Mrs. Willingham, the same!
Harold Warnell!—listen, "Slicker,"
Don't expect that prewar liquor!
Close the door and lock it tight
Wait a second—something White—
All the brothers and their wives!
See! the troupe of Young arrives,
Youngs from Lincoln Street and Hall,
Youngs from N.Y., enter all!
Everybody's here again!
Did I hear a footstep then?
Who's that in the snowy mist?
Sam and Maggie Zimbalist!

MERRY CHRISTMAS (UNDATED)

Words and music by Ginger and Johnny Mercer.

Merry Christmas and shout thanksgiving
For the income taxes and the cost of living!
Merry Christmas to all our friends—
May the New Year bring you dividends!
Santa Claus is coming again
To R. H. Macy's and the five-and-ten—
Santa Claus is coming your way
With a full full puncheon and a raise in pay!
Merry Christmas and hi-ho-nonny
From Miss Ginger Mercer and her boyfriend
   Johnny—
Hit the ceiling and whoop-dee-doo—
Merry Christmas to all of you!

CHRISTMAS CARD (UNDATED)

A Merry Christmas to you all
And, as you older ones recall,
When you are fifty-some-odd years
And slightly in the cup that cheers
You have a different point of view
From twenty-one or twenty-two!
And lots of things that used to be
Come back to haunt your memory.
Old times, old places . . . friends . . . and songs—
To each, a part of you belongs.
And yet I'd be a fool to say
I didn't like the present day:
The architecture and the food,
The transportation—twice as good!
And constellations in the sky
Not only shine today, they fly!
And yet, what furnace, out of sight,
Can touch a fire burning bright?
A hearth beside a Christmas tree
That lights our faces rosily?
The old and new, the old and new—
My heart is torn between the two.
I love the modern, gleaming cars
But miss the sight of frosty stars;
I like the freeways' change of scene
But hate the distances between.
Wipers, defrosters, and heated hoods
Keep melting the falling snow
As over the river and through the woods
To grandmother's pad we go.
But progress reigns, you must admit,
And I'm afraid we're stuck with it—
Electric blankets, Water Piks,
And stereos of '66—
The hi is fi-er, to be sure—
It's just the music that is poor!
While wiser men than those of old
Now gaze at Telstar in the cold
And go with camels on their trips,
Their Camels all have filter tips!

Ah, well, it's not for us to beef!
The years are growing all too brief.
But still we have from up above
The best of gifts—the gift of love.
And we can wish it one to each,
Though out-of-touch and out-of-reach.
So, here's to you, my special friends—
I hope our friendship never ends.
And may your journey, all the way,
Be safe, and shine like Christmas Day!
And spare a thought for Him we honor,
Perhaps the world's most generous donor—
We've yet to learn his lesson well,
But maybe someday . . . who can tell?
A fine New Year . . . in double clef—
        The Mercers (Ginger, Johnny, Jeff)

CHRISTMAS CARD 1965

The old-time wish still ringing clear
Above the tumult and the fear,
Among the sounds that underscore
The awesome jet propeller's roar,
The hi-fi blast, the freeway's hum—
A wee, small voice for Christendom,
"I wish you joy, I wish you love,"
While snowflakes spell it out above
And angels sing it once again
The fondest hopes of gentlemen—
God rest you merry, lasses, lads,
In private thoughts, in public ads.
The traffic lights, still red and green,
Help Santa baby make the scene,
Distributing his gifts and toys
To all deserving girls and boys.
The sleigh is faster than the truck;
The doe is faster than the buck.
So lay hypocrisy aside
This blessed, joyous Christmastide
And send the old-time wish and prayer
To everybody, everywhere.
Lo! Twoscore years ago or so
I listed everyone I know
And tried to write a line or two
Incorporating all of you,
But if I tried that feat this year
On every page there'd be a tear:
So many gone, so many lost—
Too often those we love the most—
My eye grows dim, my heart despairs
To think of all the empty chairs.
So I just say to you en masse
Above the overflowing glass,
God bless you, each and every one,
God bless your daughter and your son—
I send my friends from A to Z

A kiss beneath their Christmas tree!
I'd list you singly, but, I mean,
I ain't no IBM machine!
I say the wish you may recall:
"A Merry Christmas to you all!"
I write you joy and peace and cheer
And hope to see you all this year.
We've been through wars, depressions, school—
I'd say we've been around the pool—
So I feel I've a right to say,
"A happy, holy Christmas Day."
And add this from your humble versers:
"A Happy New Year too!"

The Mercers

[*Handwritten.*]

Although the olden times can't stay—
Keep swingin', Daddy, all the way!!

CHRISTMAS CARD (UNDATED)

At Christmas time, it's hard to say
The old-time wish a brand-new way,
For fashions rise and fashions fall
But Christmas is the best of all.
So prayerfully I lift my pen
To welcome Santa once again,
Old Santa of the cherry nose,
The apple cheeks, the swirling snows,
Who yearly with his reindeer comes
To shacks and condominiums,
The only payment for his ride
The knowledge there is love inside,
For though love makes the world go round,
It's getting harder to be found
And in our riot-, war-torn land
The Scrooges have the upper hand.
We oldsters who were youngsters then
Must set examples once again
And make our fun so unalloyed
That underneath they're overjoyed!
It's like a man who walks a wire
Above a sea of molten fire
While balancing on cattail stalks
Your aunt's best china as he walks,
For how can anything be solved
If no one smiles or gets involved?
But I in my dimwitted way
Sing out, "A merry Christmas Day!"
The blessing old still ringing true
For you—and you—and you—and you!
While seated round your Christmas tree,
Think of the trees that used to be,

The happy faces of old friends
Whose roles are through, whose playlet ends.
Remember how they used to smile—
Their glow lit up the world awhile.
And welcome little ones at birth
Who've just now joined us all on Earth.
The old and new—a lovely sight!
They made almost as bright a light
As that far tree in Viet Nam
Whose one bright bauble is a bomb.
Then go to church and sing—off-key
(As every hymn in church must be!).
Against our good friends' wise advice,
We'll sing the loudest at the part:
"Still stands thine ancient sacrifice,
A humble and a contrite heart."
So, friends and neighbors, Nashville-style
I send you all a great big smile,
A great big hug that's full of love,
A great big blessing from above.
I wish you in imperfect rhyme
The perfect wish at Christmas time:
Just for a moment, now and then,
Be little children once again—
Get on the floor with all your toys
And be one of the girls and boys!
Remember when the tinsel's gone—

The Mercers—Ginger, Jeff, and John

CHRISTMAS CARD 1970

This blessed time of Jesus' birth
May there be *really* Peace on Earth.
Around the tree, amongst our friends,
Let's pray this season never ends,
And show the way for all to see
How brave and good mankind can be.
The way the world is whirling on,
I wonder where the years have gone;
But when I think—don't laugh, I do!—
What pleasant vistas come in view!
Leave It to Beaver, Dan'l Boone—
How many years of *Twilight Zone*?
Jack Paar, Jack Benny, Newhart, Hope,
Have flashed across our TV scope,
While Ozzie Nelson—how time flies!—
Has raised two boys before our eyes!
The Smothers Brothers, heads unbowed,
Were fired for speaking up too loud.
Ah, well, we'll have to find the touch
To straighten out this rabbit hutch!
The moon and Mars are now next door,
But *we're* more distant than before.
Let's hope, in God's great scheme of things,
We find why we've been given wings;
So huge and vast the infinite,

We must be just a speck in it!
So let us all raise humble eyes
To God's immeasurable skies,
Then each one pray in his own way
To do the right thing every day.

CHRISTMAS CARD (UNDATED)

Who wields the knife, who hurls the stone,
The risk be his, the neck his own.
Let retribution, fast and sure,
Revenge the innocent, the pure.
(I hope you wiser heads don't find
I tilt at windmills of the mind.)
Then may we lift the flowing glass,
Invite the strangers in who pass
And drink a toast and have a pause
And spend a while with Santa Claus.
We'll take the children on our knee
And tell them how it used to be
And let them know it's really love
That's kept us humans on the move;
Then say to God—and mean it too:
Thanks for today, and all year through—
Thanks for the good things we've all had;
Now help us overcome the bad.
Teach us, like children still in school,
The facts of life, the Golden Rule.
Teach us to know what Jesus meant,
Why we are here, why He was sent.
With brimming hearts, teach us to say,
"A merry, merry Christmas Day!
And may this Happy New Year too
Be filled with joy the twelve month through!"
For goodness, kindness, peace, and love
Beats *anybody's* treasure trove—
So God bless *you*—and everyone!

The Mercers (Ginger, Jeff, and John)

CHRISTMAS CARD 1971

The children's paintings prompt a rhyme,
A wish for you at Christmas time—
Together we, from all the earth,
Combine to honor Jesus' birth;
Each in his way, the best he can,
Proclaims the dignity of man.
Of man who cares, of man who tries,
Who loves us so, he even dies,
For though we donate while we live,

That is the most a man can give—
The best among us when life ends
Is he who gives it for his friends.
And, maybe, could we only know,
Each picks the proper time to go
The final bow, amid the cheers,
Then exits from his vale of tears.
It may not be so bad at that
To be at last where "it's" *not* at!
Not bad to leave the traffic jams,
The smog, the bulging diaphragms,
The scare technique, the old VD,
Those stale commercials on TV,
The rock and roll that blares so loud,
The pushy freaks in every crowd;
To be where breath is kissing sweet,
No indigestion when you eat,
No fights between ofays and spades,
No dandruff on our shoulder blades,
No slaughter there in Viet Nam,
No Pakistanis on the lam,
No rising crime rate every day,
No sky-high taxes left to pay,
No politicians who "polit"
And then do just the opposite . . .
Ah, well, I grow too dour apace—
You'd think I had no laughing place!
I do indeed, indeed I do,
And I'll unlock it just for you.
While we're still here, let's drink a toast
To all the friends we love the most,
Buy jewels, toys, brocade, and silk—
And leave some Scotch in Santa's milk!
Let everyone hold open house
And sing of good King Wenceslas,
Wish well to all and be sincere
And try to make another year—
They dwindle to a precious few;
I'm glad I spent my best with you!
Good fortune, friends, God bless you all,
Our door is open—come to call!
These drawings by our planet's best
Are songs to soothe the savage breast;
The words are by your humble versers:
"Love makes the world go round . . ."

The Mercers

THE LAST CHRISTMAS CARD 1972

This Christmas card, I think, may be
The last you people hear from me;

The reason being, not because
I don't believe in Santa Claus,
But I most strongly disapprove
Of how you gallivanters . . . MOVE!
A half a year is what it took
To change around my address book!
In January cards come back
All saying, "Moved," "Not here," "Lost track."
In February, one or two
Return across the ocean blue;
In March and April, people call
To say, "Your card came after all!"
In May and June I start to think
And get out paper, pen, and ink
And stew and wonder how on earth
I'll celebrate our Savior's birth;
And then, as summer wanly smiles,
I busily correct my files!
Old friends deceased, this couple wed,
That pair no longer shares a bed,
Those children now have different names—
Their parents too have different dames!
With all these different "libs" in sight
The sex is incidental, right?
So I perspire, type, erase,
Recalling some forgotten face,
And pretty soon the summer's gone
And autumn puts her colors on.
The Bears, the Lions, and the Rams
Are at each other's diaphragms;
And soon it's time to "have a Merry,"
To spike yourself a Tom and Jerry.
So, here is looking at you, pal,
Out seated on the old corral
Or in the traffic's roaring boom,
The silence of your lonely room,
Safe in your boudoir or your den,
There in your tent of oxygen—
Before the IRS men catch you,
Ol' pal o' mine, here's looking at you!
Like in your bathroom all enamely,
Amid the bosom of your family,
Be thankful that's your home address—
The world out there is in a mess.
So, bank the fire, jump in bed,
Await the reindeer overhead,
And picture Santa, cheeks aglow,
Tiptoeing through the fallen snow;
Then, down the chimney noiselessly,
To leave his toys beneath the tree.
Can you recall when all were young
And Christmas carols first were sung?
How deep the snow—and everywhere!
But now the snow is in our hair.
So . . . to the tasks we have to do
While getting kisses—and loaded too—
Remembering, thanks to the Lord,

There's one gift we can all afford,
And here it is: from these old versers
The gift of love, from all the Mercers—

Merry Christmas!

UNFINISHED CHRISTMAS CARD OF 1975

Applause, applause for Santa Claus—
The only act outgrossing *Jaws*!
A "merry masterpiece of mirth,"
The biggest giveaway on earth—
The same old roly-poly elf
Who only wants to be himself,
Old apple-cheeks and twinkling eyes,
The Henny Youngman of the skies,
Who drives his reindeer through the snow
And sings to people, "Ho, ho, ho!"
All year he's busy making toys
For all believing girls and boys,
Who never stops to slave away
Except to yell at Mrs. K;
He only slows down to a crawl
To sing "A Merry Christmas all!"
The only hymns he seems to know
Are those we all learned long ago:
"It Came Upon a Midnight Clear,"
And "Christmas Star,"
"We Three Kings of Orient are . . ."
It starts at five or six o'clock—
His rock and roll and even swing
Is "Hark, the Herald Angels Sing"!
The houses bustle with the sound
Of people hurrying around
Preparing things and trimming trees
And planning the festivities.
And then, when everyone's in bed,
The tiny footsteps overhead,
The reindeer land, the sled arrives, the scene is set
The spotlight shows the best scene yet . . .

OVERLEAF *Mercer and . . .*
Top left: *Harold Arlen*
Top right: *Hoagy Carmichael*
Bottom left: *Henry Mancini*
Bottom right: *Michel LeGrand*

JOHNNY MERCER'S COLLABORATORS

Johnny Mercer's collaborators were a large and diverse group whose number seems to surpass by a wide margin those of any other major American songwriter.

The list of men and women with whom he wrote totals 230. It includes not only his primary songwriting partners such as Richard A. Whiting, Harold Arlen, Hoagy Carmichael, and Harry Warren, whose collaborations with him produced an abundance of standards, but also people he connected with for a single song.

His collaborators were usually composers, but he also worked with other lyricists and, in a few cases, provided the music for other writers' words.

Admittedly, we are using the term collaborator loosely in some instances. You will find on this list, for example, some world-renowned composers, among them Mozart, Schubert, Liszt, and Stephen Foster, who were silent partners, long dead when Mercer set lyrics to their music. We have also included the composers and original lyricists of songs for which Mercer provided now-famous English translations ("Autumn Leaves," "Summer Wind"). While biographical details were readily available for Mercer's well-known collaborators, scant information turned up for others. And then there were those who have disappeared from the public record, leaving no trace, only their name on a song—and on our list.

Harold Adamson
(b. Dec. 10, 1906, Greenville, N.J.; d. Aug. 17, 1980) collaborated with Mack Gordon and Vincent Youmans on "Time on My Hands" for the 1930 Broadway musical *Smiles*; in 1933, with a contract from MGM, he headed to Hollywood, where he became a prolific lyricist for the movies and a five-time Oscar nominee.

Edward Albertson

Steve Allen
(b. Dec. 26, 1921, New York, N.Y.; d. Oct. 30, 2000), the multitalented TV host, comedian, and author, was also the composer and lyricist of thousands of songs.

Laurindo Almeida
(b. Sept. 2, 1917, São Paulo, Brazil; d. July 26, 1995), a composer and highly regarded classical and popular guitarist, moved to the U.S. in 1947, where he recorded with Stan Kenton, Bud Shank, and the Modern Jazz Quartet and helped introduce the music of his native Brazil to American jazz.

Louis Alter
(b. June 18, 1902, Haverhill, Mass.; d. Nov. 3, 1980), a composer and pianist, studied at the New England Conservatory of Music, accompanied Nora Bayes, Irene Bordoni, Helen Morgan, and Beatrice Lillie, and wrote music for the stage and screen.

Nestor Amaral
(b. Sept. 16, 1913, Brazil; d. Feb. 26, 1962), a composer and guitarist, played in Carmen Miranda's Bando da Lua in the U.S. in the early 1940s and appeared in Disney's salute to Latin America, *The Three Caballeros*.

Fabian Andre
(b. Jan. 8, 1910, La Crosse, Wis.; d. March 30, 1960), a composer, arranger, and orchestra leader, was best known for "Dream a Little Dream of Me," co-written with Gus Kahn and Wilbur Schwandt.

Harry Archer
(b. Harry Auracher, Feb. 21, 1888, Creston, Iowa; d. April 23, 1960) composed scores for several Broadway shows in the 1920s and 1930s, including his biggest success, *Little Jesse James*.

Eddie Arkin
(b. Aug. 20, 1949, Los Angeles), an arranger and producer of film scores and albums for Barry Manilow and other leading artists, is also a composer.

Harold Arlen
(b. Hyman Arluck, Feb. 15, 1905, Buffalo, N.Y.; d. April 13, 1986), a leading composer of the Great American Songbook and one of Mercer's major collaborators, saw his career take off in 1930 with

"Get Happy," followed by a string of hits for the Cotton Club, and went on to create a memorable body of work for both stage and screen, including the songs for *The Wizard of Oz*.

Fred Astaire
(b. May 10, 1899, Omaha, Neb.; d. June 22, 1987), the brilliant singer-dancer, began performing at age five in vaudeville with his sister, Adele; a favorite interpreter of many of the greatest Hollywood songwriters in the 1930s and 1940s, he was a composer himself.

Michael William Balfe
(b. May 15, 1808, Dublin, Ireland; d. Oct. 20, 1870), an opera singer turned composer, wrote more than two dozen operas, of which the best-known is *The Bohemian Girl* (1843).

Eddie Barclay
(b. Édouard Ruault, Jan. 26, 1921, Paris, France; d. May 13, 2005), a self-taught pianist who loved jazz and changed his name to Eddie Barclay after World War II, became famous both as a record mogul whose roster of artists included Jacques Brel and Charles Aznavour and as a playboy who hosted extravagant parties and had nine wives.

Charles Bates
(b. Sept. 17, 1897, Villisca, Iowa; d. Aug. 5, 1937), a composer-pianist and one of the co-writers of the 1924 hit "Hard Hearted Hannah," died at a young age of pneumonia.

Les Baxter
(b. March 14, 1922, Mexia, Texas; d. Jan. 15, 1996) was a conductor, composer, arranger, and, early in his career, a vocalist with Mel Tormé's Mel-Tones; he worked as a musical director in radio, scored many films and TV programs, and was a best-selling easy-listening recording artist known for numerous albums of musical "exotica."

Stephen Vincent Benét
(b. July 22, 1898, Bethlehem, Penn.; d. March 13, 1943), the American poet and writer, is best remembered for his long narrative poem on the

Civil War, "John Brown's Body" (which inspired Mercer's lyric to "Georgia, Georgia"), and for his short story "The Devil and Daniel Webster."

Alan Bergman
(b. Sept. 11, 1925, Brooklyn, N.Y.) and his wife, Marilyn, celebrated their fiftieth anniversary as a lyric-writing team in 2006; they have been nominated sixteen times for Academy Awards and have won three times.

Elmer Bernstein
(b. April 4, 1922, New York, N.Y.; d. Aug. 18, 2004), a prolific and very successful film and television composer, was nominated for fourteen Academy Awards, including one for his pioneering jazz-based score for *The Man with the Golden Arm*.

Archie Bleyer
(b. June 12, 1909, Queens, N.Y.; d. March 20, 1989) was the leader of a dance band in the 1930s that featured Mercer as vocalist; he is remembered primarily as Arthur Godfrey's musical director (1946–1953) and as the producer of hit records by Julius LaRosa, Andy Williams, and the Everly Brothers on the Cadence label, which he founded in the early 1950s.

Rube Bloom
(b. April 24, 1902, New York, N.Y.; d. March 30, 1976) was a composer and arranger who worked as a vaudeville accompanist while still in his teens, played on recordings with jazz groups, with his own band, and as a solo pianist, and wrote songs with several lyricists.

Heinz Bolten-Bäckers
(b. 1871, Chemnitz, Germany; d. 1938) wrote the original German words to "Glow Worm" and later became a theater and movie director.

Ralph W. Bolton

Bonfá, Luiz
(b. Oct. 17, 1922, Rio de Janeiro; d. Jan. 12, 2001), a Brazilian guitarist and composer and one of the leaders in the dissemination of bossa nova, is best known as the composer of "Manhã de Carnaval," the worldwide hit from the 1959 movie *Black Orpheus*.

Hal Borne
(b. Dec. 26, 1911, Chicago, Ill.; d. Feb. 25, 2000) was a composer who worked mostly in film.

Don Borzage
(b. Jan. 3, 1925, Salt Lake City, Utah) is a composer, pianist, singer, and teacher.

Hans Bradtke
(b. July 21, 1920, Berlin, Germany; d. May 12, 1997) wrote the original German lyrics for "Summer Wind."

Bertolt Brecht
(b. Feb. 10, 1898, Augsburg, Germany; d. Aug 14, 1956), a major playwright and poet, collaborated with Kurt Weill on *The Threepenny Opera* and other musical theater pieces.

Ronnell Bright
(b. July 3, 1930, Chicago, Ill.), a composer, pianist, and musical director, has accompanied and recorded with numerous jazz luminaries.

Alfredo Brito
(1896–1956) was a Cuban-American bandleader, composer, and singer who helped found the famous Tropicana nightclub in Havana and had a hit record with Ernesto Lecuona's "Siboney" in 1931.

Les Brown
(b. March 14, 1912, Reinerton, Penn.; d. Jan. 4, 2001) was a big-band leader and composer whose recording of his song "Sentimental Journey" became a hit in 1945 and propelled vocalist Doris Day to stardom; he was Bob Hope's conductor on TV and on tour for many years.

Joseph (Sonny) Burke
(b. March 22, 1914, Scranton, Penn.; d. May 31, 1980) was a dance-orchestra arranger, composer, and A&R director of Decca Records for fourteen years

Ralph Burns
(b. June 29, 1922, Newton, Mass.; d. Nov. 21, 2001) made significant contributions as pianist, arranger, and composer for Woody Herman's band in the mid-1940s and later achieved success as a Broadway and Hollywood arranger, orchestrator, and composer.

Hoagy Carmichael
(b. Hoagland Carmichael, Nov. 22, 1899, Bloomington, Ind.; d. Dec. 27, 1981), one of Mercer's chief collaborators, was at the top of his game as a Hollywood songwriter and also won renown as a singer-pianist and movie actor.

Benny Carter
(b. Aug. 8, 1907, New York, N.Y.; d. July 12, 2003) was a versatile jazz musician who had a long career both in the spotlight and behind the scenes as a composer, arranger, bandleader, and soloist; an eminent alto saxophonist, he also played trumpet, clarinet, piano, trombone, and tenor and baritone saxophones.

Saul Chaplin
(b. Saul Kaplin, Feb. 19, 1912, Brooklyn, N.Y.; d. Nov. 15, 1997) and his early collaborator Sammy Cahn's English adaptation of the Yiddish song "Bei Mir Bist du Schoen" was the Andrews Sisters' first hit; moving to Hollywood, he worked as a composer, arranger, and musical director.

Philip Charig
(b. Aug. 31, 1902, New York, N.Y.; d. July 21, 1960), a composer and lyricist, wrote for Broadway, film, and television.

Geoff Clarkson
(b. Sept. 21, 1914, Yonkers, N.Y.; d. March 10, 2009) played piano with Les Brown's band and was Bob Hope's accompanist on USO tours.

Michael H. Cleary
(b. April 17, 1902, Weymouth, Mass.; d. June 15, 1954) was a 1924 graduate of West Point who became a songwriter, rejoined the army in 1942, and had been promoted to major by the time he retired in 1946.

Del Cleveland

Mike Corda
(b. July 8, 1921, New York, N.Y.)

Bob Corwin
(b. Oct. 2, 1933, New York, N.Y.), a jazz pianist and accompanist, was Mercer's musical stenographer—and son-in-law.

Xavier Cugat
(b. Jan. 1, 1900, Catalonia, Spain; d. Oct. 27, 1990), a well-known band leader brought up in Cuba, is credited with popularizing Latin music in North America.

Charles (Bud) Dant
(b. June 21, 1907, Washington, Ind.; d. Oct. 31, 1999), a record producer, composer, arranger, and conductor for radio and TV, spent his last twenty-five years in Hawaii, a place he celebrated in many songs.

Bobby Darin
(b. Walden Robert Cassotto, May 14, 1936, Bronx, N.Y.; d. Dec. 20, 1973) was a singer, actor, and popular nightclub and TV entertainer who died at the age of thirty-seven after surgery for heart damage caused by childhood rheumatic fever.

Blossom Dearie
(b. April 28, 1926, East Durham, N.Y.; d. Feb. 7, 2009) was a singer-pianist whose interpretations of the Great American Songbook and more contemporary, humorous material reflected the influences of jazz and cabaret.

Gene de Paul
(b. June 17, 1919, New York, N.Y.; d. Feb. 27, 1988) was a composer best known for his two major collaborations with Mercer, the film *Seven Brides for Seven Brothers* (1954), renowned for its extraordinary dance sequences, and the Broadway musical *Li'l Abner* (1956).

Al Dero
(b. Armando Di Robbio, Aug. 7, 1915, Providence, R.I.; d. July 29, 1999) was a composer who earned a reputation around New England as a drummer during the big band era.

Howard Dietz
(b. Sept. 8, 1896, New York, N.Y.; d. July 30, 1983) was a wordsmith who led a double life for decades as a publicist for Goldwyn/MGM and as a lyricist, most notably as the songwriting partner for more than thirty years with Arthur Schwartz, his collaborator on "Dancing in the Dark" and "That's Entertainment."

Gene DiNovi
(b. May 26, 1928, Brooklyn, N.Y.), a jazz pianist in many well-known bands, later worked as an accompanist for Tony Bennett, Peggy Lee, Lena Horne, and other popular vocalists.

Robert Emmett Dolan
(b. Aug. 3, 1906, Hartford, Conn.; d. Sept. 26, 1972), a music director in Hollywood and on Broadway and the composer of numerous film scores, wrote two Broadway musicals with Mercer, *Texas, Li'l Darlin'* (1949) and *Foxy* (1964).

Walter Donaldson
(b. Feb. 15, 1893, Brooklyn, N.Y.; d. July 25, 1947), a composer with numerous hits in the 1910s and 1920s, moved to Hollywood in 1929 and contributed songs to many movies.

Dave Dreyer
(b. Oct. 22, 1894, Brooklyn, N.Y.; d. March 2, 1967) accompanied vaudeville greats Al Jolson and Sophie Tucker, among others, worked for many years as a staff pianist at Irving Berlin's music publishing company, and composed for Hollywood.

Al Dubin
(b. June 10, 1891, Zurich, Switzerland; d. Feb. 11, 1945) arrived in the U.S. at age two and had a very successful partnership with composer Harry Warren in the 1930s ("We're in the Money," "Lullaby of Broadway").

Joseph S. Dubin
was a Hollywood orchestrator and composer for Disney, among others, in the 1940s and 1950s.

Vernon Duke
(b. Vladimir Dukelsky, Oct. 10, 1903, Parafianovo, Russia; d. Jan. 16, 1969) settled in the U.S. in 1929, where he achieved recognition as a Broadway and Hollywood composer using the name Vernon Duke (suggested to him by George Gershwin) and wrote symphonic works as Vladimir Dukelsky.

Edwin. B. Edwards
(b. May 22, 1891, New Orleans. La.; d. April 9, 1963), an early jazz trombonist, was a member of the Original Dixieland Jazz Band, famous for its 1917 pioneer jazz recordings.

Duke Ellington
(b. Edward Kennedy Ellington, April 29, 1899, Washington, D.C.; d. May 24, 1974) was world renowned as a pianist, big band leader, and composer.

Ziggy Elman
(b. Harry Finkelman, May 26, 1914, Atlantic City, N.J.; d. June 26, 1968) played the trumpet in Benny Goodman's and Tommy Dorsey's bands.

Sammy Fain
(b. Sammy Feinberg, June 17, 1902, New York; d. Dec. 6, 1989) composed for Broadway and was a two-time Oscar winner ("Secret Love" and "Love Is a Many Splendored Thing").

Percy Faith
(b. April 8, 1907, Toronto, Canada; d. Feb. 9, 1976), an arranger, conductor, and musical director of Columbia Records, became closely associated in the 1950s and 1960s with easy-listening music.

Ted Fiorito (also Fio Rito)
(b. Dec. 20, 1900, Newark, N.J.; d. July 22, 1971) was a composer whose career got off to an auspicious start when Al Jolson introduced his "Toot Toot Tootsie Goodbye" in 1922; he was also a big band leader featured on radio broadcasts in the 1930s and 1940s and appeared with his orchestra in several films.

Elizabeth Firestone
(b. 1922, Akron, Ohio; d. Oct. 1989) a granddaughter of the founder of the Firestone Tire and Rubber Co. and a 1941 debutante, was a composer-pianist who wrote a couple of film scores prior to her marriage in 1954 to Charles F. Willis Jr., a member of President Eisenhower's White House staff.

Alexander Fogarty
wrote music for Broadway in the 1930s.

Stephen Foster
(b. July 4, 1826, Lawrenceville, Penn.; d. Jan. 13, 1864) wrote some of the best-loved songs of nineteenth-century America, including "Oh! Susanna," "My Old Kentucky Home, Good Night," and "Jeanie with the Light Brown Hair."

Gerald Fried
(b. Feb. 13, 1928, New York, N.Y.), a busy Hollywood and TV composer whose credits include the music for episodes of *Gilligan's Island*, *Star Trek*, and *Mission: Impossible*, got his start scoring Stanley Kubrick's earliest movies.

Robert Friedman

Erroll Garner
(b. June 15, 1923, Pittsburgh, Penn.; d. Jan. 2, 1977), a jazz pianist known for his infectious style of music-making, was the first jazz artist presented by the legendary classical impresario Sol Hurok.

Lewis E. Gensler
(b. Dec. 4, 1896, New York, N.Y.; d. Jan. 15, 1978) had a career as a producer and composer both on Broadway and for Paramount Pictures in Hollywood.

Billy Goldenberg
(b. Feb. 10, 1936, Brooklyn, N.Y.), the son of percussionist and Juilliard teacher Morris Goldenberg, has composed extensively for TV.

Hilda Gottlieb
(b. June 23, 1911, New York, N.Y.; d. Oct. 15, 2000) collaborated with Mercer on some lyrics in the early 1930s before marrying Edgar Sachs and becoming a member of the *House & Garden* magazine editorial staff.

Jerry Gray
(b. Generoso Graziano, July 3, 1915, East Boston, Mass.; d. Aug. 10, 1976), perhaps best remembered for his Artie Shaw and Glenn Miller arrangements, including Cole Porter's "Begin the Beguine," which Shaw's orchestra made into a hit, was also the composer of "Pennsylvania 6-5000" and "A String of Pearls."

Johnny Green
(b. Oct. 10, 1908, New York, N.Y.; d. May 17, 1989), composer of "Body and Soul" and "I Cover the Waterfront," had a distinguished career at MGM, where he contributed as a music executive, arranger, composer, and conductor for many major Hollywood musicals.

Walter Gross
(b. July 14, 1909, New York, N.Y.; d. Nov. 27, 1967) was the composer of the 1946 pop song "Tenderly" (lyrics by Jack Lawrence), which had an early popular recording by Sarah Vaughan and a million-seller recording by Rosemary Clooney in 1952.

Ted Grouya
(b. July 31, 1910, Bucharest, Romania; d. April 14, 2000), who immigrated to the U.S. during World War II, wrote the music for the song "Flamingo," which had a long-lived success starting with the Duke Ellington / Herb Jeffries recording in 1942.

Johnny Gruelle
(b. Dec. 24, 1880; d. Dec. 9. 1938) was the creator of the immensely popular Raggedy Ann and Raggedy Andy children's books and dolls.

Charles Hale
(b. May 15, 1914, London, England; d. Sept. 9, 1979) was the pseudonym of Norrie Paramor, a leading British record producer whose acts included the United Kingdom's chart-topping Cliff Richard.

Marvin Hamlisch
(b. June 2, 1944, New York, N.Y.), an Oscar winner for the score and title-song music of *The Way We Were* and his adaptation of Scott Joplin's music for *The Sting*, is perhaps most famous as the composer of the Broadway musical *A Chorus Line*.

Lionel Hampton
(b. April 20, 1908, Louisville, Ky.; d. Aug. 31, 2002), an influential vibraphonist, was a member of Benny Goodman's quartet, the first integrated jazz group, and a natural showman who became the leader of his own orchestra.

Bernard Hanighen
(b. April 27, 1908, Omaha, Neb; d. Oct. 19, 1976), a composer, lyricist, and jazz-loving Harvard graduate, wrote the lyrics for the jazz standard "Round Midnight."

Al Hansen
(b. Aksel Hansen, Nov. 9, 1919, Stavanger, Norway) was a composer who studied at the Los Angeles Conservatory and later taught there.

Vern Hansen
(b. March 17, 1918, Minden, Neb.) was working in the Promotion Department of an Iowa radio station after World War II when he sent one of his songs to Mercer; although Mercer did not record the song, it was the beginning, Hansen remembers, of a friendship.

E. Y. (Yip) Harburg
(b. April 8, 1896, New York, N.Y.; d. March 5, 1981), one of the major lyricists of Broadway and Hollywood, often wrote songs that reflected his strong social conscience ("Brother, Can You Spare a Dime?") and will always be remembered for his lyrics for the movie *The Wizard of Oz*.

Neal Hefti
(b. Oct. 29, 1922, Hastings, Neb.; d. Oct. 11, 2008) made significant contributions as an arranger and composer for the Woody Herman and Count Basie bands in the 1940s and 1950s, but they were eclipsed by his later success writing for television and film, particularly the theme for TV's *Batman* series and for *The Odd Couple* movie and TV show.

Ted Helms

Woody Herman
(born Woodrow Wilson Herman, May 16, 1913, Milwaukee, Wis.; d. Oct. 27, 1987) had a talent for organization and led a succession of notable big bands.

J. Hill (probaby James Hill)
(b. June 16, 1928, Spirit Lake, Idaho), a trombonist who played with Les Brown's band, was also an arranger and composer.

Richard Himber
(b. Feb. 20, 1907, Newark, N.J.; d. Dec. 11, 1966), the leader of his own dance orchestra in the 1930s, interpolated magic tricks into his act and also had a reputation as a practical joker.

Johnny Hodges
(b. July 25, 1900, Cambridge, Mass.; d. May 11, 1970), a distinguished alto saxophonist, was one of the mainstays of Duke Ellington's great band, which he joined in 1928.

Stan Hoffman
(b. Danville, Va.)

Rolfe Humphries
(b. Nov. 20, 1894, Philadelphia, Penn.; d. April 22, 1969) was an eminent American poet, critic, and teacher; Mercer saw his translation of a poem by fourteenth-century Welsh poet Dafydd ap Gwilym in a 1951 issue of *The New Yorker*, gave it a new title ("Nine Thorny Thickets"), and set it to music.

Dick Hyman
(b. March 8, 1927, New York, N.Y.) is a versatile composer, pianist, arranger, and jazz musician who has overseen music on numerous Woody Allen films and has also written orchestra and chamber works.

Antone (Tony) Iavello
(b. Dec. 27, 1913, Baltic, Mich.; d. Dec. 9, 1955), a composer and arranger whose television work included Danny Thomas's *Make Room for Daddy*, died at age forty-one of a heart attack.

Howard Jackson
(b. Feb. 8, 1900, St. Augustine, Fla.,; d. Aug. 4, 1966) had a long career writing music for movies.

Al Jarvis
(b. July 4, 1909, Russia; d. May 6, 1970) was a pioneering radio disk jockey who had a local Los Angeles program in the early 1930s called *The World's Largest Make-Believe Ballroom.*

Gordon Jenkins
(b. May 12, 1910, Webster Groves, Mo.; d. April 24, 1984) wrote arrangements early in his career for the bands of Isham Jones, Woody Herman, and Benny Goodman, but is best-known for his work as arranger and conductor on Frank Sinatra albums.

Donald Kahn
(b. July 17, 1918, Chicago, Ill.; d. April 11, 2008), a composer and the son of lyricist Gus Kahn, grew up knowing many of the most prominent entertainers and songwriters of the time.

Emmerich Kálmán
(b. Oct. 24, 1882, Siofok, Hungary; d. Oct. 30, 1953) was a leading composer of Viennese operetta in the early decades of the twentieth century.

Alvin (Al) Kaufman
(b. July 2, 1910, Wilkes-Barre, Pa.; d. Dec. 21, 1973) was the co-composer of the first Radio City Music Hall stage production and co-writer of the Billie Holiday classic "Me, Myself and I."

Arthur Kent
(b. July 2, 1920, New York, N.Y.; d. Jan. 26, 2009) a piano prodigy, was the composer of country singer Skeeter Davis's crossover hit, "The End of the World."

Jerome Kern
(b. Jan. 27, 1885, New York, N.Y.; d. Nov. 11, 1945) was a titan among Broadway and Hollywood composers in the first half of the twentieth century.

Joseph Kosma
(b. Oct. 22, 1905, Budapest, Hungary; d. Aug. 17, 1969) immigrated in 1933 to Paris, where he collaborated on numerous songs with Jacques Prévert and contributed music to many French films.

Helmy Kresa
(b. Nov. 7, 1904, Meissen, Germany; d. Aug. 19, 1991), Irving Berlin's principal arranger and orchestrator, started working for Berlin in 1926.

Dominick James (Nick) LaRocca
(b. April 11, 1889, New Orleans, La.; d. Feb. 22, 1961), a cornetist, founded the Original Dixieland Jazz Band, a group of white musicians from New Orleans who made the first-ever jazz recordings in 1917.

Hilton (Nappy) Lamare
(b. June 14, 1905, New Orleans La.; d. May 8, 1988), a guitarist, played in the bands of Ben Pollack (1930–1935) and Bob Crosby (1935–1942).

Archie Lebrecht
wrote the lyrics for "Stop the Presses"; Mercer supplied the music.

Florence Leftwich

Michel Legrand
(b. Feb 24, 1932, Paris suburbs, France), a versatile musician with more than one hundred albums to his credit, is also a prolific movie and television composer perhaps best known for his soundtrack for *The Umbrellas of Cherbourg* and the Oscar-winning song "The Windmills of Your Mind."

Joseph J. Lilley
(b. Aug. 16, 1914, Providence, R.I.; d. Jan. 1, 1971) composed, arranged, and conducted for dozens of Hollywood films.

Paul Lincke
(b. Nov. 7, 1866, Berlin, Germany; d. Sept 4, 1946) composed "Glühwürmchen" for his 1902 operetta *Lysistrata;* the song is well known in its English version by Mercer as "Glow Worm."

Mort Lindsey
(b. March 21, 1923, Newark, N.J.), an arranger and music director for top pop-music artists, including Judy Garland and Barbra Streisand, as well as a composer, led *The Merv Griffin Show*'s studio band in the 1960s.

Franz Liszt
(b. Oct. 22, 1811, Raiding, Hungary; d. July 31, 1886) was a great nineteenth-century composer and piano virtuoso.

Carlos Loti
is the pseudonym of Charlie Lots, a trumpeter and Belgium-based studio musician who was a member of the Chakachas, which had a hit in 1972 with the disco funk single "Jungle Fever."

J. Chalmers (Chummy) MacGregor
(b. March 28, 1903, Saginaw, Mich.; d. 1973) was a friend of Glenn Miller's and the pianist in Miller's band from 1936 to 1942.

Al Mack
(b. July 29, 1912, Milwaukee, Wis.; d. March 1985) wrote music for film and television.

Tito Madinez
is the pseudonym of Gaston Bogaert, a drummer and Belgium-based studio musician who was a member of the Chakachas, which had a hit in 1972 with the disco funk single "Jungle Fever."

Matt (Matty) Malneck
(b. Dec. 9, 1903, Newark, N.J.; d. Feb. 25, 1981), best known as the composer of pop standards,

was a violinist with Paul Whiteman's band from 1926 to 1937.

Henry Mancini
(b. April 16, 1924, Cleveland, Ohio; d. June 14, 1994), a busy recording artist, film and television composer, and conductor, won twenty Grammys and four Oscars (two of them for collaborations with Mercer).

Johnny Mandel
(b. Nov. 23, 1925, New York, N.Y.) is a multifaceted musician who started his career as a jazz trombonist and whose credits include arranging, film scoring, and songwriting, and the "Theme from *M*A*S*H*."

Barry Manilow
(b. June 17, 1943, Brooklyn, N.Y.) has achieved success as a singer-songwriter with sales of more than 75 million records, as an entertainer who plays to sold-out audiences, and as a producer for other artists, including Bette Midler (whom he accompanied on the piano when she was beginning her career).

Wingy Manone
(b. Joseph Matthews Manone, Feb. 13, 1904, New Orleans, La.; d. July 9, 1982), a composer, trumpeter, vocalist, and comic personality (who acquired the name Wingy when he lost his right arm at age ten in a streetcar accident), worked frequently with Bing Crosby.

Eddy Marnay
(b. Edmond Bacri, Dec. 18, 1920, Algiers, Algeria; d. Jan. 3, 2003) was a successful and prolific lyricist whose career took off when Edith Piaf turned his "Les Amants de Paris" into a hit in 1948.

Royal Marsh
(b. Royal Bernard Arntz, Aug. 6, 1909; South Boston, Mass.; d. Sept. 10, 1994) and his twin brother, Herb, using Marsh as their stage name, formed "Herbert Marsh and His Royal Marshals," a band popular in Boston and New England around 1931–1942. As part of a contest sponsored by the Song Hit Guild, Roy composed music for a Johnny Mercer lyric, "Holy Smoke (Can't Ya Take a Joke)," and won.

Jack Marshall
(b. Nov. 23, 1921, Eldorado, Kan.; d. Sept. 20, 1973), a leading producer at Capitol Records in the late 1950s and early 1960s, was also well-known for his own acoustic guitar albums.

Hugh Martin
(b. Aug. 11, 1914, Birmingham, Ala.,) was a successful vocal arranger for Broadway as well as a songwriter for Broadway *(Best Foot Forward)* and Hollywood *(Meet Me in St. Louis)* in his own right.

Gilbert Martinez

Michael Masser
(b. March 24, 1941, Chicago, Ill.), a songwriter and record producer, began his career at Motown, where his first hit was Diana Ross's 1973 number-one pop single "Touch Me in the Morning."

Matt (Matty) Matlock
(b. April 27, 1907, Paducah, Ky.; d. June 14, 1978), a jazz clarinetist as well as an arranger, replaced Benny Goodman in Ben Pollack's band, then continued in the group under Bob Crosby's leadership.

Henry L. Mayer

Les McCann
(b. Sept. 23, 1935, Lexington, Ky.) is a soul-jazz pianist, singer, and recording artist whose 1969 album *Swiss Movement* with Eddie Harris was a top-selling jazz recording.

Earl McCarron

Fulton (Fidgey) McGrath
(b. Dec. 6, 1907, Superior, Wis.; d. Jan. 1, 1958) was a pianist who played in the bands of many jazz greats, including Red Nichols, the Dorsey Brothers, and Artie Shaw.

Jimmy McHugh
(b. July 10, 1894, Boston, Mass.; d. May 23, 1969) enjoyed a successful stint composing songs for Harlem's Cotton Club, a productive collaboration with lyricist Dorothy Fields on the score of the all-black revue *Blackbirds of 1928* and other projects, and a flourishing career writing for movies.

Rod McKuen
(b. April 29, 1933, Oakland, Calif.), a prolific poet, composer, songwriter, and recording artist, began attracting a wide following during the Vietnam War era.

Marian McPartland
(b. Margaret Marian Turner, March 20, 1918, Slough, England) married Chicago cornetist Jimmy McPartland in Euorpe in 1946 and came with him to the U.S., where she has distinguished herself as a jazz pianist and as the host of a radio program showcasing jazz.

José Antonio Méndez
(b. June 21, 1927, Havana, Cuba; d. June 9, 1989) was a major exponent of the 1940s Cuban music style known as *filin*, which took its name from the English word "feeling" and favored romantic ballads.

Joseph Meyer
(b. March 12, 1894, Modesto, Calif.; June 22, 1987) wrote music for Broadway and Hollywood and was the composer of Al Jolson's number-one recording "California, Here I Come."

Franco Migliacci
(b. May 1, 1930, Mantova, Italy), a lyricist and record producer, wrote the original Italian words to the pop classic "Volare."

Eddie Miller
(b. June 23, 1911, New Orleans, La.; d. April 1, 1991) was a tenor saxophonist who he played with Paul Whiteman's, Ben Pollack's, and Bob Crosby's orchestras.

Everett Miller
was an early Mercer collaborator and the son of Charlie Miller, an arranger for sheet-music publisher T. B. Harms; later, as head of his own publishing company, Charlie Miller became a Mercer publisher.

Margot Millham
(b. Jan. 25, 1904, New York, N.Y.; d. November 1967) was a classical pianist during her student days.

Brian Minard

(b. April 23, 1936, Liverpool, England; d. Aug. 11, 1998) had an eclectic resumé, ranging from merchant marine to author of *Wersia Sensa Yuma* (translation: "Where's your sense of humor?"), the third volume of the Liverpool-speak guide *Lern Yerself Scouse*. He and Mercer met at New York's Plaza Hotel, where Minard was a bartender.

George Motola

(b. Nov. 15, 1919, Hartford, Conn.; d. Feb. 15, 1991) was a record producer and songwriter whose best-known composition was the 1956 "Goodnight My Love."

Wolfgang Amadeus Mozart

(b. 1756; d. 1791). The world-famous composer.

Jimmy Mundy

(b. June 28, 1907, Cincinnati, Ohio; d. April 24, 1983), one of the swing era's best arrangers, worked for many of the top band leaders, among them Benny Goodman, Tommy Dorsey, Count Basie, and Harry James.

Richard Myers

(b. March 25, 1901, Philadelphia, Penn.; d. March 12, 1977) composed songs for Broadway in the 1920s and 1930s, later became a Broadway producer, and a 1954 Academy Award nominee for the song "Hold My Hand."

Josef Myrow

(b. Feb. 28, 1910, Russia; d. Dec. 24, 1987), trained as a classical pianist, was a busy Hollywood composer in the 1940s and 1950s; his songs include "You Make Me Feel So Young," which he wrote with Mack Gordon.

Ray Navarre

Sammy Nestico

(b. Feb. 6, 1924, Pittsburgh, Penn.), in a varied musical career, was an arranger for the U.S. Air Force and U.S. Marine bands in Washington, D.C., composer/arranger for Count Basie's orchestra, orchestrator for TV specials and for the major film studios, and a music educator.

Alex North

(b. Dec. 4, 1910, Chester, Penn.; d. Sept. 8, 1991), whose diverse output included ballet scores, symphonic pieces, and more than fifty movie scores, was nominated for an Academy Award fifteen times (and finally given a lifetime achievement award in film music in 1986).

Phil Ohman

(b. Philmore Wellington Ohman, Oct. 7, 1896, New Britain, Conn.; d. Aug. 8, 1954) was one half of the duo piano team of Ohman and (Victor) Arden, who won acclaim for their keyboard virtuosity in several Gershwin musicals on Broadway in the 1920s; he later worked in Hollywood scoring films.

Alfred M. Opler

(b. Aug. 30, 1897, New York, N.Y.; d. ?) was, as described by Mercer in his autobiography, "a fine composer" who knew how to plug a song.

Tony Osborne

(b. Edward Osborne, June 29, 1922, near Cambridge, England; d. March 1, 2009) was a composer, conductor, and arranger who achieved recognition in Britain during the 1950s, 1960s, and 1970s through his recordings and work on TV and radio.

Vico Pagano

is the pseudonym of Victor Ingeveldt, a tenor saxophonist and Belgium-based studio musician who recorded with Django Reinhardt and was a member of the Chakachas, which had a hit in 1972 with the disco funk single "Jungle Fever."

Virgilio Panzuti

(b. 1919; d. 1994) was an Italian composer whose "Mandolinate a Sera" was recorded by Plácido Domingo.

Frank Perkins

(b. April 21, 1908, Salem, Mass.; d. March 15, 1988) was a film and television composer, arranger, and orchestrator.

M. Philippe-Gérard

(b. Michel Philippe Bloch, 1924, São Paulo, Brazil), a French composer, wrote the song "Pour Moi Toute Seule" for Edith Piaf in 1945; it launched his career as a songwriter for Piaf, Yves Montand, and many other popular French singers and as a composer of film music.

Jacques Prévert

(b. Feb. 4, 1900, Neuilly-sur-Seine, France; d. April 11, 1977), a popular French poet and screenwriter, collaborated with director Marcel Carné on some of the major films made in France in the 1930s and 1940s.

André Previn

(b. Andreas Ludwig Priwin, Berlin, Germany, April 6, 1929), an enormously versatile musician who immigrated to the United States in 1939, has achieved recognition in both the popular and classical music worlds as a jazz and concert pianist, symphonic conductor, and Hollywood and musical theater composer.

Lew Quadling

(b. June 7, 1908, Cedarville, N.J.; d. March 3, 1987), a pianist during the big band era, was later an arranger and conductor for recording artists such as Dean Martin and Eydie Gorme; his song credits include the hugely successful "Careless."

Henry Ragas

(b. 1891, New Orleans, La.; d. Feb. 18, 1919), the pianist in the Original Dixieland Jazz Band, succumbed to the influenza pandemic of 1918–1919.

David Raksin

(b. Aug. 4, 1912, Philadelphia, Penn.; d. Aug. 9, 2004), a composer for film and television, is best remembered for the haunting musical theme of the 1944 movie *Laura*.

Milton Raskin

(b. Jan. 27, 1916, Boston, Mass.; d. Oct. 15, 1977) was a swing jazz pianist who played in the bands of Gene Krupa, Tommy Dorsey, and others before moving to Los Angeles in the 1940s and working as a studio musician.

Don Raye

(b. Donald MacRae Wilhoite Jr., March 16, 1909, Washington, D.C.; d. Jan. 29, 1985) was a talented dancer who began his career in vaudeville and a songwriter whose "boogie" songs included the Andrews Sisters' 1941 hit, "Boogie-Woogie Bugle Boy," which he wrote with Hughie Prince.

Leon René
(b. Feb. 6, 1902, Covington, La.; d. May 30, 1982) was a songwriter ("When the Swallows Come Back to Capistrano" and "Rockin' Robin") and founder of several record labels.

Wally Ridley
(b. Feb. 28, 1913, London; d. Jan. 23, 2007), a very successful, highly respected record producer for Britain's HMV label in the 1950s and 1960s, was a song composer as well.

Nikolai Rimsky-Korsakov
(b. March 18, 1844, Tikhvin, Russia; d. June 21, 1908) was the famous Russian composer of numerous operas based on folk or fairy tales and a brilliant orchestrator.

Al Rinker
(b. Dec. 20, 1907, Tekoa, Wash.; d. June 11, 1982), a composer, singer, and radio producer and brother of singer Mildred Bailey and Charles Ringer (another Mercer collaborator), was a member of Paul Whiteman's Rhythm Boys vocal trio in the late 1920s along with Bing Crosby and Harry Barris.

Charles (Chuck) Rinker
(b. Jan. 14, 1911, Tekoa, Wash.; d. Dec. 28, 1989), the brother of Al Rinker and singer Mildred Bailey, held a variety of jobs in the music business and described himself as an entertainment writer.

Marshall Robbins
(b. Jan. 12, 1927, New York, N.Y.; d. March 6, 1990), son of music publisher Jack Robbins, was nine years old when he met Mercer and asked him why he wasn't home writing songs. Despite Mercer's first impression of him as a fresh kid, he became Mercer's publisher at Commander Music for twenty-eight years.

Willard Robison
(b. Sept. 18, 1894, Shelbina, Mo.; d. June 24, 1968) was a singer, songwriter, and band leader who had a radio program with his Deep River Orchestra on New York City's WOR for seven years in the 1930s.

Archie Rosate
was a clarinetist and sax player in numerous big bands and recorded behind Bing Crosby, Lena Horne, Judy Garland, and Johnny Mercer.

Johnny Rotella
(b. Nov. 4, 1920, Jersey City, N.J.), saxophone player, composer, and studio musician, played with Benny Goodman's and Tommy Dorsey's bands and recorded with Steely Dan and Neil Diamond.

Jimmy Rowles
(b. Aug. 19, 1918, Spokane, Wash.; d. May 28, 1996) was a jazz pianist in numerous bands, a studio musician, and a favorite accompanist of many singers.

Eddy Samuels
(b. Sept 22, 1933, Chicago, Ill.; d. 1986), a pianist and the son of Mercer collaborator Milton Samuels, was Eddie Fisher's accompanist and conductor for almost twenty years and also worked with Jimmy Rodgers and Shecky Greene.

Milton Samuels
(b. Jan. 28, 1904, Denver, Colo.; d. Jan. 29, 1990), a composer and the father of Mercer collaborators Eddy Samuels and Lorelei Trepper, also used the name Edward Ross (his son's first and middle names), which is how he was credited on his hit song "Jim."

Collen Gray (Tex) Satterwhite
(b. Oct. 17, 1920, Eastland, Texas; d. Feb. 6, 1978) was a composer and arranger.

David Saxon
(b. July 31, 1919, Brooklyn, N.Y.; d. Feb. 12, 1973) was a composer and conductor.

Victor Schertzinger
(b. April 8, 1890, Mahanoy City, Penn.; d. Oct. 21, 1941), a successful Hollywood director (including two Bing Crosby–Bob Hope "Road" movies) and composer, directed and collaborated with Johnny Mercer on the songs for *The Fleet's In*, but died before the film was released.

Franz Schubert
(b. Jan. 31, 1797, Vienna; d. 1828), although little recognized in his short lifetime, was a great and prolific composer of symphonies, German *Lieder*, and chamber music.

Robert Schumann
(b. June 8, 1810, Zwickau, Germany; d. July 29, 1856) was a leading exponent of Romanticism as a composer.

Arthur Schwartz
(b. Nov. 4, 1900, Brooklyn, N.Y.; d. Sept. 3, 1984), a major composer for both stage and screen, wrote some of his best-known songs with lyricist Howard Dietz, including "That's Entertainment" and "Dancing in the Dark."

Samuel Schwartz

Anthony (Tony) Scibetta
(b. Jan. 9, 1926, Buffalo, N.Y.; d. May 18, 1990) was a well-regarded composer who wrote many songs with John Wallowitch.

Michael Shanklin
(b. June 4, 1946, Los Angeles), son of songwriter Wayne Shanklin, is a music producer and songwriter and has worked as a sound engineer for many artists.

John Rufus Sharpe III
(b. Oct. 31, 1909, Berkeley, Calif.) was a songwriter by avocation; his collaboration with Mercer ("Dream Peddler's Serenade") was one of the rare instances where Mercer set someone else's lyrics to music.

Artie Shaw
(b. May 23, 1910, New York, N.Y; d. Dec. 30, 2004) was a brilliant clarinetist and famous big band leader whose recording of Cole Porter's "Begin the Beguine" in 1938 achieved enormous success for both himself and the song.

George Shearing
(b. Aug. 13, 1919, London, England) is celebrated in both his native England, where he was knighted by Queen Elizabeth II in 2007, and in the U.S. as a jazz pianist and composer whose credits include the jazz standard "Lullaby of Birdland."

Larry Shields
(b. Sept. 13, 1893, New Orleans, La.; d. Nov. 21, 1953), a clarinetist, was a member of the Original Dixieland Jazz Band, which made the first jazz recordings in 1917.

Nathaniel Shilkret
(b. Dec. 25, 1889, New York, N.Y.; d. Feb. 19, 1982) had been a popular orchestra leader in the 1920s for Victor Records, where a rivalry developed with Paul Whiteman; he went on to become a busy motion picture composer and musical director.

Carl Sigman
(b. Sept. 24, 1909, Brooklyn, N.Y.; d. Sept 26, 2000) was a lyricist and composer whose songs included "Pennsylvania 6-5000," a Glenn Miller Orchestra hit, "Dance, Ballerina, Dance," and the English lyrics for "Arrivederci Roma."

Frank Signorelli
(b. May 24, 1901, New York, N.Y.; d. Dec. 9, 1975), a composer and jazz pianist, was the co-founder in 1917 of the Original Memphis Five (none of whose members originated from Memphis or the South), a group that made many recordings under various names in the 1920s.

Ray Sinatra
(b. Nov. 1, 1904, Girgenti, Sicily; d. Nov. 1980), an arranger, conductor, and second cousin of Frank, was best known as Mario Lanza's music director.

Freddie Slack
(b. Aug. 7, 1910, La Crosse, Wis.; d. Aug. 10, 1965), after playing in various big bands, formed his own orchestra in the early 1940s; it became one of the first bands signed by Mercer's new Capitol Records.

Howard Smith
(b. June 17, 1949, Nashville, Tenn.) was lead singer and guitarist with the Amazing Rhythm Aces in the 1970s and a Nashville songwriter after the group broke up in 1981.

Henry Souvaine
(b. 1895, Salt Lake City, Utah; d. Jan. 30, 1954) composed some songs for Broadway but is mostly remembered as a radio producer, particularly for his work, starting in 1940, on the intermission features, such as the popular Opera Quiz, of the Metropolitan Opera's Saturday afternoon broadcasts.

Tony Spargo
(b. Tony Sbarbaro, June 27, 1897, New Orleans; d. Oct. 30, 1969) was the drummer in the Original Dixieland Jazz Band, known for its first-ever 1917 jazz recordings.

Fred Spielman
(b. Fritz Spielmann, Nov. 20, 1906, Vienna; d. March 21, 1997) composed songs for movies after arriving in the U.S. in 1939.

Harold Spina
(b. June 21, 1906, New York, N.Y.; d. July 18, 1997) wrote songs for the major Hollywood studios.

Jo Stafford
(b. Nov. 12, 1917, Coalinga, Calif.; d. July 16, 2008) sang in a trio with her sisters and worked with the Tommy Dorsey Orchestra before becoming one of the top female vocalists of the newly established Capitol Records; she also had success with her husband, musical director Paul Weston, as the comedy recording duo Jonathan and Darlene.

Franz Steininger
(b. June 12, 1906, Vienna; d. Dec. 28, 1974) was a light opera conductor and movie composer who arrived in the U.S. in 1935.

Guy Stevens

Morton Stevens
(b. Jan. 30, 1929, Newark, N.J.; d. Nov. 11, 1991) started his career as Sammy Davis Jr.'s conductor and arranger, then became a television composer whose credits included the theme for *Hawaii Five-O*.

Billy Strayhorn
(b. Nov. 29, 1915, Dayton, Ohio; d. May 31, 1967), a brilliant composer and arranger, was Duke Ellington's longtime collaborator.

Bob Swanson
(b. Dec. 1, 1920)

Doris Tauber
(b. Sept. 13, 1907, New York, N.Y.; d. Jan. 20, 1996), musical secretary to Irving Berlin for thirteen years, was a composer in her own right whose credits included "Them There Eyes," a song associated with Billie Holiday and Louis Armstrong but recorded by many other major singers.

Macy O. Teetor
(b. Dec. 31, 1898, Hagerstown, Ind.; d. Dec. 8, 1978), an engineer and executive from 1923 to 1946 at his family's Hagerstown, Ind., Perfect Circle Co., a world leader in the manufacture of piston rings, played and wrote music as a hobby.

Alfred J. Thieme
(b. Jan. 4, 1908; d.?) wrote a novelty number called "Battle Hymn of the Republican Party" to the tune of "John Brown's Body" for Herbert Hoover's 1929 campaign.

Ida Thomas
reflected her strong attachment to the barrier island off the coast of Georgia in her lyrics for "My Jekyll Island," which Mercer edited.

Peter Tinturin
(b. June 1, 1910, Yekaterinoslav, Russia; d. April 15, 2007) was a classically trained musician who arrived in the U.S. in 1929 and became a songwriter, mostly for films.

Pinky Tomlin
(b. Truman Tomlin, Sept. 9, 1908, Eros, Ark.; d. Dec. 12, 1987) recorded his best-selling song "The Object of My Affection" in 1934, and afterwards appeared in and composed for motion pictures; he also toured with his own band before retiring from the music business and becoming an oilman.

Lorelei Trepper
(b. July 10, 1930, Chicago) is a classical pianist whose father, Mercer friend and collaborator Milton Samuels, showed a tune she had composed to Mercer; while on a train ride from Los Angeles to New York, Mercer wrote three different lyrics for it and asked her to pick the one she liked best.

Bobby Troup
(b. Oct. 18, 1918, Harrisburg, Penn.; d. Feb. 7, 1999), a songwriter best known for his song "(Get

Your Kicks on) Route 66" and an actor who played Dr. Joe Early on the 1970s TV series *Emergency*, was also a recording artist and a panelist and host on TV music programs.

Jimmy Van Heusen
(b. Edward Chester Babcock, Jan. 26, 1913, Syracuse, N.Y.; d. Feb. 7, 1990), who teamed up with lyricist Johnny Burke in the 1940s and 1950s and lyricist Sammy Cahn in the 1950s and 1960s, wrote the music for eighty-five songs recorded by Frank Sinatra, composed songs for twenty-three Bing Crosby movies, received ten Academy Award nominations for Best Song, and won the Oscar four times.

Angèle Vannier
(b. August 12, 1917, Saint-Servan, Brittany, France; d. December 2, 1980), a French poet who lost her eyesight at age twenty-two to glaucoma, preferred writing pure poetry despite the early success of her words for the song "Le Chevalier de Paris," popularized by Edith Piaf and Yves Montand (and adapted by Mercer as "When the World Was Young").

Johnny Varro
(b. June 11, 1930, Brooklyn, N.Y.) was a pianist who played in jazz rooms in New York, clubs in Los Angeles, and with his own trio in Miami Beach.

Billy Vaughn
(b. April 12, 1919, Glasgow, Ky.; d. Sept. 26, 1991) was a popular orchestra leader, pop music arranger, recording artist, and musical director at Dot Records during the 1950s and 1960s.

Sadie Vimmerstedt
(b. May 29, 1904; d. December 1986) was the Youngstown, Ohio, grandmother who provided Johnny with the title and idea for the song "I Wanna Be Around."

Serge Walter
(b. July 5, 1896, Hungerberg, Russia; d. Feb. 8, 1976) immigrated in 1925 to the U.S., where he wrote songs for Broadway and the movies.

Harry Warren
(b. Salvatore Guaragna, Dec. 24, 1893, Brooklyn, N.Y.; d. Sept. 22, 1981) was the winner of three Academy Awards, but the somewhat underappreciated composer of many of the best-known movie songs of the 1930s, 1940s, and 1950s, often written in collaboration with lyricists Al Dubin, Mack Gordon, or Johnny Mercer.

Bernie Wayne
(b. March 6, 1919, Paterson, N.J.; d. April 18, 1993) was a prolific songwriter whose two most often heard pieces were the Miss America competition theme song and the "Chock full o'Nuts Is That Heavenly Coffee" commercial jingle.

Kurt Weill
(b. March 2, 1900, Dessau, Germany; d. April 3, 1950), the composer of *The Threepenny Opera*, immigrated in 1935 to the U.S., where he won acclaim writing innovative musical-theater works for Broadway.

Walter Weschler
(b. Sept. 29, 1921), pianist for the Andrews Sisters, married sister Patty in December 1951.

Paul Weston
(b. March 12, 1912, Springfield, Mass.; d. Sept. 20, 1996), in a multifaceted music career, was an arranger for the Tommy Dorsey and Bob Crosby orchestras; first musical director of Capitol Records, where he conducted for, among others, Johnny Mercer, Margaret Whiting, Jo Stafford (who became his wife in 1952); a pioneer of "mood" music; and Jonathan of the Darlene and Jonathan comedy albums.

Richard A. Whiting
(b. Nov. 12, 1891, Peoria, Ill.; d. Feb. 10, 1938), a prominent Hollywood composer in the 1930s, took Mercer under his wing, but their collaboration was cut short by Whiting's untimely death at age forty-six. His daughter Margaret became a renowned singer.

Joseph Wiess

Alec Wilder
(b. Feb. 16, 1907, Rochester, N.Y.; d. Dec. 24, 1980), championed by Frank Sinatra, jazz musicians, and classical artists, was a stylistically unique composer who wrote popular songs and concert music.

John Williams
(b. Feb. 8, 1932, Floral Park, Long Island, N.Y.) is probably the most famous American movie composer of the last quarter of the twentieth century, thanks to his scores for, among many other films, *Star Wars* and *Jaws*. He also distinguished himself as the conductor of the Boston Pops Orchestra from 1980 to 1993.

William Woodin
(b. March 27, 1868, Berwick, Penn.; d. May 3, 1934), Franklin Delano Roosevelt's secretary of the treasury in 1933, was also a composer.

Allie Wrubel
(b. Jan. 15, 1905, Middletown, Conn.; d. Dec. 13, 1973) started his career as a saxophonist and moved to Hollywood in 1934, where he composed songs for Warner film musicals and for Disney, including the Oscar-winning "Zip-a-Dee-Doo-Dah."

Vincent Youmans
(b. Sept. 27, 1898, New York, N.Y.; d. April 5, 1946), an important Broadway composer whose shows included *No, No, Nanette* (1925) and *Hit the Deck* (1927), also wrote the score for Fred Astaire and Ginger Rogers's first Hollywood film together, *Flying Down to Rio* (1933), before his career was cut short by tuberculosis.

Trummy Young
(b. James Young, Jan. 12, 1912, Savannah, Ga.; d. Sept. 10, 1984) was a trombonist affiliated with Earl Hines, Jimmie Lunceford, and, for twelve years starting in 1952, Louis Armstrong's All-Stars.

Index

This is an alphabetical index of song titles, first lines (including verses and first refrains), and alternate titles of Johnny Mercer's lyrics. When the first line begins with or is identical to the title or alternate title, it is not included. The index also includes individual song copyright information. For all lyrics: © All Rights Reserved. International Copyright Secured. Used by Permission.